A DICTIONARY OF TRAVEL AND TOURISM TERMINOLOGY

Second Edition

This is my 14th book; it is the second to be published by CAB International; I hope there will be many more!

I dedicate it to my grandchildren, Anna and Noah Beaver, Lauren and Max Blum and Poppy and Jack Taylor, in the hope that it will further encourage them in the pursuit of knowledge.

Allan Beaver

A DICTIONARY OF TRAVEL AND TOURISM TERMINOLOGY

Second Edition

_____

ALLAN BEAVER

International Centre for Tourism Research
University of Bournemouth, UK

and

Leisure and Tourism Department
Buckinghamshire Chilterns University College, UK

CABI Publishing

CABI Publishing is a division of CAB International

CABI Publishing
CAB International
Wallingford
Oxon OX10 8DE
UK

CABI Publishing
875 Massachusetts Avenue
7th Floor
Cambridge, MA 02139
USA

Tel: +44 (0)1491 832111
Fax: +44 (0)1491 833508
E-mail: cabi@cabi.org
Web site: www.cabi-publishing.org

Tel: +1 617 395 4056
Fax: +1 617 354 6875
E-mail: cabi-nao@cabi.org

A catalogue record for this book is available from the British Library, London, UK.

Library of Congress Cataloging-in-Publication Data
Beaver, Allan, 1934-
   A dictionary of travel and tourism terminology / Allan Beaver.--2nd ed.
       p. cm.
   Includes bibliographical references.
   ISBN-13: 978-0-85199-020-0 (alk. paper)
   ISBN-10: 0-85199-020-7 (alk. paper) ✓
       1. Travel--Dictionaries. 2. Tourism--Dictionaries. I. Title.

   G155.A1B38 2005
   910′.3--dc22

                                                                2005009233

ISBN-13: 978 0 85199 020 0
ISBN-10: 0 85199 020 7

Typeset by Columns Design Ltd, Reading.
Printed and bound in the UK by Cromwell Press, Trowbridge.

Contents

About the Author   vi

Preface and Introduction   vii

Acknowledgements   xii

Appendix I: World Tourism Organization *Global Code of
               Ethics for Tourism*   367

Appendix II: Recommended Tourism Syllabus Content for Higher
               Education Courses Worldwide   380

Appendix III: EC Neutral CRS Rules   387

About the Author

Professor Allan Beaver has run a travel business for over 40 years. He is a Visiting Professor at the University of Bournemouth and at Buckinghamshire Chilterns University College.

His professional qualifications are: Fellow of City and Guilds of London Institute, Master of Science, Fellow of the Chartered Institute of Transport, Fellow of the Tourism Society, Fellow of the Chartered Institute of Marketing, Fellow of the Institute of Logistics, Fellow of the Institute of Travel and Tourism and academic member of the Association D'Expertes Scientifiques du Tourisme.

He is the author of many papers, articles and books in the tourism field, including three editions of the 1820-page three volume, *Mind Your Own Travel Business* and an annual industry survey and forecast, the 100-page 27th edition of which was published in December 2004. Repeatedly, his forecasts made each autumn have come within 1% of the outcome.

Allan Beaver's professional interests particularly include the marketing of travel and tourism and its terminology. He is a member of the Professional Body Board of the Chartered Institute of Marketing (CIM), Vice Chair of the CIM Travel Industry Group and writes its monthly meeting reports. He was appointed by the British Standards Institute as the senior UK expert in the field of tourism terminology, representing the UK on several international working groups. As this dictionary was going to press, he was in Berlin, leading the UK delegation to a meeting of CEN, the grouping of European Standards Institutes.

He chaired the Travel Agents and Tour Operators Sectoral Committee of the UK government-appointed Travel and Tourism Events National Training Organization (TTENTO) and was Treasurer of that organization. He is a former Board member of the Association of British Travel Agents and was for many years a member of the Association's Travel Agents Council. He was founding chairman of the ABTA's Greater London region, which includes nearly a quarter of the Association's agent members.

Preface and Introduction

What is Covered by this Dictionary

This dictionary provides definitions of terminology and 'decodes' acronyms and abbreviations for the world's largest industry. All the Internet search engines sell their services, which result in high ranking following a user search, for those who have paid for preferment. In the travel and tourism field, this means that searches involving key words often result in commercial organizations appearing first, with the sought-after organization thousands of results behind. The comprehensive listing in this dictionary of Internet addresses makes it a crucial and invaluable research and reference source for statistics, many associations, trade bodies and other voluntary organizations. As this dictionary was going to press, registrations were taking place for the new 'dot travel' domain name to be launched in 2006; *see* www.tralliance.com/dottravel/main.htm. This dictionary contains many descriptive articles on travel and tourism concepts, which cover a wider range of topics in greater depth than other dictionaries in this field. Where comprehensive information is readily accessible from the Internet, web access points have been detailed. It expands on Allan Beaver's work in the encyclopaedic volume 3 of his book, *Mind Your Own Travel Business*. This broke new ground by its all-encompassing nature. To indicate the coverage of the present book, it is first necessary to indicate the intended parameters.

The UK Quality Assurance Agency for Higher Education has, in recent years, benchmarked degree courses, identifying in general the characteristics of programmes in specific subjects and the learning outcomes to be expected. Unit 25 includes tourism, and part of that unit is detailed in Appendix II. Having specified that a typical honours graduate should be able to demonstrate an understanding of the stated areas, this dictionary has been designed to support the learning process in those subjects. Despite the wide-ranging nature and variety of tourism courses, the intention is that this dictionary should be appropriate to the needs of all those courses.

It is important to state clearly that this book is mainly limited to tourism terminology used in the English-speaking world. Many non-English words are used by tourism practitioners in Britain, North America and Australasia, hence, not all the words explained are English.

The accent in this dictionary is on the definitions themselves. But a particular exception has been made in the case of tourism information databases, for which access details are provided. Many tourism dictionaries include substantial listings of the organizations in the field with contact information. The entries in this dictionary aim only to provide information not available from organizations' web sites. In this dictionary, having decoded an abbreviation or understood the meaning of a word, it is usually necessary to access the web site noted or go to an appropriate work of reference, for names, addresses and web sites etc. of the organizations or for more information.

This dictionary does not cover words or phrases relating to cultural, destination, location, physical, place or political geography. Most other tourism dictionaries include destination information and geography; each selection is different, according to the whims of the authors and publishers. For good measure, various descriptions of local food specialities and customs are also included. To cover, for example, 5000 areas, sites or attractions of touristic interest would require a 500-page book devoted to this aspect of terminology.

The British GNVQ (General National Vocational Qualification) in this field includes studies of both leisure and tourism but, at the advanced level, tourism and leisure are separate subjects. This dictionary does not cover leisure and sports terms. In many texts, attempts to cover the leisure field are severely detrimental to achieving complete coverage of tourism, simply because of lack of space. For example, in the Columbus Press *World Travel Dictionary*, the very first term is 'A clamp, a diving term for a connecting device between an air hose and diving cylinder'. This type of term is not found here.

In some areas, there is a very thin borderline between travel and tourism, and environmental studies. For example, while there is no doubt that acid rain has a profound ecological effect with a tourism impact, nevertheless, this is not a tourism term and has been omitted together with other material of a similar nature.

There is no attempt to include definitions of words which, although they can be applied to tourism, are not specific to it. The book you are now reading is restricted to decoding and explaining words that are particular to tourism. Thus, most business terminology in general and marketing jargon in particular has been omitted.

Another grey area faced by the author, when deciding what to include, concerns technical transportation terminology. Readers should not, for example, look in this book for an explanation of all of the parts of an aircraft engine, train or ship, although an attempt has been made to cover basic nomenclature. Furthermore, tourism is specific to people rather than goods; so no aspects of the carriage of goods are covered. Thus cargo terms and the associated insurance terms are excluded. The scope of this area may surprise readers. There are 470 closely printed pages in the second edition of *The Marine Encyclopaedic Dictionary* by Eric Sullivan, published by Lloyds of London Press Ltd in 1988.

The three letter system for coding airports and cities and similar system for coding airlines has not been reiterated in this book, for coding and decoding information is readily available in many computer systems and other reference manuals used in travel agencies worldwide. So far it has been explained what is excluded; so what *is* included?

North American and European differences – It is a particular aim of this dictionary to identify differences, each side of the Atlantic, in the meanings of many of the words or phrases defined. The author is not aware of any other publication that has covered the differences in industry and travel professionals' usage, although many have covered the differences in everyday language, which are outside the scope of this dictionary.

Operating language of the providers (the industry) of tourism services – The travel and tourism industry is very diverse, not merely limited to the providers of hospitality and transport by road, rail, air and sea. There are also a huge number of ancillary services such as the provision of car rental, travel insurance, passports and visa services, health requirements, foreign currency and traveller's cheques, the information services provided by national and local tourist boards and guiding services. There are organizations that package several of these services together and sell them either direct to consumers or via intermediaries, known as tour operators. Travel agents, the retailers of the industry, are in competition with newer intermediaries, communicating with consumers via the Internet, telephone, digital cable television, or a combination thereof. The Global Distribution Systems (GDS) and national travel computer reservation systems provide services to all of the organizations mentioned so far. Each of these aforementioned fields has an operating language. The words may have only a descriptive function or may set a specific standard.

Tourism – The dictionary explains where and why the qualitative and quantitative definitions differ. The latter are used for measuring tourism while the former are valuable because they are descriptive of the phenomenon of tourism. This dictionary is currently the only one which explains the evolutionary nature of tourism definitions. Attention is drawn to alternative definitions that are in textbooks. An explanation is given of why many have been superceded and recommendations for the most appropriate definition are justified.

Acronyms and abbreviations – This is a problem area for new entrants to tourism, be they students or people entering from other fields. Even the headlines in the trade press or titles of papers in tourism journals are a complete mystery without the ability to decode them. Many acronyms are of organizations. The worldwide nature of tourism means that the names of the trade bodies, official and regulatory bodies are from many countries. The major providers of hospitality and transport by road, rail, air and sea are all international and the letters that stand for their names are meaningless to the uninitiated. Each area of travel and tourism has its own set of acronyms; this book decodes 350 International Air Transport Association (IATA) acronyms not previously generally available until publication of the first edition of this dictionary.

Alternatives – Often, various sources offer different definitions for the same word. This dictionary is, at present, the only one which covers the alternatives; when appropriate, it discusses their merits and suggests definitions for general adoption. Definitions recommended in previous editions of this dictionary have been widely quoted in tourism journals.

IT terms – Technological change has caused a revolution in the way the tourism product is distributed to the travelling public. Many large dictionaries of technical and computer terminology have been published and it has not been the intention to compete with these works. Nevertheless, some technical computer terms are commonly used in the travel industry and for the convenience of users of this book, an explanation of the basic ones has been included.

Control language – There are a large number of governmental, official and trade bodies which lay down laws, rules and regulations applicable to travel and tourism; this dictionary identifies these bodies and their functions and includes their associated terminology.

Brand names – These are liberally strewn throughout the travel business like confetti, without any indication of the associated organization. For example, most airlines have clubs with a brand name and frequent flyer schemes, often with a different brand name. The airlines may be affiliated with alliances such as Star or OneWorld. This dictionary identifies the main organizations associated with these brand names.

Accuracy of definitions – The travel and tourism industry is always changing rapidly, in response to consumer's needs and technological advances, particularly in information technology. This dictionary aims to be correct at a date approximately 6 months before its publication date. However, some seminal papers and books on many aspects of tourism were published many years ago; to understand them, it is necessary to be able to 'decode' the acronyms, brand names and expressions that were current at those times. A selection of these obsolete terms has been included, identified as such.

Web sites – Within the currency of this dictionary, 'dot travel' Internet addresses will become available. Many web sites are featured to enable users to access more information concerning many entries. Some may change to .travel.

Disclaimer: no responsibility is accepted by the author or publisher for any errors that may have inadvertently arisen. Users are particularly recommended to check with appropriate sources, information critical to their travel arrangements.

Definitions preceded by 'The 2003 CEN/European Standard official definition is' are indicative of wording which has been published by the British Standards Institute on behalf of CEN (BS EN ISO 18513:2003 Tourism services – Hotels and other types of tourism accommodation – Terminology and BS EN 13809:2003 Tourism services – Travel agencies and tour operators – Terminology). CEN is the European Grouping of National Standards Institutes, 'Comité Européen de Normalisation'. CEN members are the national standards bodies in Austria, Belgium, Czech Republic, Denmark, Finland, France, Germany, Greece, Iceland, Ireland, Italy, Luxembourg, The Netherlands, Norway, Portugal, Spain, Sweden, Switzerland and the UK.

Committee 329 was established in 1996 and is concerned with travel and tourism; it agreed to set up two working groups to create and agree standard terminology and associated definitions. WG1 was responsible for the accommodation area; WG2 was asked to handle travel agents and tour operators. The

British Standards Institute (BSI), in common with other European standards institutes, set up a national 'mirror' group – SVS2 'Tourism Services', and invited ABTA to join this. I was asked by ABTA to represent them in view of my particular expertise on travel and tourism terminology. BSI then accredited me as the Senior UK Expert in Travel and Tourism Terminology to represent them at WG2. Subsequently, WG2 adopted English as its working language and the members of WG2 elected me to be responsible for the definitive English versions of the definitions agreed.

Tourism is inherently diverse; laws, customs and practices vary so widely in each country that agreeing internationally acceptable definitions was always likely to be difficult. This situation resulted in arguments which had not been previously experienced by the UK Expert; in order to salvage something from several years of meetings, definitions were accepted which were only 'the lowest common denominator'. Part of the introduction to the BSI standard is repeated verbatim:

> Many difficulties have been encountered in the preparation of this standard. The following are some of them:
>
> - There are concepts for which an English term does not exist.
> - There are concepts for which translation does not exist in one of the official languages.
> - There are services (or types of accommodation) that are specific to only one or a few countries.
> - There are terms for which more than one meaning is possible, depending on the context.
> - In many cases, the requirements are different, depending on the national legislation. In these cases the common minimum has been agreed as the definition for this European standard.
>
> As a result, many of the definitions agreed are rather broad and the standard represents the highest level of consensus which could be reached.

In the spring of 2005, CEN 329 agreed the proposition of AENOR, the Spanish Standards Institute, to embark on an extensive programme of standards development in the tourism field. The author of this book was appointed to lead the UK delegation to Working Group 5, which is to develop a tourist guide qualification standard.

The letters (WTO TM) after a definition indicate that the source is the series of World Tourism Organization Technical Manuals: *Concepts, Definitions and Classifications for Tourism Statistics*; *Collection of Tourism Expenditure Statistics*; *Collection of Domestic Tourism Statistics* and *Collection and Compilation of Tourism Statistics*. References to the WTO Thesaurus relate to the World Tourism Organisation and Secretariat of State for Tourism of France (2001), *Thesaurus on Tourism and Leisure Activities*.

Allan Beaver
May 2005

Acknowledgements

Many of the definitions originate from the glossary of terms in the first, second and third editions of *Mind Your Own Travel Business*, first published in 1975. This dictionary sometimes proposes alternatives expressing disagreement with definitions published in other sources; in order to explain and justify the stance taken it has been necessary to quote the original work. For this purpose advantage is taken of the Copyright, Designs and Patents Act 1988 which states that fair dealing for the purposes of criticism does not infringe copyright if accompanied by a sufficient acknowledgement. Nevertheless, the owners of the copyrights concerned have generously given their encouragement and permission to quote from their work and the author records his thanks for this, which has assisted in the pursuit of knowledge and the development of tourism as an academic discipline.

Unreserved appreciation of their permission is particularly expressed concerning:

- David Relf, Head of Aviation at solicitors Sinclair Roche & Temperley, whose annual *Aviation Handbook* has been a rich source of decoding abbreviations in the aviation field.
- John Patterson (formerly of IATA UK) who listed the meaning of many IATA acronyms and abbreviations not in the Sinclair Roche & Temperley list.
- The American Society of Travel Agents (ASTA) for the access allowed to the members-only web site, enabling data to be mined from the online agents' handbook.
- The British Standards Institute which published on behalf of CEN, the European Grouping of National Standards Institutes, two standards: BS EN ISO 18513:2003 Tourism services and Hotels and other types of tourism accommodation – Terminology and BS EN 13809:2003 Tourism services – Travel agencies and tour operators – Terminology.
- The International Air Transport Association concerning definitions in their *Ticketing Handbook and Travel Agents Handbook* (UK editions).

- Columbus Publishing Limited (*World Travel Dictionary*) concerning the alternative definitions of a few tourism terms which appear in the comparative discussions of six or so expressions.
- World Tourism Organization concerning some definitions in the 1995 technical manuals *Collection of Tourism Expenditure Statistics* and *Concepts, Definitions and Classifications for Tourism Statistics*; also the WTO's *Global Code of Ethics for Tourism*, Appendix I.
- The Quality Assurance Agency in the UK relating to part of their Subject Benchmark Statement for Hospitality, Leisure, Tourism and Sport which appears in Appendix II.
- Office of National Statistics relating to various statistics published in *Business Monitor MQ6, Overseas Travel and Tourism*.
- AC Nielsen relating to various statistics published in their *Holiday Booking Survey*.
- Extracts from several CABI publications, namely *Electronic Information Distribution in Tourism and Hospitality* by Peter O'Connor concerning HANK and HIRO and *Tourism Information Technology* by Pauline Sheldon concerning data that should be provided by a destination management system.
- UK Travel and Leisure Industry Group Kirkpatrick & Lockhart Nicholson Graham LLP concerning part of the wording used in the explanation of the Warsaw Convention.

A

100 A1 In *Lloyd's Register of Shipping*, term indicates an ocean-going vessel made of iron or steel.

à la carte Restaurant menu from which the consumer can choose freely, paying for individual items, contrasting with table d'hôte which is a set menu with limited choice for an inclusive price. *Alternatively*, when used by tour operators, refers to an independent inclusive tour (IIT), arranged to the customer's choice; also called 'tailor-made' arrangements in the UK, contrasting with a package tour, where set flights and a hotel are bundled together. *See* alternative meal choices *of* table d'hôte *and* set meal.

A to Z Travel Agents System Name of Digital Computer System Limited UK's travel agents' computerized data and accounting system introduced in August 1984; now believed to be obsolete.

A/D Aerodrome.

A/G Air/Ground (communication station).

A1 First class. In *Lloyd's Register of Shipping*, the term applies to vessels built to trade in sheltered waters such as rivers. **a1** is a navigational term, the second polaris correction; while **a2** is the third polaris correction.

A¹ In connection with car rental, indicates an automatic vehicle rather than one with gear levers.

A² As a nautical term, it indicates aft.

AA¹ Aerolineas Argentinas.

AA² Always afloat.

AA³ American Airlines. S*ee* AAdvantage.

AA⁴ Apparent altitude.

AA⁵ Automobile Association; based in the UK, it is the largest organization in the world representing motorists, providing roadside repair, recovery and other services. Worldwide, there are many organizations that use these initials, a few of which are mentioned above. *See* www.theaa.co.uk

AAA The American Automobile Association represents many US motorists and is regarded as the main non-governmental body concerned with the interests of car owners. Roadside repair and recovery services are typical of the direct benefits provided to members. AAA Worldwide Travel is the wholly-owned travel agency group. *See* www.aaa.com

AAAE American Association of Airport Executives. *See* www.aaae.org

AAAVT Asociación Argentina de Agencias de Viajes y Turismo. *See* www.aaavyt.org.ar

AAB Air Authority Board.

AAC¹ Aeronautical Advisory Council.

AAC² Association of ATOL Companies in the UK, formerly the Association of Airline Consolidators. *See* www.aac-uk.org

AACC Airport Associations Co-ordinating Council in the UK is the international organization through which other national and international bodies in this sphere cooperate, world membership currently including over 95 national airport associations and over 350 airports and airport authorities.

AACO Arab Air Carriers Organization. *See* www.aaco.org

AAdvantage Brand name of American Airlines' frequent flyer programme, the largest worldwide, established in 1981. Travel on AA's services, or use of facilities offered by scheme partners, earns 'miles' which can be exchanged for free travel. While flying is the most common way of earning miles, over 40% of miles earned by AAdvantage members each year is done so through AAdvantage's thousands of partners. These include 35 airline partners, over 30 hotel companies and seven car rental companies, as well as a range of non-travel partnerships, such as retail and financial services. Members can redeem mileage for trips on other airlines as well as for hotel stays, car rentals and holiday packages. As well as bonus miles for qualifying flights, there are automatic upgrade privileges within the USA,

Canada and Mexico, preferred check-in and boarding are provided. The awards can be used to buy membership of AA's Admiral's Club.

The level of membership earned and benefits provided under the AAdvantage scheme depend on the quantity of flying undertaken in the previous calendar year: Gold 25,000 miles/30 segments; Platinum – 50,000 miles/60 segments; Executive platinum – 100,000 miles. American Airlines is a member of the OneWorld alliance and the arrangements extend to those alliance partners, both for earning points and redeeming them (Aer Lingus, British Airways, Cathay Pacific, Finnair, Iberia, LanChile and Qantas). *See* www.aa.com *and* FFP (frequent flyer programme).

AAFRA   Association of African Airlines. *See*   www.yohannes.com/Africa/AFRAA.htm

AAIB   Air Accident Investigation Branch (of the British Civil Aviation Authority). *See* www.aaib.detr.gov.uk

AAL   Above aerodrome level.

AALA   Adventure Activity Licensing Authority in the UK. Inspects UK activity centres and other activity providers on behalf of the UK Government's Department for Education and Skills (DfES). *See* www.aala.org

AAMS   All-American Marine Slip.

AAPA   Association of Asia Pacific Airlines.

AAQUARIUS   Was a Sabre CRS subsystem. *See* Sabre.

AAR¹   Aircraft accident report (aircraft accident record in some countries).

AAR²   Association of American Railroads. *See* www.aar.org

AASA   Airline Association of Southern Africa.

AASR   Airport and airways surveillance radar.

AATTA¹   Arab Association of Tourist and Travel Agents.

AATTA²   African-American Travel and Tourism Association.

AAWG   AIRPROX Analysis Working Group. (AIRPROX is the ICAO term for air proximity which has now replaced the term 'airmiss'.)

AB   Literally able-bodied. Usually applied in term 'able (bodied) seaman', indicative of a qualified seaman with at least 3 years' experience at sea. After 9 months' experience, but without qualifications,

the title is only 'ordinary seaman'. The guidelines stated have been found to vary between cruise lines.

ABA¹   American Bus Association. *See* www.buses.org

ABA²   Air charter Brokers Association (in the UK).

ABA³   Australian Business Access Card. Obsolete; replaced in July 2000 with Short Business Electronic Travel Authority. *See* ETAS.

ABAC   Association of British Aviation Consultants is a group of professional consultants in this sphere who are neither agents nor brokers. *See* www.baac.org.uk

Abacas   Was Mycrom Computers Limited's British travel agents' computerized data accounting and ticketing system. *See* Andromeda.

Abacus   GDS serving the Far East, based in Singapore. Although stated in some reference works as being associated with Worldspan, switched to Sabre.

abaft   At the back end or stern of a ship.

abandonment   Originally a maritime insurance term but now applied generally to aircraft, ships or coaches. Perhaps because of detention abroad or partial damage, an owner may be allowed, under the terms of an insurance, to declare that there has been a constructive loss and therefore claim in full.

The same term is used in the USA when an airline no longer wishes to operate on a route for which a licence has been granted.

ABAV   Asociacao Brasileira de Agencias de Viagens. *See* www.abav.com.br

abbonement   European rail ticket allowing unlimited travel within a specified area.

ABC¹   The letters were the titles of famous British airline, shipping and rail guides which have now become part of the worldwide OAG series.

ABC²   Advance Booking Charter – obsolete term. *See* Advance Booking Charter for details.

ABCOC   The Advance Booking Charter Operator's Council in the UK (obsolete).

abeam   At an angle of 90° to the long access of a ship or aircraft. The term is commonly used to mean an angle of 90° to the direction of travel, which because of cross winds etc., may be slightly different. Loosely speaking, a location opposite the mid-part of a plane or ship is abeam, while the term 'abaft the beam' means any area behind this.

able-bodied passenger   Person designated as such by airline check-in staff, who is allowed to sit in seats adjacent to an emergency exit on an aircraft.

able-bodied seaman   *See* AB.

ABn   Aerodrome beacon.

aboard   On or in a form of transportation.

abort   To abandon an aircraft landing or take-off because of a problem.

above board   At sea, passenger accommodation above the waterline, suggests US web site www.hometravelagency.com But throughout the English-speaking world, the wording indicates legitimacy and the meaning attributed is not used in the UK.

above the line promotional media   Media paying commission to advertising agencies, such as newspapers, magazines, radio, poster hoardings and television. *See* promotional media.

ABP¹   Able-bodied passenger; a person designated as such by airline check-in staff, who is allowed to sit in seats adjacent to an emergency exit on an aircraft.

ABP²   Associated British Ports. *See* www.abports.co.uk

ABPCO   Association of British Professional Conference Organizers. *See* www.abpco.org

ABS   American Bureau of Shipping. The US organization through which ships are certified with respect to international maritime *and* safety regulations. *See* IMO *and* SOLAS.

absence flag   A small, blue, square-shaped flag which shows that a boat's owner is not on board. On larger vessels, a pennant may show that the captain is absent.

absorption   When an air carrier's revenue for its part of a joint fare is less than its own local fare for the same market.

ABT   The Association of Business Travellers (in the USA). *See* www.abt-travel.com

ABTA   The Association of British Travel Agents was founded in 1950 to establish an organization fully representative of travel agents and tour operators in the UK; it aims to promote and develop the general interests of all members. Codes of Conduct have been established between members themselves, members and the general public and members and travel principals. A controversial objective, almost impossible to implement in view of the UK Competition Act, is to 'discourage unfair competition, without interfering in any way with initiative and enterprise based on fair trading'. ABTA is ruled by an 18-member Board elected by the members, which, in turn, elects a president. As well as being the public face of the Association, the president chairs the Board.

There are 11 ABTA travel agent regions: Eastern, Greater London, Midland, North Eastern, North Western, Northern Ireland, Scotland, Southern, South Wales, South Western and Yorkshire and North Midlands, each of which has a regional committee and officers. Smaller agent members with a turnover below £10 million also elect members to an 11-person Council of the Regions. The Regional Councillor automatically becomes the Regional Chairman. The regional committees have few general powers and merely organize some activities and regional meetings, discussing national matters and recommending what they believe ought to be done about them. Propositions passed by regional meetings are not binding upon the Council of the Regions or the Board and have no real authority other than indicating a viewpoint. For more information *see* www.abt-travel.com

ABTA Accounts Rules   Members must submit accounts within 6 months of the end of their financial year.

ABTA Appeal Board   Under the Association's Articles, an independent Appeal Board exists to review decisions of the Association's Councils.

ABTA Arbitration Scheme for the Travel Industry   Customers who have complaints against ABTA tour operators and travel agents may use an independent arbitration scheme negotiated with the Chartered Institute of Arbitrators in the UK.

ABTA Conciliation Service   This free service ended in spring 1991.

ABTACHECK   Name of service enabling ABTA members to check the validity of credit cards, particularly when the cardholder is not present, identifying 90% of attempted fraudulent transactions. *See* www.abtacheck.com

ABTA Membership Requirements   All the premises and general requirements for ABTA membership have now disappeared. Any person who has at least 2 years' practical experience can become an ABTA member running a travel agency business from any premises. Only 18 months of such experience is necessary if ABTAC Level 1 and some other training has been completed and this comes down to 1 year's experience for those who have passed ABTAC Level 2 general section. A sound financial background is necessary and applicants must not have been bankrupt or run a business that failed to meet its liabilities. Parallel requirements exist for tour operators. ABTA offers consumer protection against financial loss when effecting travel arrangements through members. All member agents and operators are required to provide a bond, guarantee or some other security for the protection of the Association's funds, when fulfilling this consumer guarantee. *See* bond *and* BRF (Bond Replacement Fund).

ABTA NTB   Association of British Travel Agents National Training Board, established in July 1982. Became Travel Training Company in 1993; now known as TTC Training. Partial successor to ATTITB, using title Government Approved because the Association's scheme satisfied the government's requirements. Became a wholly owned subsidiary of ABTA in 1993. In 1999 agreed a partnership with City and Guilds of London Institute to be the awarding body for the travel courses offered. Was sold by ABTA in 2002 to NTP Group. *See* City and Guilds of London Institute. *Also see* ABTA-TTC Training; Modern Apprenticeship, *also see* www.ttctraining.co.uk *and* NVQ.

ABTA Stabiliser   *See* Stabiliser.

ABTA Tour Operator Bonding   *See* bond.

ABTA Travel Agents' Fund   Association agent members can be required to contribute up to half their annual subscription in any one year as a contribution to the Fund. Its primary purpose is to indemnify, wholly or in part, members of the travelling public against losses sustained by reason of the default or financial failure of any member who is a travel agent. The fund may also be used, at the discretion of a committee of Travel Agents' Council, to indemnify tour operators who have sustained losses.

ABTAC   ABTA Travel Agents Certificate. A national examination at two levels covering much of the underpinning knowledge expected by the Association of a travel clerk working in a leisure-based UK travel agency, after 1 year's experience (Level 1) or 2 years' experience (Level 2). But with the exception of scheduled air reservations, fares and ticketing, which are covered in NVQ (National Vocational Qualification) air units at two levels. The syllabus is carefully matched to relevant leisure travel NVQ units. An ABTAC pass at merit or distinction level exempts a candidate from Unit 1 of the Level 2 or 3 (as appropriate) of the Travel Services NVQ. But whereas these may be tested 'on the job' with copious evidential proof required, ABTAC is tested by a formal written examination. There is also a separate series of examinations at two levels covering business travel, operated by the Guild of Business Travel Agents (GBTA) in conjunction with City and Guilds of London Institute (C&GLI). For more information *see* City and Guilds of London Institute entry *also* www.city-and-guilds.co.uk; ABTA-TTC Training entry *also* www.ttctraining.co.uk; MA (Modern Apprenticeship) *and* NVQ.

ABTA-TTC Training   UK travel training organization formerly an ABTA subsidiary, sold to NTP Group in 2002. *See* TTC Training www.ttctraining.co.uk for courses and facilities offered.

ABTB   Association of Bank Travel Bureaux in the USA.

ABTECH   Was the ABTA Technology Information Service providing members with impartial advice. The ABTA service continues but ended under this name in 1999, becoming a commercial organization.

ABTEL 210   Was the name of the ABTA Prestel database, managed on behalf of the trade body by Datasolve, which ended in 1984.

ABTOC   Association of British Travel Agents Tour Operators Certificate. The syllabus, at two levels, covers the underpinning knowledge to be expected of a competent member of staff of a tour operator after 1 year's experience (Level 1) or 2 years' experience (Level 2). The awarding body is City and Guilds of London Institute; for more information *see* www.city-and-guilds.co.uk

ABTOF Association of British Tour Operators to France. A UK organization of specialist operators formed in 1992. *See* www.holidayfrance.org.uk

ABTOT Association of Bonded Travel Organisers Trust; a UK trust fund which provides bonds as required by ATOL holders and others. *See* www.abtot.com

abyssalbenthic zone That part of the ocean that is deeper than 1000 m. The arechibenthic zone relates to that part between 200 and 1000 m deep.

AC^1 Abbreviation for air conditioning, particularly used when describing accommodation or car rental. *See* air conditioning.

AC^2 (or **A/C**) Aircraft.

ACA Air Cargo Annual.

ACAC Arab Civil Aviation Council (or Commission).

ACAP Aviation Consumer Action Project. In the USA, a consumer pressure group in the field of air travel. *See* www.acap1971.org

ACARS Aircraft Addressing and Reporting System.

ACAS^1 ICAO meaning is Airborne Collision Avoidance System.

ACAS^2 Worldchoice UK travel agency consortium system for automatic collection and onward payment of money due from member agents to travel principals. Consortium members can see their accounts with individual providers of travel services on an NTL viewdata system, providing the opportunity to raise queries before amounts owing are direct debited from agent's bank accounts. *See* agents' payment systems.

ACC^1 As a shipping term, means accepted or acceptance.

ACC^2 In the cruising field, in North America, means Accredited Cruise Counsellor, a travel agency employee certified by the CLIA.

ACC^3 Airport Consultative Committee – an official IATA term. Powers vary between countries. Usually an advisory body representing the interests of users and parties affected by the airport's operations such as local authorities but in some countries may have statutory powers. Most UK airports are obliged under the Civil Aviation Act to run such a committee. New committee guidelines were issued by the UK Department of Transport in the wake of the *Future of Aviation* White Paper in December 2003. These Guidelines suggest Committees should publicise their work more widely and in anticipation of this last year launched a new web site. This provides detailed information not only about the new Guidelines but also on current airport issues at national and EU level. The Liaison Group of the UK ACCs was formed in 1980; it comprises the officers of the committees at the 22 largest UK airports. *See* www.ukaccs.info

ACC^4 As an air travel term, may mean Area Control Centre.

ACCED-I Association of Collegiate Conference and Events Directors – International (in the US). *See* www.acced-i.org

access code An alpha-numeric string which is recognized by a computer and allows entry. The most sophisticated codes are bilateral, requiring responses programmed into each computer.

access time The time it takes for a computer terminal to connect to a distant system or to retrieve information, once an operator has issued an instruction calling for that data. In the travel industry, there may be several interrelated elements of access time, including that taken to establish communication with a distant computer through the Internet, a computerized reservation system (CRS) type of interfacing device, through direct, permanently leased telephone lines or through ordinary dial-up telephone lines and a viewdata gateway. Also *see* ADSL.

accessibility *See* transport modelling.

accommodation *See* accommodation types.

accommodation bill Although it could be a list of the charges for a hotel stay, depending on the context, it is more likely to be a bill of exchange which a third party has signed, endorsing it that they accept responsibility if the designated payee does not meet the agreed payment.

accommodation categorization systems
See accommodation grading systems.

accommodation centre A place where accommodation can be booked, similar to a tourist information centre. Not in common use is the ISO (International Standards Organization) 1989 Interprofessional Vocabulary of Tourism and Leisure definition, 'A collective lodging open during holiday periods for long or short stays', derived from the French *foyer d'accueil.*

accommodation classification *See* accommodation grading systems.

accommodation grading systems Schemes, either official or commercial, which identify the quality of accommodation according to predetermined standards, so that visitors may know what to expect. The 2003 CEN/European Standard official definition designates: 'System providing an assessment of the quality standards and provision of facilities and/or services of tourist accommodation typically within five categories, often indicated by one to five symbols.' The assessment system can be organized by organizations such as international, national or regional authorities, tourist boards, trade associations, guide publishers, tour operators or owners of accommodation themselves.

Systems tend to be a mixture of judgement of three facets: statements of fact as to the nature of the services and buildings available; quantitative statements of the numbers and sizes of each of these items and sometimes the prices to be charged; qualitative judgements, by which means alone the world's best hotels stand out from their counterparts. In some countries operating official classification and grading systems, registration is not compulsory, so that a non-graded hotel is not necessarily the worst.

Burkart and Medlik in their book *Tourism* defined the terms, suggesting that categorization is the separation of accommodation into different types such as hotels, motels, guest houses and pensions. Classification is the separation of accommodation according to physical features, such as the presence or otherwise of bathrooms, showers and toilets. It is felt that 'grading' ought to be a term reserved for verifiable objective features of service, such as the availability of a night porter and meals, as distinct from subjective features, such as cuisine and atmosphere which call for a qualitative assessment. Although the definition of these terms is a laudable objective, unfortunately all the words are taken to have a similar meaning in general worldwide travel industry usage. Apart from official country grading systems, the *Michelin Guide* is well known in Europe. In the UK, the AA and RAC guides are regarded by travellers as the significant systems.

In March 2004, the Britain Review Group achieved in-principle agreement by the five assessing bodies on common standards for ratings in Britain. The Group is chaired by Alan Britten and is made up of the three national tourist boards for Britain – VisitBritain, VisitScotland and the Wales Tourist Board – as well as the AA and RAC, with its recommendations endorsed by the British Hospitality Association, Regional Development Agencies and Tourist Boards, the Local Government Association and other government bodies. Self-catering properties will be assessed under the new standards from 2005, while serviced accommodation (hotels, guest houses and B & Bs) assessments begin in 2006. At present, nearly half of all accommodation operators in England participate in either the VisitBritain, RAC or AA quality assessment schemes, and a majority of local authorities have already adopted a policy of promoting quality-assessed accommodation. The majority of the major hotel groups have also committed to joining the common standards scheme, which will mean that in excess of 80% of the group hotels will be participating. *For latest details and assessment criteria see* www.VisitBritain.com; travel industry access is via www.tourismtrade.org.uk

accommodation ladder The gangway set up for people to board or disembark from a ship, which usually has handrails as well as 'ladder' type steps. Since these are difficult (if not impossible) to negotiate for elderly or infirm passengers, their usage has declined. *See* Jacob's ladder.

accommodation layout Plan of accommodation. In hotels etc., in most countries, prominent exhibition of such plans is compulsory, showing exit routes in case of fire or other emergency.

accommodation rating *See* accommodation grading systems *and* hotels, unbiased opinions of.

accommodation spaces The spaces accessible by passengers on a vessel such as a cruise ship, liner or ferry. SOLAS regulations comprehensively list such areas covering ballrooms, cabins, cinemas, corridors, games rooms, shops and theatres.

accommodation types The 2003 CEN/European Standard official definition designates accommodation as 'The provision of at least sleeping and sanitary facilities'. However, this sets a minimum standard; accommodation may not always provide sanitary facilities; moreover, a 'day room' or any meeting room in a hotel may commonly be referred to as accommodation, although no sleeping facilities are provided. *See* all suite hotel, aparthotel, auberge, boarding house, boutique hotel, budget hotel, bungalow, cabin, camper, campsite, canal barge, caravan, caravanette holiday home, caravan park, casa de huéspedes, casita, chalet, chalet hotel, farm, folding caravan, guest house, health farm, health resort, holiday camps, holiday caravan, holiday centre, holiday club, hotel, inn, lifestyle hotel, minshuku, mobile home, motel, motorhome, pension, residence², ryokan, rural house, spa hotel, static caravan, touring camp, touring caravan, touring park, trailer tent, villa for holidays, YHA.

accommodation, unbiased opinions of *See* hotels, unbiased opinions of.

accommodations In North America, the use of the plural word can mean lodgings of any type, even tents, while in Britain, accommodation can mean a room or rooms available for rental by members of the public.

accompanied car, baggage or motorcycle etc. Where the item concerned is meant to travel on the same transport service as the passenger. In respect of air travel, checked baggage is that part of a passenger's accompanied baggage which is handed to the carrier for transport and collection at the destination airport. Unchecked baggage is referred to as hand luggage or baggage.

accompanying (companion, partner, person or spouse) A non-delegate; at conferences, conventions and events, there is often a programme for non-delegates while the formal sessions are in progress.

account, travel *See* travel account.

accountable documents Providers of travel services issue blank tickets and other documents for use by themselves or their agents. Because, upon completion, they will be valid for travel or event entry, they are numbered, and must be issued in sequence and accounted for. Travel agents' sales returns to IATA, ARC or transport companies must return voided tickets. Lost tickets may be charged at average value.

accounting systems for travel agents *See* Travel agents' computerized accounting and ticketing systems in the UK.

accreditation A formal appointment by a transportation principal or group of principals to sell their services; the associated conditions are covered in an agency agreement. Only appointed agents receive commission on sales.

accredited agent An agent who has received an appointment by a transportation principal or group of principals to sell their services. IATA publishes the names of their accredited (appointed) agents in the 'Agency List'. Thus, the official IATA definition is 'A Passenger Sales Agent whose name is on the Agency List'. The Head Office, Branch Office, and Satellite Ticket Printer locations appearing on the Agency List are known as 'approved locations', as distinct from the organization itself which may own many locations. (Note that cargo and freight handling are outside the scope of this dictionary; there is a parallel set of definitions in this field.)

Accredited Travel Professional UK qualification under development by ABTA (Association of British Travel Agents), ITT (Institute of Travel and Tourism) and People 1st (The Sector Skills Council for the hospitality, leisure, travel and tourism industry). A pilot scheme is currently being run in London. Three levels are: Bronze, for those who have attained an NVQ Level 2 or equivalent qualification, such as ABTAC Level 1 together with 2 years' experience; Silver, for those who have attained an NVQ Level 3, or equivalent qualification, such as ABTAC Level 2 together with 4 years' experience; and Gold, for those who have attained an NVQ level 3 or 4, or equivalent qualification, together with 7 years' experience. It is intended that ATP should not be a new qualification, but a recognition of the qualifications and experience already possessed, providing it is kept up to date by an ATP programme of CPD (continuous professional development).

acculturation The process by which different cultures absorb customs. Despite widespread tourism, some cultural aspects have proved remarkably resistant to change. The phenomenon of westernization is, perhaps, the most significant example. The WTO definition of acculturation is: 'Process of interaction between two societies or groups that results in some degree of cultural change. While it is recognised that the tourist may change slightly because of interaction with the residents of a destination area, the area residents usually experience greater pressure to adopt the ways of the tourists' [Source: World Tourism Organization and Secretariat of State for Tourism of France (2001), *Thesaurus on Tourism and Leisure Activities*, p. 280]. The same phenomenon is described in some tourism textbooks as adaptation, a term applicable to the behaviour of people in general when they have been subjected to a new or changed environment. Thus terms host or tourist adaptation specify which group is changing as a result of the culture of the other. Anthropological studies sometimes use the word 'passing' when referring to the absorption of tourist's values and culture by an indigenous population. *See* tourism area life cycle. *See also* demonstration effect.

ACE Association for Conferences and Events; an international coordinating body for the meetings industry with over 1000 members in more than 50 countries. Members are both suppliers to and organizers and users of conference, exhibition and travel incentive facilities. Publishes the *ACE Yearbook* – a Who's Who of the Meetings and Events industry. *See* ACE web site for more information www.martex.co.uk/ace

ACET Asociación Chilena de Empresas de Turismo. *See* www.achet.cl

ACEx Aircraft Exchange (IATA).

Acey deucy Slang at sea for backgammon.

ACH US Airlines Clearing House Incorporated. *See also* IATA Clearing House.

achieved average room sales *See* room rates.

ACI[1] Airports Council International is the international trade body for airports; it provides statistics on annual throughput of cargo and passengers for over 600 airports worldwide. *See* www.airports.org

ACI[2] Assist Card International, based in Florida USA.

ACLS Automatic carrier landing system.

ACM Agency Credit Memo, a BSP document.

ACN Aircraft classification number.

ACOND International hotel code for room with air conditioning.

ACOS Autofile Coach Operators was a British coach operators' reservation and accounting system, introduced in 1983 by Autofile Software Limited.

acoustic coupler This small device has two rubber collars matching a telephone. The coupler changes sound into digital signals recognizable by a computer. Although valuable for mobile terminals, acoustic couplers have intrinsic disadvantages and, if at all possible, laptops should be connected direct to telephone lines, bypassing the ordinary speech instrument. *See also* adaptor.

acoustic sounding Used at sea to indicate depth of seabed, by using sound waves, which travel in water five times faster than in the air, 4900 ft per s. Called an echo sounder because it records the 'echo' from the seabed.

ACP Airline control protocol; early software in the 1970s used by airline reservation systems.

ACP 80 The world's most advanced cargo inventory control and customs' facilities system operated by British Customs at London's Heathrow and Gatwick airports and at Manchester airport.

acquirer *See* merchant acquirer.

ACR Aircraft control radar.

ACRA American Car Rental Association.

ACRISS Association of Car Rental Information System Standards. European group set up in June 1989 to facilitate the use of computerized reservation systems. Initial objectives to standardize car rental vouchers, CRS screen formats and codes. *See* www.acriss.org

ACRS Accelerated Cost Recovery System.

ACSSP Air Carrier Standard Security Programme.

act of god *See force majeure.*

ACT¹ Actual time of arrival (whereas ETA is estimated time of arrival).

ACT² Association of Couriers in Tourism.

ACTA¹ Association of Canadian Travel Agents. *See* www.acta.net

ACTA² Alliance of Canadian Travel Associations, the members of which are Canadian travel associations throughout Canada. *See* www.edmc.net/butte/acta.html

ACTA³ Association of Cyprus Travel Agents. *See* www.pio.gov.cy

ACTE Association of Corporate Travel Executives. ACTE, covering Africa, the Asia Pacific region, Canada, Europe, the Middle East and the USA, has around 2500 members. In February 2005 announced merger with the Institute of Travel Managers in Industry and Commerce in the UK and Ireland. As well as UK representation on the ACTE Board, a UK Regional Advisory Council has been formed. *See* www.acte.org *Also see list of 70 other business travel related entries which follows* corporate travel contracts, *some of which lead to further entries.*

Active Travel Group A Yorkshire UK-based consortium of travel agents, member of Worldchoice.

activities host American terminology for Entertainment Organizer, known as an animateur in Europe. The World Tourism Organization and Secretariat of State for Tourism of France (2001), *Thesaurus on Tourism and Leisure Activities* states 'employee of a hotel, resort or cruise ship who arranges, oversees and sometimes encourages guests or passengers to take part in optional entertainment activities'. But the WTO is wrong to suggest that the English word 'animator' is equivalent − this is a cartoon artist!

activity holiday *See* special interest holidays.

ACTO¹ Association of Camping Touring Operators Ltd in the UK.

ACTO² Association of Caribbean Tour Operators in the USA.

ACTOA Airline Charter Tour Operators in the USA.

actual demand for tourism The distinction has been made in some textbooks between the number of people actually travelling and the potential demand. There are no generally accepted definitions so that usage of the wording 'actual demand for tourism' may sometimes be taken to mean the total potential demand. In this dictionary, the opinion preferred is that of Cooper *et al.* in *Tourism Principles and Practice* (2nd edn) that 'actual demand' should always mean the actual number of tourists travelling.

actual flying time Duration of an air journey regardless of time zone differences. Travel literature now commonly only refers to 'flight durations'. Elapsed Flying Time, terminology with the same meaning, is now obsolescent.

ACV Air cushion vehicle, commonly known as a hovercraft. ACV forms of various types are the certificates of insurance cover offered by Lloyd's on hovercraft.

AD Airworthiness Directive.

ad hoc One-off or individually arranged; for example, an ad hoc charter of an aircraft, ship, train or coach is a single arrangement, contrasting with a series charter. *See* charter.

Ad valorem Literally translated from the Latin, 'in proportion to the value'. Customs duties on items imported by travellers in excess of the duty-free allowances are often of this type while airport departure charges and taxes are more usually fixed amounts.

AD75 75% Agent's Discount. IATA resolution 880 allows each appointed IATA agency to be issued with up to two 75% rebated tickets per calendar year by each IATA airline. Normally only full-time employees involved directly in the promotion and sale of travel facilities who have been working for the IATA agency for 12 months continuously are eligible. Lists of staff eligible for reduced-rate transport are meant to be maintained in each country. Similarly, in the USA, ARC and IATAN are meant to keep lists based on information submitted by appointed agents. In the USA, an 'agent' frequently refers to a person, so that an agent eligibility list lists 'people' entitled to facilities rather than businesses.

ADA room Accommodation (or other types of room) which meets the specifications of the US Americans with Disabilities legislation.

ADAP The Airport Development Aid Program is organized by the US FAA to help communities develop their airports by giving grants of up to 50% of the cost of land acquisition and construction and up to two-thirds of the cost of airport planning.

adaptation *See* acculturation.

adaptor A connector for travellers, enabling their equipment (shavers, hairdryers and laptop computers) to be connected to telephone or electric sockets in countries where systems vary from their own. The wide range of types of sockets makes it crucial for travellers to take appropriate adaptors with them on a foreign journey, if equipment use is essential.

ADAVI Asociación de Agencias de Viajes Dominicanas.

ADC^1 Air data computer.

ADC^2 IATA abbreviation for additional collection, where, due to rerouting, upgrading or other itinerary alterations of the traveller's choice, a higher fare is due.

add-on US term for optional items that can be bought with a tour or other travel arrangements. For example, it may be as little as travel insurance or can be the rail or air fare to get to the start point of the main arrangement, such as a cruise.

add-on fare Add-on fares are used to construct through international fares to and from points not otherwise published in airline tariff manuals. Also, an amount to be added to a fare as signified by the preceding descriptive word, for example, domestic add-on. When constructed, such fares are then treated for all normal purposes in the same way as published fares, with a maximum permitted mileage being derived by the use of a mileage add-on for the domestic sector, added to the international mileage. Where the fares' rules in the tariffs for a particular journey allow for constructing mileages to or from a point, then the lowest combination principle applies.

ADF Automatic direction finding equipment.

ADI Attitude/direction indicator.

ADIZ Air defence identification zone.

adjacent rooms (or seats) *See* adjoining rooms, next entry.

adjoining rooms (or seats) Hotel rooms which are situated next to each other, typically requested by a family with young children with whom they do not wish to share. In modern hotels, such rooms are seldom inter-communicating. Adjoining seats are seats next to each other, on a mode of transport or at an event. By definition, rooms on opposite sides of a corridor, or seats either side of an aisle, are *NOT* adjoining.

ADM Agency Debit Memo, a BSP document.

ADME Association of Destination Management Executives in the USA. Qualification is DCMP (Destination Management Certified Professional). *See* www.adme.org

admeasurement The official size of a ship.

Administrative Office Official IATA definition is an office which is not an Approved Location, but which is entered in the Agency List for administrative purposes. Term in general travel industry use, for example, to indicate the head office of an ABTA member not actually functioning as a travel agency or tour operating centre.

Admiral of the Open Sea Award In America, a small silver statue of Christopher Columbus is presented annually to someone who is considered to have given outstanding service to the shipping industry. Recipients are given (and may use) the title Admiral of the Open Sea.

Admiral's Club Was the name of UK Sealink incentive scheme for regular cross-channel travellers.

Admirals Club Name of American Airlines Frequent Flyers' Club. *See* airline clubs and FFP (frequent flyer programme).

Admiralty Measured Mile Defined in *The Marine Encyclopaedic Dictionary* by Eric Sullivan (1988 Lloyd's of London) as 6080 ft or 1853.184 m compared to the nautical mile of 6076.1 ft. *See* nautical mile.

ADNS ARINC Data Network Services. *See* ARINC.

ADO[1] Agent's Debit Order. A British Airways form which replaced AXOs in 1980, itself becoming obsolete upon the introduction of BSP in autumn 1984.

ADO[2] Agency Distribution Office of IATA. *See* Agency Programme Liaison Group.

adoption rate Percentage of travellers or travel bookers in a corporate entity following an agreed corporate travel policy or taking up use of a self-booking tool. Note the misnomer that the term uses the word 'rate', implying that it refers to speed of take-up, whereas it is a proportion. For example, a survey of NBTA members found that at the end 2003, over 90% of US companies with managed travel programmes booked individual travel online. In respect of travel policy, 'compliance' is often used. Term may also apply to travel situations in a general sense of the meaning. *A list of 70 other business travel related entries follows* corporate travel contracts, *some of which lead to further entries.*

ADP Automatic Data Processing. In theory the term applies to any processing undertaken by automated machinery, but in practice, this term is used to describe work done by punched card and similar equipment, so as to contrast with EDP (Electronic Data Processing) (general technical terms).

ADR Advisory route (aviation term).

ADRM Airport Development Reference Manual.

ADS[1] Agency Data Systems, the US market leader. *See* Sabre for more information.

ADS[2] Automatic dependent surveillance (aviation term).

ADS-B ADS broadcast.

ADSL An Asynchronous Digital Subscriber Line. Normal copper telephone wires can be transformed into high-speed digital lines, which are particularly valuable to the needs of the travel industry.

ADT[1] Alaska Daylight Time *or* Atlantic Daylight Time.

ADT[2] Approved departure time (air travel).

ADTF The Agency Distribution Task Force of IATA was set up at the beginning of 1984 by the IATA Traffic Committee to review the agency distribution system for air travel worldwide.

adult fare In respect of international scheduled air transport, adult fares are charged upon passengers reaching their 12th birthday, children's fares being charged from 2 to 12 and infant's fares under 2. Reductions are often given to students and other young persons. Rates within countries and for other modes of transport vary widely; for example, for domestic rail journeys in the UK, under 5 travel free while children aged 5 to 15 travel at half fares. For international rail journeys from the UK, from 4 to 11 inclusive travel at half fare, with youth fares available up to 25.

adv Advanced (Boeing aircraft nomenclature).

Advance Booking Charter Any charter where governmental or other rules require a minimum advance booking period, in order to protect scheduled carriers. Prior to April 1973, many people travelled between Britain and America or Canada on Affinity Group charters. Any organization, provided it was not formed specifically in order to arrange travel, could become involved in the provision of charter flights for members.

Charter flights in general were given a bad name because of many disreputable incidents and, from 1973, ABCs were sanctioned by the CAA in the UK and the CAB in the USA. During the following years, relaxation of the regulations resulted in a complete range of alternative low transatlantic fares and there is now little or no difference between ABC rates and similar scheduled airlines' rates offered on APEX or other low fares.

Advance Passenger Information System From October 2003, the US Government has required comprehensive data in advance of arrival in the US for air travellers arriving from abroad. PNR (Passenger Name Record) details must be sent soon after a flight's departure. Although much of this information is provided by machine readable passports, other information such as home residence and address while in the USA is also required. From 26 October 2004, travellers from 21 countries to which the visa waiver programme applies are required to have machine readable passports and have their fingerprints and photos taken on entry to the US. *See also* CAPPS.

Advance Purchase Excursion Fare Originally, a low scheduled air fare for travel in the discount or lowest class of cabin. Passengers must book and purchase tickets a minimum period before travel, varying from some months to several days. Now, APEX type fares are offered by many transport operators.

advance timetable A transport services timetable for a future season, prepared for planning convenience of both passengers and the travel industry, often in summary form, and always likely to change when the definitive timetable is published for the period concerned.

Advanced Passenger Train *See* APT.

Advantage Travel Centres (in the UK) Brand name under which NAITA (National Association of Independent Travel Agents) operates in the UK. *See* NAITA www.advantage4travel.com

adventure Followed by words such as cruise, holiday or tourism, means trips with an element of excitement, discovery, discomfort and risk. The term is not specific, so that arrangements could be for backpacking through disease-ridden snake-infested equatorial forests or carefully guided visits causing the least possible disturbance to natural habitats.

Adventure Activity Licensing Authority *See* AALA *and* www.aala.org

adventure tourism Recreational travel which is hazardous, varying from extremely dangerous activities to involvement in thrilling but relatively safe pursuits. The World Tourism Organization and Secretariat of State for Tourism of France (2001), *Thesaurus on Tourism and Leisure Activities* is felt to be wrong in suggesting that the term only applies to 'soft' adventure activities such as rafting, hot-air ballooning, trekking, four-wheel driving, helicopter riding and mountain climbing.

Adventure Travel Society (USA) *See* www.adventuretravel.com

advertised tour Originally this was an IT (inclusive tour) meeting airline requirements, so that the operator could produce a package using ITX fares which were lower than the normal rates. In Europe, this use is now obsolescent and the term usually only means a travel arrangement described in a brochure. In the USA, however, IT numbers are still assigned to approved tours by a few airlines that still remunerate agents by commission.

advertising media *See* promotional media.

AE Via Atlantic and Eastern Hemisphere. *See* routing.

AEA Association of European Airlines. *See* www.aea.be

AEADVE Asociación Empresarial Agencias de Viajes Españolas, the Spanish Association of Travel Agents.

AECMA Association Européen des Constructeurs de Matériel Aerospatial.

AEF Aviation Environment Federation. *See* www.aef.org.uk

AEO Association of Exhibition Organisers in the UK. *See* www.aeo.org

AERO Air Education and Recreation Organisation in the UK, aims to provide a general information and advisory service in its sphere by linking education and industry. *See* www.pilotweb.co.uk

aerodrome *See* airport; an aerodrome in the UK is often a small airport for light aircraft.

Aerodrome Owners Association The trade body of UK aerodromes, which represents their interests.

aerofoil *See* airframe.

Aeronautical Radio Inc *See* ARINC.

aeronautics The study of the engineering and science of flight, derived from the word aeronaut, the original, now obsolete, name for the first pilots and balloonists.

aeroplane Now airplane. *See* aircraft.

AETA Used to be the Association of European Travel Agents. *See* www.aeta.co.uk

AETF Airline Economic Task Force (of IATA).

AETR European Agreement Concerning the Work of Crews of Vehicles engaged in Road Transport. The Agreement is in respect of the hours which commercial vehicle drivers are allowed to drive, and applies to international journeys involving travel through or to Austria, Czechoslovakia, Norway, Commonwealth of Independent States (formerly USSR), Sweden and the states which were formerly Yugoslavia.

AEVT Asociación Ecuatoriana de Viajes y Turismo. *See* www.astanet.com

AEW Airborne early warning.

AF[1] Via Africa. *See* routing.

AF[2] Airframe.

AFA Association of Flight Attendants in the USA. *See* www.afanet.org

AFCAC African Civil Aviation Commission. The objectives of the Commission are to promote coordination, better utilization, and orderly development of African air transport. Membership is open to African states, members of the Economic Commission of Africa and the Organization of African Unity. *See* www.afcac-cafac.org

AFCS Automatic flight control system.

Affinity Charter Prior to April 1973, many people travelled across the Atlantic between America or Canada and Britain by virtue of their membership of a club, company, trade body, religious or similar organization. So long as it was formed for a purpose other than merely to circumvent the law as it then was, and arrange cheap travel, the group was acceptable both by the British CAA and the American CAB.

Widespread abuse finally led to international agreements permitting Advance Booking Charters (*see* separate entry), on which any individual could make reservations. Gradual relaxation of the rules allowed the introduction of other forms of cheap transatlantic air travel, so that affinity charters now only operate on a genuine basis and are no longer a major part of the transatlantic travel market.

Affinity Group *See* Affinity Charter. The term now applies to any group of people with interests in common who get together for the purposes of travel.

Affinity Group Fares Fares restricted to *bona fide* groups of members of a corporation, club or legal entity. Individuals must have membership for at least 6 months before the date on which group is to fly. Groups can only be formed by solicitation limited to personal letters, circulars or telephone calls addressed to members of the group travel organization. Public soliciting is prohibited. Such groups must not be gathered directly or indirectly by travel agents or anyone else engaged in organizing or selling transportation services.

AFI Africa/Indian Ocean; an IATA region.

AFIS Aerodrome flight information system.

AFORR Association of Foreign Railway Representatives in the UK; now AIRC, Association of International Rail Companies.

Afos *See* car ferry CRSs in the UK.

AFRAA African Airlines Association.

AFRC Australian Family Reunion Club. *See* Reunion Clubs.

Africa Travel and Tourism Association For details of this UK-based organization *see* www.atta.co.uk

Africa Travel Association Formed to promote travel to and within Africa by official national tourism organizations together with travel service operators. *See* www.africa-ata.org

African Civil Aviation Commission *See* AFCAC.

AFS[1] Aerodrome fire service.

AFS[2] Aeronautical fixed service.

aft The rear of a vessel or aircraft.

AFTA[1] Association of Finnish Travel Agents. *See* www.astanet.com

AFTA[2] Australian Federation of Travel Agents. *See* www.afta.com.au

afterbody The back half of a ship or aircraft.

AFTN Aeronautical fixed telecommunication network.

AGAS Association of Guide Booking Agency Services in the UK.

age groups (for tourism data collection) The WTO recommends that travellers' statistics should be collected for the age ranges 0–14; 15–24; 25–44; 45–64; 65 years plus.

Agency Administrator Official IATA definition is the IATA official designated by the Director General of IATA from time to time as the holder of that office or his authorised representative. The person who manages agency affairs for IATA, often in partnership with agents, in a designated area.

agency agreement A contract between a travel agent and a principal, setting out the terms and conditions under which business is transacted on behalf of or with the principal. The IATA Passenger Sales Agency Agreement operates worldwide in various forms, except for the USA, under IATA Resolutions PAC1, PAC2 and PAC3 (22) 824. In EU and EAA countries it is PAC2 (22) 814b.

After 2 years of hard bargaining the Global Consultative Committee (GCC), which consists of eight airline and eight agency representatives, recommended a new contract because the existing agreement was thought to be too one-sided in favour of the airlines. But on Friday 28 June 2002 the new deal, which needed unanimous approval, was quashed by the airlines at the IATA Passenger Agency Conference in Miami and the meeting suspended. Agents worldwide were encouraged to call on their respective governments to review the antitrust immunity granted to IATA members to control the distribution system; initiate an urgent study into the development of an alternative to the present IATA accreditation system; establish an industry task force to immediately implement a global alternative to the IATA BSP system; actively support and participate in legal class actions against airlines; and suspend until further notice all dialogue and consultations within the IATA Agency Programme. At the time of writing nothing whatsoever has happened!

agency appointment *See* appointment.

Agency Board Official IATA definition is any of the three Agency Administration Boards established for the three traffic Conference Areas by the Passenger Agency Conference.

Agency Investigation Board *See* AIP[1].

Agency Investigation Panel *See* AIP[1].

Agency List Official IATA definition is the list more fully described in section D of the Passenger Sales Agency Administration Rules containing the names and addresses of approved agency locations and, where appropriate, the addresses of their administrative offices. In the USA, an equivalent list is published by the ARC and by IATAN.

Agency Management System In the USA, is a computer system which undertakes the full administration of an agency, as well as ticketing, while in Britain, the term is more usually applied to 'back office' administrative and accounting systems.

agency manager In general usage, the manager of a travel agency. But in the USA and some other countries, it is the person designated as such to gain or hold an airline appointment. Three years' retail agency experience and other requirements are laid down.

agency payment systems *See* agents' payment systems.

Agency Programme Official IATA definition is the various IATA Resolutions, rules and procedures adopted by airline members and approved by the regulatory authorities to maintain overall standards and industry practices for the sale of international air transportation by Approved Agents.

Agency Programme Joint Council (Liaison Group) Currently, IATA Resolution 814 has been implemented in all member states of the European Union and in 31 other countries, mainly in Europe and Africa. Under this Resolution, an APJC is set up to consider all aspects of the IATA Programme in the country concerned. Membership of the Councils is limited to 18 representatives, with agency representatives being not less than one-third nor more than one-half of the 18 members. In the UK, under IATA Resolution 808, an Agency Programme Liaison Group was set up in 1988, with nine airline and nine agency representatives. In 1990, following the adoption of IATA resolution 814 in the UK this became the Agency Programme Joint Council. This APJC now has overall control, the UK AIP having been wound down and its responsibilities having been taken over by the IATA Agency Distribution Office in London. It is this office which now makes initial decisions as to whether IATA accreditation standards have been met by applicants. Of the nine UK agency seats ABTA have the majority, together with representation from the Guild of Business Travel Agents and the Scottish Passenger Agents Association. The APLG concerns itself with policy matters. It began by establishing criteria to obtain and retain IATA passenger agency approval.

It is the Agency Distribution Office in the UK that administers applications for IATA approval and has a review programme to ensure that standards are maintained by existing approved agents, both in accordance with Resolution 814 and with APJC policies.

The APJC has established a points system for the assessment of staff qualifications and has laid down approved syllabuses at two levels. In the UK IATA agents must have at least two qualifying staff members who together achieve a minimum of 40 points. Successful completion of a Level 1 air fares and ticketing course gains 10 points, while Level 2 passes gain 20 points. Recent experience in an IATA agency can gain up to 40 points.

The APJC has also laid down financial criteria. UK agents are required to show a profit before tax and to have an excess of current assets over current liabilities, at the end of a trading period, otherwise a bond is required. Minimum fully-paid share capital levels start at £40,000 for agencies with £2 million or less of IATA sales, rising to £200,000 if sales are £10 million. Companies that have been trading for 3 or more years only need half these share capital levels.

Bonds, if required, vary from 16% of forecast or actual IATA turnover for an agency able to provide less than 3 years' audited accounts; 12% thereafter.

agency representative *See* rep.

Agency Services Manager (of IATA) IATA official designated by the Agency Administrator to head the Agency Services office in a country or area, who is responsible for agency accreditation.

agency tour A term sometimes used in the USA to describe a fam trip. *See* familiarization tour.

Agenda 21 *See* sustainable tourism.

Agenda for Research on Tourism by Integration of Statistics/Strategies for Transport *See* ARTIST.

agent *See* travel agent.

agent bypass In the USA, when travel providers deal directly with customers. In the UK this is known as booking direct.

agent eligibility list *See* AD75

agents' discount Travel agents gain a discount varying according to the form of transportation or other arrangement. 50% hotel offers are common, while coaches in the UK and buses in the USA often provide free travel to good agents. For details of the 75% reduction offered to IATA agents for international air travel *see* AD75.

agents' IATA Incentive Scheme Was terminated in the UK at the end of 1978. In autumn 1979, agents received 4% extra commission on all 1978 eligible sales which were in excess of 110% of 1977 sales. *See* commission.

agents' accounting and ticketing systems *See* travel agents' computerized accounting *and* ticketing systems in the UK.

agents' coupon Most transportation tickets have many coupons with the top copy servicing as an audit or accounting coupon. The agents' coupon of a ticket, also known as the issuing office copy, is the one an agent retains. Fraud is avoided because the other coupons are all carbon copies of the top one, unless agents resort to the practice of cardboarding, so called because a piece of cardboard or thick paper through which a carbon impression will not be created, is inserted between the coupons of an air ticket before it is written out. This enables one or more of the coupons to show different information. Provided the alternative data is entered through carbon paper of the same colour as the copy material with which the ticket coupons are impregnated, the falsification is impossible to detect unless all the coupons are compared. *See* air tickets.

agents' legal status *See* legal status of a travel agent.

agents' payment systems The way in which travel agents report sales of airline tickets and pay for them was the first to be automated. In the USA, the Interactive Agent Reporting (IAR) system and associated direct debit arrangements are described under the ARC entry while the UK Bank Settlement Plan is under BSP. Whereas in Britain the basic cycle is calendar monthly, with agents' payments being debited from their accounts on the 17th of the following month, in the USA, the basic cycle is weekly. In the UK, there is an ABTA members' scheme, 'Single Payments System' (SPS) operative for sales outside BSP; unfortunately, this has had limited success, even though package holidays account for over 50% of the sales of British agents. One of the main reasons for this is that the main tour operators in the UK all have their own direct debit systems such as Thomson's TABS, Airtours' SPACE and Kuoni's KAB. Worldchoice consortium agents use their own member's direct debit system ACAS. *See* direct debit systems.

However, despite these difficulties, SPS is still developing towards becoming the standard UK agency payment system. There is no charge to travel agents but a small charge to tour operators, less than it would cost them to handle the transaction in-house. Part of the costs of running a system such as SPS are covered by the interest earned on the money in transit between agents and operators.

How does SPS work? Operators produce weekly listings of deposits and amounts due on late bookings, together with money due for departures during the next 42 days. This information is available for viewing by agents on NTL's viewdata system from Monday to Wednesday. During this period agents can amend the account, deleting incorrect charges. After this, NTL reports to operators any changes that have been made. Agents' bank accounts are debited on Friday morning and operators' accounts are credited with the money paid on Monday morning.

In the USA agents can process service fees and other credit card payments through the ARC Travel Agency Service Fee Program (TASF). ASTA members can get a better deal through ASTA's Payment Processing Program via Chase Merchant Services.

agents' sales return   *See* ASR.

agio   17th-century term for the percentage commission charged when changing paper money into cash. No evidence can be found for the assertion in several tourism dictionaries that the word agio is used to describe the commission charged by a bank or bureau de change when exchanging one currency for another.

AGL   Above ground level.

AGNIS   Azimuth guidance for nose-in stands.

Agreement on the international carriage of passengers by road by means of occasional bus and coach services   Also known as ASOR; replaced from 1 January 2003 by the EC Interbus Agreement on the international occasional carriage of passengers by coach and bus.   *See* www.europa.eu.int/scadplus/leg/en/lvb/l24264.htm

agricultural tourism   As with many descriptors preceding the word tourism, it is not specific. May mean merely rural tourism or, at the other end of the spectrum, tourism associated with working farms. *See* farm tourism.

agritourism   *See* farm tourism.

agrotourism   *See* farm tourism.

AGT   Automated Guideway Transit, is a system where public service vehicles, currently usually rail or monorail, run unmanned to a fixed schedule along reserved track.

agt   Travel industry abbreviation for agent.

AGTA[1]   Association of Gibraltar Travel Agents.

AGTA[2]   Association of Greek-Cypriot Travel Agents in the UK.

AGTE   The Association of Group Travel Executives in the USA is a trade body for those who operate or promote group travel.

AH   Artificial horizon.

AH&MA   The American Hotel and Motel Association is the largest US trade body covering the US hospitality industry. It is a federation of state and regional accommodation industry trade bodies covering Mexico and Central and South America as well as the USA and Canada. *See* www.ahma.com

AH&MA Educational Institute   *See* www.ei-ahma.org/ei/index.htm

AHTA   Association of Hungarian Travel Agents.

AI   Artificial Intelligence systems enable intelligent activities of humans to be modelled and emulated. Work in this field was undertaken by the Open University in the development of the UK travel industry's Computer Based Learning scheme.

AIA   Aerospace industries of America.

AIAA[1]   Area of intense aerial activity.

AIAA[2]   Aerospace Industry Analysis Association (US based).

AIAA[3]   American Institute of Aeronautics and Astronauts. *See* www.aiaa.org

AIB[1]   Accidents Investigation Branch of the UK Department of Transport, Royal Aircraft Establishment is the British authority responsible for the investigation of all air accidents occurring in Britain as well as those of British registered civil aircraft abroad.

AIB[2]   In some countries means Agency Investigation Board. *See* AIP[1].

AIC   Aeronautical information circular.

AIDS Aircraft Integrated Data System aims to store in a database all the information about an aircraft.

AIH Association Internationale de l'Hôtellerie; was known in English-speaking world as the International Hotel Association. Changed its name in 1990 to International Hotel and Restaurant Association. *See* www.ih-ra.com

AIIC Association Internationale des Interprètes de Conférence. The International Association of Conference Interpreters based in France.

aileron *See* airframe.

AIM Accord International de Marchandises, the international agreement concerning the carriage of goods by rail.

AIMS¹ Agency Information Management System.

AIMS² IATA meaning is Airline Information Management Study.

AIOA Aviation Insurance Officers Association in the UK. *See* www.iua.co.uk

AIP¹ Agency Investigation Panel (in some countries called an Agency Investigation Board). A group of senior airline staff, set up by the IATA Agency Administration Board of the Traffic Conference concerned. Mainly undertakes investigation and consideration of applications for appointment of new agents and reviews existing agents. In the UK, under IATA Resolution 808, an Agency Programme Liaison Group was set up in 1988, with nine airline and nine agency representatives. This APLG was then replaced under IATA Resolution 814 with the Agency Programme Joint Council, which now has overall control, the UK AIP having been wound down and its responsibilities having been taken over by the IATA Agency Distribution Office in London. It is this office which now makes initial decisions as to whether IATA accreditation standards have been met by applicants. *See* Agency Programme Joint Council (Liaison Group).

AIP² An alternative IATA meaning is Aeronautical Information Publication.

AIPC Association Internationale des Palais des Congrès.

AIR Meaning ascribed by IATA's Information and Marketing Services division is Aviation Information Research.

Air Accident Investigation Branch (of CAA). *See* www.aaib.detr.gov.uk

air conditioning When applied to accommodation or a mode of transport, means temperature control by means of a continuous air flow. In a guest's hotel room or private vehicle, the temperature is usually adjustable by the user. Even when it is centrally controlled, the air supply to a room can usually be shut off. In public transport or public rooms, control is usually centrally operated.

air credit North American term for a reduction in the price of travel arrangements including air travel for those who do not want this element. For example, travellers joining a coach tour or cruise.

air cushion vehicle A hovercraft. *See* entry under this name.

air draft The height of a ship above the International Load Line. Differences in water salinity and the loading may cause a vessel to ride higher out of the water while decorative funnels and masts may be capable of lowering. These are some of the factors which the Master of a vessel will take into account when deciding whether his ship will be able to sail under a bridge. *See* Plimsoll line.

Air Education and Recreation Organisation *See* AERO.

air fares Official IATA definitions are: A fare means the amount charged by the carrier for the carriage of a passenger and his allowable free baggage and is the current fare which an IATA member, in the publication it normally uses to publish fares, holds out to the public, or the appropriate segment of the public, as being applicable to the class of service to be furnished. An adult fare is the fare for a person who has attained his 12th birthday and a children's fare applies to a person who has attained his second but not his 12th birthday. An infant fare applies to a person who has not attained his second birthday.

A constructed fare is a fare other than a specified fare. *An economy fare*, which is equivalent to a tourist fare, means the fare established for an economy- or tourist-class service, while *a first-class fare* is that established for a first-class service.

A joint fare is one which applies for carriage over the lines of two or more carriers and which is published as a single amount. *A local fare*, which is the same as an *'on-line fare'*, means a fare which applies for carriage over the lines of a single carrier.

A normal fare is the highest fare established for a first, or economy-/tourist-class service during the period of applicability. *A proportional fare* means a fare published for use only in combination with other fares for carriage from, to or through a specified point. *A published fare* is one for which the amount is specifically set forth in the carrier's fares tariff.

A sectional fare means a fare for travel by one class of service which is established and used by a scheduled air carrier(s), including any individual joint fares, for a section of a through route. *A special fare* is one other than the normal fare. *A specified fare* is one the amount of which is specifically set out in a carrier's tariff.

A through fare means the total fare from point of departure to point of destination. *A tour basing fare* means a fare which may be used only for air transportation and part of an inclusive tour. *Combinations of fares* means an amount which is obtained by combining two or more fares.

See also under children's fares and various types of air fare, e.g. APEX, Eurobudget, Excursion, IPEX, PEX, Superpex etc. *and* under 'airline class and fare designators' for comprehensive list of fare types and codes which designate them on air tickets.

Air, Freedoms of the   *See* Freedoms of the Air.

air hostess   Female airline cabin attendant (the male equivalent is a cabin steward).

Air League   The Air League is a voluntary body in Britain which states as its main aim, 'To inculcate among the young the realisation of the importance of successful endeavour in the air and to encourage participation in air activities.' *See* www.airleague.co.uk

air mile   same as the nautical mile of 6076.1 ft or 1842.8055 m. *See* nautical mile.

Air Miles   From launch in 1988 until October 2000 was the name of the British Airways frequent flyer incentive scheme and also the brand name of British Airways promotion scheme whereby traders, mainly not in the travel industry, offer Air Miles vouchers as a sales incentive. From October 2000, the 'currency' for British Airways Executive Club frequent flyer programme was renamed BA Miles. The vouchers are not only exchangeable for British Airways, American Airlines and other airline's flights; they can be used to buy package holidays through Thomson Holidays, Kuoni and other operators, cruises, ferry travel and Eurostar. Air Miles customers collect their vouchers by shopping with one of the 50 UK High Street and on-line partners which include Shell, NatWest and Tesco. By purchasing with a NatWest credit card, Air Miles may be obtained twice, when for example, buying petrol or shopping with Tesco. The scheme is vast in size: in 2004 over one million travellers redeemed Air Miles. For further details *see* www.airmiles.co.uk

air miss   Obsolete ICAO term which has been replaced by 'AIRPROX', meaning an incident where two aircraft avoided mid-air collision. *See* AIRPROX.

Air Operators Certificate   *See* AOC.

air passenger average weights   For many calculations, it is assumed for US domestic journeys that travellers weigh 190 lb (86.2 kg) inclusive of their free baggage allowance. For international first-class travellers from the USA, the equivalent figures are 215 lb (97.5 kg) and for tourist class 200 lb (90.7 kg). The Joint Aviation Authority which sets standards in 23 European countries, was planning to increase passengers' weight allowances from 77–84 kg. In May 2003, a US Federal Aviation Authority survey of regional airline passengers found that passenger weights averaged 88 kg. At the time of going to press, no action had been taken to increase the official figures, although airlines worldwide are understood to be working on higher norms than those stated above.

air pocket   unpredictable area of low or high pressure, causing an aircraft in flight to rise or fall suddenly. *See also* explanation of clear air turbulence under 'turbulence'.

air pressure   *See* pressurization for aircraft cabin pressure.

air rage   Non-specific term for disorderly behaviour by air passengers, often as a result of excessive alcohol intake.

air safety *See* airline safety.

air/sea interchange Agreement between shipping and air carriers allowing acceptance of each others' tickets and granting round trip rebate, if applicable, enabling a complete trip to be undertaken utilizing both types of transport.

air/sea program North American equivalent of a fly cruise programme. *See* fly cruise.

Air Services Agreement *See* ASA.

air sickness Type of motion sickness particular to air travel. Modern aircraft usually fly above the weather, avoiding a bumpy journey.

air space *See* FIRs.

Air Tariff Publishing Company *See* ATPCo.

air taxi In Europe, the term applies to any small aircraft available for private hire by organization or individuals. During the existence of the American CAB, the term applied to any aircraft carrying up to 19 passengers and operating up to a 250 mile radius of its base. CAB rules were far less restrictive for air taxi services than for ordinary scheduled or supplemental carriers.

air terminal A passenger or cargo handling building on an airport. Passenger terminals provide check-in facilities for travellers and their baggage and baggage reclaim facilities for arrivals.

air ticket revalidation Whenever there is a change in the routing of air travel, with or without a change in the fare, tickets must be reissued. Changes to reservations on air tickets are made by means of a reservations alteration sticker. It is particularly important to check that the new reservation does not contravene the applicable conditions of the fare used, such as night timings, validity, minimum stay or stopovers.

A line must be drawn through any entry in the flight/class, dates, time and status boxes of the reservation being changed on all coupons of the ticket before the completed sticker is placed over the top. The ticket must be authenticated by means of an entry identifying the issuing office. Where BSP is in operation, and stickers are printed in duplicate, the extra copy is fixed to the passenger coupon.

air tickets Air tickets sold in the UK by travel agents are accounted for through a system called Bank Settlement Plan (BSP). Sales are reported by travel agents either electronically or by post and agents are billed for the value of tickets, less any commission due, sold every month, payable by direct debit on the 17th of the following month. Most air tickets are currently issued through ticket printers, used in all major travel agencies and all airlines. ATB printers (automated ticket and boarding pass) are loaded with individual cardlike coupons, one card being printed for each sector of an air journey. TAT printers are loaded with Transitional Automated Tickets in the form of continuous stationery. Once printed, TAT and ATB coupons are almost impossible to alter; forging them by alteration would require so much time and effort as to make it not worthwhile. Because of this, ticket alteration problems usually only occur in respect of tickets issued by smaller travel agencies who have a stock of international air tickets intended for manual handwritten issue. These consist of a series of coupons backed with a red self-carboning substance. There is an audit copy sent to BSP, an issuing office copy, either two or four travel coupons and a back cover of the ticket also serving as the passenger copy. BSPs operate in many countries of the world; for USA agency reporting arrangements *see* ARC[1]. For more information on air ticket types *see* ticket *and* MPD[2].

Air Traffic Conference Until 1 January 1985, this was a part of the Air Transport Association responsible for self-regulation of American and Canadian domestic airlines, which also vetted and appointed travel agents. This latter function is now undertaken by the ARC.

Air Traffic Control The services that coordinate and control air traffic throughout the world. *See* Single European Sky.

Air Traffic Control Centre A location from which air traffic within a specified area is managed. *See* FIRs and MLS.

Air Traffic Controller A qualified person who directs and manages aircraft movements.

air traffic in Europe and forecasts up to 2015 (*See table on next page.*)

Air traffic in Europe and forecasts up to 2015.

Country	Domestic and international annual growth rate (%)		Passengers (millions)	
	1998	2015	1995–1998	1998–2015
UK	143.9	310.3	6.6	4.6
Germany	106.3	220.4	7.3	4.4
Spain	92.8	173.5	6.8	3.8
France	83.1	161.1	5.5	4.0
Italy	57.0	115.1	7.0	4.2
Holland	34.0	80.3	8.8	5.2
Switzerland	28.3	52.9	5.6	3.7
Turkey	27.8	65.9	14.5	5.1

ATAG suggests that in 2004 over 1.8bn passengers flew on the world's airlines, expected to rise to 2.3bn passengers by 2010. Adapted from *European Air Traffic Forecasts 1985–2015* Air Transport Action Group 2000 edition.

Air Transport Action Group *See* ATAG.
Air Transport Association *See* ATA².
Air Transport Association of Canada *See* ATAC.
Air Transport Licence *See* ATL.
air transport of animals *See* animals by air.
Air Transportation Stabilization Board A US $10bn fund set up following the 11 September 2001 terrorist outrages to address problems faced by the US airline industry.
Air Travel and Aviation Internet sites *See* air travel on the Internet.
Air Travel Card The general name for a credit card issued by an airline in connection with the IATA Universal Air Travel Plan. *See* UATP for full description of card types.
air travel current forecasts *See* www.boeing.com/commercial
air travel deregulation *See* airline deregulation in the EU *and* airline deregulation in the USA.
air travel on the Internet *See* www.aeroseek.com an aviation search engine; Aeronet www.aeronet.co.uk; Air International mag www.keymags.co.uk; Airlines of the Web www.itn.net/airlines/; Aviation On-line www.aviation.com.br; AeroWorld Net www.aeroworldnet.com; Aviation Internet Resources www.airlines-online.com; Check-ins airline database www.checkin.com/air-db.html; Flight International mag www.flightinternational.com; for pilots and flying enthusiasts www.pilots.co.uk The Farnborough site has information on

the theory of aircraft design and flight theory www.farnborough-aircraft.com/main.html Cranfield University in the UK has developed AERADE, an Internet gateway to aerospace information www.aerade.cranfield.ac.uk The General Aviation Awareness Council in the UK (GAAC) is at www.gaac.co.uk
Air Travel Organizer's Licence *See* ATOL.
Air Travel Reserve Fund *See* ATRF; now replaced by Air Travel Trust *See* ATT.
air travel safety *See* airline safety.
Air Travel Trust *See* ATT.
air turbulence *See* turbulence.
air waybill The shipping document used in air freight transportation by carriers as evidence of a shipment. The document contains shipping instructions, a description of the goods and the transportation charges applicable. When used internationally, an air waybill should be in the standard form denominated by the Warsaw Convention.
air web sites *See* air travel on the Internet.
airbridge A mobile pier or telescopic walkway connecting the airport runway end of a passenger terminal with an aircraft, facilitating passenger access; in North America, a jet loader or Jetway. *See* gate.
Air-Britain Founded in 1948 Air-Britain is for people interested in the history of aviation. It has around 4000 direct members and many more associated with it through a network of independent branches. It claims to be the leading organization of its kind in the world and works closely with similar organiza-

tions, museums and correspondents worldwide. *See* www.air-britain.com

AIRC Association of International Rail Companies in the UK.

aircraft Although in theory the term applies to anything man-made used for flying, in practice, the term is restricted to a heavier-than-air machine with an on-board means of propulsion, airship being the term for one that is lighter than air, and glider for a craft without any means of propulsion. Helicopters, although they have rotors instead of a fixed wing, are still referred to as aircraft. *See also* many immediately following entries, SST, VSTOL *and* VTOL *and* air web sites.

aircraft deliveries worldwide *See* GAMA web site for latest half year data.

aircraft design For theory *see* www.farnborough-aircraft.com/main.html and for engineering drawings of Boeing and McDonald Douglas aircraft *see* www.myboeingfleet.com

aircraft emissions Substances produced from aircraft engine exhausts. Carbon dioxide from aircraft is indistinguishable from that from other sources as are other emissions. Aviation contributes some 2.5% of emissions of CO_2 from fossil fuels and some 12% of all CO_2 from transport worldwide. It also produces 2–3% of man-made nitrogen oxides. Nitrogen oxides emitted at cruise altitudes have two effects; one cooling and one warming. There is uncertainty about these effects. They do not cancel as they are geographically distinct. There is equal or greater uncertainty over the effects of water vapour emitted at cruise altitudes, through the formation of condensation trails and cirrus clouds, both of which could cause significant warming. Altogether, aviation is believed to be responsible for 3.5% of the total radiative forcing (causes of global warming) by all human activities. Improvements in aircraft engine technology have resulted in the virtual elimination of carbon monoxide, unburned hydrocarbons and smoke. Information sources are ATAG (Air Transport Action Group), IATA, ICAO, IPCC and www.british-airways.com. *See also* contrails, ICAO *and* air web sites *also* radiative forcing.

aircraft engine types *See* jet aircraft engine, piston aircraft engine, propjet, turbine aircraft engine, turbofan jet, turbojet, turboprop *and* air web sites.

aircraft frame *See* airframe.

aircraft grounding *See* grounding.

aircraft leasing Hire of an aircraft with all services provided, for travel between specified points is a charter; whereas a lease implies ownership of the aircraft for a specific period, during which the lessee is responsible for it. A dry lease involves only the provision of an aircraft. A wet lease is the term applied to the provision of both aircraft and crew by the lessor. ILFC (International Lease & Finance Corporation), a wholly owned subsidiary of America International Group, is the international market leader in the leasing and remarketing of advanced technology commercial jet aircraft. In July 2000 it owned a portfolio of more than 450 aircraft, 2% of the jets and turbo prop aircraft in service, valued at US$19 billion.

aircraft manufacture For latest information access the Internet sites of the main manufacturers. *See* www.airbus.com; www.boeing.com; www.aero.bombardier.com; www.bae.co.uk; www.dasa.com (Daimler Benz); www.embraer.com; www.faidor.com (Fairchild Dornier); www.galaxyaerospace.com; www.ataircraft.com; www.cessna.textron.com; www.gulfstream.com; www.dassault-aviation.fr

aircraft noise New aircraft are around 20 dB (decibels) quieter than those of 30 years ago. Each reduction of 10 dB is perceived by the human ear as a halving of the noise experienced. International aircraft noise certification standards are contained in Chapter 16 of the Convention on International Civil Aviation, widely known as the Chicago Convention. At the time of writing, discussions were ongoing concerning further reducing aircraft noise, by phasing out current chapter 3 aircraft. *See* ICAO for explanation of chapter 2/3 aircraft.

Aircraft Owners and Pilots Association *See* AOPA.

aircraft piracy *See* hijacking.

aircraft pressurization *See* pressurization.

aircraft register www.aviation-register.com provides details of over 400,000 aircraft registered in over 50 countries.

The web site is run by the UK CAA, its Italian counterpart ENAC and French company Bureau Veritas. Information includes aircraft types, engines, certification and airworthiness details together with the operator's name and address.

aircraft sharing When two or more organizations, usually tour operators, jointly charter an aircraft, or alternatively when a main charterer subcharters a share of the aircraft seats to other organizations.

aircraft slot *See* FIRs.

aircraft stacking At busy times, there are insufficient runways for all arriving aircraft to land at the world's major airports. They are, therefore, required to fly in huge circles, each stacking level being separated to ensure absolute safety.

aircraft types *See* fixed wing aircraft, QC aircraft, regular body aircraft, STOL, VSTOL, VTOL, SST, wide body aircraft and GEM.

aircrew All the airline staff on duty on board an aircraft during a flight.

AIRDES Automated interline revenue data exchange system.

AIREP Air report form used for reporting position and weather conditions during a flight.

Airfare Brand names of Thomson Holidays' variety of minimum-rated package tours. Of course, an 'air fare' is the price charged for an air ticket.

airfield *See* airport.

airfoil North American usage for aerofoil. *See* airframe.

airframe The structure of an aircraft excluding the engines and accessories. The principal parts of an airframe are the fuselage which is the body; wings; empennage, which is the assembly of stabilizing and control surfaces at the tail; landing gear, and nacelles or pods which house the engines.

The tail fin acts like a giant sail preventing yaw, the movement of the front of the aircraft from side to side. Elevators are the movable edges of the tailplane, which alter the altitude of an aircraft up or down.

An aircraft flies because of the shape of the wings – an aerofoil. The airflow over them results in less air pressure on the top surface than at the bottom. It is this difference in air pressure that con-

tinually forces the wings of a plane upwards. The many hinged surfaces on the wings have different names according to their purpose. Ailerons cause an aircraft to bank or turn when they are operated. Those on the side towards which aircraft is turning will rise while the ailerons on the other side will turn down.

Passengers looking out of an aeroplane's window on to the wing's upper surface may see panels which come up during a landing. These are known as spoilers and they help to brake the aircraft by blocking the air flow. This also reduces the normal aerodynamic effect of the wing shape that, so because of the loss of lift, the aircraft descends quickly. Everyone who has flown is familiar with the flaps that come out of both front and back edges of the wings of an aircraft. A jet plane needs an efficient wing for high speed cruising with little drag. But this wing will not satisfactorily support the aircraft at low speeds when taking off or landing. Flaps not only hinge downwards, trapping the airflow; they also considerably increase the wings' surface area by extending outwards. Names such as blown, towler, split and zap are common types of flap on the trailing edge. An additional extension to some flaps is nominated as slotted. Flaps on the leading wing edge are even more efficient at maintaining an aircraft's altitude at low speed pushing the wing surface both further forward and angled down. Common flaps in this situation are variable camber flaps, which are also known as slats, droops and kreugers.

AIRIMP ATA (Air Transport Association) and IATA Reservations Interline Message Procedure, in the form of a code requesting or altering bookings. Also the name for the booklet incorporating this information.

airline An operator of aircraft, flying passengers and/or freight on a commercial basis.

airline alliances An agreement between airlines for business cooperation aimed at increasing revenue and achieving cost savings. The extent of integration between alliances, varies from complete marketing integration to little more than sharing income on some routes. Some alliances share equity in partner carriers and may codeshare so that journeys using several alliance carriers appear to travellers to be continuous, on one flight code. If US anti-trust immunity has been provided by the Department of Transportation, the US airlines may discuss pricing with partner airlines designated in the immunity grant. Otherwise, neither scheduling nor fares may be discussed. For full information concerning the three main alliances access the web sites following the summaries below:

Star Alliance: Established in May 1997 as the first global airline alliance. It is the biggest, handling around a quarter of all world air traffic. Operates to 772 airports in 133 countries. Is a three tier alliance with core founding members in full alliance, code-share partners in a second tier and feeder regional airlines in a third tier. United Airlines together with Lufthansa, SAS and Air Canada has had US anti-trust immunity since 2001. Negotiates purchasing agreements on behalf of members. Plans that during 2005 there will a dedicated Star area at Terminal 1 Paris Charles de Gaulle airport and at Miami International Airport South Terminal, including check-in, baggage and gate. Member airlines are Air Canada, Air New Zealand, ANA, Asiana Airlines, Austrian, bmi, LOT Polish Airlines, Lufthansa, SAS, Singapore Airlines, Spanair, Thai Airways, United Airlines, USair and Varig. There are also regional members such as Adria Airways and Croatia Airlines. See www.star-alliance.com

OneWorld: Founded in 2000. Code sharing is not a formal part of this alliance even though many of the members codeshare with partners, for which American Airlines/Finnair and American/Iberia as well as British Airways/Qantas have US anti-trust approval. Member airlines are: Aer Lingus, American Airlines, British Airways, Cathay Pacific, Finnair, Iberia, Lan Chile and Qantas. *See* www.oneworldalliance.com

Skyteam: Founded in 2000. US anti-trust exemption applies to Delta's association with Air France, Alitalia and CSA Czech Airlines. With Korean Air the exemption is transPacific. The nine member airlines are Aeromexico, Air France/KLM, Alitalia, Continental Airlines, Czech Airlines, Delta, and Northwest Airlines. Negotiation for full membership of Aeroflot and China Southern were at an advanced stage at time of going to press. Operates 14,320 daily flights to 658 destinations in 137 countries. *See* www.skyteam.com for more information.

Wings: Was the oldest airline pair alliance, Northwest and KLM having gained anti-trust immunity in the USA in 1993; it disbanded 10 years later.

Qualiflyer: Following the collapse of Swissair, this alliance disbanded in February 2002.

airline automated reservation systems for travel agents *See* CRS.

airline class and fare designators Primary codes are combined with a seasonal, part of the week, part of the day, fare and passenger type and fare level identifier code in the order stated to provide a designator with a complete description of the class and conditions applicable to a traveller.

Some typical prime codes are:

R – Supersonic (Concorde Class)
P – First Class Premium
F – First Class
A – First Class Discounted
J – Business Class Premium
C – Club or Business Class
D, I or Z – Business Class Discounted
W – Economy/Coach Premium
S or Y – Economy/Coach
B, H, K, L, M, N, Q, T, V or X – Economy/Coach Discounted

Some seasonal codes are:

H – Peak or high season of a fare with more than one seasonal level.
K – Second level of a fare with more than two seasonal levels.
J – Third level of a fare with more than three seasonal levels.
F – Fourth level of a fare with more than four seasonal levels.
T – Fifth level of a fare with more than five seasonal levels.
Q – Sixth level of a fare with more than six seasonal levels.

Y – Seventh level of a fare with more than seven seasonal levels.

L – Lowest level of a fare with more than one seasonal level.

Part of the week codes are:

W – Weekend
X – Weekday
The only part of the day code is N meaning Night.

Fare and passenger type codes associated with the other letters describe the actual fare type that the customer has paid, for example:

AB – Advance Purchase Fare (lower level)
AD – Agent (followed by percentage discount)
AF – Area Fare
AP – Advance Purchase Fare
AS – Air/Surface
AT – Attendant travelling at a discounted fare to accompany disabled passenger
BB – Budget Fare
BD – Budget Discounted
BP – Bonus Programme (Frequent Flyer Scheme)
BT – Bulk Inclusive Tour Operator Package (TOP) fare in Europe
CA – Cargo Attendant
CB – Extra Seat for Cabin Baggage
CD – Senior Citizen
CF – Cabotage Fare
CG – Tour Guide (Conductor)
CH – Child
CL – Clergy
CT – Circle Trip
DA – Discover America
DD – Discounted
DE – Discover Europe Pass
DL – Labour
DF – Government Fare
DG – Government Officials
DH – Reduced Fare when travelling to Travel Agency Commissioner hearing
DM – Discount not covered by Industry Regulations
DN – Discover North America Fare
DP – Diplomats and dependants
DT – Teacher
EE – Excursion
EM – Emigrant
GA – Group – Affinity
GC – Group – Common Interest

GE – Group – Vocational Training Trips for Travel Agents
GI – Group – Incentive
GM – Group – Military
GN – Group – Non-affinity
GO – Group – Own Use
GP – Group – School
GS – Group – Ship's Crew
GU – Group – Excursions
GV – Group – Inclusive Tour
GX – Group – Advance Purchase Fare
GY – Group – Youth Fare
GZ – Group – Pex Fare
IB – ATA Employee travelling on industry business
ID – Air Industry Employee
IE – Escort to accompany an Inadmissible passenger
IF – Introductory Fare
IG – Inaugural Guest
IN – Infant Fare
IP – Instant Purchase Fare
IS – Late Booking Fare
IT – Inclusive Tour
MA – Military – Category A
MM – Military
MR – Military Recruit
MU – Military Standby Fare
MY – Missionary
MZ – Military – Category Z
OJ – Open Jaw
OR – Orphan/Orphan Escort
OW – One Way Single
OX – Excursion One Way Fare
PD – Family Fare – family members
PF – Family Fare – applicable to both family head and family members
PG – Pilgrim
PH – Family Fare – Head of Family
PX – PEX Fare
RG – General Sales Agent
RP – Regular Passenger Fares
RT – Round Trip or Return fare
RW – Round the World
SB – Seriously Disabled Passenger Fare
SC – Ship's Crew Member (Individual)
SD – Student
SE – Special Event
SF – Bilaterally agreed First Class Entitlement
SH – Spouse Fare (husband or wife)
SR – Special Euro Round Trip Fare
SS – Super Saver Fare
ST – Spouse Fare – accompanying spouse
SX – Superpex Fare
SZ – Extra seating for stretcher

UD – National Travel Agent Association Officials and delegates to joint IATA/UFTAA meetings

UU – Standby Fare

VU – Visit USA

ZS – Youth Fare for which student certificate required

ZZ – Youth Fare

Other codes used commonly in combination with the above are figures followed by % to indicate a percentage discount; figures followed by D, M or Y, indicating validity in days, months or years, or figures on their own indicating that a fare is the highest (1), second highest fare level (2) etc. FTT means Family Travel Together and GTT means Group Travel Together, when used in an air ticket endorsements box.

airline clubs Most major airlines offer frequent flyers' membership of special clubs. Benefits include use of first-class or Club/Executive class lounges, dependent on the airline, whether or not the traveller is in possession of a first- or club-class ticket, express check-in and baggage handling, reservation priority, discounts on car rental and accommodation, emergency cheque cashing facilities and a club magazine.

Unless otherwise stated, airline clubs listed under their respective headings include all of the above benefits. *See* Admirals Club, Al Fursan, Ambassador Club, Business Club, Cedar Jet, Chieftain Club, Clipper Club, Club Affaires, Club des 2000, Club Pacific, Courtesy Card Club, Crown Room Club, Diamond Club, Empress Club, Executive Club, Finnair Club, Flight Deck, Flying Colonel, Frequent Traveller Card, Global Club, Golden Falcon Executive Club, Golden Wing, Ionosphere Club, Kanata Club, King David Club, Mabuhay Club, Maple Leaf Club, Marco Polo Club, Morning Club, Navigator Club, President's Club, Prestige Club, Red Card Club, Royal Viking Courtesy Card, Service Plus, Tara Circle, Top Traveller, Travel Club, V Club, Winged Arrow Club, Worldclub.

airline codes By international agreement, for older airlines, two-character airline designators are used in reservations, timetables, ticketing, legal documents, tariffs, schedule publications and in airline inter-line communications as well as for other industry applications. When the two character codes ran out, it was necessary to begin using three characters. For example, BA is British Airways, AA is American Airlines and QF is Qantas. These designators are different from the two-letter codes used for aircraft operating agencies, aeronautical authorities and services assigned by the International Civil Aviation Organization upon request by the State Registry concerned. ICAO designators are published in ICAO Document 8585. For accounting convenience IATA have allocated all carriers a three-figure code number to be used by members on air tickets and air waybills as a prefix to the serial numbers of the document.

The airline industry began conversion from two-character to three-letter airline designators by assigning three-letter designators to non-scheduled airlines from 25 October 1987. It was planned that the scheduled airlines convert to three-letter designators for all purposes on 26 October 1995, 2 years later than the end of October 1993 date originally agreed. For example, Aer Lingus, currently EI, is planned to become EIN.

Because there are insufficient two-letter codes, since August 1981 combinations of figures and letters have been allocated, mainly to commuter airlines. Over 160 companies now have these alphanumeric codes. The numbers 1 and 0 are not used to avoid confusion with the letters I and O. An example is Air National, whose planned three-letter designator is ANE, but which is currently 6A.

airline deregulation in the EU K.J. Button (1997) writing in *Asia Pacific Air Transport: Challenges and Reforms*, p. 170 stated, 'EU policy has changed dramatically in the last decade after a move from aviation markets being a series of heavily regulated, discrete bilateral cartels, dominated by nationally owned flag carriers to a structure.... which has become a liberalised multinational civil aviation market'. The EU has aimed for gradual evolution rather than the rapid revolution which took place in the USA; however, the result is similar.

The first stage from January 1988 was general agreement to move towards a single aviation market within the EU. The second stage from June 1990 removed 'government-to-government capacity-sharing arrangements, introduced in stages the principle of double disapproval of fares and prevented governments discriminating against airlines, provided that they conformed with technical and safety standards'. Involvement of non-EU airlines was made easier, with fifth freedom (see Freedoms of the Air) rights facilitated. The third stage was adopted in January 1993, so that by 1997, the EU was regarded as one domestic market, in which full cabotage rights applied. Fares became completely deregulated. Foreign ownership of EU airlines is now permitted in principle, although the national laws of some EU countries govern the ownership of their flag carriers and other airlines. The EU still has the right to 'intervene' in various circumstances, for example, maintenance of competition and avoidance of air fare price wars.

airline deregulation in the USA The Airline Deregulation Act of 1978 scheduled the elimination of the Civil Aeronautics Board from 1 January 1985. Originally, the Act transferred authority to grant anti-trust immunity for the US travel industry's collective agreements including travel agency programmes from the CAB to the US Justice Department.

This was altered subsequently and together with the remaining economic regulation of the US airline industry, control of anti-trust immunity rules has now been vested in the Department of Transportation. Immunity disappeared altogether on 1 January 1989. The DOT now decides on policy matters and, through the Federal Aviation Administration, regulates safety.

The DOT inherited the CAB's authority to regulate charters, overbooking, baggage liability, smoking, computer reservation bias and similar matters that concern the public. The DOT also controls international route and rate matters as well as the provision of essential air services to small communities, operating the small communities service subsidy programme. The DOT has not been given the power to directly negotiate

international air treaties. This continues to be undertaken by the US State Department. Before deregulation in the late 1970s, agent's share of US air travel was around 40%. Unexpectedly, this rapidly rose to about 80% of domestic sales and over 90% for international business; by mid-2002, despite commission rates reduced to zero, agents still handled 75% of the business. This alteration in distribution costs was one of the factors leading to commission reduction, fully described in the 'commission' entry. See opening paragraph of ARC entry for how deregulation led to the establishment of the ARC and IATAN. Also see DOT Internet site www.dot.gov

airline flight schedules Travel industry staff access comprehensive flight information through the major computer reservation systems, known as Global Distribution Systems (GDS), Galileo, Sabre, Amadeus and Worldspan. Each of these holds flight availability for over 700 airlines; but only for those airlines with which that particular GDS has an agreement. All the Internet general scheduled air flight booking systems gain their inventory from one of the GDSs. OAG (Overseas Airways Guide) publishes a unique two-volume guide to all flights worldwide. In August 2000 OAG relaunched its Internet portal, OAG.com. The site provides web access to the OAG 'Flight Engine', the most up-to-date and comprehensive global flight schedules database in the world. The site also supports OAG Mobile, which offers wireless access to OAG travel information, and OAG E-Notification, providing details about the status of a current flight. More than 800 airlines are included in the OAG database, the largest of its kind anywhere. See www.oag.com

airline hub See hub and spoke.

airline liability See Warsaw Convention.

airline losses/profits See airline.

Airline Passenger Service Commitment See explanation in 'denied boarding compensation'. An agreement between airlines to maintain minimum standards relating to service and quality.

airline plate In countries without Bank Settlement Plan, individual tickets produced by each airline are supplied to travel agents, which merely need validating with the agent's airline plate before issuance. BSP tickets and documents are, however, neutral, requiring a different type of validator which in addition to the date and agency location details also imprints air tickets with an airline logo and identification. *See* BSP for further details of Bank Settlement Plan in the UK.

airline representative   *See* rep.

airline reservations systems   There are now two main types of airline reservations system. A 'single host' system is owned and operated by one airline for the purpose of providing automated reservations and other facilities to its own offices. Inventory records are maintained solely for the airline owning the system. The schedules of other airlines, on which reservations can be made, are stored and displayed according to the selling agreements concluded between the system owner and each of the other airlines.

Some single host systems are in effect simple extensions to a number of participants. The inventory-controlled services of the participating airlines are displayed. The display of non-participating airline schedules is dependent on the agreements the system owner has with those airlines. Although the basic functions of the system are used by all participating airlines, the system is designed for each to use as though it were its own. Each hosted airline has its own compartment and can utilize the basic functions of the system to meet its own requirements. Each airline usually loads into its system the schedules to be used for that airline. The schedules of the prime host airline's services are obtained from its own scheduling departments.

Generally, other airline schedule information is obtained from an airline guide publisher on magnetic tape for automatic loading into the system of the prime host airline. Not necessarily all the city pairs published in the guides may be made available for display to users of the system. Hosted airlines select those to be displayed in accordance with their marketing requirements and the agreements they have made with other airlines.

However, with the requirement to include departure and arrival times in reservations messages requesting or selling space, there is an increasing tendency for airlines to obtain, and store in their system, the basic schedules of all other airlines worldwide. In order to be sold, a seat has to be available. Each system maintains the exact numeric availability of each inventory-controlled flight.

Additionally, as interline sales are a vital feature of air transportation, each system maintains availability information for flights of other airlines, to provide for the immediate confirmation of space to the passenger. This availability information, which is incorporated in displays, is dependent on the interline selling agreements concluded between the prime host airline and each of the other hosted airlines. Availability may be on the basis of 'sell and report' (including first posting), 'free sale', 'request and reply' or a combination of types.

For flights covered by a free sale or request and reply agreement, no availability information needs to be maintained in the system of the prime host airline, as the sale is either free of restriction, or has to be requested from the other airline. For flights under a 'sell and report' agreement, the system can sell a seat only if its records show that space is available. Keeping this availability information up-to-date becomes crucial and is achieved by the extensive exchange of availability status messages (AVS[2]).

As each prime host airline has different selling agreements with its interline partners, the availability displays vary from one system to another. Availability information may be maintained by host airlines up to 1 year in advance. The Passenger Name Record (PNR) is an integral part of the airline reservations function. It presents a record of each passenger's travel requirements, and contains information necessary to enable reservations to be controlled.

A PNR is created, filed/stored and maintained for every passenger for whom a reservation transaction has been completed. The booking airline must maintain a complete record. Every transaction or change to the itinerary is recorded so that the PNR provides a complete historical record. Other airlines involved in the itinerary need only record information associated with the passenger's travel on the flights on which they are to take action.

All modern systems offer automated fare display, fare determination and automatic fare calculation for complicated international itineraries. No existing system can automatically quote or calculate the fare for every itinerary; but in the author's experience, it is only a very complex itinerary which now necessitates manual fare calculation.

These systems are capable of facilitating automated ticket issue, and can support provision of boarding passes with the ticket. Alternatively an 'e-ticket' can be produced. This is a virtual ticket which only exists electronically, although, of course, the traveller will probably be given the trip details in a printed form. All major systems can also make reservations for hotel accommodation, car rental and, to some extent, tours; some may include ground transportation. Additionally, each system provides a comprehensive fares determination system and a large amount of supporting information such as fare rules, weather, tourism, document requirements, flight or travel restrictions etc.

Airlines have automated departure control systems which use PNRs as their database. These systems include: personal name check-in, automated seat assignment, automated issue of boarding passes and baggage tags, flight reconciliation and load control (weight and balance). *See also* CRS.

airline safety This dictionary entry concentrates on ICAO, EU and FAA activities in the sphere, although all countries have legislation in force on the subject. In October 1995, ICAO members adopted a voluntary safety oversight programme. Unfortunately, it is only instigated upon a request for help. The programme permits ICAO to identify deficiencies related to civil aviation safety and offer advice and assistance to resolve them.

EU countries already have extensive safety legislation in place concerning air travel, airports and aircraft. Common Position (EC) N037/98 was adopted by the Council on 4 June 1998 and is likely to result in an EC Directive around the time of publication of this dictionary. The purpose of the Directive will be to ensure that information is collected and disseminated so that sufficient evidence can be established to decide on measures required to ensure the safety of the travelling public, as well as those on the ground. Operation and crew of aircraft outside the control of a member state will be inspected, when there is suspicion that safety standards are not being observed, and grounded if necessary.

In September 1994, the FAA began assessing the ability of certain countries to oversee air safety; category 1 countries are designated as those with civil aviation authorities which comply with ICAO standards. Category 2 may indicate, for example, that the authority has not developed or implemented regulations in accordance with ICAO standards; it may lack the technical expertise or resources to license or oversee civil aviation; there may be concerns about flight operations or aircraft maintenance. A total of 28 'unsatisfactory' countries were listed in 2000, namely, Bangladesh, Belize, Bolivia, Colombia, Côte d'Ivoire, Dominican Republic, Ecuador, El Salvador, Gambia, Guatemala, Haiti, Honduras, Kiribati, Malta, Nauru, Saba St Eustatius, Nicaragua, St Kitts and Nevis, Pakistan, Paraguay, Russia, Suriname, Swaziland, Turks and Caicos, Uruguay, Venezuela, Zaire and Zimbabwe. It should be stressed that the FAA assessments do not indicate whether particular carriers are safe; they only identify the extent to which there is a competent civil aviation authority in those countries, overseeing air safety to the satisfaction of the FAA. *See also* next entry and following table.

airline safety scoring Overall accident rates are falling; in 1999, 674 people were killed in passenger air crashes, much under the average for 1990 to 1998 of 1326. The information in the rest of this entry was provided by FlightSafe Consultants Limited, a UK company. Their web site www. flightsafe.co.uk includes a database of air accidents going back to 1988; at the time of writing, this site covered the safety records of 477 airlines, with more information available on subscription. The concept of airline safety scoring was first devised in 1997 by John Trevett, now managing director of FlightSafe. Ten safety factors are assessed, with a theoretical maximum of ten points achievable. Fleet age and composition are considered; Russian-built planes have a worse safety record than European- or American-built planes, while the newer the technology, the less the chance of accident. Other factors include management structure; safety regulations in the airline's home country, air traffic control and airfield environments. By the time this dictionary is published, a definitive set of assessment guidelines will have been agreed – check the web page for up-to-date information, including the latest statistics. The table overleaf should only be used as illustrative of the situation.

After calculation of 'accidents per 100,000 flights', these statistics are adjusted, for example by counting an accident with fatalities as two and a minor incident as a half, so as to arrive at a safety multiplier. This multiplier is then applied to the marks-out-of-ten safety assessment to produce a final total. Under the FlightSafe scoring system, a rate of one accident per 100,000 scores 0.8; 4 per 100,000 scores 0.6; 9 per 100,000 scores 0.4; 16 per 100,000 scores 0.2 and 25 or more accidents per 100,000 scores zero. It will be seen from the table that many airlines have scored zero; this is because a multiplier of zero results in a zero total score regardless of other considerations. It is suggested that where there has been a single accident early in the life of an airline, this skews the result; readers may feel that the treatment by the scoring system of these airlines is somewhat harsh, as they must all have run fewer than 2000 return flights. (*See table on next page.*)

Are any long-term trends discernible? In a previous edition of this dictionary it was stated, 'In 1986 there were 830 accidents involving aircraft operated by commercial air transport carriers. 150 of these caused 900 fatalities. At the time of writing (June 1989), only preliminary

figures for 1987 were available, there having been 780 accidents. 200 of these caused 1600 deaths. This high number of fatalities must be viewed in the context of increasing traffic. For scheduled services, passenger deaths per 100 million passenger km were 0.09 in 1978; 0.08, 1983; 0.02, 1984; 0.09, 1985; 0.03, 1986; 0.06, 1987. For non-scheduled flights, for accidents of aircraft greater than 9 tonnes maximum take-off weight, figures were 1978, 0.17; 1983, 0.00; 1985, 0.33; 1986, 0.09 and 1987, 0.00. It can be seen that there is no recognizable trend. (Readers should note that the figures quoted from IATA sources do not include USSR.)'

There are arrangements for the reporting and investigation of 'near miss' aviation incidents. *See* AIRPROX for UK statistics.

airline seats Vary in width and pitch between seats depending on class of travel and journey length. The world's largest airline seat is currently being flown by ANA on a Boeing 747 on the Tokyo/London route, 76 x 34 inches in First Class. *See* pitch of seat and reclining seat. Fully reclining seats are often known by airline brand names, such as Dormette, Skyrecliner (JAL), Sleeperette (Finnair), Sleeperseat (BA) and Slumberette (Swissair).

Airline Tariff Automated Collection Facility *See* Genesis.

airliner A large passenger aircraft; the word is imprecise and not technical.

Airlines Reporting Corporation *See* ARC[1].

airlines statistics *See* CAA Data Unit.

airpass Generic word for multi-sector air tickets allowing random travel within a specified area, usually for a limited number of stops. Often used as part of a brand name.

airplane *See* aircraft.

AirPlus An airline credit card. *See* UATP for further explanation.

airport A modern term denoting a place where aircraft land and take off. Dependent upon the size and destination of flights, facilities vary greatly, from the vast size international airport with many passenger terminals, customs and immigration facilities and hangars for storage and maintenance of aircraft, down to the small local airport, which may be little more than several small terminal buildings and re-fuelling pumps.

The word aerodrome, the normal term for these facilities at the beginning of the 20th century, is now obsolescent. Airfield is a common term in the armed services, often reduced to the usage 'field'. Sometimes this word is used in an attempt to denote an airport with few facilities which may be little more than a landing strip.

airport art Pejorative term descriptive of the poor quality of souvenirs available for tourists' purchase at airports.

Airport Associations Coordinating Council See AACC.

airport codes Airports worldwide have been given three letter codes so as to shorten reservation communications. The codes were originally assigned by IATA in Montreal and the Canadians attempted to make most airport codes coincide with their initial or similar letters.

By the time they had concluded their work, they were not left with appropriate letters for their own airports. This is why the three letter codes for Canadian airports are so unusual, e.g. YYZ for Toronto and YUL for Montreal.

Some codes, which have not been assigned by IATA, are also in general use. There is often a general city code for a town where there are several airports, in addition to the individual codes, e.g. LON for London, LGW for Gatwick and LHR for Heathrow.

Airport Consultative Committee See ACC[3].

Airport Operators Association See AOA[3] and www.aoa.org.uk

airport passenger handling automation See SPT.

airport runway lengths A large modern jet may require a runway several miles long (more than 3000 m).

airport service charge See ASC[1].

airport tax See ASC[1] (airport service charge) and departure tax.

airport terminal Part of an airport designated to handle incoming and outgoing flights on particular routes, providing all necessary customs, immigration and passenger facilities. Some airports have separate domestic and international terminals. Others have terminals which are exclusively for the use of one airline.

airport transfer See transfers.

airport–city rail links The problems of road traffic congestion in urban areas are exacerbated by large airports; increasingly, rail links are being seen as the best solution for fast convenient access to airports. Over 70 such links are currently in operation worldwide with around 150 planned or under construction. The first link opened in 1935 between London's Victoria station and Gatwick airport. Some links are an integral part of their national railway networks, for example, Amsterdam, Berlin, Birmingham (UK), Dusseldorf, Frankfurt, London Gatwick and Paris Charles de Gaulle. Others have their own dedicated rail tracks, such as the services to London Heathrow and from Milan, Oslo and Stockholm. Some of these stations incorporate airline check-in desks, for example, Airport Express's London Paddington station for Heathrow, London Victoria for Gatwick and Hong Kong. The development of New York's Jamaica station as a virtual JFK tenth terminal makes this the largest facility of its type; AirTrain JFK began operating in 2003. In autumn 2001 AirTrain services began operating between Newark airport and New York City connecting with the airport's free internal monorail service.

Airports Council International See ACI[1] and www.airports.org

airports in America The top ten US airports in 2003 ranked by preliminary passenger traffic figures in millions were:

Atlanta	79.1
Chicago O'Hare	69.4
Los Angeles	55.0
Dallas/Fort Worth	53.2
Denver	37.5
Phoenix	37.4
Las Vegas	36.3
Houston Bush	34.1
Minneapolis/St Paul	33.2
Detroit	32.7

airports worldwide outside USA The top ten airports worldwide, outside the USA in 2003 ranked by preliminary passenger traffic figures in millions were:

London Heathrow	63.5
Tokyo Haneda	63.2
Frankfurt	48.4
Paris	48.1
Amsterdam	40.0

Madrid	35.7
Bangkok	30.2
London Gatwick	30.0
Hong Kong	26.8
Tokyo Narita	26.5

AIRPROX Air proximity; a 'near miss' aviation incident which might have resulted in a collision. This ICAO term has now replaced 'AIRMISS'. The UK AIRPROX Board (UKAB)'s fifth report states that during 2000, there were 99 AIRPROX incidents involving commercial air transport aircraft (CAT), the same number as in 1999 and just one more than in 1998. Of these 99 cases, 85 were assessed as 'no collision', eight as 'safety compromised' and six as 'collision risk existed'. Significantly, the risk-bearing rate for CAT incidents in 2000 fell to an all time low of 1.01 cases per 100,000 flying hours – down 62% on the figure for 1999. *See* www.ukab.org.uk

AIRS[1] Aircrew incident reporting system.

AIRS[2] Aviation Industry Report System (in Micronesia the equivalent is IATA ARP).

airscrew Obsolete name for an aircraft propeller; but note that 'screw' is still in usage meaning a ship's propeller.

airship A 'lighter-than-air' flying machine; distinguished from an aircraft, which is heavier than air, and a balloon, which has no means of propulsion. Also known as a blimp in the USA. Obsolescent name is dirigible. The demise of airship travel was hastened by the R101 disaster in 1930.

airside That part of an airport not accessible to the general public. After a traveller has passed through immigration controls, customs and security checks, they are designated as being airside. Conversely, public area before passing customs etc. is known as landside.

airspace *See* FIRs.

airspeed Aircraft speed in nautical miles per hour (knots).

airstream A current of air, such as a jetstream. *See* turbulence for fuller explanation.

airstrip Sometimes called 'landing strip'. Any cleared piece of ground long enough to enable aircraft to land and take off. The term does not imply the provision of any facilities.

AirTrain Originally designed as New York's Newark airport monorail system, linking the three terminals, a $650m investment extended the track one mile (1.6 km) to connect with a new Newark airport station linking the airport with regional services provided by New Jersey Transit, including Manhattan; the station is also served by Amtrak's North East corridor services from Washington, DC, Philadelphia, New York and Boston. *Also see* airport–city rail links.

AirTrain JFK New York's Kennedy Airport AirTrain runs 60 feet above the central reservation of the Van Wyck Expressway from Jamaica station in New York's south eastern borough of Queens. The $1.9 billion light-rail system provides services between the airport's nine terminal buildings and to a new subway station called Howard Beach, an interchange with Line A. Passengers can travel from the central terminal area to midtown Manhattan in about 50 minutes using Howard Beach station and in as little as 30 minutes to the much expanded Jamaica station. The service is provided by 32 driverless Bombardier trains powered by linear induction motors. The service is part of the LIRR network. *See* LIRR *and* http://www.airtrainjfk.com *and* airport–city rail links.

airways *See* FIRs.

airworthiness certificates Issued by governmental aviation authorities to denote that an aircraft or component part performs its function to the authorities' satisfaction.

AISC *See* Skal.

aisle seat A seat with open space to one side, in a means of transport, theatre or cinema etc. In wide-bodied jets, once side seats have been allocated, customers often prefer not to be seated in the centre part of five abreast seating and therefore request aisle seats.

AIT Alliance Internationale de Tourisme is a grouping of over 100 national automobile associations founded in 1898. *See* www.aitgva.ch

AITA Alliance for Independent Travel Agents in the USA. *See* Alliance.

AITAL Asociación Internacional de Transporte Aereo Latinoamericano (International Association of Latin American Air Transport). *See* www.aital.com

AITO The Association of Independent Tour Operators is the UK trade body of around 100 small tour operators, around three-quarters of which are also tour operating members of ABTA. The reason for their existence is because ABTA is dominated by its travel agent and major tour operator members, the latter also being able to exercise their voice through the Federation of Tour Operators. Membership is restricted to those who either hold a valid Air Travel Organizer's Licence or are tour operator members of ABTA. Its aims are commercial cooperation between members and the joint solution of common problems. *See* www.aito.co.uk

AIV Accord International de Voyageurs, the international agreement covering the transport of passengers by rail.

AJENTS System which connects UK domestic rail agents with ATOC's Rail Journey Information System via an Internet connection, providing an information, reservations, ticketing and accounting service. Through an appropriate printer, credit card sized rail tickets are produced, similar to those issued at rail stations in the UK. Some literature still describes an initial phase where connection was via X-TANT or Fastrak viewdata systems and ticket production was not automated.

Al Fursan Name of Saudi Arabian Airlines' airline club for frequent travellers. *See* airline clubs.

Alabama Bureau of Tourism and Travel *See* www.touralabama.org

Alaska Tourism Office *See* www.dced-state.ak.us/tourism

Alaska Travel Industry Association *See* www.alaskatia.org

alba International hotel code for a single-bedded room.

Albuquerque Convention and Visitors Bureau *See* www.abqcvb.org

alcove A small area set off from a larger room. In some European or American self-catering studio suites, there may be a main living space and separate alcoves where the kitchen and bed may be located.

ALEX Iceland's agency CRS; an Amadeus partner.

alien Any person outside the country of their nationality. The word 'alien' is becoming increasingly difficult to define. For example, freedom to travel and work anywhere within the European Community are some of many rights enjoyed by all EC citizens. Nevertheless, under the laws of each EC country, other EU member states' citizens are aliens. The WTO designates tourists as being away from their normal place of residence, disregarding their actual nationality.

all or nothing assignment *See* transport modelling.

All Purpose Ticket Issue System *See* APTIS.

all suite hotel Simplistically, a hotel where all accommodation is in suites. Unfortunately, the meaning of *suite* varies between countries both by law and custom. Increasingly, the term means an apartment hotel targeted at business travellers or other corporate staff seeking more space than usually provided in a hotel room, perhaps intending a long stay. Kitchen facilities of some type are part of the facilities. Typically, prices are 25% lower than an equivalent double room in a hotel; but there are seldom restaurants and room service. *See* suite, junior suite *and* en suite.

Allbook Name of British tour operators' reservation and accounting system introduced in 1984, developed from a Scandinavian system used since 1978.

all-expense tour US terminology for inclusive tour. *See* inclusive tour.

alleyway Passageway or narrow corridor of ship.

Alliance The ARTAC travel agents consortium in the UK changed its brand name to Worldchoice but because it started as the Alliance of Retail Travel Agency Consortia, the Alliance name is sometimes used. AITA (Alliance for Independent Travel Agents in the USA) is known as the Alliance, perhaps to distinguish it from the Association of International Travel Agents Inc.

all-in Australian term for Inclusive Tour. Mistakenly stated in several American publications as British terminology.

all-inclusive When applied to an accommodation tariff it usually means inclusion of all meals, limited drinks and other facilities; hence the addition of these words to various accommodation types, as in 'all-inclusive resort', or 'all-inclusive hotel'. When applied to a package holiday, for example a coach tour, travel facilities and excursions may be included. It is crucial that travellers identify what is *actually* included before purchasing all-inclusive arrangements. The 2003 CEN/European Standard official definition is 'Tariff in which the price includes accommodation, meals and specified beverages as well as specified facilities', conveniently avoiding actually specifying anything!

all-inclusive car rental rates This apparently clear statement offers rates which *vary*, according to the rental company and the country, including some or all of the following typical items: unlimited mileage, collision damage insurance excess waiver, local taxes, airport fees, surcharges and taxes, theft insurance excess waiver, all insurance excesses, public liability, property damage, full fire, theft and third party insurance with cover varying between countries according to local laws, bail bonds where needed, insurance cover for additional drivers, a full tank of petrol, return of vehicle out of normal hours and one-way rentals. *See also* car rental.

allocation *See* allotment.

allocentric tourists Tourists who are continually looking for new experiences and destinations; they are adventurous by nature.

allotment The provision by a travel industry principal of part of its services for onward sale to the eventual customer by another intermediary. For example, a tour operator may be given an allotment of beds throughout a season at a hotel. The contractual arrangements will determine whether part or all of the allotment is returnable without penalty, rates and other conditions. The tour operator may, in turn, give an allotment of part of one or more package holiday departures to a travel agency group, who agrees to sell them. The term is general throughout the industry. It may apply to anything from the provision of car hire, to seats on any mode of transport. It is fundamental that the granting of an allotment to a third party guarantees that space or beds have been reserved and will not be sold to anyone else until or unless the allotment is returned.

allowance of free baggage Baggage which may be carried without payment of a charge in addition to the fare. On international IATA air journeys, the allowance is either by weight or a number of pieces of defined dimensions dependent upon the route. The standard weight allowance is 20 kg (44 lb) for economy- and tourist-class passengers and 30 kg (66 lb) for first-class travellers. Many airlines have introduced within Europe an alternative of allowing one large piece of baggage, the dimensions of which do not total more than 67 in. plus a smaller case, the dimensions of which must not be more than 40 in. for tourist-class passengers. On transatlantic flights, two pieces are allowed with a dimension limitation of 62 in. Domestic air travel baggage rules vary considerably between countries.

Rail companies in the UK allow second-class travellers 50 kg (110 lb) and first-class passengers 70 kg (154 lb) with half these weights for children travelling at half adult fares. Unless, however, baggage is being sent in advance, these rules are not normally applied. Similarly, the European rail limit of 20 kg or 44 lb per person is only applied where baggage is 'registered through'. The UK coach allowance of one case is also treated flexibly by coach drivers.

aloft Above the superstructure in, at or near the masthead of a ship.

ALPA Air Line Pilots Association in the USA.

Alpha 3 Name of Air France computerized reservation and administration system. For details of travel agency terminal system in France *see* ESTEREL.

alphabet *See* phonetic alphabet.

alphanumeric Featuring of both letters and figures on a computer keyboard.

ALSSA The Air Line Stewards and Stewardesses Association is a US trade union. But the British Airline Stewards and Stewardesses Association is a branch of the Transport and General Workers Union in the UK.

ALTA Association of Local Transport Airlines in the USA.

alterations to air tickets *See* revalidation stickers.

alternate distribution systems In the USA implies a system which bypasses travel agents. *See* intermediation.

alternate restaurant US usage is a cruise ship restaurant for which a supplementary charge is payable. British usage is that any cruise ship restaurant separate from the main dining room may have this designation, whether or not there is an extra charge for its use.

alternative airport Any airport to which a flight may be diverted if a landing at the original destination is no longer possible.

alternative tourism *See* tourism, alternative.

altimeter Instrument in aircraft which indicates height (altitude). *See also* altitude.

ALTIS A guide to Internet resources in hospitality, leisure, sport and tourism. *See* LTSN *and* www.brookes.ac.uk/ltsn

altitude Height above mean sea level. *See* contour.

altostratus *See* clouds.

alumni rate US term for reduced price offered to previous cruise travellers, suggests US web site www.hometravel agency.com Term is not yet in general use.

ALVA Association of Leading Visitor Attractions in the UK. *See* www.alva.org.uk

a.m. From the Latin *ante meridiem*, meaning before noon. In most countries, the 24 h clock is used in the travel industry, in order to avoid errors; but in North America it is not uncommon to find the use of a.m. and p.m. in connection with travel timings.

Amadeus This Global Distribution System (worldwide CRS) was created by 12 European airlines: Air France, Air Inter, Adria Airways, Iberia, Icelandair, Linjeflyg, Lufthansa, Finnair, Yugoslavenski Aerotransport, Braathens, SAFE and SAS. The organization's current literature suggests only that it was created by Iberia, Air France, Lufthansa and SAS (no longer a shareholder). Following development of infrastructure, systems and software, operations began in 1992; several years later, another CRS, System One, was taken over. The corporate HQ is in Madrid, Spain; the product marketing and development office is in Nice, France, and the operations and data centre in Erding, Germany.

Hosts 220,000 agency terminals in 67,000 travel agency locations, through which can be accessed over 490 airlines, 51,000 hotels, 45 car rentals companies and other providers of tourism services.

In 2004 handled 454.1m bookings, 7.6% up on 2003. For detailed information *see* www.global.amadeus.net

Amadeus Travel Agency Advisory Board An independent international body set up and funded by Amadeus to represent agents' interests concerning the system.

AMASS Airport Movement Area Safety System, a Northrop Grumman system aimed at warning of and preventing airport runway incursions. It is a development of the same company's Airport Surface Detection Equipment (ASDE). At the time of writing installation was proceeding at 34 US airports at a cost of over US$90 million.

AMAV Asociación Mexicana de Agencias de Viajes, the Mexican Travel Agents Association.

AMAVE Asociación Mayoristas Agencias de Viajes Españolas; the Spanish equivalent of the Multiple Travel Agents Association in the UK.

Ambassador class Brand name given by TWA to passenger area immediately adjacent to first class, where passengers paying full economy fares enjoy improved service and facilities. *See* business class for full description.

Ambassador Club Name of TWA's Frequent Flyers' Club. Some guests' privileges, office and conference facilities are available in addition to the standard benefits noted under the general entry Frequent Flyer Clubs.

ambient resource The fundamental character of an area which gives it tourism potential, for example, attractive scenery or guaranteed sunshine. The difficulty with terminology of this nature is in limiting its scope. Some experts restrict the application to purely physical characteristics, while others would include interesting culture or even low prices.

amenity kit The complimentary items provided for guests in a hotel room or for first- or business-class passengers on a means of transport.

American Automobile Association *See* AAA.

American breakfast A full breakfast with a choice of hot and cold foods; also known as an 'English breakfast'.

American Bureau of Shipping *See* ABS.

American Bus Association *See* www.buses.org

American Hotel and Motel Association
See AH&MA.

American Hotel and Motel Association Educational Institute *See* www. eiahma.org/ei/index.htm

American Institute of Aeronautics and Astronauts *See* www.aiaa.org

American Plan (AP) Full pension or full board – hotel accommodation inclusive of full breakfast, lunch and dinner in the stated rate for the room. Sometimes called Full American Plan or Full Pension Plan in North America. *See also* MAP (Modified American Plan).

American Resort Development Association *See* www.arda.org

American service Type of restaurant service where meals are 'plated' by cooking staff and then served directly to customers; more usually called plate service, as distinct from silver service where waiting staff carry food in covered metal dishes to an adjacent serving table. The food is then, after heating, served individually to customers. *See also* English Service *and* Silver Service.

American Society of Travel Agents *See* ASTA[2].

AMFORHT Association Mondiale pour la Formation Hoteliere et Touristique (World Association for Hospitality Education and Training). Founded in 1969 at the same time as the WTO with the aims, 'to define, develop, promote and continuously adapt, tourism education on a world-wide basis to the evolving needs and focus on the tourism industry'. *See* www.amforht.org

AMHA American Motor Hotel Association.

amidships Middle part of a ship. Halfway between bow (front) and stern (back) of the ship.

AMP Airmail Panel; an IATA body formed in 1996, which reports to the CSC (Cargo Services Conference).

amsl Above mean sea level.

AMTA Association of Multiple Travel Agents in the UK.

AMTOS Aircraft maintenance task orientation system.

Amtrak The brand name under which the National Railroad Passenger Corporation operates 265 US intercity passenger trains daily, under contract with individual railroads. Although operating over 22,000 route miles, it only owns around 3% of US rail track, 730 miles, most of which is the line between Washington, DC and Boston. Amtrak has also successfully tendered for contracts to run commuter services, such as Caltrain in California. The organization was set up in 1970 under the Rail Passenger Service Act and began operating the following year as a federally owned railroad. Amtrak was granted the right of access to the tracks owned by the freight railroads at an incremental cost and with operating priority over freight trains. Amtrak was also granted a monopoly to provide intercity rail transport over its route system. It was intended that after a few years' initial losses, it would become profitable, but during the last 30 years, subsidies of over US$27 billion have been needed. Thus, in 1997, Congress set Amtrak the objective of operational revenue covering operation costs by December 2002. To oversee headway the 1997 Act created the Amtrak Reform Council (ARC); it also provided 5 further years of funding, ended Amtrak's rail passenger monopoly and permitted closure of lines making losses.

The traffic reductions following 11 September 2001 terrorism served to exacerbate a worsening situation. As a result in November 2001, the ARC decided that Amtrak would not achieve self-sufficiency by the end of 2002 and that Amtrak should draw up a plan for liquidation by 7 February 2002, while by the same date, the ARC would draw up a plan for a restructured and rationalized national US passenger rail system. The liquidation never happened! On 7 February the ARC submitted its restructuring plan to Congress. But readers should particularly note that, crucially, the original 1997 Act did not require either the House or the Senate to act on the ARC's plan! The scheme envisaged separating Amtrak's functions into three units, each with separate Boards of Directors. The first unit would be responsible for government programme administration and hold the statutory franchise to access freight railroad rights of way at incremental costs and with operating priority. It would maintain and improve a national reservations system and ensure joint ticketing. Insurance to train operators and limitation of their liability would be continued.

The second unit would be responsible for train operations, handling mail and express business, passenger and commuter operations and equipment and repair shops. The plan envisaged the eventual privatization of this unit. The third unit would be responsible for infrastructure; it would own and maintain the North East corridor from Washington, DC to Boston, Massachussets.

The ARC plan would permit the introduction of competition at the end of a 2 to 5 year transition period, by the train operating company offering exclusive franchises through competitive bidding. Franchises would be designed and a bidding process established. Among ideas floated in the ARC report are the creation of a passenger rail trust fund and infrastructure financing through the enactment of a Railroad Infrastructure and Development Act for the 21st Century (known as RIDE-21). The US government responded to some of the ARC proposals in July 2003 with the Bush Administration Rail Plan. This sought federal/state rail partnerships to develop passenger rail services. The plan supported proposals to divide the railroad into three separate corporations according to function. Amtrak is strongly against this.

In mid-2004 Amtrak updated its 5 year strategic plan for US railroads. This called for federal funding of capital projects of around \$1.6bn annually and continuance of the \$570m annual support for operating purposes. In furtherance of the Bush proposals, Amtrak has, together with the states involved evaluated the readiness for immediate development of busy commuter rail corridors; those meeting the study criteria have been designated Tier I corridors. Amtrak's ridership on key corridors grew from 17m in 1999 to 21m in 2004.

At the time of going to press, newspaper stories suggested that some services would be reduced as a cost saving measure. However, Amtrak has assured customers that all trains will continue to operate normally for the foreseeable future. See www.amtrak.com and North American train services.

Amtrak Reform Council Following submission of Action plan in February 2002, work concluded. See www.amtrak.reform.council.gov *and* Amtrak.

amusement park In Britain, this may be little more than a few fairground attractions but in the USA, the term implies something on a grander scale. See theme parks.

analog (analogue) Data transmission method, which is the normal way that speech goes along telephone lines. Most computers transmit data in digital format. In this mode, sometimes called binary, there is a series of on or off pulses, all symbols, alphanumeric characters or other information, being broken down into such a series. Analog is a descriptive term that can be applied widely; but it is sufficient for travel industry use merely to understand that continuously variable analog waves, for example on telephone lines, must be converted before use by digital travel computers. For explanation of conversion see modem.

Anasazi Computerized hotel reservation system.

ANATO National Association of Travel and Tourist Agents in Colombia. See www.alca-ftaa.oas.org

ANC Active noise control (systems).

anchor Apparatus which attaches a water-borne vessel to the seabed, usually by its hooks. Classically of T shape and of heavy metal. Hence the term 'anchors away', which is the layman's misunderstanding of the term 'anchors aweigh', which means that a ship has taken the weight of the anchor, so that it no longer secures the ship.

anchorage port Means a port with no quay or berthing facilities for cruise ships. But note particularly that the increasing size of cruise vessels means that at some ports the large vessels cannot dock, but smaller ships may have a berth. See tender.

Andromeda Was the name of the UK AT&T ISTEL computer system for travel agents, combining a direct permanent connection from agency to

ISTEL's central computer, Autobook, the enhanced PC-based viewdata system and Mycrom Abacas back office accounting and administration system. ISTEL is now called AT&T Business (Travel Division).

anemometer An instrument which measures windspeed, various types of which are to be found at sea or in airports.

Anguilla Tourist Board *See* www.anguilla-vacation.com

animals by air A special type of box, designated in IATA regulations, must be used when an animal is being carried by air. One end of the box has to be virtually open and covered with bars to enable the animal to breathe. There is a complicated formula for determining the size of box necessary.

For example, if it is a dog, the length of the container required is calculated by adding together the length of the dog from nose to root of the tail, to the height from the ground to elbow joint. The container has to be twice as wide as the width of the dog across the shoulders, and at least the height of the dog in a standing position.

Special containers suitable for livestock are available from British Airways and other airlines. Largest normal size available is 36 × 18 × 26 inches. Travel clerks need to obtain special labels for customers, clearly indicating that the receptacle contains a live animal, its type and a sign showing the upright position.

Because of anti-rabies rules and other regulations, dogs and many other animals will not be allowed to enter Britain without undergoing a lengthy period of quarantine, unless they are certified as rabies free on a special type of animal passport. Clients should therefore be advised not to take their animals abroad unless they are emigrating or intending to leave the animal abroad.

animateur A leisure activities coordinator. The word is not used in the UK or, generally, outside continental Europe. The 2003 CEN/European Standard official definition is: 'A person responsible for the planning and supervising of leisure and sports activity programmes who encourages travellers to participate and speaks the language understood by the majority of the travellers.' The problem with this definition is that it sets a standard in its final part; language facility is not inherent in defining the meaning of 'animateur'.

annexe Concerning a travel contract or booking conditions, a separate part, usually more detailed than the main clauses. In respect of accommodation, extra rooms separate from the main part, often without many of the services provided for guests in the main building. *See also* accommodation types.

ANO Air Navigation Order.

ANSIX12 An EDI standard of the American National Standards Institute, used by the travel industry.

Antarctic That part of the Southern hemisphere around the South Pole; technically, that part south of the line of latitude 66° 33′ S.

Antarctic Traveller's Code Ecotourism rules operated by cruise operators to the area with the aim of sustainable tourism, so that cruising does not affect the environment being visited.

Anti Trust Travel Agent Coalition US travel agents body mounting class action lawsuit against airlines opposing changes to zero commission.

Antigua and Barbuda Tourist Office *See* www.antigua-barbuda.com

antipodean day A day gained because the date goes backwards when crossing the 180th parallel of longitude, travelling in an easterly direction. *See also* International Date Line.

ANTOR[1] Association of National Tourist Office Representatives in the UK. ANTOR in the UK has a membership of 85 countries. It was established in 1952 to represent the views of its members and facilitate the development of travel outbound from the UK. Objectives are to coordinate and improve, through mutual cooperation, the services that members offer to both the travel industry and British public. ANTOR has two web sites: www.tourist-offices.org.uk and www.antor.com

ANTOR[2] Assembly of National Tourist Office Representatives with similar objectives in the USA.

ANVR Algemene Nederlandse Vereniging van Reisburo – the Dutch national travel agency organization. *See* www.touring.nl

AOA[1] Angle of attack (of an aircraft).

AOA² Aerodrome Owners' Association is the British trade body of the smaller airports.

AOA³ Airport Operators Association is the trade association that represents the interests of British airports and is the principal body with whom the UK government and regulatory authorities consult on airport matters. Membership comprises 71 airports representing all of the nation's international hub and major regional airports in addition to many serving community, business and leisure aviation. *See* www.aoa.org.uk

AOC Air Operators' Certificate from the Civil Aviation Authority is required in the UK by any person or organization wishing to start an airline or air taxi service. The Flight Operations Inspectorate investigates whether the applicant has sufficient managerial and technical resources to carry out safe operations and, once an OAC is granted, continuously monitors the holder.

AOCI The Airport Operators' Council International based in the USA is an international trade body representing various governmental bodies responsible for airport operation.

AODB Airport and Obstacle Database, created by IATA.

AOG Aircraft on ground.

AONB Area of Outstanding Natural Beauty (in the UK). The Countryside Commission, Countryside Council for Wales and Department of the Environment for Northern Ireland all have the right to declare such areas, which are on a much smaller scale than national parks. The 50 or so AONBs are conserved and protected against most commercial or private development. In Scotland, the equivalent designation is National Scenic Area.

AOPA Aircraft Owners and Pilots Association of the UK represents private pilots and aircraft owners in Britain, and has representatives on the international AOPA body, together with other national AOPAs. *See* www.aopa.co.uk

AoReCa The International Union of National Associations of Hotel, Restaurant and Cafe-Keepers is a grouping of various national and other trade bodies in this field.

AOTOS *See* Admiral of the Open Sea Award.

Ap Approach (lighting at an aerodrome).

AP Via Atlantic and Pacific. *See* routing; *also* American Plan.

AP/DF Approach and direction-finding facility.

APALS Autonomous precision approach and landing system.

aparthotel In Europe, the term usually means a hotel where all accommodation is self-catering apartments, with, at the minimum, a small kitchen area, toilet and bath or shower and bedroom. This type of accommodation varies greatly in the hotel services provided and public rooms. In Europe, the terms apartment hotel, apartment complex and residence are similar establishments. Whereas in Europe an aparthotel may be very large, in America the term is usually used to describe a small hotel providing room or bed and breakfast only, which in Britain is a guest house or boarding house. In the USA, this type of accommodation, particularly when it is meeting the needs of commercial clients, is known as a hotel garni. The 2003 CEN/European Standard official definition misses a crucial point by not mentioning self-catering or kitchen facilities in the definition.

apartment Self-catering accommodation providing sleeping and sitting facilities with a kitchenette in one large room is usually known as a 'studio apartment', to distinguish it from an apartment where the sleeping facilities are separate. The 2003 CEN/European Standard official definition of 'apartment' incorporates separation as part of the standard. It then designates aparthotels, apartment hotels, apartment complexes and residences as establishments where accommodation is provided in studios or apartments.

apartment complex *See* aparthotel.

apartment hotel *See* aparthotel.

APAVT The Portuguese Association of Travel Agents and Tourism.

APCO Association of Pleasure Craft Operators in the UK; founded in 1954, it is the trade association for operators of self-drive hire, passenger/restaurant and hotel boats on Britain's inland waterways. *See* www.canals.com/orgs/apco.htm

APD Air Passenger Duty; a UK tax on all air travellers flying from a British airport.

APEX Advance Purchase Excursion transport fare.

API[1] Air position indicator (aviation term).

API[2] Application Programming Interface; a file or group of computer files for which a non-copyright interface is available, so that other software can interact with it. This is particularly important in the travel industry so that APIs are available enabling reservation and other data from GDSs to be used in travel agents' back office systems.

APIS *See* Advance Passenger Information System.

APJC *See* Agency Programme Joint Council.

APL A Programme Language, a computer programming language designed for business planning.

APLG Agency Programme Liaison Group. *See* Agency Programme Joint Council.

APMS Automated performance measuring system (aviation term).

APN Advance Passenger Notice.

Apollo Originally was United Airlines' automated reservation and information system, operated by subsidiary, Covia, through which many US agents made general industry and airline bookings; now integrated with Galileo. The Apollo brand name is still used for Galileo, the huge global CRS, in the USA, Mexico and Japan. *See* Galileo.

APP Approach control (aviation term).

apparel Although the word means clothing in general English, in shipping, it applies to all of a vessel's equipment, including such things as anchors and ropes. When chartering a ship, the wording is often extended to state 'apparel, tackle and appurtenances', covering everything physical necessary to enable the ship to function efficiently and operate for the purpose for which it was chartered.

application packages Computer programmes tailored to handle the user's particular requirement, for example, preparation of an agent's sales returns. (A general technical term.)

Application Processing System (of ARC) *See* ARC[1].

appointment The term means both the agreement entitling a travel agent to represent a travel industry principal and the process of approval. Unless an agent is officially appointed, under the terms of a specific written agreement, major groupings such as IATA will not grant commission. Although an inaccurate use of the word, it is common in the UK to call appointments 'licences'.

approval criteria for UK IATA agents *See* Agency Programme Joint Council.

Approved Agent Official IATA definition is a Passenger Sales Agent whose name is entered on the Agency List. The term in general use in the travel industry applies to any travel agent approved by a particular travel principal to sell that principal's services.

Approved Location Official IATA definition is the Head Office, Branch Office and Satellite Ticket Printer locations appearing on the Agency List.

après ski Broadly, the leisure activities in winter sports resorts.

APRO Airline Public Relations Organisation is a British group of PR managers of most airlines operating inside and from the UK. *See* apro@onetel.net.uk

apron (or ramp) Hard surface area off the airport runways, where aircraft are parked for loading, unloading, servicing or any other handling.

APS[1] Application Processing System of the US Airline Reporting Corporation for accreditation. This now allows applications to be processed electronically. *See* ARC[1].

APS[2] Aircraft prepared for service (aviation term).

APSC[1] Airline Passenger Service Commitment, a May 2001 agreement drawn up by carriers, passengers' representatives, European Civil Aviation Conference (ECAC) and the European Commission, as a voluntary code that commits airlines to provide a clearly defined minimum standard of service and sales information to air travellers. *See* Airline Passenger Service Commitment in 'denied boarding compensation'.

APSC[2] Atlantic Passenger Steamship Conference – a rate-making conference of shipping lines operating on the North Atlantic. Dissolved with the formation of the International Passenger Ship Association.

APT Advanced Passenger Train. The prototype began trials in spring 1980, eventually coming into service several years later and then being withdrawn because of problems with the tilting mechanism. Other fast train services (*see* TGV and Bullet Train) operate on specially built tracks with only slight curves. British Rail's APT used ordinary rail track; compensating against forces while travelling around a bend by tilting the train. The APT eventually went into regular service on the London–Glasgow route in 1984 carrying 8000 passengers without mishap. On 12 December 1984, the APT broke the record from London to Glasgow with a time of 3 h 52.75 min, including a 3 min signal wait, for the 401 mile run, at an average speed of over 103 mph. The APT was capable of over 160 mph on specially prepared track. Further development work on the APT has ceased. Altogether BR is believed to have invested £50 million on the APT project. Now, British Rail no longer exists, having been split up into 25 train-operating companies, Network Rail and engineering companies etc.

APTG   Association of Professional Tourist Guides in the UK. *See* www.aptg.org.uk

APTIS   'All Purpose Ticket Issue System' was the name of British Rail's electronic ticket issuing and accounting machine. The prototype was introduced to BR stations in 1982 in the form of a unit measuring 476 mm × 182 mm. Now used by UK rail stations to sell tickets for ATOC members (Association of Train Operating Companies).

APU   Auxiliary Power Unit; planes standing on the tarmac can become very uncomfortable for passengers for lengthy periods without the engines running, particularly in hot climates, because there is insufficient power to operate the air conditioning.

aquapark   Leisure facility strongly oriented towards water sports.

aquaplaning   Phenomenon where the tyres of a vehicle suffer from lack of adhesion to the surface in wet conditions, making it difficult to steer or brake. Particularly dangerous for aircraft attempting to land in tropical rainstorms.

AQZ   Area mean sea level barometric pressure zone.

ARA   Agent Reporting Agreement (of the ARC).

Arab   International hotel code for a twin-bedded room. Also name for an inhabitant of the Kingdom of Saudi Arabia, often generally applied to the inhabitants of many Middle Eastern countries.

Arab Air Carriers Organization   *See* www.aaco.org

Arbiter   Throughout the world, there are airline/IATA agency programmes operating under IATA resolutions 808 and 814, setting up organizations through which disputes between agents and the airlines/IATA may be settled. In the USA, however, arguments between agents and the Airlines Reporting Corporation are settled by a particular person, who holds the appointment of Arbiter.

arbitrary   Alternative name for a proportional fare. *See* proportional fare.

arbitration   *See* ABTA Arbitration Scheme.

ARC[1]   The Airlines Reporting Corporation became effective in the USA on 1 January 1985. Following the Airline Deregulation Act of 1978 and the Civil Aeronautic's Board's Competitive Marketing Investigation, airlines lost their anti-trust immunity. This meant that each individual airline now had to set appointment standards, commission levels and cover a huge variety of business matters previously handled under the umbrella of their IATA membership. To achieve efficient handling of airline sales while avoiding anti-competitive activities, US domestic carriers formed the ARC, while international carriers formed the Passenger Network Services Corporation, which became the parent company of IATAN, the International Airlines Travel Agent Network.

An ARC-approved agency is open and accessible to the general public for the retail sale of air transportation. Agents must employ at least one Certified ARC Specialist (CAS). A management 'qualifier' may be a person who the ARC feel is qualified to open an agency because of past relevant experience. New agents have, since July 1999, been required to have a ticketing specialist who has become a CAS via a written examination, designed to validate the ticketing qualifier's knowledge of the *Industry Agents Handbook*. Agents exert their influence via an ARC Advisory Council. The system retained some aspects of the Air Traffic Conference travel agency programme, such as a central administrative system, accreditation, bonding, maintaining uniform standards for agents and the Area Settlement Plan by which agents pay for ticket issues. Initially the ARC did not allow travel agents to use standard ticket stock in unattended ticketing machines. Under the ARC rules, agents have the ability to operate in a dual capacity, both under an ARC appointment and outside this system on an individual basis with air carriers. The ARC has coined a new term for those accredited by them, namely Industry Agents.

The ARC enables agents to vary remittance dates with individual airlines, which may help them keep money in their accounts for a longer period of time than the normal 7-day cycle. It is to be noted that the normal payment cycle in the UK is calendar monthly on the 17th of the month following ticket issuance. In the USA, to prevent massive withdrawal errors, agents nominate a 'maximum authorized amount' that the ARC may withdraw from their account. By mid 2000, ARC had switched from manual reporting to an electronic automatic reporting system, Interactive Agent Reporting (IAR). Under this system a TAAD is a Travel Agent Automated Deduction, the equivalent of an ADM (Agency Debit Memo) in the UK. Often, US travel agents charge for their services in providing low commission or nett price air tickets. When passengers pay for their tickets inclusive of the agent's fee in a single credit card transaction, the agent can submit a Travel Agency Service Fee Document (TAF) under ARC's Area Settlement Plan. At the end of 2001, an ESAC authorization code was introduced, assigned by a carrier through a CRS when a void, refund or exchange request is made on an electronic ticket. Passenger name transmittal files have enabled agents to send details to a back-office file.

Until recently, corporate travel departments (CTDs) in the USA could only get ARC accreditation in two ways. They could operate as an agency open to the public, a route that was followed by McDonnell Douglas, now part of Boeing and Charles Schwab. Alternatively, arrangements could be made with an ARC-accredited agency to use their authorization; the CTD undertakes all the travel services, using the ARC agency number. This is known as 'Rent a plate', referring to the plates that used to be used in air ticket validation imprinters. In January 1999, following a successful Beta test, the ARC offered CTDs the opportunity to be authorized in their own right under a Corporate Travel Department Reporting Agreement (CTDRA). There are around 50 accredited CTDs. They are required to post financial performance bonds of between US$50,000 and US$100,000. The application fee is from US$850 to US$1000 plus an extra US$150 per authorized location and US$625 for each Satellite Ticket Printer. As with travel agencies, it is a requirement that a member of staff be a Certified ARC Specialist (CAS).

All ARC appointees, whether Industry Agents or CTDs have to follow strict security provisions concerning ARC Traffic Documents, for which the appointee is *absolutely* liable. Those who undertake security arrangements even more stringent than those required, may obtain relief from liability for their ARC documents. In conclusion, *it is stressed that US agents are not required to be appointed through ARC.* They can sell airline tickets, earn commission or obtain reduced-rate tickets dealing directly with individual airlines. It is, however, convenient to become automatically appointed by over 100 airlines automatically, using standard ticket stock of the ARC ASP (Area Settlement Plan). Sales and reporting for these airlines and Amtrak is much simpler than dealing with each airline. For full information about ARC *see* www.arccorp.com *also see* host agency, Restricted Access Location, TravelSellers.com number *and* TSI.

ARC² Automated Revenue Collection system was used by the Owners Abroad group. It was a UK travel agency direct banking debit system whereby the agent's bank account was automatically debited, weekly, for the value of transactions with that operator due for payment. Although the brand name is part of the First Choice UK tour operator group, there is now generic usage of the ARC acronym.

ARC³ Amtrak Reform Council. *See* Amtrak.

ARC Advisory Council *See* ARC¹.

ARC number The eight-digit code allocated to ARC-appointed travel agents, the equivalent of IATA numbers in the rest of the world. Continental Airlines and Northwest Airlines require US domestic air booking locations that are not ARC accredited, but using a GDS, to obtain an RSP (Reservation Service Provider) number from ARC. This applies to all non-ARC users of a GDS outside contractors and corporate customers. In lieu of an RSP number, non-accredited international booking locations located outside the USA, Puerto Rico and USA Virgin Islands must obtain a TIDS (Travel Industry Designator Service) number from IATA. Applications via www. arccorp.com/aguaform.htm (US$225 for 3 years) or www.iata.org/tids (US$55).

architectural bias (of CRS) Refers to the way airlines' computer reservation systems used to be designed so that the parent airlines' flights were given precedence. Bias was prohibited in the USA, prior to deregulation. It is still prevented by the EC Neutral CRS Rules (Appendix III). These are under review and likely to change within the currency of this dictionary.

architecture Term used to describe the design of a computer system which often limits software programs that can be implemented on the equipment.

archived files In general applies to files in a travel agency which are no longer current, the customers having travelled and the accounting concluded. The term is also applied to computerized information stored on a disk or tape separate from the computer system, so that it may be accessed if specifically loaded.

ARCHY Accounts and Reservations Computer Holiday System; *was* the acronym for British Airways Tours Division private Viewdata system, providing full interactive communication with UK travel agents, enabling them to make bookings direct from their office terminals. Now obsolete, having been

replaced with the PAL section of BA LINK, which itself became obsolete in 2001.

Arctic That part of the northern hemisphere around the North Pole; technically, that part north of the line of latitude 66° 33' N.

ARDA American Resort Development Association. *See* www.arda.org

Area *See* the three geographical areas delineated as IATA Traffic Conference Areas, listed under the headings TC-1, TC-2 and TC-3.

Area Bank Settlement Plan *See* BSP.

Area of Bank Settlement Plan A country or group of countries in which a BSP operates.

Area of Outstanding Natural Beauty *See* AONB.

Area Settlement Plan *See* ASP.

Argentina National Travel Agency Organization *See* AAAVT.

Argentina Secretaria de Turismo *See* www.turismo.gov.ar

ARIES Was Agents Reservations and Information and Enquiries System, the acronym for Global's private Viewdata system in the UK.

ARINC Aeronautical Radio Inc. (also known as ADNS) is a non-profit making computer communications network owned by American air carriers, which also offers facilities like other travel service providers such as hotels and car rental companies.

Arizona Office of Tourism *See* www. arizonaguide.com

ARMTA Association of Regional Multiple Travel Agents in the UK.

ARP Agents Reporting Plan (of IATA air ticket sales) in the USA.

ARR¹ Arrival (aviation term).

ARR² Average room rate.

arrival tax Payment required from travellers at their destination. Usually, but not always, applied by a few countries to international arrivals.

arrival time The 2003 CEN/European Standard official definition is 'Time when the contracted service of transport ends.' Thus, the words have been given contractual significance which may become important if this standard ever has the force of law. Most travellers, for example, regard the landing time of an aircraft as their arrival time; it may well be up to an hour later that they finally pick up their luggage, thus concluding their contract.

ARS Automatic route setting. *See* Train Describer.

ARSR Air route surveillance radar.

ARTA Association of Retail Travel Agents, a trade association of US travel agents. *See* www.artaonline.com

ARTAC Alliance of Retail Travel Agency Consortia but legally registered as Alliance Travel Ltd. Operates under the brand name 'Worldchoice'. In 2001, officially changed name to Worldchoice. Grouping of most of the local and regional UK travel agents cooperative associations, including Active, Consort, Diamond, E.F.T.A., F.O.S.T.A., Gwynedd, L.T.A.C., Sun Island, Sun West, Sussex and Unity. Alliance negotiates override commissions and other deals for members. It is as large as UK multiple travel retailers, creating sufficient national cooperative marketing effort to match their buying power. In the 1990s, the Carlton group was owner of the AT Mays UK travel agency chain; the Worldchoice brand name was acquired in return for a marketing deal with ARTAC, giving the consortium combined with the chain even bigger buying power. When Thomas Cook acquired the Carlton agencies, arrangements were made so that Worldchoice was aligned with Thomas Cook in general and its holiday brand, JMC. *See* www.worldchoice.co.uk, ACAS, travel agency consortia in the UK *and* consortium.

Articles of Association A lengthy document detailing the activities a British limited company may undertake and the rules by which that company is governed. In the USA the term Articles of Incorporation is used.

artificial beach A beach that has been man-made, usually by the transport of sand and shingle from another place.

ARTIST Agenda for Research on Tourism by Integration of Statistics/Strategies for Transport. A project funded by the European Commission under the Transport RTD Programme of the 4th Research and Development Framework Programme.

ARTS Automatic Radar Terminal System enabling air traffic controllers to monitor and organize aircraft under their control.

Aruba Tourism Authority *See* www.aruba.com

AS/PAC Asia Pacific, an IATA region.

ASA An Air Service Agreement is an agreement between two or more states, regulating the air services between them. The Bermuda Agreement was made in 1946, relating to air services between Britain and the USA. This bilateral agreement was subsequently renegotiated in 1977. The original has been used as a model for many other similar bilateral air agreements, hence the term 'Bermuda type agreement' has become generic.

The most important clause in this type of agreement states that there shall be a fair and equal opportunity for the carriers of the two nations to operate on any route included in the agreement. Most international air operations are controlled by bilateral Air Services Agreements made between the governments concerned. Sometimes traffic rights are restricted. Thus, an airline flying from A to B to C and to D, may have no traffic rights to carry passengers only travelling between B and C, but permission to pick up or set down passengers travelling between these and the other points.

A multilateral ASA is one between three or more countries. When the governments concerned have signed agreements, they do not specify fares. These are left to the airlines to decide, subject to the ratification of governments. *See also* Bermuda, Traffic Rights, Freedoms of the Air, Five Freedoms of the Air *and* Chicago Convention.

ASATA Association of Southern African Travel Agents. *See* www.asata.co.za

ASAV Asociación Salvadorena de Agencias de Viajes.

ASB Air service bulletin.

ASC¹ Airport Service Charge. Charge on all passengers leaving on an international journey from an airport under the control of certain authorities, covering airport handling charges and air traffic control fees. In some cases this charge can only be paid within the country concerned; in Europe it is now normally included in the total charge for the ticket, but shown in a separate box. In 1999, in Europe, airlines began to separate these charges from fares, denoting them in a tax box on air tickets. The effect of this was to deny agents commission on a significant part of the ticket value. Court cases against airlines in Germany and Britain in 1999/2000 found in favour of agents, forcing commission payments on passenger service charges. Now that most airline commissions have ceased, the decision is merely history. *See* APD *and* departure tax.

ASC² Airport Services Committee of IATA. *See* IATA.

ASC³ Association of Snowsport Countries. This organization was formed in 1999 by the tourist boards of nine leading winter sports countries, Andorra, Austria, Canada, France, Norway, Slovenia, Sweden and Switzerland and USA. *See* www. snowsportscountries.com

ASC⁴ Aviation Security Charge; ASCs were introduced in the light of the US airline terrorist attacks on 11 September 2001, to cover the extra costs of air travel security and insurance.

ASCII American Standard Code of Information Interchange. One of the main computer standards defining every character or figure in an 8-bit digital coding system.

ASDA Acceleration stop distance available (aviation term).

ASDE Airport Surface Detection Equipment. *See* AMASS.

ASEAN Association of South East Asian Nations.

ASFA Association of Special Fare Agents. A grouping of international air travel consolidators.

ASG Air Safety Group.

ASI¹ Air speed indicator (aviation term).

ASI² American Sightseeing International, an international trade body for local tour operators.

ASIA Airlines Staff International Association based at Geneva Airport, Switzerland.

ASK Available seat kilometres. An air term arrived at by multiplying passenger capacity (number of seats) by route distances in kilometres. *See also* RPK.

ASM¹ Available seat miles. An air term arrived at by multiplying passenger capacity (number of seats) by route distances in miles.

ASM² Ad hoc schedules message from IATA providing details of an air schedule change.

ASMGCS Advanced surface movement guidance and control system (aviation term).

ASO Agency Services Office (of IATA).

Asociacao Brasileira de Agencias de Viagens *See* www.abav.com.br

ASOR Used to be the 'Agreement on the international carriage of passengers by road by means of occasional bus and coach services'; replaced from 1 January 2003 by the Interbus Agreement on the international occasional carriage of passengers by coach and bus. See www.europa.eu.int/scadplus/leg/en/lvb/124264.htm

ASP Area Settlement Plan, the generic term for schemes which enable travel agents to use standard air ticket stock and make one payment for each accounting period, rather than dealing with a multiplicity of airlines. For a typical example *see* BSP.

ASPA Association of South Pacific Airlines.

ASR¹ Airport surveillance radar.

ASR² Agent's Sales Return, which is a listing of all the tickets sold in a particular period. Sales returns must be furnished to a travel industry principal by an agent by a date specified in the agency agreement, together with a remittance for the value of the tickets less agency commission.

ASRP Aviation Safety Reporting Programme (aviation term).

ASRS Aviation Safety Reporting System (aviation term).

assistance during travel The 2003 CEN/European Standard official definition is 'information and support for travellers during the contracted portions of their travel, including a 24 h/365 day contact number'. It is suggested that this is an example of the danger of making a group of words with an obvious meaning into a definition. It is, for example, self-evident that travellers getting information from a tourist information centre after a flight but before continuing their journey onwards by public or private transport, are being assisted during travel.

Associated British Ports (ABP) *See* www.abports.co.uk

Associated Travel Network *See* ATN[2].

Association for Conferences and Events *See* ACE.

Association Mondiale pour la Formation Hoteliere et Touristique *See* AMFORHT *also* www.amforht.org

Association of African Airlines (AAFRA) *See* www.yohannes.com/Africa/AFRAA.htm

Association of American Railroads *See* www.aar.org

Association of ATOL Companies in the UK formerly the Association of Airline Consolidators. *See* www.aac-uk.org

Association of Bonded Travel Organisers Trust *See* ABTOT; www.abtot.com

Association of British Professional Conference Organizers (ABPCO) *See* www.abpco.org

Association of British Tour Operators to France *See* ABTOF. *See* www.holidayfrance.org.uk

Association of British Travel Agents *See* ABTA.

Association of British Travel Agents Certificate *See* ABTAC.

Association of British Travel Agents Tour Operators Certificate *See* ABTOC.

Association of Business Travellers (in the USA) *See* www.abt-travel.com

Association of Canadian Travel Agents (ACTA[1]) *See* www.acta.net

Association of Car Rental Information System Standards *See* ACRISS.

Association of Collegiate Conference and Events Directors-International (in the USA) *See* www.acced-i.org

Association of Cyprus Travel Agents (ACTA[3]) *See* www.pio.gov.cy

Association of Destination Management Executives (in the USA) – Qualification is DMCP (Destination Management Certified Professional). *See* www.adme.org

Association of European Airlines (AEA) *See* www.aea.be

Association of European Community Travel Agents and Tour Operators *See* ECTAA.

Association of Exhibition Organizers (AEO) *See* www.aeo.org

Association of Flight Attendants (AFA) *See* www.afanet.org

Association of Group Travel Executives *See* AGTE.

Association of Independent Tour Operators *See* AITO.

Association of Leading Visitor Attractions *See* ALVA *and* www.alva.org.uk

Association of National Tourist Office Representatives *See* ANTOR.

Association of Pleasure Craft Operators *See* APCO.

Association of Professional Tourist Guides (APTG) *See* www.aptg.org.uk

Association of Retail Travel Agents *See* ARTA.

Association of Snowsport Countries *See* ASC[3].

Association of Southern African Travel Agents *See* www.asata.co.za

Association of Teachers and Trainers in Tourism *See* ATTT.

Association of Train Operating Companies *See* ATOC.

Association of Travel Marketing Executives *See* www.atme.org

Association of Travel Trades Clubs *See* ATTC[1].

Association of Women Travel Executives A UK organization, affiliated to the Women's Travel Club of Great Britain. AWTE London organizes a mixture of educational and social events for its members, including seminars, workshops, evening meetings and monthly lunch meetings. *See* www.awte-london.co.uk *also see* IFWTO – www.ifwto.org

ASTA Tour Operator Program Whereas ABTA rules including consumer protection are mandatory on all members, ASTA's TOP is voluntary. ASTA's tour operating members are encouraged to highlight their reliability and financial stability through adherence to standards set by ASTA and participation in a consumer protection plan. A TOP program member must be an Active or Allied member of ASTA and have been in the business of operating tours for at least the previous 3 years. US$1 million Errors and Omissions insurance must be effected naming travel agents as additional insured parties. Travel agent bookings must be accepted and commission paid; TOP participating operators must ensure their promotional material does not disparage agents. Operators agree to comply with applicable federal and state travel regulations. They must respond to Better Business Bureau and other consumer protection agency complaints within 30 days and cooperate with ASTA's consumer affairs department in resolving complaints. Compliance with the ASTA Code of Ethics and ASTA's environmental code is sought.

Under TOP, operators must participate in one of the following consumer protection plans: USTOA US$1 million bond; NTA US$250,000 bond; National City Bank Travel Funds Protection Plan (TFPP) or Federal Maritime Commission (FMC) financial indemnification. For details of these *see* entries under their respective headings. For details of operation of an escrow account and of the TFPP *see* escrow account. For more details concerning bonding, *see* ATOL, ABTA, ASTA, ATRF, BCC, BRF, FMC, NTA[1], TOP[3], TPA (obsolete), USTOA and the Internet sites associated with those entries.

ASTA[1]   Airport surface traffic automation.

ASTA[2]   The American Society of Travel Agents is a US trade organization with its headquarters in New York, founded in 1931. It represents travel agents and other travel industry businesses throughout the world. With more than 26,000 members it is the largest organization of its kind. NACTA is a wholly owned subsidiary (*see* NACTA). Classes of membership are Active, International, Individual, Allied, Travel School, Associate, Associate Independent, Senior and Honorary.

Active members must be located in the USA, Puerto Rico, the US Virgin Islands, Guam, Northern Mariana or American Samoa. They must operate with the intention of making a profit from the travel agency business and conduct the majority of their business in an agency/principal relationship with suppliers. They must not be owned or controlled by a major supplier. They must also be accredited by the ARC, or ARP, or endorsed by IATAN or hold Errors and Omissions insurance of at least US$1 million.

International members must be IATA appointees not located in the USA and be operated with the intention of making a profit from the travel agency business. Individual members must not be agency owners, but full-time employees of a retail travel agency either: (i) accredited by ARC; or (ii) accredited by ARP; or (iii) endorsed by IATAN; or (iv) be an active member of the NTA. Allied members are engaged in providing products, services or information, sold or used by agencies. Travel School members educate and train individuals for a career in the travel industry. Associate members are individuals employed by any organization in the previous categories. Associate independent members are independent outside sales representatives for one or more active member firms. There are also Senior members who have retired and Honorary members.

Apart from the above, ASTA has requirements for membership concerning finance, turnover and obedience to a code of ethics. For full information about ASTA and its activities *see* www.astanet.com; *see also* ASTA Tour Operator Program *and* Bond.

ASTAPAC   ASTA's Political Action Committee.

astern   Shipping term for travelling backwards. Also applied generally to the rear part of the vessel as distinct from forward pronounced 'forrard'.

ASTOR   Airborne stand-off radar.

ASTRA   Advanced System Training Aircraft made their first flights in 1986. Hawk training jet planes have been fitted with computers enabling them to simulate the flying characteristics of any aircraft for which software has been developed.

ASVA   Association of Scottish Visitors Attractions.*See* www.asva.co.uk

AT   Via Atlantic. *See* routing.

ATA[1]   Africa Travel Association. *See* www.africa-ata.org

ATA[2]   The Air Transport Association of America is the United States' scheduled airlines trade body, originally formed in 1936. For more information *see* www.air-transport.org

ATA[3]   The Czech Association of Travel Agents.

ATAAB   *See* Amadeus Travel Agency Advisory Board.

ATAB   Air Travel Advisory Bureau in the UK. *See* www.atab.co.uk

ATAC   The Air Transport Association of Canada is that country's airlines trade body. *See* www.atac.com

ATACF Airline Tariff Automated Collection Facility. *See* Genesis.

ATAG Air Transport Action Group, a UK lobbying organization. *See* www.atag.org

ATAS Advanced training avionics suite system (aviation term).

ATB and **ATB2** An automated ticket and boarding pass. Boarding information, seat assignment and baggage data, until the 1980s, were entered on a boarding pass as passengers checked in at the airport. IATA resolution 722c and recommended practice 1722c now govern the specification and use of a combined computer produced ticket and boarding pass. Automated tickets and boarding passes are produced in multi-coupon form by specialized air ticket printers, which became the norm in large UK travel agencies by the mid-1990s, as multi-layered carbon copy tickets were phased out. However, these continue to be used by many medium- and small-sized travel agencies. ATB2 tickets incorporate a magnetic strip enabling coupons to be passed through electronic readers, facilitating speedy check-in procedures.

IATA set a deadline of 1 April 1996, by which time all airlines must issue ATB2s instead of other types of ticket. At the time of writing, 11 years later, the changeover is still not complete. However, IATA has now set an end 2007 deadline for all paper tickets to finish. Whereas the original ATB was of one type, there is an Off Premises Automated Ticket/Boarding Pass (OPATB2) for agency use. *See also* automated ticket, bar code, bull's-eye, computer airline ticket, e-ticketing, OCR, OPTAT, OPATB2, TAT, teletype airline ticket *and* ticket (main entry).

ATC¹ Additional technical conditions (aviation term).

ATC² Air Traffic Conference (USA).

ATC³ Air Traffic Control. *See also* FIRs and MLS.

ATC⁴ Air Travel Card. *See* UATP.

ATC⁵ Australian Tourist Commission. *See* www.atc.net.au

ATC⁶ Automatic Train Control. Combined signalling and automatic control systems which automatically stop a train, if the driver fails to obey signals requiring a train to slow down or stop.

Typical early introduction was in the USA, where a US$15 million investment by CSX Transportation in the early 1990s resulted in centralization of 33 dispatch (control) centres formerly located all over America. When express rail services between Kuala Lumpur and its airport were introduced in 2002, the 160 km per h trains used the Siemens Swiss ZSL90 system used by several Swiss narrow-gauge railways introduced in 1996; however, this system is not suitable for complex networks. ATC's success has resulted in driverless trains (*see* driverless trains).

In the UK, an important aspect of ATC is now called ATP (automatic train protection). This is the system that the UK government has targeted to be fitted on all British trains by 2008; meanwhile, a less sophisticated system, TPWS is being installed (*see* TPWS). ATP is much more than ensuring that train drivers obey signal instructions. Transmitting information to a computer control unit on board a train enables heavier traffic to be carried on a line, with shorter distances between trains. (Technically this is 'running with minimum headways'.) *See also* AGT.

ATC Tour Order Was the standard form covering the sale of advertised air tours that had been authorised by the Air Traffic Conference in the USA.

ATCC Air Traffic Control Centre.

ATCO The Association of Transport Co-ordinating Officers in the UK.

ATD Actual time of departure.

ATE¹ Automatic testing equipment (aviation term).

ATE² Australian Tourism Exchange. The annual Australian Tourist Commission trade fair.

ATF Aviation Trust Fund, raised from US Federal taxes on air transport.

ATHE Association for Tourism Higher Education in the UK, renamed from the National Liaison Group in November 2000. *Also see* LTSN *and* ATTT.

Athens Convention International agreement which limits liability of shipping companies in respect of loss or damage to luggage and injury or death of passengers when travelling on international services by sea. Originally adopted in 1974, the Convention harmonized the two earlier Brussels Conventions of 1961 and 1967. There have been two major revisions, the 1990 and 2002 Protocols. The carrier is made liable for damage suffered as a result of the death or personal injury of a passenger and the loss of or damage to luggage, if the incident which caused the damage was due to the fault or neglect of the carrier, its servants or agents.

Usually, in agreements of this nature, fault or neglect of the carrier, servants or agents is presumed always, unless the contrary can be specifically proved by the carrier, where a loss of or damage to cabin baggage arises from shipwreck, collision, stranding, explosion, fire or defect of the ship. In respect of loss of or damage to other luggage, the fault or neglect is presumed irrespective of the nature of the incident.

Cabin luggage is defined as not only articles actually in a passenger's cabin, but also those in his or her possession, custody or control. Cabin luggage includes possessions in or on a vehicle.

In the case of damage to luggage which is not apparent at the time of delivery, or when a loss is involved, a claim in writing must be submitted within 15 days. Other occurrences should have been reported by the customer at the time.

The maximum liability limits of carriers were originally set in terms of gold francs. These have now been replaced by Special Drawing Rights (SDR); *see entry under this heading for an explanation of SDR.* The 2002 Protocol substantially raised liability limits. In the case of death or personal injury to a passenger, liability is limited to 250,000 SDR (about US$325,000). However, there is no liability if the carrier can prove the cause resulted from an act of war, an unforseeable circumstance outside of the carrier's control etc. When losses for which a carrier is liable exceed the limit, then negligence on the part of the carrier may raise the limit to 400,000 SDR (US$524,000). However, states may opt out of these limits and set lower ones, a matter outside the scope of this dictionary. But, they may not opt for different levels in respect of damage to baggage or vehicles. For loss of or damage to baggage, liability is limited to 2250 SDR (US$2925) per passenger. For vehicles, including associated baggage, the liability limit is 12,700 SDR (about US$16,250).

This entry is only a summary of the 'Athens Convention relating to the Carriage of Passengers and their Luggage by Sea, 2002'. Readers using this information should check that the new liability limits have been activated.

ATIDS Airport surface identification system.

ATII Association of Travel Insurance Intermediaries in the UK.

ATIPAC Air Travel Insolvency Protection Advisory Committee which replaced the UK CAA's Air Travel Trust Committee with the new group. *See* ATOL *and* ATT.

ATIS[1] Automatic terminal information service (or system).

ATIS[2] The European EDI standard for the tourism industry. *See* Electronic Data Interchange.

ATITA The Air Transport Industry Training Association is a voluntary body which advises air companies and airports, undertaking some aspects of the former role of the ATTITB.

ATK Available tonne kilometres. An air cargo term arrived at by multiplying cargo capacity by the distance involved. *See also* RTK.

ATL[1] Air Transport Licence. Required by British registered aircraft before they can operate scheduled services. Under section 22 of the Civil Aviation Act 1971, authority can be granted for the operation of seven classes of flights. 1: scheduled services; 2: carriage of charter categories other than ITCs and sole-use; 3: ITCs; 4: carriage, on the same aircraft, of ITCs and other categories other than sole-use; 5: substitute charter flights, apart from exempted operation for other airlines using UK registered aircraft; 6: charter flights for the carriage of cargo and attendants; 7: sole-use charter flights apart from exempted operations. Usually, this is for sole-use flights to and from London Heathrow or traffic to and from oil rigs. (ITC means Inclusive Tour Charter.)

The full specifications for each of the seven classes of licence are published in the CAA Official Record, Series 1. ATLs are not required for ambulance, test or training flights or official government charters.

ATL[2] Arranged total loss (aviation and maritime insurance term).

Atlantic Exellence Alliance Obsolete airline alliance. Originally formed in June 1996, bringing together Austrian Airlines, Delta, Sabena and Swissair and ended in October 1999, although the code-sharing arrangements continued until August 2000. *See* airline alliances.

Atlantis Name of TAP Air Portugal in-flight magazine.

atlas A book of maps. *The Mercator Atlas of Europe* is believed by Dr Peter Barber, Deputy Map Librarian of the British Library, to be the first to have been described as an *atlas*, so-named after the Titan forced by Zeus to support the sky on his shoulders. It was assembled by Gerard Mercator, the Flemish geographer, for his patron, Werner von Gymnich, who made a tour of Europe in 1570 with the son of William V, the Duke of Cleves. The Crown Prince of Cleves was the cousin of Anne of Cleves. This famous atlas includes the only copy of Mercator's wall map of 1554 and one of only four existing copies of his wall map of the British Isles of 1564. It was Mercator's projection that has enabled navigators to plot a course on maps in straight lines. *See* map projection.

Although the *Mercator Atlas* was probably the first to be called as such, in the same year, 1570, Abraham Ortelius published his *Theatrum Orbis Terrarum* in Antwerp, an atlas in all but name. Ortelius knew Mercator – there is evidence that they had met many years before at the Frankfurt Book Fair.

Atlas Name of Air France in-flight magazine.

ATLB Air Transport Licensing Board (obsolete).

ATM[1] Air Traffic Management.

ATM[2] Available ton miles – a US term indicating air cargo capacity, arrived at by multiplying the cargo capacity by the distance involved. More usual in Europe is Available Tonne Kilometres.

ATMA Asia Travel Marketing Association. *See* www.asiatravel.org

ATME Association of Travel Marketing Executives in the USA. *See* www.atme.org

ATN[1] Aeronautical Telecommunication Network.

ATN[2] (Obsolete) Associated Travel Network in the UK. ATN originated in the USA in the 1980s as a grouping of travel agents which recruited international associates. When the ATN consortium in the USA was bought in 1989 by the United States Travel Service (USTS), the name disappeared in America and the British ATN was established as a separate grouping. By April 1991 there were 13 members with an annual sales turnover of around £150 million, with 32 business travel locations and around 120 ordinary agency sites between them. The largest companies involved were Woodcock Travel, based in Sheffield, Sibbald Travel in Scotland and John Hilary Travel in East Anglia. Woodcock Travel failed in the 1990s, while the other two companies were taken over.

ATO Automatic train operation. *See* AGT.

ATOA Was the Air Transport Operators Association which merged into the GAMTA; this, together with the BAUA formed the BBGA – British Business and General Aviation Association. *See* www.bbga.aero

ATOC[1] Association of Train Operating Companies in the UK. During the 1990s British Rail was privatized and split up into 25 operating companies, Railtrack to manage the rail network and other companies. ATOC functions as a trade body for the operating companies but also has commercial and some statutory responsibilities. It appoints travel agents to sell UK rail travel, requiring that at least two members become rail experts, passing their 'Quality of Service' validation. Bonds are also required of them. There are currently 1200 rail-appointed agents in the UK. Agency commision was cut from 9% to 7% in 2003.

The principle has been established concerning IATA appointments in the UK and ARC and IATAN in the USA that these are not dependent on the turnover that will be produced. However, ATOC expect applicants to provide a marketing plan showing that they will produce new rail business. Agents must effect reservations and undertake ticketing through one of two computer systems. Both provide a fully integrated information, reservation, ticketing and account-

ing system. Elgar, which is also the
Eurostar system, is the alternative for
agents with Galileo or Sabre GDS, ticketing being through an ATB type printer.
AJENTS connects to ATOC's Rail
Journey Information System via the
Internet and prints credit card sized tickets through a dot matrix printer. *See*
www.rail.co.uk/atoc/public/index.htm
for comprehensive index of the extensive ATOC site; www.nationalrail.co.uk
for a comprehensive guide to all UK
national rail services; trains (this main
entry details many further references);
also rail fares in the UK; rail reservations in the UK and rail season tickets in
the UK.

ATOC² The Association of Timeshare
Owners Committees. *See* timeshare.

ATOL Air Travel Organizer's Licence in
the UK, granted by the CAA (Civil
Aviation Authority). It gives comprehensive protection from losing money or
being stranded abroad to people in the
UK who buy air holidays and flights
from tour operators, consolidators and
travel agents. It is by far the largest
travel protection scheme in the UK, and
the only one for flights and air holidays
sold by tour operators. From 8 October
2003, a loophole in the regulations was
closed, so that firms selling package holidays on the basis of split contracts were
unable to do so without holding ATOLs.
'Split contract' sales are arrangements
under which a holiday company sells a
flight (which may be ATOL protected)
and accommodation, or other travel
products such as car hire, under separate contracts which may be protected
by other means, or even not all. This
sometimes caused financial loss if, for
example, the provider of the flight failed
and the customer then either could not
find a replacement flight, or had to pay a
higher price to secure a flight that
enabled them to use the accommodation. In March 2004 the CAA made revo-
lutionary proposals recommending that
the scope of ATOLs be widened to
include all UK-originating scheduled
flights booked direct and paid for in
advance of departure. The proposals
would probably mean a contribution by
each traveller to a protection fund; tour
operators might opt for similar payments instead of being bonded as at
present. It has been pointed out that in
1996 there were 22.2m VFR (Visiting
Friends and Relatives) and holiday travellers, 96% of whom were covered by
the ATOL rules. By 2003, numbers had
risen to 39.7m but only 69% were ATOL
protected. **It is hoped to have new regulations in place by 2006.** Following
extensive consultation, amended legislation was being considered by the UK
Parliament at the time of going to press.

All tour operators selling flights and
air holidays must hold a licence from
the CAA. Before it gets a licence each
operator is examined to ensure it is
properly managed and financially
sound, and it must lodge a bond, which
is a financial guarantee provided by a
bank or insurance company. If it fails,
the CAA then uses the money to pay for
people abroad to continue their holidays
and to travel home as planned, and to
make refunds to those who have paid
but not travelled. If the bond is not
enough, any shortfall is met by the Air
Travel Trust Fund, which is managed by
the CAA and backs up the individual
bonds.

Over the past 17 years, ATOL has
managed over 300 tour operator failures,
rescuing almost 190,000 people from
being stranded and giving refunds to
more than a million others at a total cost
of £160 million. In the year to March
2003, 3,900 people were rescued or
refunded, at a cost of £1.3 million.

There is no equivalent scheme covering sales made directly by airlines. Most
passengers carried on charter airlines
buy their tickets through tour operators
and are protected by ATOL. Passengers
carried on scheduled airlines are not
protected by ATOL unless they buy the
seat, perhaps as part of a package, from
an ATOL holder.

The ATOL regulations were introduced in the UK in 1972. Number of
licensees rose in 1992 to 603, following
the introduction of the EC inspired
Package Holiday legislation; there are
currently 1862 holders. It is required by
UK law that all promoters of group
arrangements by air operating in and
from Britain obtain such a licence from
the CAA, satisfying them as to their
financial stability and providing a bond.
Other types of ATOL are for travel

agents and air travel consolidators. Licence numbers must be quoted in all literature and advertisements.

It has already been pointed out that licensees must offer a bond, guaranteeing payment of the sum required in the event of their failure; this bond is executed in favour of the Air Travel Trust Fund, which authorizes the CAA to administer use of the bond if necessary. In 2000, the CAA replaced its Air Travel Trust Committee with a new group, the Air Travel Insolvency Protection Advisory Committee (ATIPAC). However, the Air Travel Trust Fund (ATTF) continues. Originally created following the Clarksons Group collapse in the 1970s as the Air Travel Reserve Fund, it was established by a levy on holiday-makers. The aim was to provide a permanent second line of defence, should an ATOL holder's bond be insufficient to cover repayments. Then in the early 1990s, following the collapse of the International Leisure Group, a payout of £10 million necessitated borrowing money; currently (31 March 2004) the ATTF is £9.7 million in deficit, guaranteed by the UK government up to £21 million.

Originally, licence numbers were followed by a letter indicating the type of activity for which a licence had been granted. Now, however, licences authorize the holder to engage in all licensable activities for group air travel, whether on part charter, scheduled or charter air services.

The three types of licensable activities under ATOL regulations are the provision of seats: on advance booking charter flights, for the carriage by air of passengers on inclusive tours, for other forms of air travel. Operators of aircraft are not required to hold an ATOL because they already hold an Air Transport Licence, nor are agents of airlines. Travel agents who act as retail agents of airlines in selling inclusive tour and common interest travel arrangements based on specified individual or group fares on scheduled service such as ITX and GIT did not originally require a licence. However, now *all* travel organizers who make available holidays by air in or from the UK, even on scheduled services, do

require a licence. The CAA has developed a new streamlined processes for firms selling fewer than 500 seats each year. ATOLs can now be issued to small firms on the basis of protection offered by third parties. Guidance about this is available on the ATOL web site www.atol.org.uk or by telephoning 020 7453 6361.

A travel organizer, which acts only as an agent of an airline or other licensed travel organizer in making available accommodation to a passenger on an aircraft, does not itself need an ATOL. But a travel organizer which acts as a principal in making available accommodation, for example, chartering the whole or part of an aircraft and selling the seats to passengers, does need a licence.

Whether a travel organizer acts as a principal or agent depends on the contractual relationship between the passenger, the airline and the travel organizer. If the travel organizer buys accommodation from an airline or from another licensed travel organizer and makes it available for example by re-selling it to a passenger, then a licence is needed. If, on the other hand, tickets for scheduled air services are sold on a commission basis as agent for an airline or another licensed travel organizer, a licence is not normally required by an IATA-appointed ticket stock-holding agent. This is providing the tickets or an airline document are issued and given to the customer at the time they pay, in whole or in part as a deposit. Sub-agents, non-appointed agents and other agents not holding stocks of blank air tickets are not able to comply with this requirement and may need an ATOL. Special arrangements for members of ABTA have been negotiated with the CAA, which are outside the scope of this book.

At the time of writing in April 2005, the non-refundable initial application fee in the UK for an ATOL for over 500 passengers was £730 plus a further £730 to be paid on the grant of the licence and 10.99p for each one-way passenger seat authorized. Annual renewal fee was £250 plus £495 renewal grant charge. In addition a passenger charge of 10.99p applies. If organizations expect to carry more passengers than originally applied for, the licence variation fee is £48 plus £55 on granting of the application and the usual 10.99p fee per passenger.

ATOLs are only granted if the holder has entered into an agreement whereby a sum of money, will, in the event of the organizer's failure, become available to a trustee for the purpose of repatriating any stranded passengers and reimbursing any clients who have paid in whole or in part for a flight or holiday that has not yet taken place. This is usually undertaken by licence holders providing a bond. At one time ABTA member tour operators were in a privileged position, being allowed reduced-rate bonding but in 1985 rates were equalized. Existing ATOL holders *must* provide a bond of 10% of their licensed annual turnover. New applicants for an ATOL must provide a bond of 15%, normally reducing to 10% after 2 years.

UK travel agents, as can be seen from this description, often do not need an ATOL. But they *MUST pass on to customers* an ATOL holder's confirmation and account, on the ATOL holder's headed notepaper, otherwise the agent may be liable in the event of failure. In November and May each year, the CAA publishes an up-to-date-list of all ATOL holders in its *Official Record Series 3*. Up-to-date information and application guidance notes are to be found on their web site www.atol.org.uk Detailed statistics on UK tour operating and ATOL licence holders are available through the Database option of the trade information section of the web site or direct www.atoldata.org.uk/database.html The latest Air Travel Trust report and details of failures is accessible through the Publications option of the trade information section of the web site.

atomisation   Lack of coordination of economic activities in tourist resorts is the suggested meaning in the World Tourism Organization and Secretariat of State for Tourism of France (2001), *Thesaurus on Tourism and Leisure Activities*. However, the term is not in general use in the English-speaking world, and appears to be limited to France.

ATOP   Autofile Tour Operators System is a computerized British tour operators reservation and accounting system introduced in 1982. It is the UK market leader.

ATP[1]   Accredited Travel Professional in the UK. *See entry under this heading.*

ATP[2]   Advanced turboprop. *See* jet aircraft engine.

ATP[3]   Automatic train protection. *See* ATC[6] (Automatic train control).

ATPCO   The Air Tariff Publishing Company which publishes the Domestic General Rules Tariff in the USA, the main rule book guiding US air travel published on behalf of US airlines. ATPCO claims to be the world's biggest distributor of air fare data. Many airlines are considering filing all their fares through ATPCO; within the currency of this dictionary their data will probably have become the best single source of this and similar information. *See* www.atpco.net

ATRF   Air Travel Reserve Fund in the UK, which became the Air Travel Trust in 1986. Organizers of group air travel must have an Air Travel Organizers' Licence, which involves a substantial bond enabling the public to be protected against financial failure of the operator. If this bond should prove insufficient, the public is further protected against loss of their money by the ATRF. Originally all holders of an ATOL were required to contribute 2% of their turnover to the fund. It was set up in the UK after the Court Line failure in 1974. Early in 1985 it was decided to wind up the administrative body which controlled the fund, the Air Travel Reserve Fund Agency and to transfer the fund to the Civil Aviation Authority to administer it on a trustee basis as the Air Travel Trust. *See* ATT (Air Travel Trust), ATOL, ATIPAC *and* bond.

atrium   A substantial, enclosed, covered area inside a building or ship; sometimes naturally lit through a glass roof. In some modern multi-storey hotels the atrium may extend from the ground floor reception to the top floor and in some ships, through from the top to bottom deck. On Royal Caribbean International vessels, it is called a centrum.

atrium cabin   cabin on a cruise ship with a window or porthole overlooking an inside atrium.

ATRM *Airport Terminal Reference Manual*, an IATA publication.

ATS¹ Adventure Travel Society in the USA. *See* www.adventuretravel.com

ATS² Agents Ticketing System, which is software for a PC enabling UK travel agents to produce British Rail tickets and to capture ticket details for accounts purposes.

ATS³ Air traffic services.

ATS⁴ American Tourism Society.

ATS⁵ Automatic train supervision.

ATSB *See* Air Transportation Stabilization Board.

ATSORA Air traffic service outside regulated airspace.

ATSU Air traffic service unit.

ATT Air Travel Trust in the UK. Following the Court Line/Clarksons failure in the UK in 1974; the Air Travel Reserve Fund was set up the following year by a 2% levy on package holiday bookings. This enabled holidaymakers to be compensated in the event of company failure and that operator's ATOL bond being insufficient. At the beginning of 1986, the ATT was established to take over the assets and responsibilities of the ATRF. The funds were exhausted by summer 1996 and the UK government guaranteed the ATT to the extent of £21 million. The ATT accounts to end March 2004 showed an accumulated deficit of £9.7 million. The ATT trustees were supported and advised by the Air Travel Trust Committee. This was reconstituted in April 2000, its terms of reference widened and renamed the Air Travel Insolvency Protection Advisory Committee (ATIPAC). The latest Air Travel Trust report and details of failures are accessible through the Publications option of the trade information section of the ATOL web site www.atol.org.uk *See* ATOL, ATRF *and* bond.

ATTA¹ Africa Travel and Tourism Association in the UK. *See* www.atta.co.uk

ATTA² The Association of Travel and Tourist Agents in Singapore.

Attache and Royal Canadian Class Brand name given by CP Air to passenger area immediately adjacent to first class, where passengers paying full economy fares enjoy improved service and facilities. *See* business class for full details.

ATTC¹ The Association of Travel Trades Clubs is the national organization of over 40 UK Travel Trade Clubs. Similar clubs exist worldwide, the members being all levels of employees in the travel and tourism industry.

ATTC² Air Travel Trust Committee of the UK CAA, replaced in August 2000 by ATIPAC. *See* ATIPAC *and* ATOL.

ATTF Air Travel Trust Fund. *See* ATOL.

ATTITB Air Transport and Travel Industry Training Board in the UK. Was one of the many Industrial Training Boards by the Manpower Services Commission, responsible for UK industry training, except for Northern Ireland. Upon its demise in 1982, some of its main functions as far as agents and tour operators are concerned, were assumed by the ABTA National Training Board. This was designated as a non-statutory government-approved training authority and was funded by ABTA. This was then reformed into an ABTA subsidiary, TTTC (The Travel Training Company) with no statutory or other non-commercial responsibilities. The Travel Tourism and Events National Training Organization (TTENTO), which received government approval at the end of 1998, was the voluntary body responsible to government for education and training in its sector in the UK. In autumn 2002 TTENTO amalgamated with the Hospitality Training Foundation and the new body, People 1st, became one of the UK government's Sector Skills Councils.

attractions Things or activities which attract tourists, for example, the CN Tower in Toronto, the tallest man-made free-standing structure, to be contrasted with the great natural attraction Niagara Falls. *See* theme parks *also* sightseeing in Britain.

attractor An important (or the most important) tourist attraction in a locality, area or region. Word has only its ordinary language meaning outside the USA.

ATTT Association of Teachers and Trainers of Tourism in the UK was originally founded in 1975 as the ATT – an independent body, becoming a section of the Tourism Society in 1981. Membership includes most British tourism teachers as well as those involved in general travel industry teaching and training. *Also see* ATHE *and* LTSN.

ATZ Air Traffic Zone.

AUAVI Asociación Uruguaya des Agencias de Viajes Internacionales, the Uruguayan national travel agency organization.

auberge A countryside hotel or inn in a French-speaking country.

AUC Air Transport User's Council in the UK. *See* www.auc.org.uk

audioguide Hand-held device with sound volume control providing information from an audio tape when activated by visitors to museums, heritage sites or other places of tourism interest.

audit coupon All multi-part travel tickets, regardless of the mode of transport involved, have travel coupons which are collected from the passenger when the journey is undertaken, and an audit coupon, used for accounting purposes. Most tickets also have an issuing office copy and passenger coupon. The audit copy is usually the top coupon, making it more difficult to alter the carbon copies for fraudulent purposes. Audit coupons are usually attached to a travel agent's sales returns so that their accuracy may be verified.

AUKDA Association of UK Domestic Airlines.

Australian Business Access Card Obsolete; replaced in July 2000 with Short Business Electronic Travel Authority. *See* ETAS.

Australian Federation of Travel Agents (AFTA[2]) *See* www.afta.com.au

Australian Tourist Commission *See* www.australia.com *or* www.atc.australia.com

Austrian Bundesnetzkarten Known in English-speaking countries as Austrian General Season Tickets, they entitle the holder to unlimited rail travel in first or second class over the lines of Austrian Federal Railways, as well as reduced fares on certain shipping services. Prices vary according to standard validity lengths of 9 or 16 days or 1 month and dependent upon class and whether the season ticket is for an adult or child. A similar Austria Ticket is available to those aged between 6 and 25 years inclusive, giving unlimited travel in second class and certain other facilities, priced between adult and child general season ticket rates.

Austrian National Tourist Office *See* www.austria.info

Austrian National Travel Agency Organization Osterreichischer Reiseburo Verband.

Auto Drop PNR The US term for a traveller's flight booking which is automatically re-presented to an agent or an airline clerk for action to be taken. For example, when a booking made a long time before is to be ticketed, or when a requested flight on a waiting list becomes available.

autobahn German equivalent of motorway in UK, freeway or expressway in North America.

Autobook Name of UK AT&T Istel's PC-based viewdata system for travel agents.

autocue Presentation of a speaker's script so that it is moving forward and visible only to the speaker. Older forms were usually projection on to the lectern but computerized systems are now using LCD displays.

autodial The ability to dial a telephone number automatically. Telephone companies worldwide make or rent devices of this nature, enabling access and automatic dialling of hundreds of numbers with the most sophisticated equipment. Computers are programmed with the telephone number of their Internet service provider so that, upon users selecting this service, the computer autodials and establishes a connection.

autogyro Word sometimes mistakenly used as an alternative to 'helicopter'. Autogyro was originally a trade name for a flying machine where the wings were similar to a windmill, but rotating freely rather than being powered, as in a true helicopter.

automated The term that indicates computerization of any activity. For example automated travel agency accounting, automated airline ticketing, automated reservation systems. *See* information technology in travel and tourism.

automated air reservation systems for travel agents *See* CRS.

automated air tickets Computer-produced air tickets can either be single documents, necessitating individual insertion into a ticket printer, or tickets on a continuous roll, remaining in the printer throughout the working day, each ticket being torn off after production. Automated Tickets and Boarding passes (ATBs) are usually produced from hoppers of blank cards.

Each of these types of ticket can be either dedicated to a particular airline or neutral, the airline's name being printed at time of issue. Some automated tickets are pre-printed with document numbers, with or without a bar code or bull's-eye to enable machine recognition of the ticket number. Alternatively, ticket numbers can be printed at the time of ticket issue. IATA has set an end 2007 deadline for paper tickets to finish, so that within the currency of this dictionary, much of this entry may become history. *See also* ATB and ATB2, automated ticket, bar code, bull's-eye, computer airline ticket, OCR, OPTAT, OPATB2, TAT, teletype air ticket *and* ticket (main entry).

Automated Guideway Transit *See* AGT.

Automated Neutral Ticketing Scheme A scheme which enables an agent with automated ticketing equipment to issue neutral tickets on behalf of airlines participating in that scheme.

Automated Revenue Collection (ARC) *See* ARC[2].

automated ticket Official IATA definition is any form of passenger ticket and baggage check described in IATA Resolutions 722 and 722a, and Recommended Practice 1722c, designed for issue in various ticket printing devices for which data may be computer generated.

automated ticket and boarding pass *See* ATB.

Automated Ticketing Services Agreement An agreement between airlines which allows a servicing airline to issue neutral tickets on behalf of itself and a number of other airlines.

automatic guide A device providing information to tourists. In some large buildings, this is achieved by radio broadcasts which can only be received in a particular area. Static displays, in museums or similar places, often have recorded sound or video descriptions of exhibits, activated on the visitor's instructions. Guides in the form of audio tapes give directions for tours on foot or by car around interesting places all over the world, whether a trip through a nature reserve or around a world-famous art gallery.

automatic train control *See* ATC[6].

automation in the travel industry – some books In the UK, at the time of writing, the standard works on this topic are: *Electronic Information Distribution in Tourism and Hospitality* by Peter O'Connor, CAB International; *Information Technology for Travel and Tourism* by Gary Inkpen, 2nd edn, Longman. Concerning travel agency automation, readers seeking information on the historical development should consult *Mind Your Own Travel Business*, by Allan Beaver, 3rd edn, Beaver Travel Publishers. This replaced *Agency Layout Design and Equipment* by Allan Beaver, published by ABTA National Training Board in June 1989, designed to complement the 1989 2nd edn of the ABTA Technology Committee's *Survey of Computer Systems Available in the UK for Travel Agents.* In the USA, *Complete Guide to Travel Agency Automation*, by N. Godwin, published by Delmar in 1987, gave good coverage of the subject. *See* travel agents' computerized accounting and ticketing systems in the UK.

Automobile Association *See* AA[5].

automobile clubs Organizations such as the Automobile Association and Royal Automobile Club in the UK and the American Automobile Association in North America, which provide substantial services to car owners, the most well known being repair or recovery services following breakdown or accident. These clubs are of the nature of huge insurance schemes, since the costs of an unfortunate emergency sustained by one member are covered by the subscriptions of all the members. Itinerary and route planning and the provision of travel tickets are also offered by the clubs mentioned.

autopilot The computer system and associated mechanics that can control an aircraft automatically; in fog, at some airports, an assisted landing and approach system can take over control of an aircraft and land it safely.

autoqueue *See* queue.

autoroute French equivalent of motorway in UK, freeway or expressway in North America.

autostrada Italian equivalent of motorway in UK, freeway or expressway in North America.

AUW All up weight (aviation term).

availability Travel or tourism services which are unsold, and therefore 'available' for sale. Hence, an 'availability display' is a computerized reservation system screen of information, generated by the system, showing unsold services which can be booked immediately.

available seat kilometres *See* ASK.

available seat miles *See* ASM.

available tonne kilometres *See* ATK.

avalanche warning An avalanche starts off as loose snow which becomes detached on a slope. As it gathers pace, ice, earth, rocks and trees are carried down. In ski resorts, skiers are warned when conditions are dangerous; explosions are detonated to cause small, less dangerous avalanches. Off-piste skiers ignoring warnings can cause avalanches.

AVE Name of Spanish high-speed trains (it is not an acronym; it means 'bird' in Spanish). For example, between Madrid and Seville, the route is covered in less than 3 h at speeds of up to 250 kph. Eight coaches are carried, divided into three classes, first, club and tourist.

average Two meanings – in normal usage, an average is a mean of a number of figures. For example, the average rainfall, humidity or temperature for a month in a particular place is a mean of all the daily figures.

Average is also insurance terminology for the process by which an insurer assesses how much to pay to an under-insured claimant. Assume a customer has a travel insurance policy offering cover under baggage loss of £500. Now assume that the luggage was really of a value of £1000. This means that there was only insurance for one half of the real value. In the event of a complete loss, this may not have any more significance than the claim being limited to £500, although in some cases it might have the effect of voiding the whole insurance. If however, only part of the contents are lost, say for easy calculation half, then although the customer has lost £500 value, identical to the amount insured, the insurer will according to the principle of average, only be liable to pay the equivalent of half the sum insured, in this case £250.

average air passenger weight *See* air passenger average weights.

average room rate *See* hotel statistics worldwide for average rates *and* pricing of hotel rooms for calculation methods and rate management techniques.

average yield *See* yield.

AVGAS Aviation fuel (gasoline).

Aviation Consumer Action Project *See* ACAP *and* www.acap1971.org

Aviation Environment Federation *See* www.aef.org.uk

aviation fuel Turbine jet engines usually use paraffin, known in other countries as kerosene. Piston engined planes need a very high octane petrol.

aviation on the Internet *See* air travel on the Internet.

aviation safety *See* airline safety.

Aviation Security Charge *See* ASC[4].

Aviation Trust Fund *See* ATF.

Avis reservation system *See* Wizard.

AVM Airborne vibration monitoring.

AVN Aviation (not generally used – only one usage of abbreviation identified).

AVNET A joint ATA[2] and IATA project to develop EDI messages suitable for use in transactions between airlines and companies involved in the supply and/or distribution of aviation fuel and related products and services.

AVOSS Aircraft Vortex Spacing System.

AVS[1] Address verification system; when a provider of travel services accepts payment by credit card and the cardholder is not present, through AVS, the address supplied can be checked. In a high proportion of attempted credit card fraud, the correct cardholder address is unknown.

AVS[2] Availability status; a type of message exchanged constantly between airline reservation systems.

AWB Air waybill. *See* air waybill.

AWTE *See* Association of Women Travel Executives.

AWY Airway (not generally used – only one usage of abbreviation identified).

AXESS Name of JAL's CRS.

AXO Agent's Exchange Order. Terminology in general travel usage although previously applied exclusively to British Airways document utilized by agents to obtain tickets they did not themselves stock or to enable a traveller to obtain a ticket on departure at an airport. Replaced April 1980 by ADO – Agent's Debit Order. Upon the introduction of BSP in autumn 1984, agents were instructed to use MCOs instead.

AYTO Association of Yugoslav Travel Organizations (until 1991).

Azerbaijan Ministry of Youth Sport and Tourism *See* www.tourism.az *and* www.myst.gov.az

B

B & B Bed and breakfast.

B & T A cabin or room with private bath/shower and toilet.

B/L A Bill of Lading is a statement and/or description of the freight being carried by an aircraft, ship or vehicle.

BAA British Airports Authority was established in 1965. Was publicly owned but was privatized, it operates London's Heathrow, Gatwick and Stansted, Glasgow, Edinburgh, Prestwick and Aberdeen airports. *See* www.baa.com

BAAC British Association of Aviation Consultants. For more information *see* www.baac.org.uk

BAB British Airways Board (UK).

baby basket *See* bassinet.

BACA Baltic Air Charter Association (in the UK).

BACD British Association of Conference Destinations (formerly BACT – British Association of Conference Towns), a cooperative body of tourist boards and local authorities which provides a free advice and information service on venues which will meet the needs of exhibition, conference and incentive travel organizers. For more information *see* www.bacd.org.uk

back bar In the USA, term means the storage cabinets, shelving and counter situated behind the bartender in a bar.

back end rebate Also called back end deal. Incentive payment made by a provider of travel services to a corporate entity at the end of an agreed period, provided purchases exceed an agreed target. *See* front end deal *for fuller explanation and also a list of 70 other business travel related entries following* corporate travel contracts, *some of which lead to further entries.*

back of house All parts of a hotel which are never in contact with customers, for example, the kitchens and administrative office.

back office Travel trade jargon for the administrative and accounting functions of a travel agency, contrasting with the 'front' or sales part of an agency, dealing direct with customers. The term 'mid-office' now applies to software in a travel agency linking the front and back office. Similarly, in a hotel, the functions have the same names.

backdate To date a travel ticket earlier than the actual date of issue. In this way, the advance purchase regulations relating to the sale of many transportation tickets are avoided.

backhaul Principle of IATA fare construction, which prevents the ordinary application of the rules to journeys which double back on themselves. This stops the regulations being applied so as to undercut the fare to the most distant point on such a journey.

backing-up At least once a day, and in a busy office, several times a day, if at all possible, it is essential to copy all the information stored on computer disks or tape, in case something goes wrong. By maintaining two or three copies of all information, loss of vital records is prevented. In cases of some vital computers, the security risk upon loss is so great, that a back-up computer records all the activities of the main computer creating a permanent ongoing duplicate record. Dependent upon how vital the functions are, there may be a third computer acting in tandem as a back-up to the first one, in case some fault develops. Back-up media may be optical (CD), zip disks or similar, tape or removable hard drives.

back-to-back A principle of charter aircraft utilization. Planes fly out with a group of holidaymakers to a distant point, returning with another group who have just finished their holiday. Obviously, some empty flights, known as empty legs, are inevitable at the beginning and the end of a season although tour operators will do their best to coordinate winter and summer programmes so as to minimize the problem. *See also* rotation.

back-to-back ticketing Ticketing an air journey so as to cut the published fare in one of several ways, for example: some promotional fares may be uni-directional, only available from particular airports and/or not combinable with other fares; in such cases, several air tickets covering a passenger's journey may be cheaper than a through ticket. Sometimes, airlines offer promotional excursion fares between two points, requiring a Saturday night stay, in order to discourage usage by business travellers. Providing the cost is less than half of the cheapest economy fare, two tickets can be issued covering successive weeks, both including a Saturday stay; thus the later ticket is used for the outward journey and the return coupon of the earlier ticket used for the journey back, within the same week. Airlines have attempted to prevent the practice, by cancelling arrangements when the outward leg of a ticket is not used. In the UK, provided a traveller informs an airline that the inward reservation will be used, the practice has been held not to be illegal. In the USA, a pair of excursions used in the way described may be called nested excursions. If an agency knowingly issues two tickets in the way described in this entry, so that it circumvents an airline's fare rules, it is probably a violation of their rules and the agency may be justifiably debited. Where an agent has not been proactive, responsibility is in doubt.

back-up Transportation operators, offering guaranteed seats on non-reservable services, plan for the expected number of passengers, based on experience. In order to maintain the guarantee, a back-up aircraft or coach may be in waiting, which will be used if necessary. Many operators have back-up transport or staff waiting on a stand-by basis, in order to maintain scheduled services, in case of breakdown or illness. *See also* backing-up, referring to duplicating computer records.

backpacker Descriptive term for a person (usually young and with little money) travelling the world in search of adventure or varied experience of many countries and diverse cultures. Name derives from their light rucksack or backpack with which they 'travel light'. *See* STONKY.

BAe British Aerospace. *See* aircraft manufacture.

BAF Bunker adjustment factor. *See* surcharge.

baggage Equivalent to the term luggage. Official IATA definition is such articles, effects and other personal property of a passenger as are necessary or appropriate for wear, use, comfort or convenience in connection with his trip. Unless otherwise specified, it includes both checked and unchecked baggage, provided it either accompanies or is sent in advance of a paying passenger, whereas anything sent for carriage on its own, even if it be personal luggage, is counted as freight.

baggage allowance *See* allowance of free baggage.

baggage check Official IATA definition is those portions of the ticket which provide for the carriage of passengers' checked baggage and which are issued by a carrier as a receipt for passengers' checked baggage.

baggage, checked The same as registered luggage. Official IATA definition is baggage of which a carrier takes sole custody and for which a carrier has issued a baggage check.

baggage excess That part of baggage which is in excess of that which may be carried free of charge.

baggage insurance *See* travel insurance.

baggage room An area in a ship, usually the upper part of a hold, where baggage is stored and made available to passengers at certain times during a voyage.

baggage tag Official IATA definition is a document issued by carrier solely for identification of checked baggage, the baggage strap or tag portion of which is attached by carrier to a particular article of checked baggage and the baggage identification tag portion of which is given to the passenger. The term also generally applies to any personal identification attached to a piece of baggage.

baggage, unchecked Baggage of which the passenger retains custody.

Bagtrack A worldwide computerized system for tracing lost air baggage, used by over 60 of the world's major airlines. Details of unclaimed baggage are compared with the data on baggage reported missing and matched by the computer. Bagtrack is operated on the SITA computer, the airlines' data processing and communications system based in Atlanta, USA.

BAHA[1] British Activity Holiday Association. The UK private sector trade association for providers of activity holidays and educational courses. Members follow a code of practice, maintaining safety standards and are inspected every 3 years. Must also follow the DfES (UK government Department of Education and Skills) *Guide on Health and Safety of Pupils on Educational Visits* and meet the requirements of the Adventure Activity Licensing Authority which inspects activity centres in the UK on behalf of the DfES. *See* www.baha.org.uk *and* www.aala.org

BAHA[2] British Association of Hospitality Accountants. *See* www.baha-uk.org

Bahrain Tourism Information *See* www.bahraintourism.com

BAHREP British Association of Hotel Representatives, the trade body of companies representing hotels, founded in 1977.

BAIR British Airports Information Retrieval System. Ferranti computer system which not only displays flight information for passengers, but also much data for airline staff, the airport authority and many associated service companies, such as customs, catering, immigration and aircraft fuelling.

bait & switch The US term for the practice of attracting customers by low prices for goods or services which are not available, in order to make a sale of an alternative. In the UK this is called switch selling.

balance The remainder of a client's final travel account due for payment, after taking into account deposits paid and discounts due.

balance chart Form used by airlines to control distribution of cargo and passengers, having regard to the centre of gravity of an aircraft.

balance due Money owed by a traveller in accordance with their travel contract with a provider of travel services, after deducting any deposit paid initially.

balance, tourism *See* travel account[2].

balcony[1] In a theatre or cinema in Britain or America, this is one of the top tiers, sometimes an alternative name for the gallery. But in France, this is situated just above the orchestra pit.

balcony[2] In regard to hotel rooms, a balcony is an outdoor extension of a room, usually in the form of a platform protruding from the side of the building, and accessible through glass doors.

BA-LINK Replaced with an Extranet (BAROL) for non-IATA travel agents from 1 October 2001. BA-LINK was the name of British Airways' UK viewdata-based CRS, used by 4750 UK agents. BA did not accept telephone reservations from UK agents for flights that could be booked on the LINK system. Through LINK, hotels, car hire and other add-ons could also be reserved. *See* BAROL.

balloon *See* hot-air balloon.

BALPA British Airline Pilots' Association. A trade union, representing aircrew, affiliated to the TUC. For more information *see* www.balpa.org.uk

BALPPA British Association of Leisure Parks, Piers and Attractions. *See* www.balppa.com

bank buying rate *See* IATA fare construction system.

bank holiday This British term is used in the UK and in some English-speaking countries to mean a public holiday; literally, a day when the banks are closed.

Bank Settlement Plan *See* BSP.

banker's buying rate *See* IATA fare construction system.

banker's selling rate *See* IATA fare construction system.

BAR Best available rate. Providers of travel services aim to maximise income by varying their prices dependant on sales on expectation of demand. Thus the BAR is a concept applicable only to a specific time on a particular day. The same acronym is used as brand name for a Galileo hotel system which guarantees that the rate offered on Galileo GDS by participating hotel groups matches that which would be offered direct by telephone or on the hotel's own web site. However, as already explained, lack of demand may cause a rate reduction. Bookings already made stay at the level already agreed. Increased demand, on the other hand, may mean that an advantage has been gained.

bar Sandbar usually caused by tidal or current conditions near the shore.

bar code A series of vertical bars incorporating a machine-readable coding system, using a combination of thick and thin lines, alternating with blank spaces, to represent numeric characters, enabling ticket numbers to be read by computers.

Barbados Tourism Authority *See* www.barbados.org

bare hull charter agreement Also known as a dry lease. When an aircraft is hired without crew to an operator.

bareboat charter When a yacht or luxury cabin cruiser is rented without crew or any other facilities. *See* charter.

Bargain Finder Name of part of Sabre's fare system. For more details *see* Sabre.

barge The word was first used to describe a small sailing boat, e.g. the admiral's barge. Now, the term means a flat-bottomed, shallow vessel used for river or canal transport. Originally, and still mainly used for cargo, but some have been converted for passenger leisure use. Thus, although some canal barges are still used for cargo transport, most are converted to provide living accommodation during a canal cruising vacation.

bark *See* barque.

BAROL British Airways Reservations On-line, called ZUJI in the Far East and Australia. From July 2002, this was named Travel Trade Fare Explorer and was made available via www.batraveltrade.com

barque Also known as bark. Three masted sailing ship, characterized by a fore and aft rigged mizzen mast while the fore and main masts are square rigged. If the main and mizzen masts are fore and aft rigged but the fore mast square rigged, then the vessel is called a barquentine. These ships are usually square sterned.

barquentine *See* barque.

BARUK Board of Airline Representatives in the UK, represents around 95 airlines, both IATA and non-IATA, operating scheduled passenger services from and in the UK. A pressure group and forum dealing with matters difficult to act upon through the official recognized bodies such as IATA. Originally formed in 1975 to eliminate fare abuses, in which area it has had mixed success. For more information *see* www.bar-uk.org

Basic Beginners All-Purpose Symbolic Interpretive Code, a computer programming language.

basing fares If, for a given itinerary from the point of origin to point of destination, no through IATA fare is published, then a basing fare must be consulted. If a basing fare is published from the origin/destination in question, then the through fare may be calculated by combining the two-part fares shown.

basing point A master point, the fares to and from which are established, used in constructing through air fares between other points.

Bass Became Six Continents in July 2001 following sales of Bass name and brewing business. This then became InterContinental hotels, currently the world's largest hotel group. *See* InterContinental hotels group, *also* www.intercontinental.com

bassinet Name of the baby basket which folds down from an aircraft bulkhead.

Bat International hotel code for a room with private bath.

BATA British Air Transport Association. *See* www.bata.uk.com

batch processing This means entering information into a computer system only periodically. Some computers can only handle information this way, while others are real time. For example, the reservations systems accessed by agents which are automatically updated as transactions are entered, are real time. But even on such a system, it may be convenient to batch process information, for instance a daily entry of an agent's accounting information (general technical term).

Bateau a Grande Vitesse *See* BGV.

BATO British Association of Tourist Offices was founded in 1932. Membership is composed of people responsible for the development of tourism within local government and tourist boards.

batten down To secure all open hatches or equipment for seaworthiness while a ship is under way.

BAUA Business Aircraft Users' Association in the UK was founded in 1961 to represent users of business aircraft. Together with GAMTA (the General Aviation Manufacturers and Traders Association) forms the BBGA (British Business and General Aviation Association); *see* www.bbga.aero The BBGA is a member of the IBAC

(International Business Aviation Council); *see* www.ibac.org

baud The unit of measurement of data transmission speeds. One baud is one bit per second. As it takes eight bits to transmit a character plus start and stop bits, ten baud is one character per second.

BAWTA British Association of Wholesale Tour Agents. *See* www.bawta.co.uk

BBGA British Business and General Aviation Association – formed from two partner organizations BAUA and GAMTA; *see* www.bbga.aero The BBGA is a member of the IBAC (International Business Aviation Council); *see* www.ibac.org

BBR Banker's Buying Rate. *See* IATA fare construction system.

BCAA British Cargo Airline Alliance.

BCAR British Civil Airworthiness Requirement.

BCASC British Civil Aviation Standing Conference represents the interests of the British civil aviation industry.

BCC Formerly Bus and Coach Council in the UK, the successor in title to the Confederation of British Road Passenger Transport, which has reverted to this original name. *See* CPT.

BCH Bonded Coach Holiday Group. *See* CPT *and* www.bondedcoachholidays.co.uk

BCP Break cloud procedure.

BCU British Canoe Union. *See* www.bcu.org.uk

BDT Bering daylight time.

beach Land area immediately adjacent to the sea; the less steep is its gradient, the more likely it is to provide tourism amenities of wide expanse and safe bathing and/or water sports. *See* developed beaches.

beach operator Provider of tourist services on a beach, such as offering for hire deckchairs, sun beds, umbrellas, rowing boats or pedalos or facilitating water sports such as water skiing, wind surfing and paragliding etc.

beam Width of a ship (amidships) between widest point of its two sides.

bearing Compass direction, usually expressed in degrees from the ship to a particular destination or objective.

Beaufort scale Measure of wind force and likely associated sea conditions on a scale from one to 12, created 150 years ago by Admiral Sir Francis Beaufort. Force 12, a hurricane, is over 64 knots; however, in the USA where very high winds are more common, the scale has a further five levels. *See also* climate.

BECA British Exhibition Contractors Association. *See* www.beca.org.uk

bed brief A description of the accommodation required by a tour operator to fulfil the requirements of a programme to a particular destination. A contracting manager (the title varies hugely) then visits resorts seeking to contract all the rooms in a hotel or some of them. For types of contract *see* allotment.

bedienung German word meaning that service is included, so that a further gratuity is not necessary.

bed-night One person spending one night in any accommodation.

Belab International hotel code for two single-bedded rooms.

Belgian National Travel Agency Organization Union Professionelle des Agences de Voyages (UPAV). *See* www.upav.be

Belgian Tourist Office *See* www.belgium-tourism.org

Belgian Tourrail Tourist Season Ticket Valid for either 5 or 8 days in first- or second-class for unlimited rail travel within Belgium during a 16-day period. For a higher price, a Belgian Railways 16-day season ticket can be purchased, valid for 16 consecutive days.

Belize Tourism Board *See* www.travelbelize.org

bell captain US term for the head porter of a hotel.

bell hop US term for a hotel porter, responsible for carrying luggage to and from rooms and other menial tasks.

bells *See* times at sea.

below the line Promotional media which do not pay commission to advertising agencies. *See* promotional media.

beltway An American freeway or motorway surrounding a city, enabling through traffic to bypass the city.

Belvu International hotel code for a room with a good view.

benchmarking of tourism courses *See* Appendix III.

beneficiary In 1985, this word was proposed in the *Interprofessional Vocabulary of Tourism and Leisure* as the technical term to be used instead of consumer, client, traveller, passenger or guest. Not normally used in this way in the UK and never generally adopted in France where it was suggested.

benefit Insurance term for money that will be paid if particular unfortunate events occur, there being no need to substantiate details of loss; merely that the actual event occurred. For example, travel insurance delayed departure cover.

BER Beyond economic repair.

Bermuda Agreement An agreement between Britain and the USA made in 1946, relating to air services between the countries. This bilateral agreement was subsequently renegotiated in 1977. The original has been used as model for many other similar bilateral air agreements hence the term Bermuda-type agreement has become generic. The most important clause in this type of agreement states that there shall be a fair and equal opportunity for the carriers of the two nations to operate on any route included in the agreement. Other clauses included government approval of rates, adequate traffic capacity and a procedure to review carriers' operation to ensure compliance with the principles.

Bermuda plan Hotel accommodation with full breakfast included in the room rate.

berth¹ The place where a ship docks.

berth² The name of a place to sleep on a ship or train. Whereas a two-bedded cabin implies two ground-floor sleeping places, a two-berth cabin normally implies that one is above the other.

berthing centre or CBO Shipping term for the department which roughly corresponds to the reservation section of an airline or tour operator. Controls allocation of berths to passengers either direct or through an agent.

bespoke charter Suggested by Reed Travel Group's *ABCs of Travel* to be British usage for special group air charters. Ad hoc charters is a more normally encountered term in the UK.

BEST Business Enterprises for Sustainable Travel. A not-for-profit venture of The Conference Board in New York City and the World Travel and Tourism Council, with headquarters in Brussels. BEST is an initiative created to support the concept, promotion and implementation of sustainable tourism. *See* www.sustainabletravel.org *and* tourism, sustainable.

Best International hotel code meaning a superior grade room; but be careful! Bon is the code for the 'best' quality room.

best available Big difference in meaning between North American and European usage of term. Charles Metelka's *Dictionary of Tourism* states, 'Supplier's promise to provide the best possible accommodation for a client'. But in Europe, the term is used when a customer's request cannot be met and an alternative is being offered, which does not meet a customer's requirements but is the best available. Clearly, in both countries, when the client is making a request of this nature, it means what it says in the ordinary usage of the language.

Best Practice Forum UK initiative covering over 100,000 employers in the hospitality, leisure, travel and tourism industries. *See* www.bestpracticeforum.org

Best Western A non-profit-making association of 4110 (June 2004) independent three and four star hotels with 310,345 rooms covering the world, established in 1946. Seventh largest hotel group in the world and largest hotel brand. *See* PMS² for computer system. *Also see* www.bestwestern.com

BETA Was name of Courier Travel's computerized UK travel agency data and accounting system.

BEVA Was British Exhibition Venues Association; now the Exhibition Venues Association (EVA). *See* www.exhibitionvenues.com

BFE Buyer furnished equipment (in relation to aircraft).

BG Board of Governors, e.g. of IATA.

BGV Bateau a Grande Vitesse. French designed super wave-piercing trimaran ferry planned to operate in 2006 from Boulogne-sur-Mer, initially as a cargo ferry carrying 1000 lorries. Alternatively, it could carry 1200 passengers and 250 cars. It will have a top speed of 75 mph and may run at an average of 56 mph.

BH&HPA *See* British Holiday and Home Parks Association.

BHA British Hospitality Association, the recognized trade body for individual establishments, while the British Federation of Hotel, Guest House and Self-catering Associations represents various groupings. *See* www.bha-online.org.uk

BHAB British Helicopter Advisory Board. *See* www.bhab.org

BHRCA Was the British Hoteliers, Restaurateurs and Caterers Association; changed its name in 1991 to the British Hospitality Association. *See* BHA.

BHTS British Home Tourism Survey. Was replaced by the BTSM which itself, was replaced in 1989 by the United Kingdom Tourism Survey (UKTS). BHTS, statistics for which will need to be consulted to provide past information, was published by the English Tourist Board annually on behalf of all the British Tourist Boards. Thus it covered British residents' tourism spending in England, Scotland and Wales separately as well as altogether. Numbers of nights, numbers of trips, types of transportation and accommodation used and other useful statistics arose from the survey.

bias Where a terminal display in a travel agent's office is presented in such a format, that a particular airline's flights are more likely to be sold. During 1984, the US authorities requested all CRS to make their displays neutral, similar rules being enforced by the EC since 1989. The USA has now deregulated, while the EC rules are under review.

bibby cabin An inside cabin off a short alleyway leading to a porthole; named after the Bibby Line which first featured this type of cabin. The line used to sail between the UK and Burma.

BIGE Billete Internationale Groupe Etudien. Obsolete European rail ticket which used to offer cheap rates for students and has been replaced with youth fares. *See* BIJ.

BIGT Billet Internationale Groupe Travailleur. A European rail ticket offering cheap rates to foreign workers travelling between their country of temporary work residence and their homes.

BIJ Billet Internationale de Jeunesse. European rail ticket offering reduced rates for youth travel.

bilateral An Air Services Agreement between two countries. *See* Bermuda Agreement, Traffic rights, Freedom of the Air *and* Chicago Convention.

Bildschirmtext The German version of the British Prestel system, accessible from abroad by direct dialling, provided the user is registered.

bilge The lowest inside part of a ship.

bill of fare A restaurant menu.

bill of lading *See* B/L.

bin The overhead luggage container in an aircraft.

Birac International hotel code signifying two rooms, one twin bedded and one single bedded.

bird dog US term for someone who solicits business for a travel agency.

birdcage An air traffic controller's slang for the local airspace surrounding an airport; the term is not in use in Europe.

bit Computer abbreviation for binary digit, the basic electronic pulse used in computers. In the ASCII system of making digital pulses represent letters or numbers, eight bits make up a character, which is known as a byte. The sophistication of microprocessor chips is measured by how many bits they can process at the same time.

BITA-LINK Name of British travel agency data and accounting system introduced by BITA Systems (Software) Limited in 1982. (Now obsolete.)

BITE Built-in test equipment (in relation to aircraft).

BITEJ International Bureau for Youth Tourism and Exchanges based in Budapest.

BITOA Formerly the British Incoming Tour Operators Association. Changed its name in November 2004 to UKinbound. *See* www.ukinbound.org

bivouacking Camping is the suggested meaning in the World Tourism Organization and Secretariat of State for Tourism of France (2001), *Thesaurus on Tourism and Leisure Activities.* However, the term is not in general use.

black box Popular name for an aircraft in-flight recorder.

blacked out Alternatively, blackout. US term for a period when normally available cheap or specially discounted fares are not available.

blended wing Aircraft fuselage where the wings and main body are one unit.

According to the shape, this futuristic air frame may be called a 'flying wing'. Boeing, with Cranfield University in the UK, is working on the design and production of a sub-scale (21-foot wingspan) demonstrator of a blended wing-body aircraft, which is being produced by Cranfield's wholly owned commercial subsidiary, Cranfield Aerospace Ltd. *See* http://www.boeing.com

blimp *See* airship.

blind persons by air Blind persons receive rebated travel and special handling dependent upon destination and airline. For example, on British Airways' domestic flights, blind persons accompanied by their attendants are only charged half of the applicable fare. Blind persons travelling without an attendant or accompanied by a guide dog are charged the full fare, but on domestic flights the dog may be allowed to travel free.

block *See* token block.

block booking *See* blocked space.

Block Coefficient An indicator of the potential speed of a ship based upon its shape. The smaller the coefficient, the faster. Definition provided by *Lloyd's Register of Shipping* is, 'the ratio of the immersed volume of a ship to a rectangular prism of the same length, breadth and draught (depth)'. Multiply the displacement in tonnes by 35 and divide this sum by the three dimensions, to arrive at a ship's block coefficient.

block speed The average speed in miles per hour of an aircraft between the time the aircraft first moves under its own power, until it comes to rest at the next landing point. The calculation is from one airport ramp to another and so includes taxi and holding time – thus, block time. In recent years, industrial disputes and other problems involving air traffic control have resulted in significant reductions in block speeds.

block time *See* block speed.

blocked space Reservations often subject to deposit forfeiture, made with principals in anticipation of resale. Block bookings are usually for groups. This is North American terminology. In Britain, tour operators, the wholesalers of the industry, seek 'allocations' from hotels for resale.

blocking *See* block space.

blown *See* air frame.

BLRA Brewers and Licensed Retailers Association in the UK.

Blue Badge Title of British qualification for tourist guides. *See* Association of Professional Tourist Guides www.aptg.org.uk GRTG (Guild of Registered Tourist Guides) www.blue-badge.org.uk *and* ITG (Institute of Tourist Guiding) www.itg.org.uk , which carries out assessments and makes the awards.

Blue Flag beach A beach which meets the requirements of the Foundation for Environmental Education, particularly covering water quality, the environment and the services available. The award is given for a year at a time. *See* www.fee-international.org

Blue Flag Campaign International campaign to improve the environmental management and public awareness of coastal regions, based in the UK. *See* www.seasideawards.org.uk

blue period In regard to SNCF (French railways) fares, the off-peak period when low fares apply.

Blue Peter The name of a flag flown by a ship expecting to sail within the following 24 h. It is a well-known design of blue with a white square in the centre. This is one of a complete set of ship's signalling flags, which designates the letter P.

Blue Riband of the Atlantic Commonly used description of the Hales Trophy, awarded by the Trustees to the current holder of the record for crossing the Atlantic ocean by a vessel carrying passengers commercially. The Hales Trophy was donated for the Blue Riband in 1934 by Howard Hales, a former British MP, to inspire developments in marine engineering. But the Blue Riband itself is much older, dating back to 1838.

The holder is *Great Britain*, a UK Hoverspeed wave-piercing catamaran (SeaCat), operating as a cross-channel ferry. On 23 June 1990, she crossed the finishing line (the Bishop Rock lighthouse off the Scilly Isles) after a journey of 3 days, 7 h and 54 min, an average speed of 36.6 knots. She beat the previous record for the 2922-mile journey set 38 years before by the *SS United States* by 2 h 46 min.

The trust deed for the Hales Trophy clearly intends it for passenger ships, which qualifies the *Great Britain*. Other boats which did not meet the qualifications have crossed the Atlantic faster than the *SS United States*, for example, the *Virgin Atlantic Challenger II*, in 1986, which clipped 4 h 9 min off the record.

blue ski run Significant international differences in meaning. In North America this means a ski trail of moderate difficulty, and may be designated as a blue square trail. However, Europeans familiar with ski runs in Germany and Austria know that a blue run is the easiest. In the USA, Canada, France and Italy, green runs are the easiest, while blue runs are second in difficulty. In Switzerland, take care. French- and German-speaking parts tend to follow their 'language' designations.

Blue Train The famous South African service running between Durban and Pretoria.

Blue Wings Name of Finnair's in-flight magazine.

BMRB British Market Research Bureau Ltd used to produce the *Holiday Booking Index* and *Target Group Index* by analysing the sales of a panel of UK agents. Total numbers of passengers booked and their destinations as well as market shares of the major operators were the statistics available to subscribers. Now replaced by AC Nielsen's *TravelTrack*.

BNTS *British National Travel Survey* is published by the British Tourist Authority. It analyses holidays taken by the British in Britain and abroad, to some extent overlapping the former BHTS, BTSM and UKTS, but more useful when comparing holidays taken by the British abroad with those in the UK. Statistics include holiday numbers, expenditure, main destinations, transport and accommodation used.

board To go on to or enter any means of transportation.

Board of Airline Representatives in the UK *See* BARUK.

boarding house Usually a private home where the owner rents rooms and provides meals. In the UK the term is old fashioned, and seaside accommodation of this nature is now entitled guest house. The term guest house, in North America, although synonymous, has come to mean a slightly larger, better boarding house. In the USA, residents in a boarding house usually expect to receive all their meals included in the daily rate.

boarding member An IATA member on whose flight a passenger is to be carried from a boarding point.

boarding pass Some airlines allocate particular seats in smoking or non-smoking areas etc., upon check-in, giving travellers a boarding pass, entitling entry to the aircraft and designating the seat. Other airlines allow issue of boarding passes at time of booking. But these should, more strictly, be called seat allocation cards, since a boarding pass is meant to indicate that the passenger has checked in.

boarding point Official IATA definition is the point at which a passenger is scheduled to embark on a flight of the boarding member.

boarding priority Airlines board their passengers to a regular pattern. Most take mothers with babies and the disabled first. In general, the higher the fare paid, the later a passenger is boarded.

boarding time Time from which travellers may embark on a mode of transport.

boat Small sea or river vessel. Terminology is loose for it can never be defined when a dinghy is a boat and when a large sailing boat is a sailing ship. A small boat with sails is also entitled to be called a yacht, but then many large cabin cruisers owned by the very rich are also called yachts. Any waterborne craft or vessel is a boat. Although often used as an alternative term to ship, the word boat should be reserved for smaller non-ocean-going craft. *See also* barge, boatel, cabin cruiser, canoe, car ferry, catamaran, coracle, cutter, dinghy, dory, dugout, felucca, gondola[1], hovercraft, junk, kayak, ketch, launch, lifeboat, life raft, liner, lugger, narrowboat, pirogue, prau, rowing boat, sampan, schooner, skiff, skipjack, sloop, speedboat, steamboat, steamship, tender, tramp steamer, trawler, tug boat, umiak, vaporetto, yacht, yawl *and* zodiac.

boat deck *See* deck.

boat drill International regulations require passengers and crew to assemble at their emergency stations as soon as it is practical after a ship has set sail, so that in an emergency everyone knows where to assemble to gain access to a lifeboat.

boatel Hotel providing special services for water travellers or leisure users in the same way that a motel provides services for motorists or a hotel which is water-borne rather than built on dry land.

bogie One of the front wheels on a locomotive, or other type of rail engine. Originally, these were the only wheels that could be steered. Now the word 'bogies' is often used to denote any train wheelset on a carriage, particularly those which may be changed when, during a European journey, there is a change of rail gauge.

Bolivia Ministry of Tourism *See* www.mcei.gov.bo

Bon International hotel code for a best-quality room.

Bonad International hotel code for two twin-bedded rooms.

bond Literally, a promise. The purchase, for a premium of a guarantee of protection for a principal or customer. Because of financial failure of travel companies resulting in substantial losses to both principals and travellers, guarantees are required, which will prevent such losses. For example, in order to satisfy the UK Civil Aviation Authorities' Air Travel Organizer's Licence requirements, a British tour operator may obtain a guarantee from a bank against equivalent security, or pay an insurance company between 7.5% and 15% premium for a similar guarantee. Should the operator fail and the bond prove insufficient, the Air Travel Trust's funds in the UK can then be called upon to reimburse consumers against loss, following the failure of any ATOL-licensed tour operator. ABTA offers consumer protection against financial loss when effecting travel arrangements through members. All member travel agents and operators are required to provide a bond, guarantee or some other kind of security for the protection of the Association's funds, when fulfilling this consumer guarantee. The Association of British Travel Agents' own bonding system for member tour operators covers holidays by surface travel which are not covered by the ATOL bonding system. ABTA has 'captive' insurance companies based in the Channel Islands. Travel agent members can provide a bond or pay a fee under the Travel Agents Bond Replacement Scheme (TABRS). Fees were £200 in 2003; those providing a bond pay £17.50, covering the possibility that their bond may be insufficient. Tour operator members of ABTA are required to pay 'Tour Operators Shortfall Insurance' for the same reasons.

US examples: a Federal Maritime Commission Bond has been required from cruise lines since 1966, protecting passengers on US-originating cruises from loss in the event of company failure. Currently this may be up to US$15 million. In the USA, even though the CAB has now ended, operators of Inclusive Tour Charters still have to carry bonds to protect their customers against default. The switch to the Airlines Reporting Corporation also made no difference to the requirements that US travel agents must be bonded to protect the airlines against losses.

IATA-approved travel agents have to meet strict financial criteria all over the world. A typical example is those laid down by the UK Agency Programme Liaison Group. There must be profit at the end of each trading period and current assets must exceed current liabilities. Failure to meet the criteria means that agents have to provide a bond of 16% of forecast or actual turnover, reduced to 12% for agents producing 3 years' audited accounts and 8%, if there are accounts for 5 or more years. The bonds are calculated to the nearest multiple of £5000, subject to a minimum of £15,000.

In the USA the ARC requires a minimum US$20,000 bond (or irrevocable letter of credit) from agents approved for less than 2 years; after this, agents with net assets of greater than US$100,000 may have their bond reduced to US$10,000. As business grows, so does the bonding requirement up to a maximum of US$70,000. Usually agents in the USA offer bonds from surety companies or in the form of irrevocable Letters of Credit (LOC) provided by any federally insured lending institution. Sellers of Travel laws or Acts with a similar name have been legislated in most US states, with different requirements for independent agents and 'full service' agents. The bonds or sureties required vary between states.

Throughout the EU, package holiday customers are financially protected, details varying dependent on the way the required legislation has been enacted. Protection of travel agents' customers varies in the rest of the world. The scheme operated by ASTA is their Tour Operators Program, aimed at reassuring clients of an operator's reliability and financial stability. Under this, operators must comply with ASTA's TOP Code of Ethics. However, the requirements for operators to participate in one the industry's consumer protection plans has been dropped, because TOP operators are required to be members of either the NTA or USTOA, which have their own consumer protection plans backed by bonding. For details of these *see* entries under their respective headings. For details of operation of an escrow account and of the TFPP (Travel Funds Protection Plan) *see* escrow account. For more details concerning bonding, *see* ARC[1], ATOL, ABTA, ASTA[2], ATRF (obsolete), ATT, BCC, BRF[1], FMC[1], NTA[1], TOP[3], TPA (obsolete), USTOA and the Internet sites associated with those entries.

Bond Replacement Fund *See* BRF[1].

Bonded Coach Holiday Group *See* CPT *and* www.bondedcoachholidays.co.uk

bonus An alternative word for an override. *See* over-riding commission.

booking A reservation. Term believed to originate from the 17th century in the UK, in connection with stagecoach travel. The stagecoach proprietors appointed representatives at the inns en route. Tickets were issued and passengers' names recorded in a book. Some of these books have survived and can be seen in UK transport museums. *See* reservation for official IATA definition.

booking agent Alternative term for a travel agent in the UK, often particularly applied to theatre booking agents.

booking around the block When a convention or meeting delegate stays at one of the official hotels, but not one of the main ones, often because of cost.

booking fee Service charge added to the cost of a ticket by an agent. Typically, airlines either deal direct with customers and/or offer negligible commissions. If agents are asked to make arrangements with such carriers, or for any booking where the profit is low, a booking fee is charged. This has always been the case for booking theatre tickets. US web site www.hometravelagency.com suggests that the term means the fee charged to an airline by a CRS; this neologism is not helpful, as the charge (currently around US$5) is per segment rather than per complete transaction.

booking form A document which purchasers of many types of travel arrangement must complete, to provide the organizer with the full particulars of the travellers and their requirements. Signature by the traveller accepts the relevant conditions of booking and executes a legal contract between purchasers and principal supplier of the services purchased. Frequently, travel bookings are effected electronically, and there is no need for a travel agent to send the booking form to the principal. But it is still important to have the customer's written acceptance of the travel arrangements that have been made.

booking outside the block When a convention or meeting delegate stays at accommodation not officially listed, often because of cost. Sometimes, because no convention registration is made, this cost is avoided. Lax security may mean admission to official events is obtained, while invitations to private functions can be taken up regardless of a person's unregistered position.

Boomerang Fare UK National Express coach fare providing a return journey at the single price for mid-week travel.

booth *See* stand.

Bord Fáilte *See* ITB[2].

Border A low-cost British coach tour operators' computerized reservations system introduced in 1984 by Border Business Systems Limited, only suitable to companies handling up to 5000 passengers.

BOSS Balkan Holidays' UK viewdata reservation system for agents.

bot *See* robot technology.

Botswana Department of Tourism *See* www.botswanatourism.org

bottoms on seats Passenger numbers. Travel industry colloquial term referring to occupancy or load factors.

boutique hotel Meaning imprecise, definitions being constantly eroded by hotel marketing campaigns. In Europe, the term currently means a distinctive, exclusive, well-designed small hotel, less than 100 rooms, often with each room individually designed. Some North American operators use the concept up to 150 rooms, while others designate some of their larger properties as boutique. These are hotels offering exceptional service, personally delivered. Uniquely designed interiors and exteriors, particularly in keeping with the natural surroundings of the location are to be expected, as are high tech 'state of the art' rooms. Boutique hotels are often also called 'lifestyle' hotels. There is no universal agreement as to whether the 'town house' concept is also embraced. The term is believed to have arisen around 1981 with the opening of Blakes hotel in London, designed by Anouska Hempel, and the Bedford in San Francisco. In 2003 they were believed to constitute around 1% of European hotel rooms but accounted for 3% of revenue. In the USA, Starwood has used the concept for its 'W' brand, with properties of 300 plus rooms. At the time of writing, Marriott in North America was repositioning its Renaissance brand to a boutique/lifestyle concept.

boutique ship North American term for a small palatial cruise vessel; all cabins are usually full suites.

bow The front or forward portion of a ship.

bow thruster A screw or propeller at the front end of a ship. By thrusting the bow sideways, docking without tug assistance is facilitated.

box In a theatre, these are usually small private compartments, either side of the auditorium, near to the stage, which are sold at the highest prices.

BP *See* Bermuda Plan.

BPA The British Ports Association is the trade body of port and water conservancy authorities.

BPO Business process outsourcing; *see entry under this heading. A list of 70 other business travel related entries follows* corporate travel contracts, *some of which lead to further entries.*

BR British Rail – no longer in existence. *See* detailed entry for ATOC[1].

BRA British Resorts Association. *See* www.britishresorts.co.uk

Branch Office Location Official IATA definition is an Approved Agent's place of business, entered on the agency list as a Branch Office Location.

Brancker Sir Sefton Brancker was responsible for equipping the British Royal Flying Corps for the First World War, retiring in 1919 with the rank of Air Vice-Marshall. He chaired the initial meeting of airline companies which eventually became IATA and, in 1922, became UK Director of Civil Aviation. He was killed in the R101 airship disaster in 1930, aged 53. He was President of the Institute of Transport, now the Chartered Institute of Transport and Logistics, in 1928; the Institute founded an annual memorial lecture in his name, which is held in London, usually in May.

BRAVO Was a computerized non-airline reservation system, for booking British hotels and other travel facilities. It failed financially in 1992.

Brazilian National Travel Agency Organization *See* ABAV.

Brazilian Tourist Board *See* www.embratur.com.br

BRB Was British Railways Board.

Breaches Commissioner Official IATA definition is the person designated by the Director General as the holder of that office, who exercises jurisdiction over matters described in section M of IATA resolution 800.

break even point The number of sales on a particular departure, or for a hotel or other tourist service, required to cover direct costs of operating. More passengers then provide revenue to the operator to cover overheads and make a profit.

breakage US term for the change in profit or loss caused by alteration in exchange rates or number of persons booked, or when customers do not use all the services they paid for as part of an inclusive tour.

breakout session (at a conference) Large conferences take place in an auditorium. They may, as part of the programme, have a number of sessions on different topics running simultaneously in smaller rooms. These 'breakout' sessions may each involve hundreds of delegates or may be small workshops for 30. Thus, the size of the 'breakout room' is entirely a function of the size of the original conference.

BREEV British Rail Europe Exchange Vouchers. These are now obsolete and were used by non-ticket-holding travel agents to obtain European continental rail tickets and by appointed European rail agents holding stocks of through tickets from the UK to obtain sectional coupons for travel within Europe.

BREL Was British Rail Engineering Limited, one of Britain's biggest engineering companies; trains are built, maintained and overhauled for customers worldwide, as well as for ATOC rail customers.

BRETA British Rail Europe Travel Agent. (Now obsolete.)

BRF[1] Bond Replacement Fund of ABTA in the UK. From November 1993, instead of bonding, ABTA member travel agents could pay premiums to the BRF on a sliding scale, based on agents' balance sheets. *See* bond.

BRF[2] British Road Federation.

bricks 'n' clicks Bricks and clicks. In the USA clicks and mortar has same meaning. A travel company business strategy which involves maintaining a UK High Street travel agency (US storefront location) presence while at the same time offering booking facilities over the Internet, thus providing customers with a choice as to how they wish to be serviced.

bridge Control centre of a ship.

bridge deck *See* deck.

briefing tour North American term for a tourist office or hotel's road-show visiting many cities to run promotions to the local travel trade.

Britexpress card A document which provides 30 days of discounted travel (currently 50%) on the services of Britain's National Express coach network. The card is designed to promote tourism in the UK and, apart from a few specialist British retailers, it is only sold outside the UK. The 1985 card could not be used on its own, whereas the Britexpress pass, which the card replaced, allows travel free of charge for varying periods. The passes are sometimes mistakenly referred to as Coachmaster cards, the brand name first applied to this concept.

British accommodation grading systems *See* accommodation grading systems; for latest details and assessment criteria *see* www.VisitBritain.com Travel industry access is via www.tourismtrade.org.uk

British Activity Holiday Association *See* BAHA[1] *also* www.baha.org.uk

British Aerospace BAe. *See* aircraft manufacture.

British Airline Pilots Association *See* BALPA.

British Airports Authority *See* BAA.

British Airports Information Retrieval System *See* BAIR.

British Airways Link *See* BA-LINK.

British Association of Aviation Consultants BAAC. *See* www.baac.org.uk

British Association of Conference Destinations *See* BACD.

British Association of Conference Towns *See* BACD.

British Association of Hospitality Accountants *See* www.baha-uk.org

British Association of Hotel Representatives *See* BAHREP.

British Association of Leisure Parks Piers and Attractions BALPPA. *See* www.balpa.org.uk

British Association of Tourist Offices *See* BATO.

British Business and General Aviation Association Formed from two partner organizations BAUA and GAMTA; *see* www.bbga.aero The BBGA is a member of the IBAC (International Business Aviation Council); *see* www.ibac.org

British Canoe Union *See* www.bcu.org.uk

British Exhibition Contractors Association *See* www.beca.org.uk

British Federation of Hotel, Guest House and Self-catering Associations Watches the interests of its UK members at national level, and promotes and advances these when possible. Helps to raise the standards of catering and secures cordial relationships between holidaymakers and accommodation providers. The Federation represents many groups, but particularly those associations in British seaside towns.

British Helicopter Advisory Board *See* www.bhab.org

British Holiday and Home Parks Association The representative body of the parks industry including park homes, caravans, chalets, tents and all types of self-catering park accommodation, whose members run the 3000 or so caravan parks and campsites in the UK. The Association recommends a voluntary grading system for caravan and camping parks, known as the British Graded Parks Scheme, with each park in the scheme being independently inspected annually. The park is then graded on a scale of 1 to 5 ticks. 1 tick is 'acceptable'; 2 ticks 'fair'; 3 ticks 'good'; 4 ticks 'very good' and 5 ticks, 'excellent'. This quality grading scheme has been adopted by the National Tourist Boards for England, Scotland and Wales. *See* www.ukparks.com/grading_scheme.asp For general information about the BH&HPA *see* www.bhhpa.org.uk

British Hospitality Association (formerly British Hotels, Restaurants and Caterers Association) UK Trade protection association for all those proprietors engaged in running hotels, restaurants and other catering establishments. *See* BHA *and* www.bha-online.org.uk

British Hotels, Restaurants and Caterers Association now changed to British Hospitality Association. *See* British Hospitality Association.

British Incoming Tour Operators Association *See* BITOA.

British National Travel Survey *See* BNTS.

British Rail Former name of nationalized rail system in the UK; now privatized. *See* ATOC.

British reasons for holidaying abroad Rather than stay in Britain, 40% gave as their first reason, that they prefer to go abroad because of better weather, 17% because they have friends or relatives there, 6% because they like the different people/way of life, 6% because the scenery is better, 3% because of price, 2% evening entertainment, 1% accommodation and 1% food. (Source *British Tourism Survey 1985.*)

British reasons for holidaying in Britain 21% of UK residents gave as their first reason that they would rather have a UK holiday instead of going abroad, that they had friends or relatives there, 12% price, 9% pleasant scenery, 7% ease of travel, 5% accommodation, 2% evening entertainment and 1% food and drink. (Source *British Tourism Survey 1985.*)

British Resorts Association BRA. *See* www.britishresorts.co.uk

British Ship Research Association World-renowned organization concerned with marine technology.

British Tourist Authority *See* BTA.

British Travel Educational Trust *See* BTET.

British Vehicle Rental Leasing Association *See* BVRLA.

British Virgin Islands Tourist Board *See* www.bvitouristboard.com

British Visitors Passport BVP. (Now obsolete.)

British Waterways Board The nationalized company which owns and manages around 2000 miles of British inland canals and rivers. *See* www.british waterways.co.uk

Britrail Pass Rail pass for visitors to the UK. Offers unlimited standard or first class transportation (reservations and sleeping facilities extra) for specified numbers of days. Youth passes are available in second class only. Cannot be accepted or sold by UK travel agents. The US equivalent is the USA Rail Pass.

BRNAV Basic area navigation. An aviation term referring to the air corridors, plus or minus 5 nautical miles, guided by VHF (very high frequency) omnirange directional navigation beacons.

broad gauge *See* gauge.

broadband Telephone connection using existing standard copper lines which speeds transmission rates a hundred fold (or more); thus it is widely used by travel agents to connect with reservation systems. *See* ADSL.

brochure The European standard defines it as a 'publication which details the characteristics of travel destinations, travel services, prices and booking conditions'. It is suggested that this is not satisfactory; better is the ABTA definition, 'A communication in any printed, viewable, audible or other form which specifies the contents of travel arrangements in sufficient detail to allow a client to reliably book the arrangements without obtaining additional information'. But this is too specific, clearly relating to the legislative requirements of the UK Package Travel rules. Combining parts of the two provides a comprehensive definition, 'A communication in any printed, viewable, audible or other form which provides details for potential travellers such as the characteristics of travel destinations, travel and hospitality services and arrangements, prices and booking conditions'. In general worldwide commercial usage, the term means any printed folder describing goods or services. But in the travel industry worldwide, travel brochures for example, detail transport services and prices or describe tourism destinations, while the package tour brochure describes holidays that people buy. Although the reality is that the resort, hotel, air seat and transfers are the holiday product, the brochure acts as the product in the minds of the customers.

In the case of the tour operator it is a vital part of the communication process, including three essential elements: the price and departure panels defining the holiday; illustrations providing a visual description, helping to sell the resort area and accommodation, assisting the client to choose appropriately; and much other information concerning each particular holiday, as well as detailing general conditions of booking. In the EC, the range of information that must be included in a package holiday brochure is strictly defined by Package Holiday legislation (Council Directive 90/314 of 13 June 1990).

brochure racking   Both a simple common meaning and important complex industry term. The words are obviously applied to the stands and shelving that support brochures in a travel agency or carrier's office. Often quite sophisticated in design with storage space behind and springing to present brochures neatly and attractively displayed.

Brochure racking is also the marketing terminology applied to the policy adopted by an agency concerning which company's services are to be promoted, handled or 'racked'. Most travel agency groups operate a preferred supplier policy, making deals with principals for extra commission and/or marketing support. These are the brochures placed in

the most favourable position on the agency racks, at eye level near the front door, in the most prominent position. Less-favoured brochures are put on racks where customers have to 'stretch' or 'stoop' to take a brochure. Carriers or tour operators that are not well known, pay low commission, offer poor quality or are disliked for some other reason, will not be racked at all. When an agent says he intends to rack a particular service, it may merely mean that he intends to sell it.

Research shows that customers consistently move to the left when entering a shop. From a merchandising point of view there are four access levels – stretch, sight and take, take and stoop. Moving items from the top to the bottom causes an 80% reduction in uptake while movement from the bottom to the premium sight and take position in another survey showed a 43% improvement.

In the UK all multiples are believed to operate a preferred supplier list, with an associated racking policy. In contrast only 58% of the small British travel retailing groups have a preferred list and only 39% of independents. For both of these company types, around 57% have a racking policy.

brown bagging North American term describing alcoholic drinks being brought in to a non-licensed restaurant for consumption.

Brunei Tourism   *See* www.tourismbrunei. com

BSF   British Spas Federation. *See* www. britishspa.co.uk   *and*   www.bathspa. co.uk

BSP   Billing and Settlement Plan, originally called Bank Settlement Plan in the UK, but now having adopted the official IATA wording. System whereby travel agents stock one uniform type of traffic documents instead of a series from each IATA airline. Payments are made through a bank in the country concerned instead of to the individual carriers. The system is now running in many countries and the UK trial began in 1984, introduction being completed in 1985. Agents now report 'manual' airline sales twice a month, covering 1st to 15th and 16th to month-end to GSI who have been appointed to administer BSP in the UK. Most airlines sales are, however, reported electronically at the time of ticketing, through a GDS. Agents' bank accounts are debited directly with the amount calculated as owed, on the 17th day of every month, or the first working day thereafter. Agents can amend the amount up to 3 days prior to payment, while the sales analysis from GSI must be received by agents no later than the 10th of the month concerned.

Under IATA Resolution 810a, the following definitions are applied to terms used, even though they may have different meanings in the travel industry:

Accountable Transactions – Transactions for which standard traffic documents were issued or refunded by the agent. The term also includes agency debit/credit memos received by an agent.

Bank Settlement Plan Committee – A committee composed of representatives of members established at a traffic conference of IATA and having general responsibilities with respect to the BSP.

Billing – The statement issued to the agent by the Clearing Bank indicating that the net amount due shown thereon is to be remitted to the Clearing Bank in respect of the accountable transactions reported by the agent for a reporting period.

Billing Analysis – An attachment to the billing recording, in detail, the accountable transactions covered by the billing and any explanations thereof.

Billing Date – The date on which the billing is issued and which appears on the billing statement received by the agent.

BSP Steering Panel – A panel which in accordance with the instructions and directions of the Bank Settlement Plan Committee is charged with the implementation and certain supervisory aspects of a given BSP.

Clearing Bank – The bank appointed under a BSP to perform all or some of the following functions: to receive sales transmittals from agents, to render billings to agents, to receive remittances from agents, and to perform such other functions that are prescribed in the Passenger Sales Agency Rules

(Resolution 810a) and in Resolution 805 and its attachments.

Remittance Date – The latest date by which the agent's settlement in respect of the appropriate billing is to be in the possession of the Clearing Bank.

Reporting Date – The last day of a reporting period.

Reporting Period – The period covered by a sales transmittal which as a general rule is from 7 to 10 calendar days in length but for a BSP operating on a monthly remittance frequency may run to a maximum length of 25 calendar days.

Sales Transmittal – The listing and substantiation of all accountable transactions made by an approved location during the reporting period.

Submission Date – The latest date by which the agent's sales transmittal is to be in the possession of the clearing bank, such date being the third day following the reporting date. *See also* ONElink.

BSR Bank selling rate or Banker's selling rate. These currency rates are used by IATA airlines and agents to convert fares between currencies or from and to NUCs. *See* IATA fare construction system.

BSRA *See* British Ship Research Association.

BTA British Tourist Authority, which in April 2003, joined with the English Tourism Council to form a new UK government body, VisitBritain (*see entry under this heading*). Following the Development of Tourism Act the BTA assumed responsibility for promoting tourism to Britain, drawing on the expertise of the Welsh, Scottish and English tourist boards, the latter were given responsibility for promoting tourism within Britain.

Under the original Act four equal organizations were established, the BTA, English Tourist Board (ETB), Scottish Tourist Board (STB) and Welsh Tourist Board (WTB) as independent statutory bodies. Nevertheless, the BTA was also given general responsibility for British tourism, being required to advise the government on all tourism matters affecting the whole of the country in consultation with the other three boards. In July 1999, the ETB became the English Tourism Council (ETC) with a more limited role than the Welsh and Scottish Tourist Boards; their resources are mainly spent on the development of amenities, provision of welcome and information services, promotion of Scottish or Welsh tourist attractions to the home market and the sponsoring and assisting by grants of regional tourist organizations. The ETC became a strategic body, brokering partnerships, setting standards, developing policy and providing research and forecasts. The Northern Ireland Tourist Board is outside the scope of the 1969 UK Act. For UK national tourism statistics, use www.staruk.org.uk For the BTA *see* www.VisitBritain.com or the Tourism Industry Professionals BTA site www. tourismtrade.org.uk which includes market intelligence data, trends and statistics.

BTC¹ Business Travel Coalition in the USA. A large pressure group representing corporate travel managers with the mission 'to lower the long-term cost structure of business travel'; *see* www.btcweb.biz *A list of 70 other business travel related entries follows* corporate travel contracts, *some of which lead to further entries.*

BTC² Business Travel Centre; *see* heading under this name *also a list of 70 other business travel related entries which follows* corporate travel contracts, *some of which lead to further entries.*

BTD Business Travel Department. In North America it is quite specifically a company's or corporation's in-house travel department which is not an appointed travel agency. In the UK, while there are certainly company travel departments often headed by a travel manager, the term business travel department could equally well apply to the section of a travel agency specializing in business travel. *A list of 70 other business travel related entries follows* corporate travel contracts, *some of which lead to further entries.*

BTEC National Awards (in the UK) *See* Edexcel Foundation.

BTET British Travel Educational Trust was funded in 1970 by the British Travel Association, the forerunner of the British Tourist Authority. Occasional awards are made to those employed in the travel and tourism industry.

BTLG Business Travel Liaison Group. A UK 'pressure group' of 21 of the major corporate travel clients, responsible for over £300 million of air travel expenditure. The organization is limited by its constitution to a maximum of 25 members.

BTP Business Tourism Partnership; umbrella UK partnership of main organizations in field: ABPCO, ACE, AEO, BACD, BHA, DCMS, DOT, EVA, ICCA, ITMA, MIA, NITB, NOEA, UKinbound, UK Trade and Investment and VisitBritain. *See* www.businesstourism partnership.com

BTSM *See* BHTS.

BTW *Business Travel World* is a monthly trade magazine published in the UK.

BUAC British Universities Accommodation Consortium which merged at the end of 2000 with Connect, the Higher Education Accommodation Consortium and now functions as Venuemasters. BUAC included around 50 universities and undertakes joint marketing of their facilities during vacation periods to potential conference and group traffic. *See* www.britishuniversities accommodationconsortiumltd.visualnet. com

bubble car Railway observation carriage with glass roof, enhancing sightseeing ability.

bucket shop A travel retailer of low-price air travel undercutting the official rates. Expression derived from stock market where it was used as derogatory term for unlicensed dealers in questionable securities. The term originated from the small elevator lift or bucket by which members of a gambling exchange reached a Chicago office to place bets on the price of Stock Exchange securities, thus avoiding the Exchange's rules and penalties.

budget fares Term originally applied by some airlines operating transatlantic flights for cheap advance and 24 h purchase arrangements. Now generally used by transportation companies to describe discounted fares.

budget hotel Low cost hotel usually offering little or none of the usual guest facilities apart from accommodation. Often no public rooms for guests, or merely a breakfast room. Catering, if offered at all, is probably provided in a separate block. However, most budget hotels aim for high occupancy levels of short-stay guests by providing two or three star accommodation at substantially lower prices than the norm for the location. Marketing of varying concepts by different hotel groups makes precise definition impossible. Sometimes described as the accommodation equivalent of a 'no frills' airline. Motel6 is the biggest company-owned budget lodging chain in the USA, having started with one site in California. In 1999, it became one of the three Accor Economy Lodging brands. There are over 800 Motel6 locations offering nearly 90,000 rooms. Accor's Formule 1 hotels aim for the lowest cost market, providing self-cleaning bathrooms shared between two rooms. For details of budget hotel room design and other information *see* www.motel6.com In the UK budget hotel sector there are around 230 Travel Inns (Whitbread) with about 15,000 rooms and 215 Travelodges with nearly 11,000 rooms (Compass). With only 116 hotels, Premier Lodge owned by Scottish and Newcastle Breweries are a poor third.

buffer In railway termini, the sprung buffers exist for safety purposes, to prevent trains running off the end of tracks. These are only there for an emergency, whereas the buffers at the ends of train carriages, at the same heights, act as sprung cushioning so that several carriages coupled together are joined in a manner which reduces sudden movement.

buffet Food available on a self-service basis.

buffet car A railcar or carriage usually serving alcoholic beverages and light refreshments for passengers. There are many types worldwide. For example, in France, a 'Voiture-bar' serves drinks and snacks, while a 'Voiture grill-express' is more like a self-service buffet.

bug A mistake inherent in a computer program, as distinct from operator error. Although bugs commonly occur in the development of software, the term can equally be applied to a hardware problem.

Buginese schooner *See* schooner.

Bulgaria National Travel Agency Organization Balkan Tourist Office.

Bulgarian National Tourism Promotion and Information Agency A department of the Ministry of Economy. *See* www.bulgariatravel.org

bulk fare North American terminology for the rate charged by a transportation company to tour operators who block space.

bulk mail *See* mailing discounts.

bulkheads Commonly applied to the fireproof and watertight doors throughout a ship. But seamen are likely to refer to any vertical partition, such as the wall of a cabin, as the bulkhead. Similarly, partitions in aircraft and other forms of transport are called bulkheads. Under an international convention governing safety at sea, bulkheads are rated; for example an A class partition is usually of steel, fire- and smoke-resistant and insulated, so that the side not exposed to a fire will not get hotter than 139°C above the ambient temperature even after an hour. *See* International Convention for the Safety of Life at Sea (SOLAS).

bull's-eye A target symbol consisting of a circle with a centre dot, following the check digit on audit coupons, to provide optical character recognition identification of the 13-digit document number.

Bullet Train Also known by Japanese name, Shinkansen. There is now a bullet train network covering Japan operating city to city at up to 270 mph. The first dates from 1964, the Tokaido Shinkansen, between Tokyo and Osaka; it now covers the 320 miles in two and a half hours and carries 132 m passengers annually. Shinkansens are operated by the seven rail companies formed when Japanese Railways was privatized in 1987; the Tokaido is run by JR Central, which is also testing a maglev (*see* entry under this name).

Bulletin Name of Globespan's UK viewdata reservation system for agents.

bump To refuse to transport a passenger with a confirmed booking. All the American glossaries of travel terminology add the words 'in favour of someone who has a higher priority'. This disregards entirely the usual practice of US airlines of raising the compensation offer until sufficient booked passengers volunteer to be off-loaded. In the USA, CAB figures are that around 15,000 passengers a month are bumped. In Europe, AEA (Association of European Airlines) official figures up to January 2002 were that overbooking leads to 11 passengers in every 10,000 being taken off their flight. For air passenger's rights in the USA in the event of a schedule irregularity such as a delay, cancellation or misconnection or *force majeure* situation, *see* Rule 240. For details of the American laws regarding compensation for 'bumped' passengers *see* US DOT publication *Fly-Rights: a Consumer Guide to Air Travel* on the DOT web site www.dot.gov or www.1travel.com via 'Rules of the Air'.

British Airways' worldwide figures provided in April 1989, were that around 10,000 BA passengers are bumped, and 23 million carried annually. The major cause of this serious problem is that many passengers book but do not arrive for their flights. BA figures are that one in every five fails to check in. The intense competition in the industry has meant the airlines have been afraid to enforce cancellation charges. Thus they must overbook, beyond the capacity of an aircraft, if it is to take off without empty seats which could otherwise be sold. The system of asking for volunteers to stand down and catch the next flight, with compensation, when a flight is over-booked, is far less common in the UK. It was introduced as an experiment by British Airways at Terminal 1, Heathrow, early in 1984 and was subsequently extended to some flights from Terminal 3.

This has resulted in over 40% of bumped passengers being volunteers, reasonably content with the compensation paid, making way for those whose personal or business plans would have been destroyed by travel delay. At the time of writing European airlines in general were expected to adopt similar procedures. In the USA, minimum compensation that must be offered under 1983 rules, in cash, vouchers or free travel passes is up to 200% of the value of the flight, to a maximum of US$400. *See* denied boarding compensation, no show *and* overbooking.

bumpy flights   *See* turbulence.

bungalow   In general parlance, a single storey home. In respect of hotels, refers to individual self-contained accommodation buildings associated with a hotel or resort complex spread throughout the grounds. They may vary in luxury from sumptuous apartments with a swimming pool to a simple chalet with no catering facilities.

bunker adjustment factor   *See* surcharge.

buoyancy   The salt in water makes it more buoyant than pure water, so that heavier objects are easier to support. Plimsoll lines on the side of ships indicate the loads that can safely be carried under different conditions. The freshwater load line is the highest. Because of variations in salinity, there will also be seasonal variations, as well as in respect of different oceans.

burden   Sometimes called burthen, it is the total weight that a ship can carry, when loaded to the legal limit (*see* Plimsoll line). It is not the actual weight of a ship, even though it is measured in tonnes deadweight.

bureau   *See* under specific types, e.g. computer bureau, employment bureau, convention bureau. Bureau on its own is applied to a ship's information office and sometimes to a hotel reception desk.

Bureau of Consular Affairs   The US State Department which handles passport matters.

Bureau of Enforcement   Was formerly the policing department of the CAB until its demise at the end of 1984.

Bureau of Operating Rights   Was formerly, until its demise at the end of 1984, the CAB office responsible for licensing air carriers and maintaining competition between them.

burn-off weight   the fuel used by an aircraft during a flight.

bus   In North America, the term means a large road passenger vehicle providing a scheduled service for individually ticketed passengers or for groups on a charter basis. But in the UK, vehicles operating long-distance express services or tours are called coaches; the word bus, being derived from omnibus, is restricted to those road passenger vehicles operating short-stage carriage services. The use of the term motor coach is obsolete in the UK and obsolescent in the USA, where it used to apply to the self-same vehicle, when operating a tour or day excursion.

Bus and Coach Council Former name of the Confederation of Passenger Transport in the UK. *See* CPT.

bus deregulation in the USA On 20 September 1982, American anti-trust laws became applicable to the US bus business. From this day, fare levels were left to individual operators and the federal government confined its role to safety standards. This resulted in long-distance fares being cut by up to 40%. An estimated 2500 bus entrepreneurs entered the industry following deregulation. The effect on Greyhound Lines, the market leader, was dramatic, because of the lower wage costs of the small operators. It was this that led to a 47-day strike in 1983, which resulted in a 15% wage reduction for Greyhound's 16,000 employees.

bus drivers' hours *See* drivers' hours in Europe.

busboy the lowest level of restaurant waiting staff in the USA, usually responsible for table clearing.

Business Aircraft Users Association *See* BAUA.

Business and Technician Education Council Obsolete but replaced; *see* Edexcel.

business class The world's airlines have many different names for their service concept designed for full fare-paying economy-class air passengers. Where there are three or more classes of passengers on an aircraft, this type of passenger occupies the seating section or cabin immediately behind first class; if there is no first class then business-class passengers are seated at the front of the aircraft. Seat pitch and width are enhanced and there are fewer passengers per member of airline staff. Alcoholic and other beverages including champagne are usually complimentary. Priority check-in, additional baggage allowances and availability of special lounges are frequently similar to that provided to first-class passengers. Cuisine is usually a great deal better than in the discount classes but not as lavish as in first class. Amenity kits including slipperettes and eye shades are usually provided and there is no charge for passengers using headsets for in-flight entertainment facilities.

Adria Airways, Aeroflot, Air China, Air Europa, Air Gambia, Air Lanka, Air Madagascar, Air Mauritius, Air New Zealand, American, Ansett Australia, Australian Airlines, Austrian, Birmingham European Airways, British Midland, Brymon European, Canadian Airlines International, Cathay Pacific, Continental, Croatia Airlines, El Al, Emirates, Ethiopian, Finnair, Iberia, Icelandair, Kenya Airways, KLM, Lan Chile, Lufthansa, Maersk Air, Qantas, Quatar, Royal Brunei, Royal Jordanian, Ryanair, Sabena, South African Airways, Swissair, Tarom Romanian, TAT, Transavia and US Air all use the title 'business class' to designate this type of service. Air India, Avianca, Finnair, Garuda Indonesia, JAL, Northwest, and Varig call their service Executive. Aer Lingus name their business class Premier Service on transatlantic routes but call it Premier Europe within Europe, while Thai call it Royal Executive worldwide. Caribbean and Australian also use Premier.

Club class was the term originated by British Airways for this type of service – because it was one of the first, its use is often generic in the UK travel industry when referring to this type of service. British Airways now call it Club Europe on short-haul flights and Club World on longer journeys. Air Malta, Air India, All Nippon, GB Airways, Gulf Air, and Nigeria still use the term Club, while Air France, on long-haul journeys, calls this cabin section Le Club. Malaysian Airlines use the title Golden Club.

Other titles are Aerolineas Argentinas, Club Gold; Air Canada, Executive First; Air France, L'Espace Affaires; Air Lanka, Peacock Class; Air Malta, Club and Eurobusiness; Air New Zealand, Pacific; Air Seychelles, Pearl; Air UK, Sterling Service; Air Zimbabwe, Rainbow Class; Alitalia, Magnifica and Prima in Europe; AOM French Airlines, Club Opale; Austrian Airlines, GrandClass Europe and Grand; Avianca, Club Elite; Biman-Bangladesh, Rajani Ghandi; British Midland, Diamond Class; BWIA, Royal Hibiscus; Cameroon, Classe Plus; Cathay Pacific, Marco Polo Business Class, Silver; CP Air, Attache and Royal Canadian; China Airlines, Dynasty; Conti-Flug International, Gold

Class, Cyprus Airways, Apollo; Delta, Business Elite; Egyptair, Horus Class; Estonian Air, Blue Velvet Business; Ethiopian Airlines, Cloud Nine Business; Gulf Air, Golden Falcon Business; Iberia, Preference; Icelandair, Saga; JAT Yugoslav, Adriatic; Korean Air, Prestige; Kuwait, Oasis; Lauda Air, Amadeus; Lithuanian Airlines, Amber Club Business; Malaysia, Golden Club; Malev, Sky Club; Meridiana, Electa Club; Middle East, Front Business; Nippon, Club ANA; Northwest, World Business; Olympic, Olympian Executive; Pakistan International, Business Plus; Philippine Airlines, Mabuhay; PIA, Sohni; Royal Air Maroc, Zenith; SAA, Gold; SAS, EuroClass and First Business; Saudia Saudi Arabian, Horizon; Singapore, Raffles; TAP Air Portugal, Top Executive; Trans European, 12 Star; TWA, Transworld One; United, Connoisseur; US Airways, Envoy; Viasa, Special; Virgin Atlantic, Upper Class (for the Virgin/South East European Airlines' service, Hermes); Zambia, Sable.

Business Club Name of Sabena's Frequent Flyer Club, membership of which is free for travellers undertaking 12 long-haul or 36 shorter return flights a year. *See* FFP.

business house Obsolescent term used by UK travel agents to describe a company travel account. Thus, 'Business House Department' is that section of an agency dealing with business accounts as distinct from over-the-counter customers. Confusingly, some specialist agents use the term Business House when referring to their own department rather than a company that is their customer. **Business Travel Agent** or **Travel Management Company** is modern terminology which has replaced business house. *A list of 70 other business travel related entries follows* corporate travel contracts, *some of which lead to further entries.*

business process outsourcing (BPO) When organizations contract to have non-core activities such as payroll and HR supplied by third parties. One aspect of this may be the appointment of a procurement services provider (PSP) which usually takes over responsibility for the procurement of indirect supplies,

including travel services. *A list of 70 other business travel related entries follows* corporate travel contracts, *some of which lead to further entries.*

business tourism Voluntary or optional travel for a commercial purpose. Thus, a person running a stand at an overseas trade exhibition is a business traveller. But visitors to that exhibition are business tourists. Similarly, a distinction may be made between the organizers of a conference and the delegates who have 'chosen' to attend. *A list of 70 other business travel related entries follows* corporate travel contracts, *some of which lead to further entries.*

Business Tourism Partnership Umbrella UK partnership of main organizations in field: ABPCO, ACE, AEO, BACD, BHA, DCMS, DOT, EVA, ICCA, ITMA, MIA, NITB, NOEA, UKinbound, UK Trade and Investment and VisitBritain. *See* www.businesstourismpartnership.com

business travel Travel for commercial or professional purposes rather than leisure. Within the broad sphere of business travel, there are associated specialist industries, regarded by some commentators as separate but by others as part of business travel. It is felt that the incentive travel market is an aspect of business travel, as is the arrangement of conferences. But consider exhibitions and events; arrangements of travel and accommodation in connection with them is clearly business travel. However organization and promotion of an event or exhibition, it is suggested, are part of an allied but separate industry. *A list of 70 other business travel related entries follows* corporate travel contracts, *some of which lead to further entries.*

business travel agent An agent specializing in handling corporate travel; modern title is a travel management company. *A list of 70 other business travel related entries follows* corporate travel contracts, *some of which lead to further entries.*

business travel centre Also known as a business travel service centre. In North America, may be merely an alternative name for a specialist division of a travel agency supplying the needs of business travel clients. But in Europe, these centres have been developed by large travel management companies aiming to reduce both ticket and transaction costs and increase productivity. With multilingual staff they handle the needs of big multi-national companies. Examples are TQ3's centre in Mechelen, near Brussels, handling the Esso account, Carlson Wagon Lit's eCentre in Warsaw, initially set up for General Electric and the American Express centre near Nice which serves IBM. *A list of 70 other business travel related entries follows* corporate travel contracts, *some of which lead to further entries.*

Business Travel Coalition *See* www.btc-online.com *A list of 70 other business travel related entries follows* corporate travel contracts, *some of which lead to further entries.*

business travel contracts *See* corporate travel contracts.

business travel department Modern title is travel management department. *A list of 70 other business travel related entries follows* corporate travel contracts, *some of which lead to further entries.*

Business Travel Liaison Group *See* BTLG.

business travel market in the UK Most (80%) business air travel starting from the UK is claimed to be handled by members of the UK Guild of Travel Management Companies. The annual Business Travel World Survey for April 2005 reports that American Express refuses to divulge turnover figures, although they are believed to be one of the leading UK travel management companies. The top ten companies handle 66% of the turnover; 13% by those ranked 11 to 20 and 6%, 21 to 30. BTI UK reported annual turnover as £1050m; Carlson Wagonlit £840m; The Travel Company £230m; TQ3 Travel Solutions UK £228m; Portman Travel £208m; P&O Travel £129m; Hillgate Travel £139m and Advanced Travel Partners £125m. Total UK business travel market was estimated as £5bn excluding American Express. For details of Guild sales *see* www.gtmc.org *A list of 70 other business travel related entries follows* corporate travel contracts, *some of which lead to further entries.*

business travel transaction fees *See* transaction fees. *A list of 70 other business travel related entries follows* corporate travel contracts, *some of which lead to further entries.*

business traveller Any person whose main reason for travel is commercial or professional rather than leisure. *A list of 70 other business travel related entries follows* corporate travel contracts, *some of which lead to further entries.*

bust out Where a travel agent's air ticket stock is fraudulently issued from 'within' the agency, often by a dishonest owner or by a person who has gained possession of the agency through an illegal change of ownership. The aim is to sell a huge number of air tickets within one reporting period by cutting prices. Since there is no intention to pay the airlines for the tickets, they may be sold at considerable discounts. The agency owners then go bankrupt, vanish or both!

buy forward Contract to purchase foreign currency for delivery on a specified date at an agreed rate. Typically, tour operators publish brochures a year or more in advance. In order to maintain the prices offered, they avoid the risk of exchange rates changing adversely. Thus, US operators who purchased currency in advance before the September 2001 catastrophe did not need to increase prices in respect of this element.

buying rate *See* conversion rate[1].

BVP Used to be a British Visitor's Passport. (Now obsolete.)

BVR Beyond visual range (in relation to aircraft).

BVRLA British Vehicle Rental Leasing Association is the trade body of car hire companies, founded in 1967. *See* www.bvrla.co.uk

bypass US term for operations of travel principals which sell direct to customers rather than through travel agents. In the UK such operations are called 'direct sell'.

byte A group of eight bits, sufficient digital pulses to communicate one character to or from a computer. A kilobyte (kb) is 1024 bytes and a megabyte (Mb) 1,048,576 bytes.

C

C Airline parlance for the control tower/operations/flight office.

C of A Certificate of Airworthiness.

C of R Certificate of Registration; a document covering the basic details of a ship, issued by the country under whose flag the ship operates.

C&GLI City and Guilds of London Institute, the awarding body for many UK travel industry qualifications. *See* City and Guilds of London Institute.

C/I Counter Indemnity Agreement. Although the abbreviation is particular to IATA Bank Settlement Plans, the concept of an agent indemnifying a principal in respect of negligence or other acts on the part of the agent is to be found in most agency/principal agreements, as well as the principal indemnifying the agent in respect of problems caused by the principal.

C/S Callsign.

CAA The Civil Aviation Authority is the UK statutory body responsible for economic, technical and operational regulation of British Civil Air Transport. Its involvement with the wider travel industry is mainly restricted to the operation of the Air Travel Organizers' Licensing System and maintaining a watching brief on behalf of government over IATA matters in general. Airport and aerodrome navigation and national air traffic services are managed jointly with the Ministry of Defence. Its central library near London Gatwick airport is the largest in its field in Britain, containing around 40,000 books and 15,000 other pieces of aviation literature. Comprehensive air traffic data is available on the web site; but it only applies to UK airlines. *See* www.caa.co.uk ATOL *and* CAP.

CAA Data Unit For airline and airport statistics. See www.caaerg.org.uk/adu/home.html

CAAA Commuter Airline Association of America.

CAAC Air China.

CAARS Sabre's car rental reservation system. *See* Sabre.

CAB Civil Aeronautics Board (USA). Existence terminated on 1 January 1985. *See* DOT[3].

cab The driver's compartment at the front of a train; also a taxi.

cabana A room in a beach or pool area, with or without beds, usually separate from a hotel's main building.

cabaret Entertainment provided for those eating meals in places such as a restaurant, night club or hotel.

cabin A sleeping compartment on board ship, passenger area on a plane, or a small building, e.g. beach cabin. In North America the term might also apply to a larger building in a country area, e.g. log cabin. On board ship, an outside cabin normally has a porthole with natural light, while an inside cabin is 'literally' inside a ship. A balcony cabin may overlook an inside atrium or be on or have access to an outside balcony.

cabin attendant An airline cabin steward or stewardess, often called an air hostess.

cabin bags At one time free cabin bags were given to all first-class passengers on long-haul IATA international flights. Their maximum value was strictly controlled under IATA regulations. These rules also restricted airlines from giving free cabin bags in other circumstances. This type of rule is no longer in force, and many airlines and tour operators now provide amenity packs and/or bags for their passengers. 'Cabin bag' is no longer definable as a specific term and commonly refers to any small bag.

cabin boy Originally a young male apprentice seaman who was the Captain's personal servant but term now applies to any youth without much experience at sea who may be undertaking menial tasks.

cabin class When travelling by sea or air, a passenger who is paying less than the first-class fare but more than the lower classes of fare. Term not now in general use.

cabin crew The purser, stewards and stewardesses who attend to the needs of air travellers, as distinct from those on the flight deck, who are responsible for flying an aircraft.

cabin cruiser A small engine-powered leisure boat which has a covered cabin with sleeping accommodation and cooking facilities. Cabin cruisers vary considerably in size and facilities dependent on the number of berths.

cabin lift North American term for a cable car by which people are transported up mountainsides for sightseeing or in order to ski down.

cabin pressurization *See* pressurization.

cabin steward¹ The maritime equivalent of a hotel chambermaid; often, on a ship, the cabin steward may also perform other duties.

cabin steward² Male aviation equivalent of an air hostess.

cabin with obstructed view Outside accommodation on a ship without a clear sea view. For example, many cabins on the boat deck will have lifeboats nearby.

cable An obsolete maritime measurement; 607.56 ft; around 100 fathoms.

cable car *See* cable transporter.

cable transporters A means of transport in mountainous areas characterized by suspension from one static cable of a cabin which is pulled by a moving cable. In the case of cable cars, these may carry 20 or more passengers at a time. In North America these are known as teleferics or cabin lifts, if they are smaller, and sometimes they are known as a funicular, although this is more correctly applied to a funicular railway. Chairlifts, rope tows, J-bars and T-bars for towing skiers may, in North America, be called teleskis. In France may be called telecabine. Following some disasters in Europe, systems with two parallel cables are appearing (funitels), where if one cable breaks, the weight of the cable car will be held by the other.

cabotage Travel between territories of the same sovereign state. This may be between a country and its colonies, or dependencies. Domestic routes are always cabotage. Cabotage routes are not controlled by the standard IATA fare agreements. *Readers should particularly note* that the word is not limited to air transport, as most other dictionaries suggest. Many countries restrict shipping services directly between their own domestic ports to vessels operating under their own national flag, for example, in the USA, the Passenger Services Act.

CAC Cargo Agency Conference of IATA.

CAEP Committee on Aviation Environmental Protection of the ICAO. *See* ICAO.

café complet A mid-morning or afternoon snack with coffee; often loosely used to describe continental breakfast.

cage Collapsible metal crate used while a ship is moored to winch up or let down passengers' luggage.

CAI Computer Aided Instruction. The GDSs offer the opportunity for travel staff to learn how to use their systems on-line. Sometimes, in North America, this is called SAI, system aided instruction.

caique Little Turkish rowing boat.

calendar The standard calendar in use worldwide is based upon the Gregorian year which was adopted in Britain in 1752, when the beginning of the new year was changed from 25 March to 1 January. It has 12 months with 365 days and a leap day on 29 February, when the year is divisible by four. This maintains stability, after refinements of omitting a leap year at certain times, when the initial figures of a year ending in 00 are not also divisible by 4. This is necessary because the earth takes 365 days, 5 h, 48 min and 45 s to revolve around the sun. The earth spins on its axis relative to the sun every 24 h and 0.59 s, called a Mean Solar Day. Of significance to astronomers is the Mean Sidereal Day, which is the time it takes the earth to spin on its axis relative to any particular star, 23 h, 56 min and 4.09 s. The term AD stands for Anno Domini, literally the year of our Lord, indicating that the current method of counting years throughout most of the world is based upon the birth of Christ. Months and normal numbers of days are: 31 January, 28 February, 31 March, 30 April, 31 May, 30 June, 31 July, 31 August, 30 September, 31 October, 30 November, 31 December.

In much of the Middle East, and some other parts of the Moslem world, the Hejira calendar is in use which starts from AD 622, the date of the prophet Mohammed's migration (Hejira) from Mecca to Medina in 1406. It is based upon the lunar year which is 10 to 11 days shorter than the Gregorian year. The Hejira calendar dates of the seasons change from year to year, with cycles recurring every 32.5 years. 'Common' years have 354 days, the months alternating between 30 and 29 days. 'Kabishah' years have 355 days, with the last month having 30 days. There are 19 Common and 11 Kabishah years in a 30- year period. Of the 12 months, two are repeated: Muharram, Safar, Rarabia 1, Rarabia 2, Jumada 1, Jumada 2, Shaaban, Ramadan, Shawwal, Dhul Qa'da, Dhul Hijja. (All spelled phonetically here.)

The Jewish year is also based upon lunar months, *but on a solar year*, alternating between 29 and 30 days each except for Cheshvan and Kislev which may have 29 or 30 days, producing a total of between 353 and 355 days per year. The lunar year of 12 months is matched with the 365.25 day solar year by adding an extra 13th month seven times in every 19 years, in the 3rd, 6th, 8th, 11th, 14th, 17th and 19th years. In order to further rationalize the system, ordinary years may have 353, 354 or 353 days and leap years, 383, 384 or 385 days. The extra leap year 30-day period follows the month of Adar, identified by the same name. The Jewish months are Tishri, Cheshvan, Kislev, Tevet, Shevat, Adar, Adar Shayynee (in a leap year), Nissan, Iyar, Sivan, Tammuz, Av and Ellul. The Jewish year was 5746 on 16 September 1985, although as far as Jews are concerned, since their days are counted from sunset to sunset, they consider that it began on the evening of 15 September. To convert Jewish years to ordinary western calendar years, take off 4000 and add 239 between mid-September, when the Jewish new year begins, and December, and add 240 from January.

The Chinese calendar is yet another lunar dating system, the year consisting of 12 months alternating between 29 and 30 days, and the 354-day year being brought into step with the solar year by the insertion of extra months. Traditionally the names of 12 animals are associated with Chinese years in the order Snake, Horse, Sheep, Monkey, Fowl, Dog, Pig, Rat, Ox, Tiger, Hare and Dragon, the first of these relating to the Chinese year beginning in 2001.

California Tourism *See* www. visitcalifornia.com

call sign Aircraft and ships have a unique call sign used in radio communications.

CALPA Canadian Airline Pilots' Association. *See* www.cahf.ca/CALPA.htm

Cambrian Travel Association Welsh grouping of travel agents which is a part of the Worldchoice UK consortium.

camp counselor US title (US spelling) for those responsible for organizing a camp. The title is more usually applied for someone working at a young persons' summer facility rather than general employees at any campsite.

Campaign for Agents' Rights and Equality CARE. *See* commission and www. astanet.com/CARE

camper or **campervan** A motorized caravan; a mobile home for vacation use. Same meaning as a motorhome or caravanette. Also a word in general language use meaning a person who is camping; in the UK, in the 1930s, 40s, 50s and 60s, 'campers' were holiday campers, the term being made famous by Butlins. *See* RV.

Camping and Caravanning Club Ltd Association representing manufacturers, traders and park owners in the UK caravan industry.

Camping and Caravanning Club of Great Britain and Ireland *See* CCC.

campsite grading system There are many such systems worldwide in most Western countries based on assessing facilities and services. For brief details of UK scheme *see* British Holiday and Home Parks Association.

campsite, camping site or campground In Europe, the term applies both to static tented holiday facilities rented by holidaymakers and areas set aside for those who have brought their own tents. Amenities vary greatly, from a simple farmer's field to a substantial complex with clubhouse, supermarket, toilet and washing facilities. The same terminology in the USA means a site where motor homes or trailers are also welcome.

But in Europe, this is not necessarily so, and joint facilities are advertised as camping and caravan sites, with the appropriate symbols on the sign outside the site.

CAN Commission Adjustment Notice.

Canadian Institute of Travel Counsellors CITC. *See* www.citc.ca

Canadian Tourist Commission *See* www.canadatourism.com

canal barge The 2003 CEN/European Standard official definition is 'boat providing accommodation and self-catering facilities for inland water cruises'. This is not correct in the UK, where the words merely mean a large, shallow draught inland waterway vessel, often used for freight carrying. *See* barge.

cancellation charge Money lost by a customer who did not use a booked facility. Charges may be in respect of non-use of transport, theatre or event tickets, accommodation or inclusive travel arrangements. *See also* flexible ticket, non-refundable *and* void ticket. Whenever it is possible cancellation charges may be raised. An agent or travel principal requests a deposit or payment in advance, since it is often difficult to collect cancellation charges from customers who have paid no money and then cancel just before departure. The example which follows as the next entry is merely to give readers some idea of the complexity of the matter. A similar analysis covering only UK tour operators would probably cover five pages. *It is essential that travel clerks recommend comprehensive travel insurance to all travellers, including cover against cancellation charges; this being a legal requirement in EC countries for package-holiday customers.*

cancellation charges on ship passage money Varies between operators and even between different services of the same operator. At time of writing Cunard gave full refunds for cancellations received from 31 days before departure, making a charge of £25 between 15 and 30 days. Less than 15 days, the charge rose to 50%, while there were no refunds in the case of a no-show. P&O charged £30 per person for cancellations on their cruises, even if this happened only a few days after a customer had paid a deposit. Between 56 and 42 days before departure, this rose to 20%, 41 to 29 days 45%; 28 to 15 days 75%; during the last 14 days 90% and on sailing day or failure to embark, no refund at all. On round-the-world cruises, the minimum cancellation charge was £60 with similar percentage charges arising from 90 days before sailing date. It is essential that travel clerks recommend comprehensive travel insurance to all sea travellers.

canoe Shallow draught small river boat, long and narrow, the width of a person, upturned at each end. Term originated from North American Indians, but now has wide general use.

canopy walkway A bridge for tourists' use built along forest treetops, usually through dense equatorial jungle.

CANSO Civil Air Navigation Services Organisation. Based in Geneva, it represents the 20-or-so autonomous providers of air traffic services.

canx Abbreviation for cancellation.

CAP Civil Air Publication of the UK CAA. The letters are followed by a number which identifies the publication.

capacity Several meanings: The number of passengers that can be carried in a mode of transport, on a tour series or accommodated in a hotel. For example, the capacity of a Boeing 737 is 130. Airtours had a capacity on its 2001 summer charter package-holiday programme of around 3.5 million. For conference facilities, capacity will vary according to the activity taking place; a room has its smallest capacity when people are seated at round tables for a meal. More can be accommodated seated theatre-style and even more at a stand-up cocktail party. But there are also the capacity restraints imposed by fire and safety regulations. Although regulations limit numbers of people that may visit a particular tourism facility, that number may lessen the enjoyment of visitors. The practical working capacity of a site will be that maximum number of visitors who can be present without significantly affecting the quality of their experience. This theme is taken further in the entry for 'tourism-carrying capacity'. In cruise ships, often cabins have two lower and two upper berths. This cabin may be sold for occupation by two passengers or for up to four people.

However, the practice has become established of referring only to the lower-berth capacity when indicating capacity. This explains the apparent anomaly that a vessel may be operating at over 100% of capacity.

capacity control Literally, limitation of seats or space; but the essence of capacity control in the travel industry is to maximize yields. *See* yield management.

capacity limitation agreement When airlines stipulate the maximum capacity to be offered by each carrier involved on particular routes. Sometimes such agreements involve reducing the pre-agreement capacity. Such agreements are illegal in many countries. *See also* pooling.

capacity restrained assignment *See* transport modelling.

capacity ton mile A measurement of air cargo-carrying ability of aircraft. It is calculated by multiplying aircraft payload, measured in short tons of 2000 pounds, and miles flown.

capped commission *See* commission.

CAPPS Computer Assisted Passenger Prescreening Systems. US government security scheme requiring comprehensive personal data about air passengers. Following criticism from the business travel industry, lawyers and civil liberties campaigners, the 'diluted' CAPPS II scheme was announced, for example, allowing the US government to retain data for hours rather than the 50 years originally proposed and preventing use of medical, bank or credit details. APIS (Advanced Passenger Information System) is part of CAPPS. The US TSA (Transportation Security Administration) was eventually forced to withdraw CAPPS II, which classified passengers as green, amber or red, accoring to the perceived risk they posed. It has proposed a new passenger prescreening system called 'secure flight', under which the TSA will check passenger names against an expanded terrorist-watch list.

capstan Originally nautical term for a short revolving post with sockets for spars, so that manpower could turn it, winding in rope or chains to raise heavy weights such as anchors or sails. Although defined as a vertically-mounted motor-driven spindle used to wind in hawsers or cables, in some textbooks, the term is generally used for any spindles used for winding on ships decks.

capsule hotel Unique to Japan, the sleeping accommodation consists of large air-conditioned drawers in stacks.

captain On a water- or air-borne craft, by international law and custom, the person in command. But in North America the term has a more general use, designating the head waiter in a dining room or the head porter, known as a bell captain, in charge of bell hops.

captain's table It is counted as an honour to be invited to sit with the captain during the course of any meal. This honour is usually formalized on cruises. Because there may be thousands of passengers on a large cruise ship, there may be a number of captain's tables each hosted by a senior officer.

CAPTS Cooperative area precision tracking system.

CAR IATA and ICAO abbreviation for the Caribbean region.

car Throughout the world means a private motor vehicle; but in North America, a train carriage (or coach) is a car. Americans must identify this difference, as in Europe, many trains are made up of carriages going to different destinations, rather than the whole train going from one origin to one destination.

car ferry A ship that can carry vehicles. Although the term is now used only to describe the vessels specially constructed for this purpose, enabling vehicles to drive-on and drive-off, there are still some car ferries where cars are loaded and disembarked by crane. Most travellers on a car ferry are either drivers or vehicle passengers. However, car ferry companies can improve their load factors by also carrying travellers who are not accompanying a vehicle; these are known as 'foot passengers'. Ro-ro or roll on/roll off refers to a ship where vehicles drive on at one end of the car ferry, either the stern or bows, and then drive off at the other end. Thus no manoeuvring is necessary as vehicles continue in the same direction, speeding loading and unloading.

car ferry CRSs in the UK Agents can make car ferry reservations through the main GDSs, using products such as

Worldspan's Ferry Source and Amadeus Ferry; or they can access ferry companies CRSs through viewdata systems such as Istel, Imminus (Telewest) or X-TANT. Anite's Afos currently hosts 19 ferry companies; Anite's new system CarRes had only been taken up by Fjord Line at the time writing. FSS is the other major software company serving the ferry industry; its system Res2000 is being replaced by ResWeb which has been taken up by Irish Ferries and Sea France. Many systems are facilitated by the use of Unicorn, the European Electronic Data Interchange Protocol. *See* Channel, Dolphin and STARS.

car hire *See* car rental.

car hop North American term for person who parks and subsequently returns guests' cars at hotels and restaurants. This may be called valet service. The term car hop is also sometimes used to describe waitress service at a drive-in restaurant or movie in North America.

car rental Cars and other vehicles can be rented worldwide. In some English-speaking countries the term 'car hire' is used as an alternative. Effecting these provided a lucrative income for travel agents in the USA in 2001; but by 2002 car rental companies had ceased to pay commission to agents on corporate rated transactions and the trend appeared to be following airline agency commission cuts. The minimum age for rental of a car varies from country to country, may depend on car size and often varies even within a country. For example, in Washington, DC, a Europcar vehicle can be hired by a person aged 18 whereas in Denver, the minimum is 25. Basic car rental rates usually include public liability, property damage, fire, theft and third party insurance with cover varying between countries according to local laws. Rental charges are based on time and mileage or a daily or other period rate with unlimited mileage. *See* also A^1, AC^1, all-inclusive car rental rates, CDW, Central Billing, Drive Away Cheques, Hertz No. 1 Club, one-way car rental charges, PAI, PAS, SR, SW, TACO, utilization rate *and* Wizard.

car rental agency accounting systems *See* TACO, Hertz *and* Central Billing.

car rental reservations systems *See* Wizard.

car sleeping train Train with sleeping car or couchette and meal facilities for passengers while motor vehicles are conveyed on specially designed double-decker open trucks.

Cara Name of Aer Lingus in-flight magazine.

caravan A trailer in the USA. Mobile home on wheels, originally developed for towing behind a vehicle from place to place. The word implies inclusion of sleeping and catering facilities. A folding caravan usually packs down to the level of a low trailer; thus, it is easier to tow. Static caravan sites, sometimes called holiday caravan sites, where there is little difference between the caravans and fixed simple holiday chalets, have caused the term to be loosely applied to many types of temporary home. *See* caravan park *and* caravan site grading system.

Caravan Club Claims to be the premier club for touring caravanners, motorcaravanners and trailer tent campers, and the largest caravanning organization in the world with over a quarter of a million members. Offering sites and a wide range of related services in the UK, members are given access to 180 sites owned by the Club and around 4000 UK locations which the Club has certified. *See* www.caravanclub.co.uk

caravan holiday home A caravan permanently located on site with facilities. *See* caravan.

caravan park A trailer park in the USA. A site where caravans may rent a space, offering various facilities; but the same term may also mean a static caravan site. Although, in theory, such caravans are capable of being moved, they remain on a set pitch, owned as holiday homes or rented for a vacation. This term is European in usage. *See also* following entry.

caravan site grading system For brief details of the UK system *see* British Holiday and Home Parks Association.

caravanette *See* camper.

CARCS Certified Airline Reporting Corporation Specialist *See* ARC.

card mill Pejorative US slang for travel agency with many outside sales staff. Term derived from practice of some less reputable agencies who issue identification cards to these staff, claiming they will enable the holders to obtain travel perks such as reduced-rate transport and accommodation. These outside sales staff do not themselves effect travel arrangements for customers; they merely effect introductions (referrals).

cardboarding   An illegal practice where a piece of cardboard or thick paper is inserted between the coupons of an air ticket, before it is written out. This enables one or more of the audit, issuing office and flight coupons to show different information. Provided the data on each coupon is entered through carbon paper of the same colour as the copy material with which the ticket coupons are impregnated, the falsification is impossible to detect unless all the coupons are compared.

CARDS   Committee of Airline Reservations Distribution Systems, in the UK.

CARE¹   Campaign for Agents' Rights and Equality. *See* commission *and* www.astanet.com/CARE

CARE²   Cook's Automated Reservations Enquiries system in the UK was a private viewdata system enabling remote terminals in Thomas Cook travel agencies to book direct into Cook's package-holidays computer.

cargo/passenger ship   A cargo ship with accommodation. Giora Israel and Laurence Miller in *Dictionary of the Cruise Industry* suggest that this is now called a Combivessel, which by definition carries 12 or more passengers as well as cargo. The older name implied the main usage of the ship, for which it was designed, as did 'passenger/cargo ship'.

Cargo-FACT   The IATA Cargo EDIFACT message manual which contains the functional specifications for IATA EDIFACT messages relating to air cargo. *See* Electronic Data Interchange.

Cargo-IMP   Cargo interchange message procedures. Developed jointly by ATA and IATA it is their proprietary message standard, for use in the air cargo industry.

Caribbean Tourism Association¹   *See* CTA.

Caribbean Tourism Organization   *See* CTO².

Carid   International hotel code for three rooms, one twin-bedded and two single-bedded.

carnet¹   Document issued to members of motoring organizations authorizing temporary importation of touring motor vehicles, trailers and caravans into foreign countries without payment of duties. A tryptique is a similar document but not issued by motoring organizations.

carnet²   An urban transit multiple-use ticket or series of tickets, sold at a reduced price.

carousel   The equipment, usually revolving, on which travellers' checked baggage arrives at any large transport terminus such as an airport. The same word also describes the slide holder on a slide projector; speakers at conferences etc. may bring their slides in a carousel, which will fit on any standard projector. During the currency of this dictionary, this projection method may be entirely replaced by projectors which transmit digital images generated by software such as PowerPoint, and Corel Presentations.

CarRes   *See* car ferry CRSs in the UK.

carriage   Official IATA definition is carriage of passengers and/or baggage and/or cargo by air, gratuitously or for hire.

Carriage by Air (Sterling Equivalents Orders)   *See* Warsaw Convention (now obsolete).

carriage, international   Official IATA definition, except for the purpose of the Warsaw Convention, is carriage in which, according to the contract of carriage, the place of departure and any place of landing are situated in more than one state. As used in this definition, the term 'State' includes all territory subject to the sovereignty, suzerainty, mandate, authority or trusteeship thereof. Used generally, the term 'carriage' refers to the transport of passengers or cargo.

carrier   In general, a carrier is any transportation operator. Official IATA definition of this term includes the air carrier issuing the ticket and all air carriers that carry or undertake to carry the passenger and/or his baggage or to perform any other services related to such air carriage.

carrier identification plate   A metal or plastic plate supplied by an IATA member or other airline to an agent for use in the issue of traffic documents under a BSP.

carrier, issuing The airline carrier whose ticket is issued for a journey and which usually but not always carries the passenger on part or all of his journey. The passenger's fare, either direct or through an agent, is received by an issuing carrier. If other carriers are involved in the journey, the money is divided between them by a system of pro-ration. In the case of IATA and many other airlines this is done by the IATA clearing house which determines net monthly settlements between airlines as a result of these calculations.

carrier, participating Official definition is a carrier over whose routes one or more sections of carriage under the ticket is undertaken or performed.

carrying capacity See tourism-carrying capacity.

carrying member Any IATA member participating in transportation of a passenger.

carry-on baggage See hand baggage.

cartridge disc See disk.

carvery Type of restaurant service where a chef will provide slices of hot meat or poultry as part of a buffet service. See silver service for comparison with various other types of restaurant service.

CAS¹ Certified ARC Specialist See ARC¹.

CAS² Collision avoidance system.

CAS³ Controlled airspace.

CAS⁴ Close air support.

casa de huéspedes Name of guest house in Mexico.

CASE Computer-Aided Software Engineering; although appearing in lists of air industry abbreviations, this is not believed to be specific to that industry.

cash bar The term used in connection with any function where guests are invited, at no charge, to indicate that at the bar they must pay for whatever they order. Usually, although drinks must be paid for, a cash bar is nevertheless for the private use of the group concerned and is not a public bar. In North America, may be called a *no-host* bar.

cash basis Official IATA definition is the withdrawal of credit facilities and the immediate payment by the agent of monies due upon issuance of traffic documents by a member with, unless otherwise specified in the IATA rules,

continued entitlement to payment of commission. The term applies generally to this method of dealing by travel agents, where credit facilities have not been established and the agent has to forward money before being sent tickets or travel documents.

casino Gambling enterprise; typically, visitors play games such as slot machines, roulette and shooting crap (dice) and card games such as poker, blackjack (21) and baccarat. Gambling in most countries is only allowed in specifically-licensed premises. Minimum ages for admission usually apply, varying between around 18 and 21. Often, there are other controls, such as entry being restricted to members, or foreigners. The profits on gaming are high; in Las Vegas, where some of the most luxurious hotel complexes in the world are situated, big gamblers (high rollers) may enjoy free accommodation.

casita A literal translation is a small house. In Mexico and some other countries, hotels may occupy large areas, with much of the accommodation in the form of self-contained bungalows or two-storey apartments, often with small kitchens and their own swimming pool.

CASMA Computerized Airline Sales and Marketing Association in the USA; see www.casma.org

CASS Cargo Accounts Settlement System of IATA.

cassette tapes Tapes similar to those used in leisure tape recorders, but with much greater capacity, are used by to store a backup copy of information in computer systems. These are already obsolescent and during the currency of this book, will probably become obsolete, being replaced by zip disks and optical disks.

cast off Literally, to release the hawsers or ropes mooring ship to the quay.

CAT 1/2/3 Categories defined by ICAO for bad-weather landings. Each category represents a combination of decision height (DH) and runway visual range (RVR). **CAT 1** is DH 60m+; RVR 800m+ **CAT 2** is DH 60m to 30m; RVR 800m to 400m. **CAT 3A** is No DH to and along runway; 200m RVR. **CAT 3B** is No DH to and along runway; 50m RVR. **CAT 3C** is No external visibility. See also CAVOK.

CAT¹ clear air turbulence. See turbulence.

CAT² Commercial air transport.

catamaran A twin-hulled ship or boat. The largest one in commercial operation is claimed to be the cruise ship *Radisson Diamond*. For details of a fast catamaran ferry *see* SeaCat.

CATB Cargo Agency Training Board.

CATC Commonwealth Air Transport Council aims to exchange opinions and information in its sphere between members of the British Commonwealth.

catchment zone For a tourist attraction, the main areas from which visitors come.

categorization systems *See* accommodation grading systems.

catenary An overhead wire in which electric current flows and from which vehicles may derive electric power, contact either being through a sprung pole as in some trolley buses or trams, or more usually by a pantograph mounted on top of the train or vehicle.

Caterbase Was a broad-based UK programme offered by the Hotel and Catering Training Board for the development of craft skills to professional standards.

catering The act of providing food and beverages for consumption by the public. Some definitions attempt to be more precise, for example, limiting the term to the provision of prepared food or excluding food sold by retailers. But many food shops sell prepared food. The word catering is very diverse in its meaning.

CATES Obsolete: was British Rail's Computer Aided Timetable Enquiry System.

CATO Canadian Association of Tour Operators.

CATS Corporate Air Travel Survey undertaken annually by IATA.

CATW Civil Air Travel Warrants are issued by government departments to obtain air travel on credit in the UK at British Airways' offices. No commission can be claimed for tickets issued against them. Only if the warrant is drawn in favour of a travel agent and that agent bills and collects the value direct, can commission be earned.

CAVOK Cloud and visibility OK; visibility, cloud and present weather better than required, for example, as noted in CAT/1, 2 or 3 above.

CAVU Cloud and visibility unlimited.

CAWG Control Authorities Working Group of IATA.

Cayman Islands Department of Tourism www.caymanislands.ky or www.caymanislands.co.uk

CBBG Abbreviation for cabin baggage.

CBEVE The Central Bureau for Educational Visits and Exchanges is an independent organization wholly financed by the UK Department of Education, acting as the national information office for all types of educational travel and exchange. It helps both British and overseas organizations to develop educational contacts and exchanges. *See* www.britishcouncil.org/cbiet

CBIT Contract Bulk Inclusive Tour, a type of air fare made available to inclusive tour operators. Since a contract is signed irrevocably purchasing the seats, there is far more commitment than with individual ITX fares.

CBPP Cargo Businesses Processes Panel of IATA.

CBT[1] Computer-Based Training. IATA launched two CBT training programmes in November 1989. 'Introduction to the Travel Industry' covers basic sales techniques, industry terms and codes, the functioning of a travel agency and issuing air tickets. 'World Airline Geography' enables the user to name and locate countries and principal cities worldwide; apply IATA three-letter, city and airport codes, understand time differences and calculate elapsed transportation time between any given points.

Computer-Based Training for the UK travel industry was made available nationally for tour operators and travel agents in 1988 under a project jointly controlled by the Manpower Services Commission, which became the Training Agency and ABTA NTB. The latest packages are available on disks for PCs from TTTC Ltd.

CBT[2] Certificate in Business Travel in the UK run by City and Guilds of London Institute under the patronage and control of the Guild of Business Travel Agents.

CC Cargo Committee of IATA.

CCAR Abbreviation for compact car.

CCC Camping and Caravanning Club of Great Britain and Ireland. Founded in 1901, it claims to be the oldest club of its kind in the world. As well as organizing many activities for its huge membership, it directly operates over 70 campsites within the UK. *See* www.campingandcaravanningclub.co.uk

CCI Corporate client information; there is an ongoing debate as to whether these travel purchasing details should be fully revealed to airlines or hoteliers, revealing share of expenditure between competing suppliers.

CCIS Corporate Client Identity Scheme of IATA, which was withdrawn in 2001 following fierce arguments in the industry concerning data disclosure and ownership. Individual airlines' schemes have also been withdrawn, such as Continental's Corporate Identity Scheme which required its corporate customers to reveal how much they spent with other airlines.

CCITT Consultative Committee for International Telegraph and Telephone. (As is often the case with titles originally in a foreign language, in the English-speaking world it is known as the International Telegraph and Telephone Consultative Committee.)

CCP IATA abbreviation for currency of country of payment.

CCS Central Collection Service of the ARC which airlines may use to attempt to collect unanswered debit memos.

CCTE Certified Corporate Travel Executive in North America, a qualification organized by the National Business Travel Association; it is for staff in corporate travel departments rather than travel agency staff. *See also a list of 70 other business travel related entries which follows* corporate travel contracts, *some of which lead to further entries.*

CDC Centers for Disease Control, a section of the Department of Health in the USA which operates surveys of cruise vessels as part of a 'Vessel Sanitation Program'.

CDITF Cargo Data Interchange Task Force of IATA.

CD-ROM Compact Disk Read-Only Memory; so widely used in computers that further explanation is not necessary.

CDT Central daylight time in the USA.

CDU Control Display Unit (obsolescent).

CDW Collision Damage Waiver for car hirers. In the event of loss or damage to a vehicle, the hirer is liable to pay a limited sum of money to the car rental company, sometimes over £50 or more than US$100. Liability for this 'excess' amount can be waived at a nominal daily charge paid at the time when the vehicle is rented. All hired vehicles supplied by the major international car rental companies are insured at least in accordance with the minimum requirements by the law of the countries in which they operate.

CEAANS Conference on Economics of Airports and Air Navigation Services of the ICAO.

CEATS Central European Air Traffic Service; an air traffic control centre which has a proposed start date of 2007. Would cover Austria, Croatia, the Czech Republic, Hungary, Italy, Slovakia and Slovenia.

CEC Cargo Executive Committee of IATA.

CECTA Central European Countries Travel Association. Members are Austria, Czech Republic, Hungary, Germany, Poland and Slovakia. *See* www.cecta.org

Cedar Jet Name of Middle East Airlines' Frequent Travellers Club, membership of which is free, but by invitation only. *See* FFP (Frequent Flyer Programmes).

CEDOK The Czech Travel and Hotel Corporation. *See* www.cedok.cz

Ceefax BBC's Teletext service in the UK. *See* Teletext.

ceiling The maximum height for which a particular aircraft is designed to fly. *See also* clouds.

Cendant During the current decade, the Cendant Corporation has become a dominant force in travel distribution, particularly in the USA and UK. The 2004 net revenue was US$1.8bn and profit $466m. Cendant has over 5000 employees in 115 countries. It has expanded from its US real estate origins to own many of the leading travel brand names in travel distribution, hospitality and vehicle rental/leasing. These are listed below:

Amerihost Inn – www.amerihostinn.com
Avis – www.avis.com
Away Network – www.away.com *and* www.GORP.com
Budget Rent a Car – www.budget.com *and* www.budget.co.uk
Cendant Travel – www.cendant.com
Cendant Vacations – www.cendantvacations.com

Cheap Tickets – www.cheaptickets.com
Cuendet – www.cuendet.com
Days Inn – www.daysinn.com
eBookers – www.ebookers.com
Fairfield Resorts – www.efairfield.com
First Fleet – www.firstfleet.com
French Life – www.frenchlife.co.uk
Galileo – www.galileo.com *and* www.cendanttds.com
Gullivers Travel – www.gta-travel.com
Holiday Cottages – www.cottages4you.co.uk
Holiday Network – www.rciholidaynetwork.com
Hotel Dynamics – www.hotel-dynamics.com
Howard Johnson – www.hojo.com
Hotel Club.com – www.hotelclub.com
Knights Inn – www.knightsinn.com
Landal Green Parks – www.landalgreenparks.com
Last Second Trips – www.lastsecondtrips.com
Lodging.com – www.lodging.com
Neat Group, Neat on-line, Neat Source – www.neatgroup.com
Novasol – www.novasol.com
Octopus Travel.com – www.octopustravel.com
Orbitz – www.orbitz.com
Orbitz for Business – http//biz.orbitz.com
PHH Arval – www.phh.com
Ramada – www.ramada.com
Rates to Go.com – www.ratestogo.com
RCI – www.rci.com
Shepherd Systems – www.shepsys.com
Thor – www.thor24.com
Travel 2 and Travel 4 – www.travel2.com
Travelodge – www.travelodge.com
Travelport – www.travelport.com
Travelwire – www.travelwiresolutions.com
Trendwest – www.trendwest.com
Trust International – www.trustinternational.com
Welcome Holidays – www.welcomecottages.com
Wingate Inn – www.wingateinns.com
WizCom – www.wizcom.com
Wright Express – www.wrightexpress.com

Center on Ecotourism and Sustainable Development (CESD) A project of the US Institute for Policy Studies and Stanford University. *See* www.ips-dc.org/ecotourism *and* www.ecotourismcesd.org *also* tourism, sustainable for monograph on topic.

Centers for Disease Control *See* CDC.

Central Billing Avis Rent-a-Car system for ensuring that documents raised by renting locations worldwide, are processed and billed to an agent monthly. Ensures commission paid and builds up history of all rentals by a particular travel agent to enable bonus commission to be assessed.

Central Bureau for Educational Visits and Exchanges *See* CBEVE.

Central European Air Traffic Service *See* CEAANS.

centrum *See* atrium.

Cercanías Spanish suburban trains. Generally self-propelled. They have second-class seating and centre aisles. Operating frequently between cities and stopping at all stations, the most important suburban train networks in Spain are those in and around the areas of Madrid, Barcelona, Valencia, Seville, the Basque Country and Asturias. There is an extensive schedule on this service, and one of RENFE's goals is to keep improving these lines. *See* train.

Certificate in Business Travel *See* CBT[2].

Certificate in Visitor Attraction Practice UK training scheme run under the auspices of the English Tourist Board and the City and Guilds of London Institute.

Certificate of Registration *See* C of R.

certificates of vaccination *See* international health requirements.

Certified Airline Reporting Corporation Specialist (CARCS) *See* ARC.

Certified Corporate Travel Executive *See* CCTE.

Certified Meeting Professional For details of this North American qualification *see* www.conventionindustry.org/cmp

Certified Niche Specialist *See* CNS[1].

Certified Tour Professional *See* CTP.

Certified Travel Associate *See* CTA[3].

Certified Travel Counselor *See* CTC[1].

Certified Travel Industry Executive US qualification launched in 2004 by The Travel Institute 'to quantify and evaluate leadership and effectiveness of executives in all industry segments'. *See* www.icta.com *or* www.thetravelinstitute.com

CESD Center on Ecotourism and Sustainable Development. *See* www. ips-dc.org/ecotourism *and* www. ecotourismcesd.org *also* tourism, sustainable for monograph on topic.

CF IATA abbreviation for constructed fare.

CFIT Controlled flight into terrain.

CFMU Central Flow Management Unit (note Central not Control as in some publications).

CFO Chief Financial Officer (widely used in the travel industry but not unique to it).

CFP Cargo Facilitation Panel of IATA.

CG or **C of G** Centre of gravity.

CGTB Canadian Government Travel Bureau, the official tourism promotion vehicle of Canada.

CH These letters are widely used in the English-speaking world to designate Switzerland; CH stands for Confederation Helvetique.

CHA[1] Caribbean Hotel Association. *See* www.caribbeanhotels.org

CHA[2] Corporate Hospitality and Event Association Ltd in the UK. Trade association for hospitality package providers, offering a voluntary bonding scheme which financially protects purchasers. Future EC legislation could lead to bonding becoming compulsory for all hospitality package providers. *See* www.cha-online.co.uk

chain hotel *See* hotel chain.

chair lift *See* cable transporters.

chalet Accommodation usually predominantly made of wood and of small size, and separate. A self-catering chalet implies that all the usual facilities such as a kitchen are provided. But chalets may merely be sleeping accommodation, set in the grounds of a hotel or leisure complex. When all the accommodation in a hotel is in the form of chalets, the unit is called a 'chalet hotel'.

chalet girl Person who services a ski chalet, usually cooking and cleaning for the occupants.

chambermaid Room cleaner for serviced accommodation.

Chameleon LinkMaster Obsolete. MNS, Midland Network Services, Fastrak's parent, launched this UK agency reservation system at the end of 1992.

CHAMPS Crystal Holidays' UK viewdata reservation system for agents.

change of gauge[1] Aviation term meaning change of equipment/aircraft. A flight number may not change but for the final part of a route (or in other circumstances), it may be appropriate to operate a smaller/larger aircraft. So travellers should beware of a change of gauge on a code-shared flight. *See* code sharing.

change of gauge[2] The distance between railway lines, which varies between countries; so that adjustable train wheelsets or alternatives are necessary, to cope with the change when travelling between countries. *See* gauge.

Channel Until 1991, was the name of P&O's (formerly Townsend Thoresen's) private viewdata system, providing full interactive communication with UK travel agents, enabling them to make bookings direct from their office terminals. System then enhanced and renamed Dolphin. Finally, in common with many reservations systems, web branding reverted to the same name as the service, now available via www.poferries.com

Channel Tunnel *See* Eurotunnel for details of Channel Tunnel vehicle services (the brand name Le Shuttle appears to be obsolescent) and Eurostar for passenger-train services.

chapter 2/3/4 aircraft *See* ICAO.

chapter 11 A US statute which allows bankrupt organizations to continue trading, in an attempt to pay their creditors in due course. Well known in the travel industry because of the famous airlines that have sought this type of protection from their creditors.

charabanc Obsolete name for a motor coach.

charge Official IATA definition is an amount to be paid for carriage of goods or excess baggage based on the applicable rate for such baggage or an amount to be paid for a special or incidental service in connection with the carriage of a passenger or baggage. A cancellation charge may mean a service charge made by reason of failure of a passenger to use reserved accommodation without having cancelled such accommodation before the latest appropriate time for cancellation specified by the carrier. In the case of full economy and first-class fares, such charges are not currently being raised by any IATA carrier. Cancellation charge may also mean the prescribed percentage charge specified in the conditions of purchase of a ticket; these are currently always being applied. A published charge means an IATA charge, the amount of which is specifically set forth in a carrier's fares or rates tariff. A fares tariff is a list of passenger prices and a rates tariff, a list of freight prices.

charge card Payment card which instantly debits amounts charged from the payee's bank account.

chargeback When a travel company has accepted payment by credit card, and receives payment from the card merchant but, subsequently, the card company reverses the payment because they cannot get the money for the services provided. The act of recouping the money previously paid is a 'chargeback'. The word is not particular to the travel business. However, ASTA estimated that 80% of consumer payments for travel facilities are by credit card and usage is growing rapidly in Europe. The most frequent reason for chargebacks is fraud. *See* chip and pin.

CHARMS Computerized holiday, administration, reservation and marketing system for UK tour operators developed by Travellog Systems.

CHART Council of Hotel and Restaurant Trainers in the USA.

chart The extremely accurate maps on which navigators plot a course by sea or air. Also a plan on which sales of travel facilities are recorded, often known as a 'booking chart'. Nautical charts include adjacent land and provide information such as sea depth in the form of contours similar to the way hills and valleys are shown on maps of land masses. Aeronautical charts highlight land reference points.

charter The major alternative to a scheduled air service for the carriage of passengers or freight. But, more generally, an organization can contract to pay an agreed sum to a carrier or owner in return for the exclusive use of any means of transport, for example, an aircraft, ship, coach or train for the flights and dates named. The transport owner or operator will receive payment for the charter regardless of who travels, so that only the operator carries the financial risk involved. Much of the terminology is derived from the shipping industry, but the following principles can be applied to any mode of transportation including chartering of ships, trains or coaches. *See* dry lease *and* wet lease for equivalent air terms.

An inclusive tour charter, known as an ITC, is the generic term for a charter where the passengers have purchased at a single 'inclusive' price, a travel service which includes other elements in addition to the charter travel, such as accommodation.

Ad hoc charters are single or several one-off arrangements.

A time charter is where an operator charters an aircraft or ship 24 h of the day for a period of time. The operator is entitled to the exclusive use of the aircraft or vessel during the period it is chartered from the owner.

A series charter means an air carrier provides flights between specified points on a regular basis, usually weekly, so that holiday arrangements can be organized back to back.

A part charter is the chartering of only part of the capacity of an aircraft. (Sometimes called a split charter in North America.) This can mean that a number of operators have shared a charter. It is more commonly used to describe the situation where an operator has chartered part of the capacity of a scheduled service. This is sometimes also known as a block-off charter.

A single entity charter is North American terminology for a whole plane charter by a person or organization for their own use as distinct from intending to wholesale the seats to others.

The term *'affinity' charter* is obsolescent; it applied to a charter for a group which was recognizable for reasons other than having come together for the purposes of cheap travel. At one time, regulations in many countries were protective of scheduled air services; however members of a club or society could arrange travel at much lower cost by arranging a members-only charter.

Affinity charter rules were widely abused.

A bareboat charter, which used to be known as a demise charter, is where only the ship itself, together with its equipment is chartered. The charterer is responsible for crewing, running and fully maintaining it.

A charter purchase is the equivalent of the way in which some people buy their domestic equipment or automobiles, by hire purchase, sometimes called lease purchase.

A voyage charter is a single-trip ship charter.

charter party Originally term for the legal agreement between a ship's owners and the charterer; but now also used for the contract applicable to an aircraft charter.

Chartered Institute of Logistics and Transport *See* CILT.

Chartered Institute of Marketing Travel Industry Group *See* CIMTIG.

Chartered Institute of Transport *See* CIT[1].

chauffeur The paid driver of a car. The term is the same whether a chauffeur is the permanent employee of a rich person, or hired together with a rented car. The term chauffeuse to indicate a female undertaking the work is seldom used, and the term chauffeur is now usually taken to mean a driver of either sex.

cheap day return A discounted return journey transportation fare valid for a day. *See* rail fares in the UK.

Cheapies Was brand name of Cosmos Holidays' variety of minimum-rated package tours in the UK. Superseded in 1986 by the name Travjet, which is now also obsolete. But the name survives as 'cheapie', meaning a low-priced travel arrangement.

check digit Travel tickets and documents are issued in numerical sequence; but following this sequence is a further check digit, allocated by computer, such that each ticket number is then doubly unique. Transmission or entry errors of merely the basic number might be recognized by computers as valid; but because the check digit will not match, the entry will be rejected as invalid.

checked baggage *See* baggage, checked.

checker At a hotel or restaurant in North America, patrons 'check' their outdoor clothes or other items for safekeeping. The equivalent in Europe of this employee who takes care of hats and coats is a cloakroom attendant. But in the USA, this may mean the same as the washroom attendant, the person taking care of the toilets.

check-in time Minimum time before flight or journey by other transport modes, by which passengers must have reported and checked in baggage, other than hand baggage. Similarly, latest time by which a hotel will guarantee to have held accommodation, unless late arrival has been notified in advance and payment guaranteed. The same wording, check-in time, is also sometimes used in North America to describe the time from which rooms will be ready for occupation. In September 2000 the UK Office of Fair Trading introduced a requirement for airlines to inform passengers of check-in and gate closing times.

check-out time All hotels state a time, often, but not necessarily, 12.00 midday, by which guests must vacate their rooms on day of departure, otherwise there may be further charges.

checkroom North American term for a cloakroom, where hats, coats and luggage may be deposited in a restaurant or hotel.

Cheetah Was British Telecom's telex terminal combining a VDU and printer, often favoured by travel agents because of its ability to transmit messages automatically at any time, enabling international time differences to be overcome. (Now obsolete.)

chef A cook in a hotel or restaurant, but in America the term often means the chief cook. Titles are often expressed in French, worldwide. The head cook or chef is the *chef de cuisine*. Each *chef de partie* is responsible for a particular section of the kitchen. For example, the *chef patissier* is the pastry chef and the *chef poissonier*, the fish chef. In Europe, there may be *sous* or under-chefs and *commis* chefs beneath them.

chevron room set-up *See* meeting room set-up.

Chicago Convention 1944 meeting which set up the ICAO. The Convention has 96 articles covering all aspects of civil aviation from landing rights through to customs and safety. The most well known is its definition of the five freedoms of the air, a misnomer since they are really a list of types of traffic rights that might be permitted under government agreement. The first freedom is the privilege of flying across another country without landing. The second that of landing for non-traffic purposes, to refuel for example. The third freedom is the privilege of putting down passengers, mail and freight taken on board in the territory of the state whose nationality the aircraft bears. The fourth freedom of the air is the privilege of taking up passengers, mail and freight destined for the territory of the state whose nationality the aircraft bears. The fifth freedom is the privilege of taking on passengers, mail and freight destined for the territory of a state other than that of whose nationality the aircraft bears, and the privilege of putting down passengers, mail and freight taken on board in such a territory. It is this fifth freedom type of traffic right that has resulted in the proliferation of so many foreign airlines flying onward to America via the UK. The Chicago Convention does not define the situation where a country picks up passengers, mail and freight from a foreign country and transports them to another foreign country via its own territory. Some books call this the sixth freedom. A listing of the currently nine freedoms is under 'Freedoms of the Air'. The conference also resulted in Bilateral Agreement Rules, which are a framework upon which air traffic negotiations can be conducted between two nations. The Convention on International Civil Aviation came into force on 4 April 1947. Now 142 states are party to the convention. It makes no reference to fare structures. *See also* ASA (Air Service Agreement), Bermuda, Freedoms of the Air (now nine), open skies, traffic rights.

Chieftain Club Was name of British Caledonian's Frequent Flyer Club available free to those who made at least eight long-haul return flights a year, or one European flight a week, or two UK domestic return flights every 2 weeks, or a combination thereof annually. Special discounts on Gatwick car parks were available, amongst other facilities in addition to those listed under the general heading FFP (frequent flyer programme). (Now obsolete.)

child seat Small seat attached to an ordinary seat on a mode of transport, enabling secure travel for a small child.

children's reductions by air On UK domestic services carriage is free for infants under 2, and half fare 3–11 inclusive. Youth fares give 25% discount 12–21 while similar student fares may apply up to 26. On international air journeys infants under 2 are charged 10%, while children 2–11 pay half. Student and Youth reductions vary.

children's reductions by rail In Britain, up to four children under 5 years of age may travel free when with a fare-paying passenger and those aged 5 but under 16 pay half. Reductions on European rail journeys vary between the railway administrations involved.

children's reductions by sea Vary between different shipping lines and often differ on various services of an operator. Children occupying a cot in a cabin usually travel at around 20% of the normal fare, while youngsters of any age up to 11 years old, occupying a berth, usually pay 50% or 60%. Youth fares for youngsters aged between 12 and 16 usually provide 25% reductions. Southampton Port Charges are not made for children aged under 5. Similar charges in other parts of the world vary. On UK car ferry journeys children under 4 travel free, while those aged 4–13 inclusive usually pay half fare.

children's reductions on UK coach One child under 5 for each accompanying adult travels free; children aged 5 and under 16 pay two-thirds of the adult fare, with some exceptions.

Chile National Travel Agency Organization *See* ACET *also* www.achet.cl

Chile Tourism *See* www.visitchile.org

China National Tourist Organization *See* www.cnto.org

chip *See* microchip.

chip and pin Name of credit or charge card usage method introduced to lessen fraud. Purchaser enters their pin on a key pad to validate a transaction. The pin must correspond with the secret code held centrally for the card. Credit card organizations will 'charge back' fraudulent transactions to travel companies if this validation method has not been used. Thus travel agents in the UK use ABTACHECK and US agents similar systems to avoid fraud when cardholders not present are making travel purchases.

ChipCard A Lufthansa card issued to frequent travellers. *See* e-ticketing.

chit Bill used in a hotel or restaurant instead of payment. Guests may sign chits, so that items can be put on their account. At an intermediate stage, the chit serves as a control mechanism because the value of chits plus cash received by a barman must add up to the value of the food and beverages consumed.

CHME Council of Hospitality Management Education in the UK. For higher education resources or teaching information. *See* Network for Hospitality, Leisure, Sport and Tourism.

chondola Third edition of *Columbus World Travel Dictionary* suggests it is a ski lift that can carry chairs or cabins. Research was unable to establish general usage of term.

CHRD Committee on Human Resources Development of IATA.

CHRIE Council on Hotel, Restaurant and Institutional Education in the USA. *See* www.chrie.org

chronometer A reliable, very precise clock, typically used on board an aircraft or ship, where the exact time is used for plotting position.

chunnel *See* Eurotunnel.

churning Process by which a travel intermediary repeatedly cancels existing air bookings and rebooks a similar journey. This may be to obtain a better fare not previously available or to achieve extra income through a GDS productivity agreement.

chute Abbreviation for parachute; also slide attached to aircraft doors, which is inflated in an emergency to enable passenger evacuation.

CIAO CIT's UK viewdata reservation system for agents.

CILT Chartered Institute of Logistics and Transport in the UK. The Chartered Institute of Transport (CIT) merged with the Institute of Logistics (IOL) in 1998 to form an international professional body, the Institute of Logistics and Transport, for individuals employed in transport and physical distribution. This body then acquired Royal Charter status; currently there are around 32,500 members. Originally founded in 1919 as the Institute for Transport, it received a Royal Charter in 1926, 'to promote and encourage and coordinate the study and advancement of the science and art of transport in all its branches'. Though based in the UK, around 5000 of its original 50,000 members were outside the UK, mainly in the current and former British Commonwealth. Examinations leading to associate and full membership of the CILT are recognized as the equivalent of university pass degree standard. *See* www.iolt.org.uk *and* www.cilt-international.com

CIMMS Computer integrated maintenance management system.

CIMTIG Chartered Institute of Marketing Travel Industry Group in the UK. A specialist branch of the Chartered Institute of Marketing still referred to by some publications as IMTIG, Institute of Marketing Travel Industry Group, its title when formed in 1969. Its main activities are monthly London meetings and annual UK travel industry awards for excellence in various forms of marketing.

CIP[1] Carrier Identification Plate. *See* carrier identification plate for explanation.

CIP[2] Commercially Important People, Persons or Passengers, dependent upon the organization using the term. VIP is also commonly used in the travel industry.

circadian rhythm The natural bodily rhythms, normally relating to a period of sleep at night and daytime activities. When travellers change to substantially new time zones, quite apart from the change in sleeping habits required, the body needs a period of adjustment before the natural rhythm is re-established. The disorientation that travellers suffer because of this is commonly known as jetlag, medically, circadian dyschronism.

Circle Trip Minimum *See* circle trips *and* IATA fare construction system.

circle trips Journeys from a point and return thereto, by a continuous circuitous air route, not falling into the ordinary return or round-trip category. If in between any two points on the itinerary there are no practicable direct air services, then a break in the circle trip may be travelled by other forms of transport without prejudice to the allowable circle trip fare.

When the fare calculation for an itinerary is completed and the journey has been defined as being a circle trip, a minimum fare check, known as the Circle Trip Minimum Fare Check must be undertaken.

The fare for a circle trip travelled on one class of service must not be less than the highest direct normal or special round-trip fare applicable to the class of service used from the point of origin to any ticketed point on the route of travel.

The fare for a circle trip travelled partly on one class and partly on another, must not be less than the highest direct or normal special round-trip fare as appropriate, applicable to the lowest class of service involved on the journey from the point of origin to any ticketed point on the journey, plus the applicable differential/s for the sector/s travelled in the higher-rated class of service/s. Official IATA definition is travel from a point and return thereto by a continuous air route; provided that where no reasonably direct scheduled air service is available between two points, a break in the circle may be travelled by any other means of transportation without prejudice to the circle trip.

circuit tourism Sometimes used as a derogatory term for a group of tourism destinations often bundled together as a multi-centre tour. Or may allude to any multi-centre leisure arrangement to a series of well-known destinations in an area or region, whether within one country or several.

circular tour Literally any trip which begins and ends at the same place; but the wording is often used for a city sightseeing or orientation tour.

cirrostratus *See* clouds.

cirrus *See* clouds.

CIRS Confidential Incident Reporting System.

CIS[1] Corporate Identity Scheme of Continental Airlines. *See* CCIS.

CIS[2] Commonwealth of Independent States (some parts of the former Soviet Union).

CIT Formerly the Chartered Institute of Transport in the UK; now the Chartered Institute of Logistics and Transport. *See* CILT *and* www.cilt-international.com

CITC Canadian Institute of Travel Counsellors. *See* www.citc.ca

CITE Certified Incentive Travel Executive. *See* www.site-intl.org , the web site of the Society of Incentive and Travel Executives.

CITES Convention on International Trade in Endangered Species of Wild Flora and Fauna.

CITOG Channel Islands Tour Operators Group in the UK.

City and Guilds of London Institute The largest UK national and international organizer of vocational qualifications. C&G is a registered UK charity founded in 1878, granted a Royal Charter in 1900. C&G provides internationally recognized qualifications, awards, assessments and support for organizations and individuals covering the complete spectrum of industry and commerce. *See* www.city-and-guilds.co.uk

City and Guilds of London Institute travel qualifications C&G is the awarding body for many UK travel industry qualifications. In 2004 qualifications were restructured to form two diplomas in travel and tourism. These are gained from taking a combination of core and optional units from the 12 available at level 1 and from the 19 at level 2. One of three specialised routes can be chosen, Travel Agents, Tour Operations or Travel and Tourism. IATA lays down standards concerning booking air travel, air fares and their calculation and ticketing. The Air Fares and Ticketing certification at two levels meets the IATA standards. ABTAC, the ABTA Travel Agent's Certificate at two levels is described under its heading in this dictionary, as is ABTOC, the ABTA Tour Operator's Certificate at two levels. There are four levels of the business travel awards, all of which are certified jointly with the Guild of Business Travel Agents. The Introductory, Consultant and Supervisory Certificates cover air fares and ticketing and business travel practices; there is both formal written and practical assessment. The Management level includes staff management and development and managing business accounts.

NVQs (National Vocational Qualifications) and their Scottish counterpart, SVQs are qualifications that can be obtained 'on the job' by proving competence in the relevant skills. C&G are the joint certifying authority for a wide range of travel oriented NVQs together with People 1st, the Sector Skills Council. Candidates choose groups of units relevant to the sector in which they work: leisure travel; business travel; tour operations, environmental and heritage interpretation. There are also 16 units covering the events sector (exhibitions and conferences etc.). For more information *see* www.city-and-guilds.co.uk, ABTAC *and* ABTOC, NVQ, TTENTO.

city break A short vacation to a city; the arrangements may be a package of accommodation and transport. The 2003 CEN/European Standard official definition is 'Journey to a city with at least one night's accommodation, usually with a sightseeing programme, which may be optional or included in the price'. Unfortunately, this definition does not take account of the growing popularity of low-cost 'no frills' air flights which many people book as city breaks, making accommodation arrangements themselves.

city pair Literally, two cities between which passengers may fly.

city terminal May mean a coach, bus or rail station, but normally used by international air travellers to indicate a place to which arriving airport passengers may be taken and from which departing airport passengers may be collected. A terminal may be merely a place for getting on and off a bus, or alternatively a substantial building where air travellers may complete all check-in formalities as well as purchase or change their tickets.

city ticket office More commonly used in North America to differentiate between airline offices at airports and those at other locations.

city tour A sightseeing trip around a city usually by coach. Strongly to be recommended at the beginning of a visit as a means of orientation.

CIV International convention concerning the carriage of passengers and luggage by rail. (Convention Internationale Concernant le Transport des Voyageurs et des Bagages par Chemin de Fer.) The convention does not apply to US rail travel.

Civil Air Travel Warrant *See* CATW.

Civil Aviation Authority *See* CAA.

CIWLT International Sleeping Car Company. *See* European rail sleeping cars.

CL Centre line (aviation term).

claim PNR The act of an organization, taking over or claiming an airline passenger name record in a computer reservation system which it did not create. Permission from the originator must be provided when, often, travel agents ticket for other agents. The same restrictions do not apply to airlines with regard PNRs in their systems.

Classe Affaires Brand name given by Air France to passenger area immediately adjacent to first class, where passengers paying full economy fares enjoy improved service and facilities. *See* business class.

classes of travel Designations by symbols, words or numerals according to the degree of facilities and comfort provided. On modes of transport, seating or accommodation is often divided into sections dependent upon fares paid, first class usually being the most luxurious. *See also* airline class and fare designators, business class, economy class, first class and intermediate class.

classification of European international coach services *See* ASOR.

classification of hotels and other accommodation *See* accommodation grading systems.

classroom style seating Alternative name for schoolroom style seating. *See* meeting room set-up.

CLB Crash location beacon (aviation term).

CLC Convention Liaison Council in the USA.

clear air turbulence *See* turbulence.

clearing bank Official IATA definition is the bank or other organization appointed under a BSP to perform all or some of the following functions: to receive sales transmittals from agents; to extract and process data therefrom; to render billings to agents; to receive remittances from agents; and to perform such other functions as are prescribed in the sales agency rules. In the UK these functions are undertaken by an organization called GSI and not one of the UK banks.

clearing house The IATA clearing house receives accounts from all IATA members of money received. Airlines may pay into or receive from the common revenue pool following pro-ration of tickets. Pool revenue from a route under a commercial agreement may also be distributed through the clearing house. *See* IATA Clearing House for full information.

cleat Originally a wooden wedge on a ship's spar, now more generally applied to pieces of wood or metal which secure rigging cable or ropes.

Clefs d'Or Literally, keys of gold, referring to the Society of Golden Keys of which the hotel porters in the world's best hotels are members. Hall porters often have the crossed gold keys symbol on their uniform lapels.

clew On a fore and aft sail, the bottom rear corner, or the bottom corner of a square sail.

clicks and mortar In the UK bricks and clicks has same meaning. A travel company business strategy which involves maintaining US storefront location (a UK High Street travel agency presence) while at the same time offering booking facilities over the Internet, thus providing customers with a choice as to how they wish to be serviced.

clicks to bricks Creation of travel business via the Internet and servicing it through a shopping area or mall travel agency.

CLIA Cruise Lines International Association. A North American trade body with membership of almost all the cruise lines selling and/or operating their services in the area. Generic marketing of cruising is undertaken on behalf of all members; a particular strength of the organization is training and certification of travel agency staff, leading to qualification as ACC, Accredited Cruise Counsellor and MCC, Master Cruise Counsellor. For further information about the CLIA, access www.cruising.org *also see* www.ten.io.com/clia *and* ICCL (International Council of Cruise Lines).

climate Weather conditions including, for example, temperature, wind, humidity, rainfall and snow conditions. Weather information is available from a plethora of sources; the author uses www.weathercall.co.uk, www.avnet.co.uk and www.weatheraction.com both for previous averages and up-to-date information. For the UK Meteorological Office *see* www.meto.gov.uk and within that site www.meto.gov.uk/aviation for specialized information. *See also* Beaufort scale *and* clouds.

Clipper Class Was the brand name given by Pan Am to passenger area immediately adjacent to first class, where passengers paying full economy fares enjoyed improved service and facilities. *See* business class for full description.

Clipper Club Was the name of Pan American's Frequent Flyer Club. *See* business class *and* FFP for description.

CLNC Clearance.

clock face timetabling Concept introduced by German Railways in the 80s whereby 35 cities have intercity services leaving at the same minutes past each hour throughout the day. A business person in those cities knows departure times without consulting a timetable.

closed dates/periods/times Time periods during which a travel facility or service is not available to certain types of passenger. The wording is also used widely in its normal meaning, when, for example, a hotel only open during the summer, is closed during the winter. The definition 'time periods when everything available at a facility or service has been booked' appeared first in a 1981 *Dictionary of Tourism* by Charles Metalka and has been copied in other publications; it is not correct. Actual travel industry usage of the term is more subtle. Huge numbers of travellers earn frequent-flyer mileage points; but they cannot use them on certain routes during peak periods; these are 'closed' so that airlines can sell the seats to paying customers. Airline and travel agency staff are entitled to discount tickets; similarly they are not allowed these discounts during closed periods.

closed user group *See* CUG.

clouds *Stratus* is sometimes used as the generic description of clouds in a horizontal sheet but it is only correctly applied to well defined layers of cloud similar to fog and often appearing beneath some of the other formations. *Altocumulus* is a frequently occurring type. Grey or white in colour or a mottled mixture, with shapes varying, often resembling waves of rounded masses. They are usually found between 7000 ft and 18,000 ft, while similar looking *stratocumulus* clouds occur below 8000 ft. *Nimbostratus* is what are often seen when the sky is covered with low grey cloud and it is raining. *Altostratus* clouds are likely to be grey or grey/blue; the sheet is often dense covering hundreds of square miles and situated between 6500 ft and 18,000 ft. *Cirrocumulus* is a thin white cloud, often in ripples. Particularly regular formations are called a mackerel sky. *Cirrostratus* are white, high and fibrous or smooth. Being made of ice crystals, a halo is seen when viewing the sun or moon through them. White, high, fine filaments, patches or bands, often with a silky look, are *cirrus* (cirus). In the appropriate shape they are called mares' tails. *Cumulus* clouds are, perhaps, the most well known, formed as rising air currents cause the water contained to condense. The dark base is usually well defined and flat, while the rising dense top has a characteristic cauliflower shape. Cumulus mountains as they join together become *cumulonimbus*, high, huge and very dense, capable of producing heavy rain or thunderstorms. The term cloud ceiling is the altitude at which, at a given time and place, clouds begin.

CLS Cargo loading system.

Club Affaires Name of UTA Frequent Flyers Club, membership of which is free to those who take six long-haul return trips from Europe to America or three to the Far East. *See* FFP (frequent flyer programmes).

club car North American term for a public area on a train, often with comfortable seating and with refreshments available; it may be restricted to those who have paid a higher fare.

Club Class Brand name given by many airlines to passenger area immediately adjacent to first class, where passengers paying full economy fares enjoy improved service and facilities. Airlines using this title include Air France, Air Malta, British Airways, Gulf Air, Malaysian Airlines and Olympic. *See* business class for full description.

Club des 2000 The name of the Air France Frequent Flyers' Club, requiring at least 40 European flown sectors annually for membership, is Service Plus. But prominent figures in industry and the arts, and other opinion formers get the same benefits by invitation of Air France, under the name Club des 2000.

club floor Area in a hotel, often set aside for business travellers; there will usually be extra security against unauthorized access, a lounge and business or other facilities.

Club Pacific Name of Air New Zealand Frequent Flyers' Club, free to first- and business-class passengers, otherwise costing NZ$200 annually.

CMC Condition monitored check (aviation term).

CMM Component maintenance manual (aviation term).

CMP[1] Certified Meeting Professional in North America. *See* www.convention industry.org/cmp

CMP[2] Acronym for a complete meeting package.

CN Consigne de Navigabilité.

CNP Council for National Parks in the UK. The CNP is made up of over 40 local and national UK organizations representing conservation and recreation interests. These include the Ramblers' Association, the National Trust and the Council for the Protection of Rural England. Although the CNP originally began as the Standing Committee for National Parks in 1936, it was not until 1949 that the National Parks and Access to the Countryside Act led to the designation of the first ten UK national parks. *See* www.cnp.org.uk

CNS[1] Certified Niche Specialist, a validation that the holder has taken an appropriate ASTA course.

CNS[2] Communications, Navigation, Surveillance.

CNSC Cargo Network Services Corporation, an IATA subsidiary.

coach In the UK, this is a large road passenger transport vehicle, carrying passengers for long distances. Buses are similar vehicles operating stage carriage services over short distances. By UK law, minibuses are those carrying 12 passengers or fewer. The same word is also applied to a rail carriage.

coach class   US domestic passenger carriage at the international equivalent of economy.

coach drivers' hours   *See* drivers' hours in Europe.

coach licensing in Europe   *See* ASOR.

Coach Tourism Council   *See* CTC².

coach waybills for international European journeys   *See* ASOR.

Coachbook   *See* Allbook.

CoachMarque   Administered by the Confederation of Passenger Transport UK. *See* www.coachmarque.org *and* www.cpt-uk.org

Coachmaster   Was National Travel's coach ticket allowing unlimited travel for periods of eight, 15, 22 or 29 days. Restricted to overseas visitors to the UK and only available on those services indicated in National's Express Coach Guide. Was not bookable through travel agents in the UK. Now obsolete and replaced by Britexpress cards.

Coalition for Travel Industry Parity   *See* CTIP.

COBOL   Common Business Orientated Language, a computer programming language.

COC   Country of Commencement. Abbreviation normally used in connection with IATA fare construction system.

cockpit   The covered area of a small motor boat or the section on an aircraft where the controls are situated and the pilots and engineers etc. sit.

code sharing   Usually relates to an airline practice where one or more airlines agree to share a single flight code, for part or all of a flight. An airline flight code often indicates one continuous flight on the same aircraft. But in order to make it easier to sell space on journeys involving one or more aircraft changes, during the 1980s some airlines adopted the practice of giving a single flight code to some multi-sector journeys. In this way, a false impression could be created concerning the convenience and comfort of a flight. Codeshare first appeared on systems in 1986. Now, 25% of all flights and 40% of itineraries held in OAG's system are marketing rather than operational schedules; some of these partners are surface transport operators. In September 2000, the UK Office of Fair Trading introduced rules requiring code-sharing airlines to name the carrier that passengers will fly with.

codes of conduct   Membership rules of an organization regulating the behaviour of members. ASTA and ABTA are typical travel industry trade bodies with stringent codes.

COE   United Nations Committee on the Transport of Dangerous Goods.

coffee shop   Not, as might be supposed, merely a retail outlet for the purchase of coffee. The term is used loosely by travellers to describe a simple hotel restaurant where unsophisticated food and beverages are available most or all of the day and night. In Holland, the name is used for the establishments which are licensed to sell cannabis products.

cog railway   *See* rack railway.

COGES   Combined gas turbine and steam turbine integrated electric drive propulsion system; a 'manufactured' acronym for one of the power-generating systems used on large ships. Many cruise ships are now being built with diesel electric power-generating systems, providing both propulsion and general electricity supply.

Cohen's five modes of tourist experience   *See* tourist typologies.

co-host airline (carrier)   An airline whose schedules and availability are stored and displayed, on a preferential basis, in the system of another airline. A co-host arrangement may include additional features, such as sharing in the development and operation of a host-automated reservation system.

co-host carrier   *See* co-host airline.

Collective Ticket   *See* European Rail group travel.

collision damage waiver for car hirers   *See* CDW.

Colombia Fondo de Promoción Turística   Colombia Tourist Promotion Board. *See* www.tourismcolombia.com

colours   A national flag or ensign flown from the mast or stern post of a ship.

COM   Country of Origin Minimum. Abbreviation normally used in connection with IATA fare construction system.

combination fare rate or charge   Official IATA definition is the establishment of a fare rate or charge by addition of sectional fares, rates or charges.

combined taxes and user fees   *See* XT (USA only).

combivessel *See* cargo/passenger ship.

commemorative **tourism** Heritage tourism. Readers are advised to disregard this mistaken attempt in the World Tourism Organization and Secretariat of State for Tourism of France (2001), *Thesaurus on Tourism and Leisure Activities* to translate the French terminology 'tourism commemoratif'. *See* tourism, heritage.

commercial agency North American usage for travel agency mainly handling business travel; in Europe, the term 'business house' as an equivalent is obsolescent – business travel agent or travel management company are usual terms.

commercial rate North American usage for corporate rate. *See* corporate rate.

commissary A main kitchen from which food is distributed to many serving points, sometimes necessitating transport because of the distances involved.

commission A sum of money paid to an intermediary/agent by a principal in return for the service of handling, promoting and selling the principal's products or services. Whereas retailers 'mark-up' a wholesale price from a manufacturer and resell to the public, commission is characterised as being a proportion of the advertised selling price. So that, for example, an agent selling rail tickets might advertise, 'tickets sold here at station prices'. For over 100 years, until 1998, it had been normal travel industry practice that commission was a percentage of the sale price; at the time of writing, this is still the case worldwide for the sale of many travel services, such as package holidays, car rental, cruises, rail tickets, car ferries and travel insurance. The commercial arrangements between a principal and intermediary are set out in an agreement between the parties, known as an 'agency agreement' or 'agency sales agreement' in which the intermediary is appointed by the principal to represent them and be their 'agent'. Such appointments are essential to earn commission. Split commissions is the widespread but unofficial practice by which appointed agents supply tickets etc. to and share commissions with others.

But now, for air travel, commissions are sometimes 'flat rate' fee per transaction payments by a principal. Moreover, commission may be 'capped' so that it remains a percentage, but only up to a maximum for various types and values of ticket. In the past, the intention behind commission payments was that the commission should be high enough to enable an efficient agent to make a profit on handling and selling the principal's services. Now, some airlines expect agents to make service charges for their services, the commissions being insufficient to make handling air sales profitable. Whereas during the 1980s and 1990s, agents often gave large corporations discounts on their air travel accounts, now, management fees are the norm. Contrary to various sources, the current situation is not of recent origin; an 'open commission' proposal, also called a 'flat rate coupon payment' was made by airlines in 1980.

In the UK, British Airways cut agency commission, replacing it by transaction fees in April 2001; these were replaced by sector payments in June 2002; these payments were then reduced. ABTA challenged the reductions on competition grounds, complaining to the UK Office of Fair Trading. The OFT concluded that BA were entitled to reduce their commission level as agents were able to add their own mark-up or service fees to BA's fares. On 1 December 2003, BA replaced sector payments with a flat rate commission of 1%, cutting it to zero in 2005.

In the USA, with regard to air travel, in 1995, major US airlines capped the 10% domestic travel commission payments at US$50 per ticket. This was followed in 1997 by a reduction in the domestic base commission rate from 10% to 8%. In 1998, commission caps were applied to international air fares, with commissions varying between 5% and 8% and caps around US$50 per single journey. In 1999 base commission rates were cut to 5% and in 2001 were capped to US$10 single and US$20 return on domestic travel. Finally, in March 2002, US air companies cut their base commission rate to zero. In response to the US$10 and US$20 commission capping ASTA initiated CARE (Campaign for Agents' Rights and Equality) involving a 2 h strike by all US agents. Pressure was put on the Department of Transportation for this to be considered by the new National Commission to Ensure Consumer Information and Choice in the Airline Industry, set up to investigated airline marketing practices that harm consumers and travel agents. ASTA reported that in 2001 over 3000 agents had gone out of business, three times the rate in 1994 when airlines first capped commission. By mid-2002 there were 16,700 travel agencies in the USA, one-third fewer than in 1994. Evidence was provided that agents income from selling air tickets had declined by 43% between 1994 and 2001, despite selling 20% more fares. But all these protests were to no avail. It now seems likely that during the currency of this second edition of the dictionary it will become the normal practice worldwide for travel agents to charge travellers a fee for booking and issuing air tickets. Despite this situation, 10% remains the normal rate of commission paid to US agents on cruise bookings. Moreover, although the large cruise companies reduced air/sea commission rates to 5% from 15 September 2001, most others have kept it at 10%. The advent of zero commissions has led to agents charging clients for their services, see service charge. Lists of the commissions payable to travel agents are regularly updated on the members only web sites of both ABTA and ASTA. See also agency agreement; fee-based pricing; incentive commission and over-riding commission.

commission capping   See commission.

commission collecting companies   It is a common problem for travel agencies worldwide that often, hotels and other tourism service providers do not remit commissions due when referred clients pay the hotel direct. When payment is made to an agent, money may be passed on less commission, but chasing a large number of small commissions can cost more than the income receivable. In the USA, commission-collecting companies undertake collection, either charging a flat fee or a percentage commission for their services.

commission protection   Act of a provider of travel services to maintain payment of commission to a travel agent, even though the service may have been cancelled or the price reduced.

commissionable   On which commission will be paid; even those airlines still paying percentage commissions to agents do not pay commission on certain parts of the fare such as taxes. Tour operators may not pay commission on supplements; hotels often only pay commission on room rates and many hotels worldwide do not pay commission to agents. In the USA, hotels often only pay commission to ARC-appointed agents, based on their ARC number.

common carrier   US term for any organization offering transport for hire.

common interest group discounts   These reductions on European air fares were discontinued in the early 1980s, although clients still ask for 5% reductions on groups of ten or 10% on groups of 15, not realizing the fares no longer exist.

common rated currency   See IATA fare construction system.

common rated points   Two or more destinations available from an originating airport at the same fares.

common use self-service airport check-in   See CUSS kiosk.

comms   Abbreviation for communications. See immediately following entry for explanation of comms package.

communications networks   For details of major UK travel communications networks see Amadeus, Fastrak/Fastlink (now called Endeavour), Galileo, Infotrac/Istel, Prestel, Sabre, Travinet, Worldspan, Xpress and NTL Business (Travel Division), formerly X-TANT. In some literature, these were referred to as a VANS (Value Added Network Service), because by offering agents an alternative to dial-up connections for viewdata reservations, more was provided than merely a simple communications network. A 'comms' package is the software used by an agent or others to access a network. Often, the term only applies to software for accessing viewdata.

commuter airline   In general, an airline operating a regional scheduled service; hence, the renaming of the trade body, as noted in the next entry. Textbooks are confusing because terminology has evolved. In 1980, in a glossary of terms by the author of this dictionary, US rules were explained that licensed air taxi firms for planes carrying up to 19 passengers to operate within 250 miles of their home base; if they operated five or more round trips a week on a regular basis, they were classified as a commuter airline. Subsequently, in the USA, the term applied to air operators of a regional service, using aircraft with a capacity of fewer than 60 passengers; this definition appears in books published in the mid 1990s, written by the author and others. The latest definitions of commuter aircraft polarize around planes with 30 seats or fewer, although the *World Travel Dictionary* suggests 29. However, there is no unanimity that commuter airlines are only those which operate commuter aircraft.

Commuter Airlines Association of America This body has now become the Regional Airlines Association.

comp travel jargon for complimentary; but usage is not applicable to all travel services. For example a couple of 'comps' might be given for a theatre or cinema; the word would not apply to free travel tickets – but it might apply to the provision of a free hotel room.

companion way The nautical term for the stairs between decks.

Company Plus Name of Southwest Airlines' Frequent Flyer Programme. *See* FFP (frequent flyer programme).

compartment Any discreet area on a form of transport. For example, in the UK, some train carriages have corridors along their length and individual compartments seating three first-class or four second-class passengers each side of the compartment, facing and back to the direction of travel respectively.

compass Device for determining direction; a magnetic compass uses the earth's magnetic field – a magnetized bar or needle aligning itself along the north–south axis.

compass points Specific compass bearings, e.g. north-east; also name of UK frequent traveller programme promoted by Stena Line.

compatibility Where equipment or software designed for use with one computer system can be used in one or more alternative systems. The biggest selling printers are designed with compatibility in mind. Unfortunately, incompatibility is the norm in the computer industry, because manufacturers have a vested interest in making their products unique. Different operating systems and computer languages are a curse of the travel industry, for there are probably already in existence, programmes to meet most of the industry's requirements. Unfortunately, since most of them are incompatible with each other, the situation is worse than the proverbial Tower of Babel.

compensation For details of compensation payable when travellers are overbooked. *See* denied boarding compensation.

competing opportunity model *See* transport modelling.

Competition Act 1998 UK legislation which brought sales of services within competition legislation, enforcing the end of Stabiliser – *see* entry under this heading.

compliance Extent to which an organization's travellers follow the official travel policy. *See* travel policy; *see also a list of 70 other business travel related entries which follows* corporate travel contracts, *some of which lead to further entries.*

Compliance Office Official IATA definition is the department charged with the duty of investigating violations by Approved Agents of IATA Resolutions and Sales Agency Agreements.

complimentary Either a perk (UK slang for free item or service provided in connection with employment) for travel staff or an inducement or gift to customers. For example, in Britain a 'comp' may be a free theatre ticket given to booking agents. In the USA the term has more general usage than in Britain. In the hospitality sector, it is more common to describe the 'freebies' in a hotel room as an amenity or hospitality pack or basket.

computer airline ticket The term 'computer ticket', though appearing to be of general application, is the terminology used to describe a particular type of automated ticket only used in the USA. This is the only type of automated ticket that is produced one coupon at a time in sequence, the individual coupons being non-carbonized. The ticket coupons are for a specific airline. *See also* ATB and ATB2, automated air tickets, e-ticketing, OPATB2, OPTAT, TAT, teletype airline tickets *and* ticket (main entry).

Computer Assisted Passenger Prescreening Systems *See* CAPPS.

computer-based training *See* CBT[1].

computer bureau An organization that processes data sent by other persons or organizations. When first established, computer bureaux received written documentation, which they entered into their computers to analyse the material. Most popular uses originally were for wages or general accounting work. In recent years, records have been created on disk or tape, which is either posted or picked up by the computer bureau in less sophisticated systems. The most efficient systems of this type are accessed by the host computer overnight, information stored during the day being extracted automatically and processed by the main computer. The ultimate in-bureau operation, is where an organization's records are stored by a bureau, being accessed on-line and entered real time. The communication costs of this method of operation are very high, so it is not cost-effective, unless permanent connections exist from a terminal to the bureau, probably through a network established for other reasons.

computer hardware *See* hardware.

computer printers Printers which can be activated by computers to produce a paper copy of information held in the system. For the main types of computer printer used in the travel industry. *See* daisy wheel, dot matrix, dump, electrostatic, ink jet, laser *and* thermal printers.

computer program *See* program.

computer programming language The codes used to design a software program for a computer, so that when the operator gives instructions for the computer to perform a certain task, that task will be undertaken according to the codes or directions stored in the program. BASIC enables these instructions to be entered from a terminal in English, while for business uses in the travel industry, many of the more complex computer languages are utilized, such as COBOL, PASCAL and PL/1.

computer reservation system *See* CRS.

computer software *See* software.

computerized accounting and ticketing systems for travel agents *See* Travel agents' computerized accounting and ticketing systems in the UK.

Computerized Airline Sales and Marketing Association (in the USA) *See* www.casma.org

computerized reservation systems for tour operators *See* tour operators' reservation systems *and* viewdata.

Comtrac Computerized data and accounting system developed by Thompson Travel Bureau for UK travel agents.

CON Consol beacon.

concentrated hub Hub dominance by an airline. *See* hub and spoke.

concentration ratio *See* tourism-carrying capacity.

concession[1] A free or reduced rate granted to a travel company employee.

concession[2] A franchise to sell goods or provide services within an area or site operated by the granting organization; for example the concessions at airports or within hotels.

concierge May be a hall porter in Europe, for example, dealing with guests' baggage, local information and provision of theatre tickets; or may have a more senior role. *See* bell captain *and* head porter.

conciliation *See* ABTA Conciliation Service. (Now obsolete.)

Concord Was name of the ICC (Independent Computer Company) front/back office administrative and accounting computer system for UK travel agents. This co-brand leader is now called Ramesys.

Concorde World's first supersonic passenger airliner. Flying temporarily suspended in 2000 following an accident involving an Air France Concorde; services restarted in autumn 2001. Services finally terminated by Air France in May 2003 and by British Airways in October 2003. Some of the aircraft are now on display in museums. Formerly operated by British Airways and Air France, it was the only supersonic airliner ever in commercial service. Its first test flight was on 2 March 1969, but it was not until 22 November 1977 that regular New York services from Paris and London were inaugurated. Among countless records for passenger-carrying aircraft, it flew from Kennedy Airport in

New York to London Heathrow on 1 January 1983 in 2 h 56 min and 35 s.

Built by British Aerospace and Aerospatiale, Concorde had an overall length of 204 ft, a wing span of 84 ft and overall height 37 ft. It was powered by four Rolls-Royce/Snecma Olympus 593–610 turbo jets with re-heat, each of which produced a take-off thrust of 169 kN. One hundred passengers were carried at the normal cruising speed of 1340 miles per hour (2150 km per h), which is twice the speed of sound.

Concorde had a very well-known droop nose. This was because the long aerodynamic shape had to be altered to allow greater visibility to the pilot during take-off and landing. The windows were smaller than in sub-sonic aircraft only because various international requirements prevented larger windows which, in the view of the designers, would have been perfectly safe. Concorde normally cruised to around 55,000 to 60,000 ft (16,800 to 18,300 m).

Simultaneously, at 11.35 on 21 January 1976, a French-built Concorde left Paris for Rio de Janeiro and a British-built plane G-BOAA took off from London to Bahrain, commanded by Captain Norman V. Todd, the first time that these planes carried fare-paying passengers. Japan and France are developing a new supersonic aircraft, spending 200m Yen (US$5.5m) in research up to 2008. Japan has already successfully tested an engine that can reach speeds of Mach 5.5.

Concordia   Computerized hotel reservation system.

concourse   Obsolescent term in Europe for the main lobby area in an airport but still commonly used in North America.

conditional fare   Obsolete arrangement for air passengers to travel subject to space being available; if the flight was full, they could get their money back and travel free on the next available flight. This concept was replaced by 'standby' fares.

conditions of carriage   The terms established by a carrier under which passengers, their baggage and/or freight are carried. IATA define 'Conditions of Contract' to mean merely the terms and conditions shown on the Passenger Ticket and Baggage Check. Nevertheless, the terminology is general. Typically transportation companies in most countries are allowed by law to exempt themselves from many of the liabilities faced by ordinary commercial concerns. The Warsaw and Athens Conventions are the international agreements absolving air or sea carriers from many responsibilities and these conventions are usually included in Conditions of Carriage. *See* Athens Convention *and* Warsaw Convention.

condo   Abbreviation for condominium. *See* next entry.

condominium   The North American equivalent of a block of flats or apartments. The term is loose, with a great deal of variation in the availability of centralized services and the legal ownership of the individual homes. Sometimes use of the individual parts of a condominium are sold on a time-share basis for use as self-catering holiday accommodation.

conducted tour   *See* escorted tour.

conductor   The person on a mode of transport responsible for fare collection, ticket checking and often on a bus or tram, indicating to the driver when to stop and start.

Confederation of Passenger Transport   *See* CPT.

conference room set-up   *See* meeting room set-up.

conference[1]   In the UK, with regard to passenger traffic, the term is obsolete, but in North America it is still used as the generic term for a grouping of transportation companies agreeing rates, conditions of travel and travel agency appointments.

It is over a decade since shipping companies in Britain acted through Conferences to decide whether travel agents merited an appointment. In those days only appointed agents earned commission on a scheduled shipping service or cruise. The original names of the Conferences were Atlantic Passenger Steamship Conference, Australian and New Zealand Passenger Conference, British Lines Passenger Conference, Far East Passenger Conference, South American Passenger Traffic Conference and South Africa Passenger Lines Committee.

Following the substantial replacement of the ATC by ARC, it is only IATA, IPSA (International Passenger Ship Association) and PCC (Pacific Cruise Conference) that are referred to in this way in North America.

conference² The term also has a general meaning of a congress, convention or group meeting.

confidential tariff Rates published by a travel industry principal or wholesaler for an agent's use. Where these are quoted net, agents are expected to add on their profit before re-sale to the travelling public. *See* handling agent.

configuration Cabin and seat layout on a mode of transport. Many international flights have both first- and tourist-class seats, while charter flights are often all tourist class with reduced pitch and increased number of seats abreast.

CONFIRM Announced in 1990, was to be the first CRS aimed specifically at the hotel and car rental sectors combined, although many CRS also offer accommodation. AMR Information Services, then an affiliate of American Airlines, Budget Rent a Car, Hilton Hotels and Marriott Hotels were collaborating with an initial investment of US$125 million, to produce a system to be available in 1992. By autumn 1992, all development work on the project had ceased and the former partners were involved in litigation.

confirmation In the UK, often called a 'confirm'. Any document which confirms the existence of a booking. Increasingly, principals are changing administrative methods so that confirmations are now obsolescent. Bookings direct into airlines computers no longer result in any written confirmation, for example. Often confirmations of reservations are subject to conditions; for example, hotels often require notification of late arrival, otherwise having the right to cancel bookings for clients who have not arrived by 18.00.

In the UK the term has a particular significance concerning package holiday bookings, since the CAA has ruled that clients are not committed to their arrangements until they have received written confirmation. It is also important to note that it is only the reservation that is confirmed on a British package tour and not the price, which may often be subject to fuel, currency or other surcharges before a final invoice is produced.

confirmation number or location code When a booking is made with a principal, the agent or client is given a unique reference code to enable easy retrieval of the booking details.

confirmation slip Sometimes used in North America to designate a voucher or document which a traveller may offer as evidence of an accommodation or travel booking. Unlike an exchange voucher or coupon, the slip does not imply that the travel company accepts responsibility for payment, unless specifically stated.

congress Alternative word for a convention, more common in North America than Europe. *See* convention.

conjunction tickets Two or more air tickets attached to each other and issued at the same time, which cover a single itinerary and form a single contract of carriage. Official IATA definition is a ticket issued to a passenger, concurrently with another ticket or other tickets, which together constitute a single contract of carriage.

Connecticut Office of Tourism *See* Discover New England www. discovernewengland.org

connecting carrier Official IATA definition is a carrier to whose services the passenger and his baggage are to be transferred for onward connecting transportation.

connecting flights Two or more flights which in combination provide a reasonable journey from origin to required destination. In some fares' rules a maximum time between such flights is laid down, associated with a prohibition on stopovers. Thus, a flight generally described as connecting may not necessarily satisfy the rule for a particular fare.

connecting rooms Often, hotels are built with communicating doors between some adjacent rooms, so that several rooms may be sold together to a family party or used together for other purposes.

connecting time Also called MCT or minimum connecting time. Minimum time stipulated for a passenger arriving at an airport on one flight to catch another flight, based on the scheduled arrival and departure times. This will take into account check-in time if necessary, inter-terminal and inter-airport journeys and security considerations. Airport headings of various guides used by agents indicate that airlines' requirements vary concerning minimum time to be allowed.

connecting timings of buses, coaches or trains Where the timing of regular scheduled services of a mode of transport has been arranged so that passengers will arrive at a point on one service in time to catch an onward service, thus making a multi-sector journey possible.

consol fares *See* consolidation air fares.

consolidation Many meanings which causes confusion. Some are stated under this heading, with further explanations under the next entry, consolidation air fares. Some travel companies bring together individual passengers in order to make up the necessary numbers to meet with group IATA fare requirements. These passengers may be smaller groups from other travel companies, or individual members of the public. The passenger is thus enabled to benefit from a lower fare than if travelling as an individual.

The same term is applied to the practice used by tour operators when insufficient demand received for a departure or series of departures. Flights are then consolidated either with other flights to the same destination being run by the same operator, or with flights being run by another operator. The result is the economic operation of aircraft because of higher load factors. In North America, consolidation often has a more general meaning of marketing an inclusive tour through many agencies and others, enhancing sales and thereby making it less likely that the IT may have to be cancelled due to lack of support.

consolidation air fares Various European regulations or laws prevent airlines from discounting official 'filed' fares. Airlines manipulate air travel markets by maintaining published fares, while at the same time selling their surplus seats at heavily discounted prices, through sales agents, called 'consolidators'. Ordinary travel agents and the public may buy these seats. Agency purchases are usually at a net fare, to which agents add a mark-up. The rest of this explanation will probably become obsolete shortly.

This type of fare developed during the 1980s as a UK replacement for European ITX fares to the main holiday destination. British agents wishing to utilize this type of fare must have an ATOL. Consol fares, as they are called, must include return air transportation to a point; sleeping accommodation at normal commercial rates for the whole of the stay, private accommodation being expressly prohibited; and a recognized additional facility or attraction. A tour brochure must be submitted to the airline for approval, an IT code being shown in this tour literature as well as on the passenger's ticket. These tickets are supplied through British Airways' consolidation section for UK tour promoters and there are similar Consol sections of other airlines.

Despite the theoretical restrictions, Consol fares have become subject to similar wide abuse to that which caused withdrawal of many European ITX fares. Most British travel agents buy consolidated tickets through a main agent, sometimes with a spurious accommodation voucher where it is necessary, with the airlines being only too well aware of the practice. The only difference from the previous situation, is that whereas it was impossible for the airlines to control the number of seats that agents were issuing on an individual ITX basis, they are able to control the number of air seats they choose to allocate under the new Consol system at low prices.

consolidator A consolidation organizer. *See* consolidation *and* consolidation air fares.

Consort A Northern Ireland consortium of travel agents, a member of Worldchoice.

consortium In general, a group of organizations, companies and/or people, forming a grouping to achieve common interests, while maintaining their individual activities which may well be in direct competition to other consortium members. Airline alliances are one well-known type of travel consortium (*see* separate entry under this heading). There are also many national and international hotel consortia, such as Best Western and SRS World Hotels. The rest of this entry concentrates on travel agency consortia to illustrate the wide variation encountered in the way consortia operate. ASTA defines a consortium as a 'coalition of incorporated companies formed for marketing and service purposes'. While the term is commonly used in the travel industry, both in the USA and UK, it is not specific to the travel business. While in the UK, consortium is a general term for such organizations, 'joint marketing organization' or 'joint marketing company' is the generic North American wording. ASTA defines this as a 'company that markets the products of selected suppliers through its ranks of member agencies'. In the USA, around half of the travel agency community are members of a joint marketing company; in the UK, 51.6% of agency locations are part of multiple agency groups and a further 25% are members of independent agency consortia. Compare the foregoing with the ASTA definitions of similar organizations:

Cooperative – a corporation acting as a joint-stock organization for establishing and maintaining a working relationship among its members.
Consortium – coalition of incorporated companies formed for marketing and service purposes.
Franchisor – entity that grants vested right to use of a brand name with the purpose of attracting consumer recognition and expectation of consistent service. This usually includes an entire business format operational plan, business package and support services. (Franchisors may be regulated by Federal Trade Commission or State Commissions.)
Licensor – entity that grants the right to use a national brand identity in all marketing and operating activities; also provides access to proprietary service and marketing systems and programs [sic].
Network – working group of independently-owned travel agencies deriving benefits of lower operating costs and higher sales commissions.
Joint Marketing Company – Organization that markets the products of selected suppliers through the ranks of member agencies.

Individual Owned Chain – Does not own any of its retail chain member outlets. Features common signage and advertising, a total marketing concept and operates in a uniform manner.
Corporate Owned Chain – Fully owned group of retail chain member outlets featuring common signage and advertising, a total marketing concept and operating in a uniform manner.
Stockholder Licensee Group – Corporation whose members are stockholders, providing a vertically integrated format, with an elected board of directors to approve the business decisions of management and to whom management reports.

ASTA break down each of the above definitions into types according to geographic coverage of their operations, international, national or regional. They also outline the main services that a joint marketing company provides, namely: commission overrides on preferred supplier sales, consumer/agent default protection, collective advertising and promotional campaigns, special hotel rate directories, 24 h reservation service hot lines, corporate hotel and car rental rates, personal consultations to review agency financial and operational problems, back-office automation systems, discounts on computers, telecopiers, office furniture and supplies, networking with fellow members.

See travel agency consortia in the UK, Worldchoice (formerly ARTAC) and NAITA, UK examples of independent travel agency consortia. The GTMC (Guild of Travel Management Companies) in the UK is so huge with £8 billion annual turnover, that it is seldom recognized as a consortium. AAA, American Express Representative Network, Carlson Wagonlit Travel, Coast Travel Group of Napa CA, GIANTS, Leisure Travel Group, MAST (Midwest Agents Selling Travel), Riverside Travel Group, TAAWNY (Travel Agents Alliance of Western New York), nearby TASC (Travel Agents of Suffolk County), Travelsavers, Uniglobe, Virtuoso *and* WESTA (Western Association of Travel Agencies) are examples of US consortia. AITO (Association of Independent Tour

Operators) in the UK, which undertakes marketing activities on behalf of members, might be regarded as a tour operator's consortium rather than merely a trade association.

consul In modern usage, a representative of any Sovereign State residing in a foreign country to protect the interests of the state's nationals while abroad. *See* consulate below.

consulate The office location of Consular officials representing a Sovereign State in a foreign country. Nationals of the state represented are assisted while travelling abroad to the country in which a Consulate is located, which also works to facilitate travel and trade between the two countries. It is the provision of visas that is the most well-known function in the tourism industry. The way in which a Consulate works to help travellers is best explained by using Britain as an example. The services which British Consular officials provide when necessary are: issuance of emergency passports; contacting a traveller's relatives or friends requesting them to help with money or tickets; advice on how to transfer funds; in an emergency advance money against a cheque for up to £50 supported by a Banker's card; as a last resort, and provided certain strict criteria are met, make a repayable loan for repatriation to the UK; provide a list of local lawyers, interpreters and doctors, arrange for next-of-kin to be informed of an accident or a death and advise on procedures; contact British nationals who are arrested or in prison and in certain circumstances arrange for messages to be sent to relatives or friends; give guidance on organizations experienced in tracing missing persons.

British consuls cannot normally pay travellers' hotel, medical or other bills or undertake work more properly done by travel representatives, airlines, banks or motoring organizations. They cannot gain better treatment for a national in hospital or prison than is provided for local nationals; give legal advice, instigate court proceedings on behalf of a national or interfere in local judicial procedures to release a Briton from prison; formally assist dual nationals in the country of their second nationality; obtain work or a work permit. Of course, there are many other functions of British

Consulates or Embassies, the title usually given to the Chief Consulate in a country which is headed by the Ambassador. This explanation is, however, restricted to travel matters.

consultant Another name for a person selling travel in a travel agency.

consumer protection against financial loss for travel arrangements *See* ABTA, ASTA[2], ATOL, bond *and* bond replacement scheme, escrow, FMC[1], NTA[1], USTOA.

consumer protection plans *See* ABTA, ASTA, ATOL, bond *and* bond replacement scheme, escrow, FMC[1], NTA[1], USTOA.

cont Abbreviation for continuous.

contemporary cruise ship A US term for the new high quality ships which, because of their size and amenities, provide high cruising standards but at three-star prices for the mass market.

continental breakfast Breakfast consisting of beverages, usually fruit juice, tea or coffee, bread, rolls, butter and preserves. An expanded continental breakfast usually also offers a selection of cheese and cold meat.

continental plan (CP) Hotel accommodation which includes continental breakfast in the specified room rate. *See* CP.

continental rail Term 'continental rail' has been replaced by 'European rail'.

continuing itinerary Official IATA definition is 'all remaining segments or portions of itinerary beyond any designated point or gap'.

continuing space North American usage for continuing itinerary or downline. *See* downline.

contour Line on a map joining places of equal height above or below mean sea level, which is counted as zero. Mean sea level is averaged after taking into account tidal conditions. Typically, coloured maps use brown to indicate hilly areas; the darker the brown, the higher.

contra booth *See* stand.

contra stand *See* stand.

Contract Based Inclusive Tour *See* CBIT.

contractor In the UK and the equivalent in European languages, the word means a person or organization which is a party to a contract. Sometimes the term is used loosely instead of sub-contractors, for example, a tour operator may refer to hoteliers in this way.

Reed Travel Group's US *ABCs of Travel* defines this as, 'A land operator providing services to tour operators, wholesalers and travel agents; also called ground operator, independent contractor, land operator, receiving agent, reception agency and receptive operator'. But these terms are all American usage; more common in the UK and Australasia is handling agent or ground handler. Moreover, the US definition is not usually applicable in Europe. *See* handling agent for full explanation.

contrails The exhaust gases from an aircraft's engines, which turn into the long thin clouds streaming out behind the plane. Density and length of trails depend only on temperature and humidity and are not affected by aircraft speed. The layers of air above the earth vary in height according to the temperature. It is in the tropopause, between 25,000 and 35,000 ft where contrails are regular occurrences. Once above the tropopause, in the stratosphere, there are no contrails, because the air is too thin and cold. On a warm moist day, the temperature at 35,000 ft might be minus 50°C. If this is the start of a warm frontal system, the contrails will be very dense and many miles long. On a cold, clear day, with no high cloud, contrails are likely to be thin and short or even non-existent.

contremarques *See* European Rail group travel.

contribution Insurance concept that a liability be shared proportionately between insurers according to the ratio of the original risk shares. Often, travel insurance policy exclusion clauses attempt to avoid this principle by suggesting that their policy only insures any loss in addition to that already covered under any other policy.

Control Was the name of British Rail's department which controlled day-to-day train scheduling. Now there is an equivalent department in Network Rail.

control of air space *See* FIRs.

control tower Raised building at an airport, usually with 360° vision from which all aircraft movements are managed, with the aid of radio and radar.

convention A meeting, conference or rally; the term implies attendance by a substantial number of persons. The diversity of reasons for meeting makes further definition impractical. *See also* convention bureau, convention centre *and* convention group.

convention bureau Convention bureau in the travel industry are usually funded either by a local, regional or national government agency, by a cooperative of hotels and conference facilities and sometimes by a combination of both. Their function is to provide information to conference organizers about facilities and services in this field available in their countries or areas, e.g. LCB, the London Convention Bureau. Sometimes called convention and visitors bureau; it means exactly the same.

convention centre Purpose-built meetings complex.

Convention for Safety of Life at Sea *See* International Convention for the Safety of Life at Sea (SOLAS).

convention group Participants of a convention who qualify for reduced air fares to specific destinations.

conversion agency In North America, an independent travel agent that becomes part of an agency chain. Same term may be used on joining a consortium, particularly when the agency is branded with the new name.

conversion fee Joining charge raised by a consortium.

conversion rate[1] There are two main conversion rates used when exchanging one currency for another. A foreign exchange dealer seeks a profit. Thus, when foreign currency is purchased, the customer's buying rate is lower than the 'average rate', while when the customer returns foreign currency, the customer's selling rate is higher than the 'average rate'. Thus, when buying currency, less is obtained for a dollar or pound and on exchanging back, the selling rate results in further small loss.

conversion rate[2] The rate of conversion of enquiries into sales; particularly used following travel advertising and Internet site hits or enquiries. Look to book ratios are the same thing, with regard to agency footfall or TV ad watching.

convertible Car with a top which folds back, so that it can be driven 'open'. The French word 'cabriolet' with the same meaning is sometimes used as an alternative.

Cook, Thomas *See* Thomas Cook.

cook-chill *See* sous vide.

cooperating carrier In the USA, means a transportation principal that funds part of the marketing costs of an inclusive tour programme. The term is not in current UK usage.

cooperative[1] Similar to a consortium, a group of organizations, companies and/or people, forming a grouping to achieve common interests, while maintaining their individual activities which may well be in direct competition to other consortium members. But in North America, there is a critical difference, in that a cooperative implies that the organization has been set up as a more formal organization than a trade representative body. Usually, members or owners have shares in their cooperative. *See* consortium for detailed explanation.

cooperative[2] Term for a consortium. *See* consortium.

COP Country of payment. Abbreviation normally used in connection with IATA fare construction system.

COR Confirmation of reservation.

coracle Ancient British small boat shaped like a bowl. Some are still used in Wales and Ireland for river fishing.

corail train A French Railways (SNCF) passenger train with carriages with separate compartments and also carriages which are open plan.

CORDA The reservation and administration computer of the Royal Dutch Airline, KLM. Dutch travel agents are connected to CORDA and it is the equivalent of Galileo in Britain, START in Germany and Apollo, Mars, Pars and Sabre in the USA.

cork charge *See* corkage immediately below.

corkage Service charge raised by a hotel or restaurant for handling a bottle of alcoholic beverage brought into the establishment by the client, and not sold to the client from the establishment's stock.

corp rate *See* corporate rate.

corporate card A credit or charge card providing the authorized user with the same general facilities as other cards, *but* with no individual liability for payment of the expenses incurred. Bills are the liability of the sponsoring company or organization. *Also see list of 70 other business travel related entries which follows* corporate travel contracts, *some of which lead to further entries.*

corporate owned chain A travel agency group with many outlets in North America. The characteristics of such a group are that it is able to exert bulk buying power and mount a sophisticated marketing approach to selling. The equivalent of a multiple in the UK.

corporate rate A reduced price offered to the staff of big spending corporations, or often to business travellers in general. Originally, the term applied to car rental and hotel organizations; now, however, the term is generic, applicable to all travel facilities and any group deserving of a discount may be offered a corporate rate. *Also see list of 70 other business travel related entries which follows* corporate travel contracts, *some of which lead to further entries.*

corporate self booking tools Also known as corporate online booking tools. Computer software enabling company staff to effect travel arrangements through the Internet. KDS, a market leader in the provision of SBTs in Europe, estimates that it costs approx. 1% of a corporation's travel budget to implement a self booking scheme, covering training and software. Resulting savings are between 5% and 20% in Europe and up to 40% in the USA. Cost reductions arise through both lower fares and avoidance of travel management/agency fees. Forrester Research predicted that by 2004 77% of business travel would be booked online in North America, which did not happen. Self booking tools had reached around 5% penetration among European companies by spring 2003 and a significant turn in attitude from initial scepticism had occurred. In the USA corporate self booking systems were used by 20% of companies. Worldwide user figures provided by the technology companies themselves were I:FAO Cytric1, 600+; Trip Manager (Worldspan), 1100+; GetThere DirectCorporate, 800+; TRXResAssist, 500+; E-Travel Aergo, 250+; Highwire (Galileo), 235; KDS DirectCorporate, 100+; BookIt! Corporate (Datalex), 7; Yatra.MANAGER (Yatra). Corporate.Res (Sabre) did not provide figures. All of these have equivalent European systems. The major business travel management companies provide clients with their own self booking tools, for example, BTI UK Direct, Carlson Wagonlit's CWT Connect portal, Cendant's Travelport and Portman Travel's LiveWire. The major online travel agents offer facilities for smaller companies not wishing to use one of these systems. Expedia Corporate Travel in the USA charges US$5 for online bookings and US$20 for telephone bookings. Their system shows public fares, web fares and corporate negotiated fares in a single window. Travelocity has a similar system. Orbitz, the web site set up by the five largest US airlines, has an 'Orbitz for Business' service; the charge is US$5 per transaction completed online and between US$15 and US$20 if a telephone consultant is needed. A range of associated self booking tools is being developed for other facilities. For example, Maritz Travel has developed a self booking meetings tool, an electronic web-based planning and delegate management system, named Meeting HQ, available since 2003. *A list of 70 other business travel related entries follows* corporate travel contracts, *some of which lead to further entries.*

corporate travel Alternative term for business travel. *See* entry immediately below.

corporate travel contracts Travel agents must justify that they add value, if they are to charge corporations for the provision of their services. Hence the modern usage of the wording 'travel management company' that is replacing the terms business or corporate travel agent. A complete book could be written on this topic; even this very extensive entry is a summary with many errors of omission. The following list of what an agency might contract to provide does not presume to be completely comprehensive, but it outlines the enormous range involved.

- Responsibility for cost control and service delivery as outlined in an agreed contract.
- General reservations and ticketing for all modes of transport, including rail, air and sea and car rental, with negotiated reduced rates or route deals.

Hotel reservations, voucher system and corporate rates availability. In respect of all of these, instant information, reservations and booking confirmation by a global computerised reservation system (GDS), such as Galileo, Sabre, Worldspan or Amadeus. Leisure and other reservations through direct computer links where available. The alternative, at the preference of the corporate account travellers, of effecting all of the foregoing through the agent's Internet site; this may be through agency facilitated self booking tools.

- Fare monitoring of existing bookings, rebooking as necessary.
- Handling ticket cancellations and lost ticket applications; negotiating refunds for clients in respect of these.
- For smaller companies ATBs (automated tickets and boarding passes) through a GDS avoiding ticketing errors or e-tickets on routes where available (until e-ticketing becomes the norm).
- For larger companies Satellite Ticket Printing (STP) of ATBs at on-site location (until e-ticketing becomes the norm).
- Aiding the establishment of (or creating for the client's approval) a corporate travel policy, if necessary operating the travel strategy across many companies within a group and/or across national boundaries. Monitoring and maintaining that policy to ensure its effectiveness.
- Expectation that the agency will conclude contracts with transport operators and hotel groups in order to obtain beneficial rates, including e-procurement initiatives, whenever appropriate, transmitting a copy of such contracts to the corporate client. The client company may reserve the right to negotiate contracts itself, where it considers that those which have been concluded are insufficiently advantageous. Also expectation that the agency will explore alternative fares and itineraries for journeys and recommend the most cost-effective travel solutions. Demonstrating this by providing monthly statistics analysing a company's travel expenditure, showing

cost comparisons with standard fares and demonstrating savings made.
- Corporate self booking system integrated with travel management company's system, providing robot (aka bot or spider) identification of lowest logical fare available for planned trip. If Internet search tool not provided, Internet search for suitable travel arrangements at lowest cost.
- Pre-trip reports e.g. report that a booking has been made outside company travel policy sent to appropriate cost centre manager.
- Post-trip reports.
- Internet profile access.
- Special business travel insurance.
- Incentive and promotion arrangements.
- Permanent room allocations.
- Airport representation.
- Conference bookings.
- Air taxi or charter bookings.
- Theatre and special event bookings.
- Self- or chauffeur-drive car hire.
- Obtaining passports and/or visas.
- Meeting and greeting or other passenger handling at airports, or stations.
- Provision of interpreters or guide services.
- Timetables, and other travel publications including regular newsletter.
- Restaurant services.
- Provision of travellers' cheques and foreign currency.
- Individual itineraries.
- Direct telephone lines to their offices and/or minimum response time.
- Twenty-four hour 365-days-a-year service.
- Dedicated travel consultant/travel counselor [sic] handling their bookings.
- In company travel consultant/travel counselor [sic] paid for by agent, otherwise known as an implant or on-site travel agency.
- Stated minimum delivery times or once or twice daily regular delivery service, if STP not provided.
- Immediate delivery of tickets, travellers' cheques and currency.
- Representatives and associates network providing worldwide assistance.
- Management fee or transaction fee arrangement with discounts and

commissions receivable by the agency rebated to the corporate client; option of ticket-by-ticket fare approval by corporate travel manager.
- Identification of traveller's whereabouts 24/365.
- Extended credit (sought by corporations but strongly resisted by travel companies)!
- Specialized services not named above such as obtaining an international driver's licence and lost baggage claims.
- And last, but certainly not least, consideration and inclusion of safety, health and environmental issues in travel programmes.

The financial arrangements in the contract apply to the provision of any or all of the above services. In the UK there have always been rules maintaining the published price at which scheduled air travel may be sold; but there has never been any prosecution of any agent discounting that price and passing on a rebate to a traveller. A similar situation exists in the USA with regard to international air travel. Under section 403(b) of the Federal Aviation Act this is illegal, but the DOT (Department of Transportation) has indicated it will not enforce the law, unless the rebating is associated with other wrongful practices such as fraud, deceptive practices or anticompetitive activity. Rebating of domestic air fares in the USA is entirely lawful.

Until reductions in airline commission (see commission) and commission capping took place, it was common for corporate customers to demand and agents to offer to share their commission. This rebating is still the basis of some contracts, particularly where airlines are paying incentive or bonus commissions to agents, using this as a conduit for discounting the price a company pays for air travel. But the usual way agents deal with large corporate accounts is now either on the basis of a management fee or transaction fee or some combination of both.

With a monthly management fee being paid, this is usually set off against all the commissions and overrides receivable by the agency, the difference being payable in addition to the ticketed costs of the travel services supplied. Alternatively, fees are agreed for each type of transaction, for example, increasing fees for arranging and ticketing one way, two, three or four sector air travel and further fees for hotel reservations and arranging car rental. These fees, as before, are usually set off against income received by the agency. Both the management and transaction fees will be calculated by an agency so as to make a profit on the costs of providing the services.

Why should large companies use travel agents? They have their own travel departments with highly trained staff. They may have negotiated excellent corporate rates with hotel groups and car rental companies. The ARC and IATA regulations no longer prevent airlines supplying company travel departments with tickets and giving commissions. Business travel agents can only maintain their position by saving money for corporate accounts. But there is a permanent conflict. The travel manager's job is to purchase a company's travel requirements as cost-efficiently as possible. However, business travellers do not necessarily want to save their company's money. They usually prefer to travel first class and stay at the best hotels. They may regard this as a non-taxable 'perk' of the job. Airlines and hotels blatantly abuse the ethics of the situation with their frequent traveller clubs, providing free hotels and flights to many business travellers. One way in which agents satisfy business travel managers that they are cost-effective, is by supplying large corporate clients with monthly analyses detailing their travel expenditure and demonstrating the savings made by their travel agents' advice.

Corporate travel contracting is often initiated by a company every few years, sending out RFPs (request for proposals). Information is provided as to the company's travel requirements together with data as to the volume of travel involved, of which the agent is wise to insist on verifiable documentation. Tenders are usually to handle an account for between 1 and 3 years, with an agreed notice period. While the corporation may seek a monthly account, agents seek to avoid credit costs and risks by arranging for purchases through corporate credit card schemes. STPs are usually requested because as ASTA states, 'They fill a need for convenient and economical delivery to corporate clients from the agency's distant office'. A dedicated on-site travel agency called an implant in the UK, may be requested. Usually, office space is provided and the costs of a CRS connection and staffing (including covering for absences) are taken into account when agreeing a contract. Using preferred suppliers to bargain and drive down travel costs may be part of the corporate clients' travel policies.

See also ACTE, adoption rate (of an SBT or travel policy), back end rebate, BTC[1], BTC[2], business house, business tourism, business travel, business travel agent, business traveller, business travel centre (business travel service centre), business travel department, business travel market in the UK, business travel transaction fees, BPO (business process outsourcing), BTD (business travel department), CCTE, compliance, corporate card, corporate rate, corporate travel department, corporate travel manager, corporate travel policy, corporate self booking tools, corporate travel contracts (this entry, which includes list of services provided to business travellers), Cost Reimbursable Contractors, CTDRA (Corporate Travel Department Reporting Agreement) and Rent a plate in the ARC entry, every day low price (EDLP), end-to-end travel management, front end deal (or rebate), Guild of Business Travel Agents, fee-based business travel contract, fee-based pricing, General Services Administration, hotel bookings for UK business travellers, implant, ITM, location of corporate travellers, lodged account, lowest logical fare (LLF), managed travel, MTMC, outplant operations, Paragon Agreement, post-trip reporting, pre-trip authority, pre-trip reporting, procurement services provider, RFI (request for information), RFP (request for proposal), robot technology, route deal, service charge/service fee, spot buying, SBT, STP (satellite ticket printer), transaction fees, travel policy, travel procurement manager, TMC, travel relationship manager *and* unmanaged travel.

corporate travel department May refer to the travel arranging department in a large *non-travel* company or to the section in a travel agent specializing in business travel. *Also see* ARC[1] *and list of 70 other business travel related entries which follows* corporate travel contracts, *some of which lead to further entries.*

Corporate Travel Department Reporting Agreement *See* ARC[1].

corporate travel manager The person in a *non-travel* company or organization that holds the responsibility for running the travel department. In America, may be called the passenger traffic manager. In the UK, usually called merely the travel manager. *See* ITM, the UK Institute of Travel Managers, and *list of 70 other business travel related entries which follows* corporate travel contracts, *some of which lead to further entries.*

corporate travel policy ASTA defines this as a set of rules and guidelines of travel practices for the overall purpose of controlling costs. Effective travel policies can drive compliance to preferred vendors. ASTA figures are that more than half of corporations using agents have a formal written travel policy, while many of the others operate an informal one. *A list of 70 other business travel related entries follows* corporate travel contracts, *some of which lead to further entries.*

corridor train Has two meanings. Normal meaning is a train which has corridors along one side of each coach so that it is possible to walk from one end of a train to another in order to access facilities such as a restaurant car. It is usually older types of railway rolling stock which are composed of carriages or coaches with a series of individual compartments. Most newer rolling stock is open plan, enabling passengers to walk right through the coaches. The alternative meaning is of a train which runs through a 'corridor' of another country in order to take a direct route between two areas of the original country. For fuller explanation, *see* korridorzuge.

Costa Rica Tourist Board *See* www.tourism-costarica.com

cost–benefit analysis Method often applied to analyse the impact of tourism, particularly in the context of developing countries. The terminology involves no restriction as to depth of investigation, with the consequence that there is always argument as to whether a particular study has gone far enough. Normally, cost–benefit analysis is expected to go much further than merely the examination of the economic effects of increased tourist expenditure and the impact on other sectors of the economy. The opportunity cost of resources and factors of production which would be diverted from other uses must be taken into account. If spare capacity exists, the analysis should aim to identify whether or not tourism is the most efficient way of employing this spare capacity in the short term. Normally, the term implies that monetary values will be put upon the social consequences, both beneficial and disadvantageous, of a proposed investment.

The principles involved, can be applied to a much more limited decision, for example, the social and economic consequences of closing a railway line and replacing it by road transport. The term cost–benefit analysis *is not restricted to the travel and tourism industry*, although wide reading of literature in this field, might lead to this erroneous impression.

Cost Reimbursable Contractors Organizations in the USA with government contracts who request government discounts for travel facilities undertaken in connection with their contracts. Although many US hotel and car rental companies extend government discounts to CRCs, since October 1998 CRCs have not been eligible for the government air fare discounts. *See* General Services Administration. *Also see list of 70 other business travel related entries which follows* corporate travel contracts *above, some of which lead to further entries.*

COTAC Was Certificate of Travel Agency Competence; an examination administered by the City and Guilds of London Institute on behalf of ABTA. Now discontinued and replaced by ABTAC. *See* ABTAC.

COTAL The Confederation of Latin American Tourist Organizations. *See* www.cotal.org.ar

COTAM Was Certificate of Travel Agency Management in the UK. Administered by the City and Guilds of London Institute on behalf of ABTA; now discontinued.

COTICC Certificate of Tourist Information Centre Competence in the UK is administered by the City and Guilds of London Institute in conjunction with the English Tourism Council for those working in Tourist Information Centres.

COTIF Convention on International Carriage by Rail. An inter-government agreement between 40 countries which facilitates international freight and passenger rail traffic.

couchette Type of sleeping berth on European Rail trains providing less comfortable but cheaper accommodation than sleeping cars. During the day, these operate as seating compartments, three passengers travelling back to direction of travel and three facing. At night, two berths are folded down from each wall, these and the seats being made into sleeping berths by the addition of rugs and pillows. The highest berth is for the occupant of the seat nearest to the window during the day, the lowest berth the place nearest the corridor and the middle berth associated with the centre seats. In North America, similar train accommodation for one person, often with a toilet and wash basin is called a roomette.

Council for National Parks *See* CNP.

Council for the Protection of Rural England (CPRE) *See* www.cpre.org.uk

counter agent North American term for a person attending to travellers' needs in an airline office, at the airport or in a travel agency. European equivalents might be counter clerk, travel consultant or ticketing clerk. Whereas in North America an agent is a person, in Europe, an agent means travel agent and refers to the travel agency as an entity.

counter indemnity agreement *See* C/I.

counterfoil Often used loosely as a synonym for ticket coupon; but term should be more particularly reserved for any part of a coupon which may be used separately. For example, many airline boarding passes may be perforated with several counterfoils, as well as a part for the passenger to retain.

Country Potential Generation Index *See* travel propensity.

coupé May also be spelled as coup or coupe. US term for a two-door car, usually 'sporty' with little or no rear seating. Because of varying usage of word by different car makers, car renters should check on the description before hiring a vehicle.

coupon brokers Exchangers of free flight tickets. *See* FFP (frequent flyer programme) for detailed explanation.

coupon payment Proposal mooted in America in the early 1980s that agents should receive a standard commission on each air ticket sale, rather than a percentage. The theory is that an agent's costs per coupon, are the same, regardless of the amount of money involved. Flat-rate handling or sales fees were never accepted.

coupon, flight Official IATA definition is that portion of a Passenger Ticket and Baggage Check or Excess Baggage Ticket that indicates particular places between which the coupon is good for carriage.

coupon, passenger Official IATA definition is that portion of the Passenger Ticket and Baggage Check that constitutes the passenger's written evidence of the contract of carriage. This is usually the back part of a ticket, the face of which is a carbon copy of the itinerary and the back of which carries the Conditions of Carriage. More generally, of course, many travel tickets consist of several coupons.

coupon, tour An inclusive tour voucher.

courier A tour escort responsible for a party of travellers, moving from place to place with them. A tour operator's representative is the alternative term when the escort is static in a resort. The same term applies to a person carrying a package or documents from place to place on behalf of another person or organization. This work is often used to gain free or cheap travel, instead of remuneration for undertaking the job. Various associations of tour managers throughout the world insist that the word courier is obsolete and has been replaced by 'tour manager'; however, it persists in brochures and industry usage. *See* tour manager.

course Direction in which a ship is heading, usually expressed in compass degrees.

courses for tourism *See* Appendix II for standard syllabus, City and Guilds of London Institute *and* Edexcel Foundation.

court cabin An inside cabin with windows on to a small hallway or court. The court has daylight coming through windows or portholes at the side of the ship. Thus, court cabins have access to natural light and air via the hallway. Different from bibby cabins which have true access to a porthole internally despite being L-shaped inside cabins.

courtesy Means 'free' in travel parlance. A courtesy car is a free car, a service which is often provided by hotels between their establishment and airports and other facilities.

Courtesy Card Club Was name of KLM and Lufthansa's Frequent Flyer Club. KLM have renamed their FFP 'Flying Dutchman'; Lufthansa now call their FFP 'Miles and More'. *See* FFP (frequent flyer programme).

cover A place-setting in a restaurant. *See* cover charge.

cover charge In Europe, an amount charged by a restaurant per person or cover in addition to the normal charge for the meal. Sometimes, cover charges include the provision of items such as rolls, bread sticks and butter. In North America, the set charge to gain entry to a nightclub or high-class establishment is called a cover charge; in Europe, this is regarded as an admission fee.

Covia *See* Galileo[2].

CP/M Control Programme for Micro Computers. Originally developed in 1973, this system is now implemented by more than 500 major suppliers internationally, each of which has a huge software library of thousands of applications, from which to choose. CP/M is an operating system, rather than a programming language.

CP[1] Continental Plan; an accommodation tariff which includes provision of a room and continental breakfast.

CP[2] Corporate Policy, a division of IATA.

CPCP Corrosion prevention and control programme.

CPGI Country Potential Generation Index. *See* travel propensity.

CPM Common Point Minimum. Abbreviation normally used in connection with IATA fare construction system.

CPP Consumer Protection Plan; a US term. *See* ABTA, ASTA, ATOL, bond *and* bond replacement scheme, escrow, FMC[1], NTA[1], USTOA.

CPRE Council for the Protection of Rural England. *See* www.cpre.org.uk

CPS Characters per second, a measure of the efficiency with which computer printers produce their output.

CPT Confederation of Passenger Transport is the UK trade body in this sphere, having over 2500 members. The Council administers a bonding scheme to protect the travelling public from financial loss, should an operator of a holiday or tour collapse. Formerly the Bus and Coach Council. Also administers CoachMarque. *See* www.coach marque.org *and* www.cpt-uk.org *also* www.bondedcoachholidays.co.uk

CPTTF Cargo Paperless Transportation Task Force.

CPU Central processing unit, the nerve centre of a computer, controlling all the other parts of the system.

CRCs Cost Reimbursable Contractors *see* entry under this heading.

Creative Tourist Agents Conference *See* CTAC.

credit account *See* credit control.

credit cards A plastic card carrying the cardholder's details, enabling payments to be made for purchases, costs thereof being billed to the cardholder monthly; the vendor accepting payment by a credit card pays charges; while cardholders settling their monthly accounts in full incur no costs. System believed to have originated in 1950 when Frank McNamara offered a cardboard Diners Club card to a New York restaurant instead of cash. Travel services such as air, rail and car ferry tickets or holidays can usually be purchased with credit cards, with travel agents sometimes earning commission. Each air company nominates the only credit cards by which its tickets may be purchased, using a UATP or similar charge form, usually restricting the facility to itineraries where 50% of the travel is with that airline. Airlines usually pay credit card company fees or commissions on agency sales. Cards acceptable to most airlines include Access (associated with Mastercard internationally), American Express, Visa and Diners

Club. In normal use, the main Amex and Diners Club cards are 'charge cards', meaning that users pay their bills as received, without the facility of taking extended credit, although both companies have launched separate credit cards, the ability to 'buy now and pay later' being automatically available up to the credit limit granted to the user.

On the sales of travel facilities other than air tickets, in the UK agents might pay credit card companies commission, ranging from 1.2% to 4%. Under an ABTA scheme in the UK, discontinued in 1990, standard details were completed on an ABTA Credit Charge form in the travel agent's office and the form was forwarded to the principal, who received reimbursement from the credit card company, less charges, while the agent's commission paid by the principal was protected. Although this formal scheme has ended, a number of smaller tour operators still allow similar arrangements for the handling of agency customers' credit card payments. In the travel industry, credit card payments are frequently initiated when the cardholder is not present, a common source of fraudulent transactions, usually resulting in the cost being charged back to the travel company. Even when the cardholder is present, unless payment is made through a 'chip and pin' terminal, losses have to be covered by the travel company. The terminal name is derived from the cardholder details held on a chip embedded in the credit card and cardholder's pin which they must enter instead of signing for the payment.

credit control Corporations, companies or other organizations and even individuals who travel regularly, are provided with credit accounts by travel agents for administrative convenience. Airlines and railway companies require payment for tickets sold by set dates, which are strictly enforced. For example, under the UK BSP, the cost of all air tickets issued by agents are debited to their bank accounts on the 17th of the month for the previous month's issues. It follows that it is vital that an agent collects this money from account customers before this date. Credit control consists of taking up credit references before opening an account, placing a limit on the amount of credit by settling maximum figures, taking immediate action where accounts are not paid in due time and maintaining a careful watch on the financial stability of all credit account holders.

Types of credit account offered by travel agents are:

1. POI (payment on invoice) either by return of post or within 7 days, depending upon conditions laid down by the agent.
2. Monthly account, usually required to be paid by the 15th of the month in the UK, or if the business system of the corporate account is based upon paying monthly accounts on a certain day of the month, then travel agents have to accept this if they wish to handle that organization's business travel.
3. Two-weekly account or other period less than 1 month in those countries where BSP or other travel agents' airline payment and reporting system involves agency payments more frequently than monthly.
4. In respect of (1), (2) or (3) above, agents may offer discounts provided payments are received within the agreed terms, and may charge penalties or interest for late payments.
5. Payment by variable direct bank debit initiated by the agent on agreed date or dates each month.
6. Payment by corporate charge or credit card accounts, such as those offered by American Express and Diners Club. In the case of airline revenue, the airlines absorb the credit company charges and agents collect their commission on the transaction by deduction from the BSP or sales return. In the case of non-air sales there may be percentage charges paid by the agent, in return for the avoidance of all debt collection responsibility.
7. Putting all transactions on clients' personal credit or charge cards. Explanations in respect of (6) above also apply.

credit line   *See* house limit.
crew   The staff on a mode of transport.
CRIS   Central Reservation and Information System. Computer Reservations

Integrated Solution (CRIS) was also the in-house computer system for business travel formerly operated by A.T. Mays in the UK. *See* DMS.

CRM customer relationship management or customer marketing. *See* entry under this heading.

Croatian National Tourist Board *See* www.croatia.hr

cross-border selling Term usually applied to air tickets which take advantage of IATA currency rules, or unidirectional or special fares. An air ticket issued in country A, from country A to country C routed via country B may be much cheaper than a ticket issued in country B for travel from B to C. A passenger or agent, flouting the rules, may destroy or not use the first coupon from A to B, thus reducing the fare. The official IATA definition is, 'The practice of selling a ticket with a fictitious point of origin or destination in order to undercut the applicable fare'. Passengers holding tickets believed to violate the IATA rules can be prevented from travelling and asked to pay the correct fare. Agents' appointments may be discontinued if they have been involved in these practices.

On 1 July 1989 IATA introduced NUCs (Neutral Units of Construction) based on the US dollar, one NUC equalling US$1. As part of the new currency system, IATA rates of exchange are now set quarterly by IATA for conversion of local currency to NUCs and vice versa. These rates are monitored monthly, and in the case of extreme currency fluctuation, the rates are changed between the quarterly reviews. At the same time, radical changes were made in the way fares are calculated, based upon local selling fares in local currency. These changes substantially reduced but did not eradicate cross-border selling.

cross-country skiing The alternative to skiing on a prepared downhill run (piste); in effect, walking using skis.

cross ticketing Practice of an agency group concentrating its business through one outlet to gain higher commissions. The concept takes place worldwide but the term is particular to North America.

crow's nest Platform at the top of a mast used by a lookout on board ship.

Crown Room Club Name of Delta Airline's Frequent Flyers Club. *See* airline clubs and FFP (frequent flyer programme).

CRS Computerized reservation system; an electronic system holding a database of seats, space or rooms etc. and through which availability for sale and sales are recorded. A CRS may be used by any provider of travel services, such as a mode of transport, tour operator, hotel group, theatre or cinema. The 2003 CEN/European Standard official definition of a computer information and booking system is 'Electronic system by which information covering availability and prices of tourism services can be distributed and through which reservations can be made.' The term distribution usually infers making a product or service available to the public, either direct or through intermediaries; but a CRS may be internal to an organization. Thus the derivation of the term Global Distribution System (GDS) to describe the four CRSs (Amadeus, Galileo, Sabre and Worldspan) with worldwide coverage offering information, reservations, ticketing and many other facilities for airlines, hotels, car rental companies and other travel service providers.

For the first 50 years of scheduled air travel, agents' bookings were done over the telephone. At first, charts recording space on particular flights were sheets of paper. Eventually, for large airlines, space boards covered the walls in a large reservation hall, necessitating binoculars or a telescope for a clerk to see the status of a particular flight at the other end of the hall.

The legendary story of the origination of CRSs began with a chance meeting on an American Airlines' flight from Los Angeles to New York between C.R. Smith AA's President and R. Blair Smith, a senior sales representative for IBM. This led to a research project SABER (Semi Automated Business Environment Research). When this joint venture had been completed, American Airlines continued the development on its own. In 1960, it became the first travel organization to hold an inventory of its seats and record passenger's booking details on a computer, creating the Sabre system, changing the spelling to differentiate it from SABER. This situation was ripe for automation, and it was a logical development that the first travel agency electronic reservation systems should merely be terminals linked directly into airline systems, with access to sensitive information in them being suppressed.

IBM's separate development, in due course, became the basis for PARS. It was not until 1968 that Delta Airlines installed their internal computerized system and 3 years after this, in 1971, the same system was adopted by TWA as PARS; this later became Worldspan. It was also in 1971 that United Airlines introduced the Apollo system for use in their own offices. In Europe, by 1970, British European Airways' (BEA) internal CRS Beacon and British Overseas Airways Corporation's (BOAC) internal CRS Boadicea, were operating. Trials were initiated enabling 12 or so agents to access each of the BEA and BOAC systems. After the merger of these airlines in 1972, the trials were extended to the new joint CRS, BABS. Some similar arrangements in the USA were taking place; for example, Apollo was extended to North American agents in 1976. Travel agents began to be allowed to book their clients direct into airlines reservation systems. Only if an airline co-hosted another airline's reservation system, could an agent make direct bookings through more than one airline at a time, although arrangements often allowed major airlines to 'sell and record', notifying another airline of the sale. Thus, it was at this point, the CRSs became distribution systems.

During the 1980s there were many independent travel agency CRSs mainly handling air bookings; usually, each was associated with a major national airline CRS; so agents had to connect into each system to make bookings. In the UK, almost all automated agents used the Travicom multi-access system. Multi-access meant that agents from one terminal could select a direct connection to any airline, or other industry suppliers such as hotels and car rental companies, in contrast to American host computer systems, where bookings were either made only through a particular airline, being passed on automatically, or where

connections to other airlines are through the host computer. This was different from single airline systems because, through one connection from one terminal, it was possible to contact many airlines. The Travicom system acted as a giant interfacing device, directly connected to the CRSs of the world's major airlines. It was available for London travel agents in 1979/80 and gradually extended to agents throughout the UK.

By 1985, Sabre was available to European agents, but the high cost and US airline orientation meant that little market penetration was achieved. In response to the growing need for a European agency-connected CRS, in 1987, a group of European airlines (see Galileo[2]) formed Galileo; however, it was not until 1990 that it became the first European-wide fully operational agency-connected CRS and the first agents cut over to the Galileo central core. Despite the growth in air bookings over the Internet, numbers of agency terminals worldwide also continue to grow as can be seen from the following comparison of mid-1997 figures with those for April 2001: Sabre 33,453, 35% : 210,000, 37%; Galileo 36,704, 31% : 178,000, 32%; Amadeus 42,328, 35% : 154,945, 27%; Worldspan 17,415 6% : 21,000 4%.

UK market share shares of GDS mid-2002 are: Galileo 49%, Sabre 30%, Amadeus 14% and Worldspan 7%.

Typical charges to airlines for bookings made through their systems by GDS companies in mid-2002: Amadeus US$3.49; Sabre US$4.00; Worldspan US$3.70; and Galileo approx. US$4.

This explanation and brief history has concentrated on airline-based CRSs. For the story of the development, unique to the UK, of viewdata package holiday CRSs, see viewdata.

For general explanations of various systems and details of the facilities offered by the CRSs and GDSs see airline reservation systems, automated air reservation systems, automation in UK travel agencies, car ferry, inside link, reservation systems, tour operator reservation systems and viewdata. For specific details of the main global and regional CRSs see Abacas, Amadeus, Apollo, AXESS, car ferry CRSs in the

UK, CONFIRM, Datas II, ESTEREL, Fantasia, Galileo[2], Gemini, Gulliver, Infini, negotiated rate (or fare), Sabre, Southern Cross, SystemOne, THISCO, TIAS, TravelNet, Travicom, UltraSwitch *and* Worldspan.

CRS agency contracts *See* GDS agency contracts.

CRS/GDS entry modes To effect transactions quickly, skilled operatives use 'cryptic' mode which means memorizing and using coded entries such as three letter codes for the world's airports. N1Y02 might mean that one tourist class seat was being booked from line two of the display. In 'graphic' mode there are pull-down menus designed for easy navigation so that anyone can effect a reservation, without any specialist knowledge.

CRS rules for neutrality Reviews of the rules are currently taking place in Europe. The American Department of Transport dropped most of its rules governing GDSs on 31 January 2004 and eliminated the rest of them on 31 July 2004, ending 20 years of US government controls. Changes mean that airlines do not have to participate in every CRS and can choose which they use. Information may now vary between each CRS. Getting and comparing fare information has become increasingly complicated. Comment from the US DOT is at www.dot.gov *See* Appendix III *for current EC rules.*

CRSHWG CRS harmonization working group of IATA.

CRT Cathode Ray Tube. Used in North America instead of the term Visual Display Unit to describe the television type of screen or terminal used to connect to a computer.

cruise A sea voyage for pleasure which usually, but not always, returns to the starting point; thus a cruise ship is regarded by passengers as any vessel used mainly for a cruise, whether or not it has been specially designed and built for the purpose. In 1995, worldwide passenger capacity for multi-day cruises on ships with more than 50 berths was 160,000; by 2005 this had risen to 310,000. Including cruise line brands under ownership or control in 2005, the Carnival Group offered 133,500 berths, the RCCL group 62,200 berths and the Syar group 26,000

berths. Together, these organizations account for 71% of world cruise capacity and 89% of ships on order. Ninety-three per cent of cruise vessels over 1500 berths and all the ships with greater than 2000 berths have been ordered by these top three cruise operators. In 2005, the North American cruise market was around 9.25m passengers and expected to grow by 4.25% annually to 2020. The UK market of 1.1m is forecast to grow faster, up to 7% a year. The world cruising passenger total of 13.6m in 2005 could rise to 27m by 2020. More detailed information is available on the Ocean Shipping Consultants web site www.OSClimited.com

cruise broker Travel agent or other intermediary handling sales of cruise line's 'distressed' inventory near to departure date which they have been unable to sell themselves.

cruise director Person on a cruise ship responsible for organizing passengers' entertainment and other activities such as shore excursions; duties vary between cruise lines.

cruise host *See* host programme.

Cruise Line Coalition (in the USA) Joint communications initiative of US cruising organizations; hosted on the web site of the International Council of Cruise Lines. *See* www.iccl.org

cruise ship sizes In *Dictionary of the Cruise Industry* the term 'megaship' is suggested as applying to vessels over 70,000GRT while those around 50,000 are suggested to be mid-sized. *The Traveller's World* suggests the same figure but suggests it is a megaliner. The British PSA suggests a measurement based on a combination of a ship's tonnage and the maximum number of passengers that can be carried. Very small is below 10,000 tonnes; small greater than 10,000 but up to 25,000 tonnes and up to 1000 passengers; medium up to 60,000 tonnes and 2000 passengers; large above 60,000 tonnes and above 2000 passengers; and huge above 100,000 tonnes and above 3000 passengers. Research for this dictionary suggests that there is no consensus about either the terms or the figures. *Also see* ship density.

cruise to nowhere Popular name in the USA for a cruise vacation which spends a day or two at sea before returning to the originating port, having visited no other ports.

cryptic CRS/GDS entry mode *See* CRS/GDS entry modes.

CS Corporate Services; an IATA division.

CSC Cargo Services Conference.

CSCMG Cargo Services Conference Management Group.

CSG Cargo Agency Conference Steering Group.

CST Central Standard Time in the USA.

CSTF Cargo Security Task Force.

CTA[1] The Caribbean Tourism Association was set up in the USA in 1952 to develop and promote travel and tourism to the area. Its European office opened in January 1984, in Frankfurt. It owes its existence to a joint funding agreement between the EEC and CTA's 25 member countries.

CTA[2] Control area (aviation term).

CTA[3] Certified Travel Associate. A US award of professional competence made after successful completion of a course of study approved or arranged by the American Institute of Certified Travel Agents, now renamed The Travel Institute. *See* www.icta.com *or* www.thetravelinstitute.com

CTAC Creative Tourist Agents Conference in the UK, a small group of operators of European Rail ITs.

CTC[1] Certified Travel Counselor. A US award of professional competence made after successful completion of a course of study approved or arranged by the American Institute of Certified Travel Agents, now renamed The Travel Institute. *See* www.icta.com *or* www.thetravelinstitute.com An award by the same name is also made by the Canadian Institute of Travel Counsellors (Institut Canadien de Conseillers en Voyages). *See* www.citc.ca

CTC[2] The Coach Tourism Council in the UK is the coaching industry's promotional group, made up of coach operators, tourist boards, hotel groups, ferry companies/Le Shuttle and attractions; its aims are to promote the benefits and raise the image of coach tourism.

CTC[3] Canadian Tourist Commission. *See* www.canadatourism.com

CTD Corporate travel department. *See* ARC. *Also see list of 70 other business travel related entries which follows* corpo-

rate travel contracts, *some of which lead to further entries.*

CTDRA Corporate Travel Department Reporting Agreement. *See* ARC. *Also see list of 70 other business travel related entries which follows* corporate travel contracts, *some of which lead to further entries.*

CTIE Certified Travel Industry Executive in the USA offered by The Travel Institute. *See entry under this heading or access* www.icta.com *or* www.thetravelinstitute.com

CTIP Coalition for Travel Industry Parity; a US coalition of travel agency consortia and cooperatives etc. *See* ASTA web site.

CTM Circle Trip Minimum. Abbreviation normally used in connection with IATA fare construction system. *See* circle trips *and* IATA fare construction system.

CTO[1] Caribbean Tourism Organization, a body which undertakes promotion of travel to and within the area. *See* www.onecaribbean.org

CTO[2] City Ticket Office of an airline in the USA, referring to an off-airport airline office.

CTO[3] Credit Travel Order. Warrants issued to individuals or organizations who hold credit accounts with British Airways. Travel agents are not allowed to issue tickets against a CTO.

CTO[4] Cyprus Tourism Organization. *See* www.visitcyprus.org.cy

CTP Certified Tour Professional; US tour operations qualification organized by the National Tour Association and its associated charitable foundation the National Tour Foundation. On 1 January 2005, the NTF, founded by the NTA, came together with the Travelers Conservation Foundation, founded by the USTOA, to form Tourism Cares for Tomorrow. *See* www.ntfonline.org *and* www.tcfonline.org

CTRL Channel Tunnel Rail Link. *See* Eurotunnel.

Cuba Tourist Board *See* www.cuba.com

CUG A closed user group in the UK refers to a public viewdata service. By definition, any member of the public paying the standard service fee can access all the general information. Many travel organizations restrict access to their group of frames only to specified travel agents. In the case of a tour operator, these may be only that company's appointed agents. In the case of large retailers like Thomas Cook or American Express, the CUGs are composed only of their networks.

cultural tourism Writers have described this as travel for the purpose of studying the culture and way of life in the area being visited. However, general usage of the wording 'cultural tour' is taken to mean travel involving study of (or participation in) the arts. Thus, a member of the public feels that travel for the purpose of attending operas, concerts and plays, as well as visiting museums, art galleries and archaeological sites all comes under the heading of cultural tourism.

cumulus *See* clouds.

curbside check-in Where air passengers can check in for a flight and deposit their baggage adjacent to the point where they are dropped off from the vehicle that has brought them to the airport. Was common in the USA until the 11 September 2001 catastrophe, when such services were suspended for security reasons.

currency buying and selling rates *See* conversion rate[1].

currency restrictions *See* exchange control.

currency surcharge General meaning is an extra charge resulting from a change in currency exchange rates. As a result of new currency conversion methods introduced by IATA in 1989, the 1973 rules have become obsolete. Because of continuing fluctuations in exchange rates, static IATA fares could not reflect changing values. As exchange rates varied, IATA declared currency surcharge or deduction percentages to be applied to fares from each country. Tariffs are now denominated in local currencies and converted at banker's rates of exchange. IATA Fare Construction Units (FCUs) and currency adjustment factors have ended. (*See* NUC.) The same term is applied to the supplement added to any travel bill, as a result of exchange rate variations subsequent to the original cost calculation.

CURS Centre for Urban and Regional Studies in the University of Birmingham in the UK undertakes research and teaching in the fields of leisure and tourism and maintains a substantial leisure, recreation and tourism library.

cursor control The cursor is usually a small line indicating the current entry position on a computer screen. Sometimes this small line flashes for ease of location and sometimes it is a small block flashing. With most keyboards, multi-directional arrows or other commands enable movement of the cursor freely all over the screen. Often, however, travel industry computers have been programmed so as to require completion of mandatory fields in a pre-determined manner. It is a defect of these systems that, although travel agency terminals are capable of cursor movement, the host computer software will not allow alteration of part of an incomplete frame. Sometimes there is no alternative but to abort a transaction and start all over again, merely in order to change one character.

CUSS kiosk Common use self-service kiosk for use by air travellers to check-in at airports.

customer activated ticketing *See* NCR Skylink.

customer profile Information concerning individual travellers is stored by all big agencies specializing in business travel, or who handle VIPs. Smoking or non-smoking, travels first class only, requires aisle seat, pays by American Express card no. ..., are typical pieces of information concerning travel preferences. It is also useful to record all previous recent travel arrangements. Galileo in the UK have made available database facilities for this and other purposes, so that agents can access the information on their terminals at the time of making air bookings. Other major UK multiples are storing this information in their own computer databases. In the UK, airline reservation system hosts store this information on their computers.

customer relationship management/marketing Customer profiles contain full details of a client, usually stored in an electronic database. At the simplest level, in business travel, the profile has their seating preferences, smoking/non-smoking, dietary requirements and perhaps reference to a company travel policy concerning class of travel. But, for example, airlines may have databases running into six or seven figures of those in their frequent-flyer schemes. Offers can be specifically targeted to groups of these people by sophisticated management of the database. Maintenance of an up-to-date list of current and past customers for CRM purposes is not particular to the travel field; but it is widely used by travel businesses.

customs The government authority that controls the import and export of goods. On entry to a country from abroad, travellers may have to pay duties or taxes. This is because most governments add high taxes or customs duties to alcoholic drinks, tobacco products and perfumes, among other products. There may be duty-free allowances, but other products may be prohibited, for example, alcoholic drinks by Moslem countries. For US information *see* www.customs.gov and for UK HM Customs and Excise duty free allowances *see* www.hmce.gov.uk/public/yourcust

customs declaration The act of declaring to the appropriate authorities on entry to a country, either that nothing is being imported or that goods specified on a customs declaration document are being imported, on which the traveller is willing to pay tax or duty. In the USA, a 'customs declaration' is the title of the form that must be completed by every person entering the USA from another country. A customs user fee is added to the cost of air tickets for those travellers, designated by the letters YC. In the UK, HM Customs & Excise have arranged for blue, green and red channels on entry to Britain. The blue channel enables travellers from EC countries with nothing to declare to walk straight through without any inspection; the green channel is for others with nothing to declare, although Customs Officers check occasionally, to make sure the use of the blue and green

channels is not being abused. The red channel is reserved for travellers who wish to make an import declaration and pay duty.

customs duty Tax on imports. *See* customs declaration.

CUTAS Cathay Pacific's CRS.

CUTE Common user terminal equipment.

cut-off Wording of general travel industry usage; several typical examples follow: date by which the unsold part of an allocation or allotment must be returned. *See* allotment. Date by which an option will expire; commonly used in connection with hotel bookings.

cutter By strict definition, this word means a sailing vessel with one mast, rigged with two forward sails; this description will be found to be almost identical to that for a sloop; but the word is often wrongly used to describe any small motor-driven boats.

CVAP *See* Certificate in Visitor Attraction Practice.

CVB Convention and visitors bureau.

CVR Cockpit voice recorder.

CWG Catering Working Group; a joint IATA/ATA committee.

CWGN Term used by some US car rental companies to indicate a compact station wagon.

CWP Central West Pacific Ocean Region (ICAO).

CYBA Charter Yacht Brokers Association in the USA.

Cyprus National Travel Agency Organization *See* www.pio.gov.cy

Cyprus Tourism Organization *See* www.visitcyprus.org.cy

CZ Control zone.

Czech Association of Travel Agents *See* ATA.

Czech Tourist Authority *See* www.czechtourism.com www.cccr-info.cz *or* www.visitczech.cz

Czech Travel and Hotel Corporation CEDOK. *See* www.cedok.cz

D

'D' Train German term for an express train (Durchgehende Zug) which requires supplementary fare.

D/F Direction finding (aviation term).

DA Display authorization (aviation term).

DAAIS Danger Area Activity Information Service (aviation term).

dabble agent US slang used by established agents for a part-time or home-working agent seeking to attack their expertise. Readers would be correct to assume that there 'is no love lost' between these groups.

DACS Danger Area Crossing Service (aviation term).

daily rate The price for a hotel room, car or any other travel facility for a period of 24 h. Must not be confused with 'day rate', explained in the next column.

daisywheel printer Obsolescent term. Associated with a computer system, this type of printer produces good-quality type similar to that achieved by an electric typewriter. Cheaper systems use dot matrix printers, punching out characters with fine needles. The name daisywheel printer arises because the type characters are held on a flower-shaped wheel. Although this type of printer provides good reproduction suitable for letters, it is too slow for most travel agency uses. Laser or inkjet printers are now the norm.

Danid International hotel code for four single-bedded rooms.

Danish National Travel Agency Organization *See* TBAD.

Danish Tourist Board *See* www.visit denmark.com

DAR Digital aids recorder (aviation term).

dark tourism *See* thanatourism.

DART Dublin Area Rapid Transport system.

DASA DaimlerChrysler Aerospace (formerly DaimlerBenz Aerospace). *See* aircraft manufacture.

data protection The UK Data Protection Act 1984 required all data users to register with the Data Protection Registrar in 1985. Data users in the UK must take security measures preventing unauthorized access, alteration, disclosure or destruction of personal data held in their computer systems. UK travel companies must describe the personal data they hold on computers, the purpose for which it will be used, the sources from which it will be obtained, persons or organizations to whom the data may be disclosed, the countries to which data may be transferred directly or indirectly and locations responsible for dealing with requests for access to the data.

The new 1998 UK Data Protection Act came into force in March 2000, introducing even tighter controls over the use of personal records and extending regulation to written records. Details available from www.dataprotection.gov.uk There is now similar legislation in force throughout the EC.

database Term meaning information stored on a computer system. Term only meaningful when specified; for example, the reservation database of an airline consists of the details of all their flights and bookings made.

databases of tourism and transport information and statistics *See* tourism information databases.

Datas II Delta Automated Travel Account Systems was a US travel industry CRS owned by Delta Airlines, accessible by travel agents. In 1989, an alliance, between Datas II and American Airlines Sabre was blocked on anti-trust grounds. In February 1990 Datas II merged with PARS to form Worldspan, separately described under this title.

DATO The Discover America Travel Organization was one of the forerunners of the Travel Industry Association of America.

davits Arms which may be swung out over the side of ships for raising and lowering of the lifeboats.

day rate The price charged for accommodation use during the day. Businessmen often need small rooms for interviewing or meetings during the day. Such rooms can be converted back into bedrooms in time for use that night. Hotels near airports will often be able to make day-rate sales to passengers who are delayed or waiting for connecting flights.

day return A fare on a mode of transport at a reduced price for travel and return to origin; but not necessarily on the same day. Some day returns cover a 24 h period, while others are valid until a specified time in the early hours of the following day.

day tripper *See* excursionist.

days of service Many transport and other services do not operate every day of the week. To save space in many timetables, days of service are designated by code numbers. Monday being 1, Tuesday 2 and so on.

DB Junior Tourist Card *See* DB Tourist Card.

DB Tourist Card Entitles the holder to unlimited rail travel over the West German Railway network. Other concessions granted include exemption from payment of TEE or IC^2 supplements. Prices vary according to validity of 4, 9 or 16 days, first- or second-class of travel required or age of purchaser, between 4 and 11, 12 to 25 and adult.

DCA^1 Deposit Collection Advice, common in the UK as a means by which travel agents inform tour operators with whom they have credit accounts, that they have collected clients' deposits for a booking. Increasingly, as reservations are switched to electronic means, it is accepted that upon making a firm booking, an agent automatically creates a debit for the deposit in the account. However, multiple travel agents or other agency groupings with central accounting, still need systems for communicating the collection of money, to pass on to a provider of travel services.

DCA^2 Director(ate) of Civil Aviation or Department of Civil Aviation (varies between countries).

DCMS Department for Culture, Media and Sport; UK government department which has tourism in its portfolio. *See* www.culture.gov.uk

dead man's handle On trains and many rapid transit vehicles, the driver must maintain continuous pressure or movement to a handle, otherwise the brakes will be applied automatically. Thus, should the driver become ill or fall asleep, the train should come to a halt.

deadhead Air or shipping staff in transit travelling free. Same term also used to describe ship, plane or vehicle travelling empty for positioning, or any other purpose. *See* empty leg.

debark/debarkation North American terminology for disembarkation, leaving from or alighting from a mode of transport.

debug To get rid of the bugs or errors in a computer program.

deck The deck is taken to mean the top or outside deck of a vessel or ship, exposed to the elements. When decks are lettered, A is usually the top deck, with subsequent letters indicating levels in descending order. The same is often, but not always, applied when decks are numbered. Sometimes particular decks are given names associated with their nautical use making their position even more difficult to identify. There is no set pattern even between cruise liners run by the same operator. For example, on one Russian ship, the top deck with passenger cabins is the Promenade, beneath this the Main deck, then A restaurant deck and finally B. Another Russian ship provides passenger accommodation on the Bridge, Boat, Saloon, Promenade, Main, Second and Third decks. Other deck titles that may be encountered include Stadium, Verandah, Sun and Observation deck, all of which would usually be found at a high level. The Lido deck is usually that on which the swimming pool is located; the boat deck is usually the one on which the lifeboats are situated and the bridge deck is the one on the same level as the ship's bridge. The orlop deck is the one immediately above the cargo hold; thus, it is the name of the lowest deck.

deck plan Shows the location and facilities for every cabin. Unfortunately, the symbols used vary enormously between companies, making it impossible to give a standard explanation, so that the first thing the beginner must do when handling a deck plan, is to find the key list for the symbols used, in order to be able to decode the deck plans. It is then possible to identify which cabins have beds and which have upper and lower berths. Other cabins might have fold-away divan beds. Other typical symbols indicate showers, toilets, baths and washbasins.

It will be obvious from a deck plan which cabins are outside with a port-hole and which are inner cabins. In bygone years, before air conditioning was introduced, there was a greater advantage in having a porthole which could be opened to let in fresh air. Nowadays, on most decks, the portholes are securely fastened, and anyway, are too small to let in much natural light. Thus, there should be little discernible difference between the two types, adjacent to one another on the same deck, even though the outer is always more expensive. This does not apply to variations encountered on different decks. The nearer a cabin is to the engines, the more likelihood of noise and vibration. Seasoned sea travellers will tell you that they find the air conditioning does not work as well on the lower decks, especially in older vessels.

Normally, holiday bookings involving a charter flight and hotel rooms do not specify the actual room, but travel by ship is entirely different. Here the norm is to allocate a particular numbered cabin to every passenger. It is essential that a travel agent carries deck plans for all the vessels on which it is intended to book passengers. Deck plans are often included in the operator's brochures.

declared value for carriage   Official IATA definition is the value of goods or baggage declared to the carrier by the passenger for the purposes of determining charges or of establishing the limits of the carriers' liability for loss, damage or delay.

dedicated line   A telephone line permanently connected between a distant terminal and a computer. For example, Galileo Executive service in the UK involves a dedicated line between a satellite point on the Galileo network and an agent's office. This permanent connection enables instant access to all the major airlines worldwide. The alternative facility is known as dial-up because the same connection is made by dialling when required. Usage now largely replaced by broadband connection – *see* entry under this heading.

deductible   *See* excess.

deed of assignment   The legal contract by which an asset or benefit is transferred between the parties concerned. In the UK travel industry, these deeds are commonly used following the financial failure of a travel company. Under the ATOL bonding arrangements backed by the Air Travel Reserve Fund, or the ABTA retailers' bonding schemes backed by the Retailers' Fund or the Bus and Coach Council bonding schemes, members of the travelling public are protected against loss. When a company collapses, travellers usually seek immediate alternative holiday or travel arrangements and these are provided at no extra charge by other travel companies, provided the traveller assigns his right to refund to the organization effecting the replacement arrangements. Thus, the deed enables the new organizer of the trip to gain the reimbursement originally due to the customer under one of the aforementioned bonding schemes.

default protection plan   *See* DPP.

default[1]   A travel agent is in default if a sales return accompanied by a remittance for tickets issued in the accounting period concerned is not forwarded by the due date. Originally, the terminology was devised by IATA, agents being reported as delinquent for initial reporting and payment failures, eventually losing an appointment altogether when declared in default. The terminology is now in general use worldwide.

default[2]   In respect of travel technology or computers, the 'default' is the situation to which a system reverts, unless instructions are given to the contrary. For example, a computer printer may be set up to handle single-copy continuous paper of a certain size, and the computer will always assume this is loaded. When triple-copy single sheets are loaded, the computer must be notified.

Defense Travel System   *See* MTMC.

Delhi belly Slang expression for traveller's diarrhoea.

delinquent The IATA term for an agent who has failed to send in a sales report and/or remittance in due time. *See* also default[1].

delivering member Official IATA definition is the IATA member on whose flight a passenger is to be carried to an interline point or gap.

Delos Name of computerized travel agent's data and accounting system introduced by Michael Gurr Associates in December 1980 formerly used by several UK travel agents.

Delta Major American airline and Northeast England-based consortium of travel agents of same name, a member of Worldchoice.

de luxe The highest standard in accommodation or travel. Term only has a specific meaning when part of an official rating system.

demand for transport Appears to be insatiable, limited mainly by price, speed/journey time, comfort and convenience. Air travel is expected to grow by around 6% annually worldwide, at the time of writing. Economic growth in the Third World will lead to much higher growth rates for car travel than elsewhere. In the USA, private car travel is around 80% of total journeys, having fallen from the often-quoted 90% of 1960, air travel 16–17% and the rest bus and rail, the latter being less than 1%. In Europe, air travel accounts for only around 30% of journeys, and is slowly growing about 0.5% annually. Journey length in Europe appears to be particularly crucial. Eighty per cent of all journeys are by car up to 150 km falling to under 10% for travel of 700 km or more; for journeys of this length, air travel comes into its own, 75% of the total. Optimum distance as far as European railways are concerned is 350 km, involving around half of all journeys. There is currently massive investment in Europe on faster trains of high standard. This, coupled with the opening of the Channel Tunnel, can be expected to result in a lower growth for European air traffic than worldwide. *See also* transport modelling for detailed explanation.

demi-pension Hotel accommodation which includes continental breakfast and table d'hôte dinner in stated room rate. In some instances lunch can be substituted for dinner. Same as MAP.

demonstration effect Holding out to members of the host community unattainable economic aspirations, with disruptive consequences. The source of this was Rivers, P. (1973) 'Tourist troubles' *New Society* 23 (539), 250, the same meaning being ascribed by Jafari, J. (1974) in 'The socio-economic costs of tourism to developing countries' *Annals of Tourism Research* 1, 227–259.

The original intention of those who created the term is being swamped by those who suggest that the demonstration effect is the result of acculturation, where a host population absorbs or imitates the manners, customs, clothing and culture of tourists; in other words, the 'demonstrable effect of acculturation'. This view is amplified, with references, by Chris Ryan, writing in *Encylopedia of Tourism*.

denied boarding compensation (DBC) Occasionally air passengers who hold confirmed reservations for a specific flight are unable to travel because of changes in aircraft type, errors resulting in overbooking or other factors. For air passenger's rights in the USA in the event of a schedule irregularity such as a delay, cancellation or misconnection or *force majeure* situation, *see* Rule 240. For details of the American laws regarding compensation for 'bumped' passengers *see* US DOT publication *Fly-Rights: a Consumer Guide to Air Travel* on the DOT web site www.dot.gov or www.1travel.com via 'Rules of the Air'. From February 2005 new EC rules applied on compensation payments by airlines to passengers on both scheduled and non-scheduled flights who are bumped (refused travel despite having firm reservations) off overbooked flights or affected by delays and cancellations. Cancellations will cost airlines (assuming an exchange rate of 1.45 euros to the UK pound) (a) €250 (£172) per passenger on flights of less than 1500 km; (b) €400 (£276) for flights between 1500 km and all intra-community flights over 1500 km and (c) 3500 km and €600 (£414) on trips over 3500 km. If passengers are offered re-routing, then provided arrival time is not more than

2 hours later for a flight type (a), 3 hours later for (b) or 4 hours later for (c), then the compensation payable is reduced by 50%. Under the new regulations, travellers suffering delays exceeding 2 hours for type (a), 3 hours for type (b) flights or 4 hours for type (c) flights will be entitled to a full refund of their ticket cost. Airlines will also be compelled to provide meals, refreshments and hotel accommodation, as appropriate. Cancellations will also involve compensation, unless the passenger is informed 2 weeks ahead or is told in due time and re-routed at a time near the original flight. This came into effect on 17 February 2005, which is 12 months from its publication in the *Official Journal of the European Union.* The text of the *Official Journal* can be found at http://europa.eu.int/eur-lex/en/archive/2004/l_04620040217en.htm The US rules encourage voluntary negotiation with passengers and when flights are overbooked, airlines usually increase their offers until sufficient passengers have relinquished their reservations. Should a US passenger be bumped involuntarily, there is no compensation due provided the alternative flights are scheduled to arrive within an hour of the original one. If the alternative will arrive between 1 and 2 hours after the original arrival time (between 1 and 4 hours on international flights), then the carrier must pay the passenger an amount equal to the single fare, with a US$200 maximum. If the substitute transportation offered will arrive over 2 hours later on domestic flights, or over 4 hours on international flights, or if an airline were not to offer any alternative arrangements, then the compensation rises to twice the single fare, with a US$400 maximum. In addition, bumped passengers may keep their ticket and use it on another flight, or request a refund. Denied boarding compensation 'is a payment for the inconvenience' states the DOT web site. *See* http://air consumer.ost.dot.gov/publications/fly rights.htm

density *See* ship density. *Also known as* PSR (passenger space ratio).

density chart A type of hotel sales and reservation chart designed to indicate the number of rooms sold, free, on option or allocation etc. Such charts are not necessary in most large hotels for the current period, because the data is recorded on the computer. But for advanced bookings, perhaps running several years ahead, density charts are invaluable.

dep Abbreviation for departure.

Department of Transportation US governmental authority in field; *see* airline deregulation in the USA for details of responsibilities in this field *and* www.dot.gov

departure gate or **lounge** Area at a transport terminal where travellers wait until they board their mode of transport. For international travel, the departure lounge is reached after passing through customs and emigration control. For travellers by air, the lounge is usually after passing through security checks. *See* gate.

departure tax Taxes on travellers are of two main types. Ticket and sales taxes are normally collected in addition to the fare when a ticket is issued, for example, the 10% Canadian air transportation tax with a maximum of Can$50. This affords a good example of another aspect of many of these taxes in that travel within Canada paid for outside that country is excepted, provided the traveller's point of origin is outside Canada, so that travel agents should, where necessary advise customers of this. Sometimes, the taxes only apply to residents of that country, for example, the US$100 Israel travel tax. Many taxes are included in the cost of air tickets, the security charges at many airports being recovered in this way. The cost of immigration and customs officials at US airports is defrayed in the same way. Airport taxes not included in the price of air tickets are normally paid for in local currency upon departure. At the time of writing 120 countries' charges of this nature were listed in the OAG, while 70 countries' charges had to be added to ticket prices and collected at time of ticket issue. In the UK, Air Passenger Duty (APD) and, in the USA, an air departure tax are charged at different rates on domestic and international travel. At the time of researching, the charge was 10% domestic and US$6 international.

departure time The 2003 CEN/European Standard official definition is 'Time when the contracted service of transport begins.' Thus, the words have been given contractual significance which may become important if this standard ever has the force of law. Most travellers, for example, regard the departure time of an aircraft as their departure time; but their contract probably begins to have effect from the moment of check-in.

departure windows Travellers dislike starting a journey or arriving at their destination in the middle of the night. Quite apart from discomfort, public transport is not usually available. Hotel rooms are only bookable for 24 h periods from midday, regardless of time of arrival. Add to this the night flying restrictions at many airports worldwide and it can be understood why there are difficulties in scheduling long flights. A departure window is the period during which it is appropriate to schedule flights on a particular route, having regard to the considerations stated. Between London and Hong Kong, for example, this is a mere 1.5 h.

depeaking Process through which airport flight congestion is relieved and flight delays reduced by cutting the number of peak hour flights. A depeaking order is an agreement or US government order which has the object of reducing the number of flights to and from an airport during peak hours. For example, the US FAA has negotiated a voluntary agreement at Chicago's O'Hare airport: the 5% peak hour flights cut between 12.00 (midday) and 20.00 (8 p.m.) is expected to reduce delay times overall by 20%, and cut the number of delays over 2 hours by a third. This agreement was then enshrined in an FAA order, providing control over how O'Hare flights are scheduled. Although the FAA order freezes the level of arrivals by large incumbent carriers, it allows a small number of extra flights by 'limited incumbent carriers' and new entrant carriers. The FAA defines a 'limited incumbent carrier' as one with eight or fewer arrivals during peak hour periods.

deplane To alight from an aircraft.

deplaning point Official IATA definition is the point at which a passenger is scheduled to disembark from a flight of the boarding member.

deplate North American term for the act of an airline removing permission from an agency to issue tickets. For many years carbon-backed air tickets were validated with an airline stamp by plates issued by airlines. Although many air journeys are now facilitated by electronic 'virtual' tickets, the wording has remained.

deposit An amount of money paid in advance, part of the total cost of an item being purchased. The word is not particular to travel services, however, deposits are usually required to secure an inclusive tour, cruise and some air tickets. Deposits are particularly required against breakages, when renting self-catering accommodation, and to secure a hotel booking. Often, deposits are not refundable in the event of cancellation.

deposit collection advice *See* DCA[1].

deposit option date US term for the date by when a provider of travel services must receive a deposit, otherwise the traveller's booking option expires.

deposit receipt Quite apart from the normal usage, meaning a document proving that part payment has been made, the term has a specific meaning with regard to sea travel. Cruise and passenger shipping tickets are often designed in multi-coupon format. One of the top coupons, the deposit receipt shows the total cost of the trip, the deposit paid and the balance of passage money due. When this is remitted, the ticket is validated as fully paid and the same document becomes the passage ticket. Initial deposit payments and subsequent payments of the total due by clients are common in the travel industry.

deposit reservation US term for a hotel booking for which part or complete payment has been made in advance. Dependent on the hotel's rules, such reservations will be maintained whether or not the client arrives before the usual check-in time, at least for one night, and possibly for the whole period booked.

deregulation This buzz-word of the 1980s means in the travel industry, abandonment of licensing rules. For example, both Britain and the USA allow market forces to control who runs long-distance express coach services, excursion trips and coach tours. Air transport is also deregulated both within the EC and USA. *See* ARC[1], CAB, airline deregulation in the EU *and* airline deregulation in the USA; *see also* bus deregulation in the USA.

Derwent Was one of Prestel's six computers.

designation The nomination of specific airlines only to operate air services agreed between governments in an Air Services Agreement.

destination Official IATA definition is the ultimate stopping place according to the contract of carriage. This is significantly different from the general use of the term in the travel industry.

Destination Management Certified Professional *See* www.adme.org

destination management company *See* ground handler.

destination management system *See* DMS[1].

destination survey A survey aimed at establishing the volume, value and characteristics of passenger traffic to particular destinations within a country. Often this consists of two parts; an accommodation survey and visitor survey. Only when a system of recording is in operation at all hotels etc. is it possible to obtain full details of arrivals and lengths of stay.

DET A domestic escorted tour is the US terminology for an inclusive tour undertaken entirely with the USA.

detrain To alight from a train.

developed beaches Concept described in the World Tourism Organization and Secretariat of State for Tourism of France (2001), *Thesaurus on Tourism and Leisure Activities* as 'Beaches with certain facilities such as access staircases, toilets and changing rooms.' Although setting standards is a laudable objective there is no worldwide agreement as to usage of the term or what standards might constitute a developed beach. The French term 'plage amenagee' of which this is a translation does not have a meaning outside France.

DFCS Digital flight control system.

DFDR Digital flight data recorder.

DFUC Direct fare undercut check. Abbreviation normally used in connection with IATA fare construction system; the check is undertaken to make sure that a constructed fare does not undercut a published through fare, which takes precedence.

DG Director General as, for example, of IATA; or Directorate General as, for example DGXXIII (DG23) of the European Commission, which covers tourism.

DGB Dangerous Goods Board of IATA.

DGCA Directorate General of Civil Aviation (in various countries).

DGNSS Differential global navigation satellite system.

DGPS Differential global positioning system.

DGR[1] Dangerous Goods Regulations of IATA.

DGR[2] Domestic General Rules Tariff in the USA is the main rule-book guiding US air travel published by the Air Tariff Publishing Company on behalf of US airlines.

DGTTF Dangerous Goods Training Task Force of IATA.

DH Decision height (aviation term).

Dialcom Was brand name for British Telecom's Prestel service which BT attempted to introduce. Despite this and previous efforts to establish alternative names or branding, the name Prestel remained the best known.

Diamond A consortium of North London travel agents, a member of Worldchoice in the UK.

Diamond Club Name of British Midland Frequent Flyers' Club, membership of which is free to those taking 40 flights with them annually.

DICIRMS Destination Integrated Computerized Information and Reservation Management System. *See* DMS[1].

Dickens Was one of Prestel's six computers.

digital Transmission and storage method of computers. *See* analog.

dine around program In North America, arrangements which allow vacationers their choice of restaurants instead of the hotel at which they are resident.

diner US term for a rail restaurant car.

dinghy Term describes an inflatable life raft or the small boat used by a larger vessel for shore access when appropriate. In India, where the term originated, it still means any small boat.

direct access system That part of a GDS (global distribution system) computerized reservation system which enables a user to have real time direct access to other systems. The benefit to agents of using this mode is that the supplier's reservation system provides a confirmation reference instantly, usually within 7 seconds of making booking requests. In the UK also means a 'hardwire' or direct permanent dataline connection between an agency and a viewdata network such as AT&T or Endeavour's Fastrak. To enable rapid data transmission, the telephone connection will usually be broadband. Also known as 'direct connect' in the USA, where the GDS service guarantees that for participating suppliers, within 7 s of finalizing the details of a reservation, agents will receive a tourism service provider's confirmation reference (called locator code by airlines). *See* inside link (also called CRS inside availability link).

direct connect   *See* immediately preceding entry.

direct debit systems   Arrangements for a bank account to be debited with varying amounts as they fall due. Thus instructions can be given to any bank allowing debits raised by another party via their bank to be deducted from a bank account. Direct debit systems function electronically and are paperless; they are widely used in the travel industry for payments by travel agents to their principals.

direct debit travel agents' payment systems   *See* agents' payment systems.

direct fare undercut check   *See* DFUC.

direct link   *See* inside link (also called CRS inside availability link).

direct reference system   US name for the GDS supplier information database accessible to all users.

direct sell   In the UK, travel transactions which are direct between the providers of a travel service and customers, without the intervention of an intermediary. For example, most low cost airlines bypass travel agents. Massive growth in Internet usage has facilitated this.

directional fare   A fare that only applies in one direction of travel. For example, rail fares in the UK are cheaper from provincial towns to London than from London to the same places. Air fares are often different according to the direction of travel. Also known as directional tariff.

directional imbalance   Most transport users, except in rare cases such as immigration, return to their point of origin. Nevertheless, the most well-known example of this phenomenon is rush-hour traffic into the world's major cities in the morning every working day and back out again in the evening. The use of any means of transport in this way is inherently inefficient. In respect of freight, directional imbalance is the norm. For example, food moves towards centres of population, where it is consumed. The transport used must then go back empty. In respect of air freight, a much-quoted example is that only one-fifth of the freight in both directions travels from Europe to Australasia, the other four-fifths being in the other direction.

directional minimum check   *See* IATA fare construction system.

directional selling   When travel agents particularly promote the products of an operator which owns them or of any provider of travel services which is a 'preferred supplier'. Phenomenon has same name in UK and USA. *See also* preferred supplier.

directory   In a hotel, the name of the booklet or guide describing the hotel's facilities. The meaning of other uses is usually self-evident: e.g. travel trade directory, telephone directory.

dirigible   Alternative name for an airship or other type of lighter-than-air flying machine. *See* airship.

Diroh   International hotel code for four twin-bedded rooms.

DIS   Destination information system. *See* DMS[1].

disabled passengers by air   *See* invalid passengers by air.

disclaimer of liability   The law of agency in some countries, allows travel agents to avoid responsibility for acts over which they have no control, for the agent is a retailer of services, acting on behalf of a principal who operates or organizes the services sold to a traveller. In many countries, the law prevents agents exempting themselves from liability in case of negligence. In the UK, the Unfair Contract Terms Act imposes limits on the extent to which civil liability for breach of contract, negligence or other breach of duty can be avoided by means of contract terms. Should there be legal action, a test of reasonableness will be applied, which would void any conditions considered unreasonable by a court. The act emphasizes that no organizations, let alone travel companies, can avoid responsibility for their own negligent actions. The British Act also takes away any ability an agent may have had to avoid liability for negligence or breach of contract resulting in death or personal injury, but this will mainly be a problem for principals. At the time of writing, European Commission proposals in respect of package holidays, were to make tour operators/agents completely liable for all aspects of the services provided.

Discover New England   The regional marketing organization of the six US New England States: Connecticut, Massachusetts, Maine, New Hampshire, Rhode Island and Vermont. *See* www.discovernewengland.org

discriminatory pricing   In the USA when transportation undertakings set fares for groups of people such as the elderly or students, other members of the public can attack the rates on the grounds that because they are not eligible to use them, they have been discriminated against unfairly, thus frequently leading to the banning of this type of fare. Such fares are not banned in Europe or most other areas. *See* yield management.

disembark   To leave a form of passenger transport, such as a ship, aircraft or vehicle.

DISG   Data Interchange Sub Group of IATA.

DISH[1]   Data Interchange Specifications Handbook of IATA.

DISH[2]   The European EDI standard for the transport industry. *See* Electronic Data Interchange.

disintermediation   *See* intermediation.

disk or **disc**   Most small computers – PCs (personal computers), used in the travel industry store the data they handle on hard disks which are coated so that they are magnetizable like the tapes used in cassette or video recorders. Storage capacities of 100 gigabytes are now common. Floppy disks were so called because they were flexible. They were cheap but wore out quite quickly. They came in two sizes, 8 in. and 5.25 in. Double density, double-sided 3.5 in. disks were the norm; they are still called floppies although they are stiff! Optical disks/CDs with their huge capacity are now the standard.

disk drive   When associated with the computer, the equipment that physically spins the record disks and at the same time enables information stored on the disks to be read, altered or added.

dispatcher   Name given to a device which controls and organizes the running of trains on a specified area of track. The name is also used loosely, both to describe a complete dispatch centre or location, and the people who manage the device, performing the function of train dispatching. *See* ATC[6] (automatic train control).

dispense bar   In a hotel or restaurant, a bar that only services the waiting staff, rather than customers themselves; similarly, the wine waiter may get wine for customers from a dispense cellar.

displacement effect   A result of tourism development, which takes employment and other economic resources away from established local industries, such as farming and fishing.

display bias (of a CRS) *See* CRS rules for neutrality.

display status   In a CRS display, the availability status shows whether the transport or facilities requested are available, on request, or if there is a waiting list etc.

distance-learning packages   Modern name for correspondence courses.

DIT   Domestic Independent Travel is an American term for an independent inclusive tour undertaken entirely within that country.

DMC[1]   Destination management company. *See* ground handler.

DMC[2]   Directional Minimum Check. Abbreviation normally used in connection with IATA fare construction system.

DMCP   Destination Management Certified Professional. *See* www.adme.org

DME   Distance measuring equipment (aviation term).

DMS[1]   Destination management system; an accessible computerized database containing comprehensive information about a diverse range of tourism-related services offered in a distinct geographical area. This may be as small as a single resort or coverage for a whole country.

'Accessible' implies that by definition, a DMS has been designed to distribute the information it contains both to the public and the travel industry. Although often, the general term is also used for non-booking systems. DMSs may have inbuilt reservation capabilities; such a system being more correctly known as a CRIS (Central Reservation and Information System). The plethora of companies that have designed DMSs has resulted in attempts to differentiate their systems; for example, reference may be made to a DDS, a destination database system, while if the system's main purpose is to provide transport-related information, it may be a TrIS (Travel Information System). The West Virginia Division of Tourism began using the most advanced statewide tourism database system in the USA on 26 March 2001. The system allows callers to the state's 1-800-CALL WVA tourism hotline, as well as visitors to the www. callwva.com web site, to receive instant fulfilment of their information requests. It can be used to respond to any inquiry regardless of origin – web, e-mail, telephone, regular mail or fax and can respond via the same media. Dimitrios Buhalis in his book *e-Tourism* has coined the term Destination Integrated Computerized Information and Reservation Management System to designate a system providing both destination management and booking capabilities; the acronym DICIRMS, is not, however in general use. *See* www.callwva.com

Pauline Sheldon, author of CAB International publication *Tourism Information Technology*, summarizes some of the information that might be available in a DMS. 'Information on both private and public facilities. For the private sector this includes information on accommodation (types, classifications, locations, rates, facilities and availability); transportation (modes, schedules, destinations, prices and availability); tours (components, sightseeing, activities, dates and availability); attractions, events and entertainment, (descriptions, locations, prices, opening hours and availability) and restaurants (type of cuisine, location, size, price range and hours of opening). For the public sector, information should be in-

cluded on parks, museums and galleries (opening hours, descriptions, entrance fees, locations and maps); public transportation (modes, schedules, destinations, prices and availability); environmental (traffic conditions, weather reports, ski conditions and beach conditions) and legal requirements (border controls and health requirements).'

DMS² Destination marketing system. *See* DMS immediately above.

DMU Distance measuring unit (aviation term).

DNR Den Norske Reisebransforening – The Norwegian national travel agency organization.

docent North American term for a local guide for an area or at an attraction or site of tourist interest. Often unpaid.

dock A berth, pier or quay, or as a verb, the act of a ship coming alongside a berth, pier or quay.

dog watch Watches are periods of duty at sea; the dog watches are from 16.00 to 18.00 and from 18.00 to 20.00. *See* times at sea.

dome car *See* bubble car.

domestic add-on When air fares for internal travel within a country are combined with international fares, the amount to be added on in respect of the domestic sectors is usually less than the price at which those sectors are sold for independent domestic travel. Also, add-ons vary according to the type of international air fare involved. Thus, there are a series of amounts to add on to a fare from London to an international destination when the journey is based on a normal yearly first-class fare, and another series when it is tourist class. Different add-on amounts will apply to excursion or other special air fares and to ITX fares. Add-on fares are used to construct through international fares to and from points not otherwise published in an airline's flight tariff manual.

domestic escorted tour American terminology for an inclusive tour taking place entirely within the USA.

domestic excursionist A day tripper, returning to their starting point on the same day, and making their trip within one country. Typical variables of the meaning of the term, when examining statistics from different countries are: limitations concerning travel purpose, e.g. leisure travellers only included; duration e.g. trip lasting more than 3 h and less than 24 h; whether those making an overnight stay are excluded; whether for statistical purposes, only those starting from and returning to their normal place of residence or home are counted. *See* excursionist for internationally-accepted definitions.

Domestic General Rules Tariff   *See* DGR.

domestic hub   *See* hub and spoke.

domestic independent travel   *See* DIT.

domestic tourism   Tourism within the borders of one country. *See* tourism for definitions of that word.

domestic tourist   A person normally resident in a country, undertaking a journey for the purposes of tourism within the borders of that country. In some literature, the term is *not* restricted to residents.

Dominican Republic National Travel Agency Organization   *See* ADAVI.

Dominican Republic Tourism Council   *See* www.dominicana.com

door to door   A transport or other service picking up from actual departure point and concluding at the actual destination, for example, starting from a passenger's home and taking them by various means of transportation to a foreign hotel.

dormette   *See* airline seats.

dormitory   A large bedroom with sleeping facilities for many people. Many youth hostels, for example, only offer dormitory accommodation.

dory   A small American fishing boat, popular in New England. Typically, it is narrow, high sided, has pointed ends and is around 6 or 7 m long.

dot matrix printer   Associated with a computer system, this type of printer punches out characters with fine needles forming a matrix of dots. Print quality is not high, moreover print speed is not comparable to an inkjet or laser printer.

DOT[1]   Date of travel.

DOT[2]   Department of Trade in the UK.

DOT[3]   Department of Transportation in the USA, which from 1 January 1985, following the demise of the CAB, took over responsibility for the remaining parts of US Airline Industry Regulation. *See* airline deregulation in the USA for fuller explanation. The US DOT is not solely responsible for air travel matters, but also encompasses the Federal Highway Administration, Federal Railroad Administration and Coast Guard service. *See* DOT Internet site www.dot.gov

double   Abbreviation for a double-bedded room, a cause of constant trouble in the travel business. Often, a honeymoon or other couple require a double bed, but receive a room with two single beds. Wording such as 'one double bed required' must be used to avoid misunderstanding.

double-decker   A two-deck mode of transport such as a London bus.

double-double   US term for a room which can take four people; often, such a room has two double beds.

double occupancy   The normal rate for a twin or double hotel room is based on occupancy by two persons. There is usually a higher charge for single occupancy of a double room.

downgraded passenger   A passenger who travelled in a lower class of service than that to which he was entitled.

downline   North American term for the remainder of a multi-sector journey, part of which has been travelled; may also be called continuing space.

downtime   A period of time when a computer system is not operative. A curse of the travel industry because few travel principals will go to the expense of maintaining two entirely separate computer systems, one for use as a backup.

Doxey's tourist/host contact index   *See* tourist/host contact index.

DPAS   Now obsolete. Acronym stood for Document Printing and Accounting System which, following the acquisition of Computer Communications goodwill by British Airways subsidiary Travicom, became known as PAMS (President Agency Management System). This too is now obsolete, support for it having ended in 1999, even though it was the UK market leader in the field of computerized ticketing and accounting systems for travel agents with around 300 installations, more than all of the other systems put together.

DPM   Downtown people mover.

DPP   Default Protection Plan. North American term for travel insurance which covers against the possibility of financial failure of their provider of the travel services contracted.

DPTAC Disabled Persons Transport Advisory Committee in the UK. A voluntary code of practice has been introduced by the UK Department for Transport 'Access to Air Travel for Disabled People' which targets the needs of individuals with a disability from the moment they book their flight to their return journey home. Recommendations in the Code concentrate on meeting the needs of disabled people when booking their flight, travelling to the airport, using facilities within the terminal building and aircraft and provides a comprehensive resource for the travel industry to follow. The Code was developed in association with the Airport Operators Association, the Association of British Travel Agents, British Air Transport Association. *See* www.dptac.gov.uk

DR Dead reckoning (aviation and maritime navigation term).

draft *See* draught.

draught The depth of the bottom of a ship (the keel) below waterline. (The US spelling is draft.)

dressing at sea It is customary to dress informally on the first and last days of a voyage as well as during the day, and on Sundays. Evening dress is normal for both men and women for cruises ex-UK. But on cruises starting from foreign ports, often there is more informality. Some cruise brochures specify that the wearing of a jacket and tie in the evening is compulsory for men.

Drive Away Cheques Avis concept which provided vouchers entitling the holder to one day's unlimited European rental of a car, the size of which was determined by the price of the cheque. Unused cheques were exchangeable for cash at any time without loss.

driverless trains The concept has been established on the French automated metro VAL network. In Singapore, the North-East line became the first steel-wheeled heavy metro driverless service in 2002. In Germany, following tests of two driverless S Bahn trains between Pirna and Dresden, services have been introduced. In the US, Airtrain is driverless. It is a paradox that despite public safety fears, by avoiding all possibility of driver error, driverless trains are likely to avoid many of the tragic accidents of the past. For full details *see* VAL.

drivers' hours in Europe The authoritative document covering this subject in the UK was published by the Department of Transport (PSV 375(8/86). There are three sets of rules, EC, AETR and Domestic. The EC/AETR rules apply to all international journeys of passenger vehicles with ten or more seats. Regular services inside the EC on routes exceeding 50 km using vehicles with 16 or more seats have EEC rules applied to them rather than domestic and the same applies to all UK excursions, tours and private hire using vehicles with 16 or more seats.

Originally, EC drivers' hours rules were a daily limit of 9 h which could be extended to 10 h twice a week only. Furthermore, there was a continuous driving limit of 4.5 h after or during which a break of not less than 45 min had to be taken. Some reference works take no account of the 1985 change; the daily driving maximum rose from 9 h to 10 and the longest permitted continuous spell of driving without a break from 4 h to 4.5 h. Also from 1985, coach and lorry drivers were allowed to take the wheel for up to 56 h a week instead of the previous maximum of 48. In most cases, under EC rules, the use of a tachograph is required by law.

AETR rules apply if a journey goes through a non-EC country. Drivers' hours requirements are similar but there are minor exceptions; for example, the maximum period of continuous driving is 4 h, which may be increased to 4.5 h to enable a journey to be conveniently broken or completed. Daily driving is only 8 h.

UK domestic rules are less restrictive, with a daily driving limit of 10 h on any working day and a continuous driving limit of 5.5 h after which a break of at least 30 min must be taken for rest, or 8.5 h, as long as breaks totalling 45 min are taken during the driving period and a 30-min break afterwards.

This entry only summarizes a series of very detailed complex regulations; road transport professionals need to consult the actual legislation.

driving hours *See* drivers' hours in Europe.

DROM Dynamic runway occupation measuring system (aviation terminology).

droops *See* Airframe.

drop-off charges *See* one-way car rental charges.

DRS Direct Reference Systems. For details *see* Sabre.

DRV Deutsche Reiseburo-Verband; the German Travel Agents' Association.

dry lease Hire of an airplane, ship or vehicle without any other service. Vessels and aircraft are often chartered long term on this basis. *See also* wet lease.

Dryden Was one of Prestel's six computers.

DSG Federal German Sleeping and Dining Car Company. *See* European Rail sleeping cars.

DST Daylight saving time.

DTM Delegação de Turismo da Madeira.

DTS Defense Travel System. *See* MTMC.

Dubai Department of Tourism *See* www.dubaitourism.co.ae

dude ranch A ranch in the USA, the main function of which is a tourist attraction or vacation destination, rather than raising livestock. The first one was founded in Sheraton, Wyoming by brothers Howard, Alden and Willis Eaton in 1904.

dugout A type of canoe made by digging out the inside of half a tree trunk. *See* canoe.

dumb terminal A VDU (CRT) which cannot perform any functions other than displaying on-the-screen messages received from a computer and sending back messages from a keyboard, unlike an intelligent terminal or PC, which incorporates some processing capability.

dumb waiter A small lift operating between a kitchen and restaurant on different floors, transporting food, used crockery etc.

dump printer A printer attached to a VDU (CRT) which merely reproduces or dumps a copy of the information currently shown on the screen.

dump waiter Same as a dumb waiter; use of term has arisen because of misunderstanding of the English language.

dumping Selling at an uneconomic price, usually below cost. The term is usually used in a pejorative sense, by producers complaining that their sales at normal prices are adversely affected. An empty transportation seat is valueless after departure, which may mean that it could be 'economic' to sell seats at any price, rather than allow them to be empty, in some circumstances. A more clear-cut travel industry example is where countries are desperate to earn foreign currency, and 'dump' below-cost seats outside their home market.

dupe Travel industry jargon for a duplicate booking; it usually means that in error, two bookings have been made for the same person. But some travel staff use the term to mean that the same travel facilities have been double-booked for different clients. In *Authentically English*, Verite Reily Collins states that dupe means the provision of an extra coach when there are too many passengers for the regular service.

duplex A hotel suite on two levels with internal stairs between the two parts.

duplicate reservation Official IATA definition is a condition which arises when two or more reservations are made for the same passenger(s) when it is evidenced that the passenger(s) will be able to use only one, except that a request to change an itinerary, whether or not it is so identified, is not considered a duplicate reservation.

Dutch Board of Tourism *See* www.holland.com *and* www.visitholland.com

Dutch National Travel Agency Organization *See* ANVR.

duty-free sales It was estimated in March 1993 that worldwide duty-free sales were over US$15 billion, around 52% of which were in Europe and around US$2.33 billion of which was in EC member countries. The EC ended duty-free sales for journeys within the EC from mid-1999, maintaining them for trips from the EC to other parts of the world. Most governments add high taxes or customs duties to alcoholic drinks, tobacco products and perfumes, amongst other products. An airborne aircraft or ship on an international journey, is held to be outside the jurisdiction of any particular state, so that the goods on board can be sold without the duty. However, journeys within the EC are treated as domestic, for the purposes of duty-free allowances. This principle has been extended by the development of huge duty-free shops at many of the world's airports and ports, situated so that purchases can only be taken with passengers on their international journeys. *See* customs declaration.

DV   Direct vision (aviation term).

DVOR   Doppler very high frequency omni-range directional navigation beacon (aviation term).

DVWG   Deutsche Verkchrswissenschaftliche Gesellschaft, the German Institute of Transport.

dynamic packaging   Arrangement by travellers themselves of the individual elements of package holidays by booking flights or other travel and accommodation etc. through the Internet. *See also* self packaging *and* IBE (Internet Booking Engine).

E

E111 Certificate available to UK citizens for use when travelling in the EU for a 'temporary' visit, outside the member state of normal residence. It acts as evidence of entitlement to state-provided emergency free medical treatment at the same level as provided to local nationals. Can be used up to December 2005 (provided issued after 1 June 2004, when form changed), when it will be replaced with the European Health Insurance Card. For details and to download form *see* www.dh.gov.uk Forms are also available from UK post offices.

EAASY Sabre *See* Sabre.

EADI Electronic altitude display indicator.

EAG European Action Group of IATA.

EAP Experimental aircraft project.

Early Bird air fare Obsolescent term for Advanced Purchase Excursion air fare (APEX).

early bird discount The price reduction received by early bookers on, for example, a package holiday, cruise or conference. A date is specified by which a reservation must be made to gain the discount.

early booking The 2003 CEN/European Standard official definition of an early booking is 'Travel booking made within a limited period of time after the publication of the travel description, in connection with a price reduction and/or other benefits.' This is not correct! The wording is ordinary language in general use in the travel industry; it could, for example, mean a booking made a long time before departure, in contrast to a 'late booking' which has been made a short time before departure.

EAS Equivalent air speed.

EASA European Aviation Safety Agency; EC agency created in 2003, initially responsible for drafting new rules for aviation safety regarding the certification of aeronauatical products and approval of organizations and staff engaged in their maintenance. During the life of this dictionary, the EASA will gradually replace the JAA and will become responsible for approval of air operations in Europe and their safety. *See* www.easa.eu.int

EASG European Airports Steering Group of IATA.

EasyRes A viewdata-based CRS through which agents mainly book the discount classes of some scheduled airlines and charter air seats.

EAT Expected approach time.

EATA East Asia Travel Association.

EATCHIP European Air Traffic Control Harmonization and Integration Programme.

EBAA European Business Aircraft Association's stated objectives are 'To promote, develop, improve and safeguard the efficient transporting of business personnel and goods by aircraft owned/operated for that purpose'. See www.ebaa.org

EBTA European Business Travel Association, which represents travel manager's associations from 11 European countries. *See* www.pws.prserv.net/ebta.org

EC neutral CRS rules *See* European neutral CRS rules; *also* EC Code of Conduct for computerized reservation systems, Appendix IV.

ECAC European Civil Aviation Conference. Formed in 1955 following proposals by Council of Europe to achieve coordination in intra-European air transport. Twenty countries are members. Major work concerns economic aspects such as passenger fares and cargo rates. *See* www.ecac.ceac.org.uk

ECAM Electronic centralized aircraft monitor.

ECAR North American term for an economy-class rail carriage.

ECB[1] Electronic control box of an aircraft's auxiliary power unit.

ECB[2] EDIFACT Coordination Board of IATA.

ECMT European Conference of Ministers of Transport. *See* Interbus Agreement for international coach traffic agreement.

economy car   *See* ECAR.

economy class   Term for a class of air travel that has less space and is considerably cheaper than first class. Also called tourist class or coach class by some airlines.

economy European rail fares   Reduced rate rail travel available from the UK only to a limited number of destinations in West Germany, including the main towns: Bonn, Bremen, Dusseldorf, Frankfurt, Hamburg, Hanover, Munich and Stuttgart. Travel from Britain must be by the Dover or Folkestone to Ostend night service or the Harwich to Hook of Holland day service.

ecotourism   Tourism which takes account of environmental, cultural and social considerations; colloquially, 'green' tourism. *See* tourism, sustainable for further detail on topic.

Ecotourism Society   (in the USA) Now known as The International Ecotourism Society (TIES) which promotes sustainable tourism. *See* www.ecotourism.org *and* tourism, sustainable for further detail on topic.

ECTAA   The Association of European Community Travel Agents and Tour Operators national associations. Has a full-time secretariat based in Brussels and is recognized by the EC as the representative body within the EC in this sphere. The English translation of the full title is the 'Group of National Travel Agents and Tour Operators Associations in the EU'. *See* www.ectaa.org

ECU   European Currency Unit; now obsolete. In April 1975, the EEC created a European Unit of Account (EUA). Following the introduction of the European Monetary System (EMS) in 1979, this EUA was renamed the ECU. The unit was composed of specific amounts of EC member country currencies and was, therefore, much less volatile than an individual EEC currency. Since 21 September 1989 when the peseta and escudo were added, the proportions of the ECU became German mark 30.1%; French franc 19%; UK pound 13%; Italian lira 10.15%; Dutch florin 9.4%; Belgian franc 7.6%; Spanish peseta 5.3%; Danish krone 2.45%; Irish punt 1.1%; Portuguese escudo and Greek drachma 0.8% each and Luxembourg florin 0.3%. In theory, many of these proportions were taken over by the euro, in respect of those countries which joined. The ECU was widely used in the travel industry for settling foreign exchange debts.

Ecuador Ministry of Tourism   *See* www.vivecuador.com

Ecuador National Travel Agency Organization   *See* AEVT.

Edexcel Foundation   (in the UK) For up-to-date details of travel and tourism qualifications, access www.edexcel.org.uk Mainly offers sub-degree, craft- and supervisory-level courses; a substantial range is offered in the travel and tourism sphere. The letters BTEC originally stood for the Business and Technology Education Council; but following mergers, the Edexcel Foundation was formed, absorbing BTEC. These letters have been retained by Edexcel as a brand name, although the acronym no longer means anything. For example, the BTEC in Travel and Tourism is one of many UK BTEC National Awards. A 2-year college Higher National Diploma (HND) course for 17–19 year-olds, is designed to meet the skills and training needs of tour operators and travel agents. The following listing is of existing Edexcel Travel and Tourism Qualifications and those submitted to the QCA for the National Qualifications Framework:

BTEC First Diploma in Travel and Tourism

BTEC National Award in Travel and Tourism

BTEC National Certificate in Travel and Tourism

BTEC National Diploma in Travel and Tourism

BTEC Higher National Certificate & Diploma in Travel and Tourism Management

BTEC Level 1 Introductory Certificate and Diploma in Hospitality, Travel & Tourism

Level 2 BTEC Diploma in Travel Operations

Level 2 BTEC Certificate in Preparation for Air Cabin Crew Service

Level 3 BTEC Diploma in Travel Operations

GCSE in Leisure & Tourism (Double Award)

Foundation GNVQ in Leisure & Tourism
Intermediate GNVQ in Leisure & Tourism
NVQ level 2 in Travel Services (Leisure Travel, Business Travel, Call Centre Operations)
NVQ level 2 in Travel Services (Tour Operations – Head Office Operations)
NVQ level 2 in Travel Services (Tour Operations – Resort Operations)
NVQ level 3 in Travel Services (Leisure and Business Travel)
NVQ level 3 in Travel Services (Supervising)
NVQ level 3 in Travel Services (Tour Operations – Resort Operations)
NVQ level 3 in Travel Services (Tour Operations – Head Office Operations)
Advanced VCE in Travel & Tourism
Advanced VCE (Double Award) in Travel & Tourism

EDGARS Electronic Goods Airline Reference System of IATA.

EDI *See* Electronic Data Interchange.

EDIFACT *See* Electronic Data Interchange.

EDLP Every day low price; a low air fare without restrictions as to advance purchase, day or date of travel etc. – it is business travel jargon. *A list of 70 other business travel related entries follows* corporate travel contracts, *some of which lead to further entries.*

EDP Electronic Data Processing is the terminology to describe what all computers undertake.

education in tourism in the UK *See* LTSN.

educational UK industry term for a trip usually arranged by a tourist board, tour operator or transportation company in order to familiarize travel industry staff with the facilities. In North America known as a fam trip or familiarization tour.

EEC Electronic engine control of an aircraft.

EEC Memorandum 2 In 1981, the European Commission proposed the application of the Treaty of Rome Competition rules to airline agreements. The second memorandum appeared in March 1984, advocating that in the long term, the EEC should have a common air transport policy. Encouraging competition and flexibility, the EEC wanted,

'The efficient and innovative airline to benefit, encourage expansion and thus employment and better meet consumer needs.' The memorandum was historic in that there was acceptance that deregulation of air transport similar to that which has occurred in America, was not appropriate to Europe. Airline statistics showed that over 60% of total costs such as fuel, navigation and landing charges were outside airlines' control. The European Commission recommended that pooling agreements should be more competitive, some smaller airlines should be allowed to operate scheduled flights on some routes and that there should be no route or rate regulation on the operation of aircraft with fewer than 25 seats. *See* deregulation.

EET Estimated elapsed time. *See* elapsed time.

EETC Enhanced equipment trust certificate (aviation term).

EEW Equipped empty weight (aviation term).

EFAS Electronic flash approach lighting system (aviation term).

EFCT European Federation Conference Towns. *See* www.efct.com

eff In North America, sometimes used as an abbreviation for effective; for example, when followed by a date, it might mean that a rate or facility is effective or operational from that date.

efficiency North American hospitality term for a room with cooking facilities. Sometimes called a 'studio apartment'. In Europe called self-catering apartment or accommodation.

EFFS Electronic Fares Filing System for Europe. *See* SITA for more details.

EFIS Electronic flight instrument system.

EFMS Experimental flight management system.

EFP Equivalent fare paid. Abbreviation normally used in connection with IATA fare construction system, when the air fare has been paid or calculated in a currency different from the country of payment.

EFT Electronic Funds Transfer is the term describing money movement automatically. For example, modern credit cards can be read by a machine. Where the card has been used to purchase goods or services, the machine can also initiate computerized instructions to debit the card-holder's account and credit the seller's account, all without any human interference.

EFTA Essex Federation of Travel Agents, a member of Worldchoice in the UK.

EGNOS European geostationary navigation overlay system.

EGPWS Enhanced ground proximity warning system.

EGT Engine exhaust temperature (aviation term).

Egyptian National Travel Agency Organization Egyptian Chamber of Tourism and Travel Agencies.

Egyptian State Tourist Office *See* www.egypttourism.org *and* www.touregypt.net

EH Within the Eastern Hemisphere. *See* routing.

EHIC European Health Insurance Card. *See* entry under this heading *and* www.dh.gov.uk

EHM Engine heavy maintenance (aviation term).

EHMA European Hotel Managers Association. *See* www.ehma.com

EHSI Electronic horizontal situation indicator (aviation term).

EICAS Engine indication and crew alert system (aviation term).

EIS Engine instrument system (aviation term).

EL End light of an airport runway (aviation term).

El Salvador National Travel Agency Organization *See* ASAV.

elapsed time Actual time taken to travel between two points. Timetables show local times; to calculate elapsed time, time changes must be taken into account. *See* GMT *and* times at sea.

elbow Slang expression for money paid by a traveller to a transport employee for carriage, and improperly retained by that employee.

elderhostel Travel and education programmes for senior citizens (over 60s) run by US grouping of schools, colleges and universities.

Electra 225 This British train's title arises because of its 225 kph (approx. 140 mph) top speed. It was planned to enter service in 1987 between London, Glasgow and Edinburgh reducing journey times by around 30 minutes. But it was never introduced. The Electra 225 would not itself tilt, although it was designed to pull some tilting coaches based on the APT concept. Only with some tilting can reasonably smooth passenger rides be provided on the twisty London–Glasgow route.

electric vehicles *See* hybrid vehicles.

electronic airline-ticketing *See* e-ticketing.

Electronic Data Interchange Where all an organization's records are kept on computer without any printed or handwritten information and where this organization is then linked electronically to its clients and suppliers, who are also fully computerized. Thus all inter-company transactions are undertaken through a computer network.

Clearly the number of companies following an EDI philosophy in any industry or country is critical, for the greatest benefits can only be obtained when the majority of an organization's transactions are electronic. The arrival of the paperless office is being held back by the pace of the slowest. At the time of writing, in the UK travel industry, travel agents' airline sales are recorded on their computers at the time of automated ticket issue. But the ticket coupons were analysed and entered again by Bank Settlement Plan Authorities to produce an agent's sales return. In December 1989, BSP began work on a scheme to enable this information to be transferred electronically. The scheme became live in 1992.

EDIFACT (Electronic Data Interchange For Administration, Commerce and Transport) is the main EDI standard which covers basic rules governing the syntax and structure of electronic messages, which has been created under the auspices of the International Standards Organization, the United Nations and many national standards organizations. In Europe, from this main standard, many industry groups have been formed to define sector EDI standards. The most important for readers of this book are ATIS, which covers tourism in general, DISH for transport, UNICORN for vehicle ferries and TRADACOMS for retailers.

Electronic Fares Filing System for Europe *See* SITA for details.

Electronic Funds Transfer *See* EFT.

Electronic Reservations Service Provider *See* ERSP.

Electronic Ticket Delivery Network *See* ETDN.

Electronic Travel Authority System *See* ETAS.

Electronic Travel Distribution Network *See* ETDN.

electrostatic printer Associated with a computer system this type of printer uses photocopier technology. Low cost but poor quality for example, fax rolls.

Elgar Elgar provides UK Galileo and Sabre GDS users with a fully integrated information, reservation, ticketing and accounting system for both domestic and international Eurostar rail travel. *See* ATOC *and* Eurotunnel.

ELT Emergency locator transponder (aviation term).

ELVA European local vendor access is a Sabre project to provide European subscribers access to tour operators and other local suppliers.

EMA Extra mileage allowance. Abbreviation normally used in connection with IATA fare construction system.

EMAS The Eco Management and Audit Scheme of the EU.

embark To board a ship, aircraft or other passenger transport vehicle.

embarkation agent The cruise line equivalent of airline check-in staff. In the same way that an airline may appoint a servicing organization to undertake their ground handling, so a cruise line may outsource this function. This North American originating term has not crossed the Atlantic very well! In the USA it means the person who performs this task; but in Britain and Europe, an agent is an intermediary, so that servicing organizations working for a number of cruise lines may be called embarkation agents.

Emble International Hotel Code for five single-bedded rooms.

Embratur Brazilian Tourist Board. *See* www.embratur.gov.br

EMC Engineering and Maintenance Committee of IATA.

EMF The European Motel Federation is a grouping of independent hotels particularly suitable for motorists.

emigrant A foreigner entering a country to take up permanent residence or a person leaving a country to take up permanent residence abroad. Special emigrant fares sometimes apply with increased luggage allowance, e.g. emigrants to Canada travelling at economy air fares have the first-class baggage allowance.

empennage *See* air frame.

employment bureau A company that finds employees for organizations needing members of staff and which finds jobs for employees looking for work. In most countries these organizations must be registered with the local authority. There are employment bureaux specializing in locating staff or jobs in the travel industry throughout the world.

employment tourism multiplier *See* tourism multiplier.

Empress Club Formerly name of Canadian Airlines International/Wardair Frequent Flyers Club.

empty leg A positioning journey of a mode of transport; term particularly used when an aircraft or ship travels without passengers from its home base to the starting point of a revenue journey. These journeys without passengers are also referred to as 'deadhead'; sometimes, there are empty legs at the start or end of a charter series: *see* back to back.

EMS Excess Mileage Surcharge. Abbreviation normally used in connection with IATA fare construction system.

EMU[1] Eccentric Mailbox User utilizing the UK Prestel or other viewdata mailbox systems to send unsolicited amusing, obscene or stupid messages.

EMU[2] Engine maintenance unit (aviation term).

en pension Also full pension. Hotel rate inclusive of three meals daily.

en suite Refers to a hotel room with bath and/or shower and toilet facilities, usually separated from the living accommodation. But usage varies; for example, in France, en suite toilet facilities do not have to be separated from the room.

end-to-end travel management Comprehensive automated system covering both travel management and associated expense management. End-to-end systems are corporate-wide systems linking finance, human resources and travel management. Not only do systems enable trips to be planned, requested and booked, but also expenses are recorded and claimed. Adherence to company travel policies is automatically enforced.

Endeavour Telewests's travel industry communication service in the UK. Fastrak 2000 is an enhanced viewdata service allowing agents to connect to and view four or more tour operators at one time. Fastrak operates within Windows 95/98/2000/NT4. Worldspan Go and Worldspan Net, with or without ticketing, are available through an agent's Endeavour connection. Cyberes is Endeavour's real-time on-line flight consolidation system for agents. All the services are available on a dial-up basis; on a permanently connected leased line or through a fast ADSL connection. Endeavour offers Internet reservations as an alternative to viewdata; agents can search multiple tour operators' systems at once based on customer criteria, such as specific resort facilities. *See* www.endeavour.co.uk

end-on   Type of air fare construction prohibited for many excursion fares from UK. Excursion fares from Britain to a point cannot usually be combined with excursion fares from that point to another destination if the combination cuts the lowest through fare. Consult airline tariffs for full regulations.

endorsements   Authority, shown on a ticket of a carrier, to transfer traffic to another carrier (mainly IATA airlines).

EnglandNet project   Project to enable planning and booking of English holidays through the Internet. *See also* ETNA.

English breakfast   Generally served in the UK and Ireland. Usually includes fruit or fruit juice; hot or cold cereal; bacon, ham, sausages or kippers; eggs; toast; butter; jam or marmalade; and tea or coffee.

English Heritage   England's leading conservation organization responsible for over 400 historic attractions including Stonehenge, Dover Castle, Osborne House and Tintagel Castle. *See* www.english-heritage.org.uk

English service   Type of restaurant service. *See* silver service.

English Tourism Council   From July 1999 until April 2003, the UK government body responsible for promoting tourism within England. In 2003, the British Tourist Authority joined with the English Tourism Council to form a new UK government body, VisitBritain (*see entry under this heading*).

English Tourist Board   Renamed English Tourism Council in 1999. *See* BTA.

ENTAF   The Environment Task Force of IATA.

ENTER   The major worldwide annual conference concerning information technology in travel and tourism. The 12th annual ENTER conference took place in January 2005 in Innsbruck, organized by IFITT, the International Federation for Information Technology and Travel and Tourism. Typically there are 3 days of case studies, presentations, discussions and interactive workshops with approximately 100 speakers. Covers issues in IT and travel and tourism trends, emerging technologies and applications, and focus in particular on multi-channel strategies for marketing, distribution and communication. *See* www.ifitt.org

Enterprise   Was the name of one of Prestel's six computers. Also was the brand name for one of Owners Abroad's inclusive holidays brochures. Now a brand name of First Choice holidays, a UK tour operator.

entry modes for a CRS/GDS   *See* CRS/GDS entry modes.

entry tax   Official tax raised on entering a country.

entry to countries   *See* visa[2].

ENVISTAT   The European Space Agency's £1.4 billion earth observation satellite launched on 1 March 2002.

Envoy   Title of American Express special travel service provided for Amex Gold Card holders.

EOBT   Estimated off block time. *See* block speed.

EP   European plan; an accommodation-only tariff, which includes no meals.

EPIC   Electronic propulsion integrated control system (aviation term).

EPNdB   Equivalent perceived noise decibel.

EPR   Engine pressure ratio (aviation term).

EPROMS   Erasable Programmable Read Only Memory. *See* ROM.

equator   A great circle of the earth, whose plane is perpendicular to the axis. A great circle is any circumference of the earth which is of maximum size and which, therefore, includes the earth's centre in its plane. Lines of latitude are counted North or South, starting from the equator as zero.

equivalent fare paid   *See* EFP.

ERA   European Regions Airlines Association. Started in 1981 by five airlines and five manufacturers, by 2000, there were 83 members and 150 associates. *See* www.eraa.org

ERAST Environmental research aircraft and sensor technology.

Ercaj International Hotel Code for five twin-bedded rooms.

ERIC European Rail Information Circular, published by the Timetable Production Section of the European Rail Passenger Office in the UK.

EROPS Extended range operations (aviation term).

errors and omissions insurance North American term for insurance covering a travel agent's liability following mistakes. In Britain, this is called 'professional indemnity' insurance.

ERSP[1] An ARC Electronic Reservations Service Provider reference or designator indicating that the booking has been made via the Internet.

ERSP[2] An IATA Electronic Reservation Service Provider is a person or organization established on the Internet or other on-line service, promoting reservation information in the same format as that provided by an IATA member, other principal's system or CRS.

ESA European Space Authority.

ESAC Electronic Ticket Authorization Code. *See* e-ticket.

ESAC code *See* within ARC[1].

escort A person responsible for taking care of another. For example, an airline hostess may be assigned to take care of an unaccompanied child. A tour escort is an alternative name for a courier or representative taking care of the passengers on a tour. An escort service may provide a secretary, guide, interpreter, chauffeur or other facilities. The term is also used in connection with the provision of companionship or sex.

escorted tour Otherwise known as a conducted or guided tour. Term common worldwide but not in the UK. The essential characteristics of an escorted tour are payment in advance by travellers, no refund being given for any unused part. A set number of people will travel together and there may be a minimum and maximum number of passengers involved dependent upon operating economics, transport sizes or restrictions and fare rules. All the members of a group must follow a planned itinerary being accompanied by the tour leader or guide or escort.

escrow account Where customers' money is placed in the safe custody of a bank, solicitor or organization of similar standing. The money is only released after the travel services have been performed, thereby protecting the public against failure of the travel company. In Europe, tour operators and travel agents can satisfy the requirements of Package Holiday legislation by operating such a scheme. In the USA approved escrow account schemes meet the requirements under the 'Seller of Travel' laws enacted in the states of California, Oregon and Washington. In the UK, the Travel Trust Association operates this type of scheme for its travel agent and tour operator members.

In the USA, the only escrow scheme approved under ASTA's Tour Operators Program offering consumer protection is the TFPP (Travel Funds Protection Plan). It is an agreement between contracting tour operators and the National City Bank. Individual deposits are received from agents via a tour operator and are deposited in an escrow account controlled exclusively by National City Bank. An ARC account is established for automatic debiting of the air portion of consumer payments. Five days after the tour is completed, the bank releases payment covering land-related costs of a tour, covering, for example, accommodation, car rental and sightseeing, to participating vendors of these services. No consumers' money is available to the tour operator before this. Each passenger's deposit is tracked by booking number and date of return, enabling suppliers and travel agents to verify that money paid by customers is being held in escrow.

ESITO Events Sector Industry Training Organisation in the UK; run from the ACE offices.

Essential Air Services Subsidy *See* hub and spoke.

ESTEREL Ensemble Spécialise de Traitement et de Réservation Electronique, formerly a computer system for French travel agents, which interfaced with Air France, Alpha 3, UTA, Air Inter and other French travel principals' reservation systems. Was the equivalent of Galileo in Britain, START in Germany and Apollo, Mars, Pars and Sabre in the USA.

ESTI European Society of Transport Institutes was formed in October 1984. Its objectives are to make Europe better informed about the facts of transport life and possibilities for the future; to offer constructive criticism on proposals affecting European transport and to keep pressing for the action necessary to increase the effectiveness of transport for the travelling public and European industry. *See* www.citi.ie/citi_sve.htm

Estonian Tourist Board *See* www. visitestonia.com

Estrella Night trains in Spain. These trains have air conditioning in first- and second-class sections and generally have a side aisle. *See* trains.

ET Electronic ticket. *See* e-ticketing.

ET/REA Electronic ticket/refund exchange authorization.

ETA[1] Estimated time of arrival.

ETA[2] Electronic Travel Authority. *See* ETAS below.

ETAG European Tourism Action Group. Set up by the European Travel Commission to report trends in European tourism and recommend action which should be taken by ETC members to exploit market opportunities revealed. *See* ETC[2].

ETAS Electronic Travel Authority System, which enables travel agents to generate authority to travel to Australia for a short stay, electronically. From May 2001 ETAs were obtainable by members of the public over the Internet (*see* web site at the end of this entry). They remove the need for a visa label or stamp in a passport. By the end of October 2000, over 8.53 million ETAs had been issued worldwide since the system came into force in September 1996. The record of the authority to travel is stored on the Australian Immigration Authority's computer. Access to the system is restricted to IATA-appointed travel agents and is only available through Galileo, Sabre, Worldspan and Amadeus computer reservations systems. More than 70 airlines are ETA capable; their system-linked airline partners are also able to access ETAs. There are two main types of ETA; the visitor ETA and the short validity single-entry business (BS-ETA), valid for 3 months, both are free of any government charge. For members of the public, access www.eta.immi.gov.au Issue of either type of visa via this site incurs an AUS$20 service charge.

ETB English Tourist Board; obsolete as replaced by the English Tourism Council in 1999 (for explanation of role *see* BTA). *Also see* www. englishtourism.org.uk

ETC[1] English Tourism Council (for explanation of role *see* BTA). *Also see* www.englishtourism.org.uk For UK national tourism statistics *see* www.staruk.org.uk

ETC[2] The European Travel Commission was founded in 1948 and is not, as the name suggests, a section of the EEC; its coverage being somewhat wider, including representatives from the national tourism authorities of 23 European countries. *See* www.etc-europe-travel.org

ETD Estimated time of departure.

ETDN Electronic Travel Distribution Network in Europe, or Electronic Ticket Delivery Network in North America. A 'neutral' means of enabling travel agents to print tickets and documents at a distant location through a 'third party' system. For example, through such a system, Dutch travel agents can have 'tickets on departure' issued at Amsterdam Schipol Airport.

By the time these words are being read, in the USA, ARC-approved travel agents will be able to arrange for delivery of their customers' tickets on departure at airports via third-party contractors. The ARC has been very strict in deciding that an electronic ticket delivery location will have as its sole travel-related function the delivery of traffic documents on behalf of an approved agent by means of a printer. The ARC will not allow other functions such as travel promotion, counselling, reservations and sales. The ETDN will *not* generate agents' and auditors' coupons of tickets but will function as a satellite ticket printer, so that these coupons will be generated at agency locations.

ETF Was the European Timeshare Federation which ended in February 1998 with the formation of the Organisation for Timeshare in Europe. *See* www.ote-info.com *and* timeshare.

Ethiopian Tourism Commission *See* www.tourismethiopia.org

ethnic tourism *See* tourism, ethnic.

ethnic traffic Travel business which originates from a particular racial group.

e-ticketing Use by an airline of an entirely electronic transaction, covering reservation and ticketing. Travel without a paper ticket is rapidly becoming the norm and paper tickets likely to be unusual within the currency of this dictionary's second edition. IATA has set an end 2007 deadline for paper tickets to finish. The official IATA definition of an electronic ticket is 'the itinerary/ receipt issued by or on behalf of a carrier, the electronic coupons and if applicable, a boarding document'. All the data relating to the passenger's itinerary, fare, class, payment and taxes etc. are stored in an ET record in the database of the carrier that created it. Travellers do not require a paper ticket; this can cause problems when a switch to another airline is needed following a change of travel plans.

E-tickets exist only in an airline's computer system so travellers cannot lose or forget them – they cannot be stolen. As there is no paperwork, tickets can be booked, paid for, cancelled or altered at any time from anywhere. At the airport travellers must present some form of photo ID – usually their passport and a copy of their itinerary. In most cases purchase will have been by credit card – that card must be produced. Documentation for expense claims is provided by mail or fax. British Airways identifies e-ticketed passengers through the magnetic strip or chip on their credit cards, while Lufthansa has issued a smart card associated with their ETIX system to frequent travellers which they have called a ChipCard; travellers' personal and flight details are stored on the card.

It was in November 1994 that UAL introduced electronic tickets on their shuttle routes, offering them on transatlantic routes in November 1997 and 4 months later, transpacific. United achieved another first in June 2000, when, together with Star Alliance partner Air Canada, the world's first interline e-ticket was launched.

In the USA an ET/REA is an Electronic Ticket Refund Exchange Authorization notice which facilitates refunds or exchanges of an e-ticket, in the absence of any document to physically return. An ET/REA must be validated by an airline's Electronic Settlement Authorization Code (ESAC).

ETIX Name of Lufthansa's e-ticketing facility. *See* e-ticketing.

ETKT Electronic ticket record held in an airline's computer. *See* e-ticketing.

ETNA The English Tourist Board Network Automation project. A joint development of the ETB and the 12 UK regional tourist boards to encourage use of information technology throughout the UK's national network of Tourist Information Centres. Initial efforts have concentrated on producing back-office systems to meet mainstream needs of TICs, including an accommodation search facility, matching clients' requirements to their needs; attractions and events information; ETNA Mail, a direct marketing facility; word processing; management functions, including statistical analysis and communications functions allowing access to a range of videotext vehicles. *See also* EnglandNet project.

ETOPS Extended range twin engine operations (aviation term).

ETP Estimated time of penetration (aviation term).

ETTFA European Tourism Trade Fairs Association. *See* www.ettfa.org

EURACA European Air Carrier Assembly organized by the International Air Carrier Association.

Eurailpass A pass permitting unlimited first-class travel on most of Europe's rail and steamer networks, which is only available to people not resident in Europe and *must* be bought before entering Europe. Prices vary according to validity. The Youth Eurorailpass is an equivalent pass covering second-class travel for those aged under 26.

EURCAE European Civil Aviation Equipment Organisation. *See* www. eurocae.org

Euro Business and Prime Business Class Brand name given by Alitalia to passengers immediately adjacent to first class, where passengers paying full economy fares enjoy improved service and facilities. *See* business class for full description.

Eurobudget air fare A single or return tariff only available on non-stop European air services with a maximum validity of one year. Reservations, full payment and ticketing must be undertaken in one transaction at the same time. Reservations may not be changed and cancellation charges are currently around 20% (50% Scandinavian). Passengers wishing to change a Eurobudget booking must upgrade to a higher class.

EuroCity European rail network Brand name of the top European trains which replaced TEE (Trans-Europe Express) in 1987. There is a supplement for travel on almost all EuroCity trains which includes a reserved seat. Most have both first- and second-class seating. All are air-conditioned throughout. To be classed as EuroCity, a train must average at least 90 kph including stops.

Euroclass and First Business Class Brand name given by SAS to passenger area immediately adjacent to first class, where passengers paying full economy fares enjoy improved service and facilities. *See* business class for full description.

EUROCONTROL European Organization for the Safety of Air Navigation. Raises service charges dependent on the distance travelled through a participating country's airspace and the weight of the aircraft. *See* www.eurocontrol.int *and* Single European Sky.

EuroDomino Freedom Pass Name of a European rail pass launched in 1993, providing free rail travel in eight countries for 3, 5 or 8 days during a 1-month period.

Euroforum The IATA Agency Programme Joint Council's Supervisory Board responsible for all aspects of the effect of the IATA Agency Programme on travel agents within Europe.

Eurolines The brand name adopted by the International Road Transport Union in cooperation with 40 European coach operators for their regular international coach lines. A timetable is published annually in English, French, Spanish, German and Italian. *See* www. eurolines.com

Europabus The motor coach system of the European railways. This international network of tourist coach services now operates in 16 European countries. The tours and packages are by luxury coach with multi-lingual tour guides and accommodation in first-class hotels. The name is mistakenly applied to international scheduled coach services, because the brand name was introduced in 1951 to develop an extensive network of express coach services operated by subsidiary undertakings of the various European railway administrations. Overnight accommodation was usually included in the travel prices and at its peak, Europabus operated 56,000 miles of scenic scheduled service coach routes. Although now less extensive, Europabus railway-owned companies will operate in many countries; use any Internet search engine to find services operated. The main European-integrated express coach network now operates under the brand name Eurolines. For details *see* www.eurolines.com

European Aviation Safety Agency *See* EASA *and* www.easa.eu.int

European Business Aircraft Association *See* EBAA.

European Business Travel Association *See* EBTA.

European Civil Aviation Conference *See* ECAC.

European Currency Unit *See* ECU.

European Federation of Conference Towns *See* www.efct.com

European Health Insurance Card Until the end of 2005, an E111 Certificate is available to UK citizens for use when travelling in the EU, outside the member state of normal residence. It acts as evidence of entitlement to free medical treatment at the same level as provided to local nationals; similar arrangements exist in other EU member states. From the end of 2005, it will be replaced with the European Health Insurance Card. As well as all EU member states, the EHIC will be valid in Iceland, Lichtenstein, Norway and Switzerland. For details and to download application form *see* www.dh.gov.uk Forms are also available from UK post offices.

European Hotel Managers Association *See* www.ehma.com

European local vendor access A Sabre CRS project which provided European subscribers access to tour operators and other local suppliers.

European Motel Federation *See* EMF.

European neutral CRS rules Rules undergoing revision; likely to be substantially eased. On 1 July 1989, the EC introduced (and subsequently amended several times) the CRS rules recommended by the European Civil Aviation Conference, set up to agree common standards. The rules state that all carriers should be given equal rights to have flights displayed on a non-discriminatory basis; information generated by a CRS must not be used to gain unfair commercial advantage; the data must be accurate and CRS should be made available to all agents on equal terms. *See* EC Code of Conduct for computerized reservation systems, Appendix III.

European plan (EP) A hotel rate that includes bed only; any meals are extra.

European Quality Alliance Was the name of a group of airlines formed in response to the deregulation of air travel in EC countries. Austrian Airlines, Finnair, SAS and Swissair were the initial members; now they are part of other groupings. *See* airline alliances.

European Rail group travel Price reductions are available at two levels, applicable to groups between ten and 24 passengers and those in excess of 25. Lower fares are available for groups of young people and students. International Rail Collective Tickets, on which the group and journey are detailed are held by a group leader, while the members of the party hold contremarques, small brown slips of paper approximately 4 in. × 3 in. certifying the traveller is part of a group.

European Rail journey breaks Except in Spain, breaks of journey are allowed as frequently as desired without formality, within the validity of a ticket. Only certain tickets specifically limit travel to non-stop journeys. Before resuming Spanish journeys, even when making a connection, passengers must have the correct ticket coupon stamped.

European Rail reservations *See* IRRF.

European Rail services *See* train.

European Rail sleeping cars In Europe these are normally operated by the railway administrations, even though the actual sleeping cars often bear the name of a subsidiary company, such as the German Sleeping and Dining Car Company or the International Sleeping Car Company. Luxembourg, Germany, Denmark, Italy, The Netherlands, Austria, Switzerland, Belgium and France have grouped their international sleeping car services into a pool, market-ing them under the brand name EuroCity Night. (The term TEN, Trans Euro Night, was replaced in 1987, and is obsolete.) The international sleeping car services in these countries are also run under the EuroCity scheme, provided they meet the requirement of maintaining an average speed, including stops, of 90 kph.

European Rail first-class sleeping-car accommodation is in single or double compartments, while second class, usually called tourist, is in two-, three- or four-berth compartments. On many trains a smaller type of one-berth compartment, known as a 'special' is available at a cheaper price than a standard single compartment. Many European sleeping cars have convertible compartments, which can be adjusted to provide single-, double- or three-berth accommodation. First- and second-class passengers thus travel in the same car. There are many anomalies; for example, in most of Europe, a type T2 sleeping car is first or second class, according to whether it has one or two berths. But it is always first class in Spain. The standard double sleeping compartment pictured in Thomas Cook's European timetable is second class in the UK and Norway but first class in the rest of western Europe.

On longer journeys, sleeping cars are placed in a daytime position between 10.00 and 22.00 with the berths converting into seating. At the passengers' wish, berths may be made up from 21.00 or earlier, but only providing all the occupants of a compartment agree.

Sleeping car compartments are regarded as exclusively for ladies or gentlemen, unless persons of different sexes travelling together and occupying all the berths in a compartment are related, such as married couples or family groups. Smoking is forbidden in compartments made up for the night and is only allowed in compartments placed in the daytime position, providing all the other passengers in the compartment agree.

European Regions Airline Association *See* ERA.

European Society of Transport Institutes *See* ESTI.

European Tourism Action Group *See* ETAG.

European Travel Commission *See* ETC.

European Union of Tourist Officers *See* EUTO.

European Union Satellite Printer Location *See* EUSTP Location.

Euroroute One of many alternative plans considered and rejected for the link between Britain and France was the Euroroute scheme involving bridges to islands 7 miles from the British coast and 4 miles from France. Only the central part between these islands would have been linked by a tunnel. This would have carried both road and rail traffic, whereas the railway scheme actually constructed carries cars on standard flat wagons while high-speed rail services run on the same lines. *See* Eurotunnel.

Eurostar *See* Eurotunnel immediately below.

Eurotunnel The title of the company which constructed the Channel Tunnel between Britain and France, the tunnel itself, which opened in 1994, and the vehicle-carrying service.

Summary history of project
- 20 October 1986 – British PM Margaret Thatcher chose Eurotunnel out of four alternatives.
- 14 March 1986 – 55-year concession granted to operators. (Following serious financial problems this was extended to 65 years and then in December 1997 to 99 years.)
- 15 December 1987 – Construction began; tunnel-boring was completed on 28 June 1991.
- 17 May 1993 – Waterloo International rail terminal was completed.
- 20 June 1994 – The first Eurostar train went through the tunnel.
- 25 July 1994 – Freight shuttle services began; this was followed on 22 December 1994 by the start of Eurotunnel passenger shuttle services.
- February 1996 – London and Continental Railways (LCR) was selected to operate the Eurostar trains and develop a high-speed rail link between London and Folkestone. LCR's shareholders were Bechtel, SCB Warburg, National Express Group, Virgin, SNCF/Systra, London Electricity, Ove Arup and Halcrow.
- 6 May 1996 – Inauguration by Queen Elizabeth II and President François Mitterand of Eurostar passenger train service.
- 14 November 1996 – First regular commercial Eurostar passenger rail services between London/Paris and London/Brussels.
- January 1998 – LCR sought £1.2 billion help from government which was rejected; high-speed rail for UK section to be built by Railtrack. First stage of 42 miles from Folkestone to Fawkham Junction to be completed by 2003; second stage of 26 miles to St Pancras by 2007. Although Railtrack is responsible for the design, maintenance and operation, LCR continues as a shell company with legal responsibility to construct both sections of the rail link. Eurostar (UK) will remain part of LCR until 2086, from when it will owned by the UK government. Agreement made that the Inter Capital and Regional Rail Group (ICCR) consortium will assume responsibility for Eurostar. Main shareholders are 34.8% British Airways and 34.8% National Express group.
- 3 June 1998 – ICCR actually took over responsibility for Eurostar on a 12-year contract until 2010. Although LCR continues to own Eurostar, a management fee is to be paid to ICCR.
- 15 December 1998 – Since 3 September 1999, Eurostar services have been jointly operated by Eurostar UK, SNCF (French Railways) and SNCB/NMBS (Belgian Railways).

The Eurotunnel takes two types of traffic. Road vehicles are carried in specially-built trains, called shuttles, while through passenger trains link the UK with other parts of Europe. The UK terminal area for the shuttle service covers a site of around 150 h near Folkestone and the French terminal of similar size at Frethun, near Calais. There are three parallel tunnels. The twin service tunnels have a diameter of 7.6 m and between them is a 4.8 m diameter service tunnel. The tunnels are nearly 50 km long.

The rail shuttles transport all types of road vehicles including cars, caravans, coaches, lorries and motorcycles. The passenger shuttles carry up to 120 cars and 12 coaches together with their passengers. There are three types of shuttle wagon. Double-deck tourist wagons are for private vehicles of less than 1.85 m in height. Single-deck tourist wagons handle cars, caravans and coaches up to 4 m in height and single-deck freight wagons carry lorries up to the same maximum height.

The shuttles and Eurostar/SNCF use the same rail track and equipment. Initially, the train control and signalling equipment have been designed to handle up to 20 shuttles or trains per hour in each direction. When required, this will be capable of upgrading to handle 30 per hour. Journey time from terminal to terminal is 35 min. Rail journey times are currently about 3 h and improvements will cut journey times by a further 20 min. Work has now started on the final section of the Eurostar railway between London and continental Europe with the setting up of a 7.62 m diameter drilling machine which will cut an underground route from Rainham, Essex, to a new St Pancras–Kings Cross terminal. The first train is set to run on 1 January 2007. Stage 1 of the project, North Kent, near the QE II bridge to Dover, has opened bringing the existing Waterloo–Paris time down to 2 hours 40 minutes and London–Brussels to 2 hours 20 minutes. The 180 mph direct service will join the two cities in something just over 2 hours. In 2007, Eurostar services will switch from Waterloo to a new terminal at St Pancras. *See* http://www.ctrl.co.uk/building/route2.htm

The high-speed rail link is sometimes referred to as the CTRL (Channel Tunnel Rail Link), work on which finally began on 1 October 1998.

In 2004 7,276,675 passengers travelled on Eurostar, up 15% on 2003. Sales were £433m, also up 15%. Highest monthly share London/Paris was 68% Eurostar and 32% all the airlines. Between London and Brussels, Eurostar rose to 63%.

Travel agents can access fares, schedules and availability and produce ATB type tickets through the Eurostar Elgar system, via either Galileo or Sabre GDS. For more information about Eurostar, booking, services, fares or availability *see* www.eurostar.com *and* www.eurostar.co.uk

EUSTP Location European Union Satellite Ticket Printer Location. Under IATA regulations, a place where off-premises automated tickets and boarding passes may be issued which is in a different country from the host agency.

EUTO The European Union of Tourist Officers is an international professional body with several thousand members in 30 European countries, all of whom are also members of their own national associations.

EVA Exhibition Venues Association; major UK organization in its sphere. *See* www.exhibitionvenues.com

every day low price A low air fare without restrictions as to advance purchase, day or date of travel etc. – it is business travel jargon. *A list of 70 other business travel related entries follows* corporate travel contracts, *some of which lead to further entries.*

EVS Enhanced vision system (aviation term).

ex Leaving from a place, for example, ex London means departing from London.

excess Insurance term indicating that the customer has to bear the first part of any loss. Currently in the UK, excesses on holiday policies are around £25 to £50 per section. In the USA this is known as a deductible.

excess baggage That part of a traveller's luggage which is greater than the carrier's free allowance. In respect of air travel, set charges are made on routes governed by piece concept rules. On other air routes, charge is 1% of the first-class air fare per kilo of extra baggage. The 2003 CEN/European Standard official definition of excess baggage is 'baggage of a traveller exceeding by number of pieces and/or size and/or weight the allowance included in the price of transport'. This does not take into account that a traveller may declare that the value of their baggage exceeds that which is normally covered; thus an excess baggage ticket *see below* may be for valuation charges.

excess baggage ticket Official IATA definition is a receipt issued by a carrier to a passenger of excess baggage and/or valuation charges.

excess mileage *See* IATA fare construction system.

excess mileage surcharge *See* IATA fare construction system.

exchange control   At the time of writing, there was no restriction on the transfer of money abroad either in the UK or USA. It is common for countries with unfavourable trade balances to restrict the amount of money their residents may take abroad as tourists, or invest abroad. Some countries prohibit the import and export of their currency notes for other reasons, for example, to prevent tax evasion. Typical examples at the time of writing are that import and export of notes to many Eastern European countries are prohibited altogether.

Exchange Order (XO)   A document issued by a provider of travel services or its agent requesting issue of a ticket or provision of other specified services to the person named in the document.

exchange rate   *See* conversion rate[1].

exclusion clauses   In the travel and tourism field, term usually applied to conditions attached to travel insurance policies limiting the cover in certain circumstances. For example, many policies exclude cover for persons over 75 years of age and it is common for claims, arising as a consequence of an illness that pre-existed the insurance, to be excluded.

Unless it is a specific sports policy, skiing and other hazardous pursuits are also usually excluded from the cover provided.

excursion   In the context of an add-on to a main holiday, it is a side trip to a place of touristic interest, which may be for a day, or a longer period. In the context of a person not already on vacation, it is a short journey for touristic purposes, varying too greatly in form for more precise definition. For various associated official definitions *see* excursionist and tourism. *See also* excursion fare.

excursion fare   Usually tourist class return journey fares at a competitive price, designed by transport operators to attract additional or holiday business. There are often minimum or maximum stay requirements or restrictions preventing travel at the discounted rate during peak times. During the 1980s, the terminology has been increasingly applied to many types of discounted fare, for both single and return journeys, e.g. excursion fares valid only or a day,

week or month. Often such fares cannot be combined with other fares. Stopovers en route are seldom permitted at the basic rate. When such fares must be purchased a certain period in advance of travel, they are known as Advance Purchase Excursion Fares (APEX fares).

excursionist   Person undertaking a leisure trip for a period of less than 24 h, specifically defined as such by the 1937 Committee of Statistical Experts of the League of Nations and still has wide general acceptance. The WTO definition only relates to international travel, suggesting that excursionists are temporary visitors, staying less than 24 h in the country visited and not making an overnight stay. A day-tripper, returning to the starting point on the same day, and making that trip within one country, is a domestic excursionist. Fundamental to all these definitions is that remuneration is not received by the person undertaking the trip. Thus, a business person will not usually be classified as an excursionist, unless undertaking a leisure side-trip, but an accompanying spouse will be. Typical variables of the meaning of the term, when examining statistics from different countries are: limitations concerning travel purpose, e.g. leisure travellers only included; duration e.g. trip lasting more than 3 h and less than 24 h; whether those making an overnight stay are excluded; whether for statistical purposes, only those starting from and returning to their normal place of residence or home are counted. *See also* tourism.

Executive Card   Card given by British Airways to identify holder as a frequent and important traveller. Card holders are entitled to use special airport lounges and executive cabin. They can often use first-class check-in desks, although only holding economy class tickets. Similar schemes are promoted by most airlines.

Executive class or cabin   Brand name given by some airlines to passenger area immediately adjacent to first class, where passengers paying full fares can enjoy improved service and facilities, e.g. Aer Lingus, BWIA, Air Canada, Finnair, Air India, Japanese Air Lines,

Northwest, Thai and Varig. For details of other airlines' similar services *see* Ambassador, Business, Club, Euroclass, Galaxy, Gold, Marco Polo, Navigator, Pacific and Preference.

Executive Club Name of British Airways' Frequent Flyer Club. Standard is a 'Blue' card. More perks are offered to those who fly most with BA. The next step entitles a traveller to a Silver card, while those who travel even more with BA receive a Gold or ultimately a Premier card. British Airways also links club membership to their frequent flyer programme, giving extra Air Miles vouchers.

executive floor A hotel floor or area, not necessarily a complete floor, for which premium rates are charged for the provision of facilities appropriate to business travellers. Often the rooms are large with a writing desk etc. There may be a room on the floor reserved for executives' use, with complimentary tea, coffee and biscuits and sometimes other beverages.

Exhibition Venues Association *See* EVA *and* www.exhibitionvenues.com

exit permit *See* visa.

exit tax *See* departure tax.

exit visa *See* visa.

expanded continental breakfast *See* continental breakfast.

expatriate A person permanently resident in a country different from their country of birth or nationality.

exposition Often abbreviated to expo. A huge trade fair and exhibition, usually aimed to promote a single country and often attracting a worldwide support.

Express Switch Name of American Express computerized reservation system connecting with major CRSs.

Express Traveller Name of American Express ticketing and administration system associated with Express Switch.

extension ladder On a manual air ticket, one section in ladder format enables entry of the fare construction details. If there is insufficient space to show the complete itinerary and fare construction, a small form is attached: this is an extension ladder.

extension of holidays As so often with terminology in this dictionary, the wording has both an obvious sense which it is not necessary to explain and an esoteric meaning. Leisure companies, hotels or holiday centres may contact booked clients shortly before arrival, offering the opportunity to come earlier or stay longer at a bargain price. This marketing concept involves strict computerized control of the inventory, to maximize use of unsold space without reducing prices and without publicizing the discounts generally.

extension tour An optional extra tour which can be booked in addition to the basic arrangements for an inclusive tour, for an extra charge.

Extra Name of National Express viewdata-based CRS in the UK. The acronym stands for Express Travel Reservations and Advice system.

extra bed An additional bed placed in a hotel room, enabling more people to use the room than normally occupy it. For example, an extra bed may be put in a twin-bedded room, to enable a child to share with parents. A substantially reduced rate is normally charged for the person using the extra bed. *See* rollaway bed.

extra mileage allowance *See* IATA fare construction system.

extra section US term for an extra transportation service arranged in addition to previously published schedules. In the UK, an airline, for example, merely refers to an extra or supplementary flight.

extras Hotel extras are items charged for in addition to the inclusive terms agreed. Thus, a guest paying full board/pension terms does not pay for normal meals, but must pay for telephone calls and newspapers as extras. A guest paying on a room-only basis, would pay for all meals as extras.

F

F   First class.

F & B   Food and beverage; the hotel section which runs the kitchens, restaurants and bars.

FAA   The US Federal Aviation Administration is a section of the US Department of Transport responsible for the promotion, regulation and safety of civil aviation and for the safe and efficient use of air space. The FAA licenses pilots and other air crew and issues Certificates of Airworthiness to aircraft. The FAA has established a US National Airport System Plan to identify where airports are needed and suggest those airports which should be further developed; for FAA assessments of foreign compliance with air safety standards *see* www.faa.gov *and* airline safety.

FACETS   Fully Automated Customer Enquiry and Travel System; was ATOC's UK rail information and reservation system using a Galileo Focalpoint workstation. FACETS enabled up-to-date train schedules to be checked without consulting printed timetables. Automatic fare quotes were provided for a selected journey, stating on-screen, the applicable travel restrictions. Through FACETS, seat and sleeper availability could be accessed and reservations made. Initially, agents with a Galileo or Sabre GDS were switched to Elgar and in 2000, other UK travel agents were switched to AJENTS. *See* Elgar *and* AJENTS.

FACT   Fully automatic control of trains. *See* ATC[6] *and* AGT.

FADEC   Full authority digital engine control (aviation term).

FAF   Final approach fix (aviation term).

FAI   Fédération Aeronautique Internationale. *See* www.fai.org

Fair Savers   Was the brand name of Grecian Holidays' variety of minimum-rated package tour.

fair wind   A following wind at sea.

fairway   Navigable route immediately outside a port or harbour.

FAL[1]   Aviation jargon for facilitation.

FAL[2]   Facilitation of International Maritime Traffic; an important maritime convention introduced in 1997 which regulates shipping practices when arriving and leaving a port and during their visit.

Falcon Business Class   Brand name given by Gulf Air to passenger area immediately adjacent to first class, where passengers paying full economy fares enjoy improved service and facilities. *See* business class.

fam trip   *See* familiarization tour.

familiarization tour   General industry term for a trip usually arranged by a tourist board, tour operator or transportation company in order to familiarize travel industry staff with the facilities.

family cabins   Cabins with four or more berths, sold at a reduced price, when all the berths are occupied.

family fares   Reduced-rate air fares are available to family groups travelling together within Europe between many places, but not generally applying to travel from the UK. Main family air fares which concern British agents are to and from the Middle East and India. Reduced-rate UK rail travel is available to Family Rail Card holders.

family holiday houses   Translated from the French 'maison familiale de vacances' this is described in the World Tourism Organization and Secretariat of State for Tourism of France (2001), *Thesaurus on Tourism and Leisure Activities* as 'collective housing for families who share the housework'. The concept has no equivalent in English-speaking countries and appears to be a French phenomenon.

Family Holidays Association   *See* FHA.

family plan   Reduced accommodation rate for family parties, which is often offered by hotels and others.

Family Rail Card   *See* rail fares in the UK.

family room The 2003 CEN/European Standard official definition is 'room with sleeping facilities for three or more persons, at least two of which are suitable for adults'. However, the major hotel groups designate as such only larger rooms, capable of accommodating at least two adults and two children.

family service US name for type of meal service where dishes of food are offered at the table or where the food is placed on the table by the serving staff, for patrons to help themselves. *See* silver service for comparison with various other types of restaurant service.

fan jet Turbo-fan jet. *See* jet aircraft engine for full explanation.

FANS Future air navigation system based on automatic control through the precise positioning provided by satellite tracking systems.

fantail May mean all of the rear of a ship above the waterline, and behind the point where the waterline crosses the stern. Term is often applied when designating the location of particular facilities in US cruise ships.

Fantasia An Australian CRS jointly owned by JAL, QANTAS and American Airlines which has a technical and marketing association with Sabre.

FAP[1] Final approach point (aviation term).

FAP[2] Full American Plan. *See* American Plan.

FAR Federal Aviation Regulation of the US FAA. For example, FAR 121 concerns large airlines and FAR 135 commuter airlines.

fare The price of travel on a mode of transport. *See also* under appropriate transport mode, i.e. air fares, rail fares etc.

fare basis Information regarding the type of fare paid by a traveller, such as category of traveller, class of entitlement, minimum and maximum validity, reservations entitlement, seasonality and days of travel. For a comprehensive list of the IATA class and fare designators for use on air tickets, *see* airline class and fare designators. The 2003 CEN/European Standard official definition is 'criteria set by a provider of transport for the management of its capacity, dependent on various factors such as the period of the year, length of the journey, number of travellers, conditions of payment and cancellation'. The opening part of this definition strays into yield control, rather than sticking to defining the term.

fare break point *See* FBP.

fare construction of air fares *See* IATA fare construction system.

Fare Construction Unit *See* FCU[1]. (Now obsolete.)

Fare Deal Monitoring Group A US group set up as part of the airlines' Yield Improvement Programme.

fare reductions Rates on modes of transport may be discounted for various types of traveller. Typical examples are infants, children, young people, students, senior citizens, members of the armed forces, ships' crews, families travelling together and groups of travellers. Reductions may also be provided for standby travel, advance booking, low season, off peak or night travel.

Fare Shares Brand name of Thomas Cook's variety of minimum-rated package tour.

farm house In Britain and North America means a house on a farm, usually where the farmer lives. But within Europe, their translation into English of holiday accommodation on a farm is often 'farm house'.

Farm Stay UK Cooperative of 1100 British farmers providing serviced and self-catering accommodation on working farms. *See* www.farmstayuk.co.uk

farm tourism That which involves visits to working farms for 'broadly' leisure purposes. Thus, some farms promote themselves as 'open farms', inviting the public to visit a working farm as a tourist attraction; educational visits from parties of schoolchildren are also encouraged. Accommodation may also be available, either self-catering or serviced. In the USA may be called vacation farm tourism, agritourism or agrotourism. The *World Travel Dictionary* is incorrect to restrict the meaning of agritourism to holidays spent working on a farm. *See also* Farm Stay UK.

fartifacts Tourist junk sold as souvenirs and meant to represent typical craft or culture of an area.

FAS Federal Aviation Service in the USA. *See* www.faa.gov

FAST Was Thomas Cook's own UK travel communications network. The acronym stood for Fast Access Service for Travel Agents.

Fast Track Provision of superior facilities for premium-class air travellers, for example: The British Airports Authority in the UK allows first-, club- and business-class passengers a separate channel to clear security and passport control. There are seldom queues so qualifying travellers find the amenity valuable.

fastest train in the world in commercial service *See* TGV.

Fastlink and Fastrak A communications/viewdata service provided in the UK by Telewest under the general brand name Endeavour. Fastrak is one of the major viewdata communication networks for UK travel agents, enabling agents to connect reservation terminals to systems of service providers, such as tour operators, airlines, hotels, ferry and car hire companies. Ordinary service is on a dial-up basis using ordinary telephone lines. Fastlink was the brand name of the 'direct connect' service, using permanently-connected telephone data lines, now called 'Endeavour connect'. For full details *see* Endeavour.

FAT Final approach track (aviation term).

fathom A water depth of 6 ft (1.8 m).

FB Full board. *See* full board.

FBL Fly by light; an aviation term used to qualify icing, turbulence, interference or static.

FBO Fixed-based operator or fixed-base operation with reference to an airline.

FBP Fare break point. Abbreviation normally used in connection with IATA fare construction system. Often the cheapest air fare is constructed by calculating fares for several parts of the itinerary, 'breaking' the journey at FBPs.

FBU Flight briefing unit.

FBW Fly by wire, meaning to fly an aircraft on autopilot.

FCA Free carrier as defined in Publication 460 of the International Chamber of Commerce.

FCB Frequency control board (aviation term).

FCC Flight control computer (aviation term).

FCCA Florida Caribbean Cruise Association; for details *see* Cruise Line Coalition web site hosted by International Council of Cruise Lines www.iccl.org

FCL Flight crew licensing.

FCO Flight crew orders.

FCOM Flight crew operating manual.

FCS Flight control system.

FCSS Flight control sight system.

FCTWG Flight Crew Training Working Group of IATA.

FCU[1] Until July 1989 meant Fare Construction Unit of IATA when it was replaced by the NUC. This obsolete term is included in order to identify that many other reference sources fail to mention this.

FCU[2] Fuel control unit (aviation term).

FDAI Flight director attitude indicator (aviation term).

FDAU Flight data acquisition unit (aviation term).

FDC Flight director coupler (aviation term).

FDI Flight director indicator (aviation term).

FDO Flight data operations in respect of air traffic flow (aviation term).

FDR Flight data recorder – colloquially known as 'the black box' (aviation term).

FDS Flight director system (aviation term).

Federal Aviation Administration *See* FAA.

Federal Maritime Administration *See* FMA.

Federal Maritime Commission *See* FMC.

Federal Railroad Administration *See* FRA.

Federal Travel Regulation *See* FTR.

Fédération Aeronautique Internationale (FAI) *See* www.fai.org

Federation of English Language Course Organizations *See* FELCO.

Federation of Tour Operators *See* FTO.

FEE Foundation for Environmental Education. A non-governmental, non-profit organization promoting sustainable development through environmental education, best known regarding Blue Flag awards for beaches, marinas and boats. *See* www.fee-international.org

fee-based business travel contract Where a travel agent charges a corporation or other organization for the handling services provided. This may, for example be an agreed annual fee or more usually fees per transaction. These may be flat fees, percentage based or a mixture of both. Commission and fees receivable by the agents may, as part of the contract, be rebated wholly or in part to the corporate account holder. *A list of 70 other business travel related entries follows* corporate travel contracts, *some of which lead to further entries.*

fee-based pricing North American term for way an inclusive tour or other travel service is usually costed by a travel agency. The costs of all items to be provided are added together and a mark-up is added. Sometimes taxes are added afterwards, sometimes before the mark-up. In the UK, this is cost-plus pricing. Because transportation does not include VAT, while foreign hotel rates put in the costing are inclusive of local tax, VA Tax is only charged on the mark-up. *A list of 70 other business travel related entries follows* corporate travel contracts, *some of which lead to further entries.*

feeder airline Airline operating a service on a local, restricted or secondary basis to a central point, node or hub, from which the main, primary or long-distance services operate. *See* hub and spoke.

feeder service Transportation service operating on a local, restricted or secondary basis to a central point, node or hub, from which the main, primary or long-distance services operate. *See* hub and spoke.

FEG Federation of European Guides.

FEGS Fixed electrical ground supply. Replacing ground power supply units, electricity generators supplying power to static aircraft without their own engine power.

FEL Flight Engineer's Licence.

Felaf International hotel code for six single-bedded rooms.

FELCO Federation of English Language Course Organisations. Membership is restricted to those organizations planning English courses for overseas students, which the British Council recognizes as efficient. Objectives, when established in 1972, were to ensure the highest possible standards of teaching, administration and welfare.

felucca General name for small boat in Mediterranean; may only have oars or also a lateen sail. Found along coasts and river deltas; particularly on the Nile

in Egypt. *See* boat for other types of small vessel.

fender Anything serving as a cushion between the side of a boat and a dock or other craft.

Feral International hotel code for six twin-bedded rooms.

ferry Although originally meaning a small water-borne vessel operating across a narrow stretch of water, the term has become interchangeable with car ferry and a specific meaning can no longer be attributed to the term.

ferry flight *See* ferry mileage.

ferry mileage The distance that has to be travelled, without passengers, in order to position a ship, aircraft or vehicle, so that the intended passenger-carrying service can be operated. Typical of the procedures used to avoid this, is to integrate a flying pattern between several destinations. For example, suppose an aircraft is based in Los Angeles (LAX), but the airline wants to operate flights between San Francisco (SFO) and Las Vegas (LAS.) If the plane flies LAX–LAS–SFO–LAS–LAX, known as a W pattern, the aircraft will have returned to base having served both routes without undertaking a positioning flight.

Ferrybook *See* Allbook.

FET Foreign escorted tour is an American term for an inclusive tour abroad.

FF Fuel flow (aviation term).

FFP Frequent flyer programme. Schemes through which travellers receive credits or mileage points every time they travel enabling them to obtain free flights or other awards. Thus, the aim is to enhance loyalty towards an airline. *See* end of this entry for FFP facts and figures.

The development began with Southwest Airlines 'sweetheart stamps' scheme in the 1970s aimed at enabling business travellers to give free flights to their spouses. As can be seen from the 'airline' entry in this dictionary, airline load factors are around 71%. The concept was designed around using this 'spare' capacity of non-used seats. But the concept has run into problems; recently, it was widely reported that some flights were full for several weeks in the summer, because of passengers using their free tickets. Controls on popular destinations such as Hawaii alienate mileage point holders. Lack of controls means loss of revenue passengers or extra flights to accommodate points holders, negating the original idea of raised load factors at little or no extra cost to an airline. Frequent travellers are often members of five or more FFPs – so much for their loyalty effectiveness. Relationship marketing is now a vital selling tool of all airlines and the possession of a frequent flyer's details is regarded as highly prized information.

Antagonism from companies is widespread; they pay for business travel but the airlines give the mileage points to travellers individually. A corporate travel manager is, in effect a special type of purchasing manager, responsible for procurement. FFPs often obstruct corporate travel policies.

Most large US airlines operated frequent flyer schemes throughout the 1980s; in the 1990s, relaxation of competition restrictions in Europe, resulted in similar European schemes. Business travellers consider the attractiveness of a carrier's frequent flyer programme second only to flight scheduling when choosing a carrier. The ultimate development of this phenomenon is that often credits are now gained for hotels, car rental and travellers cheques as well as incidental items such as travelling on an airport bus, or for having a meal at a restaurant nearby, and for much non-travel expenditure. But on top of this, credit card companies offer 'miles', so that by paying for an air ticket or these ancillaries with a card, even more are earned.

Coupon brokers are to be found around check-in desks at the largest American airports seeking to buy award certificates. Tickets obtained in this way, are then sold to other travellers at substantial discounts, despite airlines tightening their rules in order to prevent this. Although the American IRS is believed to have examined the possibility of taxing recipients on their free travel tickets, this would be very difficult. Only if the airlines could be forced to provide the names and home addresses of all those to whom awards were made, would it be possible to verify tax returns.

To summarize this entry, it is apparent that no major airline or alliance grouping of airlines can afford the catastrophic losses that would follow being the first to drop its FFP scheme. The average US frequent traveller is a member of three FFP schemes; the more frequently a person travels, the more likely is a traveller to be a member of four or five schemes; questioning whether these schemes enhance loyalty! However, these travellers certainly appear to restrict their choice of airline to the few for which they possess FFP membership. Even gradual change would immediately become obvious to travellers, who would choose the carriers with the best scheme. Thus, airlines appear to be locked in to providing FFP benefits and making the best of the relationship marketing opportunities these present. For details of a typical programme *see* AAdvantage. There are more than 120m members of FFP schemes worldwide; 74m US residents, 24m European and 21m Asian. But only 28% are current collectors of FFPs. AAdvantage, American Airlines' scheme (*see* AAdvantage entry for more details), is the biggest with nearly 50m members; it is still growing at 10,000 new members daily. InsideFlyer.com suggests that loyalty programmes are growing by 11% annually. There are nearly 100 schemes. 14m free tickets were given through them in 2001. There were believed to be 7.8 trillion (7,800,000,000,000) miles of travel unredeemed by the end of 2001 out of 9.77 trillion issued. Cost to an airline is estimated at US$13.93 per free ticket, based on extra fuel, food, drink and other costs.

FFP1 Free Flight Phase 1 (US terminology).

FH Flight hours.

FHA Family Holiday Association; UK charity which provides holidays for the disadvantaged. *See* www.fhaonline.org.uk

FIATA International Federation of Freight Forwarders Associations. *See* www.fiata.com

FIAVET Federazione Italiana della Associazioni delle Imprese Viaggi e Turismo, the Italian Federation of Travel Agents.

FIC Flight Information Centre.

FICC Federation Internationale de Camping et de Caravanning. *See* IFCC[1].

fiche *See* microfiche.

fictitious fare construction *See* hypothetical fare construction points.

Fidelio An integrated automated management system for the hospitality industry.

FIDO Fog investigation and dispersal operation.

FIDS Flight information display system at an airport.

field A particular area of a computer screen or VDU, as well as normal everyday uses of the word.

FIFOR Abbreviation for flight forecast.

fifth freedom rights *See* Chicago Convention.

FIJET Fédération Internationale des Journalistes et Écrivans du Tourisme, known in the UK as the International Federation of Tourism Journalists and Writers. Founded in 1954, there are now over 1600 members from 35 countries. *See* www.world-tourism.org

filing Lodging of a proposed fare and its associated conditions with an appropriate authority, usually governmental for approval.

FIM Flight interruption manifest; an IATA form which may be a full sheet of paper or ticket size, used where, due to flight interruption en route, passengers must be 'involuntarily' re-routed and, which will usually be the case, the flight coupon for that part of the journey will have been uplifted by the carrier at check-in. Under IATA Resolution 735d, alternative onward transport may be provided with other carriers. The FIM details the circumstances.

fin *See* airframe.

final leg *See* last leg.

financial protection for consumers *See* bond for outlines of some typical UK and US schemes covering purchasers of travel services.

FIND Ferranti's Flight Information Display system for British Airways at London's Heathrow Airport is one of the largest distribution networks designed for any airport worldwide. The system comprises over 40 input terminals and over 1100 staff monitors, linked by a 15 km cable network.

Finland National Travel Agency Organization AFTA[1]. *See* www.astanet.com

Finnair Club Name of Finnair's Frequent Flyers' Club.

Finnish Tourist Board *See* www.finland-tourism.com

Finnres Name of the Finnish agency CRS.

firming Official IATA definition is a procedure whereby a member airline at a boarding point contacts passengers holding definite reservations to ensure that they actually intend using this space.

FIRs Flight Information Regions. For air traffic control purposes, Europe is divided into a number of large areas known as Flight Information Regions. Each has within it, one or more Air Traffic Control Centres. For instance, air traffic over England and Wales is controlled from the London ATC Centre at West Drayton. France has four centres and Spain, three. At each centre, there are a number of controllers, each with a private radio frequency and each responsible for a section of air space within the FIR. Inside each information region, are sections of controlled air space. These are known as airways and they are the routes followed by aircraft.

Before starting a flight, a pilot or his company, must file a flight plan, which is an international document setting out the route planned for the aircraft and which includes details such as its preferred height and speed. This is sent to all ATC units which will be dealing with the aircraft and each allocates a block of air space to it. When a block of air space free of all other traffic has been found right through to the destination, the aircraft will be given a suitable take-off time or slot. It can take off 3 min either side of that slot, but if it misses, then the aircraft has to go to the back of the queue and start again. *See* MLS for brief description of equivalent US plan.

first class Usually the best service provided on transport services, but for hotels, often second best, top being de luxe category.

first floor In the USA, this is the ground-level or entrance floor of a hotel or building. In the UK, the first floor is the next floor above the ground floor.

first sitting On cruise ships, there is often insufficient room in the restaurants for all the passengers to be seated at once. Thus, first and second meal sittings are necessary (some cruise lines refer to these as early or late sittings).

first tour operator   *See* Thomas Cook.

first-class cabin   The area of a mode of transport reserved for those passengers who have paid a higher fare. Also, the best accommodation where there is more than one class. For example, in an aircraft, in return for the greater price, they have wider seats, with greater pitch between their seat and the one in front. Beverages, alcoholic or otherwise, are complimentary. Food is of a high standard and there is a much greater ratio of cabin staff to passengers.

first-class differential   Amount of an air fare arrived at by standard fare calculation methods, assessing sectors flown first class and tourist class in a multi-sector itinerary.

FIS   Flight information service.

FIT   Fully inclusive tour is a North American term for an independent inclusive tour (an IIT in the UK). However, the acronym is decoded in other ways in other texts, as: foreign independent tour; foreign independent travel; foreign individual travel; fully independent traveler [sic]; and frequent individual traveler [sic]. In New Zealand and Australia the acronym is decoded as free independent traveller.

five freedoms of the air   *See* Chicago Convention *and* Freedoms of the Air (currently nine).

fixed inventory   Where a package tour operator allocates specific accommodation to each flight seat, featuring the total availability in a computer system as a package. The tour operator using a completely inflexible fixed inventory system may have a request from a potential purchaser for travel to a particular resort on a specific date, which cannot be fulfilled, even though there are seats available, because the hotel requested is full. Often, in such circumstances, the tour operator will have made a firm contract for the accommodation, which might result in charges if unsold. *See also* free inventory.

fixed-wing aircraft   Aircraft with wings fixed to the fuselage, which are outspread in flight and are non-rotating, i.e. aircraft other than helicopters.

FIYTO   Federation of International Youth Travel Organizations. *See* www.fiyto.org

FL   Flight level.

flag carrier   Any carrier designated by its government to operate international services. In the case of shipping, the 'flag' flown is highly significant, designating country of registration, which might not be the same as the country from which a vessel operates. Hence the pejorative term 'flag of convenience' indicative of a vessel operating under the administration of a country where employment legislation, taxes or safety and other legislation is less strict than that of the actual home base.

flag of convenience   *See* entry immediately above.

flap   *See* airframe.

flat rate   Price or rate that is not discounted in consideration of frequency or volume of use.

flat-rate coupon payment   *See* coupon payment.

flat-rate fees   *See* coupon payment.

flats   Open rail freight wagons for carrying cars on Motorail services in Europe.

FLCC   Flight control computer.

FLCS   Flight control system.

fleet   Group of aircraft, ships, trains or vehicles; perhaps under the same ownership, type or otherwise differentiated.

flexible ticket   Concept applicable to non-refundable air tickets first introduced by US carriers, Delta, Northwest and Continental in 2003. Holders of non-refundable tickets are given 1 year from the ticket's original issue date to reschedule their travel without losing its value, provided the reservation is cancelled prior to the scheduled departure time of the original flight.

flight   A journey by air or hovercraft.

flight attendant   A steward or stewardess on board an aircraft.

flight code   Worldwide, all flights are assigned an exclusive code, comprised of letters designating the carrier and figures for the particular flight. Unfortunately, marketing agreements between airlines have blurred the simplicity of this explanation. *See* code sharing.

flight coupon   That part of an air ticket which is utilized by a passenger to travel between the points outlined. Tickets normally contain a maximum of four flight coupons together with issuing office and airline audit copies. Multi-sector itineraries involve tickets being stapled together in order to achieve the necessary number of flight coupons. *See* conjunction tickets *and* coupon, flight for official IATA definition.

flight deck The name for the cockpit of larger aircraft, from which pilots and engineers operate the aircraft.

Flight Deck The name of TAA's Frequent Flyers Club. For other benefits *See* FFP (frequent flyer programme).

flight engineer The chief mechanic and systems operator on an aircraft flight deck.

flight, first Orville and Wilbur Wright, bicycle craftsmen from Dayton, Ohio, are credited with the first controlled passenger-carrying powered flight by man. Orville was airborne for 12 s and covered 120 ft on the morning of 17 December 1903 at Kitty Hawk, on the coast of North Carolina. By the afternoon of the same day Wilbur had managed 852 ft in just under 1 min.

Flight Information Regions *See* FIRs.

flight interruption manifest *See* FIM.

flight numbers World airlines have each been allocated a two- or three-letter code for identification purposes. Many international flights are composed of these letters followed by three figures to identify particular flights. British Airways' domestic flights often have four figures. It is often customary to precede a small flight number by zeros. Flight numbers BA1 to BA299 are mainly long-haul journeys, BA300 to BA999 are shorter journeys. *See* airline codes for plans to phase introduction of three-letter codes.

flight path The route stated in a flight plan or the route actually taken by an aircraft.

flight plan *See* FIRs.

flight recorder Device which it is compulsory for aircraft to carry, recording basic technical information in a form which should be recoverable in the event of accident. Also known as an in-flight recorder and popularly called the 'black box'.

flight schedules *See* airlines flight schedules.

flight simulator A reproduction aircraft flight deck, with similar characteristics to those which aircrew would normally experience in flight. Flight simulators have become so realistic, that it may soon be practical to undertake most advanced pilot-training on them.

Worldwide leader in the manufacture of the equipment is a British company, Rediffusion, which sells 45% of the simulators used at prices ranging between £5 million and £8 million each.

flight time Airline timetables and tour operators' brochures mean the expected time from scheduled take off to scheduled landing. The 2003 CEN/European Standard official definition is 'the total time from the moment an aircraft first moves under its own power for the purpose of taking off until the moment it comes to rest at the end of a flight'. This technically appears to be similar to 'block time' rather than flight time. *See* block speed.

FLIR Forward-looking infrared radar.

float plane US term for a seaplane. *See* flying boat.

floatel *See* boatel.

floor limit Term applied to maximum amount of a credit card sale, above which authorization must be sought, regardless of any general limits in force for the type of transaction involved.

floor plan Map or diagram of rooms, facilities or exhibition stands etc.

floor show Cabaret at a night club or restaurant.

flop house Derogatory term generally applied to a run-down poor hotel, but accurately used, meaning a brothel.

floppy disk *See* disk.

Florida Caribbean Cruise Association *See* FCCA.

Florida Tourism (Visit Florida) *See* www.flausa.com

flotel A floating hotel, permanently moored at one location.

flotilla sailing holiday Where a group of yachts travel together on a planned itinerary, providing a much safer environment than individual travel.

flotsam Anything floating or washed up on a beach, although term often applied to manufactured objects or wreckage.

FLT Airline jargon for flight.

fluid pricing The practice of UK tour operators to change prices according to demand, rather than publishing a brochure price and maintaining that price until departure date. Prices may be reduced to stimulate early or late sales. But if demand appears to be exceeding availability prices are raised. *See* yield management for fuller description.

fly acts Cruise ship entertainers working on more than one ship at a time, necessitating flying between ports to connect different cruise itineraries.

fly cruise Holiday journey involving charter or scheduled flight to a distant (usually foreign) point, cruising for a period and then return by air.

fly drive Usage of term varies within the travel trade. It may mean merely car hire, booked at the same time as making a scheduled flight booking. Alternatively it may mean an inclusive package or charter or scheduled air travel together with car hire at one inclusive price. Costs of these latter arrangements may show considerable saving compared with the purchase of individual elements.

fly rail May mean a combination ticket covering an air and rail sector; or it may be a holiday journey involving a charter or scheduled flight to a distant (usually foreign) point and a rail pass providing unlimited rail travel in a nominated area for a set period.

Fly Rail Package to Austria or Switzerland consisting of an ITX, normal or excursion air fare combined with a rail pass offering unlimited rail travel, either for the duration of the trip or at least 8 days. At least two adults must travel together to qualify.

flying boat An aircraft that can take off from and land on water, by means of floats or pontoons instead of wheels. Seaplane is a more modern term.

Flying Colonel Name of Delta Airlines' Frequent Flyers' Club, membership of which is free but by invitation only. Main benefits are those listed under the general heading FFP (frequent flyer programme).

Flying Dutchman Name of KLM's Frequent flyer Club. *See* FFP (frequent flyer programme).

flying wing *See* blended wing.

FM Flight manual or fan marker.

FMA Federal Maritime Administration, a section of the DOT in the USA. Whereas the FMA has responsibility for Federal matters, the Federal Maritime Commission is an entirely independent body with powers to supervise shipping. *See* www.marad.dot.gov

FMC¹ Federal Maritime Commission in the US. *See* above for explanation of difference between FMA and FMC. The Federal Maritime Commission is the US regulatory body both controlling international passenger and cargo carriage by sea. With regard to consumer protection, FMC regulation 46 CFR Part 540 applies to owners, operators and charterers of vessels with a capacity for 50 or more passengers and embarking passengers at US ports. The requirements are that financial responsibility be demonstrated sufficient to indemnify passengers, 'in the event of non-performance of water transportation'. The evidence of financial responsibility may be in the form of a surety bond, financial guarantee, self-insurance or an escrow account. For outline of consumer protection measures *see* www.fmc.gov, bond *and* escrow account.

FMC² Flight management computer.

FMD Flight management display.

FMP Flight management position.

FMS Flight management system.

FMU Flow management unit (aviation term).

FNL Flight navigator's licence.

FOB Cargo which is free on board.

FOC¹ Free of charge.

FOC² Flight Operations Committee of IATA.

FOD Foreign object damage (aviation term).

FOI The Flight Operations Inspectorate of the CAA in the UK. *See* AOC.

folding caravan *See* caravan.

folio Was US wording for a guest's account at a hotel. Now sometimes applied to the equivalent computer record.

food and beverage The hotel section which runs the kitchens, restaurants and bars.

foot passengers *See* car ferry.

FOP Travel jargon for form of payment.

force majeure An act of God, to which all contracts are subject, not merely travel contracts. European package-holiday legislation suggests 'Unusual and unforeseeable circumstances beyond the control of the party by whom it is pleaded, the consequences of which could not have been avoided, even if all due care had been exercised.' The term or its synonym is defined in the law of every country. For air passenger's rights in the USA in the event of a schedule irregularity or *force majeure* situation, *see* Rule 240.

foreign escorted tour American term for an inclusive tour abroad.

foreign exchange rate *See* conversion rate.

foreign independent tour An American term for an independent inclusive tour abroad.

foreign workers' fares Reduced fares are available for some foreign employees returning home to their own countries on single or return journeys. Discounts vary according to country.

forfait or *à forfait* French term for inclusive package of transport, accommodation and meals etc.

form of indemnity *See* indemnity *and* lost tickets.

form of payment Many travel tickets have a 'form of payment' box, in which an entry is made indicating method of payment, such as a credit card, cash or cheque. An entry in this box of 'agt non ref' explains that an agency-issued ticket is non-refundable without reference to the issuing office. This enables agents to protect themselves in respect of tickets issued on a credit account basis.

FORTRAN Formula Translation, a computer programming language.

Fortres Was Forte Hotels' CRS; Forte ceased to exist as a major worldwide hotel brand name in June 2001.

fortress hub *See* hub and spoke.

forward Front section of the ship or aircraft, usually pronounced 'forrard'.

FOSTA Federation of Southern Travel Agents a member of Worldchoice in the UK.

Foundation for Environmental Education A non-governmental, non-profit organization promoting sustainable development through environmental education, best known regarding Blue Flag awards for beaches, marinas and boats. *See* www.fee-international.org

fowler *See* airframe.

foyer Entrance hall of a cinema, hotel, restaurant, theatre or any large building.

FP Full pension, a hotel rate inclusive of three meals daily.

FRA The Federal Railroad Administration is the US regulatory body controlling American passenger and freight train operation. *See* www.fra.dot.gov

fractional ownership of aircraft Concept initiated in 1986 for shared ownership of business jets. By 1999 *AvData* estimated that there were 329 aircraft run in this way by 1567 customers. Known as 'fractionals', the FAA in the USA has agreed guidelines for their operations.

France Vacances Pass Gives unlimited rail travel over the lines of French Railways, free travel on the Paris Metro, regular bus services of the RATP, train services of the RER and on Paris suburban rail services, with rates varying according to 7- or 15-day or 1-month validity, class of travel and whether adult or child.

franchise Grant to retailer or operator of sole selling or operational rights, usually within a specified area. The granting organization is the 'franchisor'. The term 'franchise operation', is applied to a group of independently-owned businesses operating under the same name and sharing in the advantages of national marketing, advertising, branding, bulk purchasing power and other central services provided by the franchise operator; for more information on this alternative term for a consortium *see* consortium.

free baggage allowance On air routes where baggage is weighed, free allowance is 20 kg (44 lbs) tourist class and 30 kg (66 lbs) first class. Overweight charged at 1% of first-class fare per kilo. European piece concept involves a two-case limit. For British and European rail baggage rules, and more details, *see* allowance of free baggage.

free hits In a North American contracts between a CRS/GDS and an agent, the number of times that the system can be accessed for information, without incurring extra charges. During the currency of this dictionary, with access via the Internet increasing rapidly, this type of contract term is expected to cease.

free inventory Where a tour operator sells flight seats and accommodation freely from computer stock, associating particular hotels serviced by a flight or other means of transport with seats on demand. *See also* fixed inventory.

freebie Colloquial travel industry term for educational or familiarization (fam) trip.

Freedom to Fly UK pressure group; a coalition of air users, business, tourism, trade unions, airlines and airports which promotes sustainable growth of air transport. Formed in 2002 in response to extensive government consultation concerning airport development necessary to meet forecast demand. *See* www.freedomtofly.co.uk

Freedoms of the Air In effect, these are a list of the flying rights which are the subject of agreements between countries (bilaterals) or between a number of countries (multilaterals).

First – The right to fly over the territory of a contracting state without landing.
Second – The right to land on the territory of a contracting state for non-commercial purposes.
Third – The right to transport passengers, cargo and mail from the state of registration of the aircraft to another state and to set them down there.
Fourth – The right to take on board passengers, cargo and mail in another contracting state and to transport them to the state of registration of the aircraft.
Fifth – The right to transport passengers, cargo and mail between two other states as a continuation of, or as a preliminary to, the operation of the third or fourth freedoms.
Sixth – The right to take on board cargo passengers, and mail in one state and to transport them to a third state after a stopover in the aircraft's state of registration and vice versa.
Seventh – The right to transport passengers, cargo and mail between two other states on a service which does not touch the aircraft's country of registration.
Eighth – The right to transport passengers, cargo and mail within the territory of a state which is not the aircraft's state of registration. (Referred to as full cabotage rights.)
Ninth – The right to interrupt a service.

See also Chicago Convention for details of original Five Freedoms of the Air; ASA (Air Service Agreement, Bermuda), open skies *and* traffic rights.

freeport/free port A port or any place free of customs duty and most customs regulations.

freesale (FS) or sell and record/report A system whereby reservations can be confirmed immediately to a client. Notification of the sale is forwarded to the reservations control office after the sale has been made and confirmed to the client. (Such systems generally have conditions and time limits governing the transactions.)

freeway A motorway or autobahn in North America.

French Government Tourist Office *See* www.francetourism.com *and* www.franceguide.com

French National Travel Agency Organization *See* SNAV.

French service *See* family service. *Also* sometimes means table laying with a 'show' plate between the cutlery.

Frequency Plus Name of the Air France frequent flyer programme. *See* FFP.

frequent corporate traveller Definition used by Reed Travel Group, publishers of *OAG World Airways Guide*, *Travel Weekly* and many other industry titles is 'a business traveller taking five or more flights a year'. There is much variation in the criteria applied by various airlines in their frequent flyer programmes. The term may, of course, be applied to any mode of transport.

frequent flyer programmes *See* FFP.

frequent guest programmes Also known as frequent lodger programs in the USA. Generic title of hospitality industry loyalty or promotion schemes. Similar to the frequent flyer programmes operated by airlines, many of which offer mileage points for hotel stays as part of their schemes.

frequent traveller A regular traveller on a mode of transport. Frequent flyer progammes are described above; similar schemes are run by other transportation companies. *See* Compass Points, Frequent Corporate Traveller *and* Frequent Traveller Card. 'Frequent Traveller' is also the name of US Air's frequent flyer programme. *See* FFP (frequent flyer programme).

Frequent Traveller Card As a generic term, the name of the identification card issued to people who have enrolled in any particular airline's frequent traveller programme. Also the name of Air New Zealand's frequent traveller club, membership of which is free in the USA and UK to any traveller making at least two round trips a year to NZ. A seating area is reserved for members; other details as listed under FFP.

frequent traveller programmes Generic title of loyalty or promotion schemes offered by a mode of transport.

Friendly Fours 10% reduction of fare offered by P&O to parties of four sharing the same four-berth cabin.

front end deal May also be called a front end net rate or a front end rebate. Agreement between a provider of a travel service and a corporate travel department for reduced rates, based on an estimate of annual usage. It is implied that it is net of commission. Typically, an airline may attempt to introduce a threshold level of annual business before the reduced rate operates, which is resisted by the companies, particularly because the airlines then attempt to increase the threshold every year, as part of the renegotiation process. The intense competition between airlines means that there is a huge 'spot market' where airlines attempt to unload surplus seats or merely the last few seats on a flight. A company travel department's travel policy and their appointed travel management company need to strike a fine balance between using the cheapest deal available and providing insufficient business to justify renewal of a front end deal. A back end deal is an agreement that a travel service provider will give a rebate of a proportion of fares or hotel room payments paid, provided a stated level of business has been transacted in a given period. Such deals are always the fall back position if a front end rebate cannot be negotiated. Large corporations usually set travel policies nominating preferred carriers on specific routes or groups of routes, e.g. transatlantic. *A list of 70 other business travel related entries follows* corporate travel contracts, *some of which lead to further entries.*

front of house All parts of a hotel which have customer contact.

front office The reception and porter's desk of a hotel and their control sections. In some hotels these parts may be associated with reservations and cashier's departments, causing the term to be loosely defined. Whatever is included, the title 'Front Office Manager' is the hotel executive responsible for control of the section. In an agency the term is loosely applied to administration directly concerned with sales, while 'back office' administration is more concerned with functions such as administration and accounting. This artificial terminology falls down when attempting to describe a computer with a CRS connection, also producing tickets and invoices and incorporating an accounting system. The term 'mid-office' now applies to software in a travel agency linking the front and back office. A full description of Micros Fidelioxpress hotel front office management system is available at www. micros.com/products/hotels/hotel_ management This also serves as a comprehensive listing of the functions of a hotel front office.

FSC Flight service check.

FSS Franek Software Services, a UK travel industry computer system provider.

FTA Freight Transport Association in the UK.

FTAA Federation of Tourist Attraction Associations restricts membership to groups which represent four or more tourist attractions.

FTAV Fédération Tunisienne des Agences de Voyages, the Tunisian national travel agency organization.

FTI Fast tactical imagery (aviation term).

FTL Flight time limitations.

FTO Federation of Tour Operators in the UK; formerly, the Tour Operators Study Group. An organization representing the interests of all the large-scale British tour operators. The FTO Health Safety and Hygiene preferred Code of Practice has been widely adopted by many operators worldwide. *See* www.fto.co.uk

FTP Fuel Trade Panel of IATA.

FTR Federal Travel Regulation; rules governing travel and transport for federal civilian employees in the USA. An electronic version of these regulations is on the Internet *see* www. policyworks.gov

FUAAV Fédération Universelle des Associations d'Agences de Voyage.

fuel adjustment factor *See* surcharge.

fuel stop *See* refuelling stop.

fuel surcharge   *See* surcharge.

fulfilment centre   In the 1990s, term meant a place where tickets were issued for air bookings made on the Internet. Now that air travel is often undertaken on an electronic ticket, the automated handling service for online bookings has the same name. For example, the American Express Miami fulfilment centre handles around 2m bookings a year, each one taking only 9 s, compared to an average 10 min for handling a manual air reservation. The same term also means a location which handles the supply of an incentive when goods or services are promoted by means of a premium incentive promotion. The promotional item is often merchandise but may be a travel product.

full board   Same as full pension. *See* full pension.

full house   In the UK normally designates that a theatre or cinema is full; in North America, sometimes used when a hotel is full.

full pension   Also en pension. Hotel rate inclusive of accommodation and three main meals daily.

fully appointed   Agents advertise this description to indicate that they have been appointed by most transportation and travel companies in their country to sell their services and, where appropriate, hold ticket stocks.

functional specification   The objectives of a computer program. In other words, what it will do for an end-user.

functionality   *See* functional specification.

funicular   *See* cable transporter *and* rack railway.

funitel   Type of ski lift gondola. *See* cable transporters.

funnel   The chimney of a ship.

funnel flight   It may be a feeder airline flight taking passengers to a hub, for an onward main flight, perhaps operating as a code-sharing flight, operated by more than one airline. It may be any series of flights sharing one code so as to appear to be a single flight. Term more common in USA than UK. *See* feeder airline *and* hub and spoke.

fuselage   *See* airframe.

FUSS   Flap-up safety speed (aviation term).

FX   Travel jargon for foreign exchange.

G

GA General aviation.

GAAC General Aviation Awareness Council in the UK. *See* www.gaac.co.uk

Gabriel Luxembourg's agency CRS, associated with Amadeus.

GAIN Global analysis and information network. A US accident reporting system.

gala dinner A special dinner aimed to be the high spot of a group or incentive tour. This description is rapidly becoming out-of-date, because the term is now applied very generally.

Galaxy Class Brand name given by UTA French Airlines to passenger area immediately adjacent to first class, where passengers paying full fares can enjoy improved service and facilities. *See* business class for full description.

Galileo[1] Name of the European Global Navigation Satellite System (GNSS). Specification was defined in 2000, with the aim of bringing Galileo into service in 2008. For names of existing systems *see* GNSS.

Galileo[2] One of the the four major GDSs. A Cendant subsidiary, the cornerstone of Cendant's travel distribution business. Company began in 1971 when United Airlines introduced its Apollo CRS, for use in their own offices; it was not until 1976 that Apollo Travel Services division was created and marketed to travel agencies, initially, in North America and Japan. This division was renamed Covia in 1986, 50% being sold to British Airways, KLM, Swissair and US Air. The company became Galileo in 1987, although it was not until 1993 that Galileo and the Covia Partnership were merged. Apollo became the organization's national distribution company for USA and Mexico. Galileo distributes travel inventory from multiple supplier sources, mainly to travel intermediaries but also to others including corporate travel departments. This distribution is facilitated by e-ticketing, machine ticketing

and booking products. Galileo connects with over 43,000 travel agency locations, 480 airlines, 60,000 hotels, 430 tour operators, 26 car rental companies and the major cruise lines. *See* www.galileo.com *and* www.cendanttds.com/galileo *also* CRS *and* GDS.

Galileo Users' Association (GUA) UK trade association of travel agency users of the Galileo CRS, which protects the interests of agency users, negotiating the quality of service, costs and enhancements etc. The Galileo airline user's group is a less formal UK body, organized under the auspices of Galileo, with which the GUA communicates. The GUA is the largest user group of its kind in the world. *See* www.galileo.com

galley The kitchen, on board a ship or aircraft.

GAMA General Aviation Manufacturers Association, the American national trade association, publishes aircraft deliveries every half year. *See* www.generalaviation.org

Gambia National Tourist Office *See* www.visitthegambia.gm

game lodge *See* entry below.

game park or **reserve** A managed protected area rich in wildlife operated as a tourist attraction; for example, in Africa, tourists may be accommodated in game lodges and see animals in their natural habitats. Also known as a safari park or wildlife park. For information on the facilities offered by a typical game park *see* www.KrugerPark.co.za

GAMTA General Aviation Manufacturers and Traders Association in the UK; is the British trade body in its sphere. Together with the BAUA forms the BBGA – British Business and General Aviation Association; *see* www.bbga.aero The BBGA is a member of the IBAC (International Business Aviation Council); *see* www.ibac.org

gangplank *See* gangway.

gangway The staircase on wheels used to load and unload an aircraft; also the staircase or access platform leading from a dockside to a ship's deck so that passengers may board or disembark, also known as a gangplank.

gap Official IATA definition is that part of an itinerary, except the distance between two airports serving the same city, involving transportation by means other than a scheduled air service. *See also* open-jaw.

garden room Hotel room overlooking a garden. US web site www. hometravelagency.com suggests that by definition, a 'garden-side room' has access to a garden while a 'garden view' room does not. This distinction is neither generally accepted in the USA nor in the rest of the world.

gasthof *See* inn.

GAT[1] General air traffic.

GAT[2] Guernsey Association for Tourism. *See* GHTA.

gate The area at an airport where passengers assemble before boarding an aircraft. A gate will have a waiting lounge for passengers and telescopic covered access piers or ramps, called an airbridge, which can be manoeuvred so as to connect directly with aircraft doors. In North America, this is known as a jet loader, and also as a Jetway, the brand name of the most well-known jet loader, use of which is becoming generic. The area on which the aircraft is parked for embarkation and disembarkation of passengers, refuelling etc. is the apron or loading apron. *See* airbridge.

gate agents The ground handling staff of an airline or their handling agents responsible for facilitating boarding of passengers from the departure lounge.

gate check-in Passengers with hand luggage who already have a seat number allocated may, with some airlines and in some terminals, be able to walk straight to their departure gate before checking in, thus formally notifying the airline of their arrival for the flight.

gateway[1] A main city of access for any country at which travellers go through customs and immigration formalities, and on which some international air fare constructions are based. Mainly applies to continental USA. *See also* hub and spoke.

gateway[2] A terminal user can make an onward connection through a computer

to any third-party computer for which a gateway access exists. Although originally used in the UK in respect of Prestel connections, the terminology is now generic and is applied in general where connections are made to a third party computer through a communications network computer. The terminology is not specific to the Internet, where gateways are usually called portals.

gauge The distance between the rails on a rail track. This is particularly important in land masses where several countries have adopted different rail widths. For example, the lines of the Australian, Portuguese and Spanish railways and the former USSR are 167.2 cm apart and are known as broad gauge. Many South American countries fit into this category. In Europe, 143.5 cm is more common, so that passengers have to change trains at border points between France and Spain apart from on specially designed trains where wheel widths are adjustable. If the distance between rails is less than the European standard, the term narrow gauge is applied to the track, common in South Africa, and some local trains in Switzerland. Examples of narrow gauges are 106.6 cm and 100 cm. 'Change of gauge' in the context of rail travel merely means changing from one rail width to another. However, it is also an aviation term meaning change of equipment/aircraft. *See also* wheelset.

GAVCCL Groupement Agences de Voyages, Confédération du Commerce Luxembourgeois, the Luxembourg travel agents association.

gazetteer A hotel guide which provides unbiased opinions of hotels; *see* hotels, unbiased opinions of *and* www. dggtravelinfo.co.uk for details of the series of six gazetteers published by a division of Reed Business Information in the UK.

GBCA UK Guild of Professional Cruise Agents.

GBCO Guild of British Coach Operators. *See* www.coach-tours.co.uk

GBTA Was the Guild of Business Travel Agents; renamed in 2005 Guild of Travel Management Companies. *See* GTMC; *also a list of 70 other business travel related entries which follows* corporate travel contracts, *some of which lead to further entries.*

GCA Ground controlled approach.

GCBS General Council of British Shipping.

GCN An alternative to passenger cruise day. *See* PCD.

GCSE in Travel and Tourism General Certificate of Secondary Education in Travel and Tourism in the UK. This examination, which is taken at school by pupils around the age of 16, is offered by the Southern Examining Board in the UK. The course comprises eight modules of which students must be assessed in five to qualify for a GCSE grade. There are three compulsory modules, which are Tourist Destinations, Cultures and Tourism and Work Environments. There are five optional modules, namely, Technological Aspects of Travel and Tourism, Travel and Leisure Links, Design, Food Service and Communication Strategies.

GDS Global Distribution System. The title accorded to the four major worldwide computerized airline-based reservation systems (CRS), Amadeus, Galileo, Sabre and Worldspan. At the time of writing a new GDS, TRUEConnect, is being developed in the USA. *See* under their respective headings or CRS for a general explanation. *See also* Global Distribution System New Entrants (GNEs).

GDS agency contracts Global Distribution System standard contracts in both the USA and the UK are usually productivity based, costs being based on a minimum number of bookings, with rebates dependant on volume. Within the currency of this dictionary, this may change, as airlines seek to reduce GDS charges, passing costs to agency users of GDSs. At the same time, agents are being offered Internet-based access to some GDSs free of charge. The new US-based GDS, TRUEConnect, that is being developed plans that distribution will be free to agents, while fees to airlines will be less than 20% of the rates charged by the four existing GDSs. Full contracts cover communication costs as well as essential operating hardware. In the USA communication may be by ISDN, DSL or cable-modem connection, each being faster than a simple dial-up modem. In the UK, fast connections use a broadband service; alternatively, dedicated leased tele-phone lines may be provided. In both countries there are variations as to leasing or owning PCs as terminals and printers. Alternatively, Internet connections are available to GDSs; for example, in the USA, no minimum turnover Internet-connected services include Amadeus' EasyAccess; Galileo's Select and Connect; Sabre's Simplicity; and Worldspan's Home Free. These systems provide software for a PC including a specialised Internet browser facilitating encryption and including a firewall enabling sending and receiving of sensitive data using public communication lines. Terms of contracts are currently regulated by codes in Europe that are under review and may be deregulated.

GDS resellers In the USA, several companies now contract with GDSs and then sell GDS access to travel agents on flexible and competitive terms. For example Peragis, which offers both Galileo and Sabre connections, while GRSNetwork only offers Galileo connectivity, Solartis, Cytric, InnoSys, Nexion, Magellan and Lanyon.

GEBTA Guild of European Business Travel Agents. *See* www.users.skynet.be/gebta

GEM Ground effect machine such as hovercraft or any other type of air cushion vehicle.

Gemini A regional CRS which was owned by Air Canada, Cal and Galileo International, acting as the local distribution company for Galileo in Canada; now absorbed into the GDS, Galileo.

General Sales Agent *See* GSA[1].

General Services Administration US federal government department undertaking contracting services in most spheres and in particular, for all air fares, hotel and car-rental rates and travel charge cards for US federal government employees. Together with the MTMC has joint competitive bidding arrangements for the supply of travel services to the federal government. In 1993, following a review, the Defense Travel System was established, with the MTMC acting as the sole procurement agency. Whereas the MTMC does not add a fee for its contracting services, only seeking straight rebates, travel agencies awarded contracts through the GSA not only have to cover the rebate negotiated but also 0.56%

GSA fee for its contracting services throughout the duration of any contract agreed. *A list of 70 other business travel related entries follows* corporate travel contracts, *some of which lead to further entries.*

generating country   *See* tourism generating country.

Genesis   Was an electronic air fares filing system developed by ABC Reed Travel Group in the UK. The system marketed and distributed fares on behalf of the airlines; a complementary computer system at the UK Civil Aviation Authority enabled the CAA to handle fares lodged through ABC Genesis to be approved electronically. The matching Airline Tariff Automated Collection Facility enabled airlines to automatically update fares information into the ABC database, through direct links between airlines' mainframe computers and Genesis. ABC's guides are now part of the world-wide OAG series.

Genie   Name of TUI's agency front office selling system. TUI is the largest tour operator in Europe; the system is used by their UK agency subsidiary Lunn Poly, currently being rebranded Thompson Holidays. It enables searches by customer's criteria such as price, date, destination, accommodation, free child places, discounts, and flight only or cruises and other holiday types. Other operators are included as well as parent company TUI. Information is provided on visa or health requirements based on the customer's passport details. Customer folders will enable clients to be recognized through all UK distribution points including call centres and the web site.

George   Nickname of the automatic pilot on board an aircraft.

Georgia Department of Industry, Trade and Tourism (USA)   *See* Travel South USA *and* www.georgia.org

geotourism   Alternative for ecotourism. Tourism that sustains or enhances the geographical character of the place being visited, such as the environment, culture, aesthetics, heritage, and the well-being of the residents. *See* ecotourism.

German Democratic Republic Travel Agency Organization   Reiseburo der Deutschen Demokratischen Republik. Name is now obsolete, having merged with the DRV.

German Federal Republic National Travel Agency Organization   (DRV) Deutsche Reiseburo-Verband.

German National Tourist Office   *See* www.germany-tourism.de   *and   also* www.germany-tourism.co.uk

GES   Ground earth station (aviation term).

Getaway   Name of computerized data and accounting system for UK travel agents designed by Getaway Travel and introduced in November 1983.

GETS   The CRS set up by SITA. *See* SITA.

GHA   Guernsey Hotels Association. *See* GHTA.

Ghan   The Australian transcontinental rail service between Adelaide and Darwin via Alice Springs. For further information about rail travel, *see* train.

Ghana Tourist Board   *See* www.ghanatourism.com

GHTA   The Guernsey Hotels and Tourism Association was formed in October 1984 by the merger of the long established Guernsey Hotels Association and breakaway group Guernsey Association for Tourism formed in 1983. Whereas the GHA only represented hoteliers, the new group also represents travel agents, tour operators, car-hire companies, carriers and self-catering accommodation. Current membership is around 300.

GI   Global indicator; an IATA fare construction term, used where the rate is unidirectional, to stipulate the direction of travel. For example, many RTW (round-the-world) fares.

GIA   Government and Industry Affairs section of IATA's External Relations Division.

GIANTS   The Greater Independent Association of National Travel Services in the USA.

Gibraltar National Travel Agency Organization   (AGTA) Association of Gibraltar Travel Agents.

Gibraltar Tourist Board   *See* www.gibraltar.gov.uk

Gin palace   Colloquial name for large sized, lavishly equipped cabin cruisers owned by rich people.

GIT   Group inclusive tour.

gîte   The French name for a holiday cottage, flat, apartment or part or all of a house, situated in the countryside and rented on a self-catering basis. Some certainty as to the standards that may be expected is provided if accommodation is described as a 'Gîte de France' or 'Gîte Rural de France', indicating that the standards prescribed either by the Fédération National des Gîtes de France, or of the Gîtes Ruraux de France have been met.

giveaway IATA definition is anything given gratuitously by a carrier, whether or not paid for by the carrier, to a passenger, other than air carriage from airport of departure to airport of destination.

GLAMER Group Leaders of America Travel Show. *See* www.glamer.com

Global Club Name of Japan Airlines' Frequent Flyer Club, membership of which is free for those travelling over 50,000 miles a year. *See* FFP (frequent flyer programme).

Global Code of Ethics for Tourism Adopted by WTO on 1 October 1999. *See* Appendix I.

Global Distribution System An alternative name for a worldwide CRS. For further details *see* CRS.

Global Distribution System New Entrants Web-based GDS aiming to reduce airline distribution costs. Launches planned for 2007 include G2 Switchworks, Farelogix and ITA Software.

global indicator *See* GI.

global navigation satellite system *See* GNSS.

global positioning system *See* GPS.

Global price rail tickets Combined price European rail tickets available on many routes, offering transportation, sleeping car/couchette and/or cabin/berth on board ship, at an inclusive fare, which usually incorporates a reduction on the normal separate charges. On some services, a meal may be included. Five separate coupon tickets must be issued for each person and for each direction of travel.

global warming *See* radiative forcing.

GM Gentil membre. Guest at a Club Méditerranée (Club Med) resort. *See* GO.

GMC Ground movement control (aviation term).

GMP Ground movement planning (aviation term).

GMT Greenwich Mean Time. Although 'officially' the name has changed, to Universal Time, general usage of GMT persists. Historically, zero degrees line of longitude was based on the naval centre at Greenwich, England. For accurate navigation worldwide precise timekeeping was realized to be essential. The standard time established at Greenwich was adopted worldwide. Around each 15 degrees of longitude, local times change by an hour. As a traveller goes westward it is necessary to turn the clock back. For example, the eastern side of America is around 5 h behind Britain. When travelling east, clocks go forward. An International Dateline was established which approximately follows the 180th parallel of longitude. On crossing the International Dateline travelling westward, the date goes forward a day, but on crossing the line going eastward, it reverts to the previous day's date.

GNAVE Grupo Nacional de Agencias de Viajes Espanolas, the Spanish national travel agency organization.

GNE *See* Global Distribution System New Entrants.

GNR Guest name record; an entry in a hospitality industry computer or CRS. In airline systems, the term PNR (passenger name record) is used, but perversely, some hoteliers still call it a GNR.

GNS Global navigation system.

GNSS Global navigation satellite system. The US global positioning system is currently in wide use. Its Russian equivalent is Glonass. It is hoped to provide precision navigation in Europe by enhancing the American system with Egnos, planned to come into service imminently. Specification was defined in 2000, for a European GNSS called Galileo, with the aim of bringing it into service in 2008.

GO Gentil organisateur; activity coordinator/sports coach at a Club Méditerranée (Club Med) resort. *See* GM.

Go USA A grouping of many US principals and suppliers working together with the TIA and USTAA to promote tourism to the USA.

Gold Card Name of the membership card for Cathay Pacific's Marco Polo Club, an airline frequent flyers' club. Also name of American Express credit card, the ordinary green one being the standard, Gold Card more exclusive and Platinum, the top of the Amex range. During recent years other credit card companies have introduced gold cards and during the currency of this book, the term may become generic.

Gold Class Brand name given by South African Airways to passenger area immediately adjacent to first class, where passengers paying full fares can enjoy improved service and facilities. *See* business class for full description.

Golden Age Passport This is only available to US citizens and residents. Permit allowing unrestricted access to US National Park Service parks, properties and sites, available to those aged 62 or over.

Golden Eagle Passport A US National Parks pass which is for any age and allows the bearer and other people in the vehicle into all national parks. Also includes entry to other facilities such as wildlife refuges, Forest Service and Bureau of Land Management sites. *Also see* www.nps.gov

Golden Falcon Executive Club Gulf Air's Frequent Flyers' Club.

Golden Rail Holidays Was brand name of British Rail's inclusive tour operations covering both UK domestic, Channel Islands and Continental holidays, which changed its name to Gold Star Holidays and which was sold to Superbreak, a UK tour operator, in May 1989.

Golden Wing Name of Ansett's Frequent Flyers' Club. Members receive insurance covering lost or delayed baggage, a quiet work area in airport lounges, shower facilities, priority seating, temporary membership of health clubs and reciprocal rights to some other airline clubs. For further details *see* FFP (frequent flyer programme).

gondola[1] Name of the narrow boat with a high prow and stern, plying for hire on the canals of Venice. It is propelled by a 'gondolier' wielding a single oar.

gondola[2] The passenger basket suspended beneath a hot air balloon.

gondola[3] The passenger cabin beneath an airship.

gondola[4] The name of a cable car cabin.

goodies bag Slang term for the amenity kit of complimentary items often supplied to first- or business-class passengers or in hotel rooms.

go-show US term for an airline standby passenger.

government revenue tourism multiplier *See* tourism multiplier.

Government Transportation Request (GTR) US government document acting as an exchange order or travel warrant.

GP Glide path (aviation term).

GPS Global positioning system; sometimes expressed GPSS which is global positioning satellite system. Aviation and maritime dictionaries both claim it as their own. But this is the same system originally developed by the US Defense Department which is now in wide use in private cars for location identification.

GPU Ground power supply unit. An electricity generator supplying power to a static aircraft without its own engine power. These are being phased out in favour of a fixed electrical ground supply (FEGS).

GPWS Ground proximity warning system (aviation term).

grading systems *See* accommodation grading systems.

grand tour This European phenomenon reached its height in the 18th century and was the means by which the wealthy young became educated and civilized. They travelled on an extensive tour of Europe, particularly visiting the major centres of art, culture and learning. The Industrial Revolution in the UK and the many associated social changes, brought to an end the classic grand tour, although the terminology survives to this day to describe any long, luxurious tour.

graphic CRS/GDS entry mode *See* CRS/GDS entry modes.

gratuity The practice of giving a 'tip', 'pourbois' or some money to reward excellent service. Unfortunately, this has now been institutionalized and become a strange way of paying staff in the hospitality industry. Thus, 10% or 15% of the cost of a restaurant meal is almost invariably added to bills, regardless of whether or not the customer is satisfied with the service provided. On package holidays, gratuities are not normally expected, nor is one expected to tip airline staff. Sometimes all restaurant gratuities and service charges are held centrally and distributed to staff, known as a 'tronc'. On some cruises, the amounts of the gratuities expected have become so notorious that Seabourn have banned their staff from accepting any! Other cruise companies avoid the problem by indicating an appropriate level which travellers can pay in advance, while some pool all tips, operating a tronc system.

gravity model *See* transport modelling.

Great Circle A route round the surface of the Earth with its plane cutting through the centre, resulting in the route being the shortest distance for navigation of a plane between any two points. Because of the various projections used, most world maps do not give a correct view, when looking at a flat map, of the likely appropriate shortest distance between any two places.

Greek National Tourism Organization *See* www.gnto.gr *and also* www.gnto.co.uk

Greek National Travel Agency Organization *See* HATTA.

Greek Tourist Card Is available to individual passengers, family and other groups up to five in number, entitling the holder to unlimited rail travel in second class over the Greek railway network and also bus services operated by Greek Railways.

green card In the UK, a certificate proving a vehicle's insurance has been extended to cover travel abroad, essential when making car ferry or Channel Tunnel bookings out of Britain. In the USA, it is a document allowing a non-US citizen to obtain employment.

Green Globe *See* tourism, sustainable.

green tourism *See* tourism, alternative.

Greenland Tourism *See* www.greenland.com

Greenwich Mean Time Term for the world basis of time, originating from the zero line of longitude running through Greenwich, to the east of London, UK. Now, the world standard is known as Universal Time. Although 'officially' the name has changed, general usage of GMT persists and a full explanation is provided under GMT.

greeter US term for the restaurant employee that meets customers and takes them to a table.

Gregorian calendar *See* calendar.

Grenada Board of Tourism *See* www.grenadagrenadines.com

grey tourism Tourism undertaken by senior citizens, who often have high disposable incomes, time available and high propensity to travel. Some textbooks and statistics refer to over 55s, while others either refer to over 60s or over 65s.

grill room An informal hotel restaurant. Title arose in the early 1900s because it was normal in Britain for diners to wear evening dress when eating dinner in a public restaurant. In grill rooms, formal dress attire was not a requirement.

gross registered ton Unit of passenger ship measurement. A GRT is 100 cubic feet of enclosed space.

gross travel propensity *See* travel propensity.

ground arrangements That part of a passenger's itinerary that does not involve travel by air or sea. The term is loosely used in the travel industry in connection with package holidays etc. to designate the arrangements at the destination, after flight arrival, usually consisting of transfers and accommodation. Often called land arrangements in the USA.

ground handler A provider of local services for travellers, usually on behalf of a travel service provider such as a tour operator. Also called a 'destination management company'. May cover some or all of a range of services such as contracting accommodation, arranging transfers to and from accommodation, local tours, sightseeing, acting as local representatives or merely provision of a meet-and-greet service. The same term 'ground handler' is also applied to an organization acting on behalf of an airline at an airport where that airline does not have their own staff, undertaking check-in and other passenger handling.

ground power supply unit *See* GPU.

ground power unit Generator supplying electricity to a static aircraft before the engines have been started, thus enabling lighting and air-conditioning etc. to function.

Ground Service Voucher Title of an airline voucher used in conjunction with an air ticket as a value document to be issued for car hire or hotel accommodation.

grounding When an appropriate authority requests that aircraft should not fly. In poor weather, aircraft without automatic landing and take-off equipment must be grounded. Several years ago, the FAA in the USA, CAA in the UK and other governmental bodies were responsible for the grounding of DC10s, because of a serious defect which was put right before the aircraft went back into service. More recently, in 2000, following an accident, Concorde was grounded.

Group 2 Used to be a UK Advanced Booking air fare to Spain. Withdrawn from 1 November 1979, being replaced by other low-priced rates.

Group Leaders of America Travel Show *See* www.glamer.com

Group of National Travel Agents and Tour Operators Associations in the EU *See* www.ectaa.org

group rebates by sea Varies between operators. P&O offer 10% rebate for groups of 15 adults with a free ticket as well for 21 persons. For a party of 42, two free tickets are provided.

Group Travel Organisers Association UK body of mainly non-travel trade members. *See* www.gtoa.co.uk

growth factor model *See* transport modelling.

GRT *See* gross registered ton.

GRTG The Guild of Registered Tourist Guides is a professional association of registered tourist guides in the UK, often referred to as 'Blue Badge' guides. *See* www.blue-badge.org.uk However, the officially recognized body for setting standards, is the Institute of Tourist Guiding.

GS Ground speed (aviation term).

GSA¹ General sales agent. When an airline is not represented fully in a country a GSA is appointed to handle that airline's promotion, reservations, ticketing and enquiries. The same term is applied to other similar situations in the travel industry. For example, consolidation arrangements and sale of group fares from the UK to India and Pakistan are handled by travel agent GSAs working on behalf of different airlines.

GSA² General Services Administration of the US Federal Government which administers travel services contracting. *See* General Services Administration.

GST Goods and services tax in the USA.

GTB Guernsey Tourist Board. *See* www.guernseytouristboard.com

GTI The Galileo, Thomson and Istel technology initiative was launched in the UK in 1992 to replace viewdata sets with personal computer automation in British travel agencies and standardize the formats used for data transmission and screens. Subsequently, Airtours and Owners Abroad became partners. This initiative collapsed in May 1993.

GTMC Guild of Travel Management Companies; changed name in 2005 from Guild of Business Travel Agents (GBTA). Grouping of many of the most important UK travel agents specializing in travel management. Established in 1968 as the BHTAG (Business House Travel Agents Guild), it was renamed the GBTA in 1976. It handles over 80% of business air traffic generated through UK agents; combined annual turnover of members over £8bn. In 1991, together with City and Guilds of London Institute as the examining body, set up the syllabuses for a new series of UK trade examinations. The Certificate in Business Travel, (CBT) has three levels, Consultant, Advanced and Management; CCBT, ACBT and MCBT. *See* www.gtmc.org *A list of 70 other business travel related entries follows* corporate travel contracts, *some of which lead to further entries.*

GTO Government tourist office; more common usage is NTO (National tourist office). These terms are used for the tourism information offices situated in foreign countries, to promote tourism into the NTO's country.

GTOA Group Travel Organisers Association. *See* www.gtoa.co.uk

GTR Government Travel Request; in the USA the term is applied specifically to an official voucher authorizing a travel purchase.

GUA *See* Galileo Users' Association.

Guadalajara Convention Agreement supplementing the Warsaw Convention. *See* Warsaw Convention.

guarantee policy (of hotel) Otherwise known as room-holding policy. Hotels' rules concerning times up to which booked rooms will be held for occupation that night. *See* late arrival.

guaranteed payment reservation An hotel booking, made on the understanding that should the client not arrive, the travel company will be responsible for payment. Often, indemnity is restricted to first night's accommodation. Frequently, the client's credit card details are provided for this purpose. The precise conditions laid down by each hotel are known as their *guarantee policy*.

guaranteed share Where a group organizer, tour operator or cruise company assures non-attached persons that they can have the price normally available to couples sharing, whether or not another person of the same sex is found to complete the shared accommodation.

guaranteed upgrade An upgrade is the provision of a better travel service than that for which a client has paid, at no extra charge. Members of frequent traveller clubs and others involved in customer loyalty promotions are offered 'guaranteed' upgrades, for example, by being provided with a higher class of travel, better hotel room or larger car, at no additional cost.

guarantees of no surcharges During recent years, there have been big fluctuations in the exchange rates of the UK pound against other currencies. Thus, the rates on which ground arrangements, or the cost of aviation fuel, may have been costed in an operator's brochure, published a year or more before departure, frequently become unrealistic. To continue to operate at the published prices would produce losses. In the UK tour operators and other travel companies have protected themselves against the extra costs they might incur by appropriate booking conditions, which allow them to 'surcharge' customers. Increasingly, in the late 1980s, many operators guaranteed their advertised prices, either promising not to raise any surcharges or that they would only raise them in exceptional circumstances. A number of UK shipping lines and tour operators offer customers the chance to protect themselves against any possible surcharges, by paying their fares in full within a couple of weeks of receiving their initial invoice. It is always a gamble whether the potential interest on the money is more or less than the surcharge, when customers have booked ahead.

guard In times past, the railway employee occupying the rear of a train, the guard's van. Responsible for security, for example, checking all doors were shut and signalling to the driver that it was in order to start. Now, while there may be conductors and ticket collectors on board trains, often there will not be a guard.

Guatemala City Protocol Agreement supplementing the Warsaw Convention. *See* Warsaw Convention.

Guatemala Tourist Commission *See* www.guatemala.travel.com.gt

Guernsey Hotels and Tourism Association *See* GHTA.

Guernsey Tourist Board *See* www.guernseytouristboard.com

guest cruise night *See* PCN[3].

guest history A client profile, usually kept on a hotel's computer.

guest house In the UK, small hotel providing room only or bed, breakfast and evening meal. The term is synonymous with boarding house, although it has overtones of being considered slightly better. In the UK, there is an important legal difference between a hotel and guest house. Whereas the former, under the 1956 Hotel Proprietor Act, has an obligation to accept travellers 'in a fit state' as long as there are empty rooms, guest houses can be selective. Proprietors may (and often do) behave as they would towards visitors to their home. In the USA, the term guest house may mean the provision of rooms for the public in someone's private home. Nevertheless, somewhat confusingly, some American guest houses are not in private homes.

guest name record *See* GNR.

guest night Same as a bed night; one person spending one night in any accommodation.

guest services manager *See* animateur/activities coordinator.

guide Someone who is employed to take tourists on local sightseeing excursions, or around sites of archaeological or other interest. Guides are often licensed by the local government authority in the area in which they work or authorized. *See* tourist guide for details of controversy that surrounds this definition.

guided tour In general use in the travel industry, often means escorted or conducted vacation travel. *See* escorted tour. However, the 2003 CEN/European Standard official definition is 'tour of a specified length covering cited elements of the cultural or natural heritage of a city and/or an area, conducted by a tourist guide'.

guides to hotels worldwide *See* hotels, unbiased opinions of.

Guild of British Coach Operators (GBCO) *See* www.coach-tours.co.uk

Guild of Business Travel Agents Now renamed Guild of Travel Management Companies. *See* GTMC. *A list of 70 other business travel related entries follows* corporate travel contracts, *some of which lead to further entries.*

Guild of European Business Travel Agents Eight-country grouping of travel agents specializing in business travel.

Guild of Guide Lecturers The professional body of British tourist board registered guides, founded in 1950 with over 600 members, on behalf of whom it operates Tour Guides Limited,

through which members' services may be booked.

Guild of Registered Tourist Guides *See* GRTG.

Guild of Travel Management Companies Formerly Guild of Business Travel Agents in the UK. *See* GTMC.

Guild of Travel Writers A group of around 100 UK journalists, authors, TV and radio broadcasters in the travel field, not restricted to those who are members of National Union of Journalists or Institute of Journalists. Membership is barred to anyone with a commercial involvement in organizing travel and tourism facilities.

Gulliver Name of the Irish Tourist Board's CRS.

Guyana Tourism Authority *See* www.guyana-tourism.com

Gwynedd A Welsh-based consortium of travel agents, member of Worldchoice.

H

H24 or **24/7** or **24/7/365** Service continuously available or operated, all day, every day.

HACC Heathrow Airport Consultative Committee in the UK.

Hague Protocol to the Warsaw Convention *See* Warsaw Convention.

Hales Trophy *See* Blue Riband of the Atlantic.

half board Same as MAP or demipension; bed, continental breakfast and another main meal, usually dinner. Note that term is not used in some English-speaking countries, for example, Australia.

half pension Same as MAP or demipension; bed, continental breakfast and another main meal, usually dinner.

half round trip or half return Whenever return air fares are cheaper than single fares, fare constructions may in many circumstances permit the use of half the return fare rather than the full single fare. European excursion air fares are the best example, where rates change during seasonal periods and fares may be constructed by combining lowest possible half return excursion fares.

hall porter *See* concierge.

halo effect Suggested by US web site www.hometravelagency.com to be the extra business travel agents give to airline owners of their CRS. Usage not common either in the UK or USA; moreover, separation of the major GDSs from obvious airline ownership makes this obsolescent. *See* CRS rules for neutrality.

HALO[1] High altitude long operation (aviation term).

HALO[2] High altitude low opening with reference to parachuting.

HALO[3] High agility low observable (aviation term).

hand baggage Luggage limited by number of pieces and/or size and/or weight which travellers may keep with them during conveyance on a mode of transport; being 'unchecked', such baggage is the responsibility of the traveller. Word-

ing improved from the 2001/BSI/CEN proposed standard definition.

hand luggage *See* hand baggage.

handling agent Many travel agents, particularly those located in major gateway cities, provide services to incoming visitors. These include meeting and greeting at airports or seaports, interpreter services, transfers, arranging hotel accommodation, sightseeing tours and assisting the incoming tourist in any other way that is needed. A handling agent's rates are, by travel industry custom, listed in 'Confidential Tariffs', which are sent to travel organizers in foreign countries enabling the cost of handling to be estimated in advance and priced into inclusive arrangements to be offered as a package to travellers from that country. *See* contractor for some alternative American terminology for the same concept.

handling fees Handling fee for IATA agents is US$5 for the ticketing agents if another agent took the money for a prepaid ticket advice. IATA airlines will only pay out full commission on the sale of an air ticket to one agent. If therefore an agent takes the money for a PTA effecting definite flight reservations, an agent in the issuing country cannot also receive commission and instead small handling fees at the official IATA rates are awarded (IATA Resolution 864). Of course, all of the foregoing is theoretical! With most airlines not paying commission, the only income agents receive is the fees charged to customers.

hand-off tape A magnetic tape supplied to a BSP airline containing all the data for that airline raised from the tickets and other documents in a periodic sales transmittal.

hangar Large shed for aircraft, in which they may be kept under cover, maintained or repaired.

HANK Hotels Automated Network Knowhow. An artificial acronym for Utell's database and reservation system named after Hank Utell, the organization's founder. He started Utell in the early 1930s and it has now become the largest hotel representation company in the world, handling reservations for around seven million room nights annually. Utell is the hotel industry's largest third party marketing and reservations provider representing one million rooms. It was acquired by Pegasus Solutions Inc. in 2000 and is now a wholly owned subsidiary. *See* www.pegs.com *and* www.utell.com

hard disk *See* disk.

hardware[1] (computer) The physical and mechanical elements of a computer system (something you can stub your toe on!). To be contrasted with the software, which are those unseen untouchable electronic signals that tell the hardware what to do. A disk is in itself hardware, but the data stored on its surface in the form of signals, as a program, is software. Just to confuse matters, instructions that would normally be called software are sometimes actually burnt into a computer and become an integral part of the equipment. So, since they are strictly speaking, neither hardware nor software, they are sometimes called firmware, halfway between the two.

hardware[2] (maritime parlance) May refer to the structure of a ship, while the software is an intangible item such as service.

hardwired *See* computer memory for general worldwide meaning. In the UK, the term is applied to travel agency computer terminals that are directly connected to central national computer systems by permanent data lines rather than accessing those systems on demand on a telephone dial-up basis.

HARP Helicopter Airworthiness Review Panel.

HARS Heading/altitude reference system (aviation term).

hash The symbol # which appears on many computer keyboards, and which may initiate a variety of actions according to the software programme into which the # entry is being made. In the UK the symbol has very wide application in viewdata. For example a number preceded by a star or asterisk and followed by a hash requests the computer to go to that page number.

hash through In the UK, to press the # key on a computer keyboard, thus moving through parts of a viewdata screen or a form, the ends of the sections being designated by #. Thus, to 'hash through' is to go over parts of a screen offering the chance to make entries, leaving the entry fields blank.

hatch Any opening in the deck on a ship, which during storms is securely fastened (battened down).

HATTA Hellenic Association of Travel and Tourist Agents. *See* www.hatta.gr

Hawaii Visitors and Convention Bureau *See* www.gohawaii.com

HBAA Hotel Booking Agents Association in the UK. This 51-member trade body of hotel booking specialists is unique to Britain; in the USA and in the rest of Europe there are few specialists in this field. Around 70% of US business hotels are owned by one of the big groups, while in the UK, the figure is about 30%, one of the reasons for the difference. *See* www.hbaa.org.uk

HCA Holiday Centres Association in the UK.

HCC Hotel Clearing Corporation. *See* THISCO.

HCF High cycle fatigue (aviation term).

HCIMA Hotel, Catering and Institutional Management Association, which was formed in 1971 by the amalgamation of the HCI and IMA. Although it is the UK professional body for managers and potential managers, its extensive series of membership examinations at all levels are recognized and studied for on a worldwide basis. *See* www.hcima.org.uk *and also* Hospitality Assured.

HCITB Was the Hotel and Catering Industry Training Board in the UK, established in 1970, which was replaced by the Hospitality Training Foundation in 1997. This, in turn, has now become People 1st, a Sector Skills Council.

HCS Holiday Care Service in the UK handles the special needs of disabled people, the elderly, single parents and others who find holidaymaking a problem, by providing free information. It is a charity funded by the travel industry, aiming to promote the development and inclusion of facilities for the aforementioned groups. *See* www.holidaycare. org.uk

HEAC Higher Education Accommodation Consortium in the UK, which merged with the British Universities Accommodation Consortium at the end of 2000 to form Venuemasters. Undertakes joint marketing of their facilities during vacation periods to potential conference and group traffic.

head Maritime parlance for a toilet.

head office location Official IATA definition is an approved agent's place of business entered on the agency list as a head office location.

head porter UK hotel equivalent of US bell captain; but in both countries, a person with wide ranging front of house responsibilities for guest servicing.

head sea Where the sea current and/or waves directly oppose a ship's progress, reducing headway; often associated with a headwind, which is when the wind is blowing against the direction of travel.

head tax *See* departure tax.

heads Toilets on board ship.

headwind When the wind direction is opposite to the direction of travel; this may lengthen the duration of journeys at sea. *See also* headsea.

health certificates *See* international health requirements.

health club Usual name for the exercise facilities in hotels, otherwise known as a fitness room or gym. Where a hotel has a swimming pool, this is often part of the health club.

health farm *See* health resort.

health insurance within EU An E111 Certificate is available to UK citizens for use when travelling in the EU, outside the member state of normal residence. It acts as evidence of entitlement to free medical treatment at the same level as provided to local nationals; similar arrangements exist in other EU member states. Can be used up to December 2005, when it will be replaced with the European Health Insurance Card (*see entry under this heading*). For details and to download form *see* www.dh.gov.uk Forms are also available from UK post offices.

health requirements for travellers *See* international health requirements.

health resort May be a substantial tourism area or a single unit providing facilities such as a fully equipped fitness centre, dieting/weight reduction, steam/turkish baths, saunas, massage, bathing in mineral or hot spring water, mud or earth external treatment and thalassotherapy. In the UK and North America, such complexes may be called health farms.

hearing Rulemaking, licensing or adjudicatory proceedings for the taking of evidence in the form of testimony or documents and the presentation of arguments to governmental aviation authorities, such as the CAA in Britain or the CAB in the USA.

heated swimming pool A facility sought after in cold climates, where it is necessary to heat a pool well above the ambient temperature for the comfort of users.

heave A vertical motion of a ship as it responds to waves.

HEDNA The Hotel Electronic Distribution Network Association is a not-for-profit trade association whose worldwide membership includes executives and managers from over 200 of the most influential companies in the hotel distribution industry. Founded in 1991, HEDNA strives to stimulate the booking of hotel rooms through the use of GDSs, the Internet and other electronic means. HEDNA brings all segments of the hospitality industry together to determine how to most effectively evolve their systems and services, in order to contribute to the success and revenue growth of electronic distribution for hotels. For further information see www.hedna.org For further information on booking accommodation by electronic means, *see* hotel statistics worldwide.

heel When a ship inclines to port or starboard.

Hejira Calendar *See* calendar.

helicopter A type of aircraft that derives lift from revolving wings or blades driven by an engine about a vertical axis. The small propeller revolving around a horizontal shaft of some helicopters is to provide stability. Both forward movement and lift come from the revolving rotor blades. Helicopters can hover and land or take off vertically. Horizontal movement is achieved by the pilot by slight inclination of the rotor blades so that they then pull the helicopter along. In 1986, Sikorsky, the world's leading helicopter manufacturer unveiled its

X-Wing helicopter. So named, because after take-off, the X-shaped rotor is fixed with all blades at an angle of 45° to the helicopter body. The rotor blades are hollow and movement is achieved by jets of air blown backwards through the four trailing edges of the rotor blades. The same technique has been used successfully in some military aircraft and is called the coanda effect. Sikorsky are also investigating the use of the Advancing Blade Concept, utilizing two rotor blades, one on top of the other, but rotating in opposite directions.

heliport An area from which helicopters can take off or land.

Hellenic Association of Travel and Tourist Agents (HATTA) *See* www.hatta.gr

helm Term usually refers to a ship's steering wheel – but by definition is the entire steering apparatus.

heritage tourism *See* tourism, heritage.

herringbone room set-up *See* meeting room set-up.

Hertz No. 1 Club A computerized system which maintains car rental information about Hertz customers in order to provide them with fast counter service. There is no application fee, annual fee or renewal charge and the same applies to the Hertz credit card when this is combined with No. 1 Club membership. Other car hire companies have similar but less well-known systems.

HF High frequency. Used as an aviation technical term in relation to communications but the abbreviation is *not* used as an indication of a regular service with short intervals.

HFTP Hospitality Financial and Technology Professionals. *See* www.hftp.org

HHA Historic Houses Association. Membership is restricted to private owners of houses and gardens listed by UK authorities as of particular historic interest, and which therefore are protected for posterity. Founded in 1973 it has around 1000 members. *See* www.hha.org.uk

Hi Line Was a Scottish hotels reservation system which went into liquidation in October 1992.

hidden city ticketing Issuing an air ticket to a place further than a traveller's intended destination because the fare is lower, when the flight itinerary has intermediate stops. Thus the passenger can alight where they actually wish to go, discarding the rest of the itinerary. This practice is prohibited by the airlines; however, it is difficult to prevent knowledgeable passengers making the bookings or to prove that the ticket was issued with the intention of undercutting the fare. Also known as 'point beyond ticketing'.

HIF Higher intermediate fare. *See* higher rated intermediate points for explanation of this IATA fare construction principle; *also see* IATA fare construction system.

high density ship *See* ship density.

High Life Name of British Airways' in-flight magazine.

high risk guest Hotels place limits on the maximum amount of bills they will allow clients of various types to run up, before requiring payment. This term indicates a guest that has approached or passed the maximum.

high seas At one time most countries abided by the 3-mile limit from their territory, beyond which territorial waters ended and high or open sea began. There is now little unanimity over the distance within which countries exercise their rights. Maritime law declared *mare clausum* as that area of sea subject to the laws of a country and *mare liberum* as that area subject to international maritime laws.

high season The busiest time for the use of any travel facility. The most popular travel time, in contrast to low season and the 'shoulder' period. In the Mediterranean, this is July and August, while in a ski resort, it will be in the winter. This is when fares and hotel rates are at their highest.

High Speed Trains *See* train *and* TGV.

Higher Education Academy Network for Hospitality, Leisure, Sport and Tourism (in the UK). Formed in May 2004 from a merger of the Institute for Learning and Teaching in Higher Education (ILTHE), the Learning and Teaching Support Network (LTSN) and the Teaching Quality Enhancement Forum National Co-ordination Committee (TQEC/TQEF NCT); separate centres have been established covering the main higher education study areas. The Network for Hospitality, Leisure, Sport and Tourism is located at Oxford Brookes University. Its mission is 'to be the primary information and advice resource for all staff involved in learning and teaching in the hospitality, leisure sport and tourism subject areas of higher education on subject specific and generic learning and teaching practice'. It identifies current issues within subject areas and responds to community needs. It encourages research activities and is a source of information and advice to funding bodies and bidding institutions. Accessible through the HEAN web site www.heacademy.ac.uk or www.hlst.ltsn.ac.uk is a guide with links to over 100 Internet resources in hospitality, leisure, sport and tourism. Sites have been selected for their academic quality and subject relevance. *See* www.hlst.ltsn.ac.uk/resources/resources.html

higher education in tourism in the UK *See* Higher Education Academy Network for Hospitality, Leisure, Sport and Tourism.

higher intermediate fare *See* higher rated intermediate point.

higher intermediate points *See* higher rated intermediate points.

higher rated intermediate points Occurs on multi-sector air itineraries. Fare from UK to fare breakpoint may be less than the fare to some of the points en route. The air ticket price must then be increased at least to minimum fare of these higher cost points. European excursion air fares which involve a stop in Italy en route are a very good example of this principle. *See* IATA fare construction system.

highway Throughout this book the term 'road' has been preferred to the North American term. However, Interstate Highways which may stretch for thousands of miles facilitate all long journeys by road in the USA. They are labelled Interstate (usually in red) at the top of a shield, on which the number is written in white on a blue background. They are even numbered if they run generally along an east–west axis and odd numbered, north–south. The main Interstates have a two figure number. Where there are three, the last two indicate the main highway to which the subsidiary links.

hijacking The act of violently taking over control of a mode of transport. Occasionally this is by common criminals for ransom or other monetary gain, but more usually, it is an international terrorist activity.

HIMG Hotel Industry Marketing Group, a specialist branch of the Chartered Institute of Marketing in the UK. Generally known in the UK travel industry as the Hotel Marketing Association (HMA).

hinge account IATA term for a bank account into which agents' remittances are paid and then distributed to airlines.

HIP Higher intermediate point. *See* higher rated intermediate point *and* HIF; *also see* IATA fare construction system.

hire car *See* car rental.

HIRO Holiday Inn Revenue Optimizer. *See* yield management.

Historic Houses Association *See* HHA.

HITEC An annual trade fair in the USA covering hospitality industry automation, sponsored by the IAHA/HFTP.

HITIS Hospitality Industry Technology Integration Standards in North America. *See* www.hitis.org

HJ Sunrise to sunset (aviation term). *See also* HN.

HKHATA Hong Kong Association of Travel Agents. *See* www.hata.org.hk

HKTA Until April 2001, Hong Kong Tourist Association, the official tourist organization.

HKTB Since April 2001, Hong Kong Tourist Board, the statutory tourist organization, although many textbooks, having been published before the change, still refer to the HKTA. *See* www.discoverhongkong.com

HMA Hotel Marketing Association in the UK. One of the eight interest groups of the Chartered Institute of Marketing.

HMAC Hazardous Materials Advisory Council of IATA.

Hmr Homer (aviation term).

HMU Hydro-mechanical unit (aviation engine term).

HN Sunset to sunrise (aviation term). *See also* HJ.

HO Hours of operation (aviation term).

hold A place on a ship for the storage of cargo and other items not required 'en voyage'.

hold baggage Luggage, generally of a heavy nature, which is stored in the ship's hold, and which is not available to a passenger during the voyage.

Holiday Booking Survey Comprehensive monthly analysis of UK package holiday market produced by AC Nielsen.

holiday camps *See* holiday centres.

holiday caravan A caravan permanently located on site with facilities. *See* caravan.

Holiday Care Service *See* HCS.

holiday centre The 2003 CEN/European Standard official definition brackets together holiday centres, holiday camps and holiday villages: 'holiday establishment, usually providing accommodation in chalets, bungalows or caravan holiday homes and providing on-site entertainment facilities, shops and restaurants'. In the UK usually refers to a derivative of the holiday camp phenomenon resulting from the 1935 Holiday Pay Act that provided British employees with paid holidays. Butlins, the pioneers, achieved millions of visitors annually and were still attracting around 1 million in 1988. The spartan chalets without bathrooms or toilets contrasted with the excellent entertainment and sporting facilities for family holidays. Now however, accommodation is usually of high standard.

holiday club Usage of the term has evolved. In the period until the 1960s, in the UK, a holiday club was a group of people who saved money weekly to purchase an annual holiday; so that they were best described as holiday savings clubs. During the 1970s in Europe, holiday clubs were established as complexes which today might be called all-inclusive resorts. Club Med was an example. Although usage of these two concepts continues, now in the new century, holiday clubs are also a timeshare product where holidaymakers buy points instead of a specific slot at a particular resort. The Organization for Timeshare in Europe explains that these points then act as a holiday currency. Each time a timeshare apartment is chosen, the number of 'points' that will be paid varies according to the quality, season and duration required. Because membership of a club is not linked to any rights in any particular property, consumers are not protected by the extensive legislation covering timeshare purchase. This has led to some unscrupulous holiday club operators

getting round the effective laws about timeshares by rebranding their products as holiday clubs, as described by the British DTI in July 2001. *See* timeshare for more information. *See also* VOICE.

holiday frequency *See* travel propensity.

Holiday Guide Published twice yearly by DG&G Travel Information (Reed Business Information), gives immediate access to the information contained in all major UK holiday brochures. The brochure information is broken down into various sections including Summer (or Winter) Sun, Winter Sports, Long Distance, Car Ferries and Cruises and UK Holidays, with resorts sequenced within respective countries and the hotels used by operators listed below each resort. Information given includes a brochure page reference, reservation telephone number, holiday duration, basic price, mode of travel and departure airport.

holiday insurance *See* travel insurance.

holiday propensity *See* travel propensity.

holiday savings plans Schemes whereby consumers are encouraged to open accounts with banks, finance houses, building societies and other similar organizations in order to save money for leisure travel. Despite considerable efforts on both sides of the Atlantic, schemes of this nature have not become popular.

holiday village *See* holiday centre.

Holidaymaker Was the name of Thomas Cook's private viewdata system, enabling UK travel agents to make bookings direct from their office terminals. In November 1985 Thomas Cook changed their marketing policy, deciding that in future, Thomas Cook's holidays would only be sold through their own travel shops and the system was renamed CARE, standing for Cook's Automated Reservations and Enquiries system. This policy has been reversed and Cook's-owned JMC Holidays is now a major UK Overseas holiday brand.

Holidaymaker On-line Transaction Service This service was a UK travel agency direct banking debit system whereby the agent's bank account was automatically debited, weekly, for the value of transactions with that operator due for payment. The operator failed in 1993.

Holidaymaster A computerized British tour operators' reservation and accounting system introduced in 1982 on a bureau basis by ICL Network Services. Also was the brand name of Baric's gateway service enabling UK travel agents to access tour operators' reservation and information computers through Prestel.

Holidex Holiday Inn's international information and computer reservation system. *See* yield management.

Holland Board of Tourism *See* www.holland.com *and* www.visitholland.com

Holland Herald Name of KLM Royal Dutch Airlines' in-flight magazine.

hollow square room set-up *See* meeting room set-up.

Hollywood bed Suggested in S. Medlik's *Dictionary of Travel and Tourism* to be US hotel room style of single headboard but twin beds, while a Hollywood-length bed is 80 to 82 in. instead of the normal 75. Research has not found the terms in use.

home exchange In the tourism field, means swapping homes for leisure or vacation purposes for short periods. Home exchange agencies facilitate this for fees, usually operating between countries.

home port bonus Used to be extra agency commission given to some US east-coast agents because they missed out on associated air travel bookings. *Source* suggests US web site www.hometravelagency.com

Honduras Institute of Tourism Although name suggests otherwise, official government organization responsible for tourism promotion. *See* www.explorehonduras.com

Hong Kong National Travel Agency Organization (HKHATA). *See* www.hata.org.hk

Hong Kong Tourism Board *See* www.discoverhongkong.com

Hong Kong Tourist Board *See* HKTB.

honour system (US honor system) Trust placed on guests to record their own consumption. For example, in a small guest house, the bar may be left open and guests invited to help themselves, noting what they take. This system used to work for minibars in hotel rooms, with guests recording what they consumed. Repeated dishonesty has caused an honour system to be replaced with daily checking in most hotels.

horsepower Standard way of rating the power an engine can produce. 1 HP raises 550 pounds, 1 ft in 1 s.

horseshoe room set-up *See* meeting room set-up.

Hospitality Assured A British national quality benchmarking scheme sponsored by the HCIMA facilitating external validation of UK hospitality businesses.

hospitality desk At a hotel or other venue, an information facility for members of a specified group; the term is misleading as it suggests provision of rather more than information.

Hospitality Financial and Technology Professionals For detail of this US-based organization *see* www.hftp.org

hospitality higher education in the UK *See* Higher Education Academy Network for Hospitality, Leisure, Sport and Tourism.

hospitality industry The hotel and catering industry; broadly the provision of accommodation, food and beverages. Some texts also include the meetings industry and attractions. Although readers will find these usages common, the UK *Standard Industrial Classification* leaves no doubt as to what should be included. Under the general heading of hotels and catering and sub-heading restaurants, snack bars, cafés and other eating places are to be found both licensed and unlicensed premises supplying food for consumption on the premises. These include public houses, bars, night clubs, licensed clubs, canteens and staff messes, and the catering contractors that might be running them. Catering services to hospitals and educational establishments are an obvious inclusion. But less obvious are the complete operation of running social and residential homes, convalescent and rest homes. Another section covers takeaway food shops. The hotel trade is included in all its forms, as well as camping and caravan sites, whether static or otherwise, holiday camps and villages; any other tourist or short-stay accommodation not specified also falls under the aegis of the hospitality industry.

All of the above leads to an alternative definition of the hospitality industry, 'a commercial activity centred around the provision of food, drink and accommodation'. From the perspectives of both suppliers and consumers, cost-effective quality service delivery is the aim; but this is not implicit in the proposed definition.

Hospitality Industry Technology Integration Standards *See* www.hitis.org

hospitality suite At a convention, conference or similar gathering, this is a room or area set aside for the use of any particular organization, for the purpose of entertaining invited guests. It is fundamental to the meaning of the term, that visitors to a hospitality suite are provided with free refreshment, paid for by the host who usually seeks to use the opportunity to sell the products or services manufactured or organized.

Hospitality Training Foundation Has now become a UK government Sector Skills Council for the hospitality, leisure, travel and tourism industry. *See* www.people1st.co.uk

host The North American alternative for a tour operator's representative or tour manager. *See* tour manager, tour operator's representative *and* courier. There is a semantic problem in that the word 'host' is not the male equivalent of the word 'hostess'; consider an air hostess, for example. The male is an air steward. But a hostess in the travel industry may undertake a range of activities. A hostess may greet and assist travellers at transport terminals and hotels; but there is no standard name for the male and the 2003 CEN/European Standard official definition is not helpful in its attempt to designate host as an alternative for hostess.

host agency US travel company providing services to non-accredited travel agents. Typically, a host agency might provide access to all four GDSs and process documents with ARC. Major host agencies, such as Nexion, also form their agents into a consortium, enabling extra commission to be gained through override agreements with preferred suppliers. There is a list of host agencies on the NACTA (National Association of Commissioned Travel Agents) web site www.nacta.com

host computer Terminals in travel agencies are connected to one or more GDSs or CRSs which hold or have access to the inventory that the agents book and sell. Thus, these GDSs and CRSs are the host computers.

host-escort North American wording for the tour manager of a tour operator's organized tour.

host programme Also known as escort programme. Because there are usually rather more unaccompanied women on cruises than men, cruise lines enhance their enjoyment by providing male escorts; they are sometimes rudely (and wrongly) referred to as gigolos!

hostal The name for a small hotel or guest house in Spain.

hosted tour *See* host.

hostel Low-priced residential accommodation at a university or other institution. The term has wide use, often resulting in confusion. For example, a hostel for armed services officers can be expected to be of high grade; one for the senior nursing staff of a hospital of medium grade; and another for students to be quite basic. Whereas all the examples so far mentioned are to provide accommodation for a static population, hostels provided by organizations such as the Youth Hostels Association and associated bodies throughout the world are meant to provide the cheapest possible sleeping place for travellers, usually in dormitory form, with some self-catering facilities available.

hostelry A general term which can include many types. In the UK, it might mean a local public house, a series of bars with no accommodation. In North America, it is more likely to refer to a small inn, but may refer to a hostel.

HOT *See* hand-off tape.

hot-air balloon A huge fabric envelope inflated with air heated by gas burners. As the hot air is lighter than the surrounding cooler air, lifting power is created to carry passengers in the compartment slung below. Used as a tourist attraction; for example, because it is almost noiseless, a viewing platform is created for viewing wildlife (balloon safaris). Balloon movement is subject to the vagaries of the wind.

hot dogging Acrobatic skiing.

hotel A building providing residential accommodation and food to members of the public. The term hotel usually denotes a superior type of accommodation in a property of substantial size offering a range of other services, contrasting with a boarding house or guest house. This, at the lowest end of the scale, may offer little more than a few guest rooms in a private house, either with or without some meals. In 2002 Peter Jones and Andrew Lockwood in their standard work, *Understanding Hotel Operations* suggested that a hotel is 'an operation that provides accommodation and ancillary services to people away from home'. Disagreement is expressed because many hotels have permanent residents who have made it their home. In Australia and New Zealand, a hotel can also be an establishment which does not offer accommodation, similar to a bar in North America, tavern in Europe or public house (pub) in the UK. *See also* accommodation grading systems, accommodation types, aparthotel, boarding house, guest house, hostal, hostel, motel *and* pension.

Hotel and Catering Industry Training Board *See* HCITB (obsolete).

Hotel Booking Agents Association (in the UK) *See* www.hbaa.org.uk

hotel bookings for UK business travellers An estimated 45% of all hotel rooms for business travellers in the UK (around £1500m annually) are made through specialist hotel booking companies or travel agents. Volumes are split between agents and specialists. Market leader is Expotel, booking over 1.5m rooms a year www.expotel.com – other leading specialists are Bedfare www.bedfare.net ; BSI, claiming to book 1m bednights annually www.bsi.co.uk ; The Corporate Team www.corporateteam.com and First Option reserving over 0.5m nights a year www.first-option.co.uk In the USA, Hotels.com, Expedia and Travelocity are responsible for 75% of on-line travel agency sales. Hotel groups have successfully responded by seeking to cut out these Web intermediaries by creating Travelweb in February 2002, a joint venture between Hilton Hotels, Hyatt, Marriott and Six Continents (now InterContinental) facilitated by technology provider Pegasus. This example is being emulated in Europe with the late 2003 launch of WorldResEurope which sell rooms for Accor, InterContinental and Hilton through various web sites including Placetostay.com, All-hotels.com, hotel.de and Opodo. Within the currency of this dictionary, these developments can be expected to affect the business of hotel booking companies. *A list of 70 other business travel related entries follows* corporate travel contracts, *some of which lead to further entries.*

Hotel Catering and Institutional Management Association *See* HCIMA.

hotel chain A group of hotels promoted through one or more brand names, under the same ownership or within the same cooperative or commercial franchise. The ten largest groups are listed below under hotels worldwide. Operative arrangements are often mixed within a particular brand. Best Western is an example of a brand where the partners cooperate but own their individual hotels.

hotel classification and grading systems *See* accommodation grading systems.

hotel computer systems *See* THISCO *and* PMS^2 (Property Management Systems).

Hotel Electronic Distribution Network Association *See* HEDNA.

hotel garni A hotel with no dining room or restaurant service, although occasionally, continental breakfast may be offered. The wording came into use in Britain in the early 1760s. Term is common in North America; in Europe, usually called an aparthotel.

hotel guides *See* hotels, unbiased opinions of.

hotel management system *See* PMS^2.

hotel register In old or unsophisticated small hotels, this continues to be a huge ledger, in which visitors write their name and address, passport number, nationality and sign. More common is for visitors to sign an individual slip of paper, providing the same information as well as method of payment. This is then computerized.

hotel rep *See* hotel representation below.

hotel representation Organizations or individuals may offer a service to foreign hotels to represent them. The services offered may be merely to supply information if requested, to undertake advertising of the hotel to the public or agents, to seek contracts with tour operators, to accept bookings and pass them on, or perhaps, as for example, Utell, the largest company worldwide in this sphere, to offer full CRS reservation services, as well as a complete range of other marketing and distribution services.

hotel room access   *See* keycard.

hotel room rates   *See tables on opposite page and on page 188.*

hotel room rate types   consortia, corporate, day use, group, government, opaque, internet, prepaid, promotional, special, travel industry and weekend are typical words used; but the meanings vary greatly between hotels. Associated conditions also vary such as cancellation charges or change charges which may be applicable.

hotel, tallest in Europe   Europe's tallest building, London Bridge Tower, will in 2009 be the location for a 195-room Shangri-La hotel, the first new build, five star to open in the capital for over a decade.

hotel voucher   A document providing evidence of payment to a third party, presented by a guest on arrival in exchange for accommodation and other services as specified in the voucher.

Hotelcall   A UK telephone service providing information concerning hotel room availability and rates.

hotelier   The proprietor or any senior executive employee of a hotel.

hotels, unbiased opinions of   In the USA, STAR service is the Sloane Travel Agency Report, which also covers cruise ships, and is published by Reed. In the UK, the six Gazetteer publications provide candid reports on holiday destinations and worldwide accommodation, published by DG&G Travel Information. Both are widely used within the travel industry to provide information to clients. *See* www.dggtravelinfo.co.uk

hotels worldwide   *See table below.*

HOTS   *See* Holidaymaker On-line Transaction Service. (Now obsolete.)

house limit   The amount of credit or 'credit line' that a hotel will extend to guests before account payment will be requested.

housekeeper   The person in a hotel responsible for room cleaning and linen changing including all aspects of room servicing except meals.

housing bureau   North American term for an accommodation booking centre, but in the UK, is the local authority office responsible for council housing and the homeless. *See* accommodation centre.

hovercraft   Sea-going vessel supported above the water by a cushion of air contained within a flexible skirt, produced by the craft's engines. Propulsion is by propellers mounted on the deck. From the late 1960s until the end of 2000, there was a regular hovercraft passenger/car ferry service between Dover and Calais. There is no longer an international service but there is still a hovercraft service running in the UK between Southsea and the Isle of Wight. The cross-channel hovercraft, Princess Anne, holds the record for the fastest ever seaborne passenger-carrying service across the Channel of 22 min, achieved in 1995.

HP[1]   Holding point (aviation term).

HP[2]   *See* horsepower.

HPC   High pressure compressor (aviation term).

The ten largest hotel groups worldwide.

Hotel group	Units	Rooms	HQ in	Web site
InterContinental	3,520	536,318	UK	www.intercontinental.com
Cendant	6,399	518,435	USA	www.cendant.com
Marriott International	2,655	479,882	USA	www.marriott.com
Accor	3,894	453,403	France	www.accor.com
Choice	4,810	388,618	USA	www.choicehotels.com
Hilton Corporation	2,142	344,618	USA	www.hiltonworldwide.com
Best Western	4,110	310,445	USA	www.bestwestern.com
Starwood	774	237,934	USA	www.starwood.com
Carlson Hospitality	879	147,478	USA	www.carlson.com
Hilton International	409	102,602	UK	www.hilton.co.uk

Source: *MKG Consulting Database* June 2004; for more information and details of brands offered by each group, see web sites above.

Hotel room rates – HotelBenchmark Survey Summary Report (Deloitte & Touche LLP 2004).

1/2003 to 12/2003	Occupancy		Average room rate		RevPAR	
	2003 %	Change	2003 US$	Change	2003 US$	Change
Asia Pacific (HotelBenchmark sample represents approximately 1000 hotels across the region)						
Auckland	71.8	0.2%	79	28.0%	56	28.2%
Beijing	55.8	−24.7%	81	4.3%	45	−21.5%
Hong Kong	62.1	−21.5%	111	−2.1%	69	−23.1%
Singapore	60.8	−13.8%	79	−6.9%	48	−19.7%
Sydney	75.0	4.7%	110	29.3%	83	35.3%
Tokyo	78.2	−2.5%	173	7.6%	136	4.9%
Caribbean & Latin America (HotelBenchmark sample represents approximately 120 hotels across the region)						
Buenos Aires	55.0	36.1%	74	−1.4%	41	34.2%
Mexico City	65.8	1.3%	120	−2.3%	79	−1.0%
Quito	61.4	9.5%	70	−2.1%	43	7.3%
Sao Paulo	49.9	9.3%	70	−17.5%	35	−9.8%
Santiago	55.7	8.1%	91	−6.9%	50	0.7%
Europe (HotelBenchmark sample represents approximately 3500 hotels across the region)						
Amsterdam	73.5	−5.8%	148	10.8%	109	4.3%
Berlin	63.8	1.6%	97	9.2%	62	10.9%
Brussels	64.0	−1.2%	108	17.4%	69	16.0%
London	73.6	−1.6%	159	5.6%	117	3.9%
Madrid	68.2	−3.3%	151	16.1%	103	12.3%
Paris	65.2	−8.3%	202	14.5%	132	5.0%
Rome	65.0	−3.3%	190	17.3%	123	13.5%
Vienna	71.4	6.4%	102	23.3%	73	31.2%
Middle East (HotelBenchmark sample represents approximately 500 hotels across the region)						
Cairo	64.7	−0.5%	61	−3.9%	40	−4.4%
Dubai	77.7	−0.4%	120	10.5%	93	10.1%
Jerusalem	34.6	21.9%	81	8.6%	28	32.5%
Riyadh	55.6	−9.6%	114	−0.4%	63	−10.0%

Source: *HotelBenchmark Survey* by Deloitte. © Deloitte & Touche LLP 2004. All rights reserved.

Hotel room rates – 2003 Annual Profitability Survey (Deloitte & Touche LLP 2004).

	Asia Pacific	Europe	Middle East	USA
		Per available room (US$)		
Revenues				
Rooms	23,930	33,744	19,270	29,161
Food and beverage	19,561	19,338	14,521	14,449
Other	4,058	3,666	4,025	4,159
Totals	**47,549**	**56,748**	**37,816**	**47,769**
Departmental costs				
Rooms	6,723	9,804	3,188	7,903
Food and beverage	13,849	14,738	8,905	11,117
Other operating departments	1,609	1,489	1,221	2,296
Total departmental costs	**22,180**	**26,032**	**13,315**	**21,316**
Operated departmental income	**25,368**	**30,716**	**24,501**	**26,453**
Undistributed operating expenses				
Admin and general	3,768	5,102	3,180	4,106
Marketing	2,680	2,854	1,496	3,329
POM	2,033	2,578	1,727	2,442
Energy	2,655	1,701	2,081	1,927
Total undistributed operating costs	**11,135**	**12,234**	**8,485**	**11,804**
Income before fixed charges	**14,233**	**18,482**	**16,016**	**14,649**
Average number of rooms	323	238	274	298
Occupancy %	64.2%	62.7%	63.0%	63.8%
Average room rate	102.05	145.09	84.05	125.58
Rooms yield	65.49	90.97	52.92	80.12

Source: Europe, Middle East and Asia – HotelBenchmark Survey by Deloitte; USA – Smith Travel Research.

HPT High pressure turbine (aviation term).

HR Human resources.

HRL High intensity runway edge lighting.

HSCT High Speed Commercial Transport (some textbooks suggest High Speed Civil Transport). Term usually applied to supersonic and hypersonic aircraft.

HSI Several alternative aviation terms: Hot section inspection; or Hours since inspection; or Horizontal situation indicator.

HSMAI Hotel Sales and Marketing Association International in the USA. *See* www.hsmai.org

HSS High Speed Service by a 375-car-capacity catamaran between Holyhead and Dun Laoghaire taking 1 h and 45 min for the journey.

HSST High Speed Surface Transport, a maglev train. *See* maglev.

HST[1] High speed turn-off (aviation term).

HST[2] High Speed Train. *See* train *and* TGV.

Ht Abbreviation for height.

HTCL Hard time component limit (aviation term).

HTF Hospitality Training Foundation. Has now become a UK government Sector Skills Council for the hospitality, leisure, travel and tourism industry. *See* www.people1st.co.uk

HTH Host to Host protocol; ATA/IATA term.

hub and spoke This is the classic method of airline development; to establish a main central servicing and engineering centre and run many routes in and out of that centre, arranging coordinated schedules, so that travellers can conveniently fly in on one spoke and then out on another. This development then proceeds by the creation of more hubs linked to each other by long-distance trunk routes supported by high traffic density for which the spokes provide the feeder services. One of many alternatives, is to service a series of destinations in a continuous circular chain; but places providing few passengers tend to get more services than are necessary or economically viable. Time taken and costs incurred by each landing mean that mean that linear stopping services similar to surface transport routes are also not viable.

A 'domestic' hub is one serving a route network within one country. But an international hub is more usually titled an international 'gateway' airport. A 'fortress' hub is one where, apart from the dominant carrier, no other airline has been able to establish their operations. Hub 'dominance' is the phenomenon where one airline carries most of the traffic in and out of a particular airport, having established that airport as a network hub. In 12 of the 22 (USA) hub cores as of 1993, one carrier accounted for more than 60% of their traffic and nine hubs reported more than 70% concentration. Concept may also be called 'concentrated hub'. Goetz, A and Sutton, C (1997) The Geography of Deregulation in the US Airline Industry. *Annals of the Association of American Geographers* 87(2), 244. Of 514 non-hub American communities with an air service in 1978, 167 had lost their service by 1995, with only 26 communities gaining a new service. This was despite the fact that in 1995, 77 communities received an Essential Air Services subsidy, as provided for under the Airline Deregulation Act.

HUD Head up display (aviation term).

hull The frame of a ship exclusive of masts, superstructure or rigging. The body or frame of a ship; in respect of a small boat, obviously means from the deck downwards. However, some of the superstructure of modern cruise vessels might be regarded as part of the hull.

Hungarian National Tourist Office *See* www.hungarytourism.hu

Hungarian National Travel Agency Organization *See* IBUSZ.

hybrid vehicles Vehicles powered both by electricity from batteries and an internal combustion engine. Because of the very high weights of batteries at present, there are severe difficulties in the utilization of electric power for both public and private transport. In Germany, 20 hybrid buses are involved in an experiment. Their propulsion unit is a separately excited DC motor and they have both a diesel engine and 3200 kg of battery.

The benefit is that these buses are operated as electric vehicles in city centres, thus avoiding pollution, while the engine is used in less populated areas. Waste energy from the engine is stored, together with regenerated energy from braking and it is this aspect of the system that provides good acceleration.

hydrofoils Foils or wings attached by struts to a ship's hull. As the ship gathers speed this raises most of the vessel out of the water enabling much higher speeds. The word is generally used to describe this type of ship, as well as the device.

hydroplane A water-borne vessel using hydrofoils.

hypersonic Five or more times the speed of sound in air. Term usually applied to aircraft. Five US companies are known to have ongoing contracts to design such aircraft from the US Department of Defense.

hypothetical fare construction points Points not actually flown to by a passenger, but which only serve to construct the fare. Such points are usually circled in the fare construction boxes of IATA airline tickets, but no flight coupon ever exists for them. Also called fictitious fare construction points. Such points are utilized in order to arrive at a reduced air fare.

I

IA Industry associate (of IATA).

IAAPA International Association of Amusement Parks and Attractions. *See* www.iaapa.org

IAATC International Association of Air Transport Couriers. *See* www.courier.org

IACA International Air Carrier Association. *See* www.iaca.be

IACC International Association of Conference Centers in the USA. *See* www.iacconline.org

IACVB International Association of Convention and Visitor Bureau, which has around 300 members. For the purposes of membership, a bureau is defined as a non-profit-making organization which represents and promotes a city or other defined urban area. *See* www.iacvb.org

IAF Initial approach fix (aviation term).

IAFE International Association of Fairs and Expositions. *See* www.iafenet.org

IAG Infrastructure Action Group (of IATA).

IAHA¹ International Association of Hospitality Accountants; a chapter of HFTP (Hospitality Financial and Technology Professionals). *See* www.hftp.org

IAHA² International Aviation Handlers' Association has been established as a forum for the world's major ground handling companies, representing the industry worldwide. Forming the basis of the association is the existing European alliance which has been incorporated in the new group. *See* www.iaha.info

IAL International Aeradio Limited.

IAMAT International Association for Medical Assistance to Travellers in the USA. *See* www.iamat.org

IAMS Information and Marketing Services – an IATA division.

IAMTI The International Aviation Management Training Institute in Montreal, fully supported by IATA and ICAO, is an aviation university, the first of its kind in the world, which does not duplicate work undertaken elsewhere. It is an IATA Education Services department.

IAOPA International Council of Aircraft Owner and Pilot Associations – a European representative organization. *See* www.iaopa.org

IAP¹ Instrument approach procedure (aviation term).

IAP² International Airline Publications which functions as a unit of IATA's External Relations division.

IAPA International Airline Passengers Association. *See* www.iapa.com

IAPCO International Association of Professional Congress Organizers. Established in 1968; the 39th General Assembly will be held in Mexico City from 16–19 February 2006. It is based in London. *See* www.iapco.org

IAR Interactive agent reporting, the electronic airline sales reporting system of the ARC. *See* ARC.

IARO International Air Road Organization; founded in 1997 to promote airport-to-city rail links.

IAS Indicated air speed.

IASA International Safety Assessment Programme of the FAA.

IASC *See* Skal.

IATA At a meeting at the Hague on 28 August 1919, representatives of Danish, German, British, Norwegian and Swedish airlines agreed to form the International Air Traffic Association. This lasted until December 1945, when an Act of the Canadian Parliament created the International Air Transport Association, following the rapid expansion of civil services after the Second World War.

The aims of IATA, as set down in its Articles of Association, are: '*to promote safe, regular and economical air transport for the benefit of the peoples of the world, to foster air commerce and to study the problems connected therewith; to provide means for collaboration among air transport enterprises engaged directly or indirectly in international air transport services; to co-operate with the International Civil Aviation Organization and other international organizations'.*

Membership is open to any airline which has been licensed to operate scheduled air services by a government member of ICAO. On 1 October 1979, a two-tiered IATA structure became effective. Membership of IATA as a trade association, embracing all the non-commercial aspects of civil aviation, was established as a standard minimum. In addition, airlines can opt for participation in tariff coordination involving negotiation and agreement of international passenger fares and cargo rates. IATA literature suggests that this restructuring followed its own internal 1975 review, aiming to strike a balance between the two types of activity. But quite apart from worldwide commercial pressures resulting in airlines wanting complete freedom of action to set their own fares and rates, there was the American CAB decision.

In June 1978, when the situation had been evolving for some years, the CAB, which ended its existence on 31 December 1984, issued its famous 'show cause' order. This meant that IATA was required to defend itself against the accusation that its functions were against American anti-trust laws and, apart from this, not in the best interests of American citizens. The establishment of the present structure was vital for the continuance of IATA if it were to survive, with the major American airlines as Members.

IATA has two main offices, one in Montreal and the other in Geneva. Most of the Association's work is concerned with coordination, resulting in basic operational and technical procedures, systems, agreements and manuals without which an integrated worldwide public air service could not function smoothly. The IATA clearing house system enables financial settlements between airlines, dividing the revenue between them, no matter how complicated the passenger ticket or cargo waybill. This, together with uniform documentation, has facilitated enormous growth in international air travel and, without the existence of IATA, this may never have taken place.

The main committees of IATA cover the following fields:

Technical: Airline safety procedures, flight operation, engineering and maintenance, communications systems and procedures, meteorological services, airport terminal systems, aircraft noise emissions, and medical and hygiene matters.

Legal: International government conventions, interline agreements, general conditions of carriage, agency agreements and air navigation and users' charges.

Government affairs and policy coordination: Coordination of monitoring activities in the aeropolitical field, tourism and airmail.

Industry research: Financial and economic research and studies, commercial research and analyses, and cost studies and analyses.

Traffic services: Passenger and cargo systems procedures, baggage-handling systems, container control, restricted articles procedures and standards, live animals regulations, airport handling procedures, coding systems and multilateral interline agreements.

Agency: Travel agency accreditation, training and bank settlement plans.

Financial: Revenue accounting systems, currency transfers and transactions, and the Clearing House.

Public information: Dissemination of material on issues affecting the airline industry, particularly as regards relations with users of the system, and on how these are being tackled internationally.

Facilitation: Simplification of clearance documentation and procedure at airports – for customs, immigration and health regulations.

Security: Counteracting fraud, counterfeiting and misuse of revenue documents, such as tickets and theft, stolen tickets, cargo, mail, baggage and the protection of aircraft and airports.

Tariffs are coordinated by seven conferences, one covering each of the three main Traffic Conference Areas (*see* TC-1, 2 and 3.) In addition there are four joint conferences covering routes between them. These are respectively, numbers 1 and 2, 2 and 3, and 3 and 1, and finally concerning round-the-world routes, all three meeting together.

The seven groupings are sub-divided into 57 smaller areas enabling Tariff Coordinating Conferences to be responsive to local market conditions.

The IATA decision making authority for the Agency Programme is the Passenger Agency Conference which senior managers of all IATA member airlines attend. Resolutions must be adopted by unanimous vote. They do not, however, become binding on all IATA airlines and appointed agents until approval by individual governments. The Association's Travel Agents' handbook listing IATA Resolutions applicable to approved Agents, features many governmental reservations, making all or part of a particular Resolution non-applicable in the country concerned.

Day-to-day operation of IATA Agency programme is controlled by three Agency Boards, each of which is responsible for one IATA TC Area. These Boards receive recommendations from local Agency Investigation Panels in most countries, to whom agents have to apply for IATA appointment. In the UK, this function is undertaken by the Agency Distribution Office, following guidelines agreed by the Agency Programme Liaison Group. *See also* www.iata.org, ADO², Agency Programme Joint Council, bond, Bagtrack, IAMTI, IATA Clearing House, IDEC, ISIS, METEO, Onelink, PDNA, SITA *and* SPSC.

IATA airline designator   *See* Airline code.

IATA Breaches Commissioner Official IATA definition is the person designated by the Director General and the holder of that office, who exercises jurisdiction over matters described in IATA Resolution 800.

IATA Clearing House The section that handles intra-airline payments in respect of tickets involving the services of more than one airline. Began operations in London in January 1947. Established a single, industry-wide, monthly settlement, instead of large number of bilateral payments and receipts made in a variety of currencies to and from many airlines. Covers both passenger ticket coupons and air way-bills. The system through which revenue from a multicarrier ticket is divided between the carriers is known as proration.

Airlines participating in clearance are classified into three groups: Members that have pounds sterling as currency of clearance; Members that have US dollars as currency of clearance; and Airlines that are not members of the Clearing House but participating by virtue of their membership in the US Airlines Clearing House Incorporated (ACH).

Each month, the Clearing House is notified of the claims the participating airline has against every other such airline, sorted into groups. The claims are processed for clearance. In the manual accounting system, claims by and against each member were converted into the currency of settlement and offset by means of a series of giant matrices. Today, in the new, computerized system, this is a programmed process. Each member is automatically notified by teletype of the balance payable to or by the Clearing House. Three days later, the statements of account and supporting documentation must be dispatched to each participating airline. To balance the sterling and dollar settlements, forward purchase or sale of dollars and sterling, has to be made.

Settlement is made 1 week after clearance is completed. To bridge the gap between receipt and payments caused by debtors defaulting, the Clearing House has available overdraft facilities. These facilities act as a buffer for creditor members against abatement of settlement and as a safety valve for debtor members against emergency foreign exchange shortages and banking errors.

All transactions between member airlines may be settled through the Clearing House – for example, catering, mail, ground handling and maintenance services – in addition to passenger and cargo interline sales. The efficiencies of clearance are such that some members prefer to clear even single, very large transactions, such as aircraft leasing charges and sales of assets. The greater the number of transactions submitted for clearance, the greater the chance of offset approaching 100%, when no money at all would change hands. On average, the offset ratio approaches 90%, although airlines individually have experienced 99.9% offset.

IATA designators   *See* airline codes.

IATA fare construction system   If there is no routing for a particular published air fare, or if the published routings do not include all the places to which a passenger wishes to fly, then the fare may be calculated on the mileage principle. Tariff manuals of all major airlines set out the maximum permitted mileages between various points of departure and arrival, as well as the actual mileages between points, known as TPMs (Ticketed Point Mileages). This enables travellers to deviate from the direct route between any two points without extra payment, providing the MPM (Maximum Permitted Mileage) is not exceeded. An addition of the TPMs between the places to which the client is flying, where it does not exceed the maximum permitted mileage, is usually indicated by an M written into the fare calculation box on the flight coupon immediately above the fare. In this case there is no surcharge. But if the permitted mileage is exceeded, a percentage surcharge on the fare is assessed, with extra payments of 5%, 10%, 15% or 25% resulting in 4%, 8%, 12% or 20% extra mileage being gained. This is usually expressed as 5M, 10M and so on, as may be appropriate, in the fare calculation box of an air ticket.

Obviously, it is impossible to add together a series of fares expressed in different currencies. Tickets where the journey starts outside the country of ticket sale present another currency conversion problem. To facilitate a solution of this type of problem, Neutral Units of Construction (NUC) are used, into which all currencies may be converted, the fare calculated using the above and other more complex rules, and finally converted into the currency in which the ticket is being sold. Under the IATA fare construction alterations introduced in 1989, rates became based on the country of issuance of and/or payment for an air ticket. The procedure involved the use of four four-character international sale indicators, so that fares varied for a specific journey, dependent on where the ticket was issued or paid for. Now, a change to the rules in January 2005 means that the agreed *only* rate for a journey is based on the price of it when ticketed and paid for in the country of origin of the first flight.

The introduction of NUCs was the first major overhaul of IATA currency conversion methods since 1973, making international fare calculations much simpler. IATA have changed to a system where all tariffs are denominated in local currencies and converted at bankers' rates of exchange. Until July 1989, Fare Construction Units were associated with unrealistic special IATA exchange rates, corrected, to some extent, by the application of currency adjustment factors. Now IATA rates of exchange are set quarterly for conversion of local currencies to NUCs and vice versa. These rates are monitored monthly, and if there are extreme fluctuations, rates are changed in between the quarterly reviews. At the time of writing, one NUC is equal to one US dollar.

In 2000, the Pricing Unit Concept was introduced, a method of breaking a journey into stand-alone pricing units. It must be stressed that the basic 'journey concept' pricing system described above is still in operation. IATA intends that the pricing unit concept system should complement the journey concept 'in order to provide consistency throughout the industry'. Whereas 'journey' in this context means from origin to destination of an entire ticket, a pricing unit is defined as 'a journey or part of a journey which is priced as a separate entity; i.e. it is capable of being ticketed separately'. *It is fundamental that the results of both pricing methods must be compared and the lower price charged!*

This dictionary does not provide a full explanation but defines the pricing unit terminology. Whereas 'origin' means the initial starting point of an air journey as shown on the ticket and destination, the ultimate stopping place, 'unit origin' and 'unit destination' mean the start and end of the pricing unit.

OSC is the acronym for 'one-way subjourney' defined as 'part of a journey wherein travel from one country does not return to such country and for which the fare is assessed as a single pricing unit using one-way fares'.

RSC is the acronym for 'return subjourney' defined as 'part of a journey wherein travel is from a point/country and return thereto and for which the fare is assessed as a single pricing unit using half round-trip fares; either round trip, circle trip or normal fare open-jaw'. In these contexts, 'turnaround open-jaw means where the outward point of arrival in the country of unit turnaround and in the inward point of departure in the country of unit turnaround are different'; 'origin open-jaw' means where the outward point of departure in the country of unit origin and in the inward point of arrival in the country of unit origin are different.

See also APEX, backhaul, excursion, fictitious fare construction points, half round trip, higher rated intermediate point, hypothetical fare construction point, ladder fare construction, linear fare construction, lowest combination principle, MPM, more distant point, open-jaw *and* TPM.

IATA Industry Settlement System Methods by which travel agents remit money received for tickets sold, such as a BSP (Billing and Settlement Plan). The ISS manager is the person managing a BSP. IATA's IDFS (Industry Distribution and Financial Services department) has responsibility for BSPs.

IATA international sale indicators Now obsolete. Used to be SITI, SITO, SOTI and SOTO. *See* IATA fare construction system.

IATA member profits *See* airline.

IATA passenger agents numeric code Every IATA-approved travel agency location worldwide has been assigned a numeric code which consists of a 2-digit country designator, a 1-digit area designator separated from the first two figures by a dash, a 4-digit approved location number separated from the other figures by a space and a further check digit calculated on an unweighted modulus 7 system separated from the previous figures by a further space. For example 91 is the country designator for the UK and since this is in IATA area 2, the next digit for all agents in Britain is the figure 2.

Continental Airlines and Northwest Airlines require US domestic air booking locations which are not ARC accredited, but using a GDS, to obtain an RSP (Reservation Service Provider) number from ARC. This applies to all non-ARC users of a GDS outside contractors and corporate customers. In lieu of an RSP number, non-accredited international booking locations located outside the USA, Puerto Rico and US Virgin Islands must obtain a TIDS (Travel Industry Designator Service) number from IATA. Applications via www.arccorp.com/aguaform.htm (US$225 for 3 years) or www.iata.org/tids (US$55).

IATA Ticketing Handbook Contains detailed instructions for the issuance or reissuance of passenger tickets, miscellaneous charges orders and pre-paid ticket advices. It also covers the handling of UATP sales and IATA currency procedures.

IATA TID IATA Travel Industry Designator. In March 1992, IATA launched a new service to streamline CRS and communication systems between non-IATA agents and non-airline travel industry suppliers. Non-IATA agents are allocated unique code numbers, on the recommendation of any participating principal, which will identify the agents worldwide for many reservation and administrative purposes. Although the new scheme is similar to IATA agency identification numbers, the prefix immediately indicates whether an agency is IATA appointed. *See* www.iata.org/tids

IATA Traffic Conference Areas *See* TC-1, 2 and 3.

IATA traffic documents The following are forms issued manually, mechanically or electronically for air passenger transportation over the lines of the member or airline and for related services, whether or not they bear a pre-printed individual member's identification:

- Passenger ticket and baggage check forms, miscellaneous charges orders and on-line tickets supplied by members to approved agents for issue to their customers, and
- Standard passenger ticket forms, standard miscellaneous charges orders and other accountable forms

supplied to approved agents for issue under the bank settlement plan.

IATA Travel Agents' Handbook Sets out all the IATA Resolutions and other requirements of interest to IATA Passenger Sales Agents detailing their rights and obligations. Many of the official IATA definitions in this book are taken from the glossary of commonly used terms at the end of the Agents' Handbook.

IATA/UFTAA International Travel and Tourism Training Programme Comprehensive home-/office-/web-based study courses: Foundation, Consultant, Management, Senior Management, GDS Fares and Ticket Marketing designed for travel agents worldwide. *See* www.iata. org/training/travel_tourism

IATAN International Airlines Travel Agent Network in the USA. The IATA organization responsible for agency accreditation in the USA. The Passenger Services Network Corporation, entirely independent of IATA and IATAN was founded following airline deregulation to control commercial relationships between agents and airlines and the IATA network in the USA.

IATAN card Card identifying the holder as a travel agency employee entitled to concession rate transport from IATA carriers and other discounts negotiated with travel service providers.

IATED IATA's Edifact database. *See* EDIFACT.

IATF International Airline Training Fund.

IATM International Association of Tour Managers. *See* www.iatm.co.uk

IATO The International Association of Travel Officials was a forerunner of the Travel Industry Association of America.

IAV Interactive video.

IAWT International Association for World Tourism. *See* www.uia.org

IBA International Bureau of Aviation; publishes quarterly *The Maintenance Cost Journal. See* www.ibagroup. com

IBAA *See* EBAA.

IBAC International Business Aviation Council is the US-based international grouping of associations in its sphere. *See* www.ibac.org

IBE Internet Booking Engine; computer system which allows access via the Internet to a travel provider's inventory of travel services. An IBE may enable booking by consumers of a principal's own travel arrangements or it may be an intermediary's system supplying travel and/or hospitality services as an agent. Language in this field is currently developing; thus a 'web agent' may be an IBE computer system which automatically performs the functions of a travel agent over the Internet. But a Web agent may also be a travel agent which acquires clients via the Internet, not ncessarily transacting or fulfilling traveller's requests over the Internet. *See* self packaging *and* dynamic packaging.

IBTA Formerly the International Business Travel Association, now defunct. A new European association now represents travel managers, the European Business Travel Association.

IBTS International Baggage Tracing System.

IBUSZ Hungarian National Travel Organization.

IC¹ Independent contractor; an outside sales representative for a travel agency in the USA. *See* outside sales representatives.

IC² Inner city, particularly regarding rail travel in Europe.

ICAO The International Civil Aviation Organization is the inter-governmental body which provides the machinery for the achievement of cooperation in the air. Its constitution was drawn up in 1944, the Convention on International Civil Aviation. Its chief activities are the establishment of international standards, recommended practices and procedures covering all the technical fields of aviation. These include licensing of air crew, rules of the air, meteorology, charts, units of measurement, operation of aircraft, nationality and registration marks, airworthiness, telecommunications, air traffic services, search and rescue, aircraft accident inquiry, aerodromes, aeronautical information service and aircraft noise. Amendments to the ICAO Convention are continually being made. The standards adopted are put into effect by over 140 ICAO contracting states. *See* web site www.icao.org for extensive information; for ICAO safety standards and Oversight Programme *see* airline safety.

A mini-library covers all the detailed agreements and work of the ICAO; the rest of this dictionary entry, as an example of the work of the ICAO, covers some of Annex 16 to the Convention about environmental protection; volume 1 concerns aircraft noise and volume 2 aircraft engine exhaust emissions. Aircraft which produce more than certain recommended levels of pollution and noise were designated chapter 2 aircraft in the 1990s (sometimes referred to as stage 2). The ICAO and EU suggest these aircraft should be phased out by the beginning of 2002; the USA granted waivers to airlines, particularly those with 85% or more of their fleet meeting chapter 3 so that they should phase out chapter 2 aircraft by end March 2003. Some countries have imposed restrictions earlier; for example Belgium, which has banned all chapter 2 aircraft since end March 2001. Thus, aircraft such as the Boeing 707, Douglas DC8, BAC 1–11 and the Russian IL76 and AN124 cannot now land in Belgium. Countries not signatories to the Convention or not following its recommendations will still be operating chapter 2 aircraft during the currency of this dictionary.

Many aircraft meeting chapter 3 standards also meet the so-called chapter 4 standards, which have still not been officially agreed. In January 2001, the Committee on Environmental Protection of the ICAO proposed a new noise standard to be implemented on all new aircraft from 2006, reducing permitted noise levels by 10 decibels from chapter 3 recommendations. This is not as great a reduction as that proposed by the UK Airport Operators Association together with the Airports Council International, based in Geneva, of a 14-decibel reduction.

ICC Interstate Commerce Commission in the USA was, until terminated in 1995, responsible for control and monitoring of long-distance rail and bus (coach) travel.

ICCA¹ International Civil Airports Association; merged with Airport Operators Council International to form Airports Council International. *See* www.airports.org

ICCA² International Congress and Conventions Association based in Holland. *See* www.icca.nl

ICCL International Council of Cruise Lines, the cruising lines trade body. For information access www.iccl.org

ICCR Inter Capital and Regional Rail Group. *See* Eurotunnel.

ICCS IATA's currency clearance service. *See* IATA Clearing House.

ICE German Inter-City Experimental Train which on its first journey in November 1985 reached a speed of 317 kph (198 mph); however during regular service they have been operating at 230 kph. Tests are taking place to increase this to 330 kph (205 mph) on some high-speed lines. In 1988, an ICE set the German train speed record of 407 kph.

Icelandic Tourist Board *See* www.icetourist.is

ICH IATA's Clearing House. *See* IATA Clearing House.

ICS¹ International Chamber of Shipping; the trade body of major ship owners worldwide. *See* www.marisec.org

ICS² Institute of Chartered Ship Brokers. *See* www.ics.org.uk

ICTA Was The Institution of Certified Travel Agents of America, renamed The Travel Institute in September 2003. *See* www.icta.com *or* www.thetravelinstitute.com

ID Identity, usually in the form of a code number or password. The term may apply to various similar situations, for example, the name of the document used to gain access to security-protected buildings; the code needed by an individual to log on to a computer system or the 10-figure ID with which a viewdata set must be programmed in the UK so that it automatically answers back with this, upon being connected with a central computer. In North America, **ID** also means industry discount, particularly relating to the discounts given by airlines to their staff and travel agents, but often more generally applied.

IDA Integrated Digital Access. *See* ISDN.

IDEC The IATA Interline Data Exchange Centre – In operation since January 1981, now has over 50 participants. Data preparation from interline bills received is eliminated. Carriers carry the data of their passenger and cargo billings on computer tapes to IATA and, by the end of a series of input runs from this information, one output tape for each participating carrier is produced. The successor system to TAPEX.

IDL[1]   *See* International Date Line.

IDL[2]   International Driving (Driver's) Licence, required in some countries to permit holders of foreign driving licences to drive vehicles.

IDP   International Driving (Driver's) Permit, required in some countries to permit holders of foreign driving licences to drive vehicles.

IDS   IATA's Distribution Services division.

IES   IATA's Education Services department.

IESG   IATA's interactive edifact sub-group.

IF   Intermediate fix (aviation term).

IFALPA   International Federation of Airline Pilots' Associations. *See* www.ifalpa.org

IFAPA   International Foundation of Airline Passenger Associations.

IFATCA   International Federation of Air Traffic Controllers' Associations. *See* www.ifatca.org

IFCC[1]   International Federation of Camping and Caravanning. (*See also* FICC.) This international body is composed of the national organizations in this field of 30 countries.

IFCC[2]   IATA/FIATA Consultative Council.

IFE   In-Flight Entertainment is the provision of audio and audio-visual entertainment to airline passengers, usually in the form of films, video and multi-channel tape output.

IFEA   International Festival and Events Association, based in the USA. *See* www.ifea.com

IFF   Institute of Freight Forwarders in the UK.

IFITT   International Federation for Information Technology and Travel and Tourism. The leading worldwide body which runs an annual conference called ENTER. The 12th was held in Innsbruck in January 2005. *See* www.ifitt.org

IFR   Instrument flight rules.

IFTAC   Inter-American Federation of Touring and Automobile Clubs based in Argentina.

IFTO   International Federation of Tour Operators. Based in Denmark, its membership is restricted to operators in 11 countries who are members of their national trade bodies.

IFTTA   International Forum of Travel and Tourism Advocates. *See* www.travellaw.com

IFWTO   *See* International Federation of Women's Travel Organizations.

IGHC   IATA Ground Handling Council.

IGS   Instrument guidance system (aviation term).

IGTA   International Gay Travel Association.

IHA   The International Hotel Association was established in 1946; it changed its name to the IHRA in 1990. *See* www.ih-ra.com

IHCI   Irish Hotel and Catering Institute. Offers joint Certificate in Hotel and Catering Management awarded by IHCI, Irish Hotels Federation and CERT. For details *see* www.cert.ie/S3P31.htm *or* www.ait.ie/courses

IHEI   International Hotels Environment Initiative; an educational charity established in 1993. Has concluded a benchmarking exercise designed to help hotels measure and improve on their environmental performance, leading to cost savings at the same time. *See* www.benchmarkhotel.com *and* www.un.org/esa/sustdev/viaprofiles/IHEI.htm *also* tourism, sustainable.

IHF   Irish Hotels Federation. *See* www.ihf.ie

IHRA   International Hotel and Restaurant Association. *See* www.ih-ra.com

IHT   Institution of Highways and Transportation in the UK. *See* www.iht.org

IIT or FIT   Individual Inclusive Tour tailor-made for the requirements of a particular customer.

ILAM   Institute of Leisure and Amenity Management – a UK professional body formed in 1983 by the amalgamation of four former bodies in this field, the Association of Recreation Managers, Institute of Recreation Management, Institute of Parks and Recreation Management and Institute of Municipal Entertainment. *See* www.ilam.co.uk

ILC   IATA Learning Centre – a unit of the Education Service.

Illinois Trade Office   *See* www.enjoyillinois.com

ILS   Instrument landing system in use at all the world's large airports. A radio beam identifies a glide path to a particular runway from a point between 3 and 5 miles (10 and 15 km) away.

IM   Inner marker (aviation term).

IMA Industry Monetary Affairs, an IATA division.

IMC Information Management Committee of IATA.

IMIS IATA's Management Information Service.

Immigration and Naturalization Service (USA) *See* INS[3].

IMO International Maritime Organization; the major worldwide body in this field. *See* www.imo.org *and* SOLAS.

implant A UK travel agency employee working outside the agent's own office inside a client's business location, servicing a corporate account. In North America, this type of operation is known as an on-site travel office. Sometimes, implant operatives' work is interwoven with the company's business travel manager and staff. Alternatively an implant's work may be entirely separate. *See* outplant operations for comparison between two methods of business travel management. There are no longer premises requirements for ABTA membership. Thus, an agent in Britain now has the choice of registering implants as branch office locations with ABTA, selling holidays and other products. *A list of 70 other business travel related entries follows* corporate travel contracts, *some of which lead to further entries.*

implant agency An agency established on the premises of another corporate organization for the purposes of servicing the travel needs of that organization and its employees. *See also* implant immediately above.

IMTIG Was Chartered Institute of Marketing Travel Industry Group in the UK, formerly known as the TIMG and is now CIMTIG.

INATUR In 2003 became the new Venezualan tourism organization. *See* www.inatur.gov.ve

inaugural In theory, the first departure of any travel service, often widely publicised and carrying press, publicity and VIP passengers. For a ship, this may be called its maiden voyage. But if it is carrying non-paying passengers for the purpose of trying out all the facilities and correcting faults, the term 'shakedown' voyage or cruise is more appropriate. IATA rules restrict the invitation of guests and payment for their ground arrangements to inaugural flights involving new routes or equipment, suggesting that only the initial two flights can be so categorized. Normally, an inaugural flight will take place within 6 months of the establishment of the new facility. The term is now in general use in the travel industry.

inbound agent A travel company specializing in ground handling, usually incoming from abroad.

inbound tour operator Tour operator specializing in arrangements for foreigners into the country in which it is based.

inbound tourism Tourism incoming from another country, as distinct from domestic tourism, arising from a country's own residents or outbound tourism to a country abroad. *See also* tourism balance of trade, tourism generating country, tourism receiving country *and* travel account[2].

incentive commission An extra commission or profit paid to agents or others by a principal in order to motivate the sales outlets to produce more business. Incentive commission schemes pay an additional rate, either on achieving sales levels applicable throughout the industry or, maybe, related to individual targets set for each outlet. All the major car hire companies, such as Avis and Hertz, operate such schemes, which may increase an agent's income from 15% to over 30%. Many UK tour operators run schemes which may increase an agent's income from 10% up to around 15%.

The term 'over-riding commission' is sometimes loosely used as an alternative, this practice having been encouraged following its use in the 'IATA Over-riding Commission Scheme'. This was inaccurate, however, for over-riding commission is that which is paid to a middle man or wholesaler by a principal, so that the product or service can, in turn, be sold at the standard commission rate to an agent. Nevertheless, users of this book should take care, for they may find the term over-riding commission used generally to mean any extra commission. This is particularly so in the USA. For example, a market share over-ride programme is based on an analysis of an agent's sales. A supplier may give extra commission if their market share of that agent's sales considerably exceeds the market share of that supplier, nationally or regionally. *See also* Air Miles, commission, Compass Points, FFP (frequent flyer programme) *and* Latitudes.

incentive groups   General IATA rules are that incentive air travel groups must be comprised of employees and/or dealers and/or agents, including spouses of the same firm, corporation enterprise, but excluding non-profit organizations, travelling under an established travel programme which rewards the persons concerned for past work or provides an incentive for future activities. Such groups qualify for much reduced air fares on certain routes.

incentive tour   An incentive travel package. *See* incentive travel.

incentive travel   Definition adopted by trade bodies in this sphere is: 'Management tool that uses tourism to motivate and/or recognize participants for increased levels of performance in support of organizational goals.'

Incentive Travel and Meetings Association   *See* ITMA.

incidentals   North American term for extras bill, to be paid in addition to the agreed hotel room rate, package holiday or cruise cost. *See* extras.

inclusive resort   In North America, a large-scale hotel and leisure complex attempting to supply as many as possible of the requirements of visitors on vacation within one site.

inclusive tour   Official IATA definition is a pre-arranged combination of air transportation and surface arrangements, other than solely public transportation, which is designed to encourage air travel and which conforms to certain minimum standards as defined in the applicable Resolution. On approval, an airline provides an IT number; this reference must appear on air tickets, as they do not show any price. In the UK, the term is applied to any package holiday arrangement including transportation and accommodation, sold together at a single price. Inclusive Tours (ITs) are organized by tour operators for sale either direct to the public or through agents. Breakdown of the elements which make up a typical UK short-haul overseas inclusive tour is: accommodation 38%; flying 40%; transfers and other overseas costs 2%; basic agency

commission 10%; marketing 3%, (between 1.5% and 2% of which is incentive commission); contribution to overheads including profit 7%. *See* package holiday for definition in EC Directive 90/314/EEC on package travel.

inclusive tour fares   *See* ITX *and* inclusive tour.

income tourism multiplier   *See* tourism multiplier.

incoming handling agent   *See* handling agent.

incoming tour operator   Tour operator specializing in arranging tours and holidays within their own country for foreign travellers. *See* handling agent, tour operator *and* UKInbound.

incoming tourism   Tourism that is coming from abroad, bringing foreigners into a particular country. *See also* handling agent.

incompatibility   *See* compatibility.

incremental assignment   *See* transport modelling.

indemnity   Most sections of travel insurance policies are contracts of indemnity. That means that the policy will make good the insured's loss. Clients cannot expect to make a profit by use of insurance. When a traveller's baggage and contents are lost or damaged, insurance companies will bear in mind the total possible useful life of an article and, only if the travel insurance policy involved specifically so states, will the original cost of an item be refunded. Some sections of a policy may, however, be expressed in terms of specific benefits. In these cases there is no need to prove actual loss; merely that the event covered actually occurred. A '*form of indemnity*' is the type of form completed by passengers when a travel ticket has been lost or stolen and a replacement or refund is sought. On the form, the passenger must indemnify the carrier against losses, should the missing ticket subsequently be used.

independent contractor   *See* IC.

independent tour   *See* IIT.

independent travel   The 2003 CEN/European Standard official definition is: 'journey organized by a traveller, either personally or with the help of a provider of tourism services, a tour operator or a travel agency'. Unfortunately, this definition does not capture the essence of a growing market, namely that travel is not together with an organized group; the definition adopted could equally well apply to a person selecting and booking a package holiday!

Indian Government Tourist Office *See* www.tourismofindia.com

Indian National Travel Agency Organization Travel Agents Association of India (TAAI).

Indiana Tourism Division *See* www.enjoyindiana.com

indirect air carrier North American term for an organization or individual that operates no aircraft, but charters seats from airlines and sells them either within the travel industry or direct to the public.

indirect route principle Passengers travelling on IATA airlines are always entitled to the lowest possible fare. Maximum permitted mileages exceed actual sector mileages by about 20%. Thus, providing the MPM is not exceeded, air travellers can use an indirect route at no extra charge. *See* IATA fare construction system.

Indonesia Tourism *See* www.goindo.com

Industry agent The title by which an agent accredited by the USA Airlines Reporting Corporation (ARC) is known.

Industry Agent's Handbook An operating manual for US agents recognized by the ARC; the US equivalent of the IATA Travel Agent's Handbook.

inf Industry abbreviation for infant.

infant On international scheduled air flights a child under 2 years of age. Normally qualifies for rate of 10% of adult fare. Other means of transport are usually free.

Infini Japan-based CRS owned jointly by All Nippon Airways, with 60% of the shares and Abacus with 40%. Abacus is itself jointly owned by Cathay Pacific Airways, China Airlines, Malaysia Airlines, Philippine Airlines, Royal Brunei, SIA, Northwest, TWA and Delta.

in-flight entertainment Usually film show, video or multi-channel audio systems. *See* also IFE.

in-flight magazine A publication usually placed in the seat pocket in front of air passengers. Research shows that almost all passengers read part or all of the magazine. Production is usually outsourced; because of the high advertising

revenue, in-flight magazines usually make considerable profits for airlines. For the names of some typical magazines *see* Atlantis, Atlas, Blue Wings, Cara, High Life, Holland Herald, Let's Go, Logbook, Motion, Ronda, Scanorama, Sphere, Ulisse 2000.

in-flight recorder *See* flight recorder.

in-flight service Around 75% of in-flight service costs are the cabin crew. International safety rules require a minimum number of trained cabin staff, in order to handle possible emergencies. Although there are more stewards and stewardesses in first class, it is mainly in the provision of superior meals, beverages (alcoholic or otherwise) and some free gifts, that in-flight service varies according to the amount passengers have paid. Most airlines now provide in-flight entertainment to all grades of passenger.

information databases *See* tourism information databases for details of main international computerized sources of travel and tourism publications, information, statistics *and see* CRS for a list of the systems named in this book.

information provider *See* IP.

information technology in travel and tourism *See* Amadeus, ATB, autocue, automated air tickets, automatic guide, automation in the travel industry – some books, CARE, CBT[1], Concord, CRS, CRS rules for neutrality, DMS[1], EDIFACT, Endeavour, ENTER, e-ticketing, Fast-link, Fastrak, Galileo[2], GDS, HIRO, Holidex, IDEC, IFITT (International Federation for Information Technology and Travel and Tourism), inkjet printer, ISTEL, Orbitz, Opodo, Sabre, tour operators' reservation systems, travel agents' computerized accounting and ticketing systems in the UK, viewdata, Worldspan, yield management *and* X-TANT.

Infotrac Was the brand name of the UK travel industry communications network utilizing Istel, the largest private videotext network covering the whole of the UK.

infrastructure The various amenities and facilities required to support tourism in an area. Some writers, from the manner in which the term is used, clearly believe that 'infrastructure' does not include the basics, such as accommodation. Others use the term as all embracing.

inkjet printer Associated with a computer system, this type of printer, silent in operation, offers good quality reproduction, but laser printers are probably lower in ongoing costs for heavy duties.

Inland Waterways Association *See* IWA.

inn A simple hotel in a rural setting. The 2003 CEN/European Standard official definition is an attempt to translate the meaning of the French word 'auberge' or its German equivalent 'Gasthof'. The wording is: 'establishment, often in the countryside, offering food and drink, where some accommodation is also provided'.

innkeeper Literally, a person owning or managing an inn; but the word is used in legal systems to designate the person legally responsible for running a hospitality industry establishment.

innkeeper's lien Assertion by hoteliers worldwide that they may keep a visitor's baggage, or other property, if the bill is not paid.

inplant Used to be a US ARC term designating an agency location within the premises of the organization being serviced, limited to 3% commission. *See* implant.

INS pass A permit facilitating entry to the USA for US citizens arriving from abroad. Frequent business travellers from and to the USA can take a fast track through US immigration. The US Immigration and Naturalization Service (INS) offers the INSpass to business travellers who can demonstrate three or four visits to the country per year. The initial application involves filling in a form and submitting an electronic palm print, which is used alongside a plastic card – the PortPASS – for identification in the future. Once registered, cardholders use a special INSpass channel to speed through immigration in around a minute. They simply insert their PortPASS, present their palm and key in their flight number to receive the appropriate immigration card and an advantage over the other passengers to reach the baggage reclaim area or the taxi stand. In June 2001, the scheme only covered eight US gateways (New York JFK, Newark, Washington, Miami, Los Angeles, San Francisco, Seattle and Honolulu) plus Toronto. Other international airports at Atlanta, Boston, Chicago, Dallas and Houston were planned for inclusion. The service is currently free.

INS¹ Inertial Navigation System for aircraft.

INS² Title of US computer database of international air travel statistics. *See* tourism information databases.

INS³ The US Immigration and Naturalisation Service, a unit of the Department of Justice. *See* www.usdoj.gov/ins

inside cabin One without porthole or window to the outside.

inside link A CRS inside availability link. Where at the time of making a reservation through a CRS or GDS, a direct connection 'real-time' is established to the airline, hotel or other travel services provider, generating a confirmed booking reference from that provider's system. Infrequently, a booking made into a CRS, which automatically notifies the provider's CRS, is rejected due to lack of availability, schedule changes or another reason. In North America, the same facilities may be called 'direct access' or 'direct link', the facility being advertized as provision of the airline's own locator (reference number) within 7 s of an agent completing a reservation.

insolvency protection The 2003 CEN/European Standard official definition is: 'financial guarantee provided in order to secure a refund of money paid by travellers and/or their repatriation in the event of insolvency of a provider of tourism services'. Types of protection include those provided under national rules and/or European Council Directive 90/314 of 13 June 1990 on Package Travel, Package Holidays and Package Tours.

Instalink *See* Prestel.

Institute of Leisure and Amenity Management *See* ILAM.

Institute of Logistics and Transport *See* ILOT.

Institute of Tourist Guiding UK body formed in 2002 with over 1500 members. As the recognized national body, it sets standards across the guiding, commentaries and heritage interpretation sector. *See* www.itg.org.uk

Institute of Travel Agents *See* ITT.

Institute of Travel and Tourism *See* ITT.

Institute of Travel Managers *See* ITM.

Institution of Certified Travel Agents Renamed The Travel Institute in September 2003. *See* www.icta.com *or* www.thetravelinstitute.com

Institution of Highways and Transportation *See* IHT.

Institution of Railway Operators *See* IRO.

instrument landing system *See* ILS.

insurance *See* travel insurance.

INTA Until its demise in March 1991, was the name of the International Leisure Group's and Intasun's private viewdata system, providing full interactive communication with UK travel agents, enabling them to make bookings direct from their office terminals.

intensity of tourism *See* tourism intensity.

Interactive Transaction Processing System(s) *See* ITPS.

interactive video Fully integrated combination of computer and videodisk system. Although the terminology was of general technical application, it was of significance in various travel industry spheres, for example, Sabre Vision. Now obsolete as superseded by DVD technology.

Interbus Agreement EC Agreement on the international occasional carriage of passengers by coach and bus, which replaced ASOR from 1 January 2003. *See* www.europa.eu.int/scadplus/leg/en/lvb/124264.htm

interchange flight Official IATA definition is a flight that gives passengers the benefit of a through service and is operated by two or more airlines from the boarding point to the deplaning point using the same aircraft.

interchange point In general, it means a public transportation terminus where passengers may change services, to make onward journeys, this often being facilitated by convenient timetabling and the availability of several transport modes. National Express Coaches have established in main interchange coach stations throughout the UK for this purpose. British coach companies, particularly those providing express coach, tours or holidays to Europe, may establish interchange points at motorway areas or other places not conveniently accessible to the public. For example, passengers may start their journey from any pick-up point in the UK. On arrival at the interchange, passengers change coaches as necessary, for their onward journey. Within Europe, a similar process may occur in the destination country. A few lucky passengers may find that their 'feeder' service becomes their correct onward coach and perhaps even their final 'feeder' coach. Sometimes, the feeder services are operated by different coaches from those used for central part of the journey. For equivalent air travel concepts *see* hub and spoke.

Inter-City Savers Obsolete BR fare name; now known as Savers. *See* ATOC *and* rail fares in the UK.

InterContinental hotels group Largest hotel group in the world. Bass Hotels became Six Continents in July 2001 following sales of Bass name and brewing business. This then became InterContinental hotels following acquisition of that brand. Based in the UK, in June 2004 the group had 3520 hotels offering 536,318 rooms. Includes Holiday Inn, the second largest hotel brand and Express by Holiday Inn, 9th largest; Crowne Plaza hotels and resorts, Staybridge Suites and Candlewood Suites. *See* InterContinental hotels, *also* www.intercontinental.com

interface A translation function between a user and a computer system, or between a user and a number of systems, or between two or more systems. By this means a multi-access airline reservation system enables many airlines' systems to be accessed.

interim expense allowance When airlines lose a passenger's luggage, they pay an interim expense allowance to cover the cost of the immediate purchase by the passenger of essential toiletries and a change of underwear, even though the luggage may have been located and be on its way to the passenger.

interline Official IATA definition when used in conjunction with another word to describe anything involving two or more members, such as interline itinerary, interline reservation, interline stopover, interline point, interline transaction etc.

interline agreements Only if an interline agreement exists will an airline allow its tickets to include the services of another airline. Airlines will only accept the travel documents of other airlines with whom they have an interline agreement.

interline point Official IATA definition is any point in the itinerary at which the passenger is to change from the flight of one airline to the flight of another, whether a connection or stopover at such point is involved (all airports through which a city or adjacent cities are served by an airline being considered as a single interline point).

interline representative A member of an airline's sales staff whose responsibility is interline sales.

interline traffic Passengers or cargo transported over the routes of two or more airlines as a single journey with an interline connection. Seldom used is the term *intraline traffic*, applicable where the transportation occurs over the routes of only one carrier.

interliner Despite the generality of the all of the above definitions, this is airline jargon used when airline staff are travelling by air, usually on a concession basis, on other than their own airline.

interlining The facility whereby passengers can undertake a trip transferring between carriers while using one ticket. The revenue resulting from such interlining is then pro-rated.

intermediary Person or organization in the travel distribution chain operating between providers of travel services and the public – colloquially 'middleman'. The term is not indicative of contractual position; an intermediary may be acting as a 'principal' as far as a consumer is concerned. Textbooks differ as to whether a tour operator should be regarded as a travel intermediary. *See* IATA term 'travel service intermediary', intermediation, travel agent *and* tour operator.

intermediate class IATA definition is a class of service with eating standards which may be superior to those provided on economy/tourist class but less liberal than standards provided in first class; provided that the intermediate class seat pitch shall not exceed 41 inches.

intermediation Providing a service as a person or organization in the travel distribution chain operating between providers of travel services and the public – colloquially 'middleman', often a retailer. In the travel business, the intermediary is a travel agent. The term is not indicative of contractual position; an intermediary may be acting a 'principal' as far as a consumer is concerned. Textbooks differ as to whether a tour operator should be regarded as a travel intermediary; *see* tour operator. Thus, disintermediation is the process by which travel principals cut out the middleman and deal direct with the public. For example the Orbitz web site launched in June 2001, owned by Delta, United Airlines, Northwest, Continental and American Airlines, which together handle over 85% of US air traffic. This has not alone taken business from travel agents in general; it has significantly affected web travel agents such as Expedia and Travelocity. Reintermediation is the process by which intermediaries reassert their business by offering customers the opportunity to purchase through the full range of distribution channels, colloquially called the 'bricks and clicks approach'.

An example is afforded by Thomas Cook, the UK travel agency group, which has extensive web sites, call centres and 700 British high-street travel agencies. Only 3–5% of Thomas Cook customers book on-line without recourse to their call centre and most of those few per cent are booking point-to-point flights. This has profound implications for all the new channels of distribution – Internet – iDTV – WAP. In the UK, the more expensive or complex is a product or service, the more likely it is not to be purchased on the web.

The UK travel market will continue to grow and business through UK high-street retailers will continue to expand. However, trade through alternative distribution channels will grow at a faster rate, so that sales 'over-the-counter' will become an increasingly smaller proportion of an expanding market. Many agents, by utilizing the new technologies, will take a large share of this new business. This is because the growing plethora of distribution channels in general, and web sites in particular, has weakened the development of branding, providing an opportunity for well-known travel industry names, which they are seizing.

In the UK, the Internet has been very successful for those customers looking for point-to-point and very easy-to-book products, literally click and book. Operators like easyJet and Ryanair are to be congratulated because they are doing over 90% of their business across the Internet. It is also successful for specialists. Information provision is and will continue to be the big success story of the Internet. But usage is growing rapidly. For example in 2005, several of the largest UK Package Tour operators expect to book 25% of their volume over the Internet.

intermodal A journey using several types of transport, for example a fly/cruise. An intermodal terminal, usually called an interchange, provides the opportunity to change between forms of transport. *See* interchange.

Intermodal Surface Transportation Efficiency Act (in the USA) *See* www.dot.gov/ost/govtaffairs/istca

International Air Carriers Association IACA. *See* www.iaca.be

International Air Passengers Association IAPA. *See* www.iapa.com

international air safety *See* airline safety.

International Air Traffic Association *See* IATA.

international air transport (from and to the USA) *See* definition of 'uninterrupted international air transport'.

International Air Transport Association *See* IATA.

International Association for Medical Assistance to Travellers IAMAT. *See* www.iamat.org

International Association for World Tourism IAWT. *See* www.uia.org

International Association of Air Transport Couriers IAATC. *See* www.courier.org

International Association of Amusement Parks and Attractions IAAPA. *See* www.iaapa.org

International Association of Conference Centers IACC. *See* www.oacconline.com

International Association of Convention and Visitor Bureaux *See* IACVB.

International Association of Fairs and Expositions IAFE. *See* www.iafenet.org

International Association of Hospitality Accountants *See* HITEC.

International Association of Tour Managers IATM. *See* www.iatm.co.uk

International Bureau of Aviation *See* IBA.

International Business Aviation Council *See* IBAC.

International Business Travel Association *See* IBTA.

International Certificate of Vaccination *See* international health requirements.

International Chamber of Shipping The trade body of major ship owners worldwide. *See* www.marisec.org

International Coach Services in Europe *See* ASOR.

International Congress and Conventions Association *See* ICCA.

International Convention Concerning Carriage of Passengers and Luggage by Rail *See* CIV.

International Convention for the Safety of Life at Sea Usually called SOLAS, it was established in 1914, prompted by the Titanic disaster. It is continually being updated; for example, in 1997, one of many amendments required cruise ships to install lighting strips along floors to guide passengers to exits through smoke-filled corridors.

Since 1998, cruise lines have been required to operate a Safety Management System, as part of Chapter 9 of SOLAS rules which instituted the International Safety Management Code. Each vessel is required to carry details in a Safety Manual. Further information is available via www.imo.org

International Convention on the Travel Contract Little-known convention adopted in Brussels in 1970 concerning contracts between the public and tour operators/travel agents. The major tourism-generating countries did not ratify the convention, so that there is still no international harmonization of regulations in this field.

International Council of Aircraft Owner and Pilot Associations *See* IAOPA.

International Council of Cruise Lines *See* ICCL.

International Date Line As a traveller goes westward it is necessary to turn the clock back. For example, the eastern side of America is around 5 h behind Britain. When travelling east, clocks go forward. On crossing the International Date Line travelling westward, the date goes forward a day, but on crossing the line going eastward, it reverts to the previous day's date. The International Date Line approximately follows the 180th parallel of longitude. *See also* GMT.

International Departure Tax US Federal tax charged to all international air travellers leaving the USA.

International Driver's Licence or **Permit** *See* IDL[2].

International Ecotourism Standard Announced in Cairns Australia in October 2002. The International Ecotourism Standard has been developed by the Ecotourism Association of Australia in conjunction with the Cooperative Research Centre (CRC) for Sustainable Tourism of Australia. The International Ecotourism Standard is based on the Australian Nature and Ecotourism Accreditation Programmme (NEAP), Agenda 21, and guiding principles for sound ecotourism certification (Mohonk Agreement) developed by a gathering of ecotourism certification experts at Mohonk Mountain, New York State, USA in November 2001. Green Globe 21 has the exclusive licence for the distribution and management of the International Ecotourism Standard. Green Globe 21 is the global Affiliation, Benchmarking and Certification program for sustainable travel and tourism. *See* www.ecotourism.org.au *and* tourism, sustainable for monograph on topic.

International Federation for Information Technology and Travel and Tourism *See* ENTER.

International Federation of Air Traffic Controllers' Associations IFATCA. *See* www.ifatca.org

International Federation of Airline Pilots Associations IFALPA. *See* www.falpa.org

International Federation of Camping and Caravanning *See* IFCC[1].

International Federation of Tour Operators See IFTO.

International Federation of Women's Travel Organizations Founded in 1968, it now numbers over 60 affiliated clubs worldwide. *See* www ifwto.org

International Forum of Travel and Tourism Advocates IFTTA. *See* www.travellaw.com

International Foundation of Airline Passenger Associations IFAPA.

international health requirements These can be checked in the general information pages of airline reservations systems and GDSs, in *TIM* or the electronic equivalent TIMATIC, in the DG&G *Guide to International Travel* and in other travel reference manuals. Smallpox having been eradicated, vaccination against it is no longer officially required. According to the traveller's origin or itinerary, many countries require an International Certificate of Vaccination to be produced against yellow fever before the traveller is allowed entry into the country concerned. The certificate proving vaccination against yellow fever is valid from 10 days after vaccination and for 10 years. Some countries require a general health certificate and/or X-ray proving absence of tuberculosis. There are no rules concerning malaria, but travellers visiting or passing through malarial areas should take prophylactic measures in the form of tablets at least 10 days beforehand, while in the area of danger and for 4 weeks afterwards. WHO provides information as to areas where resistance has been reported to various drugs for treating malaria. Typhoid, paratyphoid and hepatitis immunization, though not compulsory, should also be recommended for areas where sanitation is considered poor. Information on international travel and health is published annually in the World Health Organization publication by the same name, *International Travel and Health* updated by the *Weekly Epidemiological Record*. *See* www.who.int/ith *also* information online www.intmed.mcw.edu/travel

International Hotel and Restaurant Association IHRA. *See* www.ih-ra.com

International Hotel Association Changed name in 1990. *See* IHRA *and* www.ih-ra.com

International Hotels Environment Initiative *See* IHEI.

International Maritime Organization The major worldwide body in this field. *See* www.imo.org *and* SOLAS.

International Passenger Survey *See* IPS.

International Reservation Request Form *See* IRRF.

International Road Transport Union *See* IRU.

international sale indicators Now obsolete. Under the IATA fare construction alterations introduced in 1989, rates became based on the country of issuance of and/or payment for an air ticket. The procedure involved the use of four four-character international sale indicators, so that fares varied for a specific journey, dependent on where the ticket was issued or paid for. Now, the agreed *only* rate for a journey is based on the price of it when ticketed and paid for in the country of origin of the first flight. *See* IATA fare construction system *and* SITI, SITO, SOTI *and* SOTO.

International Sanitary Convention *See* ISC.

International Ship and Port Facility Security Code Rules which became operative on 1 July 2004 applying to port facilities, all ships over 500 tonnes and the companies that unload them, requiring appointment of security officers, alarm systems, automatic identifications systems and methods of checking the identity of people boarding. Involves conducting a ship security assessment and developing from this a ship security plan and associated procedures. An ISPS practical pack can be downloaded from Lloyd's Registers web site www.lr.org following the path 'Marine Services' and selecting 'Marine Security'.

International Ski Federation *See* ISF.

International Snowboard Federation *See* ISF.

International Student Identity Card A recognized document in many countries for gaining reduced-rate travel for students.

International Traffic Engineering Vocabulary Was published by the World Touring and Automobile Organization and the Permanent International Association of Road Congresses with financial assistance from UNESCO in 1957. Several definitions published in this text are acknowledged to be from this source by referring to ITEV.

International Union of Public Transport *See* UITP.

International Union of Railways *See* UIC.

International Youth Hostels Federation *See* IYHF.

Internet An alternative name for the world wide web; also a worldwide business travel management organization.

As this dictionary was going to press, registrations were taking place for the new 'dot travel' domain name to be launched in 2006. *See* www.tralliance.com/dot travel/main.htm

Internet Booking Engine *See* IBE.

Internet usage in Europe Comprehensive coverage concerning Internet usage for travel planning and booking throughout Europe is available at www.etcnew media.com/review

InterRail European railways sell Inter-Rail Travel Authority Cards valid for a month to young people under 26, entitling travel at 50% of ordinary fares over the lines of the issuing railway and free travel over the rest of the European system. The UK rail network, Coras Iompair Eireann and Northern Ireland Railways are considered as one railway. Free travel is gained on other participating European railways, except for Stena and other shipping services, where the reduction is 50% regardless of country of purchase. Twenty-seven European countries and Morocco now participate in the scheme. *See* www.interrailnet.com

Interstate Commerce Commission *See* ICC. (Now obsolete.)

Interstate Highway *See* highway.

Interurbano A Spanish train, self-propelled, with all cars having a middle aisle. Seating is made up principally of second-class sections. The Interurbano makes stops only at major population centres. *See* trains.

intervening opportunity model *See* transport modelling.

Intex System operated in conjunction with Diners Club credit cards – *see* UATP.

Intourist The Russian national travel organization.

Introduction to Tourism in Britain A UK examination syllabus, City and Guilds Scheme 480, which focuses on an awareness, rather than an in-depth study, of tourism together with the personal skills needed in handling visitors. As such, the scheme is suitable for new entrants to the industry as well as those who wish to enter it. It is also of interest to those working in hotels or other sectors related to tourism and is suitable to be run in-house by employers. The scheme was developed in association with the Tourist Boards and designed to link with the Open College tourism course and associated video and learning materials.

Intuitive Sabre   Name of Sabre system for new or inexperienced users. *See* Sabre for more information.

invalid passengers by air   Airlines must be consulted first before arrangements can be made for carriage of stretcher cases or other immobile persons. Walking passengers who are in poor health or suffering from a disability need completion of airline medical forms. British Airways' form gives guidance on the reverse as to which conditions make flying inappropriate. However, it should be noted that BA no longer carry stretcher passengers.

inventory   The 'stock' of available hotel rooms or seats on a mode of transport. A fixed inventory reservation system for a package tour operator means that each aircraft seat is associated with a bed in particular accommodation. A free inventory system means that flight seats can be associated with any accommodation near the distant airport.

invisible exports/imports   *See* tourism balance of trade.

involuntary changes   Changes in an air journey brought about by circumstances outside the passenger's control. Usually concerned with airlines' alterations or cancellations of flights. The passenger does not lose benefit of excursion fare applicable had journey scheduled actually taken place. For air passenger's rights in the USA in the event of a schedule irregularity or *force majeure* situation *see* Rule 240.

involuntary denied boarding   *See* denied boarding compensation *and* bump.

IoE   Institute of Export in the UK.

IOLT   The Institute of Logistics and Transport. The Chartered Institute of Transport in the UK merged with the Institute of Logistics in 1998 to form an international professional body for individuals employed in transport and physical distribution. Originally founded in 1919 as the Institute for Transport, the CIT received a Royal Charter in 1926, 'to promote and encourage and coordinate the study and advancement of the science and art of transport in all its branches'. Though based in the UK, around 5000 of the original CIT's 50,000 members are outside the UK, mainly in the current and former British Commonwealth. Examina-

tions leading to associate and full membership of the IOLT are recognized as the equivalent of university pass degree standard. *See* www.iolt.org.uk

IOMTB   Isle of Man Tourist Board. *See* www.gov.im/tourism

Ionosphere Club   Was name of Eastern Airline's Flyer's Club. *See* FFP (frequent flyer programme) for general details.

IOTA   Institute of Transport Administration in the UK.

IP   An information provider is an organization, making pages of information available on a public viewdata service or Internet service. Any renter of frames is an IP, but some are known as umbrella information providers. This is because they take a substantial number of pages and rent them to others, who may not have the expertise to develop, maintain and update their own series of frames.

IPDM   Institute of Physical Distribution Management in the UK.

IPEX   Instant Purchase Excursion Fare.

IPS   The International Passenger Survey is carried out for the UK government's Department of Trade and Industry by the Office for National Statistics. Interviews are undertaken with a large sample of those entering and leaving Britain at the main airports and seaports. The results are published quarterly in MQ6 – *Overseas Travel and Tourism – Business Monitor Quarterly Statistics*, covering both visits abroad by UK residents as well as visits to Britain by overseas residents. Comprehensive analyses include numbers and expenditure quoted by destination or origin. These statistics are available in full on line via www.statistics.gov.uk

IRAN   Inspect and repair as necessary (aviation term).

IRIS   Internal Reservation and Information System; was the in-house computer system for travel operated by A.T. Mays, one of the largest UK travel agency groups, part of the international Carlson Travel Group; A.T. Mays agencies were bought by Thomas Cook.

Irish Hotel and Catering Institute   *See* IHCI.

Irish Hotels Federation   IHF. *See* www.ihf.ie

Irish Tourist Board   *See* ITB[2].

Irish Travel Agents Association *See* ITAA.

IRO Institution of Railway Operators in the UK, founded in 2000. *See* www.railwayforum.com/factfile/institute

IRRF International Reservation Request Forms are the official four-part document used to apply for European Rail reservations by post, enabling applicant travel agents or rail stations to provide full details of a desired reservation, part A of which is returned with the reservation allocation. It is strongly recommended that seat reservations are obtained for all long-distance European rail journeys. Reservations are not available until 2 months before date of travel. All the West European rail networks possess electronic reservation systems whereby seats, EuroCity, couchettes and sleeping cars may be reserved through the use of computer terminals located at main offices.

IRS Inertial reference system (aviation term).

IRTE Institute of Road Transport Engineers in the UK.

IRU The International Road Transport Union was founded in 1948. Its stated objectives are to contribute to the promotion and prosperity, in all countries, of national and international passenger and freight transport by road, and to safeguard the interests of professional and own-account road transport. The IRU has over 100 active and associate member associations in 50 countries. A worldwide organization representing road transport, it enjoys consultative status with the United Nations and the Council of Europe and has a permanent delegation to the EEC. The IRU is responsible for the editing of the Eurolines multi-lingual European international scheduled coach service timetable. *See* www.iru.org

IRVR Instrumented runway visual range (aviation term).

ISA International standard atmosphere (aviation term).

ISC The International Sanitary Convention is the international agreement which prevents the spread of disease. The format of vaccination certificates and by whom they may be authorized is laid down as well as period after vaccination before certificates become effective and the length of the certificate's validity. The convention originated in 1933 was added to in 1944 and elaborated by a 1946 protocol. *See* international health requirements.

ISDN Integrated Services Digital Network; name used by British Telecom for their Broadband ADSL service.

ISDR In service difficulty report (aviation term).

ISES International Special Events Society in the UK.

ISF International Ski Federation or International Snowboard Federation, two Swiss-based organizations sharing same secretariat. For information on the former, www.fis-ski.com ; concerning the latter, www.isf-ch

ISIC An International Student Identity Card is the recognized document in many countries for gaining reduced-rate travel.

ISIS The IATA Statistical Information System is a joint SITA/IATA project, undertaking the collection, analysis and dissemination of information concerning airlines' traffic, capacity, revenue and cost and consumer information in historical, current and forecast terms. *See also* tourism information databases. ISIS also stands for IATA Software for Industry Settlement, the BSP software.

Isle of Man Department of Tourism *See* www.visitisleofman.com

ISMP International Society of Meeting Planners. *See* www.iami.org/ismp.cfm

isochrones Lines of equal travel time on maps showing the boundaries of equal travel time to a destination.

Isolax Name of French Railways' (SNCF) seat which can be altered to a reclining position.

ISP Industry Settlement Plan, generic title of the many BSPs in operation worldwide. *See* IATA Industry Settlement System.

ISS Industry Settlement System. *See* IATA Industry Settlement System.

ISPS *See* International Ship and Port Facility Security Code.

Israel Government Tourist Office *See* www.infotour.co.il

Israel Tourist and Travel Agents Association ITTAA. *See* www.ittaa. org.il

issuing office coupon The coupon of a multi-part ticket which a travel agent retains when sending off the auditor's coupon, together with agent's sales return and remittance.

ISTAT   International Society of Transport Aircraft Trading.

ISTEA   Intermodal Surface Transportation Efficiency Act in the USA. *See* www.dot.gov/ost/govtaffairs/istea

ISTEL   (Istel)   Was correctly named AT&T Istel, subsequently known as X-TANT but now known as NTL Business (Travel Division). *See* X-TANT *and* NTL Business (Travel Division).

ISTTE   International Society of Travel and Tourism Educators. A US-based organization with over 300 member educators in travel, tourism and related fields, representing all levels of educational institutions from professional schools and high schools to four-year college and graduate degree-granting institutions. For more information *see* www.istte.org

ISWL   Isolated single wheel load (aviation term).

IT[1]   *See* inclusive tour.

IT[2]   Information technology. *See* listing under information technology in travel and tourism.

ITA[1]   Institut du Transport Aerien, known in Britain as the Institute of Air Transport. This is the organization which represents all the major international groups in this field, as well as the national groups in 75 countries.

ITA[2]   Institute of Travel Agents. *See* ITT.

ITA[3]   Incentive Travel Association. *See* ITMA.

ITA[4]   Internet travel agency, also known as an online travel agency. A travel intermediary which, in theory, conducts all its business over the Internet. However, these organizations have found it essential to operate substantial telephone call centres to back up their electronic service. Thus their operations are often 'low' touch rather than 'no' touch.

ITAA   Irish Travel Agents Association is the trade body of tour operators and travel agents in the Irish Republic, most agents in Northern Ireland belonging to ABTA. ITAA has organized a bonding scheme to protect the public against financial loss should a member collapse, and is affiliated to UFTAA. *See* www.itaa.ie

Italian National Travel Agency Organization   *See* FIAVET.

Italian State Tourist Board (ENIT)   *See* www.enit.it

ITB[1]   Formerly Industry Training Board in the UK. Replaced by National Training Organizations (NTOs) which have themselves been replaced by Sector Skills Councils.

ITB[2]   Irish Tourist Board (Bord Fáilte). *See* www.ireland.travel.ie *also* for the travel trade www.bftrade.travel.ie

ITB[3]   ITB Berlin (International Tourism Bourse), which claims to be the largest annual international tourism exchange and exhibition.

ITC   American term meaning inclusive tour charter.

ITEV   *See* International Traffic Engineering Vocabulary.

ITG   *See* Institute of Tourist Guiding.

ITI   International-to-international; used in connection with a US immigration programme allowing air passengers making international journeys to transit US airports; this permission to transit without visa was suspended on 1 October 2003 for security reasons.

itinerary   The term used for a succinct list of a traveller's or group's travel arrangements, in the form of places, times and dates when everything is planned to occur. This usually begins with initial latest check-in time, followed by the time of departure and arrival of the mode of transportation involved for the first leg of the journey, and including any flight number, train number and necessary information to locate the place of check-in or boarding, as there may be more than one terminal/departure gate/platform. All the activities planned for the trip should be stated in a full itinerary. Official IATA definition is the sum of all portions from beginning to ending of passenger's trip, even though separated by gap(s).

ITIX   International Travel Industry Exposition in the USA, a huge annual travel industry event, also open to the public.

ITM   Institute of Travel Managers in Industry and Commerce in the UK and Ireland has around 1000 members with a corporate expenditure of £6bn. In February 2005 announced merger with ACTE (Association of Corporate Travel Executives). As well as representation on the ACTE Board, a UK Regional Advisory Council was formed. In July 2005, the merger was abandoned. *See* www.acte.org *Also see list of 70 other business travel related entries which* *follows* corporate travel contracts, *some of which lead to further entries.*

ITMA   The Incentive Travel and Meetings Association of the UK. Successor to the UK Incentive Travel Association. *See* www.itma-online.org

ITour   Name of a tour operator's reservation system in the UK; it is a web-based browser, using technology that overcomes the restraints of viewdata based systems.

ITP   IATA Taxation Panel.

ITPS   Interactive Transaction Processing System(s). Equipment and software enabling the public to do business direct with vendors of goods or services, without personal contact. For example, the cash dispensers to be found outside banks worldwide, the self-ticketing and reservation machines to be found at some US airports and the ticketing machines on most British railway stations. Touch sensitive, waterproof keyboards are essential. Obviously, intuitive (user friendly) software is also necessary.

ITS   Information Technology Services – an IATA department.

ITT   The Institute of Travel and Tourism in the UK. In 1948, the Institute of Travel Agents was a UK travel agents trade association and in no sense, a professional institute. Because of dissatisfaction by larger agents with the way it was run, they led the formation of the Association of British Travel Agents in 1950. For 5 years, both trade bodies continued, until they amalgamated. At the Folkestone Convention of ABTA on 19 October 1955, proposals for re-establishing an Institute of Travel Agents, now as a professional body were approved and the ITA came into being on 2 January 1956. Although running examinable qualifications in its own right, it was the Association's training arm, until on 1 July 1972, it separated from ABTA and became an autonomous body.

In December 1976, it was decided to aim for a wider membership than travel agents, and the name of the Institute was changed to the now existing one, namely the Institute of Travel and Tourism. Nevertheless, for most of the 1970s, the ITT continued to handle the ABTA National Training Plan acting as the Association's training arm and receiving substantial financial support both from the trade body and the ATTITB. Following termination of the contract to handle training for the ABTA NTB, the Institute abandoned examinations adopting Business Education Council awards and standards. Subsequently, as they were introduced, COTAC, NVQs and SVQs, Edexcel, ABTAC and ABTOC awards were recognized as entry qualifications.

In 2000, a new constitution was adopted and instead of the previous regional structure, the Board of Directors was elected to represent membership sectors of tourist boards, airlines, ground transport, tour operators, travel agents, hospitality, tourism training, sea transport and domestic tourism, together with seven general directors. The aims of the ITT include: raising and maintaining professional standards in the travel industry through the development and training of individuals; providing a platform and guidelines for the formal recognition of individual travel industry progress, supporting and guiding it; representing and lobbying on behalf of the rights and views of individuals in the travel industry.

The grades of membership of the ITT are student, Affiliate, Associate, Full Member and Fellow. These grades can be attained by passing the various industry examinations already mentioned; alternatively full membership is available to those with 5 years' experience in the travel and tourism industry at management level and fellowship after 10 years at director or senior executive level. Applicants can also submit a professional paper to become a member; a distinction means election to fellowship. *See* www.itt.co.uk

ITTA   Formerly Independent Travel Technology Association in the USA, now called the TTA (Travel Technology Association).

ITTAA   Israel Tourist and Travel Agents Association. *See* www.ittaa.org.il

ITX   Inclusive tour fares. These air fares are specially reduced to enable travel companies to utilize them as the air fare element to create package tour arrangements by scheduled air flights. The rates are only available to agents or operators producing 2000 copies of an approved brochure. ITX fares are confidential to the travel trade. Minimum selling prices for inclusive tour arrangements utilizing ITX fares are laid down by IATA. Because of abuses, airlines have withdrawn most individual ITX rates. *See* CBIT, consolidation air fares, and SGIT.

IULDUG Interline Unit Load Device Control User Group of IATA.

IUR International Union of Railways. *See* UIC www.uic.assoc.fr

Ivory Coast National Travel Agency Organization *See* Syndivoyages.

IWA Inland Waterways Association in the UK – concerned with the restoration, retention and development of UK inland waterways for both commercial and pleasure use. *See* www.waterways.org.uk

IWAAC Inland Waterways Amenity Advisory Council in the UK, which is required under the Transport Act 1968 to advise the Secretary of State for the Environment and the British Waterways Board on certain matters.

IWG Internet Working Group of IATA.

IYHF The international body of which national Youth Hostels Associations in around 50 countries are members. *See* www.iyhf.org

IYMS IATA Yield Management System.

J

J Class Brand name given by VIASA to passenger area immediately adjacent to first class, where passengers paying full economy fares enjoy improved service and facilities. *See* business class.

JAA Joint Aviation Authorities (in Europe). *See* www.jaa.nl During the currency of this dictionary will be replaced by the EASA.

Jacob's ladder Rope ladder with wooden rungs, hung over the side of ships to allow access to and from small boats. No longer used for passengers.

JACOLA Joint Airports Committee of Local Authorities in the UK.

jacuzzi Bath often offered as a hotel or health club facility in which heated water is circulated or bubbled by means of jets, usually also with an aeration device; called a spa bath or whirlpool bath in some countries.

JAG Japan Action Group (of IATA).

Jamaica Association of Transport and Travel Agents JATTA. *See* www.discoverjamaica.com

Jamaica Tourist Board *See* www.visitjamaica.com

JANSC Joint Air Navigation Services Council.

Japan Association of Travel Agents JATA. *See* www.jata-net.or.jp/english

Japan National Tourist Organization *See* www.japantravelinfo.com *also* www.jnto.go.jp

JAR Joint Aviation Regulation.

JATA Japan Association of Travel Agents. *See* www.jata-net.or.jp/english

JATO Jet assisted take-off, a system which provides extra power during take-off of aircraft powered by piston engines.

JATTA Jamaica Association of Transport and Travel Agents. *See* www.discoverjamaica.com

JCPC Joint Cargo Procedures Conference (of IATA).

JDGB Joint ATA/IATA Dangerous Goods Board.

jeepney *See* jitney.

Jersey Government Tourist Board *See* www.jersey.com

jet aircraft engine The term jet is now synonymous with the name of the aircraft as well as its motive power. A jet engine is a gas turbine which powers an aircraft because of the enormous thrust generated by the jet of air and gases forced out of the back of the engine. The world's first commercial jet aircraft, the de Haviland Comet, made its first flight on 27 July 1949, although it was 2 years later before BOAC became the first airline in the world to operate jet services with the Comet 1 aircraft, which cut many flight times by up to 50%. The Comet 1 carried 36 passengers and four crew at a cruising speed of 490 mph. The title 'turbojet' is merely another name for a jet aircraft engine. Air is sucked in, compressed and mixed with high-octane aviation fuel and the jet produced is the propellant force. Turbofan jet engines have an air intake fan at the front increasing a jet engine's efficiency, while the most sophisticated turbofan engines improve performance by ducting some of the air intake around the combustion chamber. The term ramjet is a jet engine where forward velocity of the airplane pushes air into a jet engine, rather than it being sucked in and compressed by a fan.

Developed in the 1990s were propfan engines. A new-style propeller with many sickle-shaped blades was placed to the rear of the jet engine. This arrangement enabled planes to fly at similar speed to earlier models, but with a fuel saving of at least 35%. General Electric described their new engine as a UDF (Unducted Fan.) Other aircraft manufacturers interposed reduction gearing between jet engine and new propellers to reduce noise and improve efficiency, for example, the former British Aircraft Corporation's ATP (Advanced Turbo Prop).

jet loader *See* gate.

jet/ship Originally a brand name, now a generic term applied to low-priced journey partly by sea, and partly by air, utilizing low-cost charter or group IATA fares.

jetfoil   A fast seagoing vessel of hydrofoil type, powered by water jets. In Europe, a passenger service between Dover and Ostend is currently operated by jetfoil.

jetlag   *See* circadian rhythm.

jetsam   Anything thrown overboard at sea (jettisoned); but, once overboard, it might be called flotsam, because its origin becomes unknown.

jetstream   *See* turbulence.

JetTrain   Name of new high speed train (HST) launched by European company Bombardier Transportation at Union Station, Washington, DC in 2003. The innovative JetTrain has been developed in cooperation with the United States Federal Railroad Administration (FRA). Planned to travel at 150 mph (240km/h), it uses an aircraft type gas turbine engine which drives an electrical generator to power the train. The train has been designed to offer the same speed and acceleration as electric. As it is 20% lighter than conventional diesel units, it has twice the acceleration.

jetty   Alternative name for a quay, landing stage or pier.

Jetway   The name of the best-selling passenger loading and unloading motorized pier or ramp in America, which is often used generally to describe all such devices.

JHIC   Joint Hospitality Industry Congress; a UK umbrella organization representing trade and professional bodies which encourages cooperation between SMEs and larger companies.

JICTOURS   Joint Industry Committee for Tourism Statistics in the UK. A Tourism Society initiative established in April 1991.

JISC   The Joint Information Systems Committee is an independent UK advisory body that supports further and higher education by providing strategic guidance, advice and opportunities to use information and communications technology (ICT) to support teaching, learning, research and administration.

jitney   US terminology usually applied to a small bus which, although operating on a scheduled basis along a particular route, may pick up or drop passengers within that area. Often, a set fare is paid and the service is known in some countries as dial-a-bus. In the Philippines called a jeepney.

Johnson Act   An American Act of significance to the cruise industry empowering US states to exercise authority over gambling on ships which embark from and return to their state, without visiting another state or country within 3 days. In 1993, California banned much cruise ship gambling. But the ruling was subsequently overturned in 1996 by the California Cruise Ship Revitalization Act.

Joint Automated Agency Ticketing Agreement   An agreement between airlines, enabling agents operating automated ticketing systems to issue neutral tickets on their behalf.

joint fare   A through rate approved by two or more airlines, often, but not necessarily, for a main journey with a local connection.

joint marketing company or **organization** North American equivalent terms for a consortium. *See* consortium.

joint notice of change   US form on which the vendors and purchasers of a travel agency provide full details and formally request the agency's appointments to carry on.

Jordan Tourism Board   *See* www.see-jordan.com

JPSC   Joint ATA/IATA Passenger Services Conference.

jumbo   Jumbo jet is the name commonly used for all types of the Boeing 747; at the time of writing, the name is increasingly being used for all large aircraft.

jumboizing   The act of inserting an extra section in the middle of a ship, thus lengthening it and increasing its capacity by 20% or more; it is usually associated with modernization of the vessel. This process is less expensive than building a new ship. Also called lengthening or stretching.

jump seat   Seat folding down from side or bulkhead of an aircraft for the use of crew during take-off or landing, when everyone must be strapped in.

junior suite   A large hotel room with a bathroom/toilet, and with two separate areas, one for sleeping and the other for daytime use. Term is used to distinguish this from an ordinary suite, which is composed of separate rooms rather than areas. *See* suite.

junk A typical Chinese sailing vessel, of varying size, with up to five masts and a high stern. Sails may be of traditional bamboo matting or panels of more modern material.

junket A travel trade 'educational' (*see* educational) where the accent is hedonistic.

JVS French Railway's young travellers' service. SNCF provide this service on certain TGV's for children aged 4–13 years travelling alone. A hostess takes charge of the children during the whole TGV journey, subject to payment of a supplement.

K

k Stands for kilo, which normally means 1000. However, in computer terminology, 1 kB means 1024 bytes. Kilo is also short for kilogramme (kg), the standard measurement used for baggage and cargo weights by air. A kilo is about 2.2 UK pounds.

KAB Kuoni Automatic Banking system. It is a UK travel agency direct banking debit system whereby the agent's bank account is automatically debited, weekly, for the value of transactions with that operator due for payment.

Kanata Club The name of CP Air's Frequent Flyers Club, membership of which is free, but by invitation only. For further details *see* FFP (frequent flyer programme).

KATA Kenya Association of Travel Agents. *See* www.kenyatourism.org

kayak A type of long, narrow-single-seat canoe, of Eskimo origin, widely used for sporting and leisure activities. Both hull and deck are completely enclosed, except for the space for the oarsman. A kayak is propelled by a double-bladed paddle.

Keats Was one of Prestel's six computers.

keel The backbone of a ship.

Kenny Travel System Was name of computerized British tour operator's reservation and accounting system introduced in January 1984 by Kenny Computer Systems Limited. The same name and company also produced a computerized accounting system for travel agents first introduced in November 1982.

Kentucky Tourism (Visit Kentucky) *See* www.kentuckytourism.com

Kenya Association of Travel Agents KATA. www.kenyatourism.org

Kenya Tourist Board *See* www.magicalkenya.com

kerbside check-in *See* curbside check-in.

ketch A two-masted ship, with main and mizzen masts. By definition, the rudder must be aft (to the rear) of the mizzen mast, otherwise the vessel is a yawl.

keycard In modern hotels, room entry is controlled by insertion of a credit card-sized plastic card. The magnetized strip is encoded at the time of check-in; thus attaining a high level of security. Types of client room access may include a standard where the lock only remains open for a short time after card insertion; an extended time for disabled persons; and an over-ride card for family rooms enabling access even if it has been deadbolted from inside. A huge range of staff access permutations is also possible. For a typical description of a keycard's specifications, *see* www.vingcard.com/Products/VC2100/extra.htm (The continual development of products means that users of this dictionary should seek a description of the latest keycard.)

King David Class Name of El Al's first class.

King David Club Name of El Al's Frequent Flyers Club. *See* FFP (frequent flyer programme).

king room A room containing a king-sized bed.

king-sized bed A large-sized double bed; S Medlik in his *Dictionary of Travel and Tourism* suggests greater than 72 in. × 80 in.

Kipling Was one of Prestel's six computers.

knots – nautical miles per hour As a rough approximation a speed of 20 knots is equivalent to 23 mph. *See* nautical mile for definition.

Korea National Tourism Organization *See* www.knto.org.kr

korridorzuge Literally a corridor train, which is somewhat misleading. This is the name given to Austrian and other similar trains which leave their country of origin for a short distance, traversing another country before returning to the original country, taking that routing because it is more direct. For example, many Austrian trains traverse parts of Germany in order to avoid circuitous routings. Such trains are travelling through a 'corridor' of another country, within which they may not stop, and passengers may not leave or embark on the train. There are no customs or immigration formalities since such a train is treated as if it had remained in its country of origin.

kreugers *See* airframe.

KUDOS Name of Kuoni's viewdata travel agency reservation system in the UK.

Kuoni Automatic Banking system (KAB) *See* KAB.

L

L-shaped cabin   *See* bibby cabin.

La Bed   Formerly the name of the hotel booking system of Hogg Robinson, largest UK business travel management company, now known as BTI. Their system has been renamed HotelBooker.

LACAC   Latin American Civil Aviation Conference.

ladder fare construction   The fare calculation is written on a manual IATA-style air ticket vertically. The term arises from the fact that the figures are listed in ladder form, as opposed to linear horizontal fare calculations produced by computers.

LAN   Local area network; a group of computers and/or peripheral equipment linked together, often in the same building.

lanai   American terminology for a veranda. Hence, a room with a balcony or patio, perhaps overlooking a garden or swimming pool, is referred to by the same term.

land arrangements   That part of a passenger's itinerary that is not by air or sea. In North America, where the term land arrangements is often substituted for ground arrangements, this may mean everything that is provided to a passenger at their destination.

land operator   In North America, the equivalent of a European ground handling agent, providing a comprehensive range of services, particularly for the clients of inclusive tour, group and conference operators.

landing card   Immigration form which aliens may be required to complete on arrival at a foreign destination.

landing charges or **fees**   The payments airlines make to airports for their services.

landing gear   *See* airframe.

landside   That part of an airport accessible to the general public. After a traveller has passed through immigration controls, customs and security checks, they are designated as being airside.

language   *See* computer programming language.

LAPB   Live Animals and Perishables Board (of IATA).

LAR   Live Animals Regulations (of IATA).

larboard   The port or left-hand side of a ship facing the bows (front end); the opposite of starboard.

largest hotel group in the world   *See* InterContinental hotels group, *also* www.intercontinental.com

last leg   The final sector of an itinerary. On cruises, specifically refers to the journey from the penultimate port to the home port.

last room availability   Sometimes, when a GDS is accessed, a hotel may be shown as fully booked, but when that hotel group's own CRS is accessed, rooms may be available. Increasingly, all hotels are offering travel agents last room availability through the GDSs.

last seat availability   Sometimes, when a GDS is accessed, a flight may be shown as fully booked, but when that airline's own CRS is accessed, seats may be available. Increasingly, all airlines are offering travel agents last seat availability through the GDSs.

LATA   Latin American Travel Association. *See* www.lata.org

late arrival   Hotels will only hold booked rooms up to a certain time, after which they will sell them if they can. But if a booking specifies a late arrival, the rooms are held until the time stated, which is a 'late check in'. If the reservation is guaranteed, for example, by an agent's assurance that the first night's accommodation will be paid for, then the room will also be held. The same principle also applies to other tourism services.

late booking   Travel reservations or facilities reserved shortly before departure. Package tour operators require full payment immediately for such bookings. Other typical characteristics are that a fax, telex or telephone confirmation of the ground arrangements may be necessary, and the travellers may be ticketed on departure from an airport. Some travel agents specialize in providing a late booking service.

late cancellation Official IATA definition is a reservation cancelled after the latest appropriate time prior to scheduled departure time specified by the member.

late charges Charges for items not put on a client's account on leaving a hotel, but raised subsequently. Often, these are added to a corporate account or credit card charge, and are disputed.

late check-in *See* late arrival.

late show A transportation passenger who checks in late, similarly, a person who arrives at a hotel after the latest time, up to which it was guaranteed that the room would be held.

Latin American Travel Association LATA. *See* www.lata.org

Latitudes Name of British Airways' Frequent Flyer Programme. *See* FFP (frequent flyer programme).

Latvian Tourism Development Agency *See* www.latviatourism.lv

launch Small motor boat. Same word is commonly used in the travel field in different contexts which being ordinary language need no definition here, e.g. brochure launch; programme launch; launch of new cruise ship.

layout *See* meeting room set-up.

layover Compulsory stop during a journey, usually overnight, due to there being no immediate connection between the arriving and onward transport services. For many air services, the layover costs are included in the ticket price.

LCB London Convention Bureau is a service provided by the London Tourist Board.

LCC Low cost carrier. *See* no-frills airline.

LCD Liquid Crystal Display. One of the ways of displaying alphanumeric and other symbols on a screen in response to electronic messages. The method is very versatile, screen sizes ranging from the small screen on a laptop personal computer to the world's largest at the time of writing, the departures and arrivals board at Euston rail station, London, UK.

LDW Loss damage waiver is an insurance premium paid when renting a car, which covers the hirer in the event of damage to the car. Usually, the term is synonymous with collision damage waiver. *See* CDW.

Le Shuttle Brand name of the Channel Tunnel car-carrying services. *See* Eurotunnel.

lead agent North American term for the supervisor of group of reservation, check-in or agency counter staff.

league A measure at sea of three nautical miles. Used to be the distance from a shore that the 'high seas' began.

Lebanese National Travel Agency Organization Syndicat des Agences de Voyages et de Tourisme au Liban.

Lebanon Ministry of Tourism *See* www.lebanon-tourism.gov.lb

LED Light Emitting Diode. One of the ways of displaying alphanumeric or other symbols, resulting from electronic messages.

leeward The direction toward which the wind blows.

leg A sector of an itinerary. This does not have to be a multi-sector journey for the term to be used; 'outward leg' and 'inward leg' imply obvious meanings in respect of a return journey. Official IATA definition is the space between two consecutive scheduled stops on any given flight. But the word 'leg' applies to journeys by all transport modes. *See also* sector.

legal status of a travel agent An agent is a party authorized by another party, to act for them in the conduct of their business. Most countries accept that agents are not the owners or operators of, for example, modes of transport, rental vehicles or accommodation. These owners or operators are the principals; that is, they contract directly with the traveller to provide a specified tourism service. Booking forms with associated booking conditions, which travellers are often required to sign, are always meant to establish a direct contract between a principal and a consumer. Agents facilitate the purchase of these typical tourism services but do not themselves hold any stock. The view is expressed strongly that dependent on the circumstances, a travel agent may be acting on behalf of a client, on behalf of a principal or as a neutral intermediary or broker between the two, bringing buyers and sellers together. In the USA and Britain, for which this dictionary has been particularly written, the Courts have shown this ambivalence by making decisions according to the context. During the course of any particular transaction, a travel agent may take on each of these three roles. Agents provide advisory, reservation and ticketing services for travellers; clearly they owe duties of care to these travellers and also have responsibilities to their principals, on behalf of whom they are contracted to act through an agency agreement. The best-known such agreement in the travel industry is the IATA Passenger Agency Sales Agreement. *Also see* travel agent *and* travel principal.

leisure   The personal time available for discretionary use after undertaking work and attending to essential needs such as sleeping and eating. Activities pursued during leisure time are broadly described as recreation. Hence, leisure travel is travel for pleasure, as distinct from business travel, which is undertaken in connection with work; the terms 'business travel agent' and 'leisure travel agent' refer to travel retailers specializing in either of these activities.

leisure park   *See* theme parks.

leisure travel agent   *See* leisure.

length overall   *See* LOA.

lengthening   *See* jumboizing.

Let's Go   Formerly the name of British Caledonian's in-flight magazine.

Lexique Général des Termes Ferroviaires   The standard dictionary of specialist rail terminology.

liability of airlines   *See* Warsaw Convention.

licences   It is suggested that the term should only be used to describe an official licence, for example, granted by a government authority. But the word is commonly, although wrongly, applied to commercial franchise agreements; so that references may be made to an 'ARC licence', an 'IATA licence' or an 'ATOC licence' (ATOC = Association of Train Operating Companies in the UK). *See* ATL[1], ATOL *and* Interbus Agreement.

licensing of coach journeys in Europe   *See* Interbus Agreement.

licensor   The authority or organization granting one of the many licences mentioned in this dictionary; but in North America, may be an alternative term for a consortium. *See* consortium.

lido   The swimming pool area in a European resort. Now almost obsolete, as is the use of the word lido after a resort area to indicate high quality.

lido deck   *See* deck.

life cycle   May mean an individual's life cycle (*see* market segmentation) or may mean product life cycle, the theory that any brand or product will have a growth period, become established and then eventually demand will cease.

life jacket   A sleeveless inflatable jacket carried on board aircraft or ships to save life in the event of a catastrophe. The number and type and their placement on a ship are governed by the SOLAS regulations; similarly civil aviation rules lay down requirements. *See* International Convention for the Safety of Life at Sea.

life-preserver   Generic term for a lifebuoy, life ring, life jacket or similar device.

lifeboat   Small boat carried on the 'boat' deck of large ships, which can be launched in an emergency. Strict laws govern them, making sure that there is sufficient space for passengers and crew and that they are properly equipped. The number and type and their placement are governed by the SOLAS regulations. *See* International Convention for the Safety of Life at Sea.

lifeboat drill   As soon as is practical after putting to sea, laws require that passenger-carrying vessels practise emergency procedures, which might involve escape from a sinking ship by lifeboat.

lifebuoy   Also called life ring because it is a ring shaped. Made of buoyant material they are intended to be thrown to anyone who has been swept or fallen overboard at sea. The number and type and their placement are governed by the SOLAS regulations. *See* International Convention for the Safety of Life at Sea.

life-raft   An alternative to a lifeboat, a raft may be of any shape, providing it is buoyant. Some life-rafts are inflatable with a cover and containing a survival package; others are little more than many pieces of cork sewn together with canvas. The number and type and their placement are governed by the SOLAS regulations. *See* International Convention for the Safety of Life at Sea.

lifestyle hotel   *See* boutique hotel.

Light Rail Transit   *See* LRT.

limited incumbent carrier Defined by the FAA, with respect to depeaking orders to relieve airport congestion as one with eight or fewer arrivals during peak hour periods.

limited purpose card A restricted usage credit card. Typically, corporations providing employees with credit cards may state that they are only to be used for travel and related items, or travel and entertainment.

limited service agency US term for a travel agency location that undertakes reservations but not ticketing, either because it is not an ARC-approved company, or because it is a non-approved branch being supplied from the head office.

limo North American abbreviation for a limousine, a chauffeur-driven hired car. If a hotel advertizes a *limousine service*, this usually runs between the hotel and the nearest airports.

linear fare construction Automated IATA-style air tickets produced by a printer associated with a computer, show a horizontal linear fare construction. Whereas, with ladder vertical fare calculations employed on manually produced tickets, it is possible to associate parts of the itinerary by symbols to the side of a ladder, on a computer-produced ticket, symbols and explanatory codes must precede points or groups of points on an itinerary.

liner Term is now loosely applied to any large ship. Its origin is from the famous 'lines' or companies such as Cunard and P&O which owned the ships carrying passengers and cargo between worldwide ports on a scheduled basis. Now, it is common to refer to organizations specializing in cruising as 'cruise lines', so that the term is no longer restricted to scheduled service shipping.

link span The combined companion way and bridge which links the quay to a vessel, to enable embarkation and disembarkation. Because of the rise and fall of tides, and differences in height from the water of access points for passengers, very complicated link spans are necessary. Link spans must enable vehicles to drive on or off car ferries, regardless of tidal conditions. In North America, a passenger boarding bridge is the same term, but restricted to passenger access and usually fully covered.

linkman Title of the outside doorkeeper at a British hotel. Word is obsolescent.

liquid crystal display *See* LCD.

liquidated damage clause Typical US contract term between agents and computer system suppliers covering payments in lieu of notice in the event of early cancellation. By contract, in the case of CRS/GDS contracts in the EC, the Neutral CRS Rules specifically allow for easy termination.

LIRR Long Island Rail Road. North America's busiest and oldest railway; serving New York, it was founded in 1834 as part of a boat and train route between Manhattan and Boston. It carries nearly 90m passengers a year, including large numbers of commuters to Penn Central station on the west side of Manhattan. Under construction with a target date of 2011 is a US$4.7bn link to Grand Central station on the east side of Manhattan. LIRR is a subsidiary of the publicly owned New York Metropolitan Transportation Authority (MTA).

Lithuanian State Department of Tourism Since 1993 the Lithuanian Tourism Fund has been responsible for promotion of tourism. *See* www.tourism.lt *and* www.travel.lt

Little Metro *See* VAL.

LLF Lowest logical fare; the lowest fare that can be used for a business traveller, after taking into account the client's travel policy including preferred suppliers – it is business travel jargon. *A list of 70 other business travel related entries follows* corporate travel contracts, *some of which lead to further entries.*

LLL Low-level lighting. The type and its placement on a ship is governed by the SOLAS regulations. *See* International Convention for the Safety of Life at Sea.

LOA Literally, 'length overall' with regard to a ship, including projections such a bowsprit or even stern flagpole.

load factor Percentage of occupancy of seats in an aircraft or other means of transport. Average number of passengers travelling on a series of flights or other transport or tourism service compared with total number of seats available. The equivalent for a car rental company is the percentage of the vehicles that are on hire, or for a hotel, the room occupancy percentage.

loading apron *See* gate.

loading bridge A covered passageway from a terminal building to an aircraft.

local operator North American alternative term for a ground handling agent or land operator.

local representative Meaning varies according to which organization is being represented. *See* tour operator's representative *or* rep or representative for sales representative. Sometimes travel companies appoint persons or organizations to represent them abroad; the capacity in which they are appointed varies so that a definition of the term is not appropriate.

local selling fare *See* LSF.

local time Timetables are normally based on actual local times. To calculate 'elapsed time', which is the actual time taken to travel on a particular journey, time changes must be taken into account. *See* GMT *and* times at sea.

location of corporate travellers It is becoming increasingly important for companies to be able to identify the whereabouts of their employees 24/365. Business travel management company (TMC) Rosenbluth offers TrackPoint, which in 2003 operated for over 33,000 travellers daily. Information is available through a web interface and interactive map. The Travel Company, a British TMC, calls its equivalent system Online Locator. *A list of 70 other business travel related entries follows* corporate travel contracts, *some of which lead to further entries.*

locator code The alphanumeric reference given by a travel computer upon concluding a reservation, acting both as confirmation that the booking has been satisfactorily concluded and a means of accessing or retrieving it. For air reservations, called a passenger name record (PNR).

locomotive The traction engine and power unit which pulls or pushes railway carriages.

lodged account A centrally billed account covering all an organization's travellers held by a travel management company (business travel agent) and facilitated by a corporate credit card provider. Became popular around 1985 because the accounts provided corporations with detailed information concerning travel expenditure. At the time of writing, in 2004, payments for travel through individual cards had overtaken lodged cards, but usage of them is predicted to continue. Typical names are Diners Club TravelPASS, American Express Corporate Card and Visa Corporate Card.

lodging industry North American term for the accommodation industry, as distinct from the hospitality industry, which is wider. *See* hospitality industry.

logbook Name of Lufthansa in-flight magazine.

logit model *See* transport modelling.

log-on To enter an identity into a computer, enabling recognition and permission to operate.

London Tourist Board (LTB) *See* www.londontown.com

long haul Travel jargon which usually refers to intercontinental travel, whereas short-haul routes are within a continent. In the UK the Consumer's Association publication *Holiday Which* has adopted the definition of flights over 5 h; while Vérité Reily Collins in *Dictionary for the Tourism Industry* suggests over 6 h.

Long Island Railroad *See* LIRR.

longest airplane The longest airplane in the world currently operating is the Airbus A340–600, 75.3 m. It has a fuselage diameter of 5.64 m and a wingspan of 63.5 m; typical passenger load is 380; it can fly non-stop up to 14,600 km. This will be dwarfed by the new Airbus A380–800 due to be delivered in 2006. It has a horizontal fuselage diameter of 7.14 m and a wingspan of 79.8 m; typical passenger load is 555; it can fly non-stop up to 15,000 km. However, it will be only 72.7 m long in the basic version. Within the currency of this dictionary, a stretched version may be announced that becomes the longest aircraft.

longest flight Singapore Airlines flight from Singapore to New York Newark USA departs at 12.05 and is scheduled to arrive at 18.30 the same day, a flying time of 18 h 25 min. The return journey leaves New York at 23.00 arriving in Singapore at 05.35 two days later, a flying time of 18 h 35 min. Flights are operated by the ultra-long range Airbus A340–500, travelling nearly 9000 nautical miles.

look to book ratio *See* conversion rate[2].

loss damage waiver *See* LDW.

lost tickets   If a customer loses or mislays an IATA air ticket, a duplicate may be issued for travel providing an airline Form of Indemnity has been completed. This indemnifies the airline against improper use of the lost ticket. If a document is lost and a refund claimed, an airline may still be able to reimburse the passenger, although there may be a wait of between 6 months and a year. Lost rail, car ferry and coach tickets are often non-refundable.

Louisiana Office of Tourism   *See* www.louisianatravel.com

low cost carrier   *See* no-frills airline.

low density ship   *See* ship density.

low fare search program   Computer program which regularly checks (usually overnight) all the air bookings held by an agency, seeking better fares, rebooking when possible at the most advantageous rate.

low level lighting   *See* LLL.

low season   The least popular travel time, in contrast to high season and the 'shoulder' period; as it is the least popular, fares are at their lowest, in order to attract custom.

low track force   *See* LTF.

lowest combination principle   *See also* indirect route principle. Under IATA rules, the traveller is always entitled to lowest possible combination of air fares allowed by the rules, whenever no through fare is published and the mileage has been calculated separately from the starting point to a fare construction point, and from that point onwards to the destination. *See* IATA fare construction system.

lowest logical fare   The lowest fare that can be used for a business traveller, after taking into account the client's travel policy including preferred suppliers – it is business travel jargon. *A list of 70 other business travel related entries follows* corporate travel contracts, *some of which lead to further entries.*

loyalty schemes   Frequent flyer programmes are the best known incentive reward marketing strategy in the tourism field, encouraging repeat business by aiming to persuade customers to restrict their purchasing choices in order to gain rewards; FFPs are described and discussed fully under that heading. However, loyalty schemes are not unique to air travel; they also operate in other general commercial and tourism fields. For example, Hilton initiated its 'Honours' scheme in 1987, claiming one million members a year later. Frequent travellers are encouraged to use a Hilton through membership of the Gold Passport club. For more details *see* www.hiltongroup.com

lozenge   A rectangular symbol with curved-in sides following the check digit on flight coupons, to provide optical character recognition identification of the 13-digit number.

LPB   Loss Prevention Bulletin (of IATA).

LRA   *See* last room availability.

LRT   Light rail transit. Urban mass transit systems of this type opened in Baltimore, USA, and Paris, France in 1992.

LRV   Light rail vehicle.

LSA[1]   *See* last seat availability.

LSA[2]   Leisure Studies Association in the UK, a society of researchers, planners, administrators and practitioners in this field who come together to exchange opinions and experiences and to disseminate information of common interest. Founded in 1975, has around 300 members.

LSF   Local selling fare. Abbreviation normally used in connection with IATA fare construction system.

LTAC   Leicestershire Travel Agents' Consortium in the UK, a member of Worldchoice.

LTB   London Tourist Board. *See* www.londontown.com

LTF   Low track force, a term applied to the technology allowing smaller wheels to operate on trains without damage to rail or wheel.

LTSN   Formerly the Learning and Teaching Support Network in the UK. Now renamed the Higher Education Academy Network. *See* details under this heading of the Network for Hospitality, Leisure, Sport and Tourism in the UK.

luggage   *See* baggage.

luggage, registered   *See* baggage, checked.

lugger   Boat with one, two or three masts rigged obliquely with four cornered sails.

Luxembourg National Tourist Office   *See* www.ont.lu

Luxembourg National Travel Agency Organization   *See* GAVCCL.

LYNX   *See* PMS.

M

MA¹ Via Mid Atlantic. *See* routing.

MA² *See* Modern Apprenticeship.

Mabuhay Class Brand name of Philippine Airlines' business class, available without a surcharge to all full fare passengers on a first come, first serve basis at the time of booking. *See* business class.

Mabuhay Club Name of Philippine Airlines Frequent Flyers' Club. *See* FFP (frequent flyer programme).

MAC Mean aerodynamic cord (aviation term).

Macedonian Tourism Department Part of the Republic's Ministry of Economy; *see* www.economy.gov.mk

mach numbers A means of measuring speed by comparison with the speed of sound. This varies according to the height and therefore thinness of the air. For example, in the stratosphere at around 55,000 ft, the speed of sound, Mach 1 is 670 mph and Mach 2, 1340 mph. This was approximately Concorde's cruising speed.

Machine Interface Record *See* MIR.

machine readable passport *See* passport.

MAD Major operated departments *See* Uniform System of Accounts for the Lodging Industry in hotel statistics worldwide.

Madeira National Travel Agency Organization (DTM) Delegacao de Tourismo de Madeira.

maglev Literally 'magnetic levitation', the concept by which a train may be suspended above its track by the repelling forces of electrically induced magnetism. Because actual contact between train and track is avoided other than when the train is at rest, friction between track and train is avoided. In the UK a maglev shuttle ran between Birmingham International rail station and the airport until 1995, when it was replaced by buses and subsequently in 2003 by skyrail. Work is about to begin on building a cable shuttle similar to that operating between some Las Vegas hotels. Similar maglevs run to distant terminals at London's Gatwick airport. The HSST (High Speed Surface Transport) runs on a twin track, powered by a linear induction motor. A joint venture between Japan Airlines and Sumitomo Electric, the HSST, is planned for use as a fast link between Japanese city centres and airports. Top speed achieved was 307 kph (192 mph). The German Transrapid maglev train has travelled faster. In December 1985 it achieved a new record for passenger maglevs of 355 kph (222 mph). The German consortium, after being rebuffed at home, in 2004 introduced a 270 mph maglev train between Shanghai Airport and the city outskirts in China. At the time of writing the fastest maglev train is running on a 20-mile test track at Yamanishi, 60 miles from Tokyo, at over 500 kph (310mph). It is owned by the Central Japan Railway Company; they plan to operate it between Tokyo and Osaka. It is suggested that building costs would be 30% more than a conventional high speed line, while it would use three times as much electricity per passenger as the Shinkansen, Japan's Bullet Train.

magnetic stripe A strip of magnetic material on a ticket, document or plastic card which can be encoded with information and which is machine readable. This is usually by 'swiping' the document or card. Within the currency of this dictionary edition, magnetic stripes on cards are likely to have been replaced by chips.

magrodome A ship's transparent pool cover which may be opened or closed, dependent on the weather.

maiden voyage *See* inaugural.

mailing discounts Travel industry users of UK Royal Mail Services gain bulk rebates provided second-class letters are pre-sorted into post towns and counties and each given mailing consists of items of the same size and weight. Up to 4999 letters may be posted for the cost of only 4250, the minimum. From 5000 to 23,529 letters, discount is 15% of the postage paid rising through various rebate levels up to 30% on 1,000,000 or more. In the USA, pre-sorted third-class mail qualifies for bulk discounts. Similar bulk discount rates are available in most countries.

main deck *See* deck.

Maison de la France Partnership between the French government, French regions and tourism service providers, promoting France as a destination. *See* www.franceguide.com

maître d'hôtel French term meaning head waiter in a restaurant, which is commonly used worldwide.

major operated departments *See* Uniform System of Accounts for the Lodging Industry in hotel statistics worldwide.

Malawi Ministry of Tourism, Parks and Wildlife *See* www.tourismmalawi.com

Malaysian Tourism Promotion Board *See* www.tourismmalaysia.gov.my

Maldives Tourism Promotion Board *See* www.visitmaldives.com

Malta Tourism Authority *See* www.visitmalta.com

MAM Maximum allowable mass (aviation term).

MAN Minor Adjustment Notice.

managed travel That travel which is arranged by a travel management company (TMC) as distinct from unmanaged travel, where an individual books travel arrangements (business or leisure) direct with travel operators. It is business travel jargon. *A list of 70 other business travel related entries follows* corporate travel contracts, *some of which lead to further entries.*

management fee *See* commission *and* fee-based pricing.

managerial qualifier US term for a travel agency employee who by experience and/or qualifications, satisfies the airline's criteria to manage an appointed agent.

manifest The official list of passengers or cargo being carried in a particular vessel, aircraft or other means of transport.

MANIS Was British Rail's manpower information system, on which all BR's personnel records were kept.

Manpower Services Commission *See* MSC. (An obsolete UK body.)

map projection The means by which the spherical earth is converted to a flat map. Where true compass bearings are vital, for example, in navigational charts, a version of Mercator's projection is valuable. This, however, does not produce a map to the correct scale, particularly at the poles, where land masses become exaggerated. Nordic projections are 'area true' but distorted. Some other typical map projections that might be encountered are Bonne, Chamberlin Trimetric, Conic, Lambert Azimuthal Equal Area, Lambert Conformal Conic, Lambert Zenithal Equal Area, Modified Polyconic, Secant Conic, Simple Conic, Transverse Mercator (centred on a particular meridian), Winkel's Tripel and Zenithal Equidistant. For definitions, a geography textbook should be consulted. *Also see* atlas.

MAP[1] Missed approach point (aviation term).

MAP[2] Modified American Plan. Hotel accommodation that includes a full breakfast and either lunch or dinner in the specified room rate.

Maple Leaf Super apex air fare to Canada operated by Air Canada.

Maple Leaf Club Name of Air Canada's Frequent Flyers' Club. *See* FFP (frequent flyer programme).

MAPTA Metropolitan Association of Professional Travel Agents covering New York, USA.

MARAS Middle airspace radar advisory service (aviation term).

Marco Polo Business Class Brand name given by Cathay Pacific to passenger area immediately adjacent to first class, where passengers paying full economy fares enjoy improved service and facilities. *See* business class.

Marco Polo Club Name of Cathay Pacific's Frequent Flyer Club, membership of which is free to travellers of 25,000 miles a year, who complete at least eight Cathay sectors annually. Also known as Cathay's Gold Card scheme. For further details *see* FFP (frequent flyer programme).

mare clausum or ***mare liberum*** *See* high seas.

margin squeezing Act of a provider of tourism services by cutting prices when dealing direct to customers, to a lower level than the net price to travel agents after deduction of commission. Thus, there is no profit margin for agents and they must charge fees and justify them by the added value offered to customers that agency services provide.

marina   A harbour for leisure craft such as yachts and motor cruisers, usually purpose built with servicing facilities.

mark up   The amount of profit a travel company adds to net rates to arrive at a selling price. A travel agency in the UK might add between 17% and 22.5% profit to the actual costs of the elements of an individual inclusive tour. UK tour operators usually add similar amounts.

market segmentation   Satisfying the demand for travel and tourism is achieved by breaking down that demand into many sub-markets. Services appropriate for each sub-group are then devised for and promoted to them. In the USA, VALS (values and lifestyles segmentation) analysis integrates consideration of many of the variables described in this entry. The most well-known categorization of the population in the UK is into socio-economic groups of A, B, C1, C2, D and E. Simple division into age groups is associated with life cycle stages such as childhood, teenager or young adult living at home and then away from home, marriage or involvement in a 'relationship' with another adult, various stages of family life with children and 'empty nesters'. Ethnic groups often have differing needs, while varying lifestyle or type of personality creates alternative groupings. Obviously markets can be segmented geographically; sophisticated systems now include the whole population of many western countries analysed on huge databases. *See also* tourist typologies *and* yield management.

market share incentives   Not usual in UK. In the US Market Share Override Programs (MSOP) give agents extra commission. The base figure is the percentage market share held by a supplier in an area or region. Achievement of a higher percentage for that supplier of an agency's sales than the base may attract an override payment, dependent on the terms of the MSOP.

Marketing Information Data Tape   Global Distribution Systems collate bookings, so that detailed information can be purchased by airlines, for example, on a specified route, identifying passenger numbers for each airline.

marquee value   Enhanced marketability conferred on a cruise by inclusion of a popular port or place in the itinerary. Thus, it is hoped that more customers will be attracted.

Marriott   Marriott International is the world's third largest hospitality company with 2655 units offering 479,882 rooms. Brands include Marriott hotels, resorts, suites and executive apartments; Ritz-Carlton; Renaissance Hotels and Resorts; Ramada; New World; Residence Inn; Courtyard; TownePlace Suites; Fairfield Inn; SpringHill Suites and Marriott Vacation Club International. *See* www.marriott.com

MARS   Reservation system for tour operators in the UK from Mach Associates.

Maryland Office of Tourism Development   *See* www.mdisfun.org

mass tourism   *See* tourism, mass.

Massachusetts Office of Travel and Tourism   *See* www.massvacation.com *also see* Discover New England.

mast   A tall pole rising vertically from the deck of a ship, to which sails and rigging may be attached. In a sailing vessel, masts are usually 'stepped' from the keel. In a three-masted vessel, that in the middle is the main mast, the forward one is the foremast and that to the aft, the mizzen mast.

MAST   Midwest Agents Selling Travel; a US agents consortium. *See* www.mast.org *and* consortium.

MASTA   Was Multiple Accounting Services Travel Agents system. Was first offered as a bureau service to UK travel agents in the mid-seventies, but was then upgraded with the provision of a microcomputer. *See* Microstretcher.

master   Alternative name for a ship's captain.

master bill   Meeting industry term for the final invoice covering all costs presented following a conference or event.

Master Cruise Counselor   *See* MCC.

MATZ   Military aerodrome traffic zone.

Mauritius Tourism Promotion Authority   *See* www.mauritius.net

maximum authorized amount   *See* ARC[1].

maximum number (and minimum number) of participants Package holiday departures are always limited in size by the space available on the mode of transport and in the accommodation contracted; but small special interest groups are often restricted to enhance the enjoyment of the participants; the actual maximum numbers are seldom stated. However, in all cases, there is a minimum number below which it will not be profitable for the holiday or tour to be operated. A scheduled transport operator runs services regardless of some low load factors, but a tour operator often states in the booking conditions that departures are subject to minimum numbers; seldom is that minimum number declared. This explanation has served to explain why the definitions in the CEN/BSI 2003 standard are unsatisfactory: 'Minimum number of travellers – number of travellers required for the tourism service to take place, stated in the travel offer and in the booking confirmation.' 'Maximum number of travellers – number of travellers stated in the travel offer and in the conditions of the travel contract to which the size of the group is limited.'

maximum payload capacity The maximum take-off weight of an aircraft that governmental authorities allow, less the empty weight, all justifiable aircraft equipment, and the operating load including such items as fuel, oil, flight crew and stewards' supplies. Modern jets are certificated for larger payload than usually are carried on short-haul European holiday routes. Strict baggage regulation is necessitated for profitable operation of aircraft. The weight of the fuel carried is a critical element; for example, an average aircraft passenger with luggage on a full plane between UK and Majorca will cause the use of about the same weight of fuel.

maximum permitted mileage *See* MPM.

maximum stay Varies according to particular fare for the number of days passengers are required to stay at destination, excluding day of travel.

maximum take-off weight The critical weight above which an aircraft is unable to become airborne, which varies according to airport altitude and temperature etc. Rather than restricting passenger numbers, where the maximum weight must be reduced, less fuel may be taken on board, or some passengers and their luggage may be offloaded.

MBRGW maximum brake release gross weight (aviation term).

MCBT Magnetically coded baggage tags, enabling baggage to be automatically sorted at airports and routed to the correct aircraft.

MCC In the cruising field, in North America, means Master Cruise Counselor, a travel agency employee certified by the CLIA.

MCD Multiple carrier designator (aviation term).

MCO Miscellaneous Charges Order. Both an ARC and IATA document. An all-purpose airline voucher which, subject to certain restrictions and limitations, can be used to cover collection of funds for all types of services or charges which may arise in connection with the air transport covered by a passenger ticket. MCOs may be drawn on any IATA member carrier, or on any air or surface carrier with whom the carrier issuing the MCO has interline agreement, or on any organization willing to accept as prepayment for services. MCOs have replaced exchange orders as far as airlines are concerned. Official IATA definition is a document issued by a carrier or its agents requesting issue of an appropriate passenger ticket and baggage check or provision of services to the person named in such document. IATA MCOs are being replaced with MPDs (Multi-Purpose Documents).

MCT Minimum connecting time. *See* connecting time.

MDA Minimum descent altitude or minimum decision altitude (aviation term).

MDCLS Main deck cargo loading system (aviation term).

MDH Minimum decision height or minimum descent height (aviation term).

meal sittings at sea On many cruise vessels, there is insufficient restaurant space to accommodate all the passengers; thus, there will be two sittings. Typically, the early or first sitting for dinner is from 18.00 to 20.00 and the late or second sitting from 20.00. Where there are no restrictions, this is known as open sitting.

meals Airlines and shipping companies can make arrangements to provide a variety of special meals and diets, providing these are requested in sufficient time. Medical meal requests may be for diabetic, salt-free, dairy-free, gluten-free or low-calorie diets. Vegetarian, vegan, Hindu, kosher, Moslem, oriental, seafood or childrens' meals may be requested. Consult manuals for full facilities offered by various airlines.

MEC Main engine control (aviation term).

MEDA Military emergency diversion aerodrome.

Medallion Class Brand name given by Delta to passenger area immediately adjacent to first class, where passengers paying full economy fares enjoy improved service and facilities. *See* business class for full description.

media *See* promotional media.

medical services at sea Ships that carry more than 12 passengers must, by international maritime law, carry a doctor. Passenger lines are exceptionally well equipped medically, usually with a ship's hospital and nursing staff.

meet and greet Service offered to passengers arriving by any form of transport, when they are welcomed, helped to reclaim their luggage, assisted through customs and immigration if appropriate and taken to their connecting onward service, often a transfer to a hotel etc. The French 'assistance requise' translates as 'meet and assist', which is a much better description of what is usually offered.

Meeting Professionals International (MPI) The world's largest association of meeting professionals. *See* www.mpiweb.org

meeting room set-up Theatre-style (also known as classroom or schoolroom style) means rows of chairs parallel to the top table, usually with aisles between columns of 12-or-so seats. Staggering means that alternate rows are set up so that each seat is immediately behind the gap between the seats in the row in front. Dining style means separate tables, usually round, set out in the room. Masonic style means a top table with at least three sprigs, running from the two ends of the top table and from the middle. Herringbone, chevron or V-style means that theatre-style seating is set up at an angle towards the top table from the middle aisle, thus automatically providing staggering and improving vision for the audience. Hollow square-style means tables form a square with seating around the outside; this is wasteful of space and unless the room acoustics are good, audio amplification may be necessary. Horseshoe style is similar, but with one end of the square missing. This is also called an open or closed U seating plan, depending on whether the top of the horseshoe has seating.

Meetings Industry Association Main UK body in the sector shares name with similar organizations in many English-speaking countries. *See* www.mia-uk.org

mega agency US term for a large travel agency group.

megaliner *See* cruise ship sizes.

megaship *See* cruise ship sizes.

MEL Minimum equipment list.

memory *See* computer memory.

meonscrubly Virgin habitat or scrubland, completely unaffected by outside influences, including tourism.

Mercator *See* map projection.

merchant acquirer UK credit and charge card intermediary that processes retailers transactions. Of their retail fees, around 1% of a transaction is passed back to the credit or charge company whose card was used by the purchaser. In the UK, merchant acquirers are subsidiaries of the banking organizations that run the card companies.

meridian day A day gained because the date goes backwards when crossing the 180th parallel of longitude, travelling in an easterly direction. *See also* GMT *and* International Date Line.

MET Aviation term abbreviation for anything to do with the weather (meteorology).

METAR Aerodrome meteorology report.

METEO The worldwide weather data system stored on SITA, the airlines' data processing and communications system.

Metro Name of the Paris underground railway system.

Metroliner A fast luxury Amtrak service operating between many US cities. Reservations are necessary. Like the European equivalent, TEE trains, there are no sleeping facilities, these being daytime services.

MEW Manufacturer's empty weight (aviation term).

Mexican National Travel Agency Organization (AMAV) Asociación Mexicana de Agencias de Viajes.

Mexico Tourism Board *See* www.visitmexico.com

mezzanine floor In a hotel in Europe, a floor between the ground floor and the first floor; this can cause confusion in the USA, where the ground floor, usually reception and entrance level, is known as the first floor.

MFD Multi-function display (aviation term).

MHA Marine Hotel Association.

MIA Meetings Industry Association; *see* www.mia-uk.org

MICE (sector) The travel sector covering Meetings, Incentives, Conferences and Events. Some texts suggests the acronym MICE stands for Meetings, Incentives, Conferences and Exhibitions. In 2004, US-based Meeting Professionals International estimated that $102.3bn was spent globally each year on meetings and events; for more information *see* www.mpiweb.org For details of the annual UK Conference Market Survey undertaken by the UK Meetings Industry Association *see* www.mia-uk.org

microchip A tiny slice of silicon, seldom bigger than half a centimetre square on which microscopic electrical circuits are embedded. Usually, they either act as the processors that make up a computer or are the memory devices, although it is possible for some chips to act as both, in which case, they are acting as a complete microcomputer in their own right.

Micro-COBOL A version of COBOL, a computer programming language.

microcomputer The rapid development of computers in the 1990s has made this term of little definitive value; it is now obsolete; desktop computers are generally referred to as PCs (personal computers). It was previously taken to mean a device of lower cost than a mini-computer or main frame. The hardware for a micro was usually a combination of keyboard, screen, central processor unit on a single microchip, printer and storage unit. When microcomputers were first developed, storage was always on floppy discs, although subsequently, Winchester hard discs were used. The control unit was usually on a single board.

microfiche Microfilm, usually reducing A4 pages down to half or one centimetre square, presented in the form of film cards, which contain a large amount of information. Microfiche readers enlarge these tiny film squares back to A4 size on a viewing screen.

Microspace Name of Micro Scope Limited computerized tour operators' reservation and accounting system particularly designed for operators wishing to make their systems accessible to travel agents by viewdata. Currently there are around 30 UK users of the complete system, while the company has also been responsible for the development work of many of the major British operator systems now run independently.

Microstretcher Was Multiple Accounting Services bureau system offering computerized data and accounting for UK travel agents at low costs.

microwave landing system *See* MLS.

Mid Consort Midlands Consortium of Travel Agents, a member of Worldchoice in the UK.

Midlands Independent Travel Agents *See* MITA[3].

mid-office Software in a travel agency linking the 'front office' sales functions and back office administrative and accounting systems.

midship *See* amidships.

MIDT[1] Marketing Information Data Tape, passed by GDSs to airlines.

MIDT[2] Marketing Information Data Transfer; concerning airline bookings, a system through which market shares of CRSs or GDSs in regions or countries can be established.

midweek May mean a fare which only applies to travel on Tuesday, Wednesday or Thursday, or a fare which applies to any weekday. It is not possible to be certain of the meaning without checking the actual fare rule.

mileage equalization Point which is not on an air passenger's itinerary, but used for comparative mileage purposes. *See* IATA fare construction system.

Mileage Plus Name of United Airlines' Frequent Flyer Programme. *See* FFP (frequent flyer programme).

mileage surcharge *See* IATA fare construction system.

mileage system *See* IATA fare construction system.

Miles and More Title of the Lufthansa and Austrian Airline's Frequent Flyer Programme. *See* FFP (frequent flyer programme).

military fares Reduced air, rail and car ferry fares available to military and associated personnel. From UK usually applies to US military staff going to America or members of the British, Canadian or Maltese armed forces travelling between the UK and Germany. The reduced ATOC rail fares available to members of the Armed Services and their families are normally only available to holders of Forces Railcards.

Military Traffic Management Command *See* MTMC.

mini-bar Hotels and similar establishments often provide a refrigerator or cupboard in each room containing a selection of alcoholic and other beverages. This is known as a mini-bar; the word is trademarked in some countries. Guests are charged for items consumed. In North America, the term servi-bar is the same thing.

minimum connecting time *See* connecting time.

minimum land package US term for an inclusive tour providing the minimum of services such that the air travel cost can be based on a special low fare.

Minimum Level of Training for Seafarers (EC) The European Parliament and Council directive on the minimum level of training for seafarers was published in the Official Journal of the European Communities, L136, of 18 May 2001.

minimum number of participants *See* maximum number of participants.

minimum rated package tours UK term for inclusive tours by charter flight providing only nominal accommodation in order to comply with regulations. In effect, a package tour that is really a low-cost return charter flight. *See* seat only.

minimum stay When a return air fare has a minimum stay at destination requirement, it can vary from time after leaving country or origin to actual time of minimum stay at destination. The 2003 CEN/European Standard official definition does not take account of this variation; it is: 'Minimum/maximum stay – shortest/longest stay of a traveller at a destination required for the applicable

rate fixed by a provider of tourism services'.

minimum use clause Contracts in the USA for the provision of air-based CRS services often used to require a certain volume of transactions; this practice was banned by the Department of Transport, just as many years before, abandonment of the 'need' clause concerning business volume was enforced in respect of IATA appointments and other agreements for agents selling air travel. Control of CRSs in the USA has now been deregulated.

minor operated departments *See* Uniform System of Accounts for the Lodging Industry in hotel statistics worldwide.

minshuku An inexpensive Japanese country hotel or wayside inn offering few amenities and little or no service.

MIR Machine interface record. An alternative name for a transmittal file enabling transfer of information from a CRS to an associated back-office system.

MIS IATA's monthly international statistics.

Miscellaneous Charges Order *See* MCO.

misconnection Official IATA definition is a passenger who, due to late arrival or non-operation of his original delivering flight, arrives at the interline point by his original delivering flight, an alternative flight, or surface transport, too late to board his original receiving flight. (In other words, a missed connection.)

Missouri Division of Tourism *See* www.visitmo.com

MITA[1] Multilateral Interline Traffic Agreements between airlines.

MITA[2] Membership of Individual Travel Agents, a US organization.

MITA[3] Midlands Independent Travel Agents is a consortium of travel agents in the English Midlands that is a member of Worldchoice.

Mixed Rewards Name of the Star Alliance Frequent Flyer Programme. *See* airline alliances *and* FFP (frequent flyer programme).

MKR Marker beacon (aviation term).

MLG Main landing gear (aviation term).

MLS Microwave landing system for aircraft. During the 1990s, the FAA in the USA implemented a US$12 billion National Airspace System Plan. Twenty computer centres were established; but a vital part of the development was integration with MLS, and airlines were reluctant to install FAA MLS receivers on their aircraft. *See* FIRs for equivalent description of European system and explanation of principles of Air Traffic Control.

MLW Maximum landing weight (aviation term).

MM Middle marker of an instrument landing system (aviation term).

MMEL Minimum equipment list (aviation term).

MMR Multi-mode receiver (aviation term).

mobile home *See* camper, caravan *and* caravan park.

mobile lounge A very wide-bodied airport bus operated at some airports, used to ferry passengers between their departure lounge and an aircraft, when gate boarding is not available.

MOD major operated departments. *See* Uniform System of Accounts for the Lodging Industry in hotel statistics worldwide.

Model control documents for European coach travel *See* ASOR.

modem An abbreviation of the words modulator–demodulator, which is a piece of computer equipment that changes normal digital computer output to analogue form, so that it can be transmitted along telephone lines. The data is changed back to digital format at the other end of the line. Modems are particularly important in the travel industry because ticketing and other data emanating from reservations computers arrive at an agency by telephone lines before activating a local ticketing device.

Modern Apprenticeship UK vocational training scheme applicable to those aged 16–19 (up to 24 in some areas). Currently involves 243,600 young people but set to rise 320,000 by 2003/2004. Foundation and advanced levels linked to NVQ qualifications (SVQs in Scotland). One of the largest and most comprehensive Modern Apprenticeship training schemes in the UK is run by TTC Training. For employer or potential trainee information *see* TTC Training www.tttctraining.co.uk. The UK's travel, tourism and hospitality skills council, People 1st, has also approved a vast range of MAs and NVQs; 57 MA lists are accessible from the web site www.people1st.co.uk *Also see* NVQ or for details of some travel industry NVQs; *see* City and Guilds of London Institute; or *see* www.city-and-guilds. co.uk

Modified American Plan *See* MAP[2].

Modulas Was the name of the British travel agency computerized data and accounting system marketed by Tourism Technology Limited. This was the computer system originally backed by ABTA and British Telecom, both of whom withdrew.

Monaco Government Tourist and Convention Authority *See* www. monaco-congres.com *also* www. monaco-tourisme.com

monitor Another name for a dumb terminal, VDU or CRT. A monitor is usually just a display screen. The same term is also used by computer technologists to describe one of the fundamental pieces of software, required by end-users to operate a system following menu selection.

Montenegro National Tourism Organization *See* www.visit-montenegro.com

Montezuma's revenge Slang expression for traveller's diarrhoea.

Montreal Additional Protocol concerning the Warsaw Convention *See* Warsaw Convention.

Montreal Agreement concerning the Warsaw Convention *See* Warsaw Convention.

Montserrat Tourist Board *See* www. visitmontserrat.com

Moot Brand name used by the English Tourist Board for annual travel trade fair. The term is an old English word for a meeting.

MOR Mandatory occurrence report (aviation term).

more distant point In effect, a hypothetical air fare construction point, further away than the actual break point, or mid-point of a journey. It means that under IATA fare construction rules, an air fare will be based upon the mileage and cost to this more distant point. *See* IATA fare construction system.

Morning Club Name of Korean Airline's Frequent Flyers Club. *See* FFP (frequent flyer programme).

Moroccan National Tourist Office *See* www.visitmorocco.com

MOT   In many countries, means Ministry of Transport.

motel   A hotel particularly designed for car travellers; usually suitable for short-stay travellers with reduced amenities and public rooms. In the USA may also be called a motor court or motor hotel.

Motion   Name of Olympic Airways' in-flight magazine.

motion sickness   First symptom is usually abdominal pain followed by rapidly increasing nausea. The victim then breaks out into a cold sweat, mainly on the face and hands. Excess salivation, general apathy, a 'lightness of the head' and sooner or later, vomiting, follow in quick succession. Cause is overloading of the body's balancing and position sensing organs, the semi-circular canals in the inner ear. These three loops are set at right angles in all three planes. The position and movement of fluid in them is registered by sensory hairs and with far too many messages being sent by them, the control mechanism fails.

MOTNE   Meteorological Operations Tele-communications Network Europe.

Motor Caravanners' Club Ltd   A leisure club devoted to the interests of motor caravanners and motor caravanning in the UK.

motor coach   Obsolete name for a coach, originating from the time when it was necessary to distinguish this mode of travel from a coach and horses. Now, unless otherwise stated, a coach is presumed to be driven by an engine. In North America, the word is sometimes used to describe a de luxe coach.

motor court   *See* motel.

motor hotel   A hotel which particularly caters for car travellers – *see* motel.

Motorail   UK brand name of British ATOC's car-carrying services.

motorhome   A motorized caravan. On a large vehicle chassis, complete living accommodation is built, producing a mobile home for vacation use. Same meaning as a camper.

moving sidewalk   *See* travelator.

MP   Maintenance period (aviation term).

MP4   Montreal Protocol 4. *See* Warsaw Convention.

MPD¹   Maintenance planning document (aviation term).

MPD²   Multi-Purpose Document. An IATA passenger traffic document, which can be used for any of the purposes currently served by MCOs which are being phased out. For example, an MPD can be issued to cover excess baggage charges, deposits, PTAs (Prepaid Ticket Advices), TODs (Tickets on Departure) or the cost of stopover packages. In June 2001, Amadeus, one of the four main GDSs, announced the introduction of an automated version of an MPD.

MPI   Meeting Professionals International in the USA. The world's largest association of meeting professionals. *See* www.mpiweb.org

MPM   Maximum Permitted Mileage. Under IATA fare construction rules, each through air fare is given a maximum permitted mileage which allows a passenger a choice of routings and carriers within that mileage to a particular destination. The mileage system has been withdrawn for travel wholly within IATA TC1 except Canada. MPM is 20% above sector distance in Europe, 15% elsewhere.

MPWMS   Multi-purpose waste management system; on cruise ships, environmentally acceptable practices are now followed for handling and if necessary storing waste.

MQ6   *Overseas Travel and Tourism – Business Monitor Quarterly Statistics* are the published results of the UK International Passenger Survey, the most useful single source of UK information about incoming tourism and travel abroad. These statistics are available online via www.statistics.gov.uk *See* IPS for more details.

MRC   Member and Communications division of IATA.

MRL   Medium intensity runway edge lighting (aviation term).

MRO   Maintenance repair overhaul (aviation term).

MRP¹   Machine readable passport.

MRP²   Maximum ramp weight (aviation term).

MS   Motor ship, when used as a prefix to a ship's name.

MSA   Minimum safe altitude.

MSC   The Manpower Services Commission in the UK was renamed the Training Agency; which itself changed subsequently. Its support for the UK travel industry mainly through the former ABTA National Training Board is detailed under CBT, UVP and YTS.

MSL Mean sea level.

MSP Maintenance service plan (aviation term).

MTBUR Mean time between unplanned removal (aviation term).

MTGW Maximum taxi gross weight (aviation term).

MTMA Military terminal control area (aviation term).

MTMC Military Traffic Management Command; the US Military and Defense [sic] section that handles travel contracts. Together with the US GSA (General Services Administration) has joint competitive bidding arrangements for the supply of travel services to the Federal Government. In 1993, following a review, the Defense Travel System was established, with the MTMC acting as the sole procurement agency. *A list of 70 other business travel related entries follows* corporate travel contracts, *some of which lead to further entries.*

MTOW Maximum take-off weight (aviation term).

MTWA Maximum total weight authorized (aviation term).

MUISZ Association of Hungarian Travel Agents.

Multi Purpose Document *See* MPD².

multi-access/multi-tasking Simultaneous use of a computer by two or more operators, possible because the computer has been designed to undertake more than one task at a time.

multi-access system A CRS which enables a user to have real-time access to a variety of reservation systems through a common switching centre and/or interface.

multi-access ticketing A system whereby an agent with a visual display unit and a ticket printer has access to the reservations and ticketing functions of two or more airlines. The agent can use tickets of those airlines on its ticket printer.

multi-host system A CRS that provides more than one airline with the facility to process, on an inventory basis, reservations and other passenger-related functions.

multilateral An Air Services Agreement between three or more countries. *See* Bermuda Agreement, Chicago Convention, Freedoms of the Air *and* traffic rights.

multi-path assignment *See* transport modelling.

multiple In the UK travel industry, used in the context 'multiple travel agent', meaning a travel agency group with many outlets. The characteristics of such a group are that it is able to exert bulk buying power and mount a sophisticated marketing approach to selling. In this dictionary, the definition used is that a multiple is a travel agency group with ten or more outlets.

In December 2004 there were 6247 ABTA member travel agency outlets in the UK and 1926 non-ABTA outlets. Thomson (formerly Lunn Poly) had 844 locations; MyTravel (Going Places) 736; Thomas Cook 623; First Choice 429 and Co-op Travelcare 370, although they are associated with another 318 members of the Co-operative Travel Trading Group. Smaller multiples included Bath Travel 74 and American Express 86, although over half of these locations specialize in business travel. Agents specializing in business travel include BTI Hogg Robinson 128 and Carlson Wagonlit 91. Small multiples, sometimes called miniples, include Wardle 48, Lets Go 35, Althams 32, Dawson and Sanderson 25, Premier 14 and Personal Service Travel 11. Wardle has since failed.

multiple travel agents *See* multiple.

multiplier effect *See* tourism multiplier.

murphy A hotel room bed that can fold into a wall recess, cupboard or closet.

MV Motor vessel, when used as a prefix to a ship's name.

MZFW Maximum zero fuel weight (aviation term).

N

N/A Not applicable, not available.

NA Via North Atlantic. *See* routing.

NAATO National Association of Adventure Tour Operators in the USA. *See* www.travelvue.co.at/to.htm

NABTA National Association of Business Travel Agents in the USA.

NACA National Air Carriers Association. A US grouping of airlines at the cheaper end of the market.

nacelles *See* airframe.

NACOA National Association of Cruise Only Agencies in the USA. *See* www.nacoa.com

NACTA National Association of Commissioned Travel Agents in the USA, a wholly owned subsidiary of ASTA for home-based, independent, outside sales, cruise-oriented travel professionals. Information about NACTA is hosted on the ASTA web site www.astanet.com and on its own site www.nacta.com

NAHC National Association of Holiday Centres is the UK trade association for holiday camps.

NAITA National Association of Independent Travel Agents; trade as Advantage Travel Centres. Originally restricted to non-multiple companies with IATA appointments and sales turnover above £1 million. Although restrictions no longer exist, most members still meet these requirements. *See* www.advantage4travel.com, travel agency consortia in the UK *and* consortium.

Namibia Tourism *See* www.namibia tourism.com.na

narrow-body aircraft Commonly applied to older jet aircraft. When the term was first introduced, it meant that the aircraft passenger cabin had only one aisle whereas wide-bodied aircraft have two aisles. But it should signify jet aircraft with a fuselage diameter not exceeding 200 in., with a per engine thrust less than 30,000 lb.

narrow gauge *See* gauge.

narrowboat Name of the long barges originally used for carrying cargo on Britain's canal network. Most cargo traffic has now ceased and the majority of narrowboats are now purpose-built leisure craft. Many companies offer these for hire.

NASP National Airspace System Plan. *See* MLS.

NATA[1] National Air Transportation Association in the USA. *See* www.nata-online.org

NATA[2] Nepal Association of Travel Agents.

national Official IATA definition is a person who has the citizenship of a country, either by birth or by naturalization.

National Air Carriers Association *See* NACA.

National Air Traffic Services *See* NATS.

National Airspace System Plan *See* MLS for details of this US initiative.

National Association of Adventure Tour Operators NAATO.

National Association of Business Travel Agents (NABTA) USA.

National Association of Commissioned Travel Agents *See* NACTA.

National Association of Cruise Only Agencies (NACOA) USA. *See* www.nacoa.com

National Association of Holiday Centres *See* NAHC.

National Association of Independent Travel Agents *See* NAITA.

National Association of Travel Organizations (NATO[1]) USA.

National Business Aviation Association NBAA. *See* www.nbaa.org

National Business Travel Association *See* NBTA.

National Caravan Council Ltd UK association representing manufacturers, traders and park owners in the caravan industry. *See* www.nationalcaravan.co.uk

National Carrier Worldwide, probably means a flag carrier (*see* entry under this heading). In the USA, the DOT has designated a national carrier as an airline with annual sales of between US$100 and US$1 billion.

National Commission to Ensure Customer Information and Choice in the Airline Industry US commission set up in 2001 to investigate airline marketing practices that harm consumers and travel agents. Also responsible for reporting to Congress whether airlines are blocking consumer access to information.

National Council Was, until April 2000, the controlling body of ABTA in the UK consisting of ten members, five each from TAC³ and TOC¹.

National Council of Hotels Association Represents approximately 10,000 small independently owned hotels and guest houses throughout the UK. Aims to ensure their views are represented with a united voice and to identify, organize and coordinate action on a national scale. *See* www.bed-and-breakfast.org

National Council of State Tourism Directors (in the USA) An industry council of the TIA. *See* www.tourstates.com

National Express Name of the main national express coach service network covering the UK.

National Federation of Site Operators *See* NFSO.

National Mailbox (Now obsolete.) *See* Prestel.

National Outdoor Events Association UK organization in field. *See* www.noea.org.uk

national park Country area officially designated as broadly for leisure for which purposes public access is facilitated and development strictly controlled. The relative importance placed on conservation, education or recreation varies between parks and between countries. The concept began with the establishment of Yellowstone National Park in 1872. Subsequently the US National Parks Service was created, which now has a wider role maintaining, for example, historic sites. *See* www.nps.gov/parks.html *and* Golden Eagle Passport.

In the UK, the situation was not formalized until the 1949 National Parks and Access to the Countryside Act. However, the National Trust performs what is in many respects a similar function in Britain. *See* The National Trust www.nationaltrust.org.uk and the National Trust for Scotland www.nts.org.uk

National Railroad Passenger Corporation The actual train-operating arm of Amtrak. *See* Amtrak *and* North American train services for further details.

National Scenic Area *See* AONB.

National Tour Association (in the USA) *See* NTA.

national tourism accounts *See* TSA.

National Tourism Foundation Founded in 1982 by the National Tour Association, on 1 January 2005 it amalgamated with the Travelers Conservation Foundation, founded by the USTOA to form Tourism Cares for Tomorrow. *See* www.ntfonline.org *and* www.tcfonline.org

National Tourist Office *See* Tourist Office; *also see* entries for National Tourist Office and US State Tourist Office web sites under country and state names; *also see* Tourism Offices Worldwide Directory www.towd.com

National Transportation Safety Board *See* NTSB.

National Trust Full name is 'National Trust for Places of Historic Interest or Natural Beauty'. A UK charitable body founded in 1895 to maintain the national heritage of buildings and land in England, Wales and Northern Ireland. Several million members support a huge range of activities and vast landholding described in its web site www.nationaltrust.org.uk

National Trust for Historic Preservation Leading US organization in field. *See* www.nthp.org

National Trust for Scotland Formed in 1931, it is the Scottish equivalent of the English body. *See* www.nts.org.uk

National Vocational Qualification *See* NVQ.

NATO¹ National Association of Travel Organizations in the USA.

NATO² The National Association of Travel Officials was one of the forerunners of the Travel Industry Association of America.

NATS National Air Traffic Services; its function is to secure the safe, orderly and expeditious flow of air traffic within UK air space. The services were established in 1962 as a civil and military partnership. In March 2001, the Airline Group, a consortium of Airtours, Britannia Airways, British Airways, British Midland, easyJet, Monarch Airlines and Virgin Atlantic, agreed with the UK government to acquire a 46% controlling stake in NATS for around £800 million, forming a public/private partnership. The arrangements will mean an investment of over £1 billion in NATS over the next 10 years. For more information *see* www.nats.co.uk

nature reserve Classic definitions suggest that it is an enclosed area within which flora and fauna are protected and preserved. But the term has been hijacked by countries offering safari experiences to areas within which the wildlife population and habitat are controlled (farmed?) for the main purposes of sustainable tourism. (This definition neither defames nor praises the situation – it merely identifies it!)

nature tourism Described by the prestigious Southeast Tourism Society in the USA as travel to unspoiled places to experience and enjoy nature. However, throughout Europe, this means travel by people following the practice of nudity. US travellers not understanding this may get a big surprise!

nautical mile By air or sea, nautical miles equal to about 1.15 statute miles are normally used for measurement. Defined as the length of a minute of arc of a great circle around the earth, but because the earth is not a perfect sphere, there is some disagreement over the actual distance on the earth's surface, resulting from this angular measurement. Most common in the UK is 6076.1033 ft, while several American sources suggest 6076.115 ft; this is the 'international nautical mile', sometimes called the air mile in the USA. The *Dictionary of the Cruise Industry* states 6080 ft, which is the version using an arc at 48°N. Around the equator, it would be 6087 ft.

NAVAIDS The system of aircraft navigation aids which has been installed and is operated and maintained by the US FAA.

Navigator class Former name of Air Portugal's business class, now renamed Top Executive class.

Navigator Club Name of TAP's (Air Portugal) Frequent Flyers' Club. *See* FFP (frequent flyers programme).

NBAA National Business Aviation Association in the USA. *See* www.nbaa.org

NBL No Berth List is the UK terminology applied to travellers between Harwich and Hook of Holland across the North Sea using the night service, who do not have any sleeping accommodation. The number of passengers that may be carried on any vessel is strictly limited by both national and international maritime regulation. On this route, on the night service, reservation of berths or other sleeping accommodation is normally essential. However, at peak times passengers may be given an NBL card, to allow them to travel on the service, but of course still only up to the maximum number of passengers that may be carried.

NBTA National Business Travel Association in the USA, the successor to the National Passenger Traffic Association. A grouping of corporate travel managers in *non-travel* companies or organizations who are responsible for running a travel department. *See* www.nbta.org

NCC National Caravan Council is the trade association of the UK caravan industry. *See* www.microsoft.com/uk/yourbusiness/success/ncc.htm

NCP Navigational Control Point. Such points are used by pilots to steer an accurate course.

NCR Skylink A type of self-service travellers' air ticketing terminal which was in use at several US airports. In the UK, pressure from travel agents prevented its introduction, although similar NCR equipment, adapted for selling rail tickets, was introduced at many UK rail stations.

NCSTD National Council of State Tourism Directors in the USA – an industry council of the TIA. *See* www.tourstates.com

ND Navigation display (aviation term).

NDB Non-directional radio beacon.

negotiated rate (or fare) In a GDS a hotel or car rental rate or an air fare restricted by the vendor to certain system users. Such agents or other users are given passwords or authorization codes to enable access to the restricted information and to make reservations at the special rates or fares.

Nepal Tourism Board *See* www. welcomenepal.com

Nepalese National Travel Agency Organization *See* NATA[2].

NEST Network of Entrepreneurs Selling Travel; US marketing group for home-based travel agents. *See* www. jointhenest.com *or* www.traveltrade.com

nested excursions *See* back-to-back ticketing.

net fare The fare less commission; any rate for transport to which an agent must add a profit before resale. The concept has been widely discussed following air industry deregulation as a means of abandoning agency commission systems. Similarly a net rate is any rate stated by a provider of tourism services to which an agent must add a profit before resale.

net per diem *See* PCD.

net rate *See* net fare.

net remittance The amount a travel agent pays a provider of tourism services after deducting commission from the amount originally received from a traveller. Thus payments for air ticket sales to the ARC in the USA or under Bank Settlement Plans in many other parts of the world are always net remittances. *See also* commissionable.

net sea revenue *See* PCD.

net travel propensity *See* travel propensity.

Netherlands Board of Tourism *See* www. holland.com *and* www.visitholland.com

Netherlands National Travel Agency Organization *See* ANVR.

Netherlands Railways Season Tickets Entitle the holder to unlimited rail travel in first or second class for periods of 3 or 7 days over The Netherlands Railways network. Adult rates only, no further reductions being granted to children or groups.

network In general terms, a travel network may mean the routes operated by an operator of a mode of transport. In North America, it may particularly mean a consortium (*see* consortium). A network is also a series of computers and peripheral equipment linked together as in a LAN (local area network). Multiple travel agency groups in the UK operate nationwide networks while the global CRS (GDS) companies operate international networks. The same term is also applied to communication networks, for example, in the UK, British Telecom's X25 network, NTL's (Fastrak) viewdata networks.

Network of Entrepreneurs Selling Travel US marketing group for home-based travel agents. *See* www.jointhenest.com *or* www.traveltrade.com

Network Rail In 2001, following the financial failure of Railtrack, owner of the railway infrastructure in the UK, the Government purchased it from the shareholders and reinstituted a nationalized organization to own and maintain a system on which the franchised TOCs (train operating companies) run their services. Thus, Railtrack has been renamed Network Rail, being fully established as such as Railtrack came out of financial administration in 2002.

neutral CRS rules *See* European neutral CRS rules and Appendix III.

neutral ticket Official IATA definition is the form of automated ticket (governed by Resolution 722a) intended for use by agents, not bearing any pre-printed airline identity.

Neutral Unit of Construction *See* IATA fare construction system.

Nevada Commission on Tourism *See* www.travelnevada.com

New England Tourism *See* Discover New England www.discovernewengland.org

New Hampshire Division of Travel and Tourism *See* www.visitnh.gov

New Jersey Travel and Tourism Office *See* www.visitnj.org

New Mexico Department of Tourism *See* www.newmexico.org

New York State Division of Tourism *See* www.iloveny.com

New Zealand National Travel Agency Organization (TAANZ) Travel Agents Association of New Zealand.

New Zealand Tourism *See* www. purenz.com

Nevis Tourism Authority *See* www. nevisisland.com

next generation seamless Term for technology operated by a CRS/GDS enabling an end user to have direct access to a travel service provider's inventory through the interface offered by the CRS/GDS.

NFSO Was the National Federation of Site Operators, the UK trade body composed of the operators of sites for both fixed and touring caravans, chalets, tents and apartments. Now renamed British Holiday and Home Parks Association. *See* www.bhhpa.org.uk

NGS Next generation seamless; term for technology operated by a CRS/GDS enabling an end user to have direct access to a travel service provider's inventory through the interface offered by the CRS/GDS.

NIBS Neutral Industry Booking System. Name given to US attempt to establish a non-biased reservation and information system covering all tourism and transport services. NIBS is seldom now used as a generic term.

Nicaraguan Institute of Tourism *See* www.intur.gob.ni

Nigerian Tourism Development Corporation *See* ntdc@metrong.com

night flight Some air fares are designated as applicable only to flights taking off or landing between particular times. Some airports restrict the number of flights between particular times. Thus, in these cases, the term has a particular meaning, while travellers in general regard the wording as merely being descriptive of flying at night.

night manager Used to be the person responsible for running a hotel at night; increasingly, modern hotels appoint assistant managers who take it in turns to act as 'duty manager' for a period including night-time. The duty manager will only be awakened if a problem arises that the night porter cannot handle.

night stop An alternative name for a layover.

Nightstar/Nightstock The name of a fleet of seven de luxe sleeper trains with 139 carriages between them, which were intended to operate through the Britain/France Channel Tunnel as a consortium of Dutch, German, British and French Railways from June 1994. The twin-bunk sleeper cars were finished with maple wood and equipped with a shower, WC, video, telephone, hot-drink dispenser, work desk, full-length mirror and wardrobe; they could best be described as 'four-star hotels on wheels'. Each train was to have a dining car, bar and mobile office.

Nightstock scheduled service trains were planned to start from Glasgow and Swansea, picking up passengers from British cities en route and scheduled to arrive the following morning, after breakfast, at rail terminals in Paris, Frankfurt and Amsterdam. *The service never operated!* Many of the trains are in store on UK Ministry of Defence land at Kineton, in Britain's Midlands.

NINA Non-IATA Non-ABTA was the name of the trade body of the UK cut-price air ticket retailers formed on the initiative of Riaz Dooley who became its first chairman, at the end of June 1980. At that time, it was believed that between 50,000 and 100,000 discounted airline tickets a week were being sold to British travellers. Despite the continuing use of the pejorative term Bucket Shop, this business has continued to boom and the IATA Yield Improvement Plan has only been marginally successful in regularizing air fares on some routes. *See* consolidation air fares.

NITB The Northern Ireland Tourist Board is the statutory body created by the Development of Tourist Traffic Act (NI) 1948 to promote development of tourist traffic in Northern Ireland and to encourage persons who reside elsewhere to visit the area. The Board has statutory responsibility for the registration and inspection of all catering establishments in NI and it organizes a grading system for hotels and guest houses. As part of the 'peace' initiative, an all-Ireland tourism promotion vehicle may be in existence during the currency of this dictionary. A series of web sites are quoted: www.interknowledge.com/Northern-Ireland ; www.tourist-offices.org.uk (Northern Ireland) *and* www.bluebadge.org.uk/NorthernIreland.html

NLA New large aircraft.

NLG[1] Nose landing gear (aviation term).

NLG[2] Was the National Liaison Group for Higher Education in the tourism field in the UK; changed its name to the Association for Tourism Higher Education in November 2000.

NM Via North and Mid-Atlantic. *See* routing.

No Berth List *See* NBL.

no record Sometimes shortened to 'no rec'. Official IATA definition is a condition which exists whenever a passenger presents a ticket for reserved space but the boarding member has no record of ever confirming or receiving a booking for that reserved space.

NOEA National Outdoor Events Association; UK organization in field. *See* www.noea.org.uk

no-frills airline An airline that competes with others and markets itself as offering a low-cost basic service. Thus there is abandonment of complimentary on-board services of food and beverages and other facilities usually expected when flying with a 'full service' airline.

no-host bar *See* cash bar.

no-show When passengers who have reserved transport, accommodation or other travel facilities do not 'show up' for their booking. Official IATA definition is a failure to use reserved accommodation for reasons other than misconnections. Up to 15% of British Airways' passengers booked on long-haul flights do not use their reservations. On shorter journeys, the figures are substantially higher. No-shows may be deliberate (*see* scattershot) or are unintentional. Travel difficulties may delay a previous connecting flight or cause late arrival at an airport and a missed flight; illness and domestic or business emergencies often cause last-minute changes in travel plans.

For airlines to fly with empty seats is not cost-effective, raising passenger fares and lowering carrier's profits. But while an airline's records suggest the appropriate percentage of no-shows to be expected, the statistics are only ever valid over a large number of flights. This is why an over-booking policy, intended to closely match no-shows, sometimes results in passengers being offloaded (*see* bump). When BA was prosecuted under the UK Trade Descriptions Act, it stated that to give up over-booking altogether would result in a 6% fall in average load factors, highlighting the importance of the problem. *See also* denied boarding compensation *and* overbooking.

non-carrying member Official IATA definition is a Member who will not participate in itinerary but may handle a passenger's reservation.

non-commissionable *See* commissionable.

non-name *See* TBA.

non-participating member Official IATA definition is same as a non-carrying member.

non-ref Not refundable. *See below*.

non-refundable That money paid by a traveller that will not be returned to them upon voluntary cancellation, alteration or abandonment of a travel service, depending on the conditions of the applicable contract between the parties. However, consumer pressure will continue to attempt to reduce the applicability and enforceability of the concept. Money paid may be deposits, part payments or total costs and travellers are always advised to effect travel insurance to cover themselves against cancellation losses. Frequently, deposits paid on booking inclusive tours are not refundable in the event of cancellation. Advanced Purchase Excursion transport fares are usually not refundable. When a travel agent supplies tickets to a holder of a credit account, it is standard practice to endorse all the ticket coupons 'non-ref' which has the effect that the traveller can only get a refund via the agent rather than direct from a transport company.

Contractual conditions for groups and conferences always have a non-refundability clause; *nevertheless*, it is the custom of the industry to take into account cancellations, booking changes, late extra bookings etc. to arrive at a final account which may involve an *ex gratia* (voluntary) refund by the travel agent or conference-organizing company as a matter of good faith. In September 2000, the UK Office of Fair Trading announced that it was insisting on changes to the standard IATA terms and conditions of carriage. Consumers with non-refundable tickets who miss their flights as a result of unforeseen circumstances are to receive credit vouchers. Airlines' rights to cancel return tickets where one portion is unused were withdrawn, provided that the traveller informed the airline in advance. Passengers were given the right to transfer non-refundable tickets to another person when prevented from travelling by unusual or unforeseen circumstances such as illness; they were also given the right to cancel if flight times changed significantly.

The foregoing text has attempted to be definitive; however, historically, airlines and others have always abused their own rules! In the USA, in the autumn of 2002, airlines introduced new policies, preventing use of non-refundable tickets other than for flights booked. Alterations before planned travel dates were allowed, but only on payment of fees. Large travel management companies warn business travellers before travel that a non-refundable ticket has been issued, and that a 'no-show' will mean loss. World Travel BTI's system is called Non-refundable Tracker; Navigant International's is RescueFLYR; while Rosenbluth (American Express) offer their SmartTicket service. This situation is also covered in cancellation charge, flexible ticket *and* void ticket.

non-revenue Refers to a journey from which there is no income, for example, positioning flights and empty legs at the start and finish of a back-to-back charter series. Non-revenue passengers are those who have not paid for their journey, or only paid a token sum, such as agency and airline staff. *See* revenue passenger.

non-smoker seating In many countries, smoking is banned on public transport; in the USA it depends on city or state law. At the time of writing there is a growing trend in the UK towards minimizing seats on public transport where passengers may smoke. Most airlines now designate their flights as non-smoking. London Transport has banned smoking. On UK trains and coaches between 50% and 75% of seating is for non-smokers. In November 1984 British Rail increased the non-smoking compartments on Inter City 125 trains from 60% to 70%. On suburban and short distance trains, this rises to 75%. ATOC, successors to BR have continued the practice. Smoking is banned on all Newcastle Metro trains and underground stations, and on Glasgow's underground railway.

non-stop When a passenger's trip is continuous from beginning to end. The Air ABC and OAG indicate the number of stops en route made on each flight; without checking, it cannot be assumed that any particular flight is non-stop.

non-stop sector mileage (Now obsolete.) Now replaced by ticketed point mileage in the IATA fare construction system.

non-transferable For security and other reasons, air tickets and many international travel tickets are only valid for travel by the person for whom they were issued.

Nordic Tourist Card Gives unlimited rail travel for 21 days over the lines of the Danish, Finish, Norwegian and Swedish State Railways, as well as unlimited journeys on the ferry services between Helsingor and Helsingborg, Rodby Faerge and Puttgarden and Gedser and Warnemunde. A 50% reduction is also granted for travel on certain other shipping services, including Stockholm to Helsinki. Price varies according to first or second class, adult or child aged between 4 and 11.

Nordturist Med Tag *See* Nordic Tourist Card.

North American train services Amtrak serves 500 cities across the USA. Only two classes of service are offered in North America, first and coach. First Class or Parlor Cars offer superior accommodation, swivelling individual chairs and dining-car facilities. On some trains, meals may be served at a passenger seat. Coach Class passengers have individual reclining seats. Most coaches have now been modernized with full air-conditioning, fluorescent lighting and efficient toilets. Sleeping cars are of three main types. Roomettes are usually for one passenger and contain a bed which can be folded into a seat for daytime travel. Each roomette has its own washbasin and toilet. Bedrooms, sometimes called compartments, are larger with two berths in addition to the enclosed washbasin and toilet. Bedroom suites are the most expensive accommodation, usually featuring separate apartment for daytime use.

Via Rail Canada has embarked on a 5-year project to revitalize their passenger rail service. A notable first for Amtrak has been the launch of the Acela Express, the first high-speed rail service in North America. This connects New York and Washington in 2.5 h. Two comprehensive Internet sites are likely meet the needs of all users of this dictionary including bookings, routes, schedules and fares. *See* for Amtrak www.amtrak.com and for VIA Rail Canada www.viarail.ca

North Carolina Division of Tourism *See* www.visitnc.com

Northern Ireland Tourist Board *See* www.discovernorthernireland.com

Norwegian National Travel Agency Organization (DNR) Den Norske Reisebransforening.

Norwegian Tourist Board *See* www. visitnorway.com

nosub Not subject to load.

Notam Notice to airmen.

Notice of Proposed Rulemaking An announcement to the public by governmental civil aviation authorities that amendments to their regulations are being considered. Interested persons are given an opportunity to comment or otherwise participate in developing the nature of the amendments, sometimes resulting in their withdrawal.

NOVA *See* PMS².

NP Via North or Central Pacific. *See* routing.

NPF National Park Foundation in the USA. *See* www.nationalparks.org

NPRM Notice of proposed rulemaking from the US FAA.

NPTA Was the National Passenger Traffic Association in the USA; now renamed the National Business Travel Association. *See* NBTA.

NRPC National Railroad Passenger Corporation. *See* Amtrak.

NSR *See* PCD.

NT National Trust. *See* National Trust.

NTA¹ National Tour Association in the USA. The NTA Consumer Protection Plan (CPP) enables reimbursement of clients should a member operator fail financially. The CPP's limit for losses is US$250,000 per bankrupt NTA tour operator member. For further details of the CPP and about the NTA in general *see* www.ntaonline.com

NTA² National Tourism Administration.

NTBA¹ Was the National Tour Brokers Association in the USA, which has now been renamed the National Tour Association.

NTBA² Name to be advised. *See* TBA.

NTF National Tourism Foundation, founded in 1982 by the National Tour Association. On 1 January 2005 amalgamated with the Travelers Conservation Foundation, founded by the USTOA to form Tourism Cares for Tomorrow. *See* www.ntfonline.org *and* www.tcfonline.org

NTHP National Trust for Historic Preservation. Leading US organization in field. *See* www.nthp.org

NTIS National Technical Information Service in the USA.

NTL Business (Travel Division) Major UK viewdata provider to travel industry. Formerly known as AT&T Istel, Istel and X-TANT. Currently using brand name NTL Traveleye.

NTO National Tourist Office. *See* entries for National Tourist Office and US State Tourist Office web sites under country and state names; UK Regional Tourist Boards are listed under the 'Regional Tourist Boards' headings; *also see* Tourism Offices Worldwide Directory www.towd.com

NTSB The National Transportation Safety Board is the US authority responsible for investigating and establishing the cause of accidents and setting safety standards.

NUC Neutral Unit of Construction. *See* IATA fare construction system.

NVI Nederlands Vervoerswetenschappelijk Instituut, the Dutch transport institute.

NVQ National Vocational Qualification, a UK standard at various levels usually achievable by practical work-based assessment. The title NVQ is not particular to the travel industry, although there are many travel NVQs. For details of some travel industry NVQs *see* City and Guilds of London Institute; or *see* www.city-and-guilds.co.uk

NWCA North West Cruiseship Association in the USA; hosted on the web site of the International Council of Cruise Lines. *See* www.iccl.org

NYO Not yet operating.

NZRC New Zealand Reunion Club. *See* Reunion Clubs.

O

O&D Origin and destination. *See* transit or transfer passenger *and* TRWOV.

O&I Operations and Infrastructure division of IATA.

O/R On request.

OAC Oceanic Area Control Unit.

OAG Official Airline Guide. The most well-known printed guide to international air travel with details of all international air flights. Data is also supplied to all four major GDSs from the OAG 'Flight Engine', justifiably claimed to be the most up-to-date and comprehensive global flight schedules database in the world. This gives access to information on millions of direct and connecting flights, updated daily, providing the most extensive air travel options available on the Web. First published in 1929 listing 35 airlines, the OAG database now covers over 950 airlines. *See* www.oag.com In Microsoft Office software 'Smart Tags' enable flight numbers to be recognized in just the same way that web addresses are recognized in most word-processed text. The user can link directly from a flight number to the appropriate part of the OAG site. OAGTIS is the OAG Travel Information System used by corporate travellers to save time and money.

observation car *See* bubble car and dome car.

observation deck *See* deck.

obstructed view *See* cabin with obstructed view.

OCA Oceanic Control Area.

OCA or OCH Obstacle clearance altitude or obstacle clearance height (aviation term).

occupancy *See* occupancy rate.

occupancy rate The ratio, expressed as a percentage, of bed nights sold to the total offered for sale, during a specified period, by a hotel or group of hotels.

Ocean Travel Development *See* PSA².

oceanfront Accommodation directly facing the sea. North American wording which avoids the way in which the wording sea view is abused in the UK.

oceanview Accommodation facing the sea, usually providing only a side view.

OCL Obstacle clearance limit.

OCR Optical Character Recognition. *See* bar code and bull's-eye.

ODS Origin and destination statistics produced by IATA.

OEM Original equipment manufacturer (aviation term).

OEW Operation empty weight (aviation term).

official travel policy *See* travel policy.

Off Premises Automated Ticket/Boarding Pass *See* ATB and ATB2, automated ticket, bar code, bull's-eye, computer airline ticket, OCR, OPTAT, OPATB2, TAT, teletype air ticket *and* ticket (main entry).

off-line¹ Countries/cities through which a carrier does not operate or have traffic rights to pick up passengers are said to be off-line.

off-line² Describes the state of a computer terminal when not connected to its network or to the Internet.

off-load To refuse to carry firmly booked passengers, usually because of overbooking. *See* bump, denied boarding compensation *and* overbooking.

off-peak Low season, the least popular travel time.

off-piste A ski slope or area that is unmarked and neither maintained or supervised.

off-season Period of lowest demand for a tourism service. This is not necessarily the winter; for example, this is peak season for a winter sports area.

OGL Outlet guide vane (aviation term).

OH Overhaul (aviation term).

OM Outer marker – instrument landing system (aviation term).

Oman Directorate General of Tourism *See* www.omantourism.gov.om

On Line Travel Portal Was the temporary name for the European Airlines reservation Internet site, branded 'Opodo' in July 2001. *See* Opodo.

one class Description of a mode of transport where all the passengers have equal access to all parts and amenities. Despite the title, on board a ship, there may be substantial differences between cabins and the price charged for them.

One Pass Name of Continental Airlines' Frequent Flyer Programme. *See* FFP (frequent flyer programme).

One Stop Inclusive Charter Now obsolete. In North America, was an air charter, the seats on which were being sold to the public, which met certain criteria.

One Trip Air Travel Order Document issued by corporate or official bodies enabling credit accounts to be charged for the issue of specified air tickets to named persons. *See* UATP.

One way subjourney *See* IATA fare construction system.

ONElink A worldwide IATA BSP financial settlement system for agents booking accommodation, car rental or rail services introduced in 2003. It enables online purchase and settlement through similar systems already successfully used for air travel by IATA's 55,000 international travel agency network.

one-way backhaul *See* backhaul *and* IATA fare construction system.

one-way car rental charges When a vehicle is hired but not brought back to the journey origin on termination of the rental, there is sometimes an additional fee known as a 'drop-off charge'. Often this is waived when the rental terminates at another station within the same country or state in the USA. The vehicle's documents are then transferred between rental stations and there is no wasted return journey involved. For international trips, however, this is not usually possible and it is necessary for vehicles to be returned to the originating country.

OneWorld *See* airline alliances.

on-line[1] The state of a computer terminal when it is connected to its network. Universally used to describe the state of being connected to the Internet.

on-line[2] or intraline IATA term used in conjunction with another word to describe anything involving carriage over one carrier only, such as on-line itinerary, on-line reservation, on-line stopover, on-line connection etc. Countries or cities through which a carrier operates with rights to pick up traffic are said to be on-line.

online corporate self booking tools *see* corporate self booking tools.

Online Locator *See* location of corporate travellers.

ONS Omega navigation system (aviation term).

on-site travel office Travel agency-managed facility located at a corporate account customer. *See* implant.

OPATB2 Off Premises Automated Ticket/Boarding Pass. *See* also ATB and ATB2, automated ticket, bar code, bull's-eye, computer airline ticket, OCR, OPTAT, TAT, teletype air ticket *and* ticket (main entry).

open bar A complimentary bar, the costs of which are being borne by the event host.

open date ticket When a passenger has a ticket but has not made a reservation, or has effected payment for a facility or service to be provided which is still subject to the passenger's decision concerning date of travel.

open pay *See* coupon payment.

open rate If governments fail to agree on IATA recommended fares, or if IATA airlines fail to agree, then an 'open rate' situation exists. Tariffs have then to be agreed between the countries concerned. The IATA regulations do not operate in such circumstances. In the current atmosphere of deregulation worldwide, the term is obsolescent.

open return or **open-dated return** A return ticket, often priced at a reduced return rate, for which the traveller has made no inward reservation.

open seating The alternative to seat allocation on a mode of transport; passengers may occupy any available seat.

open sitting *See* meal sittings at sea.

open skies By definition is a US Department of Transport policy; *but* the theoretical concept is of allowing freedom to airlines to operate as they wish, to and from any destination. Lack of take-off or landing slots at busy airports and politics mean that implementation of such a policy on a multi-lateral basis is often impractical. Talks between the USA and the European Union to establish an agreement broke down in March 2004. The USA offered to allow foreign companies to own up to 49% of a US airline and also to drop some of the restrictions on landing rights. The EU sought 50% ownership and for its carriers to fly US domestic routes in exchange for US carriers being allowed to fly intra-European routes.

The USA currently has 51 open skies agreements with countries worldwide and more limited agreements with 25 others. The US criteria for the concept are:

- open entry on all routes with no restriction on the number of carriers who can fly such routes
- unrestricted capacity and frequency on all routes, unrestricted route and traffic rights (e.g. no restrictions on flights to intermediate or beyond points, no restrictions on equipment changes, route flexibility, co-terminalization on fifth freedom rights)
- double disapproval pricing in third/fourth freedom markets and intra-EU markets; price matching rights in third country markets and non intra-EU; price leadership in third country markets to the extent that third/fourth freedom carriers in those markets have it
- liberal charter arrangements
- liberal cargo regime
- conversion and remittance arrangements for earnings
- liberal code-sharing opportunities
- rights to control/perform own support functions at airports
- pro-competitive provisions regarding commercial opportunities, user charges, fair competition and intermodal rights
- neutral CRS rules (both in terms of access to CRS systems and in their operation).

See also Chicago Convention *and* Freedoms of the Air.

open station concept The absence of a ticket inspector at a barrier checking rail passengers before entry to or leaving from the stations concerned. The concept is operated in Britain by ATOC/Network Rail and now applies to large parts of the network. Passengers must still purchase tickets before boarding a train, except at totally unstaffed stations, or other stations where the ticket office may be closed.

Open Travel Alliance *See* OTA *and* www.opentravel.org

open-jaw A return journey that has different originating and terminating points, or a return journey where the distant arrival and departure points are different, fall into the category of single open-jaw journeys, e.g. London/New York/Paris or London/New York and Miami/London. IATA regulations allow some transatlantic single open-jaw air journeys to qualify for excursion or other return fare rates. Open-jaw half return air sectors may undercut single fares. *See* IATA fare construction system.

operator Commonly means 'tour operator', but increasingly the word also applies to the 'operator' of any form of transport, hotel group or other touristic enterprise.

opinions of hotels *See* hotels, unbiased opinions of.

Opodo The Internet site of the major European airlines launched in 2001. A joint venture between Aer Lingus, Air France, Alitalia, Austrian Airlines, British Airways, Finnair, Iberia, KLM and Lufthansa together the GDS Amadeus.

Ops Abbreviation for operations.

OPTAT Off Premise Transitional Automated Ticket. Official IATA definition is the ticket described in Resolution 722a, and intended for use by agents, whether or not this bears a preprinted individual airline identity. *See also* ATB and ATB2, automated ticket, bar code, bull's-eye, computer airline ticket, OCR, OPTAT, OPATB2, TAT, teletype air ticket and ticket (main entry).

Optical Character Recognition *See* bar code and bull's-eye.

option or **optional reservation** When a reservation is offered by a provider of travel services, but only held for a strictly limited period of time, at the end of which time the option must be taken up and the booking made firm or the reservation is cancelled.

optional excursion A side trip for touristic purposes, offered as an extra of choice to a travel group. The term has wide variation of usage: e.g. shore excursions for cruise passengers; spouse excursions for a convention, conference or incentive group; excursions that may be booked in advance or in resort by members of an inclusive tour group etc.

OR Over run (aviation term).

Oracle Independent Television's UK Teletext service. *See* Teletext.

Orbis The Polish National Tourist Enterprise.

Orbitz Name of the highly successful air booking web site founded by the five largest US airlines, American, Continental, Delta, Northwest and United, which began operating in June 2001. Original working title had been T2.

Ordin International hotel code for a simple room without running water.

ordinary singles *See* ATOC rail fares.

Organization for Timeshare in Europe *See* OTE.

orientation tour A short non-stop tour intended to familiarize tourists with a city. When applied generally, it means any tour intended to familiarize participants with the relevant site or facility.

origin open-jaw *See* IATA fare construction system.

originating member Official IATA definition is Member transporting passenger over first portion of itinerary.

orlop deck *See* deck.

orographic windflows *See* turbulence.

ORV Osterreichischer Reiseburo Verband, the Austrian National Travel Agency Organization.

OSC One-way sub-journey. *See* IATA fare construction system.

OSI Other supplemental information. When making a booking on a GDS, a free format area used to communicate a wide range of information pertinent to the passenger.

OSSN Outside Sales Support Network Association in the USA. *See* www.ossn.com

OST Operations Standards Team of IATA.

OTA Open Travel Alliance. Comprises worldwide airlines, hoteliers, car rental companies, leisure suppliers, travel agencies, GDSs, technology providers and others, working together to create and implement industry-wide open e-business specifications using the information language XML. *See* www.opentravel.org

OTATO One Trip Air Travel Order. *See* UATP for explanation.

OTD Ocean Travel Development in the UK, was an organization set up in 1958 by some shipping companies to foster travel by sea and to simplify and unify shipping procedure and documentation. Now changed name to PSA. *See* PSA[2].

OTE The Organization for Timeshare in Europe was created in February 1998 following a decision taken by the 15 national timeshare industry associations who were members of the European Timeshare Association (ETF). Instead of a federal structure, the new body was formed on the basis of individual international membership, covering Europe, the Middle East and North Africa. Their web site provides outstanding information concerning the timeshare industry. *See* www.ote-info.com *and* timeshare.

OTMC Online travel management company. *A list of 70 other business travel related entries follows* corporate travel contracts, *some of which lead to further entries.*

OTP On-Line Travel Portal – was the temporary name for the European Airlines reservation Internet site, branded 'Opodo' in July 2001. *See* Opodo.

OTTS Organization of Teachers of Transport Studies in the UK.

OU Open University, who were contracted to develop artificial intelligence and interactive video systems for the UK travel industry's Computer-Based Learning scheme.

outplant operations Usage and meaning of the word outplant is currently changing. In the USA at first and then in the UK, it used to mean provision of a satellite ticket printer serviced by corporate staff. This was in contrast to having an implant, a travel agency operative working at the corporate site but paid for by the agency. As contracts to supply travel services have increasingly become fee based, the costs of provision of implant services are taken into account in the negotiations. In the UK, Business Travel Management (BTM) companies have established outplant offices, where the needs of one or more corporate accounts may be serviced, all by staff dedicated only to the corporation concerned. A switch of costs is involved because, whereas corporations provide the accommodation and normal office services for implants, the BTM has to cover the costs. In an extensive European survey into how travel is managed, published in *Business Travel World* August 2001, the percentage ratios between implant, outplant and business travel centre were found to be France,

33:42:42; Germany, 86:10:21; UK, 44:47:33; Sweden, 47:47:47; Belgium, Denmark, Italy, the Netherlands, Norway, Spain and Switzerland, 46:23:51. The totals are greater than 100% because many companies use a combination of methods. By the end of 2003, a substantial trend from implant to outplant arrangements had developed. For example, the largest UK travel management company BTI had 47 implants and 75 outplants, while Carlson Wagonlits had 28 implants and 41 outplants. *A list of 70 other business travel related entries follows* corporate travel contracts, *some of which lead to further entries.*

output tourism multiplier *See* tourism multiplier.

outside sales representatives Travel agencies in the UK and USA often sell their services with the help of qualified travel consultants whose status is not that of a normal employee; there are many variations. For example, in the UK, a highly successful company, Travel Counsellors, has hundreds of travel consultants working from their own homes, effecting bookings through the central office. In the USA, a desk may be 'rented' in a travel agency together with full agency facilities.

Until the conclusion of the UK Restrictive Practices Court hearings between 1978 and February 1984, the circumstances in which ABTA members could utilize outside sales representatives to sell direct to the public were severely restricted. Most of the rules have now been lifted except for simple bonding requirements. Representatives also need to be trained to standards, which at the time of writing, had not been designated by ABTA other than acceptance that any person meeting the minimum standards as a qualified member of staff for ABTA membership requirements, automatically reaches the minimum standards of knowledge required for outside sales representatives.

ASTA has produced a helpful checklist to help identify the circumstances in which an outside sales representative may be regarded as an employee or an independent contractor for tax purposes. The various criteria below indicate why this entry has avoided a meaningful definition of a phenomenon that is widespread; it must, therefore be mentioned, but cannot be precisely defined.

Outside sales representatives may: be engaged in independent employment, not under the control of the sponsoring agency or under that control; furnish their own supplies, equipment and place of work or have these provided by the agency; pay their own expenses, receiving only commission on sales or have their expenses partially or wholly defrayed and may make a profit or loss independently of the agency; entirely complete any bookings initiated or have administrative services provided by the agency; work hours of their own choosing or work the hours laid down by the agency; employ assistants to whom work is delegated. The relationship with the agency is likely to be specified in a contract.

In the USA, outside sales representatives may be known as independent contractors.

overbooking The sale of more seats on a mode of transport, rooms in a hotel or places on a tour than are actually available. The practice is commonly used by airlines in order to allow for that historical percentage of passengers who fail, for some reason, to use their reservations. In Britain and the USA, passengers unable to fly because of airline overbooking, may be eligible for denied boarding compensation. The term 'bumped' is sometimes used to describe such passengers. *See also* denied boarding compensation, no-show *and* bump.

overfly To fly over a country without landing; nevertheless, permission from the local air traffic control authorities is essential and possibly from other governmental organizations.

over-ride *See* over-riding commission.

over-riding commission Originally meant the commission allowed by principals to their general sales agents on bookings originated by an ordinary agent. Now generally used to describe all extra or incentive commissions paid above the standard rate. For full explanations *see* incentive commission.

overstays Hotel guests that continue to occupy their hotel room after the period for which they booked, sometimes causing hotels to be overbooked.

OWE Operating weight empty (aviation term).

P

P and D panel The price and departure panel in a tour operator's brochure.

P&S Products and Services department of IATA's Information and Marketing Services division.

P/L Payload (aviation term).

PA Via Pacific. *See* routing.

Pacific Area Travel Association *See* PATA.

Pacific Class Brand name given by Air New Zealand to passenger area immediately adjacent to first class, where passengers paying full fares can enjoy improved service and facilities. *See* business class.

package An inclusive tour.

package holiday An inclusive tour. Defined in EC Directive 90/314/EEC on package travel, package holidays and package tours as 'the pre-arranged combination of not fewer than two of the following when sold or offered for sale at an inclusive price and when the service covers a period of more than 24 h or includes overnight accommodation: (i) transport; (ii) accommodation; (iii) other tourist services not ancillary to transport or accommodation and accounting for a significant proportion of the package'. *See also* inclusive tour, for further definitions.

Packet Switch System *See* PSS.

paddle steamer A ship driven by paddle wheels. Whereas the paddle wheels of watermills are driven round by water flow, thus turning machinery, the process was reversed for the first steam-powered boats, with the paddle being driven round to provide propulsion. Although there were experiments throughout the 17th century, it was not until William Symington developed a crank, converting linear to rotary motion, that steam power was successfully applied to turning a paddle wheel. The first successful paddle steamer, the Charlotte Dundas, operated in Scotland from 1801. For nearly 50 years, until the development of propellers (screws),

paddle steamers ruled the waves! In the USA, because the paddle was often mounted on the stern of a vessel, paddle steamers are called sternwheelers.

PADIS-APTS Passenger and Airport Data Interchange Standards Airport Services sub-group of IATA.

PADIS-RES Passenger and Airport Data Interchange Standards Reservations sub-group of IATA.

PAI Personal Accident Insurance for car hirers which often also covers loss of baggage. If a traveller has no other insurance this is to be strongly recommended.

PAL Was Poundstretcher Agents Link, the acronym for British Airways' Poundstretcher cut-price air seats agents' view-data system, providing full interactive communication with UK travel agents, enabling them to make bookings direct from their office terminals. This is now a sub-system of BA-LINK.

Palestine Ministry of Tourism and Antiquities *See* www.visit-palestine.com

PAMS President Agency Management System. *See* DPAS.

Panama Tourism Bureau *See* www.visitpanama.com

panoramic tour The BSI/CEN 2003 Standard definition is: 'Overview of a city or area, normally without visits'. This definition attempts to distinguish it from a 'guided tour' or an 'orientation tour'; a worthy objective which, unfortunately, does not appear to have the support of the copywriters of tour operators' brochures. *See* guided tour *and* orientation tour.

PANS Procedures for air navigation services.

pantograph The sprung device, usually on top of a train, enabling electrical connection with the overhead power line.

pap Airline abbreviation for a single passenger.

paper a theatre Alternative wording is 'paper the house'. To give free tickets so as to mislead critics and others as to a play's popularity.

PAPIS Precision approach path indicating system (aviation term).

PAR[1] Passenger account record. The term used by Galileo and other CRSs for customer details, alternatively named 'customer profile'. The computer record acts as a convenient accessible file of the information which can be transferred instantaneously into bookings.

PAR[2] Precision approach and runway monitor (aviation term).

parador Spanish state-owned country hotels that have often been created from castles or other large buildings. They offer a high standard of accommodation at reasonable prices.

Paragon Agreement Links the National Business Travel Association (NBTA) in the USA with the UK and Ireland's Institute of Travel Management (ITM), the Canadian Business Travel Association (CBTA), Verband Deutsches Reismanagement (VDR) in Germany, the Australian Business Travel Association and other similar national organizations. *A list of 70 other business travel related entries follows* corporate travel contracts, *some of which lead to further entries.*

PARCA Pan-American Railway Congress Association and Latin American Railway Association (ALAF) based in Argentina. *See* www.alaf.int.ar *or* via www.railway-technology.com

parents' room Room at transport terminals and other public places providing for the needs of young children, such as nappy changing and feeding. Because of the desire for privacy by women when breastfeeding, parents' rooms are often part of female toilet facilities.

Paris Agreement The 1919 international agreement which designated that any country had complete rights over its own air space. For later development *see* Freedoms of the Air.

park A public recreation open space usually providing grass and trees. *See* national park.

parkway When part of a rail station name in the UK designates an edge of city station with ample parking facilities. In the USA designates a main road or freeway either in open country or merely one where the central reservation and/or verges have been planted with flowers and shrubs.

parlor car In North America, a type of rail restaurant car with a bar and food service.

parlour (parlor) When sold as hotel accommodation, a living room not used as a bedroom.

PARM Precision approach radar (aviation term).

PARS Programmed Airline Reservation System; formerly TWA's automated airline reservation system through which many US agents made air bookings. In February 1990 Datas II merged with PARS to form Worldspan, separately described under this title.

part charter A charter covering only a portion of an aircraft in regular scheduled service. *See* charter.

Participating Member Same as Carrying Members (IATA).

partner fare A spouse fare. *See* spouse fare.

Partners in Responsible Tourism (in the USA) *See* www.pirt.org

PAS In connection with car rental indicates power-assisted steering.

PASCAL A computer programming language.

PASOLP Products Analysis Sequence for Outdoor Leisure Planning.

pass International Hotel Code for a one-night stay.

passenger Official IATA definition is any person, except members of the crew, carried or to be carried in an aircraft with the consent of the carrier. The term is, of course, applied generally to people travelling on or in a form of transport, but not operating or controlling it.

passenger average weight *See* air passenger average weights.

passenger boarding bridge *See* link span.

passenger cruise day *See* PCD.

Passenger Enquiry Terminals *See* PET.

Passenger Facility Charge A charge raised by US airports to pay for improvements to facilities.

passenger handling at airports *See* SPT.

Passenger Network Services Corporation US travel agency distribution organization for air travel.

passenger service agents US term for airline staff who handle passengers, mainly on check-in and boarding.

passenger space ratio PSR is the gross registered tonnage (GRT) of a vessel divided by the passenger capacity. *See* ship density for further explanation.

passenger transport market segmentation
The three classic reasons why people travel are: on business, in connection with their employment, for leisure reasons such as a holiday and for personal reasons. In most modes of transport, personal trips include journeys to and from work, since these are not being paid for by their employers, although some consider this to be a fourth market segment. It is considered that the demand for most business travel, excluding incentives and conferences etc., is inelastic, so that it will not grow greatly in response to normal marketing methods. Thus, much of the advertising in the business travel sphere tends to be diversionary, attempting to persuade travellers to switch between alternative transport modes or companies. By contrast, leisure market demand for transport seems very elastic, dependent upon price and consumer spending power. *See* demand for transport *and* transport modelling.

passenger vehicle drivers' hours *See* drivers' hours in Europe.

passenger weights *See* air passenger average weights.

passenger/cargo ship *See* cargo/passenger ship.

passing *See* acculturation.

passive booking or **segment** Details of onward travel entered in the computer record of an air booking but *not* entered as part of the booking request, because arrangements have already been made direct, with the other transport company/ies involved.

passport An official identification document issued by sovereign states to their nationals for travel purposes. It may be required to authorize leaving the home country. But more usually, it is the main permit to enter a country foreign to the holder. Many countries also require specific entry authorization in the form of visas, which are stamped or attached to passport pages. Most modern passports are now machine readable, facilitating immigration checks. A machine readable passport is with an inbuilt magnetic strip or chip enabling the details to be read electronically, facilitating emigration and immigration procedures. Cost of a UK passport valid for 10 years was £42 in 2003; cost of a 10-year US

passport was US$65. *See* travel.state.gov/ passport-services.html to download the application form (DSP-11) and for US passport information; for more information about UK passports phone their advice line on 0870 521 0410 or go to www.passport.gov.uk *also see* visa.

PATA The Pacific Area Travel Association includes industry principals as well as official tourist organizations and other industry associations in the Pacific area. Chapters throughout the world include all those involved in promoting travel to this region. *See* www.pata.org

PATCO The Professional Air Traffic Controllers Organization in the USA. *See* www.patcounion.org

pavillion *See* stand.

PAWOB Passenger arriving without bag.

PAX or **pax** Travel industry abbreviation for passenger.

payload Strictly speaking is the actual weight of passengers or cargo, arrived at by deducting the empty operating weight of an aircraft including fuel and other items from the loaded weight. However, industry usage designates payload as the income or revenue producing element on a mode of transport. Although usually applied to aircraft, the term applies to any load on transport, referring either to the number of passengers, amount of freight, or combination of both, that can be carried. In respect of transport by water, rail or road, fuel weight is not very important. But in the case of aircraft, the longer the flight, the greater proportion of the total weight is taken up by the weight of the fuel carried. Thus, for any particular aircraft type there will be a payload weight/ range relationship which determined the aircraft's suitability for operations on a particular route. *See* air passenger average weights, *also* maximum payload capacity.

payment systems for travel agents *See* agents' payment systems.

PCC Pseudo city code; the unique GDS reference, usually of five alphanumeric characters given to every travel agency.

PCD Passenger cruise day; a measurement unit for budgeting and accounting purposes; but it is based on a night rather than a 24 h period. Thus, it equates to 'bed night' or in shipping parlance 'berth night'. The term NSR (net sea revenue) includes all income for a cruise including passage money less taxes, commissions on access transport ticket sales and profit generated on board during a cruise. The term 'net per diem' is arrived at by dividing the NSR by the total PCDs for a cruise.

PCHM Perishable Cargo Handling Manual of IATA.

PCM Project certification manager (aviation term).

PCMA Professional Convention Management Association in the USA. *See* www.pcma.org

PCN[1] Pavement classification number (aviation term).

PCN[2] Passenger cruise night; sometimes called a guest cruise night. An alternative to passenger cruise day. *See* PCD.

PCO Professional conference organizer.

PDM Possible duplicate message (aviation term).

PDNA IATA's Programme for Developing Nations' Airlines.

PDR Predetermined route (aviation term).

PDU Power drive unit (aviation term).

PDW Physical damage waiver; an alternative to collision damage waiver, referring to car rental. *See* CDW.

Peacock Class Brand name given by Air Lanka to passenger area immediately adjacent to first class, where passengers paying full economy fares enjoy improved service and facilities. *See* business class.

peak Highest fare when two or more seasonal fare levels operate. Off-peak is lowest fare.

peak season Time of the year when travel to a particular destination is most popular, as distinct from low season, when it is least popular and shoulder season, periods between the two.

Peanut Air Fares US terminology for cut-price travel offered on certain flights.

Pearl Class Brand name given by Air Seychelles to premium passenger area of their two class system, where passengers enjoy improved service and facilities. *See* business class.

PEC Personal effects coverage; appears in some North American car rental insurance but often specifically excluded elsewhere. *Also see* personal effects insurance in entry for travel insurance.

PED Period ending date. ARC weekly sales reporting periods which are up to and include Sunday.

penalty fare Fee charged to travellers in Britain found not have a valid ticket, in an attempt to discourage the practice.

Pendolino Name of Virgin tilting trains introduced on the UK West Coast line in 2002. Although they were intended to run at 140 mph, the track is not good enough to allow this; date for completion of upgrading is uncertain.

Pennsylvania State Tourism, Film and Economic Development Marketing Office *See* www.experiencepa.com

pension[1] European term for a small hotel. Some official accommodation grading systems in Europe require a minimum level of services for residents and public rooms before a pension may apply to be regraded as a hotel.

pension[2] In many European countries means a tariff type as well as an accommodation type; for example, full pension means full board, (accommodation, breakfast, lunch and dinner).

pension trois quart Three-quarter pension. *See* three-quarter pension.

People 1st (People First) The Travel Tourism and Events National Training Organisation in the UK merged with the Hospitality Training Foundation in 2002, forming People 1st, a UK government Sector Skills Council (SSC), formally launched in 2004 as an SSC for the hospitality, leisure, travel and tourism industry; *see* www.people1st.co.uk NTOs (National Training Organizations) began in 1997. They took over the role of 180 Industry Training Boards (ITBs), Lead Bodies and Occupational Standards Councils. In 2001 there were 73 NTOs which the UK Government decided to reduce to a small number of SSCs. SSCs are responsible for setting skills standards in their sector and assessing future needs and should actively promote good practice and ensure the availability of high quality qualifications.

people mover *See* travelator.

per capita Per person.

per diem Per day, literally translated from Latin. An example of common usage in the travel industry is 'per diem expense allowance', meaning that a set daily expense allowance will be reimbursed, regardless of the actual expenditure.

period ending date *See* PED.

peripheral The computer jargon for any piece of hardware other than the central processing unit, which operates the peripherals. For example, a screen, printer or disk drive.

permit Foreign-registered aircraft operating to and from the UK require a 'permit' from the Department of Trade. But, of course, the word has the general meaning applying to a licence, pass or permission.

personal accident insurance for car hirers *See* PAI.

Personal Vacation Planner In the USA, a person working for a transportation company such as a cruise line, selling direct to customers, bypassing travel agents.

Peru Tourism *See* www.peru.org.pe

Peruvian National Travel Agency Organization Touring y Automóvil Club del Peru.

PES Passenger entertainment system (aviation term).

PET Passenger enquiry terminal. A terminal in a public place such as a rail, bus or coach station, hotel foyer or airport enabling access to travel and timetable information. Often terminals also provide ticket-issuing facilities.

Pet Passport *See* quarantine.

Pet Travel Scheme *See* quarantine.

PETS Pet Travel Scheme for the import of cats and dogs into the UK. *See* quarantine.

PF Private facilities. In general, concerning a hotel room or in shipping terminology indicating a cabin, which has attached or built-in washing and toilet facilities, either a shower and toilet or a bath and toilet.

PFC Passenger facility charge. A charge originally raised by US airports to pay for improvements to facilities but now is often merely for the usage of an airport's services.

PFD Primary flight display (aviation term).

PFE Passenger furnished equipment (aviation term).

PFPC Passenger Forms and Procedures Committee of IATA.

PFR Permitted flying route (aviation term).

PHARE Programme for Harmonised Air Traffic Management Research.

Philippine Travel Agencies Association *See* PTAA.

Phobos A computerized tour operators' reservation and accounting system introduced by Harrison Computer Services Ltd in 1979.

phonetic alphabet For clarity of oral communication in the travel industry, the same words are used throughout the world in order to make spellings clear. This is as follows: Alpha, Bravo, Charlie, Delta, Echo, Foxtrot, Golf, Hotel, India, Juliet, Kilo, Lima, Mike, November, Oscar, Papa, Quebec, Romeo, Sierra, Tango, Uniform, Victor, Whisky, X-Ray, Yankee, Zulu.

physical tourism carrying capacity *See* tourism carrying capacity.

PIC or **P1** Pilot in command.

piece concept Where free baggage allowance depends upon number of pieces of luggage rather than their weight.

pilgrimage A journey to a holy place for religious reasons; undertaken by millions of pilgrims annually, pilgrimages are a significant part of the tourism phenomenon. For example, devout Moslems may wish to visit Mecca and Medina for the 'Haj' at least once in their lives, as it is one of 'the five pillars' of their religion; an 'Umrah' involves visiting the main holy cities. Christians may wish to visit Jerusalem; there are many other Christian pilgrimage sites throughout the world such as Santiago de Compostela in Spain.

PIP Performance improvement programme (aviation term) *or* personal injury protection, alternative wording for personal accident insurance. *See* travel insurance.

PIR Property irregularity report. Used by airlines when baggage is damaged or missing. (Some airlines decode the acronym as property incident report.)

PIRATES Was the Passenger Information, Reservation, Accounting and Ticketing for Europe System permitting British agents and rail stations to access fares, computers and reservation systems for international rail journeys. *See* Elgar.

pirogue Small boat, originally little more than a dugout canoe, but now often found in a variety of more sophisticated forms in Spanish-speaking countries.

PIRT   Partners in Responsible Tourism in the USA. *See* www.pirt.org

piste   A marked ski slope, supervised and maintained by patrolling ski resort staff. On maps of ski runs, those marked in green are for beginners; blue runs are easy, for inexperienced skiers; red runs are more difficult, for the intermediate skier while black runs are the most difficult. *See* winter sports. Note, however, significant international differences in meaning. In North America blue means a ski trail of moderate difficulty, and may be designated as a blue square trail. However, Europeans familiar with ski runs in Germany and Austria know that a blue run is the easiest. In the USA, Canada, France and Italy, green runs are the easiest, while blue runs are second in difficulty. In Switzerland, take care. French and German speaking parts tend to follow their 'language' designations.

piston aircraft engine   An internal combustion engine where the vertical movements of pistons within cylinders create rotational movement by means of a crankshaft or some other device. Aircraft engines of this type use the rotational power to turn a propeller or helicopter rotor.

pitch of propeller   The angle of a propeller blade in respect of the direction of travel, known as 'the angle of attack'. Modern airplane propellers are usually variable pitch, allowing the angle to change to optimize performance at varying speeds and in different ambient conditions.

pitch of seat   The distance between the front edge of one seat in an aircraft and the front edge of the seat immediately in front, measured when both seats are in the upright position. In first class, on 747 intercontinental routes, Air NZ, BA, Iberia, KLM, Northwest, Swissair and Thai have 62 in., Air Canada 61 and Air India, JAL, Lufthansa, Qantas, Singapore and Varig only 60 in. On other aircraft, first-class seat pitch may vary from as little as 40 in. in UTA DC-10s, up to 62 in. in an Iberia DC10.

In the business class, called executive or club by some airlines, on European routes, average is around 34 in. flying with BA or AF and varies from 32 in. with Aer Lingus to 39 in. with Olympic. In this class on long-haul routes, average is 38 in. with Air NZ, KLM, Lufthansa, SAS, Swissair, TAP, TWA, UTA and Varig. A 39 in. business-class pitch is offered by Aer Lingus, AC, Qantas, Singapore and on some UTA flights. A pitch of 40 in. is offered by Air India, BA, Northwest and Thai and 42 in. on Finnair, Iberia DC10 flights and MAS. *Readers should note that although these figures were provided by airlines, aircraft configurations are always changing.*

pitching of a ship   The rise and fall of a ship in rough seas. Pitching will vary according to the length of the ship, the distance between waves (the reach) and the pitch or height of the waves.

PKO/PKU   PKO is the abbreviation for passenger kilometres offered by an airline, while PKU refers to the passenger kilometres utilized. The ratio between these is an economic indicator.

PL/1   Programming Language/1, a computer programming language.

PLA¹   Port of London Authority. *See* www.portoflondon.co.uk

PLA²   Power level angle (aviation term).

plain   International Hotel Code for an ordinary room.

Plan management   Official IATA definition is the department of IATA responsible to the Agency Administrator for the administrative management and development of the Bank Settlement Plan in the different areas where it is applicable, and includes the local BSP Manager in the area of a Bank Settlement Plan.

Planefair   In the UK, was brand name of Rank's variety of minimum-rated package tour. (Now obsolete.)

PLASI   Pulsed light approach slope indicator (aviation term).

plate   An air carrier plate used in manual air ticket validators to produce an impression of the airline's logo and other details on a neutral air ticket. Similarly, an agency identification plate contains agency details. *See also* plating rules.

plated service   Type of restaurant service where meals are portioned and plated in the kitchen. *See* silver service for comparison with various other types of restaurant service.

platform   A raised area. Rail carriages are usually 2 or 3 ft above the ground, so a rail platform enables passengers to get on or off trains without a significant height difference.

plating away   *See* plating rules.

plating rules   The explanation above mentions the use of airline plates in ticket validators. IATA and other airlines have formed BSP or similar groupings in many countries to enable neutral ticket documents to be used and have developed rules concerning which carrier's plate should be used in given circumstances. For example, normally, a ticket should be plated on the first carrier in an itinerary. The use of a plate may significantly affect an airline's revenue, and so it is a sensitive area. Plating away is the agency practice of plating in order to avoid a particular carrier. Perhaps there is a commission difference or threatened insolvency. The widespread use of automated ticketing equipment has meant that printed tickets are now more frequently produced than manual ones in many countries. But the rules governing the carrier to be designated on these tickets are still called 'plating rules'. At the time of writing, delicate negotiations are proceeding worldwide, with the aim of liberalizing these rules.

Plimsoll line   Correctly called the International Load Line, it is an indication on the hull of the maximum depth to which a ship may be loaded.

plus plus   In North America alludes to adding taxes and tips to a rate.

p.m.   The Latin words '*post meridien*' are universally shortened to p.m. to mean the 12 h after midday. Usually, in the travel industry, the 24 h clock is used, but in North America, travel timings might be expressed a.m. (*ante meridien*) or p.m.

PMC   Power management control (aviation term).

PMS[1]   Performance management system (aviation term).

PMS[2]   Property management system. A comprehensive computerized hotel administration, management system; some PMSs have associated reservation systems while others incorporate this function. Examples are Best Western's LYNX system which runs NOVA PMS software and the Marriott systems Holidex and HIRO described in 'yield management'. *Also see* THISCO. A full description of Micros Fidelioxpress front office management system is available at www.micros.com/products/hotels/hotel-management

PNR[1]   Passenger name record. The airline jargon word for a booking stored in a reservations computer.

PNR[2]   Prior notice required (aviation term).

PNSC   Passenger network services corporation. Negotiations in the USA because of anti-trust legislation led to the establishment of an organization entirely separate from IATA to organize the travel agency distribution system for air travel. *See* IATAN.

PO   Via Polar route from Europe to Japan or Korea or vice versa. *See* routing.

Pobab   International Hotel Code for Sunday in the morning.

Pocun   International Hotel Code for Monday in the morning.

Pods   *See* airframe.

Podyl   International Hotel Code for Tuesday in the morning.

Pogok   International Hotel Code for Wednesday in the morning.

Pohix   International Hotel Code for Thursday in the morning.

Poincare gold franc   *See* Warsaw Convention.

point beyond ticketing   Issuing an air ticket to place further than a traveller's intended destination because the fare is lower, when the flight itinerary has intermediate stops. Thus the passenger can alight where they actually wish to go. This practice is prohibited by the airlines; however, it is difficult to prevent knowledgeable passengers making the bookings or to prove that the ticket was issued with the intention of undercutting the fare. Also known as hidden city ticketing.

point of no return   Point during a flight, when, if an aircraft gets into difficulties, the nearest airport is no longer that of original departure.

point-to-point air fare   A rate that does not allow an intermediate stop en route, and for which, often, the fare rules do not allow combination with other fares.

point-to-point European rail tickets   *See* sectional coupons.

Pojaw   International Hotel Code for Friday in the morning.

Pokuz International Hotel Code for Saturday in the morning.

policy *See* travel policy.

Polish National Tourist Enterprise Orbis.

Polish National Tourist Office *See* www.visitpoland.org

Polish National Tourist Organisation *See* www.polandtour.org in the USA *and* www.pot.gov.pl

Polyp International Hotel Code for Sunday in the afternoon.

Pomel International Hotel Code for Monday in the afternoon.

Ponow International Hotel Code for Tuesday in the afternoon.

pool deck *See* deck.

pooling Two or more airlines may agree to pool the revenue to be obtained on a particular route. This is banned by US law, which is why this type of agreement is most prevalent in Europe. A pooling agreement does not necessarily share the revenue on a 50:50 basis. Such a commercial agreement may also involve spreading of flights, so as to provide a more even service throughout the day or week.

Popup International Hotel Code for Wednesday in the afternoon.

Porik International Hotel Code for Thursday in the afternoon.

port The left-hand side (facing forward) of a ship.

port charges or **taxes** Charges on all passengers leaving a port, covering port handling charges and government departure taxes. In some cases this charge can only be paid within the country concerned.

port tax Tax charged to ships' passengers, usually by port authorities, to help defray the cost of running the port. Mostly collected by the shipping company at the time of payment of the fare and is non-commissionable.

Portion Official IATA definition is one segment or consecutive segment, even though a gap intervenes, via any one Member.

portion control The procedure by which restaurants control and maintain the size of food and beverage portions with the joint aims of economic operation and customer satisfaction.

portpass *See* INS pass.

portside The left side of a vessel when facing forward. Navigation lights on this side of the bridge are red.

Portuguese National Tourist Office *See* www.portugalinsite.pt

Portuguese National Travel Agency Organization Associacao Portuguesa das Agencias de Viagens e Turismo.

Posev International Hotel Code for Friday in the afternoon.

positioning cruise A one way cruise, usually inclusive of return air travel, operated so that the ship can move from the end of one series to the start of another. Often, vessels will operate in Europe during the summer months and move to a warmer area during the European winter.

positioning flight *See* ferry mileage.

positive space A definite booking confirmed by the supplier.

post-convention tour A trip or inclusive tour following a convention, congress or meeting which has been arranged by or in association with the organizers, for which there is usually an extra charge.

post-trip reporting Any reports required by company travel departments after travel has been concluded. *A list of 70 other business travel related entries follows corporate travel contracts, some of which lead to further entries.*

Poundstretcher Brand name of British Airways, used to promote many reduced-rate fares.

Povah International Hotel Code for Saturday in the afternoon.

Pow Wow Annual US tourism promotional event for the travel industry, to which many organizations promoting and selling travel to and within the USA are invited, together with foreign journalists. *See* TIA.

powder (snow) Undisturbed snow, containing much trapped air, ideal for skiers. *See* winter sports.

POWER Term now obsolete. Was Planefair/OSL/Wings/Ellerman Reservation Systems, the acronym for the Rank tour operating group's agency viewdata booking system. Absorbed into Horizon's reservation system, which itself vanished following the takeover by Thomson group.

powerboat Name of a small speedboat used for inshore water racing at high speeds.

Powis International Hotel Code for today in the morning.

Pozum International Hotel Code for today in the afternoon.

PP Partnership Programme of IATA.

pp Per person; sometimes pppd, meaning per person per day; some dictionaries suggest this is expressed as ppd.

PPI Plan position indicator (aviation term).

PPO Prior permission only (aviation term).

PPR[1] Prior permission required (aviation term).

PPR[2] Passenger profile record: full details of a regular traveller including Frequent Traveller Club memberships, seating preferences and much personal information.

prau Malayan long narrow rowing or sailing boat, with a sharp prow. Often with the aid of one or two sails, the prau is built for speed.

pre-clearance Checking of travellers for customs and/or immigration purposes before arrival at destination, usually en route.

pre-convention tour A trip or inclusive tour prior to a convention, congress or meeting which has been arranged by or in association with the organizers, for which there is usually an extra charge.

predatory pricing Where an organization dominant in a market seeks to restrict or remove competition by aggressive low prices. The most famous proved travel industry case of this behaviour was during the 1970s, when the Laker Skytrain transatlantic air service was forced out of business.

pre-existing conditions See travel insurance.

Preference Class Brand name given by Iberia to passenger area immediately adjacent to first class, where passengers paying full fares can enjoy improved service and facilities. See business class.

preferred supplier A provider of tourism services that has a formal agreement or arrangement with a retailer that their services will be particularly promoted and sold in preference to competitors. Travel agents, particularly multiple agencies, choose their suppliers carefully, dealing with those companies offering high quality, marketing support and incentive commission. Where possible, deals of this nature are negotiated with market leaders. Travel agency employees are expected to promote and sell preferred suppliers in preference to other companies. Often large travel retailers categorize their preferred suppliers into groups; those which should be offered first to the customer and those which may be offered as an alternative, prohibiting business being transacted outside those groups.

pregnant passengers by air Regulations vary between airlines. Normally such passengers are accepted up to the 28th week of pregnancy. After this, a medical certificate confirming passenger's fitness to travel and expected confinement date is required. British Airways will not accept pregnant travellers for flights of under 4 h for travel less than 4 weeks before expected confinement. For flights of more than 4 h, such travellers will not be accepted for travel less than 5 weeks before confinement.

Premier Class Brand name given by many airlines to passenger area immediately adjacent to first class, where passengers paying full economy fares enjoy improved service and facilities. See business class.

Premium Class Was People Express' name for business class.

premium fares The higher rates of a range of fares.

premium traffic Travellers at the higher rates who generate more profit for a transport provider.

prepaid ticket advice Official IATA definition is the notification by teletype, commercial wire or mail that a person in one city has requested issuance of prepaid transportation as described in the authority, to a person in another city. See handling fees and PTA.

pre-registration[1] In the UK the term is used to describe registering a customer's requirements with a tour operator or other travel company before the brochure for that season has been published, in order to be one of the first in booking a scarce service, perhaps because it is a peak date, or a popular hotel or cruise ship.

pre-registration[2] The term applies generally worldwide to the checking-in of large groups at hotels, where for ease of handling, allocation of rooms and other formalities may be undertaken before arrival.

President Agency Management System See DPAS.

President's Club Name of Continental Airline's Frequent Flyers Club.

pressurization Above approximately 10,000 ft, too little oxygen is available in the low pressure conditions for comfortable breathing by normal passengers. In order to avoid the need to supply oxygen continuously, and yet at the same time fly at high altitudes, aircraft cabins are usually kept at a pressure equivalent to around 8000 ft which should cause no discomfort to passengers.

Prestel Was British Telecom's viewdata system, the first public service worldwide on trial in the late 1970s, enabling registered users in Britain and abroad to access the huge database of information held on Prestel's computers. A specially adapted television set or terminal and keyboard were required. Communication was by telephone lines. At the time of development of Prestel, BT was a state-owned public service and alternative computer databases which could be accessed from the same set were termed private viewdata systems. But by 1995, there were over 20,000 terminals capable of connecting with these systems in British travel agencies. Having been the first to espouse the technology, British travel agents still book 15 million or more package holidays annually using viewdata. *See* viewdata.

Prestige Club Name of South African Airway's Frequent Flyers Club, membership of which is free to those who buy either two first class, three gold class, or six excursion intercontinental return air tickets annually. For further details *see* FFP (frequent flyer programme).

pre-trip authority Corporate travel requirement that permission from a superior or company travel department is granted before travel arrangements are made. May apply only to travel above stated limits or travel in a class or on a carrier outside company travel policy. *A list of 70 other business travel related entries follows* corporate travel contracts, *some of which lead to further entries.*

pre-trip reporting Any reports required by corporate travel departments in advance of travel. For example, sometimes means reporting that arrangements specified by travellers can be achieved at lower cost or are in contravention of company travel policy. May cover fare monitoring of existing bookings. *A list of 70 other business travel related entries follows* corporate travel contracts, *some of which lead to further entries.*

price discrimination *See* discriminatory pricing *and* yield management.

price grid The list of prices in a travel brochure, usually showing varying rates for different seasonal dates of travel, class of travel and accommodation etc. and usually indicating supplements payable for various optional facilities.

pricing of hotel rooms A difficulty faced by accommodation providers when pricing is that their calculations have to be based on a forecast of the expected percentage occupancy. All bar, restaurant or other costs and profits are obviously related to customer numbers. Another important factor is the current market price for the grade of accommodation under consideration in that location. Prices need to be competitive to attract custom. There are several well-known calculation methods. 1000-to-one means dividing the capital cost per room by 1000 and making that charge per night, exclusive of any meals and taxes, e.g. US$150,000 construction cost = US$150 per night. This method assumes a 60% occupancy rate, on which basis a satisfactory rate of return on the investment should be achieved. The Hubbart formula takes into account all hotel income and expenditure, an occupancy forecast and a rate of return required on the investment. The *average room rate achieved* for a period (night, month or year etc.) is calculated by dividing the total room income, less taxes and gratuities, by the number of rooms occupied. Because average room rates do not take occupancy levels into account, they are of limited value in assessing a hotel's performance. The accuracy of sales forecasts is always a crucial factor if profits are to be made. *See* hotel statistics worldwide.

pricing unit *See* IATA fare construction system.

principal *See* legal status of a travel agent *and* travel principal.

printer *See* computer printers.

priority boarding Embarkation on a mode on transport in advance of other passengers; a facility often extended to disabled or ailing passengers, pregnant women and travellers with young children.

private butler In luxurious hotels, a personal waiter may be allocated to a suite of rooms to provide room services. In North America, the term may mean the hotel employee who checks and if necessary restocks a hotel room mini-bar.

Private Settlement Tickets *See* rail Private Settlement Tickets.

private viewdata *See* viewdata.

Privilege Name of SN Brussels Airlines frequent flyer programme.

prix fixé A set price or table d'hôte menu.

PRNAV Precision navigation (aviation term).

procurement services provider Organization that undertakes the business process of procurement, outsourced to them by another business. *See* business process outsourcing. *A list of 70 other business travel related entries follows* corporate travel contracts, *some of which lead to further entries.*

professional indemnity insurance Insurance which covers travel agencies and their staff against mistakes or negligence. The wording is not specific to the travel industry.

pro poor tourism Tourism strategy which has the objective of poverty reduction.

profile system *See* customer profile.

program A computer program comprises the instructions (software) directing a computer to perform a series of functions. The functional specification details what a particular program or series of programs does for the end user.

programming language *See* computer programming language.

projection *See* map projection.

PROM Programmable read-only memory. *See* computer memory.

promenade *See* deck.

promotional media The media used by the travel (or any other) industry are divided into two types by the advertising industry. 'Above-the-line advertising' includes those means of promotion which pay commissions to an advertising agency, such as local and national press, television, radio, bus sides and some bingo halls and cinemas. Advertising agencies charge handling fees, if they do not get a commission, on what they call 'Below-the-line promotion', such as point-of-sale merchandising, direct mail, door-to-door leaflet distribution, window displays, exhibition work, incentive schemes, brochure production and exhibitions.

propeller Blades attached to a hub, which by spinning, cause aircraft and ships to move. *See* pitch of propeller.

propensity *See* travel propensity.

property irregularity report *See* PIR.

property management system *See* PMS².

propjet A propeller-driven aircraft for which the motive power is provided by a gas turbine engine. Turboprop is an alternative name for the same type of aircraft engine. *See also* jet aircraft engine.

proportional fares Add-on air fares which are used in combination with other fares to arrive at a through fare. A proportional fare is never for sale on its own.

pro-ration IATA system of dividing revenue from a multi-sector ticket between the airlines involved. When a fare is the sum of sector fares, pro-rating is not necessary. Otherwise revenue is divided in proportion to the relative theoretical sector costs.

protected commission *See* commission protection.

protecting commission When a travel principal agrees to pay commission on bookings which have not come directly from an agent, for example, when a client sends in a booking form direct to a principal which carries an agency stamp; or when the principal cancels a trip, but agrees nevertheless to pay an agent commission, even if the client gets a full refund.

protecting reservation When travel agents cannot book a traveller's requested arrangements, they may place the traveller's name on a waiting list. However, in case cancellations of other travellers do not result in a firm booking, the traveller's arrangements are protected, by also making firm alternative arrangements. Official IATA definition is 'a tentative reservation on Member other than one originally preferred by passenger and subject to cancellation or change to definite status on demand of Member holding the tentative reservation in accordance with applicable procedures'.

protection against financial loss for travel arrangements *See* ABTA, ASTA, ATOL, bond, bond replacement scheme *and* escrow account.

provider of tourism services   In this dictionary the wording means any person or organization that satisfies the needs of travellers.

provisional booking   *See* option.

prow   The front end of a water-borne vessel.

PSA[1]   In the USA, Passenger Services Act. *See* cabotage.

PSA[2]   In the UK, the Passenger Shipping Association represents the interests of around 40 car ferry, cruising and scheduled service ship owners operating from and within the UK. One of its major activities is the promotion of sea travel in general and cruising in particular. The PSA is a similar body to the CLIA in North America and Croisimer in France. It is the successor to Ocean Travel Development which was set up in 1958 to foster travel by sea and to simplify and unify shipping procedure and documentation. Now, the emphasis is more parochial, promotion of travel by sea to travel agents and their training; the latter being undertaken by PSARA, which functions as a separate PSA department. The Cruise Information Service provides agents with advice. *See* www.cruiseinformationservice.co.uk For PSARA *see* www.psa-psara.org

PSARA   Passenger Shipping Association for Retail Agents. UK organization controlled by PSA concerned with training of and promotion to British travel agents in the cruising, shipping and ferry markets.

PSC   Passenger Services Conference of IATA.

PSCSG   Passenger Services Conference Steering Group of IATA.

pseudo city code   The unique GDS reference, usually of five alphanumeric characters given to every travel agency.

pseudo PNR or reservation   An airline CRS travel booking with no air sectors.

PSR[1]   Passenger sales return, which is completed by a travel agent to report sales; the return is accompanied by ticket counterfoils and a remittance less commission and other credits.

PSR[2]   Passenger Service Representative is the North American term for an airline or airport employee attending to special needs such as taking wheelchair-bound passengers through passport control and security and boarding them on the plane, or the reverse process.

PSR[3]   Passenger space ratio (PSR) is the gross registered tonnage (GRT) of a vessel divided by the passenger capacity. *See also* ship density.

PSS   British Telecom's Packet Switch System, a fast method of communicating data through a network. The data put in at a terminal are broken up into small parts or packets. Computers control how those data are routed (switched) to arrive at their final destination, where the information is reassembled into its original sequence and format.

PST   *See* rail Private Settlement Tickets.

PSTA   Philippine Society of Travel Agents.

PSV   Public Service Vehicle licensed to carry members of the public; PSV Operators – a UK consortium of major private enterprise coach companies operating scheduled express and tour services.

psychocentric tourist   The opposite of the adventurous allocentric tourist. The psychocentric seeks familiarity, hence the Costa Brava, Spain, and advertisements 'Tea like mother makes'. Such a tourist is less likely to arrange independent travel and more likely to book through a travel agent.

PTA   Prepaid ticket advice. The notification by telephone, teletype, commercial cable, telegram, telex or mail, that a person in one city has paid for transportation for another person, usually in a different city from that in which the fare was paid if the PTA is initiated by an agent, only that agent is entitled to full commission. *See* handling fees.

PTM   Passenger traffic manager. An obsolescent North American term for a company travel manager.

PTRC   Planning and Transport Research and Computing in the UK.

PTTA   Phillipine Travel Agencies Association; part of National Travel Association composed of travel agencies, tour operators, hotels, airlines, restaurants etc. *See* www.natas.com.org

PU   Pricing unit. *See* IATA fare construction system.

public protection against financial loss for travel arrangements   *See* ABTA, ASTA, ATOL, bond, bond replacement scheme *and* escrow account.

public transport   In the UK defined in The Transport Act 1985 section 63(10) as 'those services on which members of the public rely for getting from place to place when not relying on their own private transport'. This section of the Act includes school transport but excludes excursions and tours. In section 19, Minibus Permit operations are excluded unless they are provided mainly or wholly to meet the needs of the elderly and disabled. Registered local bus services, express coaches, trains, ferries and taxis are all included. But Public Service Vehicles (PSVs) booked for private hire are excluded along with excursions and tours. In the USA, public transport is known as transit – *see* transit.

Puerto Rico Tourism *See* www.goto puertorico.com

pull factor *See* tourism pull and push factors.

Pullman A railroad company providing sleeper and seating equipment at a superior standard for which a supplement is payable. American equivalent is a parlour car. In the UK, the term is usually applied to a de luxe rail carriage with meal service at all seats. Named after an American, George Mortimer Pullman, the first Pullman service travelled from Chicago in 1858. The concept came to Europe on 21 March 1874, when four Pullman carriages travelled from St Pancras station, London to Bedford.

Pullman berth An upper berth, pulled out and folded back into the wall when not in use.

punt A small narrow boat with a flat bottom; although ideal for travel in marshy areas where there is little water depth, punting has become a leisure activity, impelling the boat with a pole rather than paddles or oars.

purser The senior officer on a passenger ship responsible for passenger handling.

push factor *See* tourism pull and push factors.

PVP Personal Vacation Planner; in the USA, a person working for a transportation company such as a cruise line, selling direct to customers, bypassing travel agents.

Q

QAR Quick access flight data recorder (aviation term).

Qatar Tourism Authority *See* www.qatartourism.gov.qa

QC aircraft Quick change aircraft. Aircraft easily convertible between passenger and freight carrying. Usually castors on the floor facilitate the removal of sections of seats, enabling the loading of cargo of the main cabin deck to be undertaken quickly within 1–2 h.

QDM Magnetic bearing or heading, zero wind (aviation term).

QEC Quick exchange kit (aviation term).

QECU Quick exchange kit unit (aviation term).

QFE Airfield barometric pressure (aviation term).

QFU Runway orientation (aviation term).

QGH Letdown procedure using very high frequency direction finding (aviation term).

QNE Landing altimeter setting (aviation term).

QNH Mean sea level barometric pressure (aviation term).

QRE Term not usually used outside North America referring to either of the *Quick Reference Editions* of the *OAG*.

QSAT Quiet supersonic aircraft technology (aviation term).

QTE True bearing (aviation term).

qualifications for UK travel staff *See* City and Guilds of London Institute *and* Edexcel Foundation. For information *see* www.city-and-guilds.co.uk *and* www.edexcel.org.uk, ABTAC *and* ABTOC.

qualifications for US travel staff *See* Institute of Certified Travel Agents of America – www.icta.com

qualifier *See* ARC[1].

Qualiflyer *See* airline alliances.

quality tourism *See* tourism, sustainable.

quarantine Literally, segregation; in the UK applies to the practice of isolating imported animals for 6 months, to ensure that they do not pass on diseases; the main target of this was to prevent rabies becoming established in Britain. Recent legislation allows cats and dogs to be vaccinated against rabies; they can then be taken in and out of the UK without quarantine. For full details access the UK Ministry of Agriculture Fisheries and Food (MAFF) Internet site at www.maff.gov.uk/animals/quarantine A summary of the relaxed rules, known as the Pets Travel Scheme (PETS), allowing quarantine exception now follows.

Countries to which PETS applies are: Ascension Island; Andorra; Austria; Australia; Barbados; Bermuda; Belgium; Cyprus; Denmark; Falkland Islands; Finland; France; Germany; Gibraltar; Greece; Hawaii; Iceland; Italy; Japan; Lichtenstein; Luxembourg; Malta; Monaco; Montserrat; The Netherlands; Norway; New Caledonia; New Zealand; Portugal; San Marino; St Helena; Singapore; Spain; Sweden; Switzerland; Vanuatu; and The Vatican.

To gain entry to the UK, the cat or dog concerned must:

- have been resident in one of the above countries for at least 6 months
- be identifiable by implanting an electronic chip (microchip)
- be vaccinated against rabies with an inactivated vaccine (booster vaccination is also required)
- be blood-tested at an approved MAFF laboratory, to prove effective protection against rabies, at least 6 months before entry to the UK
- be given a health certificate, recording all the above mentioned details. This certificate has become known in the UK as a 'pet passport'
- be treated against a range of other infections not present in the UK
- have a residency certificate declaring that the animal has not been outside any of the above-named countries within the previous 6 months.

Apart from the above, the scheme is limited to certain defined sea, rail and air routes into the UK.

Although EU rules introducing a 'pet passport' were agreed in 2003, most EU member states were not ready to implement this new system by the legislated deadline of 3 July 2004. As a temporary solution, the new system and the old will operate in parallel. This means that EU member states will have to allow the entry of pets complying with either the new rules or with existing national rules. This transitional measure, which also applies for pets coming from outside the EU, initially planned to last until 1 October 2004 has been extended. For details *see* www.europa.eu.int./comm/food/animal/ liveanimals/pets

quay A ship's berth, dock or pier.

queen room A room containing a bed of queen size.

queen-size bed A very large double bed; hotel groups vary concerning size. S. Medlik in his *Dictionary of Travel and Tourism* suggests at least 5 ft × 6.5 ft as distinct from a king-size bed, 6 ft × 6.5 ft.

Quest Was name of the Memory Computer (UK) Limited travel agency computerized data accounting and ticketing system.

queue Common usage of the term means simply a line of people waiting for a purpose, perhaps to board a bus or check-in for a flight. In airline computer jargon, the term applies to making a booking accessible by a particular location's terminals. Sending a message to an agency's queue functioned as an electronic messaging system, many years before the general use of e-mail in commerce. For example, when a requested flight, wait-listed by an agent in an airline's computer, becomes available the complete changed booking will start printing out automatically on the printer attached to a Galileo terminal in an agency. If a booking has been made by telephone, the reservation may be queued to an agent's terminal so that it becomes accessible therefrom. With British Airways reservations in the UK this happens automatically. To queue a message to an airline through its computer is to enter a message into a PNR (Passenger Name Record) which is of such a nature that it will automatically result in action.

quick change aircraft *See* QC aircraft.

R

R class   Concorde class (obsolete)

RA¹   Restaurant Association in the UK.

RA²   Resolution advisory (aviation term relating to traffic alert and collision avoidance system).

RAA   Regional Airlines' Association in the USA. *See* www.raa.org

Rabal   International Hotel Code for Sunday at nightfall.

RAC¹   Royal Automobile Club in the UK. This motoring organization, although huge, has only a third as many UK members as the Automobile Association.

RAC²   Used to mean ABTA Retail Agents' Council, at a time when ABTA affairs were governed by two councils, one representing agents, the other, operators. The RAC was renamed the TAC, standing for Travel Agents' Council, in October 1984, then being replaced in April 2000 by a single ABTA Board representing both agents and operators.

Racex   International Hotel Code for Monday at nightfall.

rack card   Instead of placing brochures in the racks lining the walls of a travel agency, a card of similar size may be put in its place, meant to cause customers to ask for the brochure or information from agency staff. In the USA, this may be called a 'teaser'.

rack hotel rates   The ordinary prices that hotels charge and advertise generally, without reduction. Various classes of customer may gain reductions, for example, group rates, corporate rates or contract rates negotiated by an operator or convention, conference or incentive group organizer.

rack railway   A railway situated on steep inclines where the adhesion between rails and train wheels would be insufficient for normal operation. Toothed wheels or cogs, powered by the train engine, work against the rack rail teeth either to power the train up the gradient or reduce the speed in the other direc-

tion. Sometimes called a funicular railway. But a cable-car may also be referred to as a funicular.

racking   *See* brochure racking.

racking policy   *See* brochure racking.

RACP   Revenue Accounting Panel of IATA.

radiative forcing   Global warming or cooling. The change to the energy balance of the earth's atmospheric system expressed in watts per square metre. A positive value implies a net warming and a negative value, net cooling. *See* aircraft emissions *and* transport emissions of CO_2.

radio token block   *See* token block.

Radius   Formerly known as the Woodside Travel Trust, which claims to be the world's largest travel company; it began trading under its new title in March 2000. Radius is composed of 110+ shareholder agencies in more than 70 countries, with over 6000 travel agency locations. It claims an annual sales turnover of US$21 billion *See* www.radiustravel.com

Radok   International Hotel Code for Tuesday at nightfall.

Rafyg   International Hotel Code for Wednesday at nightfall.

Ragub   International Hotel Code for Thursday at nightfall.

Rahiv   International Hotel Code for Friday at nightfall.

rail cards   *See* rail fares in the UK.

Rail Europ Senior   *See* RES.

rail fares in the UK   There are currently over 293 million route and fare combinations; annual sales are around £3.5 bn. Season tickets are available for regular travellers between two stated points for periods of a week, month, 3 months or a year, although these are not sold through travel agents. In the current fares structure, there are first and standard class singles valid for 1 day and open returns valid 1 month. There are savers of varying prices, according to the day and date of travel, valid for

1 month and advance purchase savers, also valid for a month. There are many types of day returns, often particular to an area. Young Persons, Senior Citizen, Family, Forces and Disabled Rail Cards enable holders to receive further discounts. The most successful site for Internet sales of UK rail travel is www.thetrainline.com through which over 15% of UK rail travel is booked.

rail Private Settlement tickets in the UK Coloured green, these differ from the ordinary red paper tickets in that there is an additional line beneath the routing at the ticket head, in which travel clerks must enter the name of a Private Settlement Company involved in a through journey.

rail reservations in the UK Travel agents are able to effect reservations for seats and sleepers. Reservations can normally be made up to about 2 h before the train leaves its first departure point or the night before, for early morning departures. On reservable trains, travellers have a choice of two classes in smoking or non-smoking sections. They can also state whether they wish to be facing or back to direction of travel; in window or gangway seats; in the restaurant car, when available; middle or end coach; airline seats (that is seats in bays of two, all facing in one direction); or individual seats (which are pairs of seats opposite each other, normally only available in first class).

Agents must effect reservations and undertake ticketing through one of two computer systems. Both provide a fully integrated information, reservation, ticketing and accounting system. Elgar, which is also the Eurostar system, is the alternative for agents with Galileo or Sabre GDS, ticketing being through an ATB type printer. AJENTS connects to ATOC's Rail Journey Information System via the Internet and prints credit card sized tickets through a dot matrix printer.

rail season tickets in the UK Seven-day season tickets are available for distances up to around 200 miles and tickets valid for any period from 1 month up to 1 year can be purchased for journeys of any distance in the UK. Season tickets permit unlimited travel between the stations specified or intermediately and are available at a considerable saving over normal tickets. All UK rail travellers with season tickets valid 1 month or longer, also in possession of a photocard, may purchase half-price day return tickets for any journey on Saturdays, Sundays and British Bank Holidays.

rail terminology For full details of trains and services worldwide, Thomas Cook's *European Timetable* or the *Overseas Timetable* should be consulted. In the USA these publications are available through Forsyth Travel Library. The *Lexique Générale des Termes Ferroviaires* lists nearly 100 different types of train. *See also the following entries which often then lead to further terms:* AirTrain, AirTrain JFK, AJENTS, Amtrak, APT, APTIS, ATOC[1], ATOC Private Supplement Tickets, ATP[2], AVE, blue period, BREEV, BREL, BRETA, British Rail, compartment, Britrail Pass, driverless trains, Electra 225, Elgar, EuroCity network, European Rail, European Rail sleeping cars, Eurostar, gauge, Global Price rail tickets, IRO, IRRF, JetTrain, Korridorzuge, LIRR, LRT, LRV, maglev, MANIS, Metroliner, Motorail, NBL, Network Rail, North American train services, pantograph, PIRATES, Pullman, Pullman berth, rack railway, rail fares in the UK, rail reservations in the UK, rail season tickets in the UK, RATP, RENFE, RER, RES, RoadRailer, RSA, RTG, Sejour rail fares, Skyrail, SRA[1], Swiss Holiday Card, TEE, TEN, TGV, TMST, token block, TPWS, train (main entry), Train Describer *and* USA Rail Pass.

railbus A standard bus body mounted on a rail chassis developed jointly by British Rail Engineering and Leyland Bus. Fuel consumption, initial capital and operating costs are all substantially lower than with ordinary trains.

railhead The end of a rail line, at which there are usually intermodal transport connections for travellers.

railpass Rail ticket providing unlimited travel for a specified period on stated parts of a rail network. Class of travel permitted is also designated. Sometimes sale is restricted to non-resident international travellers. Most railways worldwide offer rail passes; to cover all of these is beyond the scope of this dictionary. *See* Britrail Pass, Austrian

Bundesnetzkarten, DB Tourist Card, Nordic Tourist Card, USA Rail Pass *and* Swiss Holiday card as examples. Some non-quoted examples include the 14 days AlaskaPass; 12 days Austrailpass covering Australian rail travel; California Rail Pass; EuroDomino country-by-country passes; 14 days Japan Rail Pass; North America Rail Pass; Polrail and Scanrail.

railroad *See* train.

Railtrack In the UK, following franchising of parts of the former British Rail system, Railtrack became responsible for the track, signalling and other infrastructure. In 2001, following the financial failure of Railtrack, owner of the railway infrastructure in the UK, the Government purchased it from the shareholders and reinstituted a nationalized organization to own and maintain a system on which the franchised TOCs (train operating companies) run their services. This now called Network Rail.

Railtrak Was UK agents' viewdata system, through which British and European rail seats and sleepers were reserved. Superseded by Elgar via GDSs or AJENTS via the Internet.

railway *See* train.

railway track gauge *See* gauge.

Rajob International Hotel Code for Saturday at nightfall.

RAM Random access memory or read and memory.

ramjet *See* jet aircraft engine.

ramp The staircase on wheels used to load and unload an aircraft.

ramp (or apron) Hard surface area off the airport runways, where aircraft are parked for loading, unloading, servicing or any other handling.

ramp agent In North America, a member of airline staff who loads and/or unloads aircraft.

RAMS The Retail Agents' Marketing Service was formed by British Airways to provide UK agents with assistance to run their businesses better. The service ceased in 1982.

Ramyk International Hotel Code for today at nightfall.

random access memory *See* computer memory.

Ranuv International Hotel Code for Sunday at night.

rapid transit system An urban rail network capable of carrying large numbers of passengers around, into and out of a city; the word 'rapid' in the term is relative to the slower speeds of road transport, e.g. BART (Bay Area Rapid Transit) in the San Francisco area.

Rapide[1] Name of fast trains in France, which includes TGV.

Rapide[2] Name of UK National Express non-stop coach services between major cities.

Rapin International Hotel Code for Monday at night.

Raqaf International Hotel Code for Tuesday at night.

RAS[1] Royal Aeronautical Society began in 1866, before the development of heavier-than-air machines. It is regarded as one of the premier organizations of its type in the world. *See* www.raes.org.uk

RAS[2] Route area statistics from IATA.

RASA Radar advisory service available (aviation term).

RASI Regional Airline Service Initiative; set up in 2001 by regional aircraft manufacturers and suppliers to promote the role of regional airlines. Over 90 members operating over 2600 aircraft and carrying around 120m passengers annually. *See* www.regionalairservice.org

RATA Russian Association of Travel Agents.

rate IATA and aviation term for a fare or charge. Hence a joint rate is a fare offered by two or more carriers, while a local or 'on-line' rate only applies to a single carrier. A specified rate appears to be ordinary language wording; but it means a rate agreed at an IATA Traffic Conference.

rate desk An airline's fares section in North America dealing with travel agents or the public; most air fares are now calculated by the fare calculation systems of GDSs. Known as the fare quotation department or section in the UK.

rate, proportional *See* proportional fare.

RATP Régie Autonome des Transports Parisiens, the Paris transport authority.

Ratyz International Hotel Code for Wednesday at night.

Ravup International Hotel Code for Thursday at night.

Rawon International Hotel Code for Friday at night.

Raxab International Hotel Code for Saturday at night.

Razem International Hotel Code for today at night.

RBD Reservations booking designator. Abbreviation normally used in connection with IATA ticketing system.

RCC Rescue coordination centre (aviation term).

RCL Runway centre line (aviation term).

REA Refund exchange authorization. *See* ET/REA.

real time A computer with which an operator at a terminal is in full interactive communication. For example, the reservations systems which travel agents access, automatically updated as bookings are made.

reasons why people travel *See* passenger transport market segmentation.

rebated fares for travel agents *See* AD75.

rebating US term for agents reducing the selling price of travel arrangements by giving customers part of the commission earned. During autumn 2004, US cruise lines were restricting the level of discounts their agents could advertise publicly. Rebating in the cruise market has been facilitated by the high commissions paid, 18% or more for the major agencies.

receive only Pertaining to a terminal device having a printing or display mechanism but no means of transmission, e.g. ticket printer.

receiving agent US term for incoming tourism handler. *See* ground handler.

receiving member Official IATA definition is the member on whose flight a passenger is to be carried from an interline point or gap.

reception The area, desk or counter in a hotel providing the main interface between guests and the hotel and its staff. The employees working in this part of a hotel's front office operation are known as receptionists. The many functions normally carried out by reception include: welcoming arriving guests and checking them in (registration card completion and provision of key or key card); selling hotel rooms to those who arrive without a reservation; providing information (sometimes partly handled by the head porter/bell captain and their staff); handling complaints and problems; providing security services such as a hotel safety deposit box; accessing and printing out guest's bills on departure and collecting payment.

receptionist *See* reception.

receptive operator North American term for an incoming tour operator, specializing in arranging tours and holidays within their own country for foreign travellers. *See* BITOA, handling agent *and* tour operator.

receptive services agent US term for incoming tourism handler. *See* ground handler.

reclining seat A seat in a mode of transport which is not fixed in a single upright position, but may be adjusted by tilting back, to suit the comfort of a traveller. The extent to which this can be allowed without discomfort to the passenger behind depends on the distance between seats (pitch). In 2001, British Airways launched the first fully reclining air seat for first- and business-class passengers on certain long-haul routes, which will adjust to a fully horizontal position. The seating space taken up justifies the premium fare that must be charged.

reconfirmation Requirement that air travellers notify their intention to use the space reserved for the next leg of their journey. Rules do not apply to air journeys entirely within Europe. Passengers who break their journey at any point for more than 72 h may be required to reconfirm their intention to use their next reservation. A notice on air tickets points out that failure to reconfirm will result in next and any subsequent reservations being cancelled. Some airlines make reconfirmation regulations more strict, e.g. Air Canada, within Canada or continental USA, require reconfirmation if the break of journey is more than 6 h.

recreation *See* leisure.

recreational vehicle *See* RV.

Red Card Club Name of United Airline's Frequent Flyers Club. *See* FFP (frequent flyer programme).

Red Period Name given to the peak, heavy traffic times on French railways, when higher prices apply.

red-eye flight Vaguely means any night time or early morning flight; but is particularly applied to transatlantic flights which arrive at their destination around breakfast time.

reduced fares   *See* fare reductions.

reduced fares for travel agents   *See* AD75.

referral   In travel retailing, the act of making a booking for a client, arranging for them to pay directly to the provider of the travel service concerned. The 'referral' voucher identifies the customer and the agent. Many large hotel chains guarantee that they will pay referral commissions, while some car rental companies have printed referral vouchers. Ordinary usage of the word is merely making a recommendation concerning a particular travel service.

referral agency   A US travel agency doing much of its business from introductions from outside representatives. *See* card mill.

refuelling charge   Cars are rented with a full tank of petrol (gasoline). Most car rental agreements require that the vehicle be returned with a full tank; upon return, the hirer is charged for the fuel required to top up the tank.

refuelling stop   Aircraft cannot always refuel at airports where passengers are being landed or embarked. This may be due to non-availability of fuel, its high price, the high altitude necessitating take-off with a low weight of fuel, or other reasons. If insufficient aviation fuel has been taken on board to complete the journey to the next scheduled arrival point, a refuelling stop must be made. Passengers cannot normally leave the flight or commence it at this point, although in some countries, safety regulations demand that all passengers leave the plane and wait in a transit lounge until refuelling is complete.

refund   Official IATA definition is the repayment to the purchaser of all or a portion of a fare, rate, or charge for unused carriage or service.

regional airline (or carrier)   Small airline operating between secondary or tertiary airports in a given area. This definition is purposefully vague, because general usage of the concept is wide-ranging and imprecise; although the North American equivalent 'commuter airline' is more specific, this term is obsolescent. For example, the UK publication which used to be called *Commuter Airline World* is now called *Regional Airline World* while the US trade body noted in the next but one entry has also changed its name. *See* commuter airline. The US DOT has defined airlines with annual revenues of US$100 million to US$1 billion as national carriers, while those with revenues of less than US$100 million are categorized as regional carriers, regardless of the nature of an airline's operations. Agreements in the USA between regional airlines providing a feeder service to major hubs and one or more major airlines operating from that hub, known as scope clauses, limit the number of aircraft that may be flown by the regional airline and seating capacity, usually to below 50 or 70 seats. This has led to a definition of a regional airline in the USA as a carrier which only operates planes of 70 seat capacity or less. In Europe, the emergence of low cost carriers and extensions to longer routes by former regional airlines has resulted in there being no reliable definition of the term. *See* scope clause.

Regional Airline Service Initiative   Set up in 2001 by regional aircraft manufacturers and suppliers to promote the role of regional airlines. *See* www.regionalairservice.org

Regional Airlines Association   US association of regional airlines; for more information *see* www.raa.org

Regional Tourism Association of Southern Africa   *See* RETOSA.

Regional Tourist Board   An organization responsible for the maintenance and development of tourism in a specified area. Business models vary worldwide. Often RTBs are entirely state funded and are statutory bodies. Sometimes they may be wholly or partly travel industry funded. They may be entirely under the control of national tourism authorities or partly or wholly autonomous.

Regional Tourist Boards in England   At the time of writing many Tourist Boards were being wound up, their functions being operated through RDAs (Regional Development Agencies). In England www.visitengland.com   VisitEngland's tourism partners are: East of England TB covering Bedfordshire, Cambridgeshire, Essex, Hertfordshire, Norfolk and Suffolk   www.eetb.org.uk   ;   East Midlands Tourism covering Derbyshire, Leicestershire, Lincolnshire, Northamptonshire, Nottinghamshire and Rutland www.emda.org.uk ; Heart of England Tourism including the Black Country and Peak District, covering Birmingham, Herefordshire, Shropshire, Staffordshire, Warwickshire, West Midlands and Worcestershire www.visitheartofengland.com ; VisitLondon covering the Greater London Area www.visitlondon.com ; North East Tourism covering County Durham, Northumberland, Tyne and Wear and the Tees Valley www.visitnorthumbria.com ; Northwest Development Agency covering Cheshire, Cumbria, Greater Manchester, Lancashire, Liverpool and Merseyside www.nwda.co.uk ; South West Tourism covering Bath, Bristol, Cornwall and the Isles of Scilly, Devon, Dorset, Gloucestershire and the Cotswolds, Somerset and Wiltshire www.swtourism.co.uk ; Tourism South East covering Berkshire, Buckinghamshire, East Sussex, Hampshire, Isle of Wight, Kent, Oxfordshire, Surrey and West Sussex www.tourismse.com ; Yorkshire TB covering Northern Lincolnshire and Yorkshire www.ytb.org.uk

Regional Tourist Boards in Scotland In Scotland www.visitscotland.com Regional Boards in their present form are to be scrapped from 2005, with all tourism coming under the direct control of the Scottish Executive through VisitScotland. The current Regional Tourist Boards are: Ayrshire and Arran www.ayrshire-arran.com ; Dumfries and Galloway www.visit-dumfries-and-galloway.co.uk ; Scottish Borders www.scot-borders.co.uk ; Edinburgh and Lothians www.edinburgh.org ; Greater Glasgow and Clyde Valley www.seeglasgow.com ; Argyle, The Isles, Loch Lomond, Stirling and the Trossachs www.visitscottishheartlands.com ; Perthshire www.perthshire.co.uk ; Angus and Dundee www.angusanddundee.co.uk ; Kingdom of Fife www.standrews.com/fife ; Aberdeen and Grampian www.castlesandwhisky.com ; Highlands of Scotland www.visithighlands.com ; Shetland www.visitshetland.com ; Orkney www.visitorkney.com ; The Western Isles www.visithebrides.com

Regional Tourist Boards in Wales In Wales www.visitwales.com or www.wtbonline.gov.uk Four Regional Tourism Partnerships were set up in 2002: North Wales www.tpnw.org ; Mid Wales www.tpmw.org ; South West Wales www.swwtp.org and South East Wales www.capitalregiontourism.org

register Seamen often use the term to describe the tonnage of a ship. But it is strictly applied to a document fully describing a ship just like the logbook of a car. Ships are often registered in countries other than those from which they are run; the practice is known as operating under 'flags of convenience'. *See* hotel register.

registered baggage Luggage handed to the railways at certain long-distance terminals and ports for through transportation to and from European destinations. Accompanied by the passenger on the same train, yet not the traveller's responsibility until collected on arrival.

registered-traveller database Registered Traveler Smartcards in the USA contain a fingerprint and iris scan. Pilot check-in programmes are currently ongoing at Boston's Logan airport, Minneapolis, Houston and Los Angeles. *See* trusted travelers.

regular body aircraft Jet aircraft with a fuselage diameter less than 200 in., with propulsion by turbine engines with a thrust of less than 30,000 lb per engine unit, e.g. Boeing 707 or 727.

regulation ticket UK term for a ticket that 'regulates', in other words, controls the number of passengers on a train or ship, so that they are restricted to the capacity available. Regulation tickets are permissions to travel, but the holder *must* also have an ordinary travel ticket. Particular seats are not allocated in connection with regulation tickets.

REIL Runway end identifier lights (aviation term).

reintermediation *See* intermediation.

reissue Has a particular air ticketing meaning. Instead of paying for a new ticket and claiming a refund on the old ticket upon return home, in most circumstances involving a voluntary or involuntary change of a passengers itinerary, a new ticket can issued in lieu of the old one. The new ticket may involve an extra payment.

remote parking In the UK refers to 'off-airport' car parking facilities with shuttle bus services to and from the airport terminals. Such facilities are lower in cost than 'on-airport' parking. In the USA may refer to the practice of embarking and disembarking air passengers remote from terminal buildings, the runways or built 'stands'. Steps are wheeled to the aircraft and passengers travel to the terminal by coach or bus.

remote ticketing   *See* STP (satellite ticket printer).

REN   Refund Exchange Notice. A US ARC document, the name of which is self-explanatory.

RENFE   Red Nacional de Ferrocarriles Españoles, the Spanish national rail system.

rent-a-car   *See* car rental.

rent-a-plate   *See* ARC[1].

rep or **representative**   A sales representative of a travel principal such as an airline, shipping, car rental, hotel, coach or bus operator. Bigger companies employ merchandizing staff to set up window and point-of-sale displays and to deliver brochures. Smaller organizations in the travel industry may ask their reps to undertake these activities as well as persuading an agent to sell more of their services instead of their competitors' alternatives. Whereas, in the 1960s travel industry sales representatives often made courtesy calls, they are currently required to undertake hard-selling activities with the objective of meeting specified sales targets for their areas. Reps are normally given company cars and reimbursement of out-of-pocket expenses in addition to salary and bonus scheme dependent upon results. *See also* hotel representation, local representative *and* tour operator's representative.

repatriation   Passenger transport carriers have to agree to 'repatriate', in other words, bring back to the country where the passenger's journey started, anyone refused entry. Under Package Holiday legislation enacted within the EC in Europe, tour operators must lodge a bond with the authorities and/or or be insured against the possibility of bankruptcy. The bond or insurance money can then be used to repatriate clients if their operator fails while they are abroad. Travel insurance policies usually cover the cost of repatriation following illness or accident.

request for proposal   *See* RFP, *also see list of 70 other business travel related entries which follows corporate travel contracts, some of which lead to further entries.*

RER   Reseau Express Regionale, the cross-Paris commuter express rail network.

rerouting   Official IATA definition is a change of route, fare, carrier, type of aircraft, class of service, flight or validity from that originally provided in the appropriate transportation document.

RES   Rail Europ Senior is an international rail travel facility available to people over 60 years of age, who are nationals of the 19 European participating railways. Cardholders gain reductions of between 30% and 50%. RES cards, which are valid for 1 year, can only be purchased by holders of a valid national senior citizens railcard. For example, in the UK, a holder of a Senior Railcard could obtain cheap international rail travel by purchasing a £5 RES card. Participating countries are: Austria, Belgium, Denmark, Eire, Finland, France, Germany, Greece, Hungary, Italy, Luxembourg, The Netherlands, Northern Ireland, Norway, Portugal, Spain, Sweden, Switzerland, the UK and the states formerly known as Yugoslavia.

Res2000   *See* car ferry CRSs in the UK.

ResCo   A regional computerized hotel reservation service, owned by Cable and Wireless.

RESCOM   Reservations committee of IATA.

reservation   The term 'reservation' implies that a seat, space, accommodation or other service has been sold by a provider of travel services to a traveller on a definite basis, often facilitated by an intermediary. The official IATA definition is the allotment in advance of seating or sleeping accommodation for a passenger or of space or weight capacity for baggage. Reservation may be the act of making a booking or the arrangement itself. *See* bump, denied boarding compensation *and* no-show.

Reservation Service Provider number   *See* RSP.

reservations booking designator   *See* RBD.

reservations systems   Databases in which records are maintained of space availability and bookings for a mode of transport, hospitality facility and entertainment and sporting venues and events etc. Although such systems are normally electronic, they are not so by definition. *See* airline reservations systems, car ferry CRSs in the UK, CRS, tour operators' reservation systems *and* viewdata.

Reservatron Sheraton Hotel's international information and computer reservation system.

reserve *See* game park.

Reservision Formerly name of Datasolve's computerized reservation and accounting system for British tour operators. Holiday Club International (Pontins), who were the first company to use this system following its introduction in 1977, used the name Reservision as their own system name, but had no proprietary rights to it.

residence[1] Some air fares are restricted, for example, to UK or US residents. But residence may mean anything from living in a country for 3 months to permanent domicile. Air fares rules need to be checked.

residence[2] In Europe, but not in the UK, is an aparthotel, or apartment complex.

resident Official IATA definition is a person normally living in a country, whether a national or not.

resort It is important to note the context in which this word is used. Generally, it is a vacation area, place or town with various leisure facilities; e.g. a mountain resort, spa resort or a seaside resort. But the word is used in the USA to describe a large-scale hotel and leisure complex, and often, now, the word merely indicates a hotel with extensive grounds and facilities. A *resort condominium* means a block of separate apartments in a North American resort complex. In *Tourism Principles and Practice* (2nd edn) by Cooper, Fletcher, Gilbert, Shepherd and Wanhill, the definition offered is preferred to that in other textbooks, 'a place that attracts large numbers of tourists and that tourism endows with special characteristics, so that the revenue produced by tourism plays an important role in its existence'.

resort hotel Usage may merely mean a hotel situated in a particular resort. But often the term means a hotel complex including so many tourism facilities that it is a vacation resort in its own right. Readers may be familiar with a large number of such locations throughout the USA but the term now has general application. For example, the largest resort hotel complex in Europe is Disneyland in Paris, offering around 6000 rooms. Club Méditerranée operates over 100 resort hotels worldwide. UK facilities described earlier in this dictionary as 'holiday centres', operated by companies such as Butlins, Centre Parcs, Haven, Pontins and Warners may now referred to as resort hotels.

resources for teaching tourism in the UK *See* Higher Education Academy Network for Hospitality, Leisure, Sport and Tourism.

responsible tourism *See* tourism, alternative.

restaurant car The dining car. The carriage in a train where meals are served at tables.

restaurant service types *See* silver service for comparisons between this and a carvery, French service, family service and table or plated service.

Restaurateurs Association of Great Britain Trade association looking after the interests of independent restaurateurs in the UK.

Restricted Access Location An ARC agency that is not physically open to the public. US agents wishing to reclassify to this type will find a form at www.arccorp.co./forms/aas/cvr603.pdf

ResWeb *See* car ferry CRSs in the UK.

RET Rapid exit taxiway (aviation term).

Retailers' Fund Set up by ABTA to protect members of the public from financial loss, should a travel agent go out of business. During 1984, name changed to Travel Agents' Fund.

retention forecast Prediction of the number of travellers who will cancel their booking before departure. Scheduled airlines sell premium tickets on the basis of full refunds being available; consequently there are high cancellation and no-show levels. To end up with satisfactory load factors, the 'space control' and 'yield management' departments must push up occupancy levels by selling more seats than are actually available. When retention forecasts are wrong, overbooking situations arise. *See* bump *and* denied boarding compensation. Similar activities take place throughout the travel industry in respect of modes of transport, cruising and package tour operation.

RETOSA Regional Tourism Organisation of Southern Africa, responsible for the marketing and promotion of the 14 countries of Southern Africa. *See* www.retosa.org

return journey Simplistically, means a trip to a place and back to the point of origin; but there are technical travel meanings; for some examples *see* open-jaw, round trip *and* IATA fare construction system.

return subjourney *See* IATA fare construction system.

Reunion Clubs British Airways formed the clubs in the 1970s as a UK marketing device to encourage more VFR travel and facilitate the journeys of first-time or infrequent long-haul travellers. The AFRC, the Australian Family Reunion Club, is owned by British Airways and Qantas; NZRC, New Zealand Reunion Club, is shared by BA and Air New Zealand, while the SARC, South African Reunion Club is owned by BA and SAA. The American and Canadian Reunion Club was closed at the end of 1984.

revalidation sticker An attachment to a flight coupon of an airline ticket indicating a change made to the original reservation.

revenue dilution The situation that occurs when a reduced or promotional travel price is used by travellers other than those at whom the offer was targeted. Term best explained with the aid of a particular example in air transport. The demand for leisure travel is price elastic. Within certain limits, the lower the cost the more passengers would be attracted to use air transport for leisure travel. The business traveller on the other hand, is far less responsive to price change. Discounting the price of air fares will make little difference to the decision on whether an essential commercial journey will be undertaken. Because of this, airlines make it difficult for business travellers to comply with rules they have designed, which nevertheless will not prevent leisure travel. Commonly the need to book a long time in advance prevents business travellers from using many cheap air fares. The extent to which the captive business market nevertheless uses these cheap fares is described as revenue dilution. *See* yield management.

revenue management system *See* yield management.

revenue passenger An income-generating traveller on a mode of transport as distinct from a non-revenue passenger who has not paid a fare, for example, air crew on a rostering movement. Unfortunately, for many reasons, travellers who are receiving complimentary journeys are often given tickets which appear to show that they have paid; numbers of revenue passengers tend to be inflated. *See* non-revenue.

Revenue Passenger Kilometres The number of paying passengers on an aircraft, multiplied by the journey length.

Revenue Passenger Miles The number of paying passengers on an aircraft, multiplied by the journey length.

revenue per available room The actual room rate income for a hotel for a specified period divided by the number of rooms available for sale. Sophisticated computer programs are designed to help hotel sales staff maximize total revenue, balancing occupancy levels against the highest possible room rate achievable each night. Also known as revPAR. *See* yield management.

Revenue Tonne Kilometre *See* RTK.

reverse thrust When the power of an aircraft's jet engine is altered so as to be pushing it backwards, thus acting as a braking mechanism during landing. The extra noise this generates sometimes alarms travellers.

revolving replenishing fund Instead of granting full credit, a travel industry principal or agent can calculate the average monthly account over the previous year and arrange that this sum be paid regularly on a particular day of every month in respect of the previous month's transactions. A regular review ensures that the amount is approximately correct and differences from the actual account are added or subtracted monthly. Sometimes the same wording is applied to this principle, when no credit can be granted, and an account holder is required to pay the monthly sum in advance of expenditure.

REVPAR Sometimes expressed as revPAR. Revenue per available room – the actual room income for a hotel for a specified period divided by the number of rooms available for sale. This is also known as 'room Revpar' to differentiate it from Total Revpar. Some analysts suggest that 'Total Revpar' is the combined total of all hotel revenues divided by the total fixed bedroom stock. This is an oxymoron, defying the fundamental meaning of the acronym Revpar. Sophisticated computer programs are designed to help hotel sales staff maximize revenue, balancing occupancy levels against the highest possible room rate achievable each night. *See* yield management.

RFB Survey of remittances of foreign balances (IATA).

RFF Rescue firefighting ICAO category 7 (aviation term).

RFI Request for information. *A list of 70 other business travel related entries follows* corporate travel contracts, *some of which lead to further entries.*

RFP Request for proposal. When the travel departments of corporations or other organizations request tenders from travel agents, transport and accommodation providers. For US federal government contracts and in other cases, may be expressed as 'invitation for bid'. *A list of 70 other business travel related entries follows* corporate travel contracts, *some of which lead to further entries.*

riblets *See* airframe.

RITA Reservations, Information, Tourist and Accommodation. Was a viewdata system enabling travel agents to book UK resort accommodation accessible through the Datasolve section of Prestel.

RJ Regional jet. *See* regional airline.

RJIS Rail Journey Information System of ATOC in the UK.

RLCE Request level change en route (aviation term).

RMA of GB Recreation Managers' Association of Great Britain was established in 1956 and has around 700 members. *See* www.rma-of-gb.org

RMS Revenue management system. *See* yield management.

RO *See* receive only.

road average density ITEV definition is: 'The average number of vehicles per unit length of roadway over a specified period of time'.

road critical density ITEV definition is: 'The density of traffic when the volume is at the possible capacity on a given roadway. At a density either greater or less than the critical density the volume of traffic will be decreased. Critical density only occurs when all vehicles are moving at or about the optimum speed.'

road design speed ITEV definition is: 'A speed selected for purposes of design and correlation of those features of a highway, such as curvature, super elevation and site distance, upon which the safe operation of vehicles is dependent'.

road passenger drivers' hours *See* drivers' hours in Europe.

road traffic capacity Definition in the *Vocabulary of Traffic Engineering Terms* by J.T. Duff is: 'The maximum number of vehicles which has a reasonable expectation of passing over a given section of a lane or a roadway in one direction or in both directions for a two-lane or three-lane highway, during a given time period under prevailing roadway and traffic conditions'. In *The World Cities* by Peter Hall, it is suggested that on a normal street, each traffic lane could carry around 1300 persons an hour, based on an average of 1.75 persons per car. On an urban motorway, the figure rises to around 3200 in each traffic lane. There will be substantial variation from these figures, dependent upon the mix of vehicle types. A medium-sized lorry might count as two cars, while a bus, coach or heavy lorry might count as three or more cars from the point of view of a capacity calculation. Nevertheless, a motorway carrying only coaches would carry a great deal more than 3200 people an hour.

RoadRailer A semi-trailer with both road and rail rear wheels, so that it can run on rail track or road. For rail operation, roadrailers have to be capable of grouping many units together, and suitable for independent operation on roads.

robot technology Software that systematically accesses travel-provider web and other databases collecting and collating up-to-date fares. Also called bots or spiders. *A list of 70 other business travel related entries follows* corporate travel contracts, *some of which lead to further entries.*

Rocare Name of airline sleeper seats used in first class by Air New Zealand.

ROE   Rate of Exchange. The abbreviation is commonly used on air tickets.

roll (of a ship)   *See* stabilizers.

roll on/roll off   *See* car ferry.

rollawaybed   A hotel guest bed that can be moved easily between rooms, in North America. Some hotels call this a 'roll away bed'. Moreover, there is variation in what is meant. Some hotels designate a child's cot as a rollaway while others mean an adult bed.

Romanian National Tourist Office   *See* www.romaniatravel.com *and* www.romaniatourism.com

Ronda   Name of Iberia in-flight magazine.

room count   How much of a hotel's accommodation has been sold for a particular night; advance knowledge of this may instigate corrective action. *See* yield management.

room inventory   *See* inventory.

room keys   *See* keycard.

room layout   *See* meeting room set-up.

room night   *See* bed-night.

room rates   *See* 'hotel statistics' worldwide for average rates *and* 'pricing of hotel rooms' for calculation methods and rate management techniques.

room service   Usually refers to the delivery of food or beverages to a hotel room but can refer to any services that a hotel offers direct to the room.

room set-up   *See* meeting room set-up.

roomette   In North America, a sleeping compartment including a toilet, on a train.

rooming house   US term for a private house with furnished rooms to rent.

rooming list   The list a tour operator sends to a hotel detailing the clients they are sending for a particular arrival date and naming, where appropriate, individual persons to whom particular rooms are to be allocated.

Roomwatch   Formerly the name of the English Tourist Board's electronic room booking system for travel agents, enabling them to make bookings direct from their office terminals.

ro-ro   Roll on/roll off. *See* car ferry.

rotation   Several travel industry meanings, apart from the obvious ordinary connotation. During a coach tour, participants often rotate each day, so that they move between the more attractive window seats, and less comfortable seats over wheels. In a back-to-back air charter operation, a rotation is one complete return journey.

ROTO   Roll out and turn off (aviation term).

Round the World   *See* RTW.

round trip   A return journey. Official IATA definition is: (i) travel from one point to another and return by the same air route used outbound whether or not the fares outbound and inbound be the same; or (ii) travel from one point to another and return by an air route different from that used outbound for which the same normal, through one-way fare is established.

rounding-up unit   Under IATA fare construction rules, fares in each currency may only be expressed in minimum steps. For example, a fare calculated and sold in UK pounds, euros or US dollars must be rounded up or down to the nearest whole pound, euro or dollar.

route assignment   *See* transport modelling.

route deal   Also known as strategic airline deal. An offer by a transport provider (usually an airline) to agents and corporate customers of reduced rates or incentive commission in return for agreement to place most or all of their business on the route concerned with that airline. An agency or company has bargaining power if it provides heavy traffic on a route where an airline seeks to expand its market share. Analysis now suggests that it is often cheaper for corporations to switch from route airline deals to dynamic purchasing of the lowest logical fare at the point of service. Information systems are becoming more effective at trawling through airline sites to locate lowest available fares, often substantial savings over a route deal. Typical deal types may involve front end deals and/or back end rebates; *see entries under these headings. A list of 70 other business travel related entries follows* corporate travel contracts, *some of which lead to further entries.*

route, direct   Official IATA definition is the shortest route operated between two points.

route, indirect   Official IATA definition is any other route other than the direct route operated between two points.

route, through Official IATA definition is the total route from point of departure to point of destination.

routing Many fares are restricted to travel in a particular global direction within a certain area. *See* individual entries for AP, EH, PO etc. Airline manuals and timetables show complete routings for every flight. Thus, although a timetable may only show departure and arrival times between two points, the routing section may show that the flights actually touch down at a number of other airports en route.

rowing boat A small boat propelled by oars.

Royal Aeronautical Society *See* RAS¹.

Royal Automobile Club *See* RAC¹.

Royal Viking Courtesy Card Name of Scandinavian Airlines System's Frequent Flyer Club, membership of which is free, but by invitation only. *See* FFP (frequent flyer programme).

RPC Restrictive Practices Court. *See* Stabiliser for effect on UK travel industry.

RPK Revenue Passenger Kilometres. The number of passengers on an aircraft, multiplied by the journey length.

RPM Revenue Passenger Miles. The number of passengers on an aircraft, multiplied by the journey length.

RPS Regional pressure setting (aviation term).

RQ Request. Abbreviation is used to designate any items requested but not yet confirmed, whether it be car hire, accommodation or a flight. The same letters, however, designate a flight or class that has been wait-listed, so that an important distinction needs to be understood by travel clerks between items requested which are expected to be confirmed, and items requested where there is some doubt from the outset.

RS Registered supplier (IATA).

RS 232 In theory, a worldwide standard for communication between computers and peripherals, such as printers, keyboards etc. While the shape of the plug and position of the pins is standard, unfortunately, it is often necessary to specify the equipment being joined together so that the lead is correctly wired, quite apart from the basic compatibility of the two pieces of equipment which may necessitate intervention of a software driver.

RSA¹ Railway Study Association in the UK.

RSA² Receptive Services Association in Spain. *See* www.rasan.com

RSC Return subjourney. *See* IATA fare construction system.

RSP Reservation Service Provider number in the USA. Continental Airlines and Northwest Airlines require US domestic air booking locations which are not ARC accredited, but using a GDS, to obtain an RSP (Reservation Service Provider) number from ARC. This applies to all non-ARC users of a GDS outside contractors and corporate customers. In lieu of an RSP number, non-accredited international booking locations located outside the USA, Puerto Rico and US Virgin Islands must obtain a TIDS (Travel Industry Designator Service) number from IATA. Applications via www.arccorp.com/aguaform.htm (US$225 for 3 years) or www.iata.org/tids (US$55).

RSR Route surveillance radar (aviation term).

RT Round Trip; a return journey. Defined by IATA as: 'A return journey'; official IATA definition is: (i) travel from one point to another and return by the same air route used outbound whether or not the fares outbound and inbound be the same; or (ii) travel from one point to another and return by an air route different from that used outbound for which the same normal, through one-way fare is established.

RTCA Radio Technical Commission for Aeronautics.

RTF Radio telephone.

RTG A French Railways (SNCF) train hauled by a gas turbine type of engine, which in some countries, is called a turbo train.

RTK Revenue Tonne Kilometre; the quantity of paid cargo on an aircraft multiplied by the journey length.

RTO Regional Tourist Office or Regional Tourism Organization.

RTPA¹ Restrictive Trade Practices Act 1956 (in the UK). *See* Stabiliser for effect on UK travel industry *and* Appendix II.

RTPA² Was the Rail Travel Promotion Association in the USA, its functions were taken over by Amtrak.

RTW Round the World. There are four basic round-the-world IATA routings, and certain standard construction points, which, regardless of the actual itinerary, will always produce the lowest fare. These construction points are listed in most major airlines' tariff manuals.

Rule 240 US airline rule in the Domestic General Tariff (DGR-1) published by ATPCo covering air passengers' rights in the USA in the event of a schedule irregularity such as a flight delay, cancellation or misconnection or *force majeure* situation. For details of the American laws regarding compensation for 'bumped' passengers *see* US DOT publication *Fly-Rights: A Consumer Guide to Air Travel* on the DOT web site www.dot.gov or www.1travel.com via 'Rules of the Air'.

Rule 240 outlines individual airlines' rules specifying the amenities offered to affected passengers following the involuntary events already stated; but *it does not* cover overbooking. Under Rule 240, passengers may receive pre-paid telephone cards, meals or accommodation and may be able to cancel their trip and receive a full refund. *See* bump, denied boarding compensation *and force majeure.*

run of the house A flat rate at which a hotel agrees to offer any of its rooms to a group regardless of the location of the rooms. Sometimes term also applied to all the standard rooms with similar facilities in a particular hotel.

runway lengths *See* airport runway lengths.

rural house A literal translation of several European languages; it means a holiday cottage in the country.

Russian Federation Tourism Department Part of the Ministry of Economic Development and Trade. *See* www.russiatourism.ru (in the USA www.russia-travel.com)

Russian National Travel Organization Intourist. *See* www.intourist.ru *see also* Russian National Tourist Organization www.russia-travel.com

RV Recreational vehicle such as a caravette or camper van; term mainly used in North America.

RVI Residual value insurance (aviation term).

RVR Runway visual range (aviation term).

RVSM Reduced vertical separation minima (aviation term).

Rwanda Tourism Board *See* www.rwandatourism.com

RWM Round the world minimum. Abbreviation normally used in connection with IATA fare construction system. *See* RTW.

RWY Abbreviation for runway.

ryokan A country hotel or wayside inn in Japan.

S

S & T Shower and toilet, usually refers to ships' cabins with private shower and toilet.

S class In the USA, means Jet, one class or standard service; in Europe applied to various types of discounted fare.

SA¹ Via South Atlantic. *See* routing.

SA² Service available; in a GDS indicates that the required service is active or available.

SA³ Space available.

Sabre (Also known as STIN, Sabre Travel Information Network.) The leading GDS handling over US$70bn travel sales annually. The Sabre® system was the first CRS, an American Airlines investment, installed on two IBM 7090 computers in 1960. The initial effort took 400 man-years costing nearly US$40 million, a huge sum in those days. It took 56 months to prepare and complete functional requirements, program specifications and coding. Sabre was the first reservation system for any mode of transport that combined in a centralized electronic unit the two basic reservation records: passenger name record (PNR) and a seat inventory. But despite this early lead, it was not until May 1976 that its system was made available to US travel agents and 1983 to those outside the USA, at first, in Canada and in 1985, Europe.

Sabre is organized into three main divisions. SabreTravelNetwork is the world's largest GDS network, providing over 60,000 travel agency locations with access to the inventory of airlines, hotels, car rental companies, cruise lines and other travel service providers. It handles half of all airline tickets sold through travel agencies in North America. Travelocity is the world's most popular on-line travel service, handling US$4bn sales annually. Sabre airline solutions provides management tools for every facet of airline operations. The latest passenger management system is called SabreSonic. GetThere corporate self booking tool is a Sabre market leader, used by over 2500 corporations, including over half of Fortune 200 companies. *See* www.sabre.com www.sabreTravelNetwork.com www.travelocity.com *and* www.sabreairlinesolutions.com *also see* CRS, GDS and inside link.

SAC Safety Committee of IATA.

SAD Shared Airline Designator.

safari Originally meant a hunting expedition (in Kiswahili the word simply means journey). Now usually means any leisure trip for the purpose of seeing and/or photographing large animal wildlife. *See* game park.

Safety Assessment Directive (EU) *See* airline safety.

safety deposit box Metal drawer or compartment in a rack behind or adjacent to hotel reception used by guests for safe storage of valuables. Usually there are two locks for each box, one of which is given to the hotel guest renting the box and the other only available to hotel reception staff. Thus, possession of one of the keys will not necessarily gain access to a box, if the person is unknown to reception staff. Various electronic systems are being introduced as alternatives to keys. For example, boxes may be operated with a programmed pin number chosen by the guest.

safety in the air *See* airline safety.

Safety of Life at Sea *See* International Convention for the Safety of Life at Sea (SOLAS).

Saga Class Brand name given by Icelandair to its business class. *See* business class.

SAGTA School and Group Travel Association in the UK. Information available via www.martex.co.uk

SAHARA SITA Airline Hotel Advanced Reservations Automation. The world's airlines hotel booking system available through the GDSs in 154 countries. Is the hotel booking package for the Gets GDS.

SAI   System aided instruction. *See* CAI.

sailing list   A shipping line's timetable. The term is obsolescent; most shipping companies now only refer to their 'timetables'.

sailing permit   Although term is in general usage worldwide, it has a specific meaning in the USA. American residents who are not US citizens must possess an income tax clearance certificate before they may leave the USA.

sailing tickets   Control tickets on certain specified boat services at peak holiday periods, limiting the number of passengers who may board.

sailing time   The time at which a vessel will depart.

SAL   Supplementary approach lighting (aviation term).

sales agency agreement   Official IATA definition is: an Agreement in the form prescribed in Resolution 800b, as may be amended from time to time and includes, where the context so permits, a Supplementary Agreement to the Passenger Sales Agency Agreement in the form prescribed in Resolution 832a. Of course, agency agreements are common worldwide between principals and their agents, setting out the conditions under which an agent may represent a principal, sell products or services and receive remuneration.

sales tour   Has a specific meaning in Germany (Werbefahrt) and some other European countries. An inclusive tour or short package holiday where the focus of the trip is selling something, such as art.

sales tourism multiplier   *See* tourism multiplier.

salon   When sold as hotel accommodation, a living room not used as a bedroom.

saloon deck   *See* deck.

same day visitor   *See* 'internal' and 'international same day visitor' under the heading of 'tourism'.

sampan   General name applied to many types of small boat throughout East Asia. In Chinese waters, a sampan is indistinguishable from a small junk, with traditional matting sails and a raised stern.

SAPHIR   Name of Zurich airport's information system based on a Ferranti UK FIDS.

Saphir   The Belgian agency CRS, associated with Galileo.

SAR¹   Search and rescue.

SAR²   Synthetic aperture radar (aviation term).

SARC   South African Reunion Club. *See* Reunion Clubs.

SATA   South American Tourism Association.

SATCOM   Satellite communications system.

Satellite Account   *See* TSA.

Satellite Ticket Printer   *See* STP.

SATH   Society for Accessible Travel and Hospitality; founded in 1976 as the Society for the Advancement of Travel for the Handicapped in the USA. *See* www.sath.org

SATO   Scheduled Airline Traffic Office. In the USA, airlines are encouraged to set up joint services in government buildings.

Sato Travel   Official United States government departments obtain their travel requirements from this organization owned by many American airlines.

SATOUR   South Africa Tourism. *See* www.satour.org

SATTA   Syrian Association of Tourist and Travel Agents. *See* www.syriatourism.org/travel.htm

saturation tourism   *See* tourism carrying capacity *and* tourism, sustainable.

SATW   Society of American Travel Writers. *See* www.satw.org

saver fares   British Airways brand name for all the discounted air fares they offer.

saver ticket   *See* rail fares in the UK.

savers   *See* rail fares in the UK.

Savia   The Spanish agency CRS, associated with Amadeus.

SAVTL   Syndicat des Agences de Voyages et de Tourisme au Liban.

SB   Service bulletin (aviation term).

SBAC   Society of British Aviation Companies. For more information contact www.sbac.co.uk

SBRO   Sleeping Berth Reservation Office.

SBT   self booking tool. *See* corporate self booking tool.

sc   Self-catering. Provision of facilities enabling travellers to cook for themselves and eat their meals. In effect, usually means an equipped kitchen together with crockery, glassware and cutlery. Hence obvious meanings of self-catering apartment or accommodation, which in North America, are called an efficiency.

SCA Scottish Conference Association.

Scanorama Name of the SAS in-flight magazine.

SCAT 1 Special category 1 (aviation term).

scattershot Official IATA definition is the procedure of handling reservations transactions by dealing with one or more airline offices independently of other airline offices and which results in one or more airline offices not having knowledge of the passenger's complete remaining itinerary including the current status of each remaining segment.

schedule change Official IATA definition is any modification to the operation of a flight which may require passenger notification. This may be a change in arrival or departure times, flight numbers or class of service, frequency of operation or airports served etc. Thus, there is no change when the only factor is conversion to or from Daylight Saving Time, with departure and arrival times remaining the same in terms of local time.

scheduled service or **transport** A series of journeys on a passenger transport mode on a defined route according to a published timetable. The 2003 CEN/European Standard official definition is: 'Transport of travellers on a defined route and according to a timetable'. It can be seen why the definition here suggested for this important term differs from the BSI/CEN standard. The following wording was agreed by ICAO in 1952: 'A scheduled international air service is a series of flights that possesses all the following characteristics. It passes through the air space over the territory of more than one state. It is performed by aircraft for the transport of passengers, mail or cargo, for remuneration, in such a manner that each flight is open for use by members of the public. It is operated, so as to serve traffic between the same two or more points, either according to a published timetable, or with flights so regular or frequent that they constitute a recognisably systematic service.'

schedules Timetables. Because of major seasonal differences in traffic, summer schedules usually start on 1 April and winter timetables extend from 1 November, in the northern hemisphere; the reverse in the South.

schoolroom style seating See meeting room set-up for details of alternative conference and meeting seating plans.

schooner A small fore- and aft-rigged sailing ship which originally, by definition, had two masts; term now often applied to similar vessels with three or four masts. Tour operators to the Indonesia area offer arrangements on board 'Buginese schooners' as a sailing experience.

SCMP Society of Corporate Meeting Professionals in the USA. See www.scmp.org

SCN Stock Control Number.

scope clause Part of a code-sharing or franchise agreement between a regional airline providing a feeder service to major hubs and one or more major airlines operating from that hub. Scope clauses agree a ceiling on the number of aircraft that may be flown by the regional airline and limit seating capacity, usually to below 50 or 70 seats.

Scottish Passenger Agents Association See SPAA.

Scottish Tourist Board See STB.

Scottish Vocational Qualification See SVQ.

SCP Supplemental Compensation Plan. See Warsaw Convention.

SCR Specific commodity rate (aviation term).

Screw Maritime word for a propeller. See propeller.

SDF Simplified directional facility (US aviation term).

SDR Special Drawing Rights were proposed at the beginning of the decade as an international airline currency, to avoid directional fare imbalances; whereby, as currency rates change, fares become different according to the direction of travel. Unfortunately, the world's airlines were not able to agree on the introduction of the SDR for fares, inventing instead Neutral Units of Construction, mistakenly referred to as Neutral Units of Currency in some publications, for fare construction purposes from 1 July 1989. SDRs have, however, become accepted for the purposes of defining airline liability under the Warsaw Convention.

When it was originated, it was defined in terms of gold as being equal to 0.888671 g of fine gold for one US dollar. After many currencies were floated in 1973, the value of the SDR in terms of other currencies began to fluctuate violently. Thus, the system in use today was developed, with the value fluctuating daily according to the movement of the standard basket of 16 currencies belonging to countries which had more than 1% of total world export of goods and services during the 5 years between 1968 and 1972. Each currency is given a weight according to its relative share in the total, although the 33% given to the dollar is to allow for its importance in the international monetary system. The British pound has a weight of 9% in this basket. Unfortunately, there is no longer parity with the dollar, which was the value of an SDR for many years.

sea   The sea covers about 70.92% of the earth's surface, just under 140 million miles^2 (361.7 million km^2). At its deepest, the Mariana Trench, it is 35,840 ft (10,942 m), but averaging around one-third of this. Contains 3.5% salt, although weaker than this around the Arctic and Antarctic and stronger in the Mediterranean.

sea route codes   Two-figure codes written on European Rail tickets between Britain and Europe, indicating the Channel crossings route involved.

sea sickness   *See* motion sickness.

sea view   Much abused term for a room from which a hotel guest can see the sea. Sometimes, this may only be a side sea view, and rarely, the sea can only be seen from the room's balcony.

SeaCat   Hoverspeed's wave-piercing catamaran. *See* WPC for fuller details.

Sealynx   Stena Sealink's wave-piercing catamaran, introduced on their Irish Sea route in 1993.

seamen's fares   Seamen are usually entitled to reduced air fares whether travelling individually or as a group. A shipping company is required to fully detail the ship being joined or from which a crew member is leaving. Discounts vary according to route, nationality of ship's crew and other matters are fully explained in airline tariffs.

seamless connectivity   Facilitation of direct access to a travel service provider through a GDS. This enables any data stored in the provider's computer system to be viewed by agents, such as hotel descriptions and photographs. GDS reservations are made using inventory within the system; but there is not the capacity to store all the data held on the computer systems of the travel service providers. Thus, for example, when requesting full details of a hotel, the GDS may act as a communication system, facilitating access direct into a hotel system.

season tickets   *See* rail fares in the UK.

seasonal rates   Pricing structure allowing for variation for the same service, depending upon the time of the year.

seasons   Travel seasons are times during which demand fluctuates, usually described as low, shoulder or intermediate and high season; thus high season for a winter sports resort will be in the winter, while for the bulbfields area in Holland, it will be the spring. In the USA, low season may be referred to as 'value season'.

seat only   UK term for air charter seat sales without any other facilities actually provided. Wording arose because many countries only allow air travel services to operate to them from the UK as licensed scheduled air services or as inclusive package holidays, usually incorporating an accommodation element and transfers or car hire, as well as an air charter seat. In the case of UK/North America traffic, Advance Booking Charters (*see* separate entry) were agreed between governments to stamp out abuses of the regulations. In Europe, from the UK, 'seat only' air charter seat sales are mainly 'minimum-rated package tours' (*see also* in a separate entry) utilizing the regulations allowing for package holidays to operate between the UK and various countries, providing vouchers for very low grade dormitory, or even non-existent accommodation, together with an air seat, so as to comply with the rules.

 This twisting of the regulations, means that 'seat only' air charter seat sales are competing with scheduled air services on many European routes where there is substantial leisure traffic.

seat pitch   *See* pitch of seat.

seat regulation ticket   *See* regulation ticket.

seat reservation Booking by a traveller of a specified seat on a mode of transport, at a theatre or sporting or other event. Seats for scheduled air passengers are allocated at check-in or, in many cases can be booked in advance from an on-screen seat map available for many flights on GDSs. Travellers can arrange to sit together, choose smoking or non-smoking (in the rare cases where smoking is still allowed) and an aisle or window seat. For other typical examples *see* rail reservations in the UK or *see* IRRF for details of seat reservations on European railways.

seat rotation On a coach tour, some seats are above the wheels, resulting in a less comfortable ride, while other seats may have a restricted view, or the best view. Because of this, it is common for passengers to be moved around the coach, each day or half-day.

seating styles *See* meeting room set-up for details of alternative conference and meeting seatings plans.

SEC Special Event Charter or Security Committee of IATA.

second class Class on a mode of transport is an indicator of service level provided and in respect of a seat, the width, pitch (distance from next seat behind/in front), reclinability and other features concerning comfort. There is such a huge variety of class systems in use on transport worldwide and for categorization of accommodation, that the term is arbitrary, without association with a particular system. Obviously, it is inferior to de luxe and first class and superior to third class.

second sitting On cruise ships, there is often insufficient room in the restaurants for all the passengers to be seated at once. Thus, first and second meal sittings are necessary (some cruise lines refer to these as early or late sittings).

sectional coupons Not all clients want a European rail ticket for a journey starting or terminating in the country in which they are purchasing the ticket. For example, they may be intending to undertake a rail journey following an air sector. Tickets for such point-to-point journeys within Europe are issued on sectional coupons (TCVs). A separate coupon must be issued for travel over the lines of each railway administration involved and the tariff provides the kilometric distance and fare converted to the currency of country of purchase.

sector, segment or leg A sector is, by definition, a portion of an itinerary or journey, which may consist of one or more legs or segments. A leg is the portion of a journey between two consecutive scheduled stops on any particular flight. A segment is that portion of a journey, from a boarding point of a passenger, to a deplaning point on a given flight. Although the passenger may not leave the plane, it may touch down to take on or let off passengers at several points, so that a segment may be made up of a leg or group of legs.

secure electronic transactions *See* SET.

secure flight *See* CAPPS.

security charge or **tax** A tax imposed on air travellers to cover the costs of security measures. With the growth in recent years of international terrorism, transport terminals in general and airports in particular have been forced to install sophisticated equipment and security staff, the costs of which are recovered from passengers.

Sefton Brancker *See* Brancker.

segment *See* sector, segment or leg.

segmentation *See* market segmentation.

Sejour rail fare Reduced-rate European rail fares are available for journeys where the total rail travel in France is at least 1000 km or payment is made for that distance. Travel on both outward and return journeys in France must start on a Tuesday, Wednesday, Thursday or Saturday. In case of overnight journeys, or a break of journey, travel in France started on one of those 4 days may be continued on an unauthorized day. The return journey cannot be started before the sixth day from the date of entry into France, that day included. Sejour fares are available on through journeys to Austria, Italy, Morocco, Portugal, Spain and Switzerland with routings via France, as well as journeys terminating in France. Sometimes called Holiday Return rail fares in English-speaking countries because of the translation of the French term.

SELCAL Selective calling system (aviation term).

Selective Prices Manual *See* SPM. (Now obsolete.)

self booking tool *See* corporate self booking tool.

self-catering *See* sc.

self-drive   The basis on which rented cars are normally hired, with the renter driving the vehicle themself.

self-drive tour   In North America, this term refers to an inclusive holiday by car, whether or not the traveller uses their own car or rents it. In the UK, for those using their own car this is called a motoring holiday. Most inclusive arrangements by car, including car hire, also involve air travel, and so are covered by the wording fly-drive package.

self packaging   Arrangement by travellers themselves of the individual elements of package holidays by booking flights or other travel and accommodation etc., rather than booking through a tour operator which arranges the package and sells it to travellers at an inclusive price. The concept is often mentioned in connection with sourcing and booking travel over the Internet, when it is also known as dynamic packaging; but self packaging is not necessarily an e-tourism concept. *See* IBE (Internet Booking Engine).

self-sale   North American term for tickets supplied by a travel agency to an organization owning the agency or with which the agency is associated. There is no equivalent wording in common use in the UK or in European languages.

self-service airport check-in   *See* CUSS kiosk.

self-service ticketing   Where a person is able to issue a ticket from a machine, without the intervention or assistance of a ticket clerk. Such machines are sited on many rail stations worldwide. Those that issue air tickets are encouraged in some countries and banned in others. The machines may accept payment with coins, currency notes/bills and credit/charge cards. Sometimes called customer ticketing in North America. *See* NCR Skylink.

sell through   When a hotel accepts a reservation, even though the customer's requirements may be fully booked or overbooked for part of the proposed stay. The reservation may be accepted according to the sales policy laid down by the hotel, in order not to lose remunerative business.

selling rate   *See* conversion rate[1].

Senior Citizen RailCard   *See* rail fares in the UK.

senior fares   In North America, this refers to tariffs only available to senior citizens.

SEO   Society of Event Organizers. *See* www.seoevent.co.uk

Serbian National Tourism Organization   *See* www.serbia-tourism.org

series charter   *See* charter.

servi-bar   Suggested in US dictionaries to be European equivalent of mini-bar; usage of the term questionable.

service available   Literally, on a CRS, the travel provider's service requested is available.

service charge/service fee   In hotels and restaurants, typically around 10% may be automatically added to a meal bill; only those with robust constitutions refuse to pay this if service was poor! Fees are now often raised by travel agents for the work they do. Historically, agents advertised 'tickets at airline and station prices'. Indeed, part of the airline commission earned was often rebated to corporate clients. However, zero commissions from airlines have made it necessary for agents to raise charges for services and to demonstrate that their provision adds value to the transaction. In the USA for ASTA members a useful service fee calculation chart is available via www.astanet.com/members/center/re_agency_servicefees.asp For ABTA members, model terms can be found at www.abtamembers.org/legal/agency terms.doc Companies seeking a contract for the supply of travel services need to identify if transaction fees include the provision of these various services, by requiring them to be listed. *A list of 70 other business travel related entries follows* corporate travel contracts, *some of which lead to further entries.*

service complet or **service compris**   French wording in common use worldwide, indicating that service charges are included in the bill. Nevertheless, in a restaurant, people often still leave a gratuity. Service 'non' compris clearly indicates to customers either that they have to leave a gratuity or, more usually, that a standard charge of between 10% and 15% of the bill will be added for service.

Service Plus   Name of Air France's Frequent Flyer Club. Membership is free but by the airline's invitation only. *See* FFP (frequent flyer programme).

servicing airline Official IATA definition is an airline whose system is used to print (or to acquire ticketing data in order to print) neutral tickets, either on its own behalf, or on behalf of other airlines.

servicing airline code Official IATA definition is a four-digit code comprising a three-numeric code plus a check digit of the servicing airline system generating the ticketing transmission. This code is always transmitted by the generating system, either directly or through a third party.

SET Secure electronic transactions. A standard originally developed by Visa and Mastercard to enable Internet purchases using credit cards. This standard has been of particular importance in the development of on-line travel purchasing.

set meal A restaurant menu specifying the food, with choice. *See* alternative meal choices of à la carte and table d'hôte.

set-up *See* meeting room set-up.

Seychelles Tourism *See* www.aspureasitgets.com

SFC Specific fuel consumption (aviation term).

SFU Suitable for upgrade; an entry on an air passenger's computer record made by airline staff in appropriate circumstances which vary greatly between airlines.

SGIT Special Group Inclusive Tour fare. In the UK these low-cost European ITX fares are only available to ATOL-holding tour operators. Groups of at least ten passengers must be contracted and paid for at least 1 month before travel.

SGMP[1] Society of Government Meeting Planners – National Capital Charter; part of the Society of Government Meeting Professionals in the USA. *See* www.sgmpnatcap.org

SGMP[2] Society of Government Meeting Professionals in the USA. *See* www.sgmpkc.org

SHAARP Sabre Hotels Automated Availability and Reservations system. For further details *see* Sabre.

SHAC Small Hotel Advisory Council, set up by the Caribbean Hotel Association.

shakedown cruise *See* inaugural.

shared commissions *See* split commissions.

sharing airline codes *See* code sharing.

sharing airline designators When an airline operates flights on behalf of another airline and uses the latter's standard designator.

shell scheme stand *See* stand.

shells Brochures or brochure covers devoid of copy, but containing artwork, graphics or illustrations, provided to travel organizers to overprint with their arrangements. In North America, sometimes called tour shells.

ship A water-borne craft or vessel. Although often used as an alternative term to boat, the word ship should be reserved for larger ocean-going craft. *See also* barge, bark, barque, barquentine, boat, boatel, cabin cruiser, canoe, car ferry, catamaran, coracle, cutter, dinghy, dory, dugout, gondola[1], hovercraft, junk, kayak, ketch, launch, lifeboat, life raft, liner, lugger, narrowboat, pirogue, prau, rowing boat, sampan, schooner, skipjack, sloop, speedboat, steamship, tender, tramp steamer, trawler, tugboat, umiak, vaporetto, yacht, yawl and zodiac.

ship density Also known as PSR (passenger space ratio). The gross registered tonnage (GRT) of a vessel divided by the passenger capacity. There are ships catering for the popular cruise market where, in order to keep fares as low as possible, it is necessary to carry as many passengers as the ship can comfortably accommodate – these are known as *high-density* ships. A typical example would be a ship of 10,902 GRT carrying 790 passengers. This can be contrasted with another well-known ship of 10,720 GRT, which although of similar tonnage, only carries 400 passengers and is therefore a low-density ship.

The main difference is that low-density ships usually offer more space per passenger which means larger cabins, more deck space, less crowded restaurants and lounges. Generally a greater degree of comfort and service, which is brought about by the likelihood of a higher ratio of crew per passenger. On the most luxurious ships there is a ratio of approximately one crew member for every two passengers carried. An easy way to ascertain the density of a ship is to divide the number of passengers carried into the tonnage. At the time of writing, the largest cruise ship operating is the *Queen Mary 2*, 151,000 GRT which has 2620 berths, giving a density of 57.6. The second largest, *Voyager of the Seas* is 142,000 GRT but has around 3114 berths, a density of 45.6. *Carnival Conquest*, 110 GRT with 2794 berths has a density of 39.4. Growth in ship size has altered cruise passenger's perceptions of what they expect; so the definitions previously suggested, that a ratio of 20 was high density and over 40 low density may not be valid. The above explanation is summarized, with permission, from *ABTA NTB Cruising and Shipping, A Primer for Cotac Level 2*. *See also* passenger space ratio (PSR).

ship of the desert   A camel.

shipping conference   *See* conference[1].

ships' bells   *See* times at sea.

ships' crews by air   *See* seamen's fares.

shipside/outside cabin   A cabin with porthole or window.

shore excursion   An excursion, coach tour or other type of arranged visit ashore during a cruise.

short haul   An intracontinental journey. A loose term which in the UK is applied generally to European journeys as distinct from trips to other continents which are long haul. In North America, local journeys are likely to be designated short haul, but the term has no precise definition. *See* long haul.

short take-off and landing   *See* STOL.

shoulder   *See* shoulder period.

shoulder period   Calendar period between a peak and an off-season, to which a promotional fare or rate often applies, which is lower than peak and higher than off-season.

showroom   Modern term for the theatre on a cruise ship. In the latest vessels these are designed with tiered seating and sophisticated stages, running through many deck levels.

shuttle   A term usually denoting a no-reservation air service, although often used in a general sense for a frequent passenger transport, which may be operating continuously on a circular route or back and forth between two points, such as a bus between airport terminals. In the USA, for example between New York and Boston, 'shuttle' means a very frequent service; disappointed travellers for one flight merely wait for the next one. On some air shuttle services it is possible to pay the fare on board the aircraft.

SI   Special information field in a GDS reservation, used for communicating special requests.

sico bed   US terminology for a bed that folds away into the cupboard or wall, giving more space in a bedroom. Term is not applied to a divan bed, which achieves a similar objective by switching use into a comfortable chair or settee.

SICTA   Standard International Classification of Tourism Activities, prepared by the WTO, adopted by the Ottawa Conference on Travel and Tourism Statistics in June 1991 and approved by the United Nations' Statistical Commission in 1993.

SID   Standard instrument departure (aviation term).

side trip   In general terms, it is any leg or sector (usually return) of a travel itinerary that is off the main continuous routing. So that if a passenger is travelling A to B to C but is also travelling B to X and back to B before continuing B to C, then the B/X sector is part of a side trip. Side trips, in air fare construction, are charged extra. In connection with an inclusive tour, the concept may be called an optional excursion in the UK or an add-on in North America.

SIE   Safety information exchange (aviation term).

Siesta Dreamer   Brand name for Iberia's first-class sleeper seats.

SIG   Special interest group. *See* special interest holidays.

SIGB   Snowsport Industries of Great Britain (www.snowlife.org.uk) the trade association of the UK internal and outbound winter sports market. Snowlife is the brand name of its winter sports promotional campaign. *See also* Association of Snowsport Countries (ASC) *and* ski market in the UK and Europe.

sightseeing   Visits by tourists to places of interest. *Also see* to view.

sightseeing in Britain   Information on the subject is published annually by VisitBritain, covering trends in revenue, overseas visitors, opening hours, admission charges, new attractions, demand relative to capacity, capital expenditure and employment. Much detailed information is given on the factors influencing visitors and visitor numbers for attractions known to have at least 5000 visitors annually.

Sigma   The Italian agency CRS associated with Galileo.

SIGMET   Significant meteorological information concerning en route weather (aviation term).

sign-in message   When travel agents log on to a GDS on starting a work session, a promotional message may be screened, which may be an advertisement paid for by a third party or a GDS service announcement.

Silver Class   Brand name given by Continental to its business class. *See* business class for full details.

silver service   Type of restaurant service where waiting staff carry dishes of food with one hand, moving round a table and serving each person separately, using a spoon and fork held in the other hand. French service differs in that people serve themselves to food, from the dish held by the waiting staff. In some reference books, this is called 'English service'. When, instead, serving dishes are placed on the table by waiting staff, from which customers help themselves, this is called family service. If a meal is placed before clients having been assembled on plates in the kitchen, it is called plated service. Buffet service involves clients helping themselves from a buffet and then returning to their tables, while a carvery is where a chef will provide slices of hot meat or poultry as part of a buffet service.

Simplifying Passenger Travel Interest Group   *See* SPT.

Simplifying Passenger Travel Program   *See* SPT.

Singapore Tourism Board   *See* www. visitsingapore.com

Singaporian National Travel Agency Organization   *See* ATTA[2].

single   When applied to a journey or fare, means one way; when applied to accommodation, or, for example, a ship's cabin or a rail sleeping compartment, single means that it is only for one person. There is usually an extra charge above the price per person for a twin-bedded or double room; the single room supplement.

single access system   A system in which a user has direct access to a single airline's system, which may or may not provide reservations and/or ticketing capabilities on other airlines.

single entity charter   Chartering of an aircraft by one organization or a person. *See* charter.

Single European Sky   The EU Transport Council has agreed four regulations designed to create a 'Single European Sky'. The regulations aim to ensure more effective use of airspace and provision of air traffic services within the European Union and were meant to be implemented by the end of 2004. They pave the way for Europe's 16 different air traffic control systems to come under one new regulatory framework. Benefits are expected to include fewer delays in Europe, better air traffic communications between member states, the freeing up of airspace capacity and cuts in the costs of air traffic services. The cost of air traffic delays is substantial with Eurocontrol estimating a total cost in 2001 of €2.5–€3.6bn. Single European Sky could reduce this figure in the medium to long term by at least 25% whilst more effective routing of aircraft could reduce aircraft emissions by 5–10%. *See* http://www.europa.eu.int/ comm/transport/themes/air/english/ single_eur_sky_en.html

Single payment system   Known as SPS in the UK; it is ABTA's agency payment system. *See* agents' payment systems for full description.

single room supplement   *See* single.

SIPP   Standard Interline Passenger Procedures.

SISC   Scheduling Information Standards Committee of IATA.

SIT   Special interest tour *or* traveller. *See* special interest holidays.

SITA   Societé Internationale de Telecommunications Aeronautiques is the organization which runs the airlines' data-processing and communications system on a computer complex in Atlanta, USA. On this is stored BAG-TRAC, the IATA baggage tracing system; METEO, the worldwide weather data system for airlines; SAHARA the hotel booking system; TIMATIC, the electronic version of the *Travel Information Manual* and much other information used by airlines. Even by 1986 it covered 161 countries and SITA handled 8.3 billion messages a year. In 1992, SITA introduced Europe's first electronic fares library. *See* www.sita.int

SITE Society of Incentive and Travel Executives. Founded in 1973, has around 2000 members in 81 countries, mainly in the USA and Europe. Offers qualification of Certified Incentive Travel Executive (CITE). *See* www.site-intl.org

site inspection Visit by a group, incentive, conference or event organizer to a booked or prospective venue.

site stress *See* tourism-carrying capacity.

SITI Now obsolete – withdrawn January 2005; formerly was IATA international sale indicator, showing that both sale and issuance of an air ticket have taken place inside the country of commencement.

SITO Now obsolete – withdrawn January 2005; formerly was IATA international sale indicator, showing that an air ticket sale has been made inside the country of commencement of the journey, but that the ticket has been issued outside.

SITPRO Simpler Trade and Procedures Board. UK official body aimed at cutting red tape and boosting EDI.

SITTF Shipment Identification and Tracking Task Force of IATA.

sitting On cruise ships, there is often insufficient room in the restaurants for all the passengers to be seated at once. Thus, first and second meal sittings are necessary (some cruise lines refer to these as early or late sittings).

Six Continents Hotel name established in July 2001 following sales of Bass name and brewing business. This then became InterContinental hotels, currently the world's largest hotel group. *See* InterContinental hotels group, *also* www.intercontinental.com

SJTC States of Jersey Tourism Committee. *See* www.jerseytourism.com

Skal The international travel and tourism organization whose members are senior industry executives. Objectives are: 'To develop friendship and common purpose between the members of the staffs of the Tourist Industry and by means of International Tourism, to foster goodwill in order to increase mutual understanding between the peoples of the world.'

The first Skal club was formed in Paris in 1932. Within 2 years, there were 12 clubs in seven countries and the International Association was formed. There are now nearly 500 clubs of the Association Internationale des Clubs Skal (AICS), known in English-speaking countries as the International Association of Skal Clubs (IASC). The executive Committee is selected annually by an international general assembly of delegates of all clubs.

skeleton itinerary *See* stripped package.

ski packs Term used by winter sports tour operators and others to designate a package of items which skiers can purchase. This may include hire of ski boots and skis, ski school and lift passes.

skiff A small rowing boat, term particularly applicable if is attached to a larger vessel. Same name applies to a single crewed light narrow racing shell propelled by a pair of oars (sculls).

skipjack A type of small US fishing boat.

sky darkening and height The familiar blue of the sky is caused by the scattering effect of the earth's atmosphere on sunlight. When an airplane is flying at a high altitude, the atmosphere has become thinner, lessening the scattering, so that passengers notice the sky has become considerably darker. Astronauts, at their extreme heights, see an entirely black sky from space.

Sky Recliner Brand name for JAL's first-class sleeper seats.

Skycare Brand name of American Airlines' service, providing skilled medical companions for travellers who need limited medical attention or care during their flight. These companions are registered nurses with advanced experience, training and qualifications. The service was introduced in 2001, initially from the Chicago and Dallas/Fort Worth hubs. Under the programme, the customer buys two adjacent seats (either first class or economy) at 30% discount off the full fare and pays an hourly fee for the nurse. *See* www.aa.com

Skylounger Was brand name of BCAL's first-class sleeper seats.

Skyrail Birmingham airport now operates a new £11m people-mover operation between the airport and the international station/NEC complex. Capable of shifting over 1600 people an hour, and based on the highly successful system used to link hotels at Las Vegas, the Austrian-built cable-driven system replaces maglev, which served Birmingham for 10 years until 1995. Included in the package is a new and impressive interface with the rail station. Skyrail is fully automated with a transfer time of less than 90 s. The name of the service is less embarrassing than the acronym of Airport Rail Shuttle, the project's code name. http://www.bhx.co.uk

Skyteam   *See* airline alliances.

Skytrack   Was name of Galileo's UK agents' viewdata air booking CRS, withdrawn in 1992.

Skytrain   Was the name of Laker's low-cost daily air services operating between London's Gatwick Airport and the USA, which ceased when the company collapsed in 1982.

Skywards   Emirates' Frequent Flyer Programme. *See* FFP (frequent flyer programme).

SL   Sea level.

slats   *See* airframe.

sleeper   Name by which a rail sleeping compartment is known.

Sleeperette   Brand name for Finnair's type of first-class sleeper seat.

sleeperseat   Generic term for fully reclining airline seats, usually only provided in first-class cabin, designed specially for passengers to be able to sleep comfortably. The term is also the brand name of British Airways' facility of this type.

sleeping cars on European Railways   *See* European Rail sleeping cars.

SLFC   Supersonic laminar flow control (aviation term).

slip   US term for a place where a ship docks, instead of the UK term, berth.

SLMG   Self-launching motor gliders (aviation term).

sloop   A sailing vessel with one mast, a mainsail and jib. Often some headsails as well. Word now means the same as a cutter.

slot   An allocated time of departure and/or landing at a busy airport. At most of the world's major airports, there are requirements for more slots than are available. Night-flying may be curtailed or banned, in order to reduce noise annoyance to local inhabitants. Morning take-offs are a particular peak. Regulatory frameworks attempt to control the way in which major airlines attempt to monopolize slots at their main hub airport. Provision of opportunities for new airlines and facilitation of competition at popular airports are problem issues. When large airlines merge, the merged group may be required to give up some slots. Slots are a valuable commodity; dependent on the country and airport, airlines may be allowed to sell their slots. *See also* FIRs.

slot control   *See* FIRs.

slot-wobbler   Colloquial travel industry term for any factor which affects the use of a flight slot at an airport. Because of aircraft congestion, the loss of a slot might substantially delay an aircraft's departure.

Slovak Tourist Board   *See* www. slovakiatourism.sk

Slovenian Tourist Board   *See* www. slovenia-tourism.si

slow record   Sometimes shortened to slow rec. An air booking made in an airline's computer or a CRS which is substantially delayed in its transfer to another CRS or airline. This possibility is avoided when a CRS has arrangements for immediate transfer of data while a booking is being made, a locator (booking reference) being supplied by the second computer which is then incorporated in the booking.

SLS   Satellite landing system (aviation term).

SLST   Sea level static thrust (aviation term).

Slumbercoach   Brand name of Amtrak's economy-class rail sleeping compartment.

Slumberette   Was brand name of Swissair's fully adjustable first-class sleeper seat.

Smart Tag flight recognition   The software concept is not restricted to the travel and tourism industry; this is an application of the technology. Microsoft partner OAG Worldwide, has customized Smart Tag technology, built into Office XP, to deliver details of specific flights direct to the screens of PCs with Microsoft Office suite of applications. The Smart Tags have been developed to recognize the textual form of airline flight numbers, so when one is typed into the latest version of Word or

Outlook, it will be automatically highlighted and then a route offered into the web site OAG.com for specific information about the relevant flight. An Internet connection will allow instantaneous checks on information such as scheduled departure times, which terminal to use, arrival times and even the type of aircraft being used for a particular flight. The system will also give PC users a real-time check on whether a flight is on time or delayed. The table of information is drawn from the OAG Flight Engine.

SME Small and medium sized enterprise; the expression is not particular to tourism but the following definition is necessary because of the use of the acronym SMTE meaning either small and medium sized tourism enterprise or small and medium sized travel enterprise. In the EC an SME is an organization with up to 250 employees; some other countries set 200 employees as the upper limit, BUT, in the USA, the term SME includes firms with up to 500 employees. Small firms are generally considered as those with less than 50 employees, while the definition of a micro business ranges between five and ten employees. In the EC, SMEs must also by definition have an annual turnover of less than €40m and/or a balance-sheet valuation of less than €27m. For up-to-date SME statistics, including the travel sector, the Organization for Economic Co-operation and Development has a joint OECD/Eurostat database accessible via www.oecd.org

SMS Safety Management System, incorporated in chapter 9 of the SOLAS convention. *See* International Convention for the Safety of Life at Sea.

SMTE Small and medium sized tourism enterprise or small and medium sized travel enterprise. *See* SME for size definitions.

SMWP Specified minimum weather provisions (aviation term).

SNAV Syndicat National des Agents de Voyages.

SNCA Scottish National Camps Association.

Snowsport Industries of Great Britain *See* SIGB.

snowsports Growing in popularity as an alternative to 'winter sports'. *See* winter sports.

SOAP Spectroscopic oil analysis programme (aviation term).

Societé Internationale de Telecommunications Aeronautiques *See* SITA.

Society for Accessible Travel and Hospitality *See* SATH.

Society of American Travel Writers (SATW). *See* www.satw.org

Society of British Aviation Companies (SBAC). *See* www.sbac.co.uk

Society of Corporate Meeting Professionals SCMP. *See* www.scmp.org

Society of Event Organizers (SEO). *See* www.seoevent.co.uk

Society of Government Meeting Professionals (in the USA) *See* www.sgmpkc.org

Society of Incentive Travel Executives (SITE) *See* www.site-intl.org

Society of Travel Agents in Government *See* STAG[2].

Society of Travel and Tourism Educators *See* ISTTE (International Society of Travel and Tourism Educators).

SODA Was Eastern Airlines' automated reservation system. Acronym stood for System One Direct Access.

soft opening Prior to the 'official' opening of a hotel, the hotel may be 'run in' with some non-paying visitors. Sometimes this is a public relations exercise. The wording 'soft launch' is used generally in commerce for this type of situation.

soft tourism *See* tourism, alternative.

software A program of electronic signals that tells a computer what to do.

SOH Since overhaul (aviation term).

solarium Literally a sun room; generally used in the tourism industry for any windshielded area which is a part of the hotel building set aside for sunbathing, as distinct from a sun terrace which is not part of the hotel building. The same term also describes a room with artificial tanning equipment (usually UV light). Thus when a hotel description states that there is a solarium, it is ambiguous as to what may be provided.

SOLAS *See* International Convention for the Safety of Life at Sea.

sommelier The wine waiter.

son et lumière *See* sound and light show.

SOTI Now obsolete – withdrawn January 2005; formerly was IATA international sale indicator, showing that an air ticket sale has been made outside the country of commencement of the journey, but that the ticket has been issued inside.

SOTO Now obsolete – withdrawn January 2005; formerly was IATA international sale indicator, showing that both the sale and issuance of an air ticket have taken place outside the country of commencement of the journey.

sound and light show Also known as son et lumière; an audio-visual presentation or spectacle, usually outdoors.

sous vide[1] Vacuum or inert gas packaging followed by cook and chill method of meal preparation. Cook and chill involves cooking meals, rapid chilling within 90 min to 0°C–3°C, storage at 3°C and regeneration prior to serving to a customer. In the UK under the Food Hygiene Regulations 1995, storage up to 8°C is permissible (although a lower temperature is necessary to maintain palatability). Airline meals are often prepared cook and chill. Storage should only be for 5 days, including the day of production and consumption.

sous vide[2] Involves the use of high barrier plastic containers into which the food is placed; these are either vacuum sealed or filled with an inert gas such as nitrogen before sealing. The packs are then cooked and chilled as before; but the removal of oxygen results in stability for up to 21 days. Moreover, deterioration in food quality is reduced. Cook freeze involves the flash freezing of prepared meals to −18°C. These processes enable restaurants to offer extensive menus without wastage dependent on the vagaries of customer choice. The provision of complex dishes is facilitated at locations without highly qualified kitchen staff.

South African National Travel Agency Organization *See* ASATA.

South Africa Tourism *See* www.southafrica.net

South Carolina Tourism *See* www.discoversouthcarolina.com

South Pacific Tourism Organization A regional intergovernmental organization founded to promote tourism to American Samoa, Cook Islands, Fiji Islands, French Polynesia, Kirbati, New Caledonia, Niue, Papua New Guinea, Samoa, Solomon Islands, Tonga, Tavalu and Vanuatu. *See* www.spto.org

Southern Cross Name of regional CRS for South Pacific area owned by Ansett and Australian Airlines, which has a marketing and technical agreement with Galileo.

SP[1] Special performance (aviation term).

SP[2] Via South Pacific. *See* routing.

spa As this dictionary is going to press, usage is changing. Spa is now becoming a generic word for the health and fitness area in a hotel or resort. But the original centuries-old usage continues, referring to a place where there is a mineral spring producing water believed to have medicinal/curative properties. At these locations, often, a variety of health treatments is offered. In many countries, the conduct of spas is regulated by law. In Australasia, the word is used to describe a small heated swimming pool swirled by air or water jets, like an oversize jacuzzi.

spa hotel A hotel in Europe providing health and/or medical facilities, not necessarily located in a health spa resort, although often so sited.

SPAA Scottish Passenger Agents Association; established in 1921, the oldest travel trade association in the world. *See* www.spaa.org

space available Means 'subject to space becoming available'; it is the same as a traveller being on a waiting list or on standby for a scheduled departure of a mode of transport. Opposite to a confirmed reservation. If space fills up with full-fare-paying passengers, subject-to-load travellers (subload passengers), such as travel agents on a reduced fare, will not be able to travel. In North America, concept is usually expressed as 'space available' travel being subject to the space being available, rather than subject to load.

Spanish National Tourist Office *See* www.spain.info

Spanish National Travel Agency Organization *See* GNAVE.

SPAR Slight Provision Approach Radar (aviation term).

SPARTA Was the name of Olympic Holidays' UK agents' viewdata system.

SPC The Strategy and Policy Committee or the Scheduling Procedures Committee of IATA.

Special Drawing Rights *See* SDR.

Special Group Inclusive Tour Fare *See* SGIT.

special interest holidays Holidays for groups of persons with a particular interest, not necessarily leisure pursuits. For example, an industry group is often extremely interested in seeing how their industry operates in another country. It may be a group of sporting spectators or players and covers almost anything; for example, *sporting interests such as*: angling, archery, athletics, baseball, basketball, bowling, boxing, car-rallying, canoeing, climbing, cricket, equestrian, fencing, flying, football, golf, gliding, greyhound racing, gymnastics, handball, hockey, horse-racing, hunting, judo, lacrosse, motor-racing, parachuting, pony-trekking, rowing, sailing, shooting, skiing, skating, squash, sub-aqua sports, swimming, table tennis, tennis, volleyball, rambling, water-skiing, weightlifting, wrestling. *General interests such as*: amateur dramatics, antiques, archaeology, art, ballroom dancing, baroque architecture, birdwatching, bridge, camping, caravanning, cats, chess, dogs, festivals of all kinds, gardening, gambling, gourmandizing, inland waterways, jazz, languages, music, naturism, opera, painting, philately, photography, politics, vintage cars. As well as these specific interests and activities, there are religious minority groups, senior citizens, youth clubs, women's organizations and trade associations. The possibilities are vast. In the USA the *Speciality Travel Index* and in the UK the *Holiday Guide* series by DG&G Travel Information, both published twice a year, list the providers of special interest holiday arrangements. The term *theme cruise* is a cruise formulated to appeal to a special interest group, as described above.

special service requirement   *See* SSR[2].

SPECTRA   Facility offered by Sabre enabling selection of PNRs by category. For further details *see* Sabre.

speech recognition travel booking system   Program in the USA which enables air reservations to be made automatically by telephone, developed by Thomas Cook and American Express and designed by Bolt, Beranek and Newman.

speedboat   A small fast boat, commonly used for racing, pulling water skiers, or other leisure pursuits.

Sphere   Name of Sabena's in-flight magazine.

spider   *See* robot technology.

spinner   North American term for a traveller who finds their allocated seat already occupied. Appears to have originally applied when two passengers were given identical boarding cards; now, however, that computer systems prevent this, the term has more general application.

split   *See* airframe.

split charter   When two or more organizations jointly contract to charter an aircraft. When it is chartered by one person or organization, this is a single entity charter. This nomenclature is more common in North America than Europe. *See* charter.

split commissions   It is a custom of the travel trade throughout the world, in respect of all types of travel tickets, for non-appointed agents to obtain their tickets from appointed agents, splitting the commission between them. The term is obsolescent because few airlines now pay commission. IATA specifically prohibits this, saying: 'The agent shall retain the full amount of the commission allowed by the carrier and shall not rebate or promise to rebate directly to or indirectly, in any manner whatsoever such commissions or portions thereof … except as provided in the Sales Agency Rules.' But regardless of this and similar rules in most transportation principals' agency agreements, the practice continues.

split contract   Term for UK practice which, until 2003, avoided tour operating ATOL licensing rules by selling the holiday elements separately. Typically, flights and accommodation are sold under separate contracts, as are other travel products such as car hire. Only the flight is likely to be ATOL protected.

split ticketing[1]   The practice of undercutting the fare for a journey by issuing two or more tickets, taking advantage of lower sector or promotional fares.

split ticketing[2]   Arrangements in connection with an STP (satellite ticket printer) or other remote ticket printing; the travel coupons of the ticket are available at the remote site but the issuing office and audit coupon(s) are printed at the host site.

SPM The Selective Prices Manual was British Rail's rates book. The term arose because the customary method of charging for rail travel in the UK had been based for over half a century on deciding on a rate per mile, and charging travellers accordingly. Nowadays, the price of train travel reflects more accurately market pricing for individual journeys. The manual was renamed *National Fares Manual* on 6 January 1985, but over 15 years later, travel staff were still using the old name!

spoilers *See* airframe.

spot buying Use of the lowest fare available for a journey on any airline, at the time of booking, despite the existence of a contract or route deal by a corporate travel account with a particular carrier. Spot buying may save money on specific flights, but if it leads overall to a rebate loss, it has been counter-productive. *A list of 70 other business travel related entries follows* corporate travel contracts, *some of which lead to further entries.*

spouse fare A reduced travel rate for a person accompanying a traveller to whom they are married. The target market is business travellers, aiming to encourage an extra person to travel. There is wide variation in the definition; often airlines do not extend the fare to unmarried couples or same-sex partners.

spouse programme Leisure activities at a conference, convention or event organized for non-participants attending with a delegate partner.

SPS Single payment system (of ABTA). *See* agents' payment systems.

SPSC The Strategic Planning Sub-Committee of IATA.

SPT Simplifying Passenger Travel Program. Brings together the key parties involved with the aim of improving and automating the movement of passengers through airports. This major tourism initiative is managed by the SPT Board consisting of AUC, ACI[1], AACO, IATA and IATA's CAWG, IBIA (International Biometric Industry Association), ICAO, SITA, UFTAA and WCO. The SPT Internet site www.simplifying-travel.org details how, in the future, travellers will be able to use smart-card identification when checking-in for journeys, their details being checked by a biometric scan, such as iris recognition.

In the UK, under the aegis of IATA, an SPTIG (Simplifying Passenger Travel Interest Group) was formed by BAA, British Airways, HM Customs & Excise, UK Immigration Service and Virgin Atlantic Airways to promote, test and develop 'one-stop' passenger processing for airlines and airports. The UK trial they have set up was taking place as this dictionary was going to press. It is the first large-scale airport passenger handling trial in the world to rely entirely on biometric identification. It involves around 2000 North American Virgin Atlantic and British Airways frequent travellers.

EyeTicket Corporation's JetStream™ Passenger Processing System will enable passengers who have been enrolled and pre-cleared by the UK Immigration Service to look into a video camera when arriving at Heathrow's passport control. In less than 2 s, travellers will have their identity verified and their admission to the UK granted, based solely on their iris pattern and verification of their status.

SPTIG Simplifying Passenger Travel Interest Group. *See* SPT.

SPTO *See* South Pacific Tourism Organization.

SR In connection with car rental indicates a sun-roof; in connection with aircraft means short range.

SRA[1] Strategic Rail Authority in the UK. Following denationalization of British Rail in the 1990s, the network was split into competing operating companies (*see* ATOC[1]) and Railtrack (now called Network Rail) which owns and operates the stations, track and system. The SRA is the body which undertakes franchising of the TOCs (train operating companies) and other functions.

SRA[2] Surveillance radar approach (aviation term).

SRE Surveillance radar element (aviation term).

Sri Lanka Tourist Board *See* www. srilankatourism.org

SRM Structural repair manual (aviation term).

SRO Seat Reservation Office.

SS Steamship when used to prefix a ship's name.

SSB Single side band (aviation term).

SSCV Semi-submersible Crane Vessels are huge floating platforms equipped with giant cranes, capable of lifting 10,000 t or more.

SSID Supplementary structural inspection document (aviation term).

SSIM Standard Schedules Information Manual of IATA.

SSIP Supplementary structural repair programme (aviation term).

SSR¹ Secondary Surveillance Radar.

SSR² Special service requirement (or request). In the latter case, this could be, for example, requests for special meals for an air traveller. Although now used in reference to GDS bookings, the term has been in general usage for much longer.

SST Supersonic transport; an aircraft capable of flying faster than the speed of sound, 741 mph at sea level. *See* Concorde.

SSV¹ Scheduled shop visit (aviation term).

SSV² Supplementary Services Voucher. An accountable airline document used to make payment for items such as car hire, hotel accommodation or the hire of an air-taxi.

SSV1 Standard Software Version One for an IATA Bank Settlement Plan.

St Kitts Tourism Authority *See* www.stkitts-nevis.com

St Lucia Tourist Board *See* www.stlucia.org

St Vincent and the Grenadines Tourist Office *See* www.svgtourism.com

Stabiliser (*See next entry for ship's stabilizers*) Term was applied to the exclusive dealing arrangement in the UK whereby ABTA tour operators could only sell through ABTA retailers, who could not sell non-ABTA tour operators' arrangements.

stabilizers Usually retractable fins, coming out from the sides of a ship, like short, stubby aeroplane wings. They damp down a ship's rolling motion, but create a lot of drag, greatly increasing fuel costs. Rolling is side-to-side from port to starboard as distinct from pitching which is from the bow or stern rising and falling. Flume stabilizers transfer water in and out of, or between, huge tanks to lessen rolling.

stacking In hotels, the practice of placing more guests in a room than allowed by the regulations, or for which the room was designed. *See also* aircraft stacking.

stadium deck *See* deck.

staff bureau *See* employment bureau.

STAG¹ Society of Travel Agents in Government in the USA. *See* www.government-travel.org

STAG² Scottish Top Agents Group, formed in 2001.

stage 2/3/4 aircraft *See* ICAO.

staged authenticity *See* 'the folk'.

stand A stand or booth is an exhibition or trade fair area sold to an exhibitor for the duration of an exhibition for them to display and/or sell their products or services. The words are used both to designate the area rented and what the exhibitor builds on the space. Although dimensions vary between different exhibitions, a stand is usually the full basic size, at least 3 m × 3 m, whereas a booth is likely to be a smaller area with only enough room for a small table and one (sometimes two) chairs. Some exhibitors may negotiate an agreement for the provision of space, sometimes fully furnished, in exchange for services or other benefits supplied to the exhibitors. Such 'free' booths or stands are known as 'contra booths' or 'contra stands'. A shell scheme stand at an 'all in' price provided to exhibitors normally includes carpeting, a simple structure with the exhibitor's name, lighting or electric points and sometimes a table, desk and chairs. A collection of booths or stands occupying a large exhibition area may be called a pavillion.

stand-alone system An agent's system, which is used for recording bookings and reservations, but is not linked to principals' systems (also sometimes referred to as an agent's 'mini-system').

Standard Foreign Fare Level The US International Air Transportation Competition Act of 1979 laid down fares starting from a 1 October 1979 base, which were increased after calculating rises in operating costs periodically.

Standard Industry Fare Level The US 1978 Deregulation Act established as a base the maximum fares the CAB allowed on 1 July 1977. These fare levels are adjusted regularly to take into account changes in operating costs. The Deregulation Act allows US carriers to charge fares up to 5% less than the standard level, providing virtually complete tariff freedom in America.

Standard International Classification of Tourism Activities *See* SICTA.

Standard Load Factor Before the demise of the American CAB at the beginning of 1985, they assessed aircraft load factors on routes, using the figures to calculate appropriate fares they would allow.

standard open returns *See* rail fares in the UK.

standard singles *See* rail fares in the UK.

standard syllabus for tourism courses *See* Appendix II.

standby fare Available on certain air routes at a much reduced rate from the normal fares, for travellers willing to wait until shortly before departure time, before knowing if they will be carried. Official IATA definition is a potential revenue passenger who presents himself at a designated check-in location and who is prepared to accept space subject to availability. Standby fares are also available on other forms of transport.

STAR¹ Sloane Travel Agency Report in the USA which provided unbiased opinions of hotels and cruise ships.

STAR² Standard instrument arrival procedure (aviation term).

Star Alliance *See* airline alliances.

starboard side The right side of a vessel when facing forward. There are green navigation lights on that side of the bridge or aircraft.

StarNet The IT network of the Star airline alliance. *See* airline alliances.

STARS¹ Was Sealink's Ticketing and Reservation System (now absorbed into P&O Stena).

STARS² Special Traveller Account Record System, a client information sub-system in Sabre.

STARS³ Standard terminal automation system (aviation term).

START Was the German multi-access travel reservations and administration system used by travel agencies in that country and Austria. Acquired by Amadeus in 2003, the company became Amadeus Germany. The company used to be called Start Data Technik Fuer Reise und Touristik although the acronym arose from the original name Studient Gesselschaft zur Automotisierung Fuer Reise und Touristik, developed in the early 1970s.

stateroom A large de luxe ship's cabin; often there may be a living room and bedroom en suite.

States of Jersey Tourism Committee (SJTC) *See* www.jerseytourism.com

static caravan *See* camper, caravan *and* caravan park.

statistics *See* tourism information databases.

status of a travel agent *See* legal status of a travel agent.

STB Scottish Tourist Board. For explanation of role *see* BTA. *See* www.visitscotland.com

STC Supplemental type certificate (aviation term).

STDMA Satellite system synchronized self-organizing time division multiple access (a global navigation datalink aviation term).

steamboat *See* steamship.

steamer *See* steamship.

steamship Any water-borne vessel propelled by a steam engine. The word is in such general use that it is abbreviated to SS as a preface to ship's name. A steamboat may be the same as a steamship. But the word was particularly used in the 19th century to describe the stern-wheelers (paddle steamers) on the Mississippi in the USA. *See* paddle steamer.

Steering panel of the Bank Settlement Plan Official IATA definition is a panel which in accordance with the instructions and directions of the Bank Settlement Plan Committee is charged with the implementation and certain supervisory aspects of a Bank Settlement Plan.

stem An alternative term for the front end or bows of a water-borne vessel.

step-on guide A local guide who joins a bus or coach to impart particular knowledge of the area or a site being visited.

Sterling Equivalents Orders *See* Warsaw Convention.

stern An alternative term for the rear (aft) end of a water-borne vessel.

STICEC Special Travel Industry Council on Energy Conservation in the USA.

STIN Sabre Travel Information Network. *See* Sabre.

stock control number Official IATA definition is the unique identification number that is pre-printed on automated tickets not having pre-printed form and serial numbers.

Stockholder Licensee Group *See* consortium.

STOL Short Take Off and Landing aircraft. Simply descriptive that the machine can take off and land within a relatively short horizontal distance.

STONKY Still travelling on, no kids yet – term descriptive of a traveller who was a backpacker when younger, but whom, despite now being more affluent, still espouses the backpacker spirit of adventure and travelling with little luggage. *See* backpacker.

stop International Hotel Code meaning stay extended by the number of days stated. Also internationally agreed method for indicating a sentence end in a telex or similar type of message.

stopover Deliberate interruption of journey, agreed in advance by the carrier, at a point between the point of origin and the point of destination. Some air fare rules define a stopover as being a break in journey at an intermediate point after a certain length of time. Where description of fare type states that the official IATA description applies, this is as follows: 'Stopover means a stop at an intermediate point from which the passenger is not scheduled to depart on the day of arrival. If there is no schedule connecting departure on the day of arrival, departure on the next day within 24 h after the time of arrival will not constitute a stopover.' The 2003 CEN/European standard official definition is: 'Deliberate stop during a journey at a place between the departure point and the destination point, contracted in advance and specified in the transport document'. In North America, the travel industry often calls the situation described in this entry a layover. Thus, whereas the previous edition of this dictionary specified only one definition, some confusion is now possible.

stopover complimentary *See* STPC.

STP Satellite ticket printer. Travel ticket printer at a location that is remote from the controlling staff and computer. For example, IATA- or ARC-appointed agents may have a satellite ticket printer at the premises of a non-appointed corporate account, in some countries in Europe and in North America. To establish an STP, it is essential that printers capable of producing ATBs (Automated Ticket and Boarding Passes) are used. These enable the travel coupons of an air ticket to be issued at the satellite location while the audit and issuing office coupons are issued at the agency site. In the USA STPs have been the fastest growing type of ARC-approved location since they were first introduced in 1986 and by 1991 there were already over 6000 US STP locations, approximately 16% of the US total. Arrangements involving placement of STPs are sometimes known as outplant operations. In the US Satellite Ticket Printer Networks (STPNs) have been developed by ARC-appointed agents, sited at hotels and other places. Through these networks, delivery services are offered to other agents. *A list of 70 other business travel related entries follows* corporate travel contracts, *some of which lead to further entries.*

STPC Stopover complimentary; when an air journey consists of connecting flights, airlines usually provide complimentary accommodation and meals, if the break of journey is more than 6 hours. If there is an involuntary stopover, an STPC is often provided. *See* stopover.

STPN Satellite ticket printer network. *See* STP.

strakes *See* airframe.

Strategic Rail Authority (in the UK) *See* SRA.

stratocumulus *See* clouds.

stratosphere *See* contrails.

stratus *See* clouds.

stretcher cases by air Airlines must be contacted before any arrangements are made. Stretcher cases must always be accompanied by an escort who will be required to take care of any toilet requirements. Charges vary between airlines. British Airways charge four times the normal applicable fare on all routes, plus the single fare for the attendant.

stretching *See* jumboizing.

stripped package North American term for an inclusive tour by scheduled air, providing the minimum services necessary to qualify for ITX or other special air fares designed to promote the use of scheduled air travel as part of an IT. An alternative term is skeleton itinerary. A stripped package is *not* the same as a minimum rated package tour in the UK.

This is an IT providing the minimum of services necessary to remain within the air charter regulations of various European countries.

STS Southeast Tourism Society in the USA; founded in 1983 has 520 members from 11 regional states. *See* www.southeasttourism.org *and* www.escapetothesoutheast.com

STTE Society of Travel and Tourism Educators in the USA is wrong in some reference works. *See* ISTTE (International Society of Travel and Tourism Educators) www.istte.org

Student Rail Card *See* rail fares in the UK.

studio room A hotel room provided with couches that convert into beds. But some hotels use this term to designate a single room apartment with cooking facilities. Travellers *must* check the actual facilities being offered.

subject-to-load Sometimes written as subload. Opposite to a confirmed reservation and the same as standby. If space fills up with full-fare-paying passengers, 'subload' passengers, such as travel agents on a reduced fare, will not be able to travel. In North America, concept is expressed as 'space available', travel being subject to the space being available.

subload *See* subject-to-load.

subrogation Insurance term, indicating that if a customer's claim is successful, then he cannot take further action himself to obtain a repeat pay-out from any third negligent party. Whenever an insured person has an alternative remedy, by indemnifying the client, the insurance company takes over the benefit of such rights so that they have the opportunity of recovering in respect of the claim they have had to pay and this act of taking over these rights is subrogation.

subway Name of New York's underground railway system and generic term for such a system in North America.

SUD Stretched upper deck (aviation term).

suite or **stateroom** Usually a two-bedded or twin room with private shower/bath and toilet, separate sitting room/lounge or day room or similar. Unfortunately, usage varies; for example, in France a suite in a hotel may consist of only one room. Such a room combining a sig-

nificant lounge area, bedroom and toilet/bathroom is often called a junior suite in the rest of the world. Stateroom is the term often applied on a ship.

sun deck *See* deck.

Sun Island Holidays A Lancashire, UK-based consortium of travel agents, member of Worldchoice.

Sun West A consortium of UK travel agents, member of Worldchoice.

superjumbo Name of the Airbus Industrie A380, a 555-seat aircraft with a 79.8 m wingspan, a prototype of which has now flown. It is due to enter service in 2006 between Heathrow and Singapore; Airbus believes there will be 1000 of these aircraft flying within 20 years. The A380 will be the biggest, widest, longest and heaviest aircraft in the world, flying up to 13 hours non-stop for up to 8000 miles. Operating costs are expected to be 13% cheaper than B747.

supersonic aircraft *See* Concorde *and* SST. Japan and France are developing a new supersonic aircraft, spending 200m Yen (US$5.5m) in research up to 2008. Japan has already successfully tested an engine that can reach speeds of Mach 5.5.

supplement An extra charge for a specific tourism service, provided in addition to the basic arrangements. For example, with regard to accommodation, a single room supplement, or a supplement for a room with a bath and toilet, or with a sea view. In respect of transport, the supplement may be for travelling on a particular train, or for upgrading to first class. In the case of package holidays, basic prices from one airport are usually quoted with extra charges for departures from other airports.

Supplementals Supplementary Air Carriers authorized by the United States' CAB to carry charter traffic.

supplier A travel principal. The company that provides the actual components of travel such as an airline, coach operator or hotel.

SUPROS Name of UK-based Supranational's dedicated hotel CRS created on a distributed database.

surcharge An extra charge on a customer's bill. Term is usually applied to amounts which are additional to those agreed by the customer at the time of booking. Booking conditions may allow a provider of travel services to pass on to the contracted traveller unexpected costs. Typically, these arise from the introduction of government taxes, changes in aviation or marine fuel costs or fluctuations in the value of the destination country's currency compared with that of the originating country. For explanation of the surcharge phenomenon in the UK, *see* guarantee of no surcharges. A 'fuel surcharge' in Europe may be called a 'bunker adjustment factor' or 'fuel adjustment factor' in North America.

surface break or **sector** An interruption in a flight itinerary because the passenger is travelling a segment by rail, road or sea. The advantage of reduced-rate return air travel may still be available. *See* open-jaw.

Sussex A South-of-England-based consortium of travel agents, member of Worldchoice.

sustainable tourism *See* tourism, sustainable.

SVQ Scottish Vocational Qualification. NVQs and SVQs are a UK standard at various levels usually achievable by practical work-based assessment. The title SVQ is not particular to the travel industry, although there are many travel SVQs.

SW In connection with car rental, indicates a station wagon.

Swedish National Travel Agency Organization Svenska Resebranchens Forening, the Association of Swedish Travel Agents.

Swedish Travel and Tourism Council *See* www.visit-sweden.com

Swiss Holiday Card Entitles the holder to unlimited rail travel on a large number of rail, boat and coach services in Switzerland and purchase of an unlimited number of reduced-rate tickets for certain other services. Cards can be purchased for 4, 8 or 15 days or for 1 month, price varying according to whether first or second class, or for an adult, or child aged between 6 and 15 inclusive.

Swiss National Travel Agency Organization Association of Swiss Travel Agents.

Swiss Rail half-fare season tickets Entitle holder to purchase International Rail tickets with a 50% reduction over the Swiss sections, or an unlimited number of tickets for Swiss internal journeys at half-fare. 20% reduction is gained on the price of Regional Holiday tickets in Switzerland. At time of going to press, second-class prices are £18 for 15 days and £22.50 for 1 month.

Swiss Saver Swissair apex fare between UK and Switzerland.

Switzerland Tourism *See* www.myswitzerland.com

SYDAC A 5000 MHz instrument landing system (aviation term).

syllabus for tourism courses *See* Appendix II.

Syndivoyages Syndicat des Agences de Voyages et de Tourisme en Cote d'Ivoire, the national travel agency organization of the Ivory Coast.

Syrian Association of Tourist and Travel Agents *See* SATTA.

Syrian Ministry of Tourism *See* www.syriatourism.org

SystemOne Originally a US travel industry CRS accessible by travel agents, owned by Texas Air, Eastern Airlines and Continental Airlines, in February 1990, a 50% stake in System One was sold to US company Electronic Data Systems. In 1997/98 users were converted to Amadeus.

Systrav British travel agents' computerized accounting system developed by Hallamshire Programming Limited.

T

T   Threshold lighting (aviation term).

T bar   *See* cable transporters.

T Class   Propeller tourist, coach or economy class. Usually used in the USA.

T FACTS   Was a UK multi-user travel agent's front and back office system, providing control of client data from point-of-sale to full profit and loss accounts. Used by Trailfinders, which claims to be the largest single-site travel agency in Europe, and which marketed T FACTS.

T2   *See* Orbitz.

TA   Transition altitude *or* Traffic Advisory of traffic alert and collision avoidance system.

TAAD   Travel Agent Automated Deduction in the USA. *See* ARC[1].

TAAI   Travel Agents Association of India.

TAANZ   Travel Agents Association of New Zealand.

TAAWNY   Travel Agents Alliance of Western New York.

table d'hôte   A limited-choice menu for a stated price, from which deviations may not normally be made without incurring additional charges. This is the normal type of meal provided when the meals have been included in the price of a group tour. *See* alternative meal choices of à la carte *and* set meal.

TABRS   Travel Agents Bond Replacement Scheme for members of ABTA in the UK. *See* bond.

TABS   Thomsons' Automatic Banking System is a UK travel agency direct banking debit system whereby the agent's bank account is automatically debited, weekly, for the value of transactions with that operator due for payment.

TAC[1]   Travel Agency Commission.

TAC[2]   Travel Agency Commissioner. *See* Agency Programme Joint Council (Liaison Group).

TAC[3]   Was, until 1999, the Travel Agents Council of ABTA, the UK trade body, having previously, up to October 1984, been called the Retail Agents Council.

TACAN   Tactical air navigation (aviation term).

TACC   The Travel Association's Consultative Council, formed in 1977, represented many of the major organizations in the UK travel industry. Its objectives were to consider common definitions of policies and more effective cooperation between associations concerned with travel and tourism, to present a coordinated view in negotiations with government and to promote by concerted action legislation favourable to British interests in the field of travel and tourism. (Now obsolete.)

tachograph   Recorder on a road vehicle to ensure compliance with laws concerning maximum permitted driver's hours and speed limits.

TACO   Hertz Rent-a-Car Travel Agents Commission Order. Documents are raised by renting locations worldwide. Ensures commission is paid and builds up a history of all rentals by a particular travel agent to enable bonus commissions to be assessed.

TACS   Travel Agent Computer Society, a US organization.

TACT   The air cargo tariff.

TAD2000   UK travel agency administration and accounting system using Windows and Microsoft Access.

TAF[1]   Terminal aerodrome forecast *or* turbulence. *See* turbulence.

TAF[2]   Travel Agency Fee Document. *See* ARC[1].

TAG   Technical Assessment Group of IATA.

TAI   Thermal anti-ice (aviation term).

tail   *See* airframe.

Take a Chance   A number of shipping companies offer guaranteed waiting list reservations. There is a considerable reduction in the rate, because the actual cabin, sailing or cruise is not known in advance. For example, P&O apply this description to their offers of accommodation for passengers who travel at 1 month's notice on any cruise during a season.

TALIS   Name of Belgian SEMA group's computer system for travel agents. At the time of writing, no users in English-speaking countries, although well-known in Europe.

Talisman Was name of UK computer system marketed by Data Management Group. Different systems suitable for travel agents, inbound tour operators, flight sales and charter seat selling.

tallest hotel in Europe Europe's tallest building, London Bridge Tower, will in 2009 be the location for a 195-room Shangri-La hotel, the first new build, five star to open in the capital for over a decade.

TALON Was a UK-based CRS operated by Mercury Communications on behalf of Cable and Wireless.

Tanzania Tourist Board *See* www.tanzania-web.com

TAP Terminal area productivity, an aviation term; *also* the initials of the Portuguese national airline.

TAPEX An acronym for Tape Exchange, the term for the exchange of computer tapes by which passenger interline billing data was passed through IATA. Because of the huge increase in the number of tapes that had to be handled under this system, it was replaced by IDEC.

TAPP Travel Agents Protector Plus.

TAPS Transatlantic air passenger survey.

TAR Terminal area radar (aviation term).

Tara Circle Name of Aer Lingus' Frequent Flyer Club. *See* FFP (frequent flyer programme).

TAREX Name of Cable and Wireless Asia and Pacific area CRS.

tariff, rules Official IATA definition is the tariff concerned with the general terms and conditions of carriage.

Tariffe Conveyance Voyageurs *See* TCV.

tariffs Official IATA definition is: the published fares, rates, charges and/or related conditions of carriage of a carrier. Substitute 'travel service provider' for 'carrier' and it becomes a more general definition applicable, for example, to any mode of transport or a hotel. The official airline guides listing full details of fare rules and regulations are also known by the same name. The Air Tariff is distributed in Britain by British Airways on behalf of over 80 airlines, the Airline Passenger Tariff is produced by SAS and Swissair for 40 airlines. Lufthansa produces its own Passenger Tariff.

TARSC Travel Agency Retail System Concepts. The market-leading UK reservations, administration, accounting and communication system for travel agents. *See* www.tarsc.co.uk

TAS[1] True air speed (aviation term).

TAS[2] Was Travel Agent's System, a British computerized travel agent's accounting and ticketing system marketed by Travel Specialised Computers Limited, first introduced in 1977.

TASC Travel Agents of Suffolk County, a US agency consortium.

TASF Travel agent service fee programme for processing service charges and other credit card payments. *See* ARC[1].

TAT Transitional Automated Ticket (IATA). All automated tickets feature the same data to be found on a manual ticket, although some items are in different positions. Because of the way a computer prints out fare calculation data, there is no ladder fare calculation box to the right of an automated ticket. Instead there are lines for a print-out of the fare calculation in a horizontal linear format. The term off-premise transitional automated ticket (OPTAT) came about because of the need to develop a ticket specifically for sales agents who were 'off airline premises'. *See also* ATB and ATB2, Automated ticket, bar code, bull's-eye, computer airline ticket, OCR, OPATB2, OPTAT *and* teletype airline ticket.

Taurus Was a UK tour operator's reservation, administration and accounting system marketed by Astralogic Travel and Leisure Systems.

taxes, fees and charges *See* TFCs.

TBA or **TBN** To be advised, to be assigned or to be notified. Used when making bookings where name of passenger travelling is not yet known, or by travel principals when they can guarantee that space is available but are unable to designate it precisely. Sometimes in North America, the designation 'no name' is used.

TBAD Travel Bureau Association of Denmark.

TBO Time between overhauls (aviation term).

TC Traffic Conference or total cycles (aviation term).

TC-1 IATA Traffic Conference Area 1. The area comprising all of the North and South American Continents, and the islands adjacent thereto, including Greenland, Bermuda, the West Indies and the Islands of the Caribbean Sea and the Hawaiian Islands.

TC-2 IATA Traffic Conference Area 2. The area comprising all of Europe, including that part of the former USSR in Europe and the islands adjacent thereto; Iceland, the Azores, all of Africa, and the islands adjacent thereto; Ascension Island and that part of Asia lying west of and including Iran.

TC-3 IATA Traffic Conference Area 3. The area comprising all of Asia east of Iran and islands adjacent thereto; all of East Indies, Australia, New Zealand and islands adjacent thereto; the islands of the Pacific Ocean except those included in Traffic Conference 1.

TCA Timeshare Consumers Association. *See* www.timeshare.org.uk *and* timeshare.

TCAS Traffic Collision Avoidance System of the US FAA.

TCDS Type certificate data sheet (aviation term).

TCF Travelers Conservation Foundation, founded by the USTOA; on 1 January 2005 it amalgamated with the National Tourism Foundation, founded in 1982 by the National Tour Association to form Tourism Cares for Tomorrow. *See* www.ntfonline.org *and* www.tcfonline.org

TCN Transmission Control Number.

TCSN Total cycles since new (aviation term).

TCV Tariffe Conveyance Voyageurs. Used as both name of the tariff used for calculating point-to-point European Rail fares and the name of the actual ticket coupons which are also called TCVs. *See also* sectional coupons.

TDA Tourist or tourism destination area. An area that is a substantial receiver of incoming tourism from abroad, as distinct from a tourism-generating area, from where a large number of tourists emanate.

TDAP Tourist Development Action Programme.

TDC Tourism (or Tourist) Development Council. There are a number of organizations with this title in English-speaking countries, both statutory and non-statutory.

TDM Ticket Delivery Machine.

TDR Technical despatch reliability (aviation term).

TDS Travel Distribution System; nomenclature that may replace the term GDS within the currency of this dictionary.

TDZ Tourist or tourism destination zone. Same as tourism destination area above.

TDZE Touch down zone elevation (aviation term).

teaching tourism in the UK *See* Higher Education Academy Network for Hospitality, Leisure, Sport and Tourism.

technical stop A stop (usually planned) during an air journey which is not scheduled as a pick-up or departure point, often to take on fuel; normally, passengers may not board or leave the aircraft, or freight be loaded or unloaded. Sometimes, local laws require passengers to leave an aircraft during refuelling; in these circumstances, passengers are kept in a holding area or transit lounge, and must reboard the aircraft.

TEDIS Trade Electronic Data Interchange Systems. European community programme developing EDI standards.

TedQual Tourism education quality. The WTO certification system for quality and efficiency in tourism education, is detailed in www.themis.ad/english/products/tedqual_info.htm *and also in* www.worldtourism.org/education/tedqual.htm

TEE Trans-Europe Express trains. Obsolescent term replaced by the EuroCity brand name in May 1987. There are only a few TEE trains still operating, running entirely in France; the Faidherbe and the Watteau between Paris and Tourcoing and the Jules Verne between Paris and Nantes. TEE trains are fast day-time train services using luxury air-conditioned carriages. Travellers pay a supplementary charge, which includes a seat reservation, in addition to a first-class travel ticket.

telecabine *See* cable transporters.

teleferic *See* cable transporters.

telephone toll-free *See* toll-free telephone calls.

teleskis *See* cable transporters.

Teletext This is the transmission by broadcasting of either text or pictures, which can be picked up by television sets having special adapters. The new digital TV services, currently received by a low proportion of UK TV users, allow much more efficient teletext services to be transmitted. Thus, within the lifetime of this dictionary, the rest of this entry will become obsolescent. At present, in the UK, the non-digital service utilizes only the top few of the 625 lines broadcasts. Individual frames are transmitted at the rate of ten or more a second and are picked up by the operator of the TV receiver, choosing the number of the frame required and waiting until it is transmitted. Thus, the number of frames available on a TV channel is limited because users will generally be unwilling to wait more than 15 s to see what they require. One solution by which these services have been expanded, has been to group together five or six frames on a subject, each of which is transmitted in turn, merely giving the watcher sufficient time to read each frame. A teletext service would be capable of vast expansion, if a whole TV channel were to be devoted to it. While the great advantage is that of low cost, no interactive communication is possible, severely limiting development potential. The UK BBC teletext service is called Ceefax and the UK Independent TV alternative, Oracle.

teletype airline ticket This form of air ticket used to be issued by IATA and ATC agents in the USA. It was a multi-copy carbonized document in continuous roll form to be used only on teletype equipment, the ticketing process normally being activated by the airline.

Telex Link The UK service that used to enable Prestel users to transmit telex messages through any Prestel compatible terminal.

Telidon A Canadian and American version of UK Prestel.

TEN[1] Trans-Euro-Night. Term now obsolete having been replaced by the EuroCity Night Train brand name. *See* European Rail sleeping cars.

TEN[2] In the USA, may mean Ticket Exchange Notice.

TEN[3] or **TEN-T** In the EU means transport, energy and communications networks. In April 2004 new guidelines were adopted by the EU for transport TENs which included a list of 30 priority projects. The cost of these would be around €225bn (£150bn, US$260bn).

tender A small boat which transfers passengers from ship to shore, when it is not possible to dock adjacent to quay. The same term has the general meaning of bidding for a contract, for example, when travel agents are invited to tender for a big company's travel account.

Tennessee Department of Tourism *See* www.tnvacation.com

terminal *See* airport terminals as a typical example. The same word describes any computer screen in the travel industry.

Texas Tourism *See* www.traveltex.com

T-Facts Travel agents' computerized accounting system developed in the UK by a London-based agent/tour operator, Trailfinders. *See* T FACTS.

TFCs Taxes, fees and charges, for example regarding air travel, these include airport service charges; departure, local, sales, departure and transportation taxes; passenger facility and service charges and customs inspection fees. These can be similar to the cost of the ticket! Some of these can only be paid locally; it is, therefore, important when arranging payment for issue of an air ticket in another country that the PTA (pre-paid ticket advice) specifies INCL TFCs, so that the full costs of the ticket are covered and none has to be borne by the recipient.

TFPP Travel Funds Protection Plan. *See* escrow account.

TGC Travel group charter.

TGP Tourism growth point. A UK tourism development initiative launched in 1977, which identified a series of places away from the existing main centres of tourism with potential. Substantial sums of money were successfully invested from government sources, mainly the Tourist Projects Scheme, in cooperation with private enterprise.

TGT Turbine gas temperature (aviation term).

TGV Train à Grande Vitesse is French Railway's (SNCF) fastest train in the world. In March 1985, through-TGV services were introduced from Paris to Grenoble, the last stage in the high-speed rail network linking the French capital with the whole of south-east France. Running at 270 kph on a newly-built track from Paris to Lyons, TGV is by far the fastest train in the world, not only because of its normal operating speed but because it also holds the world rail speed record of 320 mph (515 kph), achieved near Tours on 9 May 1990. In 2001 SNCF matched the Japanese record for long-distance rail travel over the 600 miles (960 km) between Calais and Marseilles, run in 3 h 29 min, an average speed of 170 mph (272 kph). Every day 100 TGV trains run a total 41,000 km and carry an average of 36,000 passengers. Its success is such that French Railways built another TGV line which came into service in 1990, serving Brittany, the Atlantic Seaboard and the Pyrenees. TGVs first came into service on 27 September 1981 and their network is still developing; on 11 June 2001 a new section in southern France was opened with stations at Valence, Avignon, Aix en Provence and Marseille, reducing the journey time from Paris to Marseille by 80 min to only 3 h. Travellers from London on Eurostar change at Lille, achieving a journey time from London to Marseilles of 6 h 50 min.

Textbooks suggest that rail cannot compete with air travel for journeys greater than 300 miles; however, the convenience of city-centre-to-city-centre travel means that TGV is often travellers' choice for journeys up to 625 miles.

TGV operations are a testimony to the hypothesis that speed and service improvements will divert more traffic to rail. During the first 3 years of operation, annual passenger traffic between Paris and the south-east of the country increased by 51%, 48% being directly attributable to TGV. The final cost of building the high-speed line from Paris to Lyon varied by only 1% from the original estimate, being 7.8 billion francs, while the cost of the rolling stock was 5 billion francs. The cost of building one TGV train-set is 52.2 billion francs, which works out at 135,000 francs per passenger's seat offered, approximately one tenth of that of a seat on short distance aircraft. TGV revenue is sufficient to cover not only operational costs, but also interest charges and repayments on the original loan. The whole of the latter was paid off by 1990, an extremely short period in view of the scale of the operation.

TGV offers high-speed travel to everyone, whether in first or second class, the basic fare being the same as on the rest of the SNCF network. The only extra charge on TGV is during peak hours. Reservations are compulsory, seat bookings opening 2 months prior to date of travel. If a traveller possesses a ticket, a self-service reservation system is available to enable passengers to book on the first TGV with seats available, leaving within 90 min following the request at the computer terminal. This, however, is not to be recommended, since on a late booking, the computer will not assign particular seats, for example, in a smoking or non-smoking area or window, aisle or meal seats. A version of the TGV that provides the Eurostar high-speed international services between London, Paris and Brussels is called the Trans Manche Super Train (TMST). Each 18-carriage train is powered by 12 asynchronous traction motors, each rated at 1 MW.

Thailand Tourism Authority *See* www.tat.or.th

thalassotherapy Treatment available at health resorts which varies. Sometimes involves covering the body with mud or seaweed, or may merely be immersion in mineral or sea water.

thanatourism Also known as dark tourism. Visiting sites such as former battlefields, concentration camps, cemeteries and other sites associated with death and destruction.

'the folk' Travel industry pejorative name for folk dancing or any similar activities which fulfil tourists' insatiable demand for authentic local culture. This 'staged authenticity' may be only a tourism show, part of local cultural heritage but no longer normally performed.

The Hotel Industry Switch Company *See* THISCO.

The International Ecotourism Society US body which promotes sustainable tourism. *See* www.ecotourism.org

The Travel Institute Changed name from the Institution of Certified Travel Agents of America in September 2003; runs the well known CTA and CTC qualification courses. *See* www.icta.com *or* www. thetravelinstitute.com

theme cruise *See* special interest holidays.

theme parks Funfairs and pierhead amusements were the forerunners of this major tourism phenomenon of the second half of the 20th century, exemplified by

Disneyland and Disney World, and otherwise known as leisure parks. What is a theme park? It is hard to provide a definition because of their diverse nature. Displays of artefacts of the UK industrial revolution, in 'heritage museums'; safari parks, the modern equivalent of zoos; vast funfairs with extraordinary and thrilling rides; and everything aquatic, as in Seaworld in the USA. In the *Tourism Marketing and Management Handbook* Jean-Claude Corze suggests: 'A site, uniting in a single enclosure a series of attractions and activities and completed with a number of important side services such as cafeterias, restaurants, shops and lodgings'. It is felt that this definition is unsatisfactory in a number of respects; for example, the provision of accommodation is not an essential. The following alternative is offered. A theme or leisure park is a man-made tourist attraction, usually on a large scale and usually mainly in the open, providing interest and entertainment to people of all ages. Theme park is the description for a park catering to a particular market or with any overall theme or interest paramount, while leisure park is the more general or generic term.

Many readers will be surprised to learn that Coney Island, New York, USA, was established in 1887. Disneyland in California, which opened in 1955, and Disney World/Epcot in Florida are in a class of their own, each regularly attracting well over 10 million visitors annually. (Even a major tourist destination like Britain can only manage 12 million!) Original costs of US$1.5 billion at Disney World have been matched by similar investment since. But with a Disney turnover which will have reached US$1 billion annually, by the time these words are being read, the investment has been worthwhile. In the USA, at the time of writing, there were around 2000 theme parks, around 40 of which are big enough to attract over a million visitors a year. The Six Flags sites are the best known outside the USA, apart from Disney.

In the UK, the biggest development of this type has been Alton Towers in Staffordshire. Thorpe Park, by the side of the Thames, was built on the site of some old gravel pits, but many British developments are associated with stately homes, such as Windsor Safari Park, Woburn Abbey and Longleat.

On the European mainland, in mid-April 1992, a Disney complex opened near Paris, to compete with the Jardin d'Acclimatation and Mirapolis. Phantasialand near Cologne in Germany, Walibi, near Brussels in Belgium and Efteling in Holland are indications that huge sums of money are being spent on the assumption that Europeans will develop a similar taste to Americans for theme parks. For UK statistics *see* sightseeing in Britain.

Themis Foundation   Created in 1998 by the WTO and the Government of Andorra with the mission to promote quality and efficiency in tourism education and training and in general in the development of human resources in tourism. Details accessible via WTO Internet site www.world-tourism.org The WTO certification system for quality and efficiency in tourism education, TedQual, is detailed in www.themis.ad/english/products/tedqual_info.htm

thermal printer   Associated with a computer terminal, this acts as a dump printer, using special paper to produce a copy of the image shown on the screen. Slow in operation, it is unsuitable for other travel industry uses. Many fax (facsimile) machines use this technology.

THF   Obsolete. Was Trusthouse Forte in the UK, known as Forte Hotels. It was a leading hotel operator in the UK, owning over 200 hotels with around 21,000 rooms in the 1990s. But following the sale of the group and dismantling of the brands, Forte ceased to exist from June 2001.

THISCO   Acronym stands for The Hotel Industry Switch Company. A global hotel CRS formerly owned by 17 of the largest worldwide hotel companies, now part of Pegasus Solutions Inc. The Ultra-Switch Europe gateway, located in London, was activated in August 1990. HCC, the Hotel Clearing Corporation is a THISCO subsidiary created to provide centralized commission payments on hotel bookings to travel agents, worldwide, in local currencies. UltraSelect is THISCO's seamless connectivity function (*see* explanation under this heading). *See* www.thisco.com *and* www.pegasus.thisco.com

Thomas Cook Born in England in 1808, he thought of the idea of chartering trains to bring supporters to temperance meetings in the Midlands. His first excursion train ran from Leicester to Loughborough and back on 5th July 1841, with 570 passengers who each paid 1 shilling return. This excursion is regarded as making Thomas Cook, the world's first tour operator and it was only later that he also became a travel agent. It was also in 1841 that Henry Wells started a company which 9 years later merged to form Wells Fargo. Thus, American Express, the successor company and Thomas Cook both have claims to be the oldest travel company in the world.

Thomsons' Automatic Banking System (TABS) See TABS.

three-letter codes Cities and airports worldwide have been given three-letter codes for abbreviated identification purposes in ticketing and timetables.

three-quarter pension Scandinavian term for a hotel tariff which includes a meal plan of breakfast, dinner and a packed lunch which guests make for themselves from a cold table.

through fare A fare for travel between any two points which allows for stopovers en route. The fare rules may limit transport to one carrier, and may limit the number of stops allowed.

throwaway Any item in the land part of an inclusive tour which it is difficult or undesirable for the passenger to use, so that it is rarely, if ever, utilized. Such items have been included in the tour package merely to qualify the passenger for a tour-based air fare. The arrangement involving a throwaway is commonly called a minimum-rated package tour.

THWG Ticketing Handbook Working Group of IATA.

TIA The Travel Industry of America represents the interests of all 1.4 million organizations in the US travel industry. Travel to and within the USA is promoted by means of its Discover America annual Pow Wow and other marketing activities. The International Association of Travel Officials was formed in 1939, designed to encourage reciprocal travel within the Western Hemisphere. In 1941 it changed from an international to a national organization with a new name of National Association of Travel Officials to focus on promoting travel in the USA and securing favourable legislation for the travel industry. In the mid-1960s, Discover America, Inc., was formed, which in 1969 was merged with NATO to become Discover America Travel Organizations. In May 1980, the name was changed to the Travel Industry Association of America (TIA). See www.tia.org; for general US tourism information see www.SeeAmerica.org

TIAC Tourism Industry Association of Canada. See www.tiac.ca

TIAS Travel Industries Automated Systems. The main Australian airline reservation distribution system which connects over 4500 terminals and printers to over 40 airlines and tour operators. The system uses SLIQ software developed by Novus Systems Technology and is owned by QANTAS and Southern Cross.

TIBA Traffic information broadcast by aircraft.

TIBS Was Travel Industry Booking System. A UK computer system for both tour operators and agents.

TIC Tourist Information Centre. A UK term indicating an office, usually run by a tourist board or local authority, providing information about that locality to visitors. Increasingly, TICs are undertaking many travel agency functions. TICs vary greatly in the commercial activities they undertake.

ticket Document identifying the bearer as a fare-paid passenger on a mode of transport. Tickets usually mention that carriage is subject to conditions laid down by the operator. In their simplest forms, tickets merely note the price paid; however, most tickets also state the origin and destination for which travel is covered by the ticket. Official IATA definition is the document entitled 'Passenger Ticket and Baggage Check, issued by or on behalf of the carrier and includes the conditions of contract and notices and the flight and passenger coupons contained therein'. This definition must be read together with the IATA definition 'passenger ticket'. There are many types of air ticket in common use worldwide, fully described in the *IATA Ticketing Handbook*. The latest versions for manual hand-written issue are of two types – for airline use and by a billing and settlement plan agent; the previous styles of these are still in use in the USA. The Transitional Automated Ticket (TAT) is for airline use and the Off Premise Transitional Automated Ticket (OPTAT) for others; both are continually being updated. The original version of an Automated Ticket/Boarding Pass (ATB1) is designed for all users. The second version of an Automated Ticket/Boarding Pass (ATB2) is for airline use; there is an equivalent Off Premises Automated Ticket/Boarding Pass (OPATB2). ATBs incorporate a magnetic stripe for electronic reading; stapling or writing on the tickets can damage the stripe. Travel industry staff must take particular care when handling ATBs. There are no generally accepted worldwide ticket formats for other transport modes; commentary on these has been left out by design rather than accident! The word ticket also has general meanings as indicating payment for admission, for example, to cinemas, theatres and sporting events. It should be particularly noted that IATA seeks to end the use of paper air tickets in favour of e-ticketing by 2007. *See also* ATB and ATB2, air tickets, automated ticket, bar code, bull's-eye, computer airline ticket, e-ticketing, MPD[2], OCR, OPTAT, OPATB2, TAT *and* teletype airline ticket.

ticket agent In the UK, a generic term, somewhat archaic, used as alternative to travel agent or to describe a theatre ticket agent. In North America, may describe an officially authorized agency as distinct from one that docs not hold ticket stocks; ticket agent is also a member of staff of a transportation company or travel agency, although strictly speaking, it should only be used concerning someone who actually issues tickets. The term is 'creeping' into Europe in this form.

ticket collector Used to be the name of the rail official who checked the validity of disembarking passengers' tickets, charging as necessary and retaining used tickets. Now, however, most rail stations are either 'open' or have automatic barriers actuated only by correct tickets. Ticket inspection is usually done on board trains. Nevertheless, the old name sticks and these inspectors are often called ticket collectors, even though they no longer collect tickets.

ticket on departure *See* TOD[1].

ticket printer Official IATA definition is a computer-driven machine that imprints ticketing data on a traffic document in the prescribed format. But, of course, the term has general travel industry application.

ticket, conjunction *See* conjunction tickets.

ticket, excess baggage *See* excess baggage ticket.

ticket, passenger Official IATA definition is a receipt issued by a carrier which provides for the carriage of the passenger.

ticketed point mileage *See* TPM *and* IATA fare construction system.

ticketing codes IATA prescribe several series of code letters to designate various aspects of a flight on an air ticket. *See* airline class *and* fare designators for full details.

Ticketing Information Exchange Standard Official IATA definition is the ATA/IATA standard which defines specifications for the exchange of ticketing information between airlines.

ticketing systems for travel agents *See* travel agents' computerized accounting and ticketing systems in the UK.

ticketing time limit The official IATA definition is: 'the time by which the passenger must secure his ticket for a confirmed reservation as required by the carrier'. IATA lays down strict time limits for ticketing. This must be effected at least 30 days before departure date, when reservations have been made more than 2 months before travel. Bookings confirmed between 2 months and 15 days before departure should be ticketed at least 7 days before travel. If reservations are made between 14 days and 3 days before travel, ticketing should be at least 48 hours before departure, while for bookings within 3 days of a journey commencing, ticketing should be as soon as possible. These limits are often completely disregarded!

ticketing, airline selection rules Official IATA definition is the rules governing the selection, by the agent, of the airline to be designated as the ticketing airline on a neutral ticket.

ticketless travel *See* e-ticketing.

TID Travel Industry Designator. *See* IATA TID.

tides In tidal waters, the water rises to its peak about every 12 h 25 min, roughly half the time it takes the moon to circle the earth. Tides follow the moon, somewhat behind it, one high tide being at the side of the earth opposite to the moon, and the other facing it. The sun exerts a similar gravitational pull on water, thus, when sun and moon correspond, there is a bigger, or spring tide. When the gravitational pulls are at right angles, this conflict produces a small tidal range or neap tide. *See* link span.

TID Travel Industry Designator. *See* IATA TID.

TIDS Travel Industry Designator Service. Continental Airlines and Northwest Airlines require US domestic air booking locations which are not ARC accredited, but using a GDS, to obtain an RSP (Reservation Service Provider) number from ARC. This applies to all non-ARC users of a GDS outside contractors and corporate customers. In lieu of an RSP number, non-accredited international booking locations located outside the USA, Puerto Rico and US Virgin Islands must obtain a TIDS (Travel Industry Designator Service) number from IATA. Applications via www.arccorp.com/aguaform.htm (US$225 for 3 years) or www.iata.org/tids (US$55).

TIENET International Tourism Exchange Network. *See* WTIEC.

TIES¹ *See* Ticketing Information Exchange Standard.

TIES² The International Ecotourism Society in the USA, which promotes sustainable tourism. *See* www. ecotourism.org *see also* tourism, sustainable for monograph on topic.

TIM *The Travel Information Manual* features health and immigration requirements of a large number of countries to which the sponsoring airlines fly.

TIMAS Travel Industry Multi-Access System; a travel agent's CRS in the Irish Republic associated with Galileo.

TIMATIC The electronic version of *The Travel Information Manual* enabling reservation clerks automatically to access health and visa requirements for an air traveller's itinerary. Multiple destination and transit points can be taken into account as well as countries visited by the passenger in the 6 days prior to the trip in question. TIMATIC is

updated continuously with information concerning the 216 countries featured. Response time is less than 3.5 s for 90% of transactions and less than 5 seconds for 98% of the enquiries. TIMATIC is stored on the SITA, the airlines data processing and communications system in Atlanta, USA. *See* www.iata.org/tim

TIME Travel Industry Marketing Enterprises, an industry grouping in the USA.

time and mileage car rental rate A rate which is based on the period of rental, usually per day, with a charge per mile travelled. Weekly rentals are usually on an 'unlimited' mileage basis.

time charter *See* charter.

time worldwide *See* GMT *and* times at sea.

times at sea Telling the time at sea is based upon the spells of duty of a ship's crew, known as watches. The afternoon watch is from midday to 16.00. This is followed by the first dog watch until 18.00 and the second dog watch until 20.00. The first watch is from then until midnight, the middle watch lasts until 04.00, the morning watch from then to 08.00 and the forenoon watch from 08.00 to 12.00. On board ship, bells will be heard being struck every half hour. The first half hour after a watch has started, one bell will be struck, the second two bells and so on, finally reaching a maximum of eight bells. Dog watches have been designed to enable duties to rotate between members of a vessel's crew.

Timesaver Two meanings. One is the name given to British Airways' voucher tickets held by non-travel companies or businessmen. Applies to domestic travel only. Passengers can telephone BA direct to make bookings, entering reservation references on timesaver tickets. If provided to a business house through an agent the retailer's account is debited for all flights made and normal commission earned. Alternative meaning is the name of British Midland Airways' domestic flights.

timeshare A lease, usually on holiday property, for a specified part of the year for a long period or 'in perpetuity' according to the contract agreed. In EU Directive 94/47/EC, timeshare is defined as: 'Any contract or group of contracts concluded for at least 3 years under which, directly or indirectly, on payment of a certain global price, a real property right or any other right relating to the use of one or more immovable properties for a specified or specifiable period of the year, which may not be less than 1 week, is established or is the subject of a transfer or an undertaking to transfer'. 'Holiday clubs', described under this name as a separate entry, are not covered by the EC legislation, because membership of the club is not linked to any rights in any particular property.

Typically, a timeshare will be for an apartment or villa in a development for the same week or 2 weeks of every year during the summer and often a week off-season, when the developers will have found it difficult to sell. Timeshare purchasers have the right to use the accommodation, which is usually fully furnished etc., during their annual period, upon paying a capital sum to the site owners. Maintenance and other charges for the upkeep of the specified accommodation purchased as well as general amenities still have to be paid annually. The timeshare concept may vary from merely being applied to small units of accommodation, up to sharing in huge developments offering every major sporting and leisure activity.

Timeshare exchange companies service owners by providing the opportunity to exchange a fortnight's vacation with other timeshare owners all over the world. UK market leader in the exchange field is RCI which claims over 50% of British membership of exchange systems. The Organization for Timeshare in Europe (OTE) explains that the popularity of the exchange system has led to the holiday club concept, a timeshare product where holidaymakers buy points instead of a specific slot at a particular resort. These points then act as a holiday currency. Each time a timeshare apartment is chosen, the number of 'points' that will be paid varies according to the quality, season and duration required.

The timeshare concept was developed in the mid-1970s; according to the OTE, revenues of over US$6 billion are generated annually; timeshare is forecast to grow as fast as overall world travel and tourism over the next 10 years. There are currently 4.4 million timeshare owners of properties in 5300 resorts worldwide; in Europe, there are 1.2 million owners in 1600 resorts.

Although a theoretically sound concept, timeshare development attracted some unscrupulous operators in its early days as an industry, resulting in an undeserved bad name for all the honest developers. This led to legislation in most countries to control timeshare sales. Typical is the EU Directive 94/47/EC enacted in the UK on 29/4/97. This deals with the information to be provided to a purchaser and provides for a 'cooling off' period of at least 10 days during which the purchaser can withdraw from any agreement made to purchase a timeshare. Taking of deposits before the end of the cooling-off period is prohibited. Contracts must be in the language of the EU member state of residence of the purchaser. In Europe, members of the OTE must abide by a comprehensive code of ethics, which offers much more protection to timeshare purchasers.

The strong sales methods in this sphere have resulted in some unusual jargon. An OPC is an Offsite Personal Contact, who has the responsibility of approaching potential timeshare purchasers who are holidaymakers nearby, attracting them to visit a new development. The Ups are the people who go along to visit, while a 'one-legged up' is an Up without a spouse. The Line is a line of timeshare salesmen, the most successful of which are at the head of the Line and get the first chance to sell and earn their commission, when a new prospect arrives. For very detailed information *see* the Organization for Timeshare in Europe web site www.ote-info.com; for the British government consumer gateway *see* www.consumer.gov.uk/consumer_web/holiday.htm#5 For the UK government DTI Timeshare Guide *see* www.dti.gov.uk/cacp/ca/tsbulletin.htm *See below* for the Timeshare Consumers Association. *See also* VOICE.

Timeshare Consumers Association *See* www.timeshare.org.uk

Timeshare Council Was the UK timeshare industry association; in 1998 the major European trade associations in the field formed the Organization for Timeshare in Europe (OTE), abandoning independent national status. *See* OTE, timeshare and www.ote-info.com. The title 'Timeshare Council' continues to be used by a Spanish organization with a web site under that name.

timetable List of times of departure and arrival of a mode of transport between various places. Usually published in leaflet or brochure format, if it merely covers an individual operator's services. May be several volumes thick with many thousands of pages, if covering many operator's services, e.g. the *OAG*, providing comprehensive worldwide airline timetables.

TIMG Was the Travel Industry Marketing Group in the UK; title obsolete as now called CIMTIG. *See* CIMTIG.

TIP¹ Transportation Improvement Programme in the USA. Main objective is to cause implementation of planning resulting from other US groups.

TIP² May also mean Tourist Information Point. In the UK these are usually unstaffed, differentiating them from TICs (Tourism Information Centres). A TIP may be little more than a large board with a map indicating places of local interest, and other important local information, such as emergency telephone numbers and details of banking facilities.

tipping *See* gratuity.

TIPTO Truly Independent Professional Travel Organisation in the UK. Small grouping of niche market independent tour operators and their agency supporters. *See* www.tipto.co.uk

TIZ Traffic information zone (aviation term).

TL Transition level (aviation term).

TMA Terminal control area (aviation term).

TMC Travel management company; modern usage for a company specializing in handling business and corporate travel. *A list of 70 other business travel related entries follows* corporate travel contracts, *some of which lead to further entries.*

TMP Technical monitoring programme.

TMST Trans-Manche Super Train. A version of the TGV that provides high-speed international services between London, Paris and Brussels, via the Channel Tunnel.

T-NASA Taxi navigation and situation awareness.

TO Tourist Office. *See* entries for National Tourist Office and US State Tourist Office web sites under country and state names; *also see* Tourism Offices Worldwide Directory www.towd.com

to be advised/notified *See* TBA.

to view The 2003 CEN/European Standard official definition has attempted to resolve misunderstandings by travellers of this phrase and the phrase 'to visit', suggesting the adoption of definitions: 'to view – to look at items of cultural or natural interest, usually specified in the itinerary, from afar or nearby, for a short or long time, without visiting them' and 'to visit – to physically enter a site of cultural or natural interest specified in the itinerary'. It is hoped that promulgation of these simple concepts in this dictionary will result in them becoming more widely known and used.

to visit *See* to view.

TOC¹ Was ABTA Tour Operators Council. ABTA used to be governed by two councils, one representing tour operators, the other, agents. Each elected five members to form ABTA's controlling body, National Council. In 1999, this was replaced by a single unified Board consisting of both operators and agents.

TOC² Train operating company in the UK. *See* ATOC.

TOD¹ Ticket on Departure. By telephoning an airline and giving an MPD² (MCO in some countries) document number, arrangements can be made for a ticket to be available for a passenger at any departure airport. The same information may be sent electronically through a CRS to an airline. A copy of the document concerned is forwarded for accounting purposes. Some airlines, as a security check, always telephone back to the agent to prevent misuse of the system. In the USA and some other countries, non-airline independent airport ticketing organizations are being set up to handle agents' TODs for a fee.

TOD² Top of descent (aviation term).

TODA Take-off distance available (aviation term).

TODS Tourist orientated directional signage; acronym noted in US listings but not in general use in the UK.

token block Traditionally single-track railway lines have been controlled by exchanging wood or metal tokens to give a train exclusive access to a section of track. With radio token blocks, the token becomes an electronic message, transferred between a computer in the lines' control room and the train driver's cab by radio.

toll Fee for a traveller to use a bridge or road.

toll free telephone calls A huge number of the travel industries' bookings and conversations throughout the world take place on the telephone. In order to attract travel agents and customers to their particular services, travel companies have been in the forefront of introducing free or reduced-rate telephone charges. In America travel industry companies are the largest users of the 800 toll-free telephone systems, while in Europe a similar trend has developed. In the UK British Telecom introduced 0800 free-dialling facilities in 1985, mainly for travel agents, enabling them to direct dial to airlines and other travel principals, at no cost to agents. Variations to this such as 0870 numbers have resulted in increasing communications costs for UK agents, with some travel principals making substantial profits from their telephone access points.

tollway A US motorway on which users are charged for travel; commonly, a distance card is provided on entry and payment is made at the time of exit. Also known as a turnpike.

tonnage Term originally derived from number of tuns or casks of wine that a ship could carry. Later when spelling changed, it has tended to be confused with normal measures of weight. The gross tonnage of a ship is its inside volume, measured in tonnes, each of which is 100 cubic ft. Net tonnage uses the same units and is a way of expressing how much of the space can be used by passengers or for cargo, by deducting engine rooms and crew quarters etc. from the gross tonnage. Imagine putting a ship in a large bath already filled to the top. The displacement tonnage is the weight of the water that would overflow when the ship was put in the bath. By Archimedes' principle, this is identical to the actual weight of the ship, which is measured in a normal ton of 2240 pounds. But note that on the continent of Europe, outside the

UK, the term tonne probably means 1000 kg. Deadweight tonnage is the actual weight of cargo, fuel, fresh water and stores etc., when a ship is fully loaded. In other words its capacity for carrying purposes. *See also* passenger space ratio (PSR) *and* ship density.

Top Executive class Brand name of Air Portugal's business class and cabin, for the area immediately adjacent to first class, where passengers paying full fares gain improved service and facilities including use of a luxury lounge at Lisbon airport. *See* business class.

Top Flight Club Name of Northwest's Frequent Flyer Club. *See* FFP (frequent flyer programme).

Top Traveller Name of Austrian Airlines' Frequent Flyers Club. *See* FFP (frequent flyer programme).

top-up insurance Sometimes, for UK travellers renting a car in the USA, the basic travel insurance included in the rental rate is insufficient to fully cover third-party liability, the laws concerning which vary from state to state. Top-up insurance is necessary to provide this cover.

TOP[1] Tour Operators' Package fares. A type of group ITX fare. In the UK, these low-cost fares are available only to ATOL-holding tour operators. Groups of at least ten passengers (15 in Austria) must be contracted for at least 1 month before departure. TOP fares available ex-UK to Austria, France, Scandinavia and Switzerland. Similar to SGIT.

TOP[2] Thomson Open Line Programme. The acronym for Thomson Holidays' private viewdata system, providing full interactive communication with UK travel agents, enabling them to make bookings direct from their office terminals.

TOP[3] Tour Operator Program of ASTA. *See* ASTA Tour Operator Program *and* bond for outline of this scheme protecting purchasers of travel services from loss.

TOPAS Tour Operator Product Availability Standard in the UK. *See* Travel Technology Initiative.

topoguide A map or guide of particular use to walkers following marked paths, often including information about places of historical, scenic or other interest. The same word may also describe a canal or river map. The term *is not* in common usage in English-speaking countries; it is used in France and some other European countries. A cartoguide is the same thing.

TOPS[1] Brand name of two entirely different British tour operators' computerized reservation and accounting systems. The system introduced by Travel and Specialised Computers (TAS) Limited in 1978 and the Tour Operators' System available since 1979 from Hallamshire Programming Limited.

TOPS[2] Total Operations Processing System. This was a computerized system for monitoring the location of freight wagons on the British Rail network.

TORA Take-off run available (aviation term).

TORIX Tour Operator Reservation in XML; a UK standard. *See* Travel Technology Initiative.

TOS Was Tour Operators System designed by SEMA, a Belgian group, European market-leaders in the production of software systems for tour operators.

TOSG Obsolete – was Tour Operators' Study Group but is now called the Federation of Tour Operators, the organization of Britain's major tour operators.

Total Access A Sabre service mark. For details *see* Sabre.

touchdown The landing of an aircraft.

touchless rate Price or fare offered by providers of tourism services for fully automated reservations, without any human intervention.

touchless transaction A booking with a tourism service provider which is fully automated and has not required any human intervention.

tour *See* inclusive tour.

tour broker An individual or company which, not owning any transport, equipment or other facility, charters space and/or equipment required to supply the ground arrangements needed for a package tour commissioned by a tour wholesaler.

tour conductor In North America, any individual who is in charge of, or who personally escorts a group of passengers for all or any part of their journey. Many group ITX fares rules allow a free flight for one or more tour conductors. In Europe, would probably now be called a tour manager, or sometimes a guide or courier. *See* tour manager. The official IATA designation is 'an individual who is in charge of and/or who personally escorts a group of passengers for all or part of the itinerary'.

tour director *See* tour manager.

tour escort *See* tour manager.

tour leader *See* tour manager.

tour manager 'Senior conductor when more than one tour escort is involved for a large group of passengers' – is now the least likely meaning although it is still to be found in older textbooks. By 1990, Reed Travel Group in *ABCs of Travel* had designated the term as, 'a person who leads a trip from beginning to end, or at least, the land portion'. Verité Reily Collins in *Authentically English* (1996) distinguishes between a tour manager, conductor and director, suggesting a tour manager is 'a person in charge of coach tour', while a tour conductor is a tour manager in charge of a group and a tour director is a person in charge of a group of tourists. To distinguish between them, the artifice was used of suggesting that a tour manager was qualified to English NVQ Level 3 intermediate standard and tour director to Level 4. Few English tour managers are so qualified, let alone others.

Richard English in the 2nd edition of Columbus Press *World Travel Dictionary* (1999) offered a better definition, 'person who manages and supervises a pre-established tour itinerary, ensuring that it is carried out according to schedule and to standard'. However, although the source is not stated, this wording originates from the International Association of Tour Managers' (IATM) detailed definition, published in 1989 and revised in 1991 which describes the responsibilities of a tour manager as: 'To manage and supervise the pre-established itinerary, ensuring the programme is carried out in its entirety as described in the company's literature and sold to the consumer. To ensure that the standards and quality of all services included in the price of the package are maintained and that they are rendered efficiently and punctually. To care for the well-being, comfort and safety of each individual on the tour. To give all necessary help to any group in difficulty or an emergency. To furnish the group with background information en route covering the general ethnic, geographic, historic and socio-economic aspects of each country visited and customs and local practical information.'

The 2003 CEN/European Standard official definition can also be seen to have been derived from the IATM wording, 'A person who manages and supervises the itinerary on behalf of the tour operator, ensuring the programme is carried out as described in the tour operator's literature and sold to the traveller/consumer – who furnishes background information en route, covering general and particular ethnic, geographic and socio-economic aspects of the country visited, as well as local practical information'. This definition would be better if 'the operator of the tour', was substituted for 'tour operator', which has too specific a meaning.

Against the background of this lengthy entry, what is a **tour escort**? The 2003 CEN/European Standard official definition states specifically that it is a 'representative of a tour operator providing basic assistance to travellers'. Unfortunately, this is not accurate. The term 'escorted tour' is in wide use, so that it is hardly surprising that travellers often refer to their tour manager as their escort. *The Traveller's World* by Nona Starr and Sybil Norwood suggests that in North America, a tour escort is the same as a tour manager. Finally, the term, **tour leader.** *The Travel Dictionary* by Claudine Dervaes suggests this also is synonymous with a tour escort or tour manager. *See also* tour conductor.

tour operator 'A person or organization combining several elements of travel arrangements and offering them as a product for sale at a single price. Typically, tour operators arrange and sell the products known as package holidays and inclusive tours.' Inclusive Tours (ITs) are organized by tour operators for sale either direct to the public or through agents. Price breakdown of the elements which make up a typical UK short-haul overseas inclusive tour by charter flight is: accommodation 38%;

flying 40%; transfers and other overseas costs 2%; basic agency commission 10%; marketing 3%, between 1.5% and 2% of which is incentive commission; contribution to overheads including profit 7%. In simplistic terms, a tour operator is any organization or individual organizing a tour. But the rules concerning what constitutes a tour vary between different regulatory authorities. For example, the EC, ABTA, BSI/CEN and IATA definitions explained below.

The EC define as tour operators, any person or organization arranging package holidays, but clearly, the operators of other types of inclusive tour are also operators. The EC definition of an inclusive tour is in EC Directive 90/314/EEC on package travel, package holidays and package tours – 'the pre-arranged combination of not fewer than two of the following when sold or offered for sale at an inclusive price and when the service covers a period of more than 24 h or includes overnight accommodation: (i) transport; (ii) accommodation; (iii) other tourist services not ancillary to transport or accommodation and accounting for a significant proportion of the package'.

CEN is the European grouping of Standards Institutes. Between 1996 and 2003, a CEN working party devised tourism terminology applicable to travel agents and tour operators. Their definition extends the EC Directive, 'Enterprise organizing package tours and tourism services, selling them or offering them for sale whether directly or through retailers'. The associated definition of a Package Tour is: 'A pre-arranged combination of not fewer than two of the following tourism services when sold or offered for sale at an inclusive price and when the service covers a period of more than 24 h or includes overnight accommodation; transport; accommodation; other tourism services not ancillary to transport or accommodation and accounting for a significant proportion of the package tour'.

The definition used in the Association of British Travel Agents (ABTA) Articles of Association until 1999 was that an organization was considered to be engaged in the business of a tour operator, 'provided it acted as principal and not merely as agent remunerated only by commission; it organizes and offers for sale to members of the public at an inclusive price, tours, holidays, or other travel arrangements comprising at least transportation and accommodation. For this purpose, organizing includes entering into a contractual commitment with other principals for the purchase of blocks of such inclusive tours, holidays or other travel arrangements, and accommodation includes the provision of a car or other vehicle and that literature is published to market its own tours or holidays.' Note that there is no mention of 'pre-arranged', a word which features in the previous definitions. The EC Directive, for political and practical reasons, needed to exclude from the control of the Package Holiday legislation, many arrangements organized by travel agents and others for business travellers, which often involve a flight or rail journey combined with accommodation and car rental. The wording also excludes IITs (independent inclusive tours) sometimes called tailor-made packages.

In 1999, the new ABTA definition of a tour operator was adopted, 'Any person or organization carrying on business in whole or in part as a Principal to a contract with a consumer either directly or through an agent in respect of the sale or offer for sale of *travel arrangements* or who holds an Air Travel Organizer's licence to sell or offer for sale, in any capacity, travel arrangements to the general public'. *Travel arrangements* were then defined as: 'Transport, accommodation, tourist or business services and facilities, travel insurance, holidays, packages as defined in the Package Travel, Package Holidays and Package Tours Regulations 1992 or otherwise and any other arrangements designated as travel arrangements by the Board of Directors from time to time'. The effect of the very broad definition of travel arrangements is to severely lessen the usefulness of this definition for any other purpose other than membership of ABTA.

The official IATA definition of an **inclusive tour** is a pre-arranged combination of air transportation and surface

arrangements, other than solely public transportation, which is designed to encourage air travel and which conforms to certain minimum standards as defined in the applicable Resolution. In the UK, the term is applied to any package holiday arrangement including transportation and accommodation, sold together at a single price. *See also* legal status of a travel agent *and* travel principal.

Tour Operator Product Availability Standard (in the UK) *See* Travel Technology Initiative.

Tour Operator Program (of ASTA) *See* bond.

Tour Operator Reservation in XML A UK standard. *See* Travel Technology Initiative.

tour operator's representative European term for an escort and activities organizer for a static inclusive tour; sometimes called a local representative or just a 'rep'. On a coach tour, the tour operator's accompanying guide might still be called a courier, despite the insistence of tour managers that the term is obsolete. In North America, the alternatives host, escort and tour manager are more common.

tour operator's reservation systems For British viewdata systems accessible by travel agents *see* viewdata. For brief details of individual operators systems, *see* ACOS, Allbook, ATOP, Border, CHARMS, Coachbook, Ferrybook, Flightpak, Holidaymaster, ITour, Kenny Travel System, MARS, Microspace, Phobos, Reservision, TOPS[1], Tourpars, Tourplan, Tours, Travel Systems 4/11, Travelog *and* Trip.

The best of these systems carry an inventory which can be booked either as an inclusive package holiday or in individual components, such as flight only. Multi-centre arrangements, optional extras and independent inclusive itineraries can also be handled by the most sophisticated systems. Bookings are done in real time and pricing is usually provided. Both bookings and options are recorded. When reservations are not available there are extensive search facilities for offering alternative arrangements. The larger systems are accessible by UK agents direct on viewdata systems.

The biggest systems are also fully

integrated with the tour operators' accounting and management systems providing extensive statistical, management and control information, while even the smallest systems will usually provide facts such as costs of sales. Usually, these systems will automatically, produce confirmations, invoices, tickets, vouchers, itineraries, labels, letters to customers as well as general mailing facilities, receipts, airplane manifests, hotel rooming lists, transfer and coaching documentation, insurance and car hire information and releases to pay hotels.

tour order   *See* vouchers.

tour organizer   The organization or person arranging an inclusive tour, in North America, but in the UK, this is the tour operator; *alternatively* in the USA may be a person or organization assembling tour groups as an intermediary.

tour shell   *See* shells.

tour wholesaler   North American term for a tour operator selling through travel agents; tour wholesalers in the USA do not necessarily operate the package themselves. Richard English in the 2nd edition of *World Travel Dictionary* states, 'An organization that puts together an inclusive holiday for sale to the public. Tour operators are not regarded as principals in the UK travel industry, although there are occasions when they could be considered as such. Tour operators are more commonly regarded in much the same way as a wholesaler would be in the case of manufactured products.' Throughout the EC, by law, a tour operator *is* a principal, so the validity of this definition is questioned. As for the wholesaler analogy, S. (Rik) Medlik in the *Dictionary of Travel, Tourism and Hospitality* quite rightly points out that a tour operator is a manufacturer of travel products which assembles product components, just like a car manufacturer.

tour-basing fare   A creative (or normal) round-trip air, rail or sea fare used by tour operators as a basis to promote an inclusive tour and on which they qualify to obtain overriding commission only if they produce promotional literature in specified quantities.

touring camp   A campsite or caravan site. *See* campsite *and* caravan park.

touring caravan   A caravan which is mobile and moved around according to the owner's wishes, as distinct from one permanently sited in one place. *See* caravan.

touring park   A campsite or caravan site. *See* campsite *and* caravan park.

tourism   As this word forms part of the title and its use is pivotal to this reference dictionary, the entry is substantial. Most of the well-known definitions concern the demand side, the consumers. Readers are strongly reminded that there is also a supply side to tourism, the vast industry that satisfies the demands of tourists. There is a definition encompassing both sides at the end of this extensive entry. This monograph concentrates on the history of demand-side definitions. Those merely seeking the most generally used definition related to the demand side need look no further than the next few sentences.

No definitions in this field are universally accepted; the ones most frequently used are those adopted at the International Conference on Travel and Tourism Statistics held in Ottawa, Canada at the end of June 1991. These were ratified by the United Nations Statistical Commission at their 27th meeting in New York from 22 February to 3 March 1993. They agreed that:

Tourism comprises the activities of persons travelling to and staying in places outside their usual environment for not more than 1 consecutive year, for leisure, business and other purposes.
Domestic tourism is residents of a country visiting their own country; *inbound tourism* is non-residents visiting a country other then their own and *outbound tourism* is residents of a country visiting other countries.
An *international visitor* is any person who travels to a country other than that in which s/he has his/her usual residence outside his/her usual environment for a period not exceeding 12 months and whose main purpose of visit is other than the exercise of an activity remunerated from within the country visited.
An *international tourist* is a visitor who stays in the country visited for at least 1 night.

An *internal visitor* is any person residing in a country, who travels to a place within the country, outside his/her usual environment for a period not exceeding 12 months and whose main purpose of visit is other than the exercise of an activity remunerated from within the place visited.

An *internal* tourist is a visitor who stays in the place visited for at least 1 night.

A person is considered to be a *resident* in a country, if the person: (i) has lived for most of the past year (12 months) in that country; or (ii) has lived in that country for a shorter period and intends to return within 12 months to live in that country.

An *international same-day visitor* is a visitor who does not spend the night in a collective or private accommodation in the country visited.

An *internal same-day visitor* is a visitor who does not spend the night in a collective or private accommodation in the place visited.

Up-to-date information on the economic impact of tourism is available from the World Travel and Tourism Council (WTTC), 20 Grosvenor Place, London SW1X 7TT, UK. Tel: +44 (0)207 838 9400; fax +44 (0)207 838 9050; www.wttc.org Statistics now provided are intended merely to give readers an indication of the range of information available. In even greater detail, it is also accessible broken down into 13 world regions. The latest WTTC report estimated that in 2005 the travel and tourism economy accounted for 10.6% of world Gross Domestic Product (GDP). World Travel and Tourism Economy employment is estimated at 221,568,000 jobs in 2005, 8.3% of total employment. By 2015, this should total 260,556,000 jobs, 8.9% of total employment. However, Travel and Tourism industry jobs number only 74,223,000, 2.8% of total employment.

- Personal travel and tourism was US$2883 billion, 10.4% of total consumption; this included spending by residents on travel and tourism services such as air transport and hotels, and goods such as luggage, film and automobile use.

- Business travel was US$652.9 billion; this covered expenditure by companies and government agencies on travel while engaged on business.

- Capital investment by travel companies and government agencies on travel and tourism infrastructure was US$918 billion, 9.4% of total investment in 2005.

- Visitor export spending by international visitors was US$1512.5 billion in 2005, 12% of total exports.

- Thus, World Travel and Tourism is expected to generate US$6201.5 billion of economic activity (total demand) in 2005, growing in nominal terms to US$10,678.5 billion by 2015. Travel and Tourism demand is expected to grow by 5.4% in 2005 and by 4.6% per annum in real terms between 2006 and 2015.

It is hardly surprising that difficulties have been faced when attempting to define an activity of this magnitude. The definitions stated in this section arise from over 60 years of discussions. A committee report to the Council of the League of Nations in 1937 resulted in the widely quoted original United Nations definition. This defined a tourist as a temporary visitor staying at least 24 h, but less than 1 year in a country other than his own place of residence, when the purpose is either leisure, recreation, holiday, health, study, business, family affairs, convention or congress. Armed services staff, diplomats, resident students, those who accept employment in a foreign country and permanent migrants, were not considered tourists. This definition then went on to suggest that tourism was the vast worldwide industry which involves the transportation, feeding, provision of accommodation, entertainment and other facilities for the tourist.

This definition was slightly changed in 1950 at a meeting in Dublin of the International Union of Official Travel Organizations (IUOTO). It was altered again in 1953, when the UN Statistical Commission adopted a definition of the term, 'International visitor'.

The 1937 wording became obsolete, when a technical definition for statistical purposes was recommended by the UN conference on international travel and tourism held in Rome in 1963, which was subsequently approved by the 15th session of the UN Statistical Commission in New York in 1968, the same wording then being adopted by the 21st General Assembly of IUOTO in Dublin in 1969.

For statistical purposes, the term visitor describes any person visiting a country other than that in which he has his usual place of residence, for any reason other than following an occupation remunerated from within the country visited. This definition covers:

1. Tourists, i.e. temporary visitors staying at least 24 h in the country visited and the purpose of whose journey can be classified under one of the following headings:
• Leisure including recreation, holiday, health, study, religion and sport.
• Business, family, mission, meeting.
2. Excursionists, i.e. temporary visitors staying less than 24 h in the country visited, including travellers on cruises. The statistics should not include travellers who, in the legal sense, do not enter the country, for example, air travellers who do not leave an airport's transit area and similar cases.

Increasingly, definitions in this field are broad in scope and include business travel, although the argument as to whether the business traveller can properly be regarded as a tourist still continues. For example, H. Robinson, in his book, *A Geography of Tourism*, said that a tourist, 'is a person travelling for a period in excess of 24 h in a country other than that in which he normally resides'.

A paper presented at Ealing College of Technology in the UK in May 1971, suggested division of tourism into two highly artificial sectors, one dynamic and the other static. Within the former, are included the economic activities of the formation of the commodity, the motivation of demand and the provision of transport. The static sector is defined as that which looks after the sojourn part of tourism. However, the vertical integration of the travel industry world-wide, with large companies owning accommodation and transport as well as wholesale and retail organizations, draws attention to the obvious interdependence of all the elements.

The AIEST (International Association of Scientific Experts in Tourism) published a definition developed by Professor W. Hunziker in 1942, which says, 'Tourism is the sum of the phenomena and relationships arising from the travel and stay of non-residents, insofar as they do not lead to permanent residence and are not connected with any earning activity'. This definition still has wide support and is quoted in textbooks worldwide.

In January 1975, the Department of Hotel, Catering and Tourism Management at University of Surrey, distributed some notes on their approach to studies in this field. They adopted a view which is, in effect, a translation of the previous definition into simpler language.

Tourism denotes the temporary, short-term movement of people to destinations outside the places where they normally live and work and their activities during the stay at these destinations. Much of this movement is international in character and much of it is a leisure activity.

Tourism is a highly complex phenomenon; it involves the activities and interests not only of large transport undertakings, but also owners of tourists sights and attractions and of various services at the destination as well as central and local government. Each of these serves both the resident population and visitors and their management must reconcile the needs of tourists with the needs of the resident population.

The UK Tourism Society has consistently adopted a broad definition which encompasses both domestic and foreign tourism, business and conference tourism, as well as on holidays, staying with friends and relatives, staying in self-catering units or serviced accommodation, day visits and overnight stays. This definition includes some, but not all travel and may include some leisure recreation and sport. The Tourism Society admits that the borderline in these latter respects is difficult to define.

The Tourism Society's 1976 definition changed the second sentence into a much broader, all-encompassing phrase. 'Tourism is the temporary short-term movement of people to destinations outside the places where they normally live and work and their activities during their stay at these destinations; it includes movement for all purposes as well as day visits or excursions'.

A.J. Burkart and S. Medlik in their book, *Tourism Past Present and Future*, 1974 and 1981, isolated the following five main characteristics of tourism as a concept.

1. Tourism arises from a movement of people to, and their stay in, various destinations.

2. There are two elements in all tourism: the journey to the destination and the stay including activities at the destination.

3. The journey and the stay take place outside the normal place of residence and work, so that tourism gives rise to activities, which are distinct from those of the resident and working populations of places through which tourists travel and in which they stay.

4. The movement to destinations is of a temporary, short-term character, with intention to return within a few days, weeks or months.

5. Destinations are visited for purposes other than taking up permanent residence or employment remunerated from within the places visited.

Unfortunately, much of the published literature criticises Burkart and Medlik's definitions because they exclude business travel. In fact, it was only in the 1974 edition of their book that this was so. Then, the wording of the last part, was, '... destinations are visited for purposes not connected with paid work, that is not to take up employment and not for business or vocational reasons'. The 1981 second edition wording that has been reiterated satisfies most criticism.

L.J. Lickorish in *Tourism, Volume IV, Review of UK Statistical Sources*, suggested that, 'Tourism embraces all movement of people to find their own community for all purposes except migration or regular daily work. The most frequent reason for this movement is for holidays, but it will also include, for example, attendances at conferences and movement on sporadic or infrequent business purposes.'

Of many reviews of the definitions of tourism, a paper by Leiper is recommended, entitled 'The framework of tourism; towards a definition of tourism, tourists and the tourism industry' (*Annals of Tourism Research* (1979) 6(4), 390–407). This paper identifies technical, economic and holistic ways of defining tourism. It is suggested that technical definitions demarcate the tourist to provide a common base by which to collect statistics; economic definitions recognize that tourism is an industry or a business; and holistic definitions attempt to embrace the whole essence of the subject.

An alternative review of definitions was written by J. Heeley in a paper entitled, 'The definition of tourism in Great Britain. Does terminological confusion have to rule?' (*Tourist Review* (1980) 2 (May/June), 11–14). Definitions were classified into either technical or conceptual.

Some definitions are merely meant to be descriptive while others attempt precision, so as to give validity to statistics based upon a particular understanding of the term. Sir George Young in *Tourism, Blessing or Blight* utilized a broad definition, stating that a tourist is someone who travels away from home.

Of the many shorter, but more technical, definitions, the one offered by John O'Dell in the *Journal of the UK Institute of Travel and Tourism* in 1980 is preferred to many others of that vintage. 'The temporary movement of people to destinations outside the places where they normally live and work and their leisure activities during the stay at those destinations.'

Reviewing what has been stated shows that the definition of tourism has become increasingly broader since the first accepted definition in 1937. In the 1986 WTO publication *Measurement of Travel and Tourism Expenditure*, number 2 in the series concerning statistical methods and techniques, there was the following short definition: 'The term tourism refers to all trips made by residents of a country, both within the country and abroad, for non-migratory purposes'. In considering this, the question must be asked, 'Was it intended that the commuter going to work each day should be included?'

This problem was considered in the next definition offered here. This was published in 1986 in the *Bulletin of the European Communities*, Supplement 4/86, entitled 'Community action in the field of tourism'. On page 5 it states: 'Tourism includes all journeys of more than 24 h for recreation, business, study or health purposes'. Subsequently, this definition was adopted by the WTO and the OECD. A comment at a conference is well remembered, 'The protests of the day-tripper and excursionist lobby have succeeded in changing the definition yet again'.

The foregoing has mainly been an historical listing of some of the main definitions of the demand side of tourism. There is a different approach to the topic by Jafar Jafari, in his article, 'Tourism models – the socio-cultural aspects' (*Tourism Management* (1987) 8(2)). Jafari echoes part of Marshall's famous definition of economics as the study of man in the ordinary everyday business of life, suggesting, 'Tourism is the study of man, away from his usual habitat, of the touristic apparatus and networks, and of the ordinary and non-ordinary worlds and their dialectic relationship'. The second half of this uses imprecise wording, such as 'ordinary and non-ordinary worlds', lessening its usefulness as a definition, while to use the word 'touristic' defeats the objective (although, to be fair these areas were qualified and explained by Jafari). However, this definition broke new ground, in the way it introduced both the supply and demand side into one definition. However, the 1991 Ottawa definition is believed to be right to nominate the 'activities' themselves rather than the study of them, to encompass tourism. Clearly, Jafari had in mind the reality of what his students were actually being taught.

So what of the supply side, the tourism industry itself, sadly neglected by the creators of most definitions. Leiper's 1979 paper has already been mentioned. Page 400 suggests that, 'The tourist industry consists of all those firms, organizations and facilities which are intended to serve the specific needs and wants of tourists'. The WTO has analysed these; in the absence of a Standard Industrial Classification (SIC) specific to tourism, they have produced a Standard International Classification of Tourism Activities. These were published in 1995 by WTO as an appendix to *Concepts, Definitions and Classifications for Tourism Statistics*. In this, for each type of organization in the tourism industry, the ISIC Category, Group and Class are named. Two sub-classes are denominated, 'T' for those dedicated to tourism and 'P' for those types of organization with partial involvement. A column headed 'Sales to tourism', suggests percentage sales explicitly from tourism. Another headed 'Share of tourism purchases', estimates the percentage of total tourism expenditure for each industrial activity. The letter H in either of these columns suggests 'high' meaning above 60% of sales. 'M' stands for medium, between 60% and 20% while 'L' is low, below 20%.

This moves considerably forward the discussion of appropriate definitions for the supply side of tourism, as, to the best of the knowledge of the author, there has been no criticism; only praise as to how comprehensive is SICTA. It is suggested that a glaring omission is computer reservation systems. The main Global Computer Reservation Systems Galileo, Sabre, Worldspan and Amadeus as well as many smaller companies throughout the world are vital to tourism. In the case of British systems providing access to tour operators, they are a crucial link. Leaving aside this oversight, the belief is expressed that what can be identified can be defined; the foregoing discussion, has undoubtedly identified what is included in both the demand and supply sides of tourism.

As was pointed out at the beginning of this section defining tourism, the United Nations Statistical Commission approved the decisions of the June 1991 Ottawa conference on travel and tourism statistics. That conference recommended that tourism comprises the activities of persons travelling to and staying in places outside their usual environment for not more than one consecutive year, for leisure, business and other purposes. In 2003, the results of the deliberations of Working Group 2 of Committee 329 of CEN, the European Standards Institutes, was published as a national standard by each CEN member institute. Aimed specifically at the fields of travel agents and tour operators, they agreed the concept of a 'provider of tourism services', defining this as 'Enterprise providing tourism services to wholesalers, tour operators and/travel agencies as well as directly to travellers'. Why not marry this idea to the UN official definition?

Apart from Jafari, academics in this field have not dared suggest the obvious. *Surely, a definition of tourism should encapsulate both the demand and supply sides? The first edition of this dictionary suggested the adoption of the following definition:*

Tourism comprises the activities of persons travelling to and staying in places outside their usual environment for not more than one consecutive year, for leisure, business and other purposes together with organizations or persons which facilitate these activities. It includes the services which enable and support those activities and the providers of those services, both public and private, whether supplied direct to travellers or through intermediaries.

At the end of 1999, the UK Quality Assurance Agency (QAA), responsible for Higher Education Standards called together five bodies to develop a set of generic statements which could be applied to all programmes of study relevant to Unit 25, broadly speaking, the fields of leisure, hospitality, sport and tourism. The British Association for Sport and Exercise Sciences, Council for Hospitality Management Education, Leisure Studies Association, National Liaison Group for Higher Education in Tourism and the UK Standing Conference for Leisure, Recreation and Sport consulted with 91 institutions

delivering education programmes in these fields. Their definition of tourism published in January 2000 also combined both supply and demand side definitions. 'The term tourism refers to the phenomena and relationships arising from the travel and stay of people away from their normal home environments for a variety of purposes. This includes activities in the private sector such as tour operators, airlines and hotel companies, as well as public and not-for-profit bodies such as tourist boards.' Surrey University has adopted the first part of the NLG recommended definition but has replaced the second sentence with 'It includes the products, structure of and interactions in the tourism industry; the characteristics of tourists and the effect of the phenomena on communities and environments.' Despite the current awareness of the need to include in any definition of tourism both supply and demand sides, there is great reluctance to mention the supply side first, despite it being acknowledged as the world's largest industry. The second edition of this dictionary follows this theme by suggesting a further simplified definition of tourism: Tourism includes organizations and people providing services which facilitate the travel and stay of people away from their normal home for a variety of reasons; tourism also includes the study of these people (defined as tourists) and the phenomena arising from their travel.

In the 'tourism' entry in *The Encylopedia of Tourism* which Jafar Jafari edited in 2000 and subsequently, a holistic approach is now strongly supported, defining tourism as: 'The study of man (the tourist) away from his usual habitat, of the touristic apparatus and networks responding to his various needs, and of the ordinary (where the tourist is coming from) and non ordinary (where the tourist goes to) worlds and their dialectic relationships'. The *study* of tourism happens in universities and research organizations – but surely, by definition, tourism is the thing itself, the activities which it encompasses rather than the study of it. Moreover, the use of *him* rather than asexual nomenclature, is, to say the least, old fashioned. While recognizing the outstanding contribution he has made to the development of tourism as an academic discipline, it is not felt that Professor Jafari's latest definition is helpful.

Clearly the definition of 'tourism' has not yet stabilized.

See also many immediately following entries, commencing with the word 'tourism'. Part of the QAA Benchmark Statement is reiterated as Appendix II.

Tourism Alliance UK domestic tourism lobbying body formed in October 2001. First Chairman Digby Jones, Confederation of British Industry Director General. Members include CBI, ABTA and BITOA. It seeks to establish and maintain a favourable operating environment for all businesses involved in the delivery of tourism, particularly in England. It provides a forum for discussion as well as a lobby on issues of quality, competitiveness and best practice. It intends to create a united voice for tourism at the national level and work towards industry-wide cohesion; and to identify and develop policies and strategies to raise standards and promote quality within the industry.

tourism area life cycle May be referred to as TALC, as in TALC curve. Theory of how resorts develop over time, applying to tourism, the marketing theory of product life cycles. In the initial discovery phase, explorer types of tourists are attracted, numbers being limited by the lack of facilities and access difficulties. Entrepreneurs will, if unchecked, attempt to develop the resort. Textbooks refer to the second phase as involvement, assuming that local residents will be able to exert influence on the facilities to be made available and the numbers of tourists to be accommodated. All too frequently, this desirable model and reality diverge; so that a resort moves quickly through its development stage and tourist numbers grow larger than the local population. Competition from other destinations is not merely on price and facilities. Tourists are 'travel-fashion' conscious. The social phenomenon of acculturation is the way in which the cultures of different cultural groups change because of exposure to each other. As a tourism resort develops, the acculturation tends to be mostly in one direction, destroying the unusual culture that was interesting for tourists to experience. Consolidation and eventually growth stagnation may be followed by the decline of a resort or its rejuvenation. Although this concept appears in tourism textbooks, for one of the original sources, consult R.W. Butler 'The concept of a tourist area cycle of evolution' (*Canadian Geographer* (1980) 24, 5–12). Butler's graphical description of his concept showing the rise, stagnation and fall is known as a TALC curve. *See also* tourist enclave, tourist/host contact index *and* tourist trap.

tourism balance of trade Also called the travel account; concerns a country's income from foreign tourists compared with the amount that country's residents spend abroad. Tourism-generating countries have a natural tendency to have a negative balance, while tourism destination zones are likely to have positive balances. Countries in the Mediterranean and Caribbean areas typically have a big surplus on their travel accounts.

'Invisible' exports are represented by the income a country receives from services and invisible imports, the expenditure on purchasing services abroad. Thus, incoming tourism is an invisible export and money spent overseas by tourists, an invisible import. Money spent on transport, even to an overseas destination, is 'current account', being neither an import or export. UK figures below are taken from the UK *Business Monitor MQ6 Overseas Travel and Tourism*, indicating clearly how such things as increasing affluence, changing fashions in destination preference, terrorism and exchange rate fluctuations can affect a country's tourism balance of trade. All figures are in £ million (*see table*).

The figures have not been quoted because of national chauvinism! As can be seen, they illustrate the point being made. The WTO and OECD publish tourism balance of trade figures regularly, and these sources should be consulted for further information. The USA continues to have an adverse balance of

UK incoming tourism earnings and outgoing tourist expenditure 1978–2004 (£ million).

Year	Earnings from overseas visitors to the UK	Expenditure by UK residents going abroad	Balance
1978	2,507	1,549	+958
1979	2,797	2,109	+688
1980	2,961	2,738	+223
1981	2,970	3,272	−302
1982	3,188	3,640	−52
1983	4,003	4,090	87
1984	4,614	4,663	−49
1985	5,442	4,871	+571
1986	5,553	6,083	−530
1987	6,260	7,280	−1,020
1988	6,184	8,216	−2,032
1989	6,945	9,357	−2,412
1990	7,748	9,886	−2,138
1991	7,386	9,951	−2,565
1992	7,891	11,243	−3,351
1993	9,487	12,972	−3,485
1994	9,786	14,365	−4,579
1995	11,763	15,386	−3,623
1996	12,290	16,223	−3,933
1997	12,244	16,931	−4,687
1998	12,671	19,489	−6,818
1999	12,498	22,020	−9,522
2000	12,805	24,251	−11,446
2001	11,306	25,332	−14,026
2002	11,737	26,962	−15,225
2003	11,855	28,550	−16,695
2004	12,685	29,692	−17,007

Source: International Passenger Survey of UK National Statistics Office; even if the figures are adjusted to constant prices, there is still a huge gap between income and expenditure. 2004 figures were estimated at the time of going to press; 2004 earnings figures were estimated to be plus 7%, while expenditure was only plus 4%.

around US$5 billion annually, and Japan has now overtaken this figure. But both still have a long way to go to match West Germany's huge adverse balance, which is over twice as large. See also tourism-generating country, tourism-receiving country and travel account.

Tourism Canada Name of the official Canadian government tourist office.

Tourism Cares for Tomorrow On 1 January 2005, the Travelers Conservation Foundation, founded by the USTOA, amalgamated with the National Tourism Foundation, founded in 1982 by the National Tour Association to form Tourism Cares for Tomorrow. See www.ntfonline.org and www.tcfonline.org

tourism-carrying capacity In the early 1980s, environmentalists defined this as the maximum level of tourists that can be supported without causing excessive environmental deterioration and without leading to a decline in visitor satisfaction. By the mid-1980s, definitions were including, 'and the maximum level above which a negative impact is experienced by the local/host population'. The terminology is now generally applied to include social or even economic damage and appears to be developing into a comprehensive term, used loosely by the environmental lobby to indicate that areas have a low finite capacity for tourism without causing damaging effects.

Physical tourism-carrying capacity is the actual volume of the available resources or infrastructure in a resort or area. It is the simplest measure of the adequacy of an area to cope with an increase in tourism. Thus availability of accommodation will limit the number of overnight visitors while car parking spaces may limit number of car visitors.

Environmental tourism-carrying capacity is a subjective term. For the wilderness enthusiast, anyone else present spoils the beauty so that one other visitor can be said to have exceeded the local carrying capacity. Although the concept has only a limited value, a suggested usable definition is, 'That maximum level of tourists for an area, beyond which natural and other resources cannot be sustained and are unlikely to endure'. 'Saturation tourism' occurs when the maximum number of possible tourists which an area can accommodate is reached. Often, saturation of the accommodation facilities in an area results in over-saturation of the other facilities.

Dependent upon the environmentalist/political position of the user of the term, 'carrying capacity' may or may not take into account the capacity that there may be in an area for restructuring and the ongoing self-adaptation of all areas, whether they receive tourists or not. The term, 'intensity of tourism', may be used instead of 'carrying capacity', but more usually it applies to the proportion of tourists compared with the local population.

Textbooks may refer to sustainable tourism as that which does not affect ambient resources. Ambient resource is the fundamental character of an area that gives it tourism potential, for example, attractive scenery or guaranteed sunshine. The difficulty with terminology of this nature is in limiting its scope. Some experts restrict the application to purely physical characteristics, while others would include interesting culture or even low prices. In 2001, the World Tourism Organization and Secretariat of State for Tourism of France, *Thesaurus on Tourism and Leisure Activities* emphasized a different aspect suggesting 'composite early warning measures of key factors affecting the ability of the site to support different

levels of tourism'. Unfortunately, the word 'measures' introduces an alternative meaning. If the WTO were to change this to 'indicators', unanimity as to the meaning would be restored. The WTO also defines 'site stress' as 'composite measure of levels of impact on the site'. Research for this edition found no general usage of this term. 'Social impact' is defined as 'ratio of tourists to locals, peak period and over time'. This proportion of tourists to the local population is called 'concentration ratio' by Stephen Smith writing in *The Encyclopedia of Tourism*. Wording recommended in this dictionary is 'tourist/resident index or proportion' which is more obvious in its meaning and carries no pejorative implication.

Tourism Concern UK organization seeking to promote greater critical understanding of the impact of tourism. *See* www.tourismconcern.org.uk

tourism course standard degree syllabus *See* Appendix II.

tourism courses in the UK *See* City and Guilds of London Institute (CGLI), Edexcel Foundation *and* GCSE in Travel and Tourism.

tourism destination area *See* TDA.

tourism, ethnic A substantial part of VFR (visiting friends and relatives) traffic is described as ethnic traffic, particularly, for example, travel to the Indian subcontinent by expatriates and their descendants. Sometimes the term is applied to pilgrimages and it is also commonly used to describe travel to destinations believed by tourists to offer an interesting culture, substantially different from their own.

tourism expenditure WTO advocates the following definition in order to harmonize the collection of tourism statistics: The total consumption expenditure made by a visitor or on behalf of a visitor or on behalf of a visitor for and during his/her trip and stay at the destination. The following outlays or acquisitions should be excluded from tourism expenditure:

1. Purchases for commercial purposes, that is resale or use as a factor of production, made by any category of visitor and purchases made on behalf of their employer by visitors on business trips.

2. Capital type investments or transactions engaged in by visitors, such as land, housing, real estate and other important acquisitions (such as cars, caravans, boats and second houses) even though they may be used in the future for tourist travel purposes.

3. Cash given to relatives or friends during a holiday trip which does not represent payment for tourism goods or services, as well as donations made to institutions.

Tourism expenditure should be collected and presented for at least the following product categories: package travel, package holidays and package tours; accommodation; food and drink; transport; recreation, culture and sporting activities; shopping; other activities. (Source WTO TM.)

tourism-generating country Any country whose inhabitants have a substantial propensity to travel abroad. Departure statistics of residents of the main generating countries travelling abroad, broken down by country and region of destination, are to be found in Volume 1 of the WTO publication, *Year Book of Tourism Statistics*.

tourism growth point *See* TGP.

Tourism Industry Association of Canada (TIAC). *See* www.tiac.ca

tourism   information   databases Addresses, telephone numbers and web sites are provided, to facilitate research.

CABI Publishing's Internet resource www.leisuretourism.com provides comprehensive coverage of the leisure, tourism, recreation, sport and the cultural industries. A fully searchable international abstracts database in these areas covering over 400 serials is supplemented by review articles by subject specialists on the research and strategic development of these fields. This abstracts database contains links to many of the relevant journal articles online through the ingentaJournals global research gateway. www.ingenta. com hosts over 2700 journals from over 48 publishers providing registered users with access to a bibliographic database of over 1 million headers and abstracts, extending to full text on either an existing journal subscription or a

pay-per-view basis. To register for ingentaJournals readers should access www.ingenta.com For more information, in the UK contact CAB International, Wallingford, Oxfordshire, OX10 8DE UK; tel: +44 (0)1491 832111 e-mail publishing@cabi.org In the USA contact CAB International, 10 East 40th Street, Suite 3203, New York NY 10016; tel: +1 212 481 7018 (toll-free (within USA) +1 800 528 4841), e-mail cabi-nao@cabi.org

The World Tourism Organization (WTO) is an excellent source of worldwide travel and tourism statistics; the organization functions as a worldwide clearing house for all available information on international and domestic tourism, including statistical data, legislation and regulations, facilities and special events, and is responsible for its systematic collection, analysis and dissemination. Access information via www.world-tourism.org and then, for example, clicking on statistics. WTO's address is Capitan Haya 42, 28020 Madrid, Spain; tel: +34 91 567 8187.

The World Travel and Tourism Council (WTTC) is another rich source of tourism statistics. Access www. wttc.org and then, for example, tourism satellite accounting research, or contact them at 1–2 Queen Victoria Terrace, Sovereign Court, London E1W 3HA; tel: +44 (0)870 727 9882, fax: +44 (0)870 728 9882, e-mail: enquiries@wttc.org

MQ6 – *Overseas Travel and Tourism – Business Monitor Quarterly Statistics* are the published results of the UK International Passenger Survey, the most useful single source of UK information about incoming tourism and travel abroad. These statistics are now available, free of charge, on-line via www.statistics.gov.uk/products/p1905. asp ; *Travel Trends* is available via www.statistics.gov.uk/products/p1391. asp and *Travel and Tourism First Release* via www.statistics.gov.uk/ press_Release/CurrentReleases.asp or contact The Library, Office for National Statistics, 1 Drummond Gate, London SW1V 2QQ, UK; tel: +44 (0)207 533 5888.

For comprehensive coverage concerning Internet usage for travel planning and booking in 54 countries, free of charge, access the European Travel Commission's New Media Monitor site www.etcmonitor.com A world and regional overview provides figures and forecasts for the use of the Internet throughout the world and by region. There are sections on the on-line travel market, mobile devices and interactive television overall and for each country. The information is not accessible by telephone or in writing via the European Travel Commission.

In the USA, the Travel Resource Centre of the University of Colorado, Boulder, includes the Travel Reference Center which comprises the largest collection of travel, tourism and recreation research studies available at any one place in the USA. The Travel Resource Centre is a broadly based but highly specialized market research library including research material, public records, data resources and unpublished documents on travel and tourism. Access www.colorado.edu and then the Travel Resource Centre, Travel Reference Centre, Business Research Division, Campus Box 420, University of Colorado, Boulder, Colorado 80309; tel: +1 303 492 5056.

IATA Global Aviation Business Intelligence (IATA GABI) is IATA's subscription-based online service providing key air transport statistical information. Airline data is available as monthly international statistics (MIS) and world air transport statistics (WATS). Passenger data are supplemented with a passenger forecast and details of IATA's annual Corporate Air Travel Survey. Airport data includes airport capacity/demand profiles and a global airport monitor. Financial data include airline annual reports, economic results and prospects. Cargo data cover a freight forecast and air cargo annual review. For full details *see* www.iataGABI.com tel: +44 20 8607 6218 – other information is still available via www.iata.org PO Box 160, 1216, Cointrin, Geneve, Switzerland; tel: +41 22 983366.

tourism intensity Proportion of tourists compared with the local population. *See also* tourism-carrying capacity.

tourism multiplier A measurement of the impact of the extra expenditure of tourists on an economy, sometimes called 'tourism expenditure impacts'. This may be direct spending by the tourists themselves (direct or primary impacts) or associated investment on tourism in the area. In direct expenditure, it covers the successive rounds of business transactions resulting as hoteliers make purchases and the suppliers then make further purchases (indirect or secondary impacts). There is 'induced expenditure' because of the spending by employees who have provided tourism services. Sometimes, there is no multiplier effect because tourism has replaced an alternative form of expenditure or economic activity. This is known as a 'displacement effect'.

Fundamental to multiplier research is the concept of leakages from the economy under consideration to other economies or areas. Thus, the multiplier effect diminishes in successive rounds of income and employment.

There are seven types of multipliers in common use. The sales or transaction multiplier measures the extra business turnover, both direct and secondary created by an extra unit of tourist expenditure. The output multiplier is similar, but also takes into account inventory changes, such as the increase in stock levels by hotels, restaurants and shops, because of increased trading activity. Unfortunately, few published studies specify whether inventory changes have been taken into account. Thus, output multipliers are concerned with actual levels/changes in production, rather than the value or volume of sales.

An income multiplier measures the income generated by an extra unit of tourist expenditure. Sometimes income is defined as disposal income accruing to households within the area under consideration. Although salaries paid to overseas residents are often excluded, a proportion of these may be spent in the area, and should, therefore, be included. If it is a national economy under consideration, revenue accruing to the government is included.

The ratio method of expression states direct and indirect incomes, or the direct and secondary incomes, generated per unit of direct income. The more normal method of expression states the total income, both direct and secondary, generated in the study area per unit increase in final demand created within a particular sector.

Ratio multipliers give an indication of the internal linkages that exist between various sectors of the economy, but do not relate income generated, to extra sales. Hence, on their own, ratio multipliers are useless as planning tools.

Employment multipliers can also be expressed in two ways. As a ratio of the combination of direct and secondary employment generated per additional unit of tourist expenditure to direct employment generated; or as the employment created by tourism per unit of tourist expenditure.

There are two other types of tourism multiplier. The tourism imports multiplier provides an indicator of the value of imported goods or services provided to tourists. The Official or Government Revenue tourism multiplier indicates the net value of official income from tourism – i.e. taxes less subsidies.

Multiplier evaluation necessitates the use of models, a full description of which cannot be provided in this entry. There are three main types of model.

The Base Model is very simple and rarely used in practical research. It is assumed that the economy under research can be divided into export and non-export activities and that a stable relationship exists between the export and local activity sectors, with these linked by linear relationships. It is further assumed that unemployed resources are available within the economy and that the scale of the export activities is the sole determinant of the level of income and employment within the area.

The Keynesian Model is based on identifying streams of income and employment that are generated in rounds of expenditure, which diminish in geometric progression because of the leakages at each round.

The Input–Output Model enables an analysis of an economy into its sectors and expresses a relationship of these in matrix form, based on the results of research into the effects of tourist expenditure.

The size of the Tourism Multiplier depends on the nature of the local economy under consideration and the degree to which its various sectors are interlinked in their trading patterns. The wider the range of economic activities within the area, the greater the amount of trading which is likely to take place within them and hence the larger the size of the multiplier. The propensity to import goods and services from other areas, is particularly important. The higher the propensity to import, the lower the resultant value of the multiplier and hence the lower the benefit to the economy under consideration.

Pages 163 to 183 in *Tourism Principles and Practice*, 3rd edition, published by Pearson Education in 2005, written by Professor John Fletcher of Bournemouth University, are particularly recommended for readers seeking further information concerning tourism multiplier analysis.

The authors have examined many published articles and unpublished government reports, finding that Tourism Output Multipliers for medium to large industrialized economies range between 2.0 and 3.4; for a selection of US states between 1.5 and 2.20; for city/urban economies between 1.24 and 1.51; and for rural area economies betweeen 1.12 and 1.35. This book also provides ranges for tourism income multipliers and employment multipliers derived from many sources.

tourism potential Also known as ambient resource. The fundamental character of an area which gives it tourism potential, for example, attractive scenery or guaranteed sunshine. The difficulty with terminology of this nature is in limiting its scope. Some experts restrict the application to purely physical characteristics, while others would include interesting culture or even low prices.

Tourism Price Index Figure used to indicate changing prices of tourism elements over time. Full description outside the scope of this book. For more information readers should consult WTO publication *Guidelines for Constructing a Tourism Price Index*, which details: 'Elements for constructing a tourism price index. Methods of approach to the construction of tourism price indexes and description of main indexes. The basket of goods and weighting. Chaining, group indexes, choice of sales outlets and reference items. Plurality of indexes reflecting the various means of organizing travel.'

tourism, pro poor Tourism strategy which aims to reduce poverty.

tourism pull and push factors Circumstances in the locality of a person's residence which make it unpleasant are suggested to motivate people to leave it; these negative matters are called push factors. While qualities seen as positive and beneficial which people find pleasant at a receiving destination, and which, therefore, attract them to it are called pull factors. It is obvious that all factors are comparitive; for someone to be motivated to travel, the local environment is likely to be less pleasant than tourism destinations being contemplated.

tourism-receiving country Any country receiving a substantial number of tourists. Note particularly that usage *does not* imply that the number of residents of a country travelling abroad from that country is less than the number of tourists visiting the host country. Confusingly, some textbooks imply this. As an example, the UK is often listed as a tourism-receiving country, but it is also a major tourism-generating country.

Tourism Recreation and Information Package (TRIP) *See* TRIP.

Tourism Review and Implementation Group UK group set up by the Department for Culture, Media and Sport, aiming to increase Britain's annual incoming tourism from £76bn to £100bn. It will particularly examine improvements that might be delivered in marketing and e-tourism, domestic accommodation, the skill of people working in the industry and data.

tourism satellite account *See* TSA (which includes details of the WTO Tourism Satellite Accounts Project).

tourism services provider In this dictionary the wording means any person or organization that satisfies the needs of travellers.

Tourism Society A UK professional body, although it has a wider remit; general membership is concentrated on those in the field of incoming and British tourism. The Tourism Society, established in 1977, is a membership body of individual professionals working in, studying or associated with tourism. The Society is an active advocate and independent organization, often consulted by government and other official bodies on tourism and related policy matters. Members are drawn from the whole spectrum of tourism and its related bodies: public and private sector companies at international, national, regional and local levels – including visitor attractions, tour operators, carriers, hospitality and catering, educational, and consultancy sectors. Professionals from other fields who are active in tourism, such as accountants, architects and surveyors, are also represented. A separate section exists for consultants while another section is the Association of Teachers and Trainers in Tourism. *See* www.toursoc.org.uk

tourism statistics *See* tourism information databases.

Tourism Training Initiative UK scheme launched at the beginning of 1988. The Initiative focused on the tourism and leisure-related skill and training needs in all sectors with a significant involvement in the provision of tourist and leisure facilities.

tourism, alternative Usage varies. Sometimes means the same as 'sustainable tourism', 'soft tourism', 'green tourism', 'responsible tourism' or 'tourism with insight and understanding'. Some travel industry leaders apply the term to any type of speciality tourism attracting low numbers of tourists, and this is also now established as a usage. Environmentalists probably mean benign tourism which does not exploit or damage the local population, natural ecology, culture and economy of a destination country. The diversity of meaning of the words 'alternative tourism' was defined by Linda K. Richter in *The Politics of Tourism in Asia* (1989) University of Hawaii Press: alternative tourism means a variety of concerns and responses, some focused on the tourist, some on the natural environment and some on the political environment. *See also* ecotourism, meonscrubly, tourism-carrying capacity *and* tourism, sustainable.

tourism, green   *See* tourism, alternative.

tourism, heritage   Tourism inspired by, organized in connection with or visiting the cultural and/or natural heritage of an area. This heritage includes, for example, areas of natural beauty, buildings, geographical features, monuments, natural areas, sites of archaeological interest and other natural or man-made places of importance for aesthetic, anthropological, ethnological, historical, scientific or other reasons.

tourism, mass   Imprecise term indicative of large-scale tourism. By definition, an area has to be developed with an appropriate infrastructure to support mass tourism. But because of this development, tourism to that area may be sustainable. Thus, definitions of mass tourism as 'that which is not sustainable' are not correct. Many definitions use a historical basis, describing the current tourism market as mass tourism, compared with 50 years ago. Countries that restrict tourism growth are said to be against mass tourism. *See also* tourism typologies.

tourism, responsible   *See* tourism, alternative.

tourism, saturation   *See* tourism-carrying capacity.

tourism, soft   *See* tourism, alternative.

tourism, sustainable   Concept of tourism development, which preserves and harmonizes with the pre-existing economic, social/cultural and ecological situation. Because the activities of the visitors do not alter anything, the area continues without change and tourism to the area is sustainable in the long term. This theoretical aim is, in practice, not achievable. What most writers appear to mean by sustainable tourism is 'tourism that has a negligible, minimal or the least possible effect on the pre-existing economic, social/cultural and ecological situation'. There may be a wide differences between what is meant by 'negligible, minimal or the least possible'. What is meant has to be judged by the reader, each time! The BSI/CEN definition published in 2003 struck a slightly more realistic note: 'Concept of development and planning of tourism in order to protect and preserve the environment

in all its aspects and to respect the way of life of local residents'.

At the time of writing this monograph in July 2004, over 60 different voluntary certification programmes were identified which award ecotourism labels for sustainable tourism practice, while a further dozen or more countries are developing new programmes. Most of these concern accommodation, although some cover beaches, parks, tour operators and golf courses. The WTO is working with Affiliate Members from the private sector on an initiative aimed to ensure that governments get involved in these processes, supporting certification systems and overseeing their operation. WTO believes that certification systems and ecolabels in tourism are essential to inform consumers and to encourage more sustainable production and consumption patterns in tourism services. WTO suggests that these systems must follow accepted criteria in order to increase their credibility.

Four organizations, WTO, Rainforest Alliance, The International Ecotourism Society (TIES) and the Center on Ecotourism and Sustainable Development (CESD) are collaborating on the harmonization of the criteria of the large number of ecolabelling or green certification programmes within the tourism industry described above. Another component of the same project, led by the United Nations Environment Programme (UNEP) aims to survey best practices among tourism policies and strategies at the national level. A handbook will be produced with recommendations and case studies to increase environmental benefits from tourism development.

All too frequently, definitions of sustainable tourism have an unnecessary political dimension. For example, that of D.W. Pearce and R.R. Turner (1990) in *Economics of Natural Resources and the Environment* (Harvester Wheatsheaf, Hemel Hempstead, UK). 'Sustainable tourism development or growth involves maximizing and optimally distributing the net benefits of economic development, so far as these can be achieved while establishing and reaffirming the conditions of security under which the services and qualities of natural resources can be maintained, restored or improved into the foreseeable future.'

Tourism planners are constantly being urged to make developments 'sustainable'. In this field, the 1990s were marked in Europe by initiatives associated with Agenda 21. The 1992 Rio de Janeiro UN Environment and Development Conference adopted the statement, 'Only whatever can be sustained by nature and society in the long term is permissible'. The title Agenda 21 was meant to be indicative of the statement's intention to take the world into the 21st century. Although widely quoted in tourism textbooks, Agenda 21 was *not* devised specifically for tourism; that is merely one area to which it has been applied. Some associated documentation was reported by J. Lorch and T. Bausch, *Sustainable Tourism in Europe* in *Tourism and the Environment in Europe* (published by the EU in 1995). The definition provided was:

A development will be understood to constitute a sustainable tourism development where it takes into account not only aspects in visitor source countries, but the form of outward journey, on the one hand, along with the interests of visitors and residents in a region to be defined. Activities at the destination need to be based on nature's capacity to absorb, whereby consumption of all resources should be as sparing as possible. The objective of such a tourism policy is the lasting fulfilment of the ecological, economic and socio-cultural functions, judged on whatever criteria, and whilst preserving a balance between endogenous and exogenous claims to exploit it.

This statement also advocated some rules:

- The fulfilment of a need shall only be permissible provided it does not render satisfaction of the same need impossible for ensuing generations.
- In otherwise identical circumstances, a course of action where there is only a low probability that it will result in a specific evil is to be preferred to another more likely to do so.
- In otherwise identical circumstances of evils that are unavoidable, the lesser one is to be preferred to the greater, and the one of lesser duration to the one lasting longer.
- In the event of conflict, in otherwise identical circumstances, a decision should be taken in favour of many people rather than the few.
- A course of action serving a morally good objective is ethically only justified when the negative side effects involved can be reduced to a minimum. A course of action designed to serve a morally good objective is ethically only justifiable providing that the evil arising as a side effect is less than the evils that would result from refraining action.
- The rate of consumption of self-replenishing resources may not exceed their rate of regeneration. The rate of consumption of finite resources may not exceed the rate of increase of self-generation raw material resources. The rate of pollution emissions may not exceed the environment's capacity for absorbing these.

The environmentalist lobby felt that the above statement 'let tourism off the hook', while the tourism industry felt the rules were unworkable.

Gaining general acceptance is the *Global Code of Ethics for Tourism*, which was adopted by the WTO General Assembly in Santiago, Chile, on 1 October, 1999. This is repeated in full as Appendix I to this dictionary.

Terms 'alternative tourism', 'appropriate tourism', 'environmentally-sound tourism', 'ethical tourism', 'green tourism', 'quality tourism', 'responsible tourism' and 'soft tourism' may have a similar meaning. These terms may mean sustainable tourism, depending upon the context; but often, authors put their own *spin* on the meaning. Sustainable tourism has been the subject of many books, papers and articles during the last 10 years, most of which are referenced in computerized bibliographic sources. The select bibliography of earlier work found most useful by the author is that following the papers published in connection with the 41st Congress of the Association Internationale d'Experts Scientifiques du

Tourisme held in Mahé, Seychelles, in November 1991, *Editions AIEST*, Vol. 33.

Green Globe is a programme of environmental awareness launched by WTTC in 1994. In December 1995, WTTC and DG XXIII of the European Commission launched the ECoNETT site www.greenglobe21.com/econett.htm The Alliance for Sustainable Tourism (AST) web site is www.wttc.org.strat dev/sustainable.asp Both sites feature detailed case studies and references, with hotlinks to other relevant web sites.

The United Nations Environment Programme (UNEP) in 1999 identified over 100 environmental codes of conduct which had been established by national tourism organizations. Although widely quoted in tourism textbooks, UNEP's programmes were *not* devised specifically for tourism; that is merely one area in which they have been applied.

Having reviewed the literature and related opinions, what definition of sustainable tourism does a major organization in the field recommend? The International Ecotourism Society (TIES) defines ecotourism as, 'responsible travel to natural areas that conserves the environment and improves the well being of local people'. TIES feels this means that those who implement and participate in ecotourism activities should follow certain principles; however, readers should note that these are not considered by the author of this dictionary to be part of the definition; they are a TIES wish list! A consensus on defining the terms sustainable tourism aka ecotourism, may never be achieved. TIES seeks to:

- Minimize impact on local culture, economy, wildlife and environment
- Build environmental and cultural awareness and respect
- Provide positive experiences for both visitors and hosts
- Provide direct financial benefits for conservation
- Provide financial benefits and empowerment for local people
- Raise sensitivity to host countries' political, environmental and social climate

- Support international human rights and labour agreements.

See also www.sustainabletravel.org for the initiatives organized through the association between BEST and WTTC, tourism, alternative *and* tourism-carrying capacity, Antarctic Traveller's Code, Blue Flag beach, Center on Ecotourism and Sustainable Development, displacement effect, Foundation for Environmental Education, IHEI (International Hotels Environment Initiative), International Ecotourism Standard, 'the folk' (staged authenticity), tourism *and* WTO *Global Code of Ethics for Tourism* in Appendix I.

tourist   As outlined above, tourism statistics include most business travellers; however, general language usage often implies that tourists are 'holidaymakers'. Despite the 'official' designations of types of tourist above, the 2003 CEN/European Standard official definition suggests a tourist is a: 'Person travelling for leisure purposes'. *See* tourism.

tourist, allocentric   Tourists who are continually looking for new experiences and destinations; they are adventurous by nature.

tourist attraction   *See* theme parks *and* sightseeing in Britain.

tourist attractions   Normally refers to man-made attractions *See* attractions, theme parks *and* sightseeing in Britain.

tourist campsite   Collective facilities in enclosed areas for tents, caravans, trailers and mobile homes. Often tourist services are provided such as recreational activities, canteen and information services. Source: WTO TM.

Tourist Card   Document permitting a person to enter a country for leisure purposes and leave afterwards; often issued instead of a visa and sometimes issued as well as a visa. *See also* visa².

tourist class   Usually an inferior class of travel or hotel, and usually the cheapest. *See* classes of travel *and* airline class and fare designators.

tourist enclave   Sources agree that this is an area set apart from a local community for leisure visitors. But whereas some definitions suggest this is to afford tourists security, others identify that by concentrating tourists into an enclave, they are isolated from the local population. Thus the tourists are meant not to become aware of the poor conditions in which the local residents live. And equally, a usually unsuccessful attempt is being made to prevent the local population from being aware of the luxuries tourists enjoy. Those wishing to deprecate the concept call them tourist ghettos. *See also* tourism area life cycle, tourist/host contact index *and* tourist trap.

tourist expenditure impacts   *See* tourism multiplier.

tourist ghetto   *See* tourist enclave *and* tourist trap.

tourist guide   There are alternative definitions for political reasons. In some countries, such as France and Italy, qualifications of tourist guides are, by local and national law, mandatory. In others, such as the UK and Germany, there are qualifications, but no national requirements and often no local regulations concerning these, regarding entry to and employment in the guiding profession.

The latest wording published by BSI on behalf of CEN 2003 as a standard does not imply possession of a qualification as part of the definition: 'A person who guides visitors in the language of their choice and interprets the cultural and natural heritage of an area, which person normally possesses an area-specific qualification'. This 'standard' does not reflect actual practice; for example, possession of language skills is not implicit in defining the term 'guide'.

Contrast this with Columbus Press' *The Dictionary for the Travel Industry* published in 1999:

'A person who possesses an area-specific tourist guide qualification recognized by the appropriate public authority in the country concerned... .' This is followed by wording which is similar to the 1991 revision of a press release issued by the European Federation of Tourist Guides (FEG) which stated: 'The tourist guide's main role is to guide groups or individual visitors from abroad or from the home country around the monuments, sites and museums of a city or region; to interpret in an inspiring and entertaining manner, in the language of the

visitor's choice, the cultural and natural heritage and environment.' The opening wording of the FEG definition, leads the reader to believe that, by definition, a tourist guide is always qualified and licensed.

In 1986 the European Commission challenged France for preventing guides from elsewhere in the EU operating there; similar action was begun against Italy in 1987 and Portugal in 1991. That year, the European Court ruled that member states were entitled to require tour guides to have local qualifications *only* for visits to museums or historical monuments that could not be visited without a specialized professional guide. The Court laid down the principle of freedom to provide services in the case of guided tours to all other places. The EC then ruled that each member state was responsible for defining the 'regulated' sites.

In 1996, the EU reaffirmed its view that restrictions on the freedom to provide guiding services were regarded as serious infringements of EU law. FEG appeared to have succeeded in their vigorous lobbying when in May 1997 the European Commission issued its Working Document on Tourist Guides (SEC 97 final) which outlined a definition of a wholly qualified profession. However, the EC did not drop the matter completely; for example, in 1998, following EC pressure, Italy reduced the number of sites where 'official' guides had to be used from 2990 to 2540. On 6 July 1999, in a formal 'European Travel Policy' statement, the EU announced that it was dropping the cases going back to 1986 because its legal advisors cautioned against 'undertaking an impossible task on a subject where EU law is not clear... the battle has turned into a simple turf war between tour managers and tour guides, in which the EC has no place!' For details of UK recognized body *see* the Institute of Tourist Guiding www.itg.org.uk

The author of this dictionary is currently leading the UK delegation to Working Group 5 of CEN, the grouping of European Standards Institutes, which is devising a European standard for qualifications for guides. This will be published in 2007.

tourist/host contact index   Although since widely-copied, the concept was originally devised by G.V. Doxey (1976) in 'When enough's enough: the natives are restless in old Niagara' (*Heritage Canada* 2(2), 26–27). The five stages of Doxey's index are:

- The level of euphoria; the initial thrill and enthusiasm that comes along with tourism development results in the fact that the tourist is made welcome.
- The level of apathy; once tourism development is under way and the consequential expansion has taken place, the tourist is taken for granted and is now only seen as a source of profit-taking. What contact is made between host and guest is done so on a commercial and formal footing.
- The level of irritation; as the industry approaches saturation point, the hosts can no longer cope with the number of tourists without the provision of additional facilities.
- The level of antagonism; the tourist is now seen as the harbinger of all ills; hosts are openly antagonistic towards tourists and tourists are regarded as being there to be exploited.
- The final level; during the above process of development, the host population has forgotten that all they once regarded as being special was exactly the same thing that attracted the tourist. But in the rush to develop tourism, circumstances have changed. The social impact has been comprehensive and complete and the tourists will move to different destinations.

See also tourism area life cycle, tourist enclave *and* tourist trap.

Tourist Information Centre   *See* TIC.

Tourist Information Point   *See* TIP[2].

Tourist Office   An organization or specific outlet through which tourism to an area, resort, region or country is promoted. Older textbooks designate these as official or government institutions, which is still the case for the majority; but increasingly, they may be either public/private partnerships or entirely industry funded. *See* entries for National Tourist Office and US State Tourist Office web sites under country and state names; *also see* Tourism Offices Worldwide Directory www.towd.com

Tourist Project Scheme   *See* TPS.

tourist, psychocentric   The opposite of the adventurous allocentric tourist. The psychocentric seeks familiarity, hence the Costa Brava, Spanish advertisements 'Tea like mother makes'. Such a tourist is less likely to arrange independent travel and more likely to book through a travel agent.

tourist trap   Deprecatory description of shop, site, area or resort which has lost or is losing its appeal because of its popularity. *See also* tourism area life cycle, tourist enclave *and* tourist/host contact index.

tourist typologies   The most well-known which has lasted the test of time, quoted in most tourism textbooks, was devised by E. Cohen in 'Towards a sociology of international tourism' (*Social Research* (1972) 39(1), 164–182) repeated in E. Cohen's 'A phenomenology of tourist experiences' (*Sociology* (1979) 13, 179–201). Cohen's Five Modes of Tourist Experience are: in recreational mode, mental and physical powers are restored; in diversionary mode the boredom of society is escaped; in experiential mode the tourist is alienated from his centre and searches for another; in experimental mode tourists engage in alternative lifestyles without being fully committed; while in existential mode tourists become fully committed to an alternative centre.

See also tourist, allocentric *and* tourist, psychocentric. Another 'classic' analysis of tourism typologies is by Valene Smith in *Hosts and guests* (University of Pennsylvania Press, 1989). This contrasts tourism volume with adaptation to the receiving area.

tourists' experience   *See* tourist typologies.

Tourpars   Was name of System Aid (Tour Processing) Limited computerized British tour operators reservation and accounting system.

Tourplan   Was name of Tower Computer Group's UK computerized reservation and accounting system, designed particularly for inbound tour operators.

Tours   Was name of computerized tour operator's reservation and accounting system developed in 1976 and available in the UK through Infocentre Limited.

TP[1]   Travel Partner of IATA.

TP² Turning point (aviation term).

TPA The Travel Protection Association (obsolete). It was planned to offer financial protection to UK package holiday travellers by surface transport. When the EC Package Holiday laws were implemented in the UK in 1993, tour operators were required to protect holidaymakers against financial losses. The Air Travel Organizers' Licence (*see* ATOL) incorporates bonding which protects those travelling by air on an inclusive tour. UK tour operators organizing arrangements not involving air travel would have been able to protect their clients by effecting a bond through the TPA. The TPA was modelled on the ATOL department of the Civil Aviation Authority. In order to create a back-up reserve fund, in case particular bonds proved insufficient to cover the liabilities, it was suggested that £1 per traveller be levied, starting with 1993/94 winter brochures. When the reserve fund was sufficient, it was intended that the TPA took over the bonding responsibilities of the bodies which formed it: Passenger Shipping Association, Association of Independent Tour Operators, Bus and Coach Council, Association of British Travel Agents and Tour Operators Study Group.

TPACS Trip pairing for airline crew scheduling.

TPM Ticketed point mileage. The airline tariff manuals list, for fare construction purposes, tables of the shortest geographical distances between points all over the world. Sometimes, the figures may only be shortest mileage operated by airlines at the present time. The mileage of a journey for fare construction purposes is calculated by adding together all the TPMs. This is then compared with the MPM to see if there is any excess mileage, resulting in a fare surcharge. *See* IATA Fare Construction System.

TPS Tourist Projects Scheme in the UK. The major channel through which UK government money was allocated to specific tourism projects for 20 years.

TPSG Technology Planning and Strategy Group of IATA.

TPSI Transport Planning Skills Initiative in the UK, designed to address skills shortages in transport planning. Supported by four of the UK institutes in the field of transport, IHT, ICE, CILT and RTPI.

TPWS Train Protection and Warning System, the train safety system that is being installed in British trains while development work continues on a more sophisticated full Automatic Train Control System, which the British government plans to be in place on the UK network by 2008. Although the TPWS prevents driver error, for example, passing a signal at danger, it only guarantees success when trains are travelling below 75 mph. The first ATOC company on which TPWS is now operating is Thameslink, having introduced it in April 2001 after extensive trials. *See* ATC⁶.

track In the USA, a charter route on which back-to-back flights are operated. *See* back-to-back.

TrackPoint *See* location of corporate travellers.

TRACON Terminal radar approach control in New York (aviation term).

TRADACOMS The European EDI standard for retailers. *See* Electronic Data Interchange.

Trade Show Exhibitors Association (in the USA) *See* www.tsea.org

Traffic Conference Areas *See* TC-1, TC-2, TC-3.

traffic distribution *See* transport modelling.

traffic documents Official IATA definition is the following forms issued manually, mechanically or electronically for air passenger transportation over the lines of the member of airline and for related services, whether or not they bear a preprinted individual member's identification: (i) carriers' own traffic documents – passenger, ticket and baggage check forms, automated ticket/boarding passes, miscellaneous charges orders, multiple purpose documents, agents refund vouchers and on-line tickets supplied by members to approved agents for issue to their customers; and (ii) standard traffic documents – billing and settlement plan passenger ticket and baggage check forms, standard off-premise automated ticket/boarding passes, standard miscellaneous charges orders, neutral multiple purpose documents, BSP agents refund vouchers and other accountable forms supplied to accredited agents for issue under a Billing and Settlement Plan.

traffic forecasting *See* transport modelling.

traffic rights Most international air operations are controlled by bilateral Air Services Agreements made between the governments concerned. Sometimes traffic rights are restricted. Thus an airline flying from A to B to C and D may have no traffic rights to carry passengers between B and C, but permission to pick-up or set-down passengers in all other respects. *See also* Chicago Convention.

trailer US term for a mobile home on wheels, originally developed for towing behind a vehicle from place to place. In Europe, called a caravan. The word implies inclusion of sleeping and catering facilities. A folding trailer usually packs down below the level of a car roof; thus, it is easier to tow. Trailer parks offering a varying range of site facilities cater for touring vacationers. Sites for static trailers may still be called trailer parks where they may be used as simple holiday chalets or permanent homes.

trailer tent The term is not to be taken literally and does not apply to any tent which can be transported in a vehicle or trailer. It is specifically a type of tent which folds flat into its purpose-built trailer and which is easily mountable/demountable.

train A surface transport vehicle running on rails. For details of types of high-speed trains, *see* entries APT, Bullet and TGV. Mainline InterCity express rail services in the UK are called InterCity 125, named because of the speed at which they travel on the fastest stretches of track. Trains in France are classified as TEE, InterCity, TGV, Rapide (which includes TGV), Express Direct or Omnibus. Swiss express trains are called InterCity, while in Italy, the terminology is Rapido, Direttissimo (Express) and Diretto (fast).

In Spain, the supplement to travel on a Rápido is called a *suplemento expreso*, which is why foreigners often call them by the wrong name, Expresso. Correct terminology is TER, Tren Español Rápido for these fast diesel rail

cars. ELT stands for Electrotren and these, together with TER, InterCity and Talgo services are all air-conditioned, which for travel in Spain, during much of the year, foreigners find essential. AVE is the high-speed train between Madrid and Seville introduced in 1992. *See* Cercanías, Estrella *and* Interurbano for details of non-express Spanish trains. Spain now has a high-speed railway with the partial opening of a new track between Madrid and Barcelona reducing travel time from 7 h to 4 h 35 min. This first section of high-speed track runs from Madrid's Puerta de Atocha station through Zaragoza to Lleida/ Lerida in Catalunya. The second section, from Lleida to Barcelona's Sants station, is expected to be completed in 2005, further reducing the travel time between Madrid and Barcelona to just 2 h 30 min, competitive with the present air services scheduled for 80 min. Currently there are six daily services. Travel times have also been cut between Madrid and Zaragoza – from 3 h to 1 h 45 min – and between Madrid and Lleida – from 5 h to 2 h 40 min.

Internal fast trains in Denmark are of two categories, InterCity trains and Lyntog (Lightning train) which are express diesel railcar sets with limited accommodation. In West Germany, there are TEE trains, InterCityzuge, fast trains designed for business travellers, Fernexpresszuge, the longer distance express trains Schnellzuge and Eilzuge, the semi-fast services. Apart from TEE services, in Austria, International express trains are called Expresszuge with other fast services known as D trains. Slower services are called Eilzuge. In Norway, express trains are called Ekspresstog, fast services, Hurtigtog and slow, Persontog.

Many trains worldwide are well known by their names. For example, Acela Express between Washington, DC and Boston, Broadway Limited from New York to Chicago; Canadian, operating between Vancouver and Montreal; Chopin, between Moscow and Vienna via Warsaw; Simplon Express between Paris and Belgrade via Venice; Arlberg between Paris and Vienna; Rheingold between Amsterdam and Switzerland. Unfortunately confusing is

the official express service between
Paris and Bucharest known as the
Orient Express and the tourist service
introduced in 1983 recreating the
original service and style known as the
Venice Simplon Orient Express
operating between London and Venice.

High Speed Trains (HSTs) in Europe
are exemplified by the French TGVs.
But there are many other developments;
the Thalys network is a consortium of
French, Belgium and Dutch Railways
working from 1997 and operating a 1 h
25 min service between Brussels and
Paris. The Rhealys consortium
established in 2000 includes the rail
companies of France, Germany,
Luxembourg and Switzerland. They
plan HSTs between Paris and Frankfurt
and Paris/Zurich by 2007. By 2010, the
Paris/Madrid link should be operating.

For full details of trains and services
worldwide, Thomas Cook's *European
Timetable* or the TC *Overseas Timetable*
should be consulted. In the USA these
publications are available through Forsyth
Travel Library. The *Lexique Générale des
Termes Ferroviaires* lists nearly 100
different types of train. *See also the
following entries which often then lead to
further terms:* AirTrain, AirTrain JFK,
Ajents, APT, APTIS, ATOC[1], ATC, AVE,
Amtrak, blue period, BREEV, BREL,
BRETA, British Rail, Britrail Pass,
compartment, driverless trains, Electra
225, Elgar, EuroCity European rail
network, European Rail group travel,
European Rail sleeping cars, Eurostar,
FACETS, gauge, Ghan, Global price rail
tickets, IRRF, IRO, JetTrain, Korridorzuge,
LIRR, LRT, LRV, maglev, MANIS,
Metroliner, Motorail, NBL, Network Rail,
North American train services,
pantograph, PIRATES, Pullman, Pullman
berth, rack railway, rail fares in the UK,
rail Private Settlement Tickets, rail
reservations in the UK, rail season tickets
in the UK, RATP, RENFE, RER, RES, RSA,
RTG, RoadRailer, Sejour rail fares, Skyrail,
SRA[1], Swiss Holiday Card, TEE, TEN,
TGV, TMST, token block, TPWS, train
describer, USA Rail Pass, Zephyr *and* the
entries immediately below commencing
'train'. *See* www.raileurope.com
Train à Grande Vitesse *See* TGV.
train classes in North America *See* North
American train services.

train describer Computer system that
keeps track of the location of trains in
the area controlled by a particular signal
box. Train codes are displayed in their
sections on a control panel. Train
Describers in the UK have become an
information database, performing many
other functions, such as activating platform indicators. The information, combined with details of the timetable,
enables automatic route setting to operate, so that trains can be routed with a
minimum of interference.
Train Protection and Warning System
See TPWS *and* ATC[6].
training for tourism in the UK *See*
Caterbase, Introduction to Tourism in
Britain – City and Guilds Scheme,
Tourism Training Initiative, training for
work in museums and heritage sites *and*
Visitor Attraction Operations Certificate.
**training for work in museums and her-
itage sites** In the UK the RSA
Examination Board is running a diploma
scheme in Tourism in Museums and
Heritage Sites. This covers a range of
tasks from receiving and storing exhibit
items to maintaining a sales area.
Criteria for achievement of the tasks are
set out in the format familiar to those
acquainted with RSA's other integrated
awards. The same system of assessors,
accreditors and record books also applies.
tramp steamer Cargo-carrying ship
which travels to any destination according to demand; the alternative to a cargo
liner scheduled service, operating on
particular routes to a planned pattern.
The word tramp may be misleading, for
modern vessels do not deserve the name.
transaction fee A charge made by a travel
agent for performing a particular service. Also known as a service fee or service charge. The ending of commission
payments by airlines on ticket sales has
led to substantial charges by third parties for planning and booking air travel.
In the UK in 2004, typical fees for individual transactions were £15 to £20 for
domestic travel; £15 to £25 for short
haul flights and £30 to £40 for long haul,
with higher charges for complex and
multi-sector arrangements. Fees are
negotiated as part of corporate travel
contracts at lower levels than those
stated. Rates are particularly affected by
the extent to business travellers use a

self booking tool (SBT). At the end of 2003, Carlson Wagonlit suggested that a traditional business travel booking cost US$40; an assisted on-line booking, US$30; and a no-touch booking handled entirely by an SBT, US$10. *See* fee based contracts; *also see a list of 70 other business travel related entries which follows* corporate travel contracts, *some of which lead to further entries.*

transactions tourism multiplier *See* tourism multiplier.

Trans-Europe Express Trains *See* TEE.

transfer[1] Transport for a short, intermediate or connecting part of a tourism service. For example, the transport provided for travellers when they arrive at or leave a given location, taking them to or from an airport, wharf, railway station, town, terminal or hotel.

transfer[2] A type of US bus ticket (transfer ticket) enabling a passenger on a bus to continue their journey on another bus on another route. Rules restrict the break of journey to a reasonable connecting time.

transfer connections Connecting flights which, in combination, provide a continuous journey from origin to required destination with passengers' baggage being transferred between the flights by the airlines concerned.

transit US term for public transport. Entries immediately below outline British usage. Transit operators are often public bodies, although this is not implicit in the term transit. For example, the holding company for New York's transit system is the Metropolitan Transport Authority (MTA) and for the Metro, New York City Transit MTA-NYCT; in Washington, DC it is the Washington Metroplitan Area Transit Authority (WMATA) and in Chicago, the Chicago Transit Authority (CTA). Transit travel is currently growing by 5% annually, with higher growth rates in major cities; for example, in Chicago, in 1999, 50% of passengers using buses and trains did so from choice. By 2000 this figure had risen to 59% and by the end of 2001, it was the mode of choice for 68% of travellers. *See* public transport.

transit lounge *See* transit passenger.

transit or transfer passenger A passenger who has disembarked from a mode of transport at an intermediate point, but who will be continuing his journey by a connecting flight. As distinct from an O&D (origin and destination) passenger, whose journey begins and/or ends at that place. Thus, transit traffic is composed of travellers who never leave the bus terminal, rail station or airport. In the case of international journeys, many countries allow transit without visa. Such passengers are put in a transit lounge, where they are treated as if, technically, they have not entered the country concerned. These lounges are often primitive or worse! *See* TWOV.

transit without visa *See* TWOV (TRWOV is used an alternative acronym) *and* visa[2].

Transitional Automated Ticket *See* TAT.

Trans-Manche Super Train *See* TMST.

transmission control number Official IATA definition is a unique reference number generated by the ticketing system, and printed on an automated ticket.

transparent link A connection between a CRS and a supplier of travel services designed so that agents connect directly from the CRS without keying to switch from one to the other. Particularly used in the UK with regard to access to tour operators' reservation systems via larger CRS networks.

transport-carrying capacities In *The World Cities* by Peter Hall, it is suggested that a commuter railway can carry up to 40,000 passengers per track per hour with all passengers seated. Somewhat conservatively, it is suggested that an underground railway or rapid transit system, including its standing capacity can take 60,000 passengers per track per hour. Readers who have experienced the New York Subway, the Paris Metro or the London Tube in the rush-hour may feel that this is a substantial underestimate. Those who have lived in Tokyo will be sure! *See* road traffic capacity.

transport demand *See* demand for transport *and* transport modelling.

Transport Direct Internet-based UK national travel enquiry service. Funded by the British government Department of Trade, it covers rail, long distance coach and Traveline data for local bus services. Provides real-time information about services and prices, as well as journey comparisons between modes.

Transport Direct is an Internet-based one-stop-shop service for the public, providing a range of information on all forms of transport and travel. Plans for Transport Direct were first announced in the Government's 10-Year Transport Plan in July 2000. When completed, it will provide comprehensive information on all aspects of public travel, including bus and rail, road journeys, maps and other options. *See* www. dtlr.gov.uk/itwp/transdirect

transport emissions of CO_2 (carbon dioxide) The transport sector is estimated by IPCC to use 25% to 30% of the world's fossil fuel consumption. Of this share, light-duty road vehicles (cars) use around 45%; heavy-duty road vehicles (lorries, trucks, coaches and buses) use about 30%; aircraft 12%; maritime transport 7%, while rail and inland waterways account for the remaining 6%. *See* aircraft emissions *and* radiative forcing.

transport market segmentation *See* passenger transport market segmentation.

transport modelling Surveys are frequently undertaken to establish traffic by various transport modes between areas. In simplistic form, these can be recorded on an origin/destination matrix. These can be decreased or increased by multiplying by growth or other factors, taking into account estimates of the amount of future traffic. Far more sophisticated work utilizes traffic models. These establish equations concerning the relationship between some or all of the variants associated with trip attraction or generation between the area or areas concerned. For the purposes of establishing standard definitions in this field, UITP and the US Department of Transportation were co-sponsors of the 1981 *Dictionary of Public Transport*. Trip distribution is described as the actual matrix resulting from the survey initially described in this entry. The basic model is called a 'growth factor model'.

A gravity model is a formula 'that distributes trips from production zones to attraction zones in proportion to the attraction of every zone and inversely proportional to some function of the separation and/or resistance to travel between production zones and attraction

zones'. Tourism gravity models follow this principle, suggesting, for example, that tourism generated between places is proportional to their population size but inversely proportional to the distance/ travel cost between the places.

The intervening opportunity model 'is based on probability theory and distributes trips from one zone to each other zone in proportion to the probability that the trips have not found a prior destination ranked closer to the zone of origin'. A competing opportunity model 'calculates the trip attraction probabilities from the production of the probability of attraction and the probability of satisfaction'.

Traffic distribution is defined as the procedure undertaken when these models are used, 'in which the number of trips generated by any given traffic zone are distributed to all other zones in the study area in proportion to their degree of attraction'. Logit model is defined as 'a form of disaggregate mode choice modelling which calculates the probability of individuals making travel choices. Utility functions enter the model as exponentials. The model's estimates assume the maximum likelihood method. It is applied to both binary and to multi-nominal choices. In either a sequential or simultaneous structure, it may be used to calculate not only mode choice, but also trip generation, trip distribution and route assignment.'

In all of the above, accessibility is defined as 'an index of the relative ease of travel between two or more areas in terms of distance, time and cost. Specifically, the term also implies the number of opportunities available for a given amount of travel cost. For transport modelling purposes, accessibility is usually taken mathematically to be the sum of the travel times from one zone to all other zones in a region, weighted by the relative attractiveness of the destination zones involved.'

The final step in forecasting by transport modelling is route assignment, where trips on an origin/destination basis are assigned to particular routes. All-or-nothing assignment is where 'all traffic between an origin/destination paid is assigned to one route with no traffic assigned to any competing routes'. Capacity-restrained assignment is 'an iterative process by which the volume allocated to a route is compared with the capacity of that route and the speed of the route is adjusted accordingly to reflect its characteristics of speed, volume and density. New minimum time paths are calculated at the beginning of each iteration'. Multi-path assignment means that 'traffic between an origin/destination pair is divided among several competing routes in accordance with certain probability principles or linear graph techniques'.

When maps show the boundaries of equal travel time to a destination, these lines of equal travel time are called isochrones. *See* demand for transport *and* passenger transport market segmentation.

Transport Supplementary Grant *See* TSG.

transportation *See* carriage.

Transportation Improvement Programme *See* TIP[1].

transportation order Government or Official transportation orders, sometimes known as warrants, act as purchase orders, their reference numbers and dates being crucial information authorizing the expenditure. Billing agents, transport companies or providers of other travel services must quote the references when seeking payment. The IATA definition draws attention to the other type of transportation order: 'An agent's own order form authorized by a Member for use by the agent, against which the member issues its ticket and containing at least the following information: the name of a passenger, the routing itinerary, the class of travel and the fare'.

Transportation Security Administration US government body, part of the US Department of Homeland Security; not limited to air travel security – for example in 2003 $20m grants were approved to improve security on intercity bus travel; rail and sea travel are also within their remit. *See* www.tsa.gov registered-traveller database *and* trusted travelers.

Transrapid A maglev train. *See* maglev.

Travac Was name of British travel agency data and accounting system developed by Travel Computer Systems, a subsidiary of Carefree Travel introduced in 1980.

travel account[1] A corporate or business travel account between a company and a travel agent.

travel account[2] The tourism balance of trade of a country. *See* tourism balance of trade.

travel advice In the UK the Foreign and Commonwealth Office issues regular bulletins which enable travellers to decide whether it is prudent to travel to the area or country concerned. From the UK, the latest information is available on Ceefax page 470 onwards or the Internet, www.fco.gov.uk *See also* Travel Advisory.

Travel Advisory In the USA, State Department statements about the situation (usually abroad) which enable travellers to decide whether it is prudent to travel to the area concerned. On the Internet, www.travel.(country).gov/travel_warnings

travel agency automation *See* travel agents' computerized accounting and ticketing systems in the UK.

Travel Agency Commissioner *See* Agency Programme Joint Council (Liaison Group).

travel agency consortia in the UK These are travel agencies that have come together for commercial reasons to act in the same way as large travel agency groups; they establish a single nation-wide brand name, market their services as a group, contracting with and promoting sales of preferred suppliers. In December 2004 there were 8173 travel agency locations in the UK. Of these 845 were Thomson owned, 736 were owned by Airtours, 623 by Thomas Cook, 429 by First Choice Retail and 688 formed the Co-operative Travel Trading Group. North American readers should note that although the word 'co-operative' can mean a consortium, the Co-op is a major UK retailer. These figures enable information concerning the 'true' consortia of independent agents which compete with the 'multiple' travel agents to be put in context. Consortia agency location numbers are: Global Travel Group 850, Advantage 681, Worldchoice 582, Mid Consort 100 and SWIFTA 72.

Travel Agency Fee Document *See* ARC[1].

travel agency numbers in the UK *See* details incorporated in entry above for travel agency consortia in the UK.

travel agent Because the EC Package Holiday Directive concerns inclusive holidays, its definition of a travel agent is not very useful. The term 'retailer' is used to mean the person or organization which sells or offers for sale the package put together by the organizer. Thus, in the UK, retailers are travel agents and organizers are tour operators.

The Law of Agency is a veritable minefield in the UK and is equally complex, but often significantly different in other countries. The EC plan, to harmonize legislation throughout the Community may well result in some agreement. But it is most unlikely that this can cover the complete field of the law of agency even in the medium term. Differences are highly significant, concerning when and whether agents act for their customers or principals.

In the light of the foregoing, it can be seen that it is extremely difficult to identify the 'duties of care' of agents of any type, let alone travel agents. In the UK an ABTA Code of Conduct exists, details of which have been very carefully negotiated with the Office of Fair Trading, agreeing agents' responsibilities to clients and to tour operators and other principals. As these 'duties of care' vary greatly all over the world, the only solution is to omit altogether any mention of an agent's responsibilities to clients from the definition. If, for other reasons, a reader decides to add wording on this topic to a definition of 'travel agent', then it *must* be compatible with the ABTA Code of Conduct requirements, if it is to apply to the UK.

There is little distinction between travel agents and tour operators in some countries. This is why the definitions for an agent often stated outside the UK would, in Britain, also describe a tour operator.

There are many types of voluntary and other organizations who might fall within some proposed definitions, for example, the travel departments of corporate bodies. It follows that a satisfactory definition must imply that a travel agent acts for profit and offers a service to the public at large. The justification for this approach is that principals' agency agreements usually stipulate that the agent must offer a public service.

The definition proposed here has been developed from the IATA and UFTAA definitions of a travel agent, taking account of the matters mentioned above.

'A travel agent is any person or organization, (excluding persons or organizations acting as tour operators or actually providing transportation, accommodation or other travel-related services and the employees or subcontractors of such organizations) offering a public travel information, reservation and ticketing service, who for profit, solicits, obtains, receives or furnishes, directly or indirectly, passengers or groups of passengers for transportation by a carrier or the supply of other services by another travel industry principal.'

In general terms, a travel agent is a person or organization selling transportation services to individuals or groups on behalf and in the name of carriers and other principals. Although in the UK, the term is normally applied to travel retailers, in North America and many other countries the term is applied to a person rather than an organization.

The IATA definition is, 'Excluding carriers performing transportation for one of their employees or subcontractors, a travel agent is any person or organization who for compensation or profit, solicits, obtains, receives or furnishes directly or indirectly, passengers or groups of passengers for transportation by a carrier'. *See also* legal status of a travel agent *and* multiple.

Travel Agent Arbiter *See* Arbiter.

Travel Agent Automated Deduction *See* ARC[1].

Travel Agent's Handbook The official IATA publication containing the regulations agreed by the APJC (Agency Programme Joint Council) and IATA Resolutions relating to IATA Sales Agency Distribution Rules.

Travel Agents Commission Order *See* TACO.

travel agents' computerized accounting, administration and ticketing systems in the UK TARSC and Ramesys Traveller claim to be the administration system market leaders; until 2000, Ramesys was known as ICC Concorde. Other systems used substantially include Dolphin Travel Manager, Voyager and Comtec Travelcat. Associated with these systems are multi-operator search systems such as Comtec Easysell and Ramesys Sales Agent. Leading communications systems used include Telewest Endeavour, NTL Traveleye, Comtec Communications and Call Link Magic Desktop.

travel agent's legal status *See* legal status of a travel agent.

travel agents' payment systems *See* agents' payment systems.

Travel and Tourism Programme UK school level educational initiative founded by American Express; subsequently joined by partners British Tourist Authority, English Tourist Board, Forte and Crest hotels. Now organized by Springboard UK. Main activity is through the promotion and organization of the GCSE (General Certificate in Secondary Education) in travel and tourism, explained in detail under this heading. *See* www.springboarduk.org.uk/ttp

travel brochure *See* brochure.

travel bureau Another name for a travel agency.

Travel CAT Was name of UK computer system for multi-branched travel agencies.

Travel Club Was name of Swissair's Frequent Flyers Club, membership of which was free, but at Swissair's discretion. *See* FFP (frequent flyer programme).

travel consultant Another name for a person selling travel in a travel agency, who provides information and advice in order to facilitate this.

Travel Counsellors UK travel agency selling its services through home-based travel consultants. *See* outside sales representatives.

Travel Directory In Britain, the two main competing publications *Travel Trade Gazette* and *DG&G Travel Information*, provide a comprehensive listing of names, addresses and telephone numbers of most companies involved in travel and tourism in the UK. In the USA the Fairchild Publication's *Travel Industry Personnel Directory* is the equivalent publication.

Travel Distribution System Name that may replace the term GDS within the currency of this dictionary.

travel document Stateless persons in the UK who are unable or unwilling to obtain British nationality can utilize a Home Office travel document for international travel. Visas are essential in such a document for all countries to which the holder intends to travel.

Travel Funds Protection Plan *See* escrow account.

Travel Industry Designator *See* IATA TID.

Travel Industry of America *See* TIA.

Travel Information Manual *See* TIM.

Travel Information Online Has been introduced by the UK government as part of its ukonline.gov.uk Internet project. Help and advice on travelling is provided including all the latest health tips such as specific country-by-country advice on nearly 200 destinations; vaccinations required by country; and advice on getting treatment when abroad. Tips for staying healthy whilst away include advice on avoiding Deep Vein Thrombosis during flights. According to the Department of Health, two-thirds of Britons do not seek medical advice before travelling abroad and 50% of travellers to exotic locations do not take measures to prevent infectious diseases. *See* www.ukonline.gov.uk

travel insurance The contingencies against which travel insurance policies may give cover include: loss of irrecoverable deposits or payments as a result of cancellation; loss of part of a planned holiday or trip because it had to be curtailed; medical and emergency expenses with additional benefits payable where hospitalization occurs; personal accident with benefits varying according to the nature of the disablement resulting; departure delay due to reasons outside the control of the insured person and associated expenses; loss of baggage and personal effects; loss of personal money and valuables; possible claims against an insured person of a personal liability nature; expense resulting from delayed baggage; losses as a result of tour organizer or transportation company failures.

Travel insurance policies offer cover for varying periods and premiums are not only rated according to duration of cover, but also dependent upon the area of travel, the least expensive available in Britain being for UK domestic travel, then European travel, and the most expensive concerning worldwide travel. Some UK insurers charge additional premiums for North American travel. It is an important principle that travel insurance will not cover against the consequences of medical conditions known by the applicant; if such pre-existing conditions are disclosed to the insurer, travel insurance may be offered at a higher rate or under certain exceptions. Free medical treatment is available for UK citizens when travelling within the EU, at levels varying considerably between member states; some travel insurers require policy holders to obtain an E111 entitlement certificate, to be replaced by the European Health Insurance Card from the end of 2005; *for details see* www.dh.gov.uk *See also* average, benefit, contribution, excess, exclusion clauses, indemnity, subrogation *and uberrimae fidei.*

Travel Key Was name of British Rail's business charge card made available through organizations, companies, government departments and the like, to their employees. Now withdrawn.

Travel Links A British Consortium of travel agents based in Lincolnshire, members of Worldchoice.

travel management company Modern usage for a travel agent specializing in business travel. *See also the list of 70 other business travel related entries following* corporate travel contracts, *some of which lead to further entries.*

travel manager *See* corporate travel manager; *see also the list of 70 other business travel related entries following* corporate travel contracts, *some of which lead to further entries.*

travel policy Official rules concerning travel arrangements undertaken on behalf of the organization concerned. Coverage includes accommodation and sometimes entertainment expense policies are integrated. Scope usually states class of travel to which various employee grades are entitled. Where route deals, front end rebates or front end deals are in place, usage of preferred suppliers/carriers may be either recommended or obligatory. Similarly, usage of a nominated travel management company and/or a self booking tool may also be optional or mandatory. Pre-trip reporting with pre-trip authorization may be enforced by the policy. *The terms used in this entry are explained under their respective headings. A list of 70 other business travel related entries follows* corporate travel contracts, *some of which lead to further entries.*

travel principal Any individual or corporate entity in the travel industry contracting with consumers to organize or provide a facility or service directly rather than acting as an intermediary. The term is meant to differentiate agents from wholesalers. While it is abundantly clear that the operators of modes of transport are principals together with hoteliers and car rental operators, it depends upon the circumstances, as to whether a tour operator is to be regarded in this light. *See* legal status of a travel agent *and* tour operator.

travel procurement manager Person in an organization responsible for maximizing the best price and quality of travel and related services needing to be purchased by the organization. For fuller explanation *see* travel relationship manager.

travel propensity Although reference is made to travel propensity in both transport and tourism textbooks, in the former they usually mean travel by any mode of transport for any purpose; while in the latter, the analysis usually indicates relating to the likelihood of travelling for the purpose of tourism for leisure or vacation purposes. Net travel propensity is a measure of the proportion of an area's or country's population that takes a trip in a stipulated period of time, often 1 year. Gross travel propensity is the total number of trips expressed as a proportion of the population. Thus, since many people may make three or more tourism journeys a year, the gross figure may be well over 100%, while in the UK or the USA, it may be around 75%.

- Net travel propensity (NTP) = no. taking one or more trip ÷ no. of population × 100.
- Gross travel propensity (GTP) = total no. of trips ÷ no. of population × 100.
- It will be seen that GTP ÷ NTP provides an indicator of, on average, how frequently people in a country travel.

Now, to calculate a CPGI (country tourism potential generation index). Number of trips generated by a country divided by the total trips generated worldwide (A) certainly indicates relative importance. But it is difficult to make comparisons because of differences in population size; so another ratio should be ascertained by dividing the population number of a country by the total world population (B). On average A divided by B should be an index of 1. The greater the index the more likely it is that a country is at present and will continue to be a strong generator of tourism trips. (Although this index is now taught widely it is thought to originate from A.J. Burkart and S. (Rik) Medlik when they were teaching at Surrey University, UK, in the 1970s.)

Travel Protection Association *See* TPA.

travel relationship manager Person in a company or corporation charged with the responsibility for the relationships between a corporate company and travel suppliers; nevertheless, that person might be employed by a travel management company or the corporation. If the latter, the responsibilities will include management of TMC relationships. A TRM is expected to maximize service provision within agreed financial guidelines, while ensuring that the provision of travel arrangements assists meeting general company business objectives. However, most large businesses have procurement departments, responsible for maximizing the best price and quality of goods and services needing to be purchased by the organization. The person responsible for this in respect of travel may be a TRM or may be called a travel procurement manager. *A list of 70 other business travel related entries follows* corporate travel contracts, *some of which lead to further entries.*

travel seasons *See* seasons.

travel service intermediary IATA use this phrase as a generic term to describe any person or organization functioning between an IATA member airline and a traveller, facilitating a ticket sale, such as a travel agent, tour operator or Internet company.

Travel Shopper Was a Worldspan (originally PARS) CRS that competed with Eaasy Sabre for the public CRS travel booking market.

travel sickness *See* motion sickness.

Travel South USA Regional tourism promotion organization for the US southern states. *See* www.travel-south.com

travel statistics *See* tourism information databases.

Travel Technology Initiative A European industry user group, based in the UK, that promotes the development and use of open systems within travel, tourism and leisure. With a membership drawn from across the industry, the TTI continues to demonstrate that competing organizations can cooperate together for a common goal. Since 1989, the TTI has identified and delivered technology solutions in the search for open systems and shared benefits. The TTI's mission, as the travel and tourism industry continues to explore new technologies, is to provide an essential forum for pan-industry cooperation and the development of open standards. Many standards developed are based on XML (extensible mark-up language), covering message standards for package holiday bookings and use of XML for brochure, destination and event content.

TOPAS (Tour Operator Product Availability Standard), introduced in 2004, is an industry standard for the exchange of holiday availability information. It has been devised to pass product availability from tour operators to the data screening organizations that provide travel agents' product search systems.

TORIX (Tour Operator Reservations in XML) standard was also introduced in 2004, designed to overcome the severe limitations of viewdata, by providing a standard set of messages for passing between electronic systems descriptive and booking data. It will give UK agents a much more sophisticated booking methodology than was feasible through viewdata. The initial system (V1) taken up by TUI UK, Thomas Cook, First Choice and MyTravel cannot change or cancel bookings or handle complex itineraries. *See* www.tti.org

travel training in the UK *See* MA (Modern Apprenticeship); City and Guilds of London Institute (www.city-and-guilds.co.uk); TTC Training (www.ttctraining.co.uk) *and* NVQ.

Travel Transaction Processing Corporation *See* Worldspan.

Travel Trust Association *See* consortium, travel agency consortia in the UK *and* TTA.

travel vouchers *See* vouchers.

Travel Weekly Travel industry newspaper, appearing twice a week in the USA and weekly in the UK.

travel with pets *See* quarantine.

travelator A moving pavement or walkway, typically found in large airports to facilitate passenger movement to and from departure gates. In North America, also known as a people-mover or moving sidewalk.

Travelers Conservation Foundation Founded by the USTOA; on 1 January 2005 it amalgamated with the National Tourism Foundation, founded in 1982 by the National Tour Association to form Tourism Cares for Tomorrow. *See* www.ntfonline.org *and* www.tcfonline.org

Traveleye Internet-based UK agency system launched by X-TANT (now known as NTL Business (Travel Division)) in 2001. Multi-operator searching provides point-and-click searching for five operators simultaneously. The Easysell late availability provides a gateway to an hourly updated database of up to 75,000 holidays. TravelLITE is the associated travel agency management system, while Travelguide is a huge travel information resource. There are on-line brochures; a direct link to flights consolidation and links to Worldspan enabling air and other bookings via the Internet.

Traveller Activated Ticketing *See* NCR Skylink.

traveller's cheques (US **traveler's checks**) A secure means for travellers to carry money. The document is of face value, when exchanged in a country in whose currency a traveller's cheque is denominated; but when exchanged into another currency, there will be charges. Purchasers of traveller's cheques usually pay 1% or less of their value as a fee for their provision. The major organizations who sell traveller's cheques such as American Express, Thomas Cook, Citicorp and most major banking institutions worldwide, guarantee to replace lost or stolen traveller's cheques within 48 h. Although there is some variation, travel agents and others selling traveller's cheques usually keep the 1% commission customers pay.

American Express business was based on the Wells Fargo movement of valuables and following the American Civil War, it became less necessary for currency to be moved about because of the introduction of the money order. In 1882, Wells Fargo brought out its own form of money order, switching in 1891 to introduce the first travellers' cheque. Regardless of advertising to the contrary, it was not American Express that were first in this field. Companies supplying traveller's cheques make a profit from investment of their customer's money, because of the long periods of time often elapsing before customers cash their traveller's cheques. Current UK traveller's cheques sales are believed by Thomas Cook to be approximately £2000 million a year.

travellers' profiles *See* customer profile.

TravelNet Name of Telecom Singapore's CRS.

Travelog Name of a tour operator's reservation system in the UK.

Travelpack Name of British travel agents' computerized data and accounting system developed by Independent Computer Company Limited and first introduced in 1981.

TravelSellers.com number TravelSellers.com in the USA is a subsidiary of NACTA, the National Association of Commissioned Travel Agents. A number provided by them originates from IATA, thus instead of direct accreditation from ARC or IATAN, this is is an alternative method of achieving industry identification.

Travicom Was the main UK agency CRS. In 1989, Travicom, a British Airways subsidiary, was renamed Galileo UK, and in the first few months of 1990, Travicom users were switched to live operations on the Galileo CRS. Originally Travicom developed in its own right, as a multi-access airline reservation system for UK travel agents. Multi-access meant that agents from one terminal, could select a direct connection to any airline, or other industry suppliers such as hotels and car rental companies, in contrast to American host computer systems, where bookings were either made only through a particular airline, being passed on automatically, or where connections to other airlines were through the host computer. Travicom's DPAS (Document Printing and Accounting System) and PAMS (President Agency Management System) became brand names of Galileo; they were the brand-leading, fully integrated UK agency ticketing and accounting system, but were discontinued in 1999. *See* Galileo *and* DPAS.

Travicom Skytrack Was the name of the viewdata UK agents' air CRS; the name changed to Galileo Skytrack in 1990 and the service was withdrawn in May 1992.

Travicom Users' Association Renamed the Galileo Users' Association in March 1991. UK trade association of Galileo Users, which protects their interests in negotiation with Galileo concerning quality of service, price, enhancements etc. *See* GUA.

Travinet Was a UK travel industry communications network owned by Thomas Cook. This eventually became, through Cook's Midland Bank parents, and with share participation of other travel principals, Fastrak and Fastlink.

TRAVIS Was name of British Airways' Travel Industry School, a correspondence course covering the whole of the UK travel industry. Now run under the Speedwing Training brand name.

Traviswiss The Swiss agency CRS, associated with Galileo.

Travjet Brand name of Cosmos Holidays' variety of minimum-rated package holidays in the UK.

Travstar Was a UK travel agency viewdata reservation and administration computer system marketed by Tandata.

trawler A boat or ship that is a specialized fishing vessel.

trekking Term has been adopted by the travel industry to mean a walking holiday through desolate or mountainous areas. But pony trekking is often also referred to merely as trekking.

TRIG Tourism Review and Implementation Group in the UK. *See* entry under this heading.

trimaran A three-hulled ship.

Trinidad and Tobago Tourism Office *See* www.visittnt.com

trip In common usage, a trip is any journey. Was also name of Osprey Computer Services Limited computerized British tour operators' reservation and accounting system.

TRIP Tourism Recreation and Information Package; a computerized tourism database and mapping package, produced by the University of Edinburgh, UK.

trip distribution *See* transport modelling.

Trip Index Method of assessing the extent to which places on a tourist's itinerary are a main destination or day visits. The Trip Index for a particular place on an itinerary is calculated by dividing the number of nights spent there by the total nights of the trip duration, then multiplying by 100. Thus a TI of 100 would mean a holiday was spent in one place, while zero would be indicative that there was no overnight stay. The index was devised by D.G. Pearce and J.M. Elliott in 'The trip index' (*Journal of Travel Research* (1983) 22(1), 6–9).

trip, circle *See* circle trips.

trip, round *See* round trip.

triple room In theory, accommodation designed for occupancy for three people. In practice, tourism laws in some countries specifically allow the placing of an extra bed in a twin or double room during high season. Where there is no legislation, hoteliers often place an extra bed in a room; many modern hotels often have large rooms which they use for this purpose, but can use as a normal twin or double at other times.

TRIPS The name of the American Express travel agency computer system through which air bookings, tickets and administration can be effected. TRIPS is connected to Worldspan, through which reservations are made. Automatic transfer of accounting information from these bookings make it a completely integrated automated agency system. TRIPS stands for Travel Information Processing System.

triptik Documentation provided by the American Automobile Association providing a route map, directions and other information for a specified journey.

TrIS Travel Information System. *See* DMS[1].

TRM *See* travel relationship manager.

tronc *See* gratuity.

Tropic of Cancer A parallel of latitude which is 23° 7′ N of the Equator.

Tropic of Capricorn A parallel of latitude which is 23° 7′ S of the Equator.

tropopause *See* contrails.

TRRU Tourism and Recreation Research Unit, University of Edinburgh, is an inter-disciplinary research centre with a comprehensive library of references to tourism, leisure and travel.

Truly Independent Professional Travel Organisation *See* TIPTO.

trusted travelers US scheme which allows frequent flyers to undergo personal background checks, thereby minimizing their security screening at airports.

TRWOV Transit Without Visa. Alternative acronym is TWOV. Some countries waive the visa requirements for those passengers passing through in direct and immediate transit or moving on to another country (for which they have documentation to enter) within a certain time limit. *See* visa[2].

TS Trans-Siberia. *See* routing.

TSA[1] Tourism Satellite Account. A satellite account is a statistical process designed to measure the size of economic sectors that are not defined as industries within a country's national accounts. The United Nations has devised a system of national accounts, referred to as SNA in some textbooks. This standard way of presenting a country's national accounts is used by many states. A TSA is an extension to these accounts focusing on tourism as an economic activity within a country's national accounts. The WTO's Tourism Satellite Accounts Project received top-level recognition when its Recommended Methodological Framework for Satellite Accounting was adopted by the UN Statistical Commission in March 2000. Historically, the project had its foundation in a Canadian proposal for a Satellite Account and Information System in 1991. The essence of the project is validity and comparability; if all countries presented satellite accounts in the same format, the validity of international tourism statistics would be greatly enhanced. For more information *see* www.world-tourism.org or access the comprehensive satellite account worldwide annual statistics via the WTTC web site www.wttc.org

TSA[2] Transportation Security Administration in the USA. *See* entry under this heading *and* www.tsa.gov

TSEA Trade Show Exhibitors Association in the USA. *See* www.tsea.org

TSG Transport Supplementary Grant, is paid by the UK government to area authorities after consideration of an annual document entitled *Transport Policies and Programme*, covering planned investment in or subsidization of public transport and roads.

TSHI Time since hot section inspection (aviation term).

TSHM Time since heavy maintenance (aviation term).

TSI Travel Service Intermediary or Travel Sellers Intermediary of IATAN; agents in this category are able to retain their ARC-assigned IATA numeric code even though they no longer sell air travel.

TSMO Time since main overhaul (aviation term).

TSO Time since overhaul (aviation term).

TSP Travel service provider. Any organization supplying facilities for the use of the travelling public.

TSSA Transport Salaried Staff's Association. A trade union, affiliated to the TUC, to which many UK travel employees belong. *See* www.tssa.org.uk

TSSMV Time since shop maintenance visit (aviation term).

TTA[1] Travel Technology Association in the USA, formerly the Independent Travel Technology Association.

TTA[2] Travel Trust Association in the UK. Comprises around 350 independent travel agents, around 4% of the UK total and 80 tour operators. Not members of ABTA, the organization's members protect customers' money by keeping it in trust accounts until after departure.

TTAAT Travel and Tourist Agencies Association of Turkey.

TTC Training UK travel training organization formerly an ABTA subsidiary, sold to NTP Group in 2002, with agreement that TTC would continue to operate training on behalf of ABTA for 5 years. In 1982, the UK government abolished statutory training boards, including the Air Travel and Travel Industry Training Board, under whose aegis, training for travel agents and tour operators laid. ABTA formed its own National Training Board to take over the ATTITB travel industry functions, operating for many years as an ABTA department and subsequently as a trading subsidiary. In 1999, TTC and City and Guilds of London Institute formed a partnership to offer qualifications in the travel field, with C&GLI as the awarding body and TTC as the organizer of some courses, also liaising with colleges with appropriate facilities to run courses for travel agents. For more information *see* City and Guilds of London Institute entry *also* www.city-and-guilds.co.uk *also* www.ttctraining.co.uk ; Modern Apprenticeship *and* NVQ.

TTENTO Was the Travel Tourism and Events National Training Organization in the UK which merged with the Hospitality Training Foundation in 2002, forming People 1st, a Sector Skills Council (SSC), for the hospitality, leisure, travel and tourism industry, launched in 2004. *See* www.people1st.co.uk

TTGAC Travel and Tourism Government Affairs Council in the USA.

TTI Travel Technology Initiative in the UK. *See* entry under this heading, *also* www.tti.org

TTL Ticketing Time Limit.

TTP *See* Travel and Tourism Programme.

TTPC Travel Transaction Processing Corporation. *See* Worldspan.

TTRA The Travel and Tourism Research Association in Salt Lake City, USA, produces bibliographies and undertakes worldwide research in its specialist field. *See* www.ttra.com

TTSN Total time since new (aviation term).

tugboat A small, very powerful vessel used for towing larger ships.

Tunisian National Tourist Office *See* www.tourismtunisia.com *see also* www.cometotunisia.co.uk

Tunisian National Travel Agency Organization *See* FTAV.

turbine aircraft engine Where the blades of a turbine are rotated by expanding gases. Typically this type of engine has a rotary air compressor with an air intake and one or more combustion chambers. The gas expansion produced drives a turbine, finally leaving the engine through exhaust outlets. When the rotational power of the turbine is taken to drive a propeller via a reduction gear, this is known as a turboprop or propjet. When the engine is designed so that the turbine rotation creates a thrust producing a jet, this is a turbojet. A fanjet or turbofan engine is of the turbojet type, where the thrust has been increased by the addition of a low-pressure compressor. Varieties of this type of engine have a front fan or an aft fan. *See also* jet aircraft engine.

turbofan jet Aircraft powered by a turbojet engine, the thrust of which has been increased by the addition of a low-pressure compressor or fan. *See also* jet aircraft engine.

turbojet Aircraft powered by an engine incorporating a turbine-driven air compressor to take in and compress air for fuel combustion, the combustion gases and/or heated air being used both to rotate the turbine and create a thrust-producing jet. *See also* jet aircraft engine.

turboprop An aircraft powered by an engine in which the main propulsive force is supplied by a gas turbine which drives a propeller. *See also* propjet *and* jet aircraft engine.

turboshaft engine Terminology applied to a gas turbine engine driving a shaft to power a helicopter.

turbulence Aircraft and other radar can detect turbulence caused by storm clouds. Quite apart from being able to see the clouds, it is therefore, within a pilot's control, to avoid turbulence of this nature. But clear-air turbulence cannot be spotted in this way. Below a cloud base, when it is warm or in blustery or thundery conditions, turbulence is often caused by simple up or down currents of air. Instead of this convection, there may be orographic windflows. These are the airflows associated with contour changes such as mountains or valleys.

Above the cloud, in a clear sky, clear-air turbulence may be caused by the friction of two different air masses rubbing together. The turbulence may be even more pronounced when the air masses are moving in different directions. The other main cause of this type of turbulence are the jetstreams. These occur only at high altitudes and are semi-permanent tubes of fast-moving air, with speeds up to 300 mph. They move rather like a snake around the world and in the northern hemisphere, go from west to east. The speed of the jetstream is at its greatest at the centre, dropping off towards the edge, which is called the skin. Flying along the edge of the jetstream is similar to driving over cobblestones, hence the derivation of the pilots' name for this. Flying in the centre of the jetstream is likely to be very bumpy.

Turbulence is reported by and to pilots in the form of a figure from 1 to 9 indicating its severity and whether in cloud, followed by further figures indicative of its base level and height.

Turkish National Travel Agency Organization   *See* TTAAT.

Turkish Tourist Office   *See* www.tourism turkey.org *and* www.gototurkey.co.uk

turnaround   The time between an aircraft landing and taking off; low cost airline operations necessitate speedy turn-around in order to maximize aircraft usage.

turnaround open-jaw   *See* IATA fare construction system.

turndown   Literally the act of a room maid in a hotel taking off the daytime bed cover and folding down the sheets slightly. Typically, higher-class hotels leave a chocolate on the pillow, together with a breakfast order menu. The opportunity may be taken also to give the room a quick clean and tidy.

turnpike   A US motorway on which users are charged for travel; commonly, a distance card is provided on entry and payment is made at the time of exit. Also known as a tollway.

TVOR   Terminal VHF omni-range directional navigation beacon (aviation term).

twin double   *Twin-bedded room* has the same meaning worldwide, but a *twin double* is mainly used in North America to designate a large room containing two double beds.

TWOV   Alternative acronym for transit without visa. *See* TRWOV.

TWY   Taxiway (aviation term).

U

U/C Undercarriage.

UACC Upper airspace control centre (aviation term).

UAR Upper air route (aviation term).

UAS Upper airspace (aviation term).

UATP Universal Air Travel Plan. IATA's credit card facility for the purchase of international and domestic air transportation; the cards issued to travellers are called 'Air Travel Cards'. There are two categories: embossed with a 'P', a card is only valid for purchases of air travel and related services for the cardholder; embossed with a 'Q' the cardholder can make purchases for anyone. There are five types of cards. The International also has an embossed 'W' and is green; it will be honoured worldwide for purchase of air transportation and related services. The North American card is also embossed with an 'N' and is red; it will only enable purchase of travel between points in the USA and immediately surrounding area. The AirPlus card is blue and the PassAge is silver; both allow an increased range of purchases. The co-branded Air Travel Card/MasterCard Business Card allows all the usual card purchases through any merchant accepting a MasterCard. The debit slip used in travel agencies worldwide is known as a Universal Credit Card Charge Form (UCCCF). A 'Q' cardholder may complete a one trip travel order (OTATO) enabling purchase of travel by another person.

UAV Unmanned air vehicle.

UBE Ultra bypass engine (aviation term).

uberrimae fidei Insurance term meaning, 'of the utmost good faith'. It is not general law in Britain that parties to the contract disclose absolutely everything pertaining to a situation. It is only essential that neither side tells any lies. In insurance matters, however, there is a legal obligation that the insured person reveals every material fact within his knowledge concerning the policy.

In the case of travel insurance, customers at the time of taking out policies, will have 'warranted' that they and all the persons on whom the holiday depended, were in good health at the time of taking the insurance. It is common for unthinking and perhaps deceitful travellers, realizing there is a potential problem, to undertake travel insurance, believing that in this way they can cover against a risk they can foresee and travel agents should bear this situation in mind when handling policies.

UBOA Was the United Bus Association of America, now called the United Motorcoach Association.

UC Unable to confirm. Message response, for example, when a hotel reservation which is not available, is requested through a GDS.

UCAV Unmanned combat aircraft vehicle.

UCCCF Universal Credit Card Charge Form. *See* UATP.

UCP User Charges Panel of IATA.

UDF Unducted fan (aviation term).

U-Drive Advertising terminology used by some North American car rental companies.

UFD Up front display (aviation term).

UFTAA Universal Federation of Travel Agent's Associations. The main global grouping of national travel agents' associations. *See* www.uftaa.com

Uganda Tourist Board *See* www.visituganda.com

UHB Ultra bypass (aviation engine term).

UIC Union Internationale des Chemins de Fer (International Union of Railways) is the international organization to which most national rail organizations belong. *See* www.uic.asso.fr

UIR Upper flight information region (aviation term).

UIS Upper flight information service (aviation term).

UITP Union International des Transports Publics (International Union of Public

Transport) is an association promoting the interests of the public transport sector internationally. Since 1885, the organization has coordinated research in this field, and run a major congress every 2 years. *See* www.uitp.com

UK Agency Programme Joint Council   *See* Agency Programme Joint Council.

UK multiple travel agents   *See* multiple.

UKAB   UK Airprox Board. *See* AIRPROX.

UKinbound   Formerly the British Incoming Tour Operators Association (BITOA). Changed its name in November 2004. Primarily represents the interests of organizations involved in handling tourists coming into the UK. *See* www.ukinbound.org

Ukraine National Tourist Organization   *See* www.nto.org.ua

UKTS   United Kingdom Tourism Survey. *See* BHTS.

ULD   Unit load device. Equipment for loading aircraft.

ULDP   Unit load device panel of IATA.

Ulisse 2000   Name of Alitalia's in-flight magazine.

UltraSwitch   A hotel CRS. *See* THISCO.

UM   Unaccompanied Minor. Young persons, usually aged between 6 and 12 whom airlines will accept for travel without an accompanying adult. Special handling, by ground and inflight staff, takes particular care of such passengers to ensure their comfort and safety. UM forms must be completed to ensure that the children will be met on arrival. The terminology varies between airlines; e.g. until February 1985, British Airways used the wording 'unaccompanied young passengers', which then changed to 'young flyers', which, unfortunately, does not carry the vital information that no adult is travelling with them.

UMA   United Motorcoach Association, formerly United Bus Association of America. *See* www.uma.org

Umbrella Information Provider   *See* IP.

umiak   Inuit canoe similar to a kayak, but whereas in the latter, the hull and deck are completely enclosed, except for the space for the oarsman, a umiak is an open boat.

Unaccompanied Minor   *See* UM.

unbiased opinions of hotels   *See* hotels, unbiased opinions of.

unchecked baggage   *See* hand baggage.

UNCLOS   United Nations Convention on Law of the Sea.

undercutting   In no circumstances may a combination of direct or indirect sector air fares undercut a direct through fare. *See* IATA fare construction system.

underground railway   Often referred to in the UK merely as the 'Underground' or 'Tube'. An urban rail system usually running in tunnels beneath built up areas but operating above ground in the suburbs. The equivalent of the Metro in Paris, Subway in New York and rapid transit systems in many other locations, e.g. BART, the Bay Area Rapid Transit system around San Francisco.

UNEP   United Nations Environment Programme. *See* tourism, sustainable.

UNICORN   The European EDI standard for the vehicle ferry industry. *See* electronic data interchange.

Unified Vocational Preparation   *See* UVP.

Uniform System of Accounts for the Lodging Industry   *See* hotel statistics worldwide.

uninterrupted international air transport (in and from the USA)   That which does not include a scheduled stopover at any US city of more than 12 h.

Union Internationale des Chemins de Fer   *See* UIC.

Union Internationale des Transportes Publiques   *See* UITP.

Unison Travel Management System   Was name of Magnasys Limited computerized UK travel agency data and accounting system.

unit destination   *See* IATA fare construction system.

unit origin   *See* IATA fare construction system.

United States Tour Operators Association   *See* USTOA.

Universal Air Travel Plan   *See* UATP.

Universal Federation of Travel Agents Associations   *See* UFTAA.

Universal Time   Basis of time worldwide, formerly known as Greenwich Mean Time (GMT). The standard is based on the zero line of longitude, running through Greenwich to the east of London, UK. Although 'officially' the name has changed, general usage of GMT persists and the full explanation has been left under this heading.

universal time coordinates   *See* Universal Time.

university education in tourism in the UK
See Higher Education Academy
Network *and* Appendix II.

unlimited mileage car rental When a car
is rented for a period, with no extra charge
dependent on the distance travelled. *See
also* time and mileage car rental.

unmanaged travel That travel where an
individual books travel arrangements
(business or leisure) direct with travel
operators, as distinct from managed
travel, which is arranged by a travel
management company (TMC). It is business travel jargon. *A list of 70 other
business travel related entries follows*
corporate travel contracts, *some of
which lead to further entries.*

unrestricted fare A rate on a mode of
transport free of travel conditions, other
than basic; for example, air tickets are
not valid for more than 1 year from date
of first travel and are only valid for a
specified class of travel.

UNSTAT United Nations Statistical
Commission which together with the
WTO published in 1994, *Recommendations on Tourism Statistics*, details of
which are under their definitions in this
dictionary. *See* tourism.

UPAV Union Professionelle des Agences
de Voyages; the Belgian National Travel
Agency Organization. *See* www.upav.be

UPBAV Union Professionelle Belge des
Agences de Voyages.

upgraded passenger A passenger who
travelled on a flight for which he had a
ticket and a confirmed reservation, but
in a class higher than that to which he
was entitled. This may occur when it is
discovered that for some reason or
another there is no record of the passenger at the time of check-in and the class
of service to which the passenger is entitled is fully booked. Members of frequent flyer programmes often use some
of their 'miles' to 'purchase' upgrades.
The same term now applies generally in
the travel industry. For example, a customer who, for any reason, is given a
better car than that reserved, without
extra payment, or a better hotel room,
has been 'upgraded'.

Upper Class Brand name given by Virgin
to passenger area immediately adjacent
to first class, where passengers paying
full economy fares enjoy improved service and facilities. *See* business class.

Uruguay Ministry of Tourism *See*
www.uruguaynatural.com

**Uruguayan National Travel Agency
Organization** *See* AUAVI.

US Travel Data Centre A major source of
US travel and tourism statistics. *See*
tourism information databases.

US visa requirements *See* Visa Waiver
Program.

USA Rail Pass Amtrak's USA Rail Passes
are only available to international visitors. Each rail pass is valid for 15 or 30
days (except for the Northeast Rail Pass
which is also valid for 5 days) with
unlimited stopovers. Rail passes are
available for the following regions:
Northeast, East, West, California as well
as coastal areas. UK equivalent is the
Britrail Pass.

USANTO United States of America
National Tourist Office.

user group A group of users of a particular type of computer or computer service who associate in order to negotiate
from strength with the computer manufacturer; e.g. Galileo Users' Group.

USSR National Travel Organization Was
Intourist; this organization now operates
in many of the States of the Commonwealth which were formerly the USSR.

USTDC United States Travel Data Centre,
a major source of US travel and tourism
statistics. *See* tourism information databases.

USTI United States Tourism Industries.
See www.tinet.ita.doc.gov/

USTOA United States Tour Operators
Association. Although there are more
than a thousand operators in the USA,
only 33 of them belong to the
Association at the time of writing. All
the large companies are members and
they account for between 65% and 70%
of agency sales. While USTOA financial
criteria and regulations are not as stringent as ABTA in the UK, the Association
exerts a stabilizing influence on the market. A $1 million Consumer Protection
Plan protects consumers in the event of
member bankruptcy or insolvency.
Active members must post US$1 million
in security in the form of a bond, letter
of credit or certificate of deposit. The
security is held by USTOA and is used
to reimburse consumers in the event of
financial failure of a member. The security is also available to consumers if

their money is not refunded within 120 days of cancellation of travel arrangements, or other failure to complete performance obligations. *See* www.ustoa.com

USTOL Ultra-short take-off and landing.

USTS United States Travel Service; was the official American agency for the promotion of tourism to the USA. *See* USTTA *and* Visit USA Association below.

USTTA United States Travel and Tourism Administration. No longer exists; was the section of the US Department of Commerce responsible for the promotion of US tourism. Now some of these functions have been taken over by the Visit USA Association.

UTA Upper control area (aviation term).

Utah Travel Council *See* www.utah.com

UTC Universal Time Coordinates. *See* Universal Time.

UTDN Unattended Ticket Delivery Network.

Utell *See* HANK.

Utellvision Uses laser technology to depict 6500 hotels, their facilities and location. System is associated with Utell's hotel computer reservation system. The largest worldwide network not dedicated to a particular hotel chain.

UTH Unity Travel Holdings. A UK consortium of travel agents which is a member of Worldchoice.

utilization rate The equivalent for a car rental company of load factor for modes of transport or occupancy rate of a hotel. It is the percentage of the vehicles that are on hire.

UTM Universe Transverse Mercator. A map projection used in aviation charts. *See* map projection.

UTV Universal Travel Voucher. A Mastercard scheme used in the USA for intermediaries to remit money to principals, at the same time confirming bookings.

UVP Was the Unified Vocational Preparation programme in the UK, was replaced by YTS and after further name changes, is now the Modern Apprenticeship scheme used by the UK travel trade.

V

V Club Name of Varig's Frequent Flyers Club, membership of which is free, but by the airline's invitation only. *See* FFP (frequent flyer programme).

V1 Maximum speed below which a pilot can abort a take-off; **V2** is the lowest air speed indicator reading at which an aircraft can climb following one engine failure. **V3** is normal speed for take-off with all engines operating, while **V4** is the steady climb speed for first segment noise abatement.

vacation club *See* holiday club.

vacation farm tourism *See* farm tourism.

vacation savings plan *See* holiday savings plans.

vaccination *See* international health requirements.

VAD Visual approach/departure (aviation term).

VADS Value Added Data Services. Generic term for all time and cost saving means of passing information electronically, including EDI, electronic mail etc.

VAL The world's first automatic metro or Urban Rapid Transit system, based in and around Lille, northern France and which opened in May 1984. All the trains are fully automatic, with no staff such as drivers or guards, on board. Progress and location of individual trains is controlled by a central computer. Automatic glass doors on platforms match those on the trains, and open and close simultaneously. The automatic control always slows down and halts trains at the right places along the platforms. These trains run on rubber tyres along concrete channels similar to the Paris Metro. They are not as wide as normal trains (1.9 m).

valet parking Parking of a guest's car by staff of the establishment visited, such as a hotel or restaurant. The person doing the parking is known as a car hop or car valet. But confusingly, a person who cleans a car is also called a car valet.

validation Official IATA definition is the authorized stamping or writing upon the passenger ticket evidencing that it has been officially issued by the carrier or its appointed agent. The term applies generally to the imprinting of a ticket by the issuer, without which the ticket is not valid for travel.

validator Any device used to validate a travel document by imprinting an official stamp on it. Impressions are created by simple machines similar to those that used to be familiar to readers when their credit cards were imprinted on a document for signature. Now, both for credit cards and travel documents mechanical imprints are obsolescent.

validity Period of time for which a ticket is available for use.

VALS Values and Lifestyles Segmentation. *See* market segmentation.

Value Added Tax *See* VAT[1].

value season *See* seasons.

VAMP Visual anamorphic motion picture (aviation term).

VANGUARD A UK Department of Trade and Industry initiative intended to act as a catalyst in the formation of EDI communities.

VANS Value Added Network Service. *See* communications networks.

VAOC *See* Visitor Attraction Operations Certificate.

VAPI Visual approach path indicator (aviation term).

vaporetto Small motor boat serving as a water taxi in Venice; they may not be as romantic as a gondola but they are recommended for their convenience and speed.

VAR Visual/aural range **or** magnetic variation (aviation terms).

variable camber flap *See* airframe.

VASI Visual approach slope indicator (aviation term).

VASIS Visual approach slope indicator system (pronounced var-zi) (aviation term).

VAT¹ Value Added Tax is the usual form of consumer sales tax worldwide, based on taxing the value added at each stage of the manufacture or distribution of goods or services. In the UK, at the time of writing, travel is zero-rated which means that no tax is charged on air, sea or surface transport, although EC Commissioners have made proposals to tax rail and coach travel. Insurance is exempt which means that while insurance companies do not have to charge VAT to customers, they cannot recover VAT incurred in the expenditure of running their business. Since handling travel insurance is less than 5% of a travel agent's business, this factor is usually disregarded when UK agents are allowed to recover all of the VAT that they spend in running their businesses. British hotels have the standard rate of 17.5% tax charged on customers' bills. Thus, when American, or indeed any other tourist, books inclusive tours to Britain and to most European countries, the hotel element of the payment made actually includes VAT.

British tour operators are involved in charging holidaymakers a VAT element for their profit margin or 'added value' on top of the cost of the elements they use to make up a package holiday. UK agents, when collecting commission from British operators and hoteliers have also to collect an extra 17.5% VAT on that commission. This VAT is remitted to Customs & Excise every quarter (or deducted from any reimbursement claim). The tour operating principal then recovers this VAT on commission from the Customs & Excise. Thus, there is a 'money-go-round' resulting in no government tax gain and a waste of administrative time. *It is stressed that as far as Customs & Excise in the UK are concerned, a travel agent's turnover is commission income and **not** sales turnover.*

VAT² Target threshold speed (aviation term).

VAX Web-based Vacation Access technology owned and operated by TriSept Solutions of Milwaukee, USA.

Vb Design speed for maximum gust intensity (aviation term).

Vbs Maximum air brake operating speed (aviation term).

Vc Designed cruising speed or rate of climb (aviation term).

VCB Visitor(s) and Convention Bureau. Most organizations serving this function use these words in an alternative order, Convention and Visitors Bureau.

Vd Design diving speed (aviation term).

VDF¹ Very high frequency direction finding (aviation term).

VDF² Maximum demonstrated speed during certification testing (aviation term).

VDT Video display terminal. A North American term for a computer monitor or visual display unit (VDU).

VDU Visual display unit; a computer screen.

Ve Equivalent air speed (aviation term also abbreviated as EAS).

Venezuela Fondoturismo Venezuela tourism training and promotion fund. *See* www.venezuela.com/corpoturismo

Venezuela Tourism In 2003, INATUR became the new Venezualen Tourism organization. *See* www.inatur.gov.ve

Venuemasters Consortium of British universities and colleges which undertakes joint marketing of their facilities during vacation periods to potential conference and group traffic. Formed at the end of 2000 by amalgamation of the British Universities Accommodation Consortium and Connect, the Higher Education Accommodation Consortium.

verandah deck *See* deck.

verandah suite The quintessence of luxury on a ship, where the accommodation includes a small private deck area.

Vermont Tourism *See* www.1-800-vermont.com or www.travel-vermont.com

vertical integration The terminology implies the ownership by one organization of both the manufacturing and means of distribution to consumers. For example, in the UK, the German-owned Thomson conglomerate owns Britannia Airways, the second largest airline in the UK; Thomson Holidays, the biggest tour operator, the largest chain of travel shops; and an overseas hotel subsidiary.

Vessel Sanitation Programme *See* CDC.

Vf Design flap speed (aviation term).

Vfe Maximum indicated air speed with flaps extended (aviation term).

VFR¹ Visiting friends and relatives: one of the major reasons for leisure travel. In

2003 8.5m VFR travellers went abroad from the UK, 13.9% of all visits abroad.

VFR² Visual flight rules.

VFR traffic Travel business that emanates from the Visiting Friends and Relatives market.

VG Variable geometry (aviation term).

VGA Variable graphic adaptor. VGA and its enhancements are the computer industry standard for the screens of VDUs.

VGPI Visual glide path indicator (aviation term).

VGS Visual guidance system (aviation term).

VGSI Visual guide slope indicator (aviation term).

VHF Very high frequency, ranging from 30 to 300 MHz (aviation term).

VHSIC Very high speed integrated circuits (aviation term).

Vi Air speed indicated (aviation term also abbreviated as IAS).

VIA The Videotex Industry Association has over 100 members embracing the whole of the British viewdata and Teletext industry, including many of the major travel information providers, equipment manufacturers and software developers. For more information *see* www.iit.edu/departments/csep/Public www/codes/coe/Videotex_Industry_ Association.htm The equivalent US organization is the Interactive Services Association.

VIA Rail Canada The organization that combined the passenger services of Canadian National and Canadian Pacific Railways to form a single rail network throughout Canada. *See* www.viarail.ca *and* North American train services for further details.

Viatel The Australian public videotex service which is similar to, and was developed from Prestel.

video conferencing Interactive TV conference connections between distant groups, over the Internet, through phone cabling or enabled by satellite communication. In the CAB International publication *Strategic Management in Tourism* (L. Moutinho, 2000), it is suggested that in the USA, video conferencing will reduce demand for domestic air travel by 12% to 16% by 2030; in Europe, reductions are likely to be larger, between 13% and 23%.

videodisk A disk about the size of a long-playing record on which video material can be recorded and from which it can be played back through an appropriate player and television set. The advent of CDs has made videodisks obsolete.

Videotext *See* viewdata and Prestel.

Vietnam National Administration of Tourism *See* www.vietnamtourism.com

viewdata Remote terminals connected by telephone lines on a dial-up basis to computer databases from the 1970s vastly increased efficiency in the UK travel industry by enabling travel agents to book package holidays direct into tour operators' computerized reservation systems. This system is described under the heading Prestel, which was the name of British Telecom's viewdata system. Whilst the layman uses the term viewdata, technologists refer to this communication method as videotex. There are two main international videotex standards. A total of 26 countries, which make up the Committee of European Post and Telegraph, have agreed to a version of Prestel's alpha-mosaic standard. An alpha-geometric system has been adopted by the US giant ATT in concert with the Canadian Telidon system. This explains why European terminals cannot access North American systems and vice versa.

This text-based technology with a slow transmission rate may be regarded as old-fashioned, although it is still very widely used in the UK and is both low cost and effective. Increasingly, there has been travel industry migration to more modern interfaces, Internet Protocol (IP) and Transmission Control Protocol (TC/IP). During the next few years, the travel industry will probably switch to Extensible Mark-up Language (XML). In effect, these are sets of rules that govern the way computers communicate. But despite these and similar developments, viewdata remains the system of choice of UK tour operators and travel agents. Speaking in March 2001, Directors of Airtours and Thomsons, the two largest British tour operators agreed that viewdata would continue to be the main UK booking tool for another 3–5 years. Although they saw the need for an airline-style multi-access system to replace viewdata with unbiased availability and prices. Currently the two main viewdata services to British travel agents are through Endeavour/Fastrak and NTL. *See* entries under those headings.

villa for holidays A villa is generally understood worldwide to mean a luxurious private home, often in a rural setting. However, vacation accommodation, in a detached house or bungalow, for holiday use, is referred to as a villa throughout Europe. The villa may be part of a holiday complex with a range of facilities or may be entirely separate. The term is wide-ranging in its meaning and may be palatial with a private swimming pool or quite basic.

VIN Visitor Information Network.

Virginia Tourism Corporation *See* www.virginia.org

virtual reality *See* VU.

Visa[1] The huge multi-national credit card group under this brand name, under which Barclaycard and others operate throughout the world, has many products such as the Visa Travel Card and Visa Traveller's Cheques. *But* the generic meaning follows.

visa[2] Authority, usually stamped in passport by a government foreign to the holder, permitting entry to the country concerned, providing health and other normal entry requirements are observed. Although visas are usually permissions to enter, they may give permission to leave, being called 'exit visas'. Sometimes visas are endorsed when leaving a country to give aliens permission for re-entry. Visas always denominate the number of entries allowed. Russia and similar countries currently give single entry visas, usually stating date, time and method of entry and exit. Some countries give tourist-card visas for a similar purpose. Other types of tourist card are usually issued by airlines to British people travelling to South American countries.

Entry permits are a further type of visa which usually must be obtained before travel and which are often issued separately from a passport. Multiple-entry visas may allow an unlimited number of visits or may specify the number of times entry is allowed. Visas may have a limited life, specified as being valid up to a date named on the visa or for a period of time after entry,

for the life of the passport in which they are stamped, or may be for an indefinite period. Visas are also classified according to the purpose of entry of an alien. Thus, there are visitor, tourist, student, business, temporary resident and permanent immigrant visas. Transit visas allow aliens to traverse a country en route to a final destination in another country. *See* passport.

visa service Facilitation of the acquisition of visas, which is undertaken by travel agents or specialist visa companies on behalf of travellers in return for fees. Not infrequently, applicants may have to queue for many hours and then return the following day. Many consulates worldwide have agency sections that deal with applications. In the USA, a person or organization performing this service may be called a visa expediter. *See* visa[2].

Visa Waiver Program US facility allowing travellers from certain countries to enter the USA without obtaining an entry visa in advance of travel. However, since 26 June 2005, VWP travellers have been required to have a machine readable passport. Separate US legislation requires that the 27 VWP countries must issue passports containing biometric information after 26 October 2005. Most countries will be unable to meet this deadline.

VisitBritain Name of UK government body responsible for promoting tourism to Britain as a whole and also within and to England in particular. Formed in April 2003 from the British Tourist Authority (BTA) and English Tourism Council (ETC). *See* www.VisitBritain.com For UK national tourism statistics *see* www.staruk.org.uk ; travel industry access is via www.tourismtrade.org.uk which includes market intelligence data, trends and statistics.

Visit USA Association Following the termination of the USTTA by the US government, the Visit USA Association was formed by the private sector, undertaking international promotion of the USA as a tourism destination. *See* www.visitusa.org

visiting friends and relatives *See* VFR.

visitor *See* tourism for official definition.

Visitor Attraction Operations Certificate In the UK, the Visitor Attraction scheme from City and Guilds has been devised in association with the tourist boards and practising attractions managers, specifically to meet the growing demand for training leading to a nationally recognized qualification for non-specialist employees working in a variety of visitor or tourist attractions.

The scheme is suitable for running at colleges or by employers on an in-house basis to suit their own arrangements. All centres and employers must nevertheless register as approved centres with City and Guilds. It is recommended that a course consists of a minimum 100 teaching hours with extra time for visits, preparation of assignments and practical work.

The scheme aims to cover all the main subjects involved in the day-to-day operation of an attraction, as follows: Introduction to UK tourism; Local knowledge; Operating a sales outlet; Marketing and promotion; Cash handling; Office practice; Communication skills; Booking procedures; Interpretation and presentation skills; Health and safety; Security.

visitor attractions Normally refers to man-made tourist attractions. *See* attractions, theme parks *and* sightseeing in Britain.

Visitor(s) and Convention Bureau Most organizations serving this function use these words in an alternative order, Convention and Visitors Bureau.

VISTA Was, in the UK, Viewdata Information Service for Travel Agents, the acronym for Horizon's viewdata system. Name became obsolete following takeover of Horizon by Thomson group.

Vle Maximum indicated air speed with landing gear extended (aviation term).

VLF Very low frequency, ranging between 3 and 30 kHz (aviation term).

Vlg Maximum landing gear operating speed (aviation term).

Vlo Maximum indicated air speed while landing gear is extending or retracting (aviation term).

VLO Very low observable (aviation term).

Vlof Lift-off speed (aviation term).

VLR Very long range (aircraft).

Vmc Minimum control equivalent air speed, with the critical engine inoperative during take-off (aviation term).

VMC Visual meteorological conditions (aviation term).

Vmca Minimum control speed in the air with critical engine failed (aviation term).

Vmcg Minimum control speed on the ground (aviation term).

Vmcl Minimum control speed for the landing approach (aviation term).

Vmo Maximum indicated speed at which the aircraft should be flown (aviation term).

Vms Minimum stall speed (aviation term).

Vmsl Minimum speed in the stall (aviation term).

Vmso Minimum speed in a stall, flaps down (aviation term).

Vmu Minimum unstick speed (aviation term).

Vne Never exceed speed (aviation term).

Vno Normal operating speed (aviation term).

VOICE The Vacation Owners' Independent Coalition in Europe comprises the Organization for Timeshare in Europe and the Association for Timeshare Owners' Committees Ltd. VOICE will provide an information and conciliation service for consumers, and establish a code of conduct to govern post-contractual issues of timeshare.

void ticket A ticket issued by a travel agent which is reported on a sales return, whether manual or electronic, as having being spoilt, issued in error or for other reasons, is to be treated as if it had never been issued. This is different from a cancelled ticket, where, according to the fare rules associated with it, cancellation charges may be applicable. Many businesses have been avoiding refund restrictions on non-refundable air tickets, usually at low fares, when, as is often the case, travel plans are changed shortly before travel, by asking their agents to void tickets. Rosenbluth International, part of American Express, stated in 2003 that in the USA, they voided between 2% and 3% of air tickets (1500 to 2500 weekly), mainly because of alterations in travel plans. Changes in ARC reporting procedures in June 2003, requiring reporting of voids within 24 or 48 hours have been made to prevent this. Since then, overall void rates have halved from their previous level of 6.8%. Penalty fees are charged to US agents on void tickets, according to the circumstances. Some airlines have responded by offering travellers the opportunity to retain the value of theoretically non-refundable tickets. *See* flexible ticket *and* non-refundable.

VOLMET Meteorological information for aircraft in flight.

volume incentive North American term sometimes used instead of overriding commission.

voluntary changes Changes to a flight or itinerary, which are made at the traveller's own choice.

VOR Very high frequency omni-range directional navigation beacon (aviation term).

VORTAC VOR and TACAN combination (aviation term).

vouchers Documents issued by travel agents, tour operators or tour wholesalers in exchange for which travellers receive specified tourism services such as accommodation, meals, sightseeing trips and other items included in a tour. Such documents are then debited back to the original agents or wholesalers, less commission, unless a contract was arranged net. Agents mostly use vouchers in connection with hotel bookings and car rental. In the USA, an airline voucher used as described in this entry, for example, in connection with a vacation package, is called a 'tour order'.

voyage A journey by sea.

voyage charter *See* charter.

voyager[1] Literally, a person on a voyage.

Voyager[2] Name of UK travel agency accounting and administration system.

Voyager[3] Name of the new trains introduced by Virgin Trains in the UK at a cost of £1 billion. The first 34 of the trains delivered in 2001 are non-tilting, operating on various Virgin routes, these have been followed by 44 tilting trains, called 'Super Voyagers' for use on the main London–Scotland west-coast main line which is very 'curvy'.

Voyager[4] Name of Cendant-owned web-based hotel CRS.

VP Variable pitch (aviation term concerning propellers).

Vr Rotation speed; true airspeed corrected for pressure error (aviation term).

Vra Specifically recommended speed for flight in turbulent air (aviation term).

VRP Visual reporting/reference point (aviation term).

Vs1 Stalling speed, no power, flaps retracted (aviation term).

VSA By visual reference to the ground (aviation term).

VSD Vertical situation display (aviation term).

Vshb High buffet speed (aviation term).

VSI Vertical speed indicator (aviation term).

Vslb Low buffet speed (aviation term).

Vslg Minimum speed, power off, at which the aircraft can develop lift equalling its own weight (aviation term).

Vso Stalling speed, no power, flaps down (aviation term).

VSTOL Very short take-off and landing aircraft. A description applied to aircraft capable of taking off and landing vertically or in a short distance.

VSW Variable sweep wing (aviation term).

Vt Threshold speed; design aero tow speed for gliders (aviation term).

VTOL Vertical take-off and landing aircraft.

VU Virtual reality; in tourism terms, experiencing a destination artificially. Audio-visuals are complemented by smells and the appropriate temperature and humidity. Together with a body suit and moving chair, all the body's senses are fooled into believing that the far-off destination is a reality. Small-scale virtual-reality kiosks are complemented by IMAX cinemas, which show 3D large format films on special, very large wrapround screens. Viewers are literally, immersed in larger-than-life images. *See* www.imax.com

VUSA Visit USA fare offering discount on normal American domestic air fares.

Vw Maximum winch launching speed for gliders (aviation term).

Vx Best angle of climb/speed, flaps up (aviation term).

Vxse Best angle of climb/speed on one engine (aviation term).

Vy Best rate of climb/speed flaps up (aviation term).

Vyse Best rate of climb/speed on one engine (aviation term).

W

W flying pattern   *See* ferry mileage.

W&BM   Weight and balance manual (aviation term).

W/M   Weight and/or other measurements.

W/V   Wind velocity (aviation term).

WAAS   Wide area augmentation system (aviation term).

WAC   World aeronautical chart.

WACS   Wireless airport communications system.

Wagon-Lits   Sleeping cars on the railroads of Europe, consisting of a private bedroom with accommodation for one or two people.

waiting list   *See* WL.

wake turbulence spacing minima   Wake turbulence is the phenomenon that aircraft leave behind them (disturbed air), similar to the passage of a ship through water, although this is usually visible. Because of this, for example, it would not be recommended that a light aircraft take-off from the same runway position until 3 min after the departure of a heavy aircraft, such as an Airbus A300 or Boeing 747.

wake vortex separation   *See* wake turbulence spacing minima (aviation term).

Wales   Tourist   Board   *See*   www. visitwales.com

walk a guest   When a hotel is overbooked, the term means to transfer the booked person to another hotel.

walk-in guest   Customers who arrive at a hotel without booking in advance. Also known as 'off-the-street' customers.

walking tour   A vacation during which most days are spent walking (hiking). Of two main types: a centred walking tour will be based on a specified hotel or hostel, returning there each night. On a progressive walking tour, participants' luggage may be transported ahead to the next night stop or participants carry all their belongings in a rucksack.

walk-up passenger   Literally an airline passenger who walks up to a check-in desk and purchases a flight. Any traveller buying their flight just before take-off.

WAND   Wallace Arnold's viewdata reservations system for UK travel agents. The acronym stands for Wallace Arnold Network Database.

warrant   A document which may be exchanged for tickets or other travel services, for example Government Air Travel Warrants (GATWs) or the rail warrants given to military staff going on leave. *See also* voucher.

Warsaw Convention   International agreement which limits liability of airlines in respect of loss or damage to luggage and injury or death of passengers. Carriage by air in and from the UK is governed by the Warsaw Convention, which was implemented in Britain by the Carriage by Air Act 1932. The Convention was amended by the Hague Protocol (1955) implemented in 1967 by the Carriage by Air Act (Application of Provisions) Order. Other parts of the Convention relating to delays in general and delayed lost or damaged baggage were affected by a 1961 Carriage by Air Act. UK legislation enacted in 1999 brought into force Montreal Protocols 1, 2 and 4. Adoption of further Montreal protocols took place from 28 June 2004 throughout the EU. The following monograph is historical, providing details not available to readers in other publications. If details are sought as what is now applicable to air travellers within the EU and between the EU and other countries readers should turn to the end of this entry, under the sub-heading, 'New rules under the Montreal Convention 1999'. This is followed by a summary of the position for US travellers. The huge variation between countries concerning adoption of parts of the Convention means that many readers will need to seek further information about their positions.

In 1928, the Warsaw Conference met with the intention of nursing an infant industry, which could not afford the possibility of big claims. The following year a system of limitation of liabilities arising out of carriage by air came into being. Called the Warsaw Convention – WC throughout the rest of this section – it is the most widely accepted international law treaty in the transportation field, and has been ratified, or is adhered to, by over 100 nations.

If a passenger is injured or killed, while involved in an international air journey to which the WC applies in its original form, then the damages payable are limited to 125,000 French Gold or Poincare Francs. *Part of the following explanation may become unnecessary during the currency of this dictionary if all countries were to adopt the alternative of Special Drawing Rights, envisaged under Montreal Additional Protocol 4, for calculating the maximum levels of an airlines liability.*

The Poincare Franc consisted of 65.5 milligrams of gold of millesimal fineness 900. The limits of carriers' liability set out in Article 22 of the WC are converted into national currencies, by the use of a formula. The value of one Troy ounce of gold in the national currency is divided by the number of grams in one Troy ounce. This is multiplied by 65.5 and divided by 1000. This again is multiplied by 900/1000 and finally multiplied by the number of Francs.

When the world's currencies were linked to the gold standard, and while the value of gold remained fairly constant, there were no serious calculation difficulties. In recent years, however, the price of gold has depended upon the nature of the transaction, which has caused calculation difficulties. In Britain, these were solved regularly by the publication of Carriage by Air (Sterling Equivalents) orders. Thus in the UK, in March 1985, 250 Poincare Francs were valued at £13.80. This is also the limit of liability under the WC per kilo of checked baggage.

By 1955, it was necessary to revise limits upwards and passenger liability limits were doubled by the Hague Protocol (HP) to the WC. Thus, on many international flights, the limit of 250,000 Gold Francs applies, valued at £13,800 on the British system.

Unfortunately, many countries were not signatories to the WC, let alone the HP. The conditions of carriage of the individual airline are those which limit liability on routes where WC does not apply.

One of the reasons for non-adoption, has been the divergence from general laws throughout the world. Under the WC, absolute liability is imposed on an airline, regardless of fault, unless it can be proved that all necessary measures were taken to avoid the injury or death concerned. The burden of proof is shifted from the injured person to the airline.

The USA was one of the countries never to ratify the HP. Believing the limits to be too low, it forced the pace during the 1967 round of negotiations. These resulted in the Montreal Agreement, which applies to all airlines carrying passengers for reward on journeys involving a USA stop. Compensation limits were set at US$58,000 maximum, exclusive of legal fees and US$75,000 including those costs. These figures still operate today.

Both WC and the HP were supplemented by the Guadalajara Convention of 1961, but this did not significantly affect the general limits already mentioned and that many countries still accept.

The redrafting and alterations of the Guadalajara Convention greatly improved the WC from the lawyers' point of view.

The Guatemala City Protocol (GCP) of 1971, was a major step forward from the Warsaw Convention. Unfortunately, there has not been general adoption of these proposals, which were originally submitted by IATA to the ICAO legal committee in 1969.

It would clearly be to the advantage of airlines and their passengers alike, if the WC promoted speedy settlement of claims without recourse to litigation. Under the proposed Guatemala alterations, a carrier would not be able to avoid liability by disproving negligence. The carrier would virtually become an insurer of passenger in-flight safety. Thus, by removing the question of carrier's liability from contentious areas, only the size of damages may be in dispute. A further sub-section 3 of Article 22 of its amended version contains settlement inducement provisions. This carrot encourages a quick ending to negotiations on a claim.

The GCP limit of liability is 12 times the original WC, namely £82,800. Article 42 of the GCP also contains provisions for reviewing the limits every 5 years. The only way in which passengers are slightly disadvantaged by the plan, is that in the case of delay the original WC limits on carrier's liability are halved, becoming 62,500 Gold Francs, which is a limit of £3450.

At the moment, there is an unrealistic distinction between checked baggage, with a liability of 250 Gold Francs per kilo and 'objects of which the passenger takes charge himself'. In this latter case, the liability of the carrier is limited to a total of 5000 Gold Francs per passenger. The GCP proposed to abolish this, setting a new limit of carrier liability for all baggage of 15,000 Gold Francs per passenger, an equivalent to £828.

Article 3, sub-section 2 of WC, deprives the carrier of liability limitation if no ticket is issued or if a ticket is defective in certain respects. This is why air tickets always state on them words to the effect, 'Subject to conditions of contract on reverse of passenger coupon'. If the passenger's journey involves an ultimate destination or stop in a country other than the country of departure, the WC may be applicable, and the Convention governs and, in most cases, limits the liability of carriers for death or personal injury and in respect of loss or damage to baggage – see also 'Notice headed advice to international passengers on limitation of liability.' This is called the Hague Notice and the GCP suggests that non-compliance with ticket requirements should not affect the existence of validity of a contract of carriage. The GCP also recognizes any other means which would preserve a record of essential information. Thus, storage of a passenger record in a computer might be sufficient.

The alterations just discussed highlight the vital necessity, at the present time, of making sure air travellers have valid tickets containing the Hague Notice. Now that most travellers have electronic rather than physical tickets, the Hague Notice is usually provided as a leaflet, incorporated in an airline document wallet or provided in some other way. A passenger managing to board an aircraft without the Hague Notice might involve liability to pay damages on an entirely unlimited basis.

Article 25 of the WC means that an airline loses limitation of its liability if the damage is caused by its own wilful misconduct or recklessness. A sub-section deprives a carrier's servant or agent of protection in similar circumstances. It is hardly surprising that there has been much international argument concerning the proposed elimination of these articles in the GCP. On the one hand, the IATA intention is quite laudable. By providing limits of liability, which are absolute maxima, and may not be exceeded whatever the circumstances, hopefully, all litigation might be avoided. On the other hand, consumer pressure and current laws in many countries will probably make such a proposition unacceptable.

Although the GCP greatly modernized the WC, as amended by the HP and at Guatemala, carrier's liability limits were still expressed in terms of a currency unit tied to gold. This led to the most recent amendment suggestion, agreed upon at Montreal in 1975. Montreal Additional Protocol (MAP) No. 3 deals with passengers and baggage. Ratification would automatically bring into force the GCP amendments. MAP No. 4 deals with cargo and mail. MAP suggests replacement of Gold Francs by International Monetary Fund Special Drawing Rights (SDR). (See www.imf.org for daily values.)

When the SDR was originated it was defined in terms of gold as being equal to 0.888671 g of fine gold, or one US dollar. After many currencies were floated in 1973, the value of the SDR in terms of other currencies began to fluctuate violently. Therefore, the system in use today was developed, where the value of the SDR fluctuates daily, according to the movement of a standard basket of 16 currencies belonging to countries which had more than 1% of total world export of goods and services, during the 5 years between 1968 and 1972. Each currency is given a weight according to its relative share in the total, although the 33% given to the US dollar is to allow for its importance in the international monetary system. The British pound has a weight of 9% in this basket. Unfortunately, there is no longer parity with the dollar, which is why a compensation limit of 100,000 SDRs, as proposed under MAP, was, in April 1978, valued around US$127,775. The 1976 IATA Annual General Meeting passed a resolution strongly urging ratification of the MAPs. All IATA members were to urge their governments to take all necessary measures to ensure ratification at the earliest possible date, and the Director General of IATA was required to take steps 'to bring this resolution to the attention of governments and take appropriate action in conjunction with national carriers to convey to governments the benefits for passengers, shippers and carriers of early entry into force, of Montreal Additional Protocols Nos. 3 and 4'.

Since the Second World War, the USA has been greatly dissatisfied with the liability limits of the WC. In 1972, the US government said that it would only ratify the Guatemala Protocol if a plan were developed, providing at least US$200,000 extra compensation in addition to airlines' WC liabilities. This plan is now known as the proposed United States Supplemental Compensation Plan (SCP). Initially SCP would be funded by a levy of US$2 per ticket, to be collected by carriers. The surcharges are to be paid over to the Prudential, if the plan is eventually approved. They will evaluate claims and make payments up to a maximum of US$200,000 per passenger. The SCP proposals were based upon carriers voluntarily opting into agreement. The suggestion has been that carriers not wishing to become involved would be under no obligation to collect surcharges on transportation purchased in America. It has also been proposed that the plan will only come into force when

taken up by airlines who, together, carried at least 85% of all passengers departing from the USA to foreign countries by air in 1973. It now looks unlikely that an SCP will ever be introduced in the USA.

Non-British readers need to consult their own laws to find out the limits of liability within their own countries. The range of figures within the EU mentioned in the first edition of this dictionary ended in 2004 following the adoption of the Montreal Convention (see below).

The 1967 Carriage by Air Acts (Application of Provisions) Order in Britain, inserted figures similar to those applying to travel to the USA, into British domestic air travel regulations. BEA were disturbed by the differences in liability limits between domestic and international travel and so unilaterally introduced liability limits matching with both UK domestic and American regulations. When BEA merged into British Airways, the liability offered remained at the higher BEA limit, instead of the lower BOAC figures.

In 1975, the CAA introduced new conditions for holders of Air Transport Licences, reading as follows: 'The Licence holder shall enter into a special contract with every passenger to be carried under this licence on or after 1/10/75, or with a person acting on behalf of such passenger, for the increase to not less than £25,000 exclusive of costs of the limit of the carrier's liability under the WC of 1929 and under the convention as amended at the Hague in 1955'. Mainly because of inflation, the CAA considered the £25,000 limit to be inadequate and the limits were raised to those operated by British Airways, namely US$58,000.

New rules under the Montreal Convention 1999

The Montreal Convention (the Convention in the rest of this monograph) became effective within the EU on 28 June 2004, enhancing financial protection for air travellers and their luggage (and also for cargo consignors, but this is outside the scope of this dictionary). The Convention requires airlines to provide an identification tag for each piece of checked baggage. Note that the 'baggage check' previously required under the WC has ended, because liability is no longer weight dependent.

The carrier is liable for damages should checked baggage be destroyed, lost or damaged if the causation event took place on board the aircraft or during any period within which the checked baggage was in the charge of the carrier. Liability is excluded if the damage etc. resulted from a defect in the baggage. Concerning unchecked baggage and personal items, carriers are only liable if the damage, loss or destruction arises from their fault, or that of their servants or agents. On admission of loss of checked baggage, or if it has not arrived within 21 days, the passenger can rely on the Convention under their Contract of Carriage. Often, however, travellers may make a claim on their travel insurers rather than directly against a carrier. The insurers then recover from the carrier (*see* subrogation entry in this dictionary). Acceptance of checked baggage without complaint now leads to the automatic assumption that it was delivered in good condition. Any damage or loss must be reported to the carrier as soon as it is discovered, *and at the latest, within 7 days of delivery of the baggage*. If a claim is being made that baggage was delayed, the claim has to be made within 21 days of the date when it was actually put in the hands of the traveller.

The use of SDRs as a currency unit has already been explained in this monograph; they are also explained as a separate definition earlier in this dictionary. *See* www.imf.org for the daily value of an SDR. The liability of a carrier under the Convention following destruction, loss, damage or delay to a traveller's luggage is limited to 1000 SDRs, around £850. However, travellers can now declare a higher value of their luggage and on payment of a fee, this will be registered and higher liability will apply.

Apart from the higher limits on liability for baggage claims, the Convention makes a big change by abandoning financial limits on liability for injury or death of passengers. For damages up to 100,000 SDRs, carriers cannot exclude or limit liability in their conditions of carriage, although it may be possible to make passengers liable for their own contributory negligence. For claims above 100,000 SDRs, airlines can defend themselves by proving that they were not at fault. If, for example, it could be proved that the claim arose from the negligent act of a third party, then that part of the liability exceeding the 100,000 SDRs limit could be resisted. But if there was negligence on the part of the carrier, its employees, or agents, then liability would be unlimited. There is also provision for advance payment to be made of not less than 16,000 SDRs, to cover immediate economic needs, within 15 days when a passenger is killed or injured. The limitation period for bringing claims of the type just described has been set at 2 years from when the aircraft arrived (or should have arrived).

As explained at the start of this monograph, it would take a huge book to detail the way in which each country has implemented the WC. This dictionary, however, is designed for UK and US readers. It is outside the scope to comment on which rules apply and at which stage, to journeys between the EU and USA. Basic US information is in *A Consumer Guide to Air Travel* at http://airconsumer. ost.dot.gov/publications/flyrights.htm Proven damages not exceeding US$75,000 in the case of death or personal injury to air passengers are due from carriers on a journey to, from or with an agreed stopping place in the USA. Liability up to this limit does not depend on negligence on the part of a carrier. If bags are delayed, lost or damaged on a US domestic trip, the airline can invoke a liability ceiling of US$2800 per passenger. (Disregard older texts that refer to US$2500, the limit on flights before 22 October 2004.) However, on international round trips that originate in the USA, the Montreal Convention limit of 1000 SDRs applies. Both in respect of domestic and international journeys, 'excess valuation' can be bought, increasing the liability to cover more valuable baggage.

Washington, DC Convention and Visitors Bureau *See* www.washington.org

WAT Weight/altitude/temperature.

WATA World Association of Travel Agencies. *See* www.wata.net

watch *See* times at sea.

water park Use of the term varies; may be a large water-sports complex, or a tourist attraction, such as a water-based theme park, or a combination of the two.

water taxi *See* vaporetto.

WATOG World Airlines Technical Operations Glossary.

WATS World Air Transport Statistics produced by IATA.

wave Crests are the tops of the waves, separated by troughs. Wavelength is the distance between two crests, while their height is measured as the vertical distance from the bottom of a trough to the top of the crest. When a wave crest overbalances, the mass of foam is known as a white cap. The spray showering into the wind is the spindrift. The distance between waves blown over the sea is known as their fetch. The fetch normally encountered in the English Channel means that hovercraft rides tend to be very bumpy during inclement weather.

wave-piercing catamaran *See* WPC[1].

way station In the USA, a small rail station between the main stations; also called a 'whistle-stop'.

waybills for air cargo *See* air waybills.

waybills for occasional European coach journeys *See* ASOR.

WB Weather bureau (US aviation term).

WC[1] *See* Warsaw Convention.

WC[2] Letters also designate a water closet, and are generally used as an abbreviation for toilet in most English-speaking countries.

WCO World Customs Organization. *See* www.wcoomd.org

WCTR World Conference on Transport Research.

WEAA Western European Airport Association.

weather *See* climate.

weekend fares or room rates Whereas sometimes there is a surcharge for weekend travel, for example, transatlantic airfares (*see* below), the fare may be cheaper, or a hotel may charge less, in order to fill space occupied on weekdays by business travellers.

weekend surcharge Extra charge for travellers between specified times at a weekend. Definition of what constitutes a weekend not only changes between fares, but often is different in different directions between the same two points.

weigh an anchor To raise the anchor.

WESTA Western Association of Travel Agencies in the USA.

Western Travel Star Was name of the UK travel agency computerized data and accounting system designed by Western Software Limited.

wet lease The hire of an aircraft, ship or vehicle, fully provisioned, fuelled, maintained and crewed, so that it is completely operational.

WFU Withdrawn from use (aviation term).

WH Within the Western Hemisphere. *See* routing.

wheelset Set of train carriage wheels, usually four or six, which can be changed as required to cater for varying rail gauges. *See* gauge.

whistle-stop *See* way station.

WHO The World Health Organization is a United Nations agency concerned with public health. The prevalence of communicable diseases throughout the world is monitored. International travellers are prevented from spreading these diseases by the health regulations recommended by the WHO and enforced by governments. Thus, Certificates of Vaccination familiar to all international travellers are necessary in appropriate circumstances, to prove that the traveller concerned is unlikely to transmit the disease in question. Information on international travel and health is published annually in the publication by the same name, *International Travel and Health*, updated by the *Weekly Epidemiological Record*. *See* www.who.int/ith *also see* international health requirements.

wide-body aircraft Commonly applied to most of the newest generation of jet aircraft. When term was first introduced, it meant that the aircraft passenger cabin had two aisles, whereas narrow-bodied aircraft have only one aisle. But it should signify jet aircraft with a fuselage diameter exceeding 200 in., with a per engine thrust greater than 30,000 pounds, e.g. Boeing 747, Douglas DC-10, Lockheed L-1011.

wildlife park   *See* game park.

Winchester disk   Obsolete type of computer disk. *See* disk.

windward   The direction from which the wind is blowing.

Winged Arrow Club   Name of Alitalia's Frequent Flyer Club. Available free, but by invitation only. Members are given priority to the top of waiting lists and have some secretarial facilities free. *See* FFP (frequent flyer programme).

wings   *See* airframe.

Wings   *See* airline alliances.

winter sports   The word 'snowsports' as an alternative term is growing in popularity. Group of tourism/leisure activities including bobsleighing, luge/tobogganing, skiing (both cross-country and on piste), skiblading and snowboarding. Alpine skiing, also known as downhill skiing is the most important of these, accounting for around 80% of participants, suggests the SIGB. Thus the need for and existence of over 20,000 ski-lifts worldwide, to transport skiers to the point from which they can ski downhill. The industry includes the operation of dry ski slopes, provision of instruction, instructor qualification and provision of a huge range of equipment. *See* ASC³, blue ski run, cable transporters, off-piste, piste, powder (snow) *and* SIGB ski pack.

Wizard   Avis car rental reservations system. It is linked worldwide via a satellite 23,000 miles above the earth to the Avis reservations centre at Tulsa, Oklahoma. Database has information on every Avis location globally and handles reservations, check-outs/check-ins and invoicing, holding information on every Avis charge card.

Wizcom   Avis subsidiary separate from operation of Wizard offering general GDS services, started in 1987. ResAccess links hotel CRSs to GDSs; was first to develop a 'seamless' link. *See* seamless connectivity.

WL¹   Waiting list. A record of travellers wishing to join a travel service which is currently full. When a flight becomes fully booked most airlines maintain a waiting list of passengers wishing to join the flight; other travel organizations also keep waiting lists. The WL is closed at the point where the airline feels there is no reasonable chance of any further

passengers ever being confirmed. *See also* RQ.

WL²   Seaplane design landing weight (an aviation term).

WLRA   World Leisure and Recreation Association, based in Canada. *See* www.worldleisure.org

WMO   World Meteorological Organization. *See* www.wmo.ch *and* climate.

Women's Travel Club of Great Britain   Was founded in London in 1954. A Scottish Club followed in 1959, and a Heart of England branch in 1985. By 1988, the membership exceeded 450, divided into active, overseas, associate and honorary categories. A Charter (Founder) member of the International Federation of Women's Travel Organizations.

Woodside Trust   Name has changed. *See* Radius.

workers' fares   *See* foreign workers' fares.

Workplace Technology Scheme   *See* CBT¹.

World Airports   An alliance of the world's largest airport group including Aeroports de Paris (Charles de Gaulle and Orly); British Airports Authority (London's Heathrow, Gatwick and Stansted, Edinburgh, Glasgow and Southampton), Copenhagen, Dallas/Fort Worth, Houston Airport System (HAS includes George Bush Intercontinental, William P Hoby and Ellington Field), Indianapolis International, Melbourne, Pittsburgh International and Tokyo Narita. *See* www.worldairports.com covering the business to consumer sector and www.airportsmart.com an on-line airports buying exchange. *See also* large number of entries starting with the word 'airport'.

World Association for Hospitality Education and Training   See AMFORHT; *also see* www.amforht.org

World Association of Travel Agencies (WATA) *See* www.wata.net

Worldchoice   Market-leading UK consortium of independent travel agents. *See* ACAS², ARTAC, travel agency consortia in the UK *and* consortium *or* www.worldchoice.co.uk

World Customs Organization   *See* www.wcoomd.org

World Health Organization   *See* WHO.

World Heritage Site Place recognized as such by UNESCO, identified as worthy of support and/or protection/preservation because it is of unique cultural and historical interest. There are both natural and man-made sites.

World Perks Name of Northwest Airline's Frequent Flyer Programme. *See* FFP (frequent flyer programme).

world room rates *See* 'hotel statistics worldwide' for average rates and 'pricing of hotel rooms' for calculation methods and rate management techniques.

World Tourism Information Exchange Centre WTO was attempting to establish a permanent centre for the international exchange of information amongst all persons and organizations involved for the development of the tourism industry. TIENET (Tourism Information Exchange Network) was to be gradually established as a formal computerized network linking various procedures and suppliers of information currently existing at the national, regional and international levels and directly or indirectly concerned with tourism, for which WTO would constitute the focal point. Although the aim has never been officially abandoned, the project is not currently being pursued.

World Tourism Organization *See* WTO.

World Transport Institute The Institute was established in Vancouver, Canada during the World Exposition of 1986. The transport data programme became the most complete source of computer-based transport information available in North America from a single source. However, current web searches by the author reveal no information.

World Travel Agents Associations Alliance Formed on 20 April 2005. Members include AAFTA, ABTA, ACTA, ASATA, DRV, ECTAA and TAANZ. Presidency held initially by Australia; will be rotated annually in alphabetical association order, the Secretariat functions being administered by the association holding the presidency for 1 year.

World Travel and Tourism Council A council, membership of which is by invitation only, restricted to around 100 of the industry leaders, worldwide. Inaugural meeting held in spring 1990. Chairman 1996 to 2001 was Harvey Golub; he was replaced in May 2001 by Sir Ian Prosser, Chairman of Bass (now Six Continents) in the UK. *See* www.wttc.org for extensive information including a major source of tourism statistics.

World Travel Market *See* WTM.

Worldclub Name of Northwest Airline's Frequent Flyers Club.

WorldOne hotel system Name of Wagon-lit's UK computer software which is between hotel databases on CRS and booking clerks, preventing reservation of unsatisfactory hotels.

Worldspan One of the four major GDSs (Global Distribution Systems). The history of Worldspan started in 1968 when internal reservation systems were implemented for Delta Air Lines and in 1971 for Trans-World Airlines (TWA). TWA installed their PARS reservation system in travel agencies in 1976, but it was not until 1982 that Delta's DATAS II installation started in agencies.

Northwest Airlines purchased 50% of TWA's system in 1986. Then in 1990 agreement was reached between Delta, Northwest and TWA to combine NW's PTIS with DATAS II and PARS to form Worldspan. In March 2003, the company was sold to the Travel Transaction Processing Corporation (TTPC), a joint company set up between Citigroup Venture Capital Equity Partners and Teacher's Merchant Bank. At the time of the sale Worldspan had 29% of the US travel distribution business, compared to Galileo's 20.5% and Sabre's 42%. Finalization of the deal took place in June 2003. TTPC has now been renamed Worldspan Technologies Inc. (WTI).

Handles over 60% of all online travel agency airline bookings and over 65% of all US online air travel transactions. For detailed information *see* www.worldspan.com *also see* CRS, GDS *and* inside link.

worldwide hotel industry *See* hotel statistics worldwide.

WPC[1] Wave-Piercing Catamaran. The largest in the world of this type of craft, otherwise known as SeaCats, were built for the UK ferry operator, Hoverspeed, at a cost of £7.5 million each, the first one being delivered in June 1990. These vessels are able to cut through the waves, rather than riding over them, at speeds of 35 knots, or 40 knots in good conditions. Capacity is around 450 passengers and 84 cars. Used on the Dover/Calais route across the English Channel, journey times are 45–50 min. One of these WPCs, named *Great Britain*, is the current holder of the Hales Trophy, for the Blue Riband, awarded to the passenger-carrying vessel holding the record for the fastest crossing of the Atlantic. This was achieved on 23 June 1990 in the time of 3 days, 7 h and 46 min.

WPC² World aeronautical planning chart.

WPT Waypoint (aviation term).

WSI Wind shear indicator (aviation term).

WT Seaplane design take-off weight **or** wireless telegraphy.

WTAAA World Travel Agents Associations Alliance. *See entry under this heading.*

WTB Welsh Tourist Board (for explanation of role *see* BTA).

WTCGB *See* Women's Travel Club of Great Britain.

WTI *See* World Transport Institute.

WTIEC *See* World Tourism Information Exchange Centre.

WTM World Travel Market. An annual travel and tourism trade fair held at the end of November in London. *See* www.wtmlondon.com

WTO World Tourism Organization. Within the currency of this dictionary, WTO will have become a specialized agency of the United Nations. Also known as OMT (Organisation Mondiale du Tourisme) and BTO. It is the successor to IUOTO (the International Union of Official Travel Organizations) founded in 1925. Currently over 130 countries are state members while over 300 other organizations in the industry are Affiliate Members. Its mission is to promote and develop tourism as a significant means of fostering international peace and understanding, economic development and international trade. An excellent source of worldwide travel and tourism statistics, the organization functions as a world clearing house for all available information on international and domestic tourism, including statistical data, legislation and regulations, facilities and special events, and is responsible for its systematic collection, analysis and dissemination.

Its research activities cover tourism markets, plant and enterprises, physical planning and area development, promotion and marketing, economic analysis and financing techniques, documentation and facilitation. WTO keeps tourism trends under constant review and exercises vigilance over changes in world economic and social conditions affecting tourism, market fluctuations and the maintenance of standards within the tourism sector. The United Nations considers WTO as its main instrument for the promotion of tourism. *See* www.world-tourism.org , TedQual *and* www.WTOelibrary.org , an online, fully cross-searchable virtual library of the WTO, Themis Foundation, tourism information databases *and* World Tourism Information Exchange Centre.

WTS Workplace Technology Scheme for the UK travel industry. *See* CBT¹ (computer-based training).

WTTC *See* World Travel and Tourism Council.

WTTERC World Travel and Tourism Environment Research Centre.

WV Weight variant (aviation term).

WWW World Wide Web. *See* Internet for travel usage details.

X

XM Extra marker (aviation term).

XML Extensible Mark-up Language; used by Travel Technology Initiative to produce travel industry standards. *See* entry under Travel Technology Initiative.

Xpdr Transponder (aviation term).

Xpress Name of American Express UK travel communications network through which Amex travel agents can access data or effect reservations. Xpress is connected to Amex TRS (Travel Related Services) and TPM (Travel Products Marketing), TRIPS (Amex International Airline Reservation System), a Prestel CUG (a Closed User Group of data, access to which is restricted to Amex agents), CRU (The Central Reservations Unit of Amex handling hotel bookings worldwide) as well as the British Reservation systems of many inclusive tour, car ferry and other operators. Connection by agents is through a simple viewdata terminal on a dedicated line basis, connections to the other systems having been achieved by Xpress.

XS Atmospherics (aviation term).

XT Code used on air tickets in the USA to indicate that there are more taxes and/or user fees than will fit into the available airline tax boxes of an air ticket; the amounts are then denominated in the fare calculation section.

X-TANT Now known as NTL Business (Travel Division). The service was formerly known as Istel (AT&T Istel) but is now called NTL Traveleye. One of the main UK travel agency data communication networks, through which agents connect with a huge variety of travel services, to effect reservations or access information. NTL's 'direct service' is their term for the provision of service through a permanently connected pair of telephone datalines, rather than dialling each time access is required to one of the principals available through NTL. *See also* Infotrac *and* Traveleye.

Y

Y class Tourist, coach or international class. Used in the UK to designate all economy-class flights, but by the strict IATA definition should be restricted to jet travel, T applying to economy propeller flights. Within the currency of the book, Y may be restricted to passengers paying the full economy fare, occupying the second class in aircraft with three-class configuration.

yacht Originally a light fast-sailing ship. Became associated with luxury, as in a Royal Yacht. When these became motor driven, the name yacht was retained. Thus, a yacht can now be a small fore- and aft-rigged sailing vessel, particularly when used for racing or it can be a luxury leisure boat of varying dimensions.

Yatres Was Yugoslavian agency CRS, associated with Amadeus.

yaw *See* airframe.

yawl A two-masted sailing vessel, with a main and mizzen mast. By definition, the mizzen mast is stepped aft of the rudder, otherwise the vessel is a ketch.

Yemen Tourism Promotion Board *See* www.yementourism.com

YHA The Youth Hostels Association provides simple accommodation for young people away from home, in the UK.

yield The income resulting from control and allocation of passenger transport space provided at different fare levels. From this can be derived the 'average' yield per seat, or for a series of journeys. Planned yields vary from the actual yields, depending on load factors at each rate. Although airline staff believe these terms to be particular to their industry, the terms are general to transport. *See* yield management.

yield management Control and allocation of the services of a tourism provider, by offering them to travellers at different price levels to maximize income. Yield management in the travel industry used to be all about pricing; now the normal term to use is revenue management; the subtlety is that to get the best profit from a travel operation, prices and load factors must be considered together. However, at the time of writing, the two terms are used indiscriminately. Revenue management is the process of determining which products and services should be sold to which customers, through which channels and at what price, in order to maximize profits. It utilizes data-warehousing/mining techniques and methodologies, which are very complex processes whereby huge amounts of data are collected from a huge number of transactions, enabling purchasing trends and patterns to be spotted and analysed. The mathematics to achieve this is very complicated. Computer analysts would refer to 'the complex algorithms inherent in developing a revenue management system'.

Behind this concept is the underlying innate perishability of tourism services; a seat on yesterday's departure of a flight, package holiday, cruise or room in a hotel the previous night has lost all value. However, it is essential that action to improve load factors leads to increasing profit.

In the hospitality field, Holiday Inns provide a good example of the concept. Information is fed from their computerized main administration and reservation system Holidex to HIRO (Holiday Inn Revenue Optimizer), which is a very complex retail pricing model, which calculates optimum room rates for any individual property. These are continuously recalculated to arrive at the minimum acceptable rate for each guest's stay, taking into account factors such as type of hotel and distance away of its competition, the property's own location, the price sensitivity of its guests, booking lead times and occupancy levels. HIRO predicts the occupancy of a hotel on a given day and the relative daily worth of each room. If the length of stay requested is not available throughout at the same price, the system is sufficiently sophisticated to calculate whether it is advantageous to accept the booking.

No longer will all the passengers on an aircraft have paid the same fare; different fares will have been promoted to various market segments the operator has identified. On multi-leg journeys, passenger numbers must be controlled so that being full for one sector does not prevent lucrative income from through travellers. Complex computer models are used to control capacity for each leg to maximize income. The model must also take into account forecast demand from each market segment and allocate space for each segment to optimize profit. One Northern European airline is believed by the author to have spent US$10 million developing their existing revenue management system; but even when it was finished, it still can only be used for 5% of their flights because of the huge number-crunching involved. A Far East airline recently spent US$76 million on their system and are not satisfied with what they have achieved. These cases are indicative of the difficulties.

From the point of view of the traveller, they may regard yield management as 'discriminatory pricing' if they are, for example, business travellers, who book shortly before departure and have to pay high fares for the privilege. The travel industry refers to the same phenomenon in non-pejorative terms as 'price discrimination'. In the UK, tour operators sometimes refer to yield management as 'fluid pricing'. It has always been the case that operators charge more during peak season when all available space can be sold and lower prices off-season when there is spare capacity to fill; but revenue management for tour operators is much more sophisticated than this.

The system must cover transport, accommodation and transfers; and moreover consider separate brands within them. What are described as 'bid price' packages analyse multiple events and determine what the minimum acceptable price would be for each of those elements given current and anticipated demand; for this particular package request this should be the minimum price.

Has any large UK tour operator yet achieved a fully working revenue management system? To the best of the writer's knowledge and belief, no. RTS (Revenue Technology Services in Dallas) and Talus Solutions Inc. are probably the market leaders in the development of revenue management systems; it is understood they are currently working with UK technology companies to develop systems for major UK tour operators. FSS, who have much expertise in the field, have developed a working full system for the small Keycamp group offering camping/auto holidays. This, uniquely, is believed to be the only system which currently has automated the setting of prices. *See also* discriminatory pricing *and* revenue dilution. The information concerning HIRO was extracted from *Electronic Information Distribution in Tourism and Hospitality* by Peter O'Connor; CAB International.

YIP Yield Improvement Plan is IATA's attempt worldwide to regularize air ticket sales so that the public pay published fares and airlines cease selling heavily discounted tickets through unauthorized non-appointed agents. While the plan has been successful on some routes from the UK, cheap tickets continue to be available because of the huge over-capacity of airline seats. In theory, British airlines are breaking the law if they sell tickets at prices lower than those set by the CAA, sales being covered by section 21, paragraph 5, sub-section B, of the Civil Aviation Act 1971. This is a complex clause and it is not known whether it covers sales through travel agents or bucket shops, as no one has ever been taken to court since the 1971 Act came into force.

Young Flyers British Airways' term for unaccompanied young passengers aged between 6 and 12 years.

Youth Hostels Association *See* YHA.

Youth Training Scheme *See* YTS. (Now obsolete.)

YTS The Youth Training Scheme in Britain was developed by the government with the intention of ensuring a job for every school-leaver. It has changed in name and character to the

Modern Apprenticeship scheme. *See* MA.

Yugoslavian National Travel Agency Organization *See* AYTO.

Yugotel Formerly the name of Yugotours UK, travel agents viewdata system. (Now obsolete.)

Z

Zambia National Tourist Board *See* www.zambiatourism.com

ZAP *See* airframe.

ZD Zenith distance (aviation term).

Zephyr The California Zephyr; a US train service between San Francisco and Chicago. For further information about rail travel, *see* train.

ZFW Zero fuel weight (aviation term).

Zimbabwe National Travel Agency Organization Association of Travel Agents of Zimbabwe.

Zimbabwe Tourism Authority *See* www.tourismzimbabwe.co.zw

zipper principle When in a narrow road, every second car has the right of way. In Norway, a zipper road sign indicates the principle is in operation.

ZLC Zero lift chord (aviation term).

zodiac Inflatable flat-bottomed rubber dinghy used in many leisure pursuits. Although it is the brand name of a French manufacturer of such craft, the term has become generic. Used by divers and snorkellers and as a means of getting ashore to a beach from a ship of any size where there is no access other than a beach.

ZT Zero time indicator (aviation term).

ZUJI Name in Far East and Australia of British Airways' on-line reservations system.

Zulu Travel jargon for GMT.

Appendix I
World Tourism Organization
Global Code of Ethics for Tourism
Available at www.world-tourism.org

PREAMBLE PRINCIPLES ANNEX

Article 1   Tourism's contribution to mutual understanding and respect between peoples and societies
Article 2   Tourism as a vehicle for individual and collective fulfilment
Article 3   Tourism, a factor of sustainable development
Article 4   Tourism, a user of the cultural heritage of mankind and contributor to its enhancement
Article 5   Tourism, a beneficial activity for host countries and communities
Article 6   Obligations of stakeholders in tourism development
Article 7   Right to tourism
Article 8   Liberty of tourist movements
Article 9   Rights of the workers and entrepreneurs in the tourism industry
Article 10   Implementation of the principles of the Global Code of Ethics for Tourism

The General Assembly of the World Tourism Organization,

Recalling:

- that it had provided at its Istanbul session in 1997 for the formation of a Special Committee for the preparation of the Global Code of Ethics for Tourism and that this Committee met at Cracow, Poland on 7 October 1998, in conjunction with the Quality Support Committee meeting, in order to consider an outline of the said Code,
- that based on these initial considerations, the draft Global Code of Ethics for Tourism was prepared by the Secretary-General, with the assistance of the Legal Adviser to WTO and was studied by the WTO Business Council, the Regional Commissions and finally by the Executive Council at its sixtieth session, all of which were invited to formulate their observations,
- that the WTO Members were invited to communicate in writing the remarks or suggestions that they could not make at those meetings;

Noting:

- that the principle of a Global Code of Ethics for Tourism aroused great interest among the delegations that participated in the seventh session of the Commission on Sustainable Development (CSD) in New York in April 1999,
- that after the CSD session, additional consultations were undertaken by the Secretary-General with institutions representative of the tourism industry and the workers, as well as with various non-governmental organizations interested in this process,
- that, as a result of these discussions and consultations, many written contributions were received by the Secretary-General, which have so far as possible been reflected in the draft submitted to the Assembly for consideration;

Reaffirming that the aim of the Global Code of Ethics for Tourism is to establish a synthesis of the various documents, codes and declarations of the same kind or with comparable aspirations published over the years, to complement them with new considerations reflecting the development of our societies and thus to serve as a frame of reference for the stakeholders in world tourism at the dawn of the next century and millennium,

A. Adopts the Global Code of Ethics for Tourism, which reads as follows:

Preamble

We, Members of the World Tourism Organization (WTO) representatives of the world tourism industry, delegates of States, territories, enterprises, institutions and bodies that are, gathered for the General Assembly at Santiago, Chile on this first day of October 1999,

Reasserting the aims set out in Article 3 of the Statutes of the World Tourism Organization, and aware of the 'decisive and central' role of this Organization, as recognized by the General Assembly of the United Nations, in promoting and developing tourism with a view to contributing to economic development, international understanding, peace, prosperity and universal respect for, and observance of, human rights and fundamental freedoms for all without distinction as to race, sex, language or religion,

Firmly believing that, through the direct, spontaneous and non-mediatized contacts it engenders between men and women of different cultures and lifestyles, tourism represents a vital force for peace and a factor of friendship and understanding among the peoples of the world,

In keeping with the rationale of reconciling environmental protection, economic development and the fight against poverty in a sustainable manner, as formulated by the United Nations in 1992 at the 'Earth Summit' of Rio de Janeiro and expressed in Agenda 21, adopted on that occasion,

Taking into account the swift and continued growth, both past and foreseeable, of the tourism activity, whether for leisure, business, culture, religious or health purposes, and its powerful effects, both positive and negative, on the environment, the economy and the society of both generating and receiving countries, on local communities and indigenous peoples, as well as on international relations and trade,

Aiming to promote responsible, sustainable and universally accessible tourism in the framework of the right of all persons to use their free time for leisure pursuits or travel with respect for the choices of society of all peoples,

But convinced that the world tourism industry as a whole has much to gain by operating in an environment that favours the market economy, private enterprise and free trade and that serves to optimize its beneficial effects on the creation of wealth and employment,

Also firmly convinced that, provided a number of principles and a certain number of rules are observed, responsible and sustainable tourism is by no means incompatible with the growing liberalization of the conditions governing trade in services and under whose aegis the enterprises of this sector operate and that it is possible to reconcile in this sector economy and ecology, environment and development, openness to international trade and protection of social and cultural identities,

Considering that, with such an approach, all the stakeholders in tourism development – national, regional and local administrations, enterprises, business associations, workers in the sector, non-governmental organizations and bodies of all kinds belonging to the tourism industry, as well as host communities, the media and the tourists themselves, have different albeit interdependent responsibilities in the individual and societal development of tourism and that the formulation of their individual rights and duties will contribute to meeting this aim,

Committed, in keeping with the aims pursued by the World Tourism Organization itself since adopting resolution 364(XII) at its General Assembly of 1997 (Istanbul), to promote a genuine partnership between the public and private stakeholders in tourism development, and wishing to see a partnership and cooperation of the same kind extend, in an open and balanced way, to the relations between generating and receiving countries and their respective tourism industries,

Following up on the Manila Declarations of 1980 on World Tourism and of 1997 on the Social Impact of Tourism, as well as on the Tourism Bill of Rights and the Tourist Code adopted at Sofia in 1985 under the aegis of WTO,

But believing that these instruments should be complemented by a set of interdependent principles for their interpretation and application on which the stakeholders in tourism development should model their conduct at the dawn of the twenty-first century,

Using, for the purposes of this instrument, the definitions and classifications applicable to travel, and especially the concepts of 'visitor', 'tourist' and 'tourism', as adopted by the Ottawa International Conference, held from 24 to 28 June 1991 and approved, in 1993, by the United Nations Statistical Commission at its twenty-seventh session,

Referring in particular to the following instruments:

- Universal Declaration of Human Rights of 10 December 1948;
- International Covenant on Economic, Social and Cultural Rights of 16 December 1966;
- International Covenant on Civil and Political Rights of 16 December 1966;
- Warsaw Convention on Air Transport of 12 October 1929;
- Chicago Convention on International Civil Aviation of 7 December 1944, and the Tokyo, The Hague and Montreal Conventions in relation thereto;
- Convention on Customs Facilities for Tourism of 4 July 1954 and related Protocol;
- Convention concerning the Protection of the World Cultural and Natural Heritage of 23 November 1972;
- Manila Declaration on World Tourism of 10 October 1980;
- Resolution of the Sixth General Assembly of WTO (Sofia) adopting the Tourism Bill of Rights and Tourist Code of 26 September 1985;
- Convention on the Rights of the Child of 26 January 1990;
- Resolution of the Ninth General Assembly of WTO (Buenos Aires) concerning in particular travel facilitation and the safety and security of tourists of 4 October 1991;
- Rio Declaration on the Environment and Development of 13 June 1992;
- General Agreement on Trade in Services of 15 April 1994;

- Convention on Biodiversity of 6 January 1995;
- Resolution of the Eleventh General Assembly of WTO (Cairo) on the prevention of organized sex tourism of 22 October 1995;
- Stockholm Declaration of 28 August 1996 against the Commercial Sexual Exploitation of Children;
- Manila Declaration on the Social Impact of Tourism of 22 May 1997;
- Conventions and recommendations adopted by the International Labour Organisation in the area of collective conventions, prohibition of forced labour and child labour, defence of the rights of indigenous peoples, and equal treatment and non-discrimination in the work place;

affirm the right to tourism and the freedom of tourist movements, state our wish to promote an equitable, responsible and sustainable world tourism order, whose benefits will be shared by all sectors of society in the context of an open and liberalized international economy, and solemnly adopt to these ends the principles of the Global Code of Ethics for Tourism.

Principles

Article 1. Tourism's contribution to mutual understanding and respect between peoples and societies

1. The understanding and promotion of the ethical values common to humanity, with an attitude of tolerance and respect for the diversity of religious, philosophical and moral beliefs, are both the foundation and the consequence of responsible tourism; stakeholders in tourism development and tourists themselves should observe the social and cultural traditions and practices of all peoples, including those of minorities and indigenous peoples and to recognize their worth;
2. Tourism activities should be conducted in harmony with the attributes and traditions of the host regions and countries and in respect for their laws, practices and customs;
3. The host communities, on the one hand, and local professionals, on the other, should acquaint themselves with and respect the tourists who visit them and find out about their lifestyles, tastes and expectations; the education and training imparted to professionals contribute to a hospitable welcome;
4. It is the task of the public authorities to provide protection for tourists and visitors and their belongings; they must pay particular attention to the safety of foreign tourists owing to the particular vulnerability they may have; they should facilitate the introduction of specific means of information, prevention, security, insurance and assistance consistent with their needs; any attacks, assaults, kidnappings or threats against tourists or workers in the tourism industry, as well as the wilful destruction of tourism facilities or of elements of cultural or natural heritage should be severely condemned and punished in accordance with their respective national laws;
5. When travelling, tourists and visitors should not commit any criminal act or any act considered criminal by the laws of the country visited and abstain from any conduct felt to be offensive or injurious by the local populations, or likely to damage the local environment; they should refrain from all trafficking in illicit drugs, arms, antiques, protected species and products and substances that are dangerous or prohibited by national regulations;
6. Tourists and visitors have the responsibility to acquaint themselves, even before their departure, with the characteristics of the countries they are preparing to visit; they must be aware of the health and security risks inherent in any travel outside their usual environment and behave in such a way as to minimize those risks;

Article 2. Tourism as a vehicle for individual and collective fulfilment

1. Tourism, the activity most frequently associated with rest and relaxation, sport and access to culture and nature, should be planned and practised as a privileged means of individual and collective fulfilment; when practised with a sufficiently open mind, it is an irreplaceable factor of self-education, mutual tolerance and for learning about the legitimate differences between peoples and cultures and their diversity;

2. Tourism activities should respect the equality of men and women; they should promote human rights and, more particularly, the individual rights of the most vulnerable groups, notably children, the elderly, the handicapped, ethnic minorities and indigenous peoples;

3. The exploitation of human beings in any form, particularly sexual, especially when applied to children, conflicts with the fundamental aims of tourism and is the negation of tourism; as such, in accordance with international law, it should be energetically combatted with the cooperation of all the States concerned and penalized without concession by the national legislation of both the countries visited and the countries of the perpetrators of these acts, even when they are carried out abroad;

4. Travel for purposes of religion, health, education and cultural or linguistic exchanges are particularly beneficial forms of tourism, which deserve encouragement;

5. The introduction into curricula of education about the value of tourist exchanges, their economic, social and cultural benefits, and also their risks, should be encouraged;

Article 3. Tourism, a factor of sustainable development

1. All the stakeholders in tourism development should safeguard the natural environment with a view to achieving sound, continuous and sustainable economic growth geared to satisfying equitably the needs and aspirations of present and future generations;

2. All forms of tourism development that are conducive to saving rare and precious resources, in particular water and energy, as well as avoiding so far as possible waste production, should be given priority and encouraged by national, regional and local public authorities;

3. The staggering in time and space of tourist and visitor flows, particularly those resulting from paid leave and school holidays, and a more even distribution of holidays should be sought so as to reduce the pressure of tourism activity on the environment and enhance its beneficial impact on the tourism industry and the local economy;

4. Tourism infrastructure should be designed and tourism activities programmed in such a way as to protect the natural heritage composed of ecosystems and biodiversity and to preserve endangered species of wildlife; the stakeholders in tourism development, and especially professionals, should agree to the imposition of limitations or constraints on their activities when these are exercised in particularly sensitive areas: desert, polar or high mountain regions, coastal areas, tropical forests or wetlands, propitious to the creation of nature reserves or protected areas;

5. Nature tourism and ecotourism are recognized as being particularly conducive to enriching and enhancing the standing of tourism, provided they respect the natural heritage and local populations and are in keeping with the carrying capacity of the sites;

Article 4. Tourism, a user of the cultural heritage of mankind and a contributor to its enhancement

1. Tourism resources belong to the common heritage of mankind; the communities in whose territories they are situated have particular rights and obligations to them;

2. Tourism policies and activities should be conducted with respect for the artistic, archaeological and cultural heritage, which they should protect and pass on to future generations; particular care should be devoted to preserving and upgrading monuments, shrines and museums as well as archaeological and historic sites which must be widely open to tourist visits; encouragement should be given for public access to privately-owned cultural property and monuments, with respect for the rights of their owners, as well as to religious buildings, without prejudice to normal needs of worship;

3. Financial resources derived from visits to cultural sites and monuments should, at least in part, be used for the upkeep, safeguard, development and embellishment of this heritage;

4. Tourism activity should be planned in such a way as to allow traditional cultural products, crafts and folklore to survive and flourish, rather than causing them to degenerate and become standardized;

Article 5. Tourism, a beneficial activity for host countries and communities

1. Local populations should be associated with tourism activities and share equitably in the economic, social and cultural benefits they generate, and particularly in the creation of direct and indirect jobs resulting from them;

2. Tourism policies should be applied in such a way as to help to raise the standard of living of the populations of the regions visited and meet their needs; the planning and architectural approach to and operation of tourism resorts and accommodation should aim to integrate them, to the extent possible, in the local economic and social fabric; where skills are equal, priority should be given to local manpower;

3. Special attention should be paid to the specific problems of coastal areas and island territories and to vulnerable rural or mountain regions, for which tourism often represents a rare opportunity for development in the face of the decline of traditional economic activities;

4. Tourism professionals, particularly investors, governed by the regulations laid down by the public authorities, should carry out studies of the impact of their development projects on the environment and natural surroundings; they should also deliver, with the greatest transparency and objectivity, information on their future programmes and their foreseeable repercussions and foster dialogue on their contents with the populations concerned;

Article 6. Obligations of stakeholders in tourism development

1. Tourism professionals have an obligation to provide tourists with objective and honest information on their places of destination and on the conditions of travel, hospitality and stays; they should ensure that the contractual clauses proposed to their customers are readily understandable as to the nature, price and quality of the services they commit themselves to providing and the financial compensation payable by them in the event of a unilateral breach of contract on their part;

2. Tourism professionals, insofar as it depends on them, should show concern, in cooperation with the public authorities, for the security and safety, accident prevention, health protection and food safety of those who seek their services; likewise, they should ensure the existence of suitable systems of insurance and assistance; they should accept the reporting obligations prescribed by national regulations and pay fair compensation in the event of failure to observe their contractual obligations;

3. Tourism professionals, so far as this depends on them, should contribute to the cultural and spiritual fulfilment of tourists and allow them, during their travels, to practise their religions;

4. The public authorities of the generating States and the host countries, in cooperation with the professionals concerned and their associations, should ensure that the necessary mechanisms are in place for the repatriation of tourists in the event of the bankruptcy of the enterprise that organized their travel;

5. Governments have the right and the duty – especially in a crisis, to inform their nationals of the difficult circumstances, or even the dangers they may encounter during their travels abroad; it is their responsibility however to issue such information without prejudicing in an unjustified or exaggerated manner the tourism industry of the host countries and the interests of their own operators; the contents of travel advisories should therefore be discussed beforehand with the authorities of the host countries and the professionals concerned; recommendations formulated should be strictly proportionate to the gravity of the situations encountered and confined to the geographical areas where the insecurity has arisen; such advisories should be qualified or cancelled as soon as a return to normality permits;

6. The press, and particularly the specialized travel press and the other media, including modern means of electronic communication, should issue honest and balanced information on events and situations that could influence the flow of tourists; they should also provide accurate and reliable information to the consumers of tourism services; the new communication and electronic commerce technologies should also be developed and used for this purpose; as is the case for the media, they should not in any way promote sex tourism;

Article 7. Right to tourism

1. The prospect of direct and personal access to the discovery and enjoyment of the planet's resources constitutes a right equally open to all the world's inhabitants; the increasingly extensive participation in national and international tourism should be regarded as one of the best possible expressions of the sustained growth of free time, and obstacles should not be placed in its way;

2. The universal right to tourism must be regarded as the corollary of the right to rest and leisure, including reasonable limitation of working hours and periodic holidays with pay, guaranteed by Article 24 of the Universal Declaration of Human Rights and Article 7.d of the International Covenant on Economic, Social and Cultural Rights;

3. Social tourism, and in particular associative tourism, which facilitates widespread access to leisure, travel and holidays, should be developed with the support of the public authorities;

4. Family, youth, student and senior tourism and tourism for people with disabilities, should be encouraged and facilitated;

Article 8. Liberty of tourist movements

1. Tourists and visitors should benefit, in compliance with international law and national legislation, from the liberty to move within their countries and from one State to another, in accordance with Article 13 of the Universal Declaration of Human Rights; they should have access to places of transit and stay and to tourism and cultural sites without being subject to excessive formalities or discrimination;

2. Tourists and visitors should have access to all available forms of communication, internal or external; they should benefit from prompt and easy access to local administrative, legal and health services; they should be free to contact the consular representatives of their countries of origin in compliance with the diplomatic conventions in force;

3. Tourists and visitors should benefit from the same rights as the citizens of the country visited concerning the confidentiality of the personal data and information concerning them, especially when these are stored electronically;

4. Administrative procedures relating to border crossings whether they fall within the competence of States or result from international agreements, such as visas or health and customs formalities, should be adapted, so far as possible, so as to facilitate to the maximum freedom of travel and widespread access to international tourism; agreements between groups of countries to harmonize and simplify these procedures should be encouraged; specific taxes and levies penalizing the tourism industry and undermining its competitiveness should be gradually phased out or corrected;

5. So far as the economic situation of the countries from which they come permits, travellers should have access to allowances of convertible currencies needed for their travels;

Article 9. Rights of the workers and entrepreneurs in the tourism industry

1. The fundamental rights of salaried and self-employed workers in the tourism industry and related activities, should be guaranteed under the supervision of the national and local administrations, both of their States of origin and of the host countries with particular care, given the specific constraints linked in particular to the seasonality of their activity, the global dimension of their industry and the flexibility often required of them by the nature of their work;

2. Salaried and self-employed workers in the tourism industry and related activities have the right and the duty to acquire appropriate initial and continuous training; they should be given adequate social protection; job insecurity should be limited so far as possible; and a specific status, with particular regard to their social welfare, should be offered to seasonal workers in the sector;

3. Any natural or legal person, provided he or she has the necessary abilities and skills, should be entitled to develop a professional activity in the field of tourism under existing national laws; entrepreneurs and investors – especially in the area of small and medium-sized enterprises – should be entitled to free access to the tourism sector with a minimum of legal or administrative restrictions;

4. Exchanges of experience offered to executives and workers, whether salaried or not, from different countries, contributes to foster the development of the world tourism industry; these movements should be facilitated so far as possible in compliance with the applicable national laws and international conventions;

5. As an irreplaceable factor of solidarity in the development and dynamic growth of international exchanges, multinational enterprises of the tourism industry should not exploit the dominant positions they sometimes occupy; they should avoid becoming the vehicles of cultural and social models artificially imposed on the host communities; in exchange for their freedom to invest and trade which should be fully recognized, they should involve themselves in local development, avoiding, by the excessive repatriation of their profits or their induced imports, a reduction of their contribution to the economies in which they are established;

6. Partnership and the establishment of balanced relations between enterprises of generating and receiving countries contribute to the sustainable development of tourism and an equitable distribution of the benefits of its growth;

Article 10. Implementation of the principles of the Global Code of Ethics for Tourism

1. The public and private stakeholders in tourism development should cooperate in the implementation of these principles and monitor their effective application;

2. The stakeholders in tourism development should recognize the role of international institutions, among which the World Tourism Organization ranks first, and non-governmental organizations with competence in the field of tourism promotion and development, the protection of human rights, the environment or health, with due respect for the general principles of international law;

3. The same stakeholders should demonstrate their intention to refer any disputes concerning the application or interpretation of the Global Code of Ethics for Tourism for conciliation to an impartial third body known as the World Committee on Tourism Ethics.

THE WTO

B. Calls upon the stakeholders in tourism development, national, regional and local tourism administrations, tourism enterprises, business associations, workers in the sector and tourism bodies, the host communities and the tourists them-selves to model their conduct on the principles embodied in this Global Code of Ethics for Tourism and to implement them in good faith in accordance with the provisions set out below;

C. Decides that the procedures for implementing the principles embodied in the Code will, where necessary, be subject to guidelines for application, prepared by the World Committee on Tourism Ethics, submitted to the Executive Council of WTO, adopted by the General Assembly and periodically reviewed and adjusted in the same conditions;

Recommends:

(a) States Members or non-members of WTO, without being obliged to do so, to accept expressly the principles embodied in the Global Code of Ethics for Tourism and to use them as a basis when establishing their national laws and regulations and to inform accordingly the World Committee on Tourism Ethics, whose creation is provided for in Article 10 of the Code and organized in paragraph 6 below;

(b) tourism enterprises and bodies, whether WTO Affiliate Members or not, and their associations to include the relevant provisions of the Code in their contractual instruments or to make specific reference to them in their own codes of conduct or professional rules and to report on them to the World Committee on Tourism Ethics;

D. Invites the Members of WTO to actively implement the recommendations it has previously expressed during previous sessions in the fields covered by this Code, so far as the sustainable development of tourism, the prevention of organized sex tourism, as well as travel facilitation and the safety and security of tourists are concerned;

E. Subscribes to the principle of a Protocol for implementing the Global Code of Ethics for Tourism as annexed to this resolution and adopts the guiding principles on which it is based:

- creation of a flexible follow-up and evaluation mechanism with a view to ensuring the constant adjustment of the Code to the developments of world tourism and, more broadly, to the changing conditions of international relations;
- the making available to States and other stakeholders in tourism development of a conciliation mechanism to which they may have recourse by consensus of on a voluntary basis;

F. Invites the Full Members of the Organization and all the stakeholders in tourism development to submit their additional remarks and proposed amendments to the draft Protocol of Implementation annexed to this resolution within a period of six months, so as to allow the Executive Council to study, in due time, the amendments to be made to this text and requests the Secretary-General to report back to it on this point at its fourteenth session;

G. Decides to start the process of appointing the Members of the World Committee on Tourism Ethics, so that its composition may be completed at the fourteenth session of the General Assembly;

H. Urges the States Members of WTO to publish and make known as widely as possible the Global Code of Ethics for Tourism, in particular by disseminating it among all the stakeholders in tourism development and inviting them to give it broad publicity;

I. Entrusts the Secretary-General with approaching the Secretariat of the United Nations in order to study how it might be associated with this Code, or even in what form it could endorse it, in particular as part of the process of implementing the recommendations of the recent CSVC session

Annex

Protocol of implementation

I. Body responsible for interpreting, applying and evaluating the provisions of the Global Code of Ethics for Tourism

(a) A World Committee on Tourism Ethics shall be created comprising twelve eminent persons independent of governments and twelve alternates, selected on the basis of their competence in the field of tourism and related fields; they shall not receive any orders or instructions from those who proposed their nomination or who designated them and shall not report to them.

(b) The members of the World Committee on Tourism Ethics shall be appointed as follows:

- six members and six alternate members designated by the WTO Regional Commissions, on the proposal of the States Members of WTO;
- a member and an alternate designated by the autonomous territories that are Associate Members of WTO from among their members;
- four members and four alternate members elected by the WTO General Assembly from among the Affiliate Members of WTO representing professionals or employees of the tourism industry, universities and non-governmental organizations, after conferring with the Committee of Affiliate Members;
- a chairman, who may be an eminent person not belonging to WTO, elected by the other members of the Committee, on the proposal of the Secretary-General of WTO.

The Legal Adviser of the World Tourism Organization shall participate, when necessary, and in an advisory capacity, in the Committee meetings; the

Secretary-General shall attend ex officio or may arrange to be represented at its meetings.

On appointing the members of the Committee, account shall be taken of the need for a balanced geographical composition of this body and for a diversification of the qualifications and personal status of its members, from both the economic and social as well as the legal viewpoint; the members shall be appointed for four years and their term of office may be renewed only once; in the event of a vacancy, the member shall be replaced by his alternate, it being understood that if the vacancy concerns both the member and his alternate, the Committee itself shall fill the vacant seat; if the Chairman's seat is vacant he or she shall be replaced in the conditions set out above.

(c) The WTO Regional Commissions shall act, in the cases provided for in paragraphs I(d), (g) and (h), as well as II(a), (b), (f) and (g) below of this Protocol, as regional committees on tourism ethics.

(d) The World Committee on Tourism Ethics shall establish its own Rules of Procedure, which shall apply equally, mutatis mutandis, to the Regional Commissions when these are acting as regional committees on tourism ethics; the presence of two-thirds of the Committee members shall be necessary to constitute a quorum at its meetings; in the event that a Member is absent, he may be replaced by his alternate; in the event of a tie in the voting, the Chairman shall have the casting vote.

(e) When proposing the candidature of an eminent person to serve on the Committee, each Member of WTO shall undertake to cover the travel expenses and daily subsistence allowances occasioned by the participation in the meetings of the person whose nomination it has proposed, it being understood that the members of the Committee shall not receive any remuneration; the expenses incurred by the participation of the Chairman of the Committee, also unremunerated, may be borne by the WTO budget; the secretariat of the Committee shall be provided by the services of WTO; the operating costs remaining payable by the Organization may, wholly or in part, be charged to a trust fund financed by voluntary contributions.

(f) The World Committee on Tourism Ethics shall meet in principle once a year; whenever a dispute is referred to it for settlement, the Chairman shall consult the other members and the Secretary-General of WTO about the expediency of convening an extraordinary meeting.

(g) The functions of the World Committee on Tourism Ethics and the WTO Regional Commissions shall be the evaluation of the implementation of this Code and conciliation; it may invite experts or external institutions to contribute to its proceedings.

(h) On the basis of periodic reports submitted to them by Full Members, Associate Members and Affiliate Members of WTO, the WTO Regional Commissions shall, every two years, as regional committees on tourism ethics, examine the application of the Code in their respective regions; they shall record their findings in a report to the World Committee on Tourism Ethics; the reports of the Regional Commissions may contain suggestions to amend or supplement the Global Code of Ethics for Tourism.

(i) The World Committee on Tourism Ethics shall exercise a global function as a 'watchdog' for the problems encountered in implementing the Code and for the proposed solutions; it shall summarize the reports drawn up by the Regional Commissions and supplement them with the information it has collected with the assistance of the Secretary-General and the support of the Committee of Affiliate Members, which shall include, should the need arise, proposals to amend or supplement the Global Code of Ethics for Tourism.

(j) The Secretary-General shall refer the report of the World Committee on Tourism Ethics to the Executive Council, together with his own observations, for consideration and transmission to the General Assembly with the Council's recommendations; the General Assembly shall decide what follow-up action to take on the report and the recommendations thus submitted to it, which the national tourism administrations and other stakeholders in the tourism development shall subsequently have the task of implementing.

II. Conciliation mechanism for the settlement of disputes

(a) In the event of a dispute concerning the interpretation or application of the Global Code of Ethics for Tourism, two or more stakeholders in tourism development may jointly refer it to the World Committee on Tourism Ethics; if the dispute is between two or more stakeholders belonging to the same region, the Parties should refer the matter to the competent WTO Regional Commission in its capacity as a regional committee on tourism ethics.

(b) The States, as well as tourism enterprises and bodies, may declare that they accept in advance the competence of the World Committee on Tourism Ethics or of a WTO Regional Commission for any dispute concerning the interpretation or application of this Code, or for certain categories of dispute; in this case, the Committee or the competent Regional Commission shall be considered as validly referred to unilaterally by the other Party to the dispute.

(c) When a dispute is submitted in the first instance to the World Committee on Tourism Ethics for consideration, its Chairman shall appoint a sub-committee of three Members who shall be responsible for examining the dispute.

(d) The World Committee on Tourism Ethics to which a dispute has been referred shall reach a decision on the basis of the record drawn up by the Parties to the dispute; the Committee may ask these Parties for additional information and, if deemed useful, may hear them at their request; the expenses incurred by this hearing shall be borne by the Parties unless the circumstances are considered exceptional by the Committee; the failure of one of the Parties to appear even though he or she has been given a reasonable opportunity to participate, shall not prevent the Committee from making a ruling.

(e) Unless otherwise agreed by the Parties, the World Committee on Tourism Ethics shall announce its decision within three months of the date on which it was referred to; it shall present recommendations to the Parties suitable to form the basis of a settlement; the Parties shall immediately inform the Chairman of the Committee that has examined the dispute of the action they have taken on these recommendations.

(f) If a dispute is referred to a WTO Regional Commission, it shall announce its decision following the same procedure, mutatis mutandis, as that applied by the World Committee on Tourism Ethics when it intervenes in the first instance.

(g) If, within a period of two months after notification of the proposals of the Committee or of a Regional Commission, the Parties have failed to agree on the terms of a final settlement, the Parties or one of them may refer the dispute to a plenary session of the World Committee on Tourism Ethics; when the Committee has made a ruling in the first instance, the members that served on the sub-committee that examined the dispute may not take part in this plenary session and shall be replaced by their alternates; if these intervened in the first instance, the members shall not be prevented from participating.

(h) The plenary session of the World Committee on Tourism Ethics shall make its ruling following the procedure laid out in paragraphs II(d) and (e) above; if no solution has been found at a previous stage, it shall formulate final conclusions for the settlement of the dispute, which the Parties, if they agree with their contents, will be recommended to apply at the earliest possible opportunity; these conclusions shall be made public, even if the process of conciliation has not been successfully completed and one of the Parties refuses to accept the final conclusions proposed.

(i) Full Members, Associate Members and Affiliate Members of WTO, as well as States that are not members of WTO, may declare that they accept in advance as binding and, where applicable, subject to the sole reservation of reciprocity, the final conclusions of the World Committee on Tourism Ethics in the disputes, or in a private dispute to which they are party.

(j) Likewise, the States may accept as binding or subject to exequatur the final conclusions of the World Committee on Tourism Ethics in disputes to which their nationals are party or which should be applied in their territory.

(k) Tourism enterprises and bodies may include in their contractual documents a provision making the final conclusions of the World Committee on Tourism Ethics binding in their relations with their contracting parties.

Appendix II
Recommended Tourism Syllabus Content for Higher Education Courses Worldwide (based on QAA UK Benchmark Statement)

The extracts in this appendix are the copyright of the Quality Assurance Agency for Higher Education (in the UK); they are reproduced with their permission. The material is part of the UK Subject Benchmark Statement for Hospitality, Leisure, Tourism and Sport. The QAA has examined the areas taught and courses run in higher education in the UK; Unit 25 concerns Hospitality, Leisure, Tourism and Sport. The text that follows is part of what relates to the tourism curriculum. It has been created with the objective of making explicit the general academic characteristics and standards to be expected of an honours degree in the subject. A full understanding of the QAA's aims and the scope of Unit 25 can only be acquired from reading the complete document. Much of the work on tourism course benchmarking in the UK was undertaken by the National Liaison Group for higher education in the tourism field; this has been renamed the Association for Tourism Higher Education.

The discussion in this dictionary of what constitutes tourism needs to be compared with the QAA wording in its own context, which follows; clearly, this dialogue is still ongoing! Meanwhile, not alone are British universities strongly urged to take heed of the outline that has been developed. It is hoped that it will have worldwide influence. This dictionary is believed to be the first publication which has used the QAA outline to determine the scope of the coverage. Every entry is meant to be relevant to an area taught.

Some Extracts from the QAA Subject Benchmark Statement for Hospitality, Leisure, Tourism and Sport

2.5 Programmes broadly concerned with tourism

The term tourism refers to the phenomena and relationships arising from the travel and stay of people away from their normal home environments for a variety of purposes. Programmes with tourism in the title typically have their origins in providing a vocational understanding relevant for potential employment in some or all of the components of what is loosely referred to as the tourism industry. This includes activities in the private sector such as tour operators, airlines and hotel companies, as well as public and not-for-profit bodies such as tourist boards.

Most programmes have broadened from their vocational origins to embrace wider issues relating to the nature, impacts and meanings of tourism, thereby furnishing an understanding of what is now a major world phenomenon. However, most programmes still lay emphasis on career and vocational objectives. Over the past 15 years the number of programmes in tourism has proliferated. They have a wide range of titles. The most common are 'Tourism Management', 'Tourism', 'Leisure and Tourism Management' and 'Tourism Studies' but also included are other titles reflecting the focus of particular programmes such as 'Travel Agency Management', 'Sports Tourism', 'Rural Tourism', 'Sustainable Tourism'. Of the programmes with management in the title many focus particularly on business management. Others are more concerned with the management of scarce resources in the community through concepts of planning and public policy.

The study of tourism overlaps with subject domains from both within, and outside, Unit 25. To some extent, this is reflected in the trend for more recently validated tourism programmes to incorporate ideas and concepts drawn from, for example, social anthropology, sociology and cultural studies.

Degrees in tourism typically involve the following:

- a consideration of the concepts and characteristics of tourism as an area of academic and applied study
- an examination of the nature and characteristics of tourists
- a study of the products, structure, operations and interactions within the tourism industry
- an analysis of tourism in the communities and environments that it affects.

While most include some consideration of all the above areas of study different programmes have different emphases. Typical subject areas might include: accommodation for tourists, destination planning and development, geography of tourism, impacts of tourism, international tourism, operation of the tourism industry, passenger transportation, research methods, technology in travel and tourism, tourism and the environment, tourism economics, tourism marketing, tourism policy, tourism management, sustainable tourism.

3. Knowledge and skills

3.1 Introduction

In this section we identify the knowledge and skills of a typical graduate (Section 5) that we would expect to be developed as part of an undergraduate programme. The depth of knowledge, the proficiency of skills and the balance of specific knowledge and skills may differ with the particular programme. This will reflect the approach taken, the context of study and the aims and objectives of the programme. Each institution is free to decide on the content, nature and organization of the degree programme and its constituent courses/modules, but it is expected that curriculum designers will ensure that the following 'generic' knowledge-base underpins all programmes, together with the knowledge-base given in the subject-specific guidelines identified in Section 6. It is also expected that generic knowledge will be set in the subject-specific context at all levels of the programme. The intellectual skills and the key skills identified in 3.3 and 3.5 should also feature in all undergraduate programmes. The skills specific to Unit 25 in 3.4 will be developed variously, depending upon the particular context in which the student is studying.

3.2 Knowledge

Subject-specific guidelines are given in Section 6. However, graduates of all programmes in Hospitality, Leisure, Sport or Tourism will be able to demonstrate:

* a critical understanding of the development of knowledge in their particular subject domain
* an understanding of the need for both a multi-disciplinary and inter-disciplinary approach to study, drawing, as appropriate, from service, research and professional contexts
* their understanding of the subject through both academic and professional reflective practice
* their research and problem-solving abilities by critically understanding methods of acquiring, interpreting and analysing information appropriate to their context of study
* an understanding and critical awareness of the moral, ethical, environmental and legal issues which underpin best practice.

3.3 Intellectual skills

The typical graduates of programmes in Hospitality, Leisure, Sport or Tourism will have developed a range of intellectual skills including being able to:

* research and assess subject-specific facts, theories, paradigms, principles and concepts
* critically assess and evaluate evidence
* critically interpret data and text
* describe and analyse information
* apply knowledge to the solution of familiar and unfamiliar problems
* develop a reasoned argument and challenge assumptions
* take responsibility for their own learning and continuing professional development.

3.4 Skills specific to unit 25

Skills will be developed in various ways largely depending upon the subject domain within which the student is studying. The range of skills will normally include some or all of the following, with graduates being able to:

* plan, design and execute practical activities using appropriate techniques and procedures

- undertake fieldwork with due regard for safety and risk assessment
- plan, design, execute and communicate a sustained piece of independent intellectual work using appropriate media
- recognize and respond to moral, ethical and safety issues which directly pertain to the subject domain, including relevant legislation and professional codes of conduct.

3.5 Key skills

In addition to skills specific to Unit 25, all undergraduate programmes will enable students to develop the following:

- communication and presentation skills
- numeracy and C & IT skills
- interactive and group skills
- problem-solving skills
- ability to self-appraise and reflect on practice
- ability to plan and manage learning.

3.6 Approaches to programmes of study in unit 25

Where the programme title contains the word 'Management' then it should *inter alia* enable students to:

- demonstrate vocationally relevant managerial skills and knowledge by exposure to professional practice
- evaluate and apply vocationally relevant concepts associated with the operational and strategic management of financial, human and physical resources and/or understand and apply concepts associated with the allocation of resources in the community.

Where the programme title contains the word 'Science' then it should *inter alia* enable students to:

- demonstrate an understanding of the philosophical basis of scientific paradigms
- demonstrate evidence of competence in the scientific methods of enquiry, interpretation and analysis of relevant data and appropriate technologies.

Where the programme title contains the word 'Studies' then it should *inter alia* enable students to:

- critique the contributions of a range of academic disciplines that have informed the development of the subject as a field of study
- demonstrate an appropriate degree of progression within specialist fields
- display an integrated knowledge of the scope and breadth of the subject domain.

4. Learning, teaching and assessment

4.1

Unit 25 encompasses a rich variety of often diverse disciplinary cultures. It also includes a range of patterns of study including full-time, sandwich, part-time and distance-learning degree programmes. In particular, some of the programmes within Unit 25 will include as integral some form of extended placement in industry. Some placements will be credit-bearing, many will not. It is therefore considered inappropriate to be prescriptive about which specific teaching and assessment methods should be used except that programme teams should be able to justify their choices in terms of the criteria laid out in this document.

4.2

Students reading for a degree in programmes embraced by this Unit should be provided with full documentation on their programme of study and each individual component (course, field, module, unit etc.). Learning, teaching and assessment should be interlinked as part of the curriculum design and development to enable students to develop the knowledge and skills identified in Section 3 of this of this benchmark. Assessment methods should be chosen to provide evidence of the achievement of learning outcomes using the performance indicators set out in Section 5. Programmes should be delivered by staff with qualifications or experiences which are relevant to the subject domain.

4.3

The learning and teaching methods that programmes in this Unit have typically included are lectures; tutorials; laboratory practicals; other small group formats; directed reading etc. It is in applying theory to practice that these subject domains adopt distinctive learning, teaching and assessment strategies.

4.4

Learning will be structured to ensure that students are engaged in the subject-specific contexts throughout the programme. These will include, *inter alia:*

- learning opportunities in specialized facilities (sports science laboratories, training kitchens and restaurants, sports participation facilities, leisure facilities etc.)
- contact with the industry, or professional bodies (fieldwork and other activities in the external environment, visits, visiting speakers and other professionals in the field, and 'live' case studies)
- learning opportunities through the use of specialized items of equipment (HEFCE in separate studies on hospitality management and sports-related provision have identified minimum provision)
- access to relevant applied IT systems.

6.5. Tourism

A typical honours graduate in tourism will be able to demonstrate an understanding of:

- the concepts and characteristics of tourism as an area of academic and applied study including being able to:
  - understand and appreciate the potential contributions of disciplines that help to explain the nature and development of tourism
  - explain and challenge theories and concepts which are used to understand tourism
  - explain and challenge the definitions, nature and operations of tourism
  - demonstrate an understanding of the domestic and international nature and dimensions of tourism
  - utilize a range of source material in investigating tourism
  - demonstrate an awareness of the dynamic nature of tourism in modern societies
  - understand the inter-cultural dimensions of tourism.
- the products, structure of and interactions in the tourism industry including being able to:
  - demonstrate an understanding of the structure, operation and organization of the public, private and not-for-profit sectors and their activities
  - evaluate the factors that influence the development of organizations operating in tourism
  - analyse relations between consumers of tourism and the providers of tourism services.
- the role of tourism in the communities and environments that it affects and in particular:
  - have an understanding of the relationship between tourism and the communities and environments in which it takes place
  - be able to evaluate the contribution and impacts of tourism in social, economic, environmental, political, cultural and other terms
  - have an understanding of and be able to evaluate the approaches to managing the development of tourism through concepts of policy and planning
  - appreciate the ethical issues associated with the operation and development of tourism.
- the nature and characteristics of tourists and in particular:
  - be able to explain the patterns and characteristics of tourism demand and the influences on such demand
  - understand the cultural significance of tourism for the tourists and their societies.

Appendix 1. Award titles

The 'leisure' sector (in its broadest definition) is one of the largest and fastest growing sectors of the global economy. Although there is a core of recognized course titles, it is also a developing area of study with a great deal of innovation and diversity. The benchmarking group has therefore made use of the UCAS directory in identifying those course titles which properly fall within the remit of the group. The current scope of the group with respect to Tourism is degrees with the following titles:

Tourism, including: Tourism Studies; Tourism Management; Ecotourism; European Tourism; International Tourism; Rural/Countryside Tourism; Sports Tourism; Sustainable Tourism; Tourism Planning; Adventure Tourism Management; European Tourism Management; International Tourism Management; Rural Tourism Management; Tourism Business Management; Visitor Attractions Management; Tourism Operations Management; Travel and Tourism Management; Travel Management; European Travel Management; International Travel; Travel Agency Management.

Appendix III
EC Neutral CRS Rules

This document is meant purely as a documentation tool and the institutions do not assume any liability for its contents.
COUNCIL REGULATION (EEC) No 2299/89 of 24 July 1989 on code of conduct for computerized reservation systems (Official Journal L 220, 29.7.1989, p.1)
Amended by: Council Regulation (EEC) No 3089/93 of 29 October 1993, Official Journal L 278, 11.11.1993
Corrected by: Corrigendum, Official Journal L 17, 25.1.1995, p.18 (3089/93)

COUNCIL REGULATION (EEC) No 2299/89 of 24 July 1989 on code of conduct for computerized reservation systems

THE COUNCIL OF THE EUROPEAN COMMUNITIES,
Having regard to the Treaty establishing the European Economic Community, and in particular Article 84 (2) thereof,
Having regard to the proposal from the Commission (1),
Having regard to the opinion of the European Parliament (2),
Having regard to the opinion of the Economic and Social Committee (3),
Whereas the bulk of airline reservations are made through computerized reservation systems;
Whereas such systems can if properly used, provide an important and useful service to air carriers, travel agents and the travelling public by affording easy access to up-to-date and accurate information on flights, fares and seat availability, making reservations and, in some cases, issuing tickets and boarding passes;
Whereas abuses in the form of denial of access to the systems or discrimination in the provision, loading or display of data or unreasonable conditions imposed on participants or subscribers can seriously disadvantage air carriers, travel agents and ultimately consumers;
Whereas this Regulation is without prejudice to the application of Articles 85 and 86 of the Treaty;

Whereas Commission Regulation (EEC) No 2672/88 (4) exempts for the provisions of Article 85 (1) of the Treaty agreements for the common purchase, development and operation of computerized reservation systems;

Whereas a mandatory code of conduct applicable to all computerized reservation systems and/or distribution facilities offered for use and/or used in the Community could ensure that such systems are used in a non-discriminatory and transparent way, subject to certain safeguards, so avoiding their misuse while reinforcing undistorted competition between air carriers and between computerized reservation systems and thereby protecting the interests of consumers;

Whereas it would not be appropriate to impose obligations on a computerized reservation system vendor or on a parent or participating carrier in respect of an air carrier of a third country which, alone or jointly with others, owns and/or controls another such system which does not conform with this code or offer equivalent treatment;

Whereas a complaints investigation and enforcement procedure for non-compliance with such a code is desirable,

HAS ADOPTED THIS REGULATION:

Article 1

This Regulation shall apply to computerized reservation systems to the extent that they contain air transport products, when offered for use and/or used in the territory of the Community, irrespective of:

- the status or nationality of the system vendor,
- the source of the information used or the location of the relevant central data processing unit,
- the geographical location of the airports between which air carriage takes place.

Article 2

For the purposes of this Regulation:

(a) 'unbundled air transport product' means the carriage by air of a passenger between two airports, including any related ancillary services and additional benefits offered for sale and/or sold as an integral part of that product;

(b) 'bundled air transport product' means a prearranged combination of an unbundled air transport product with other services not ancillary to air transport, offered for sale and/or sold at an inclusive price;

(c) 'air transport product' means both unbundled and bundled air transport products;

(d) 'scheduled air service' means a series of flights all possessing the following characteristics:

- performed by aircraft for the transport of passengers or passengers and cargo and/or mail for remuneration, in such a manner that seats are available on each flight for individual purchase by consumers either directly from the air carrier or from its authorized agents,
- operated so as to serve traffic between the same two or more points, either;

1. according to a published timetable: or
2. with flights so regular or frequent that they constitute a recognizably systematic series;

(e) 'fare' means the price to be paid for unbundled air transport products and the conditions under which this price applies;

(f) 'computerized reservation system' (CRS) means a computerized system containing information about, *inter alia*, air carriers':

*   schedules,
*   availability,
*   fares, and
*   related services, with or without facilities through which:
*   reservations may be made, or
*   tickets may be issued,

to the extent that some or all of these services are made available to subscribers;

(g) 'distribution facilities' means facilities provided by a system vendor for the provision of information about air carriers' schedules, availability, fares and related services and for making reservations and/or issuing tickets, and for any other related services;

(h) 'system vendor' means any entity and its affiliates which is or are responsible for the operation or marketing of a CRS;

(i) 'parent carrier' means any air carrier which directly or indirectly, alone or jointly with others, owns or effectively controls a system vendor, as well as any air carrier which it owns or effectively controls;

(j) 'effective control' means a relationship constituted by rights, contracts or any other means which, either separately or jointly and having regard to the considerations of fact or law involved, confer the possibility of directly or indirectly exercising a decisive influence on an undertaking, in particular by:

*   the right to use all or part of the assets of an undertaking,
*   rights or contracts which confer a decisive influence on the composition, voting or decisions of the bodies of an undertaking or otherwise confer a decisive influence on the running of the business of the undertaking;

(k) 'participating carrier' means an air carrier which has an agreement with a system vendor for the distribution of air transport products through a CRS. To the extent that a parent carrier uses the facilities of its own CRS which are covered by this Regulation, it shall be considered a participating carrier;

(l) 'subscriber' means a person or an undertaking, other than a participating carrier, using the distribution facilities for air transport products of a CRS under contract or other arrangement with a system vendor;

(m) 'consumer' means any person seeking information about and/or intending to purchase an air transport product;

(n) 'principal display' means a comprehensive neutral display of data concerning air services between city pairs, within a specified time period;

(o) 'elapsed journey time' means the time difference between scheduled departure and arrival time;

(p) 'service enhancement' means any product or service offered by a system vendor on its own behalf to subscribers in conjunction with a CRS, other than distribution facilities.

Article 3

1. A system vendor shall have the capacity, in its own name as a separate entity from the parent carrier, to have rights and obligations of all kinds, to make contracts, *inter alia* with parent carriers, participating carriers and subscribers, or to accomplish other legal acts and to sue and be sued.

2. A system vendor shall allow any air carrier the opportunity to participate, on an equal and non-discriminatory basis, in its distribution facilities within the available capacity of the system concerned and subject to any technical constraints outside the control of the system vendor.

3. (a) A system vendor shall not:
   - attach unreasonable conditions to any contract with a participating carrier,
   - require the acceptance of supplementary conditions which, by their nature or according to commercial usage, have no connection with participation in its CRS and shall apply the same conditions for the same level of service.

   (b) A system vendor shall not make it a condition of participation in its CRS that a participating carrier may not at the same time be a participant in another system.

   (c) A participating carrier may terminate its contract with a system vendor on giving notice which need not exceed six months, to expire not before the end of the first year.

   In such a case a system vendor shall not be entitled to recover more than the costs directly related to the termination of the contract.

4. If a system vendor has decided to add any improvement to the distribution facilities provided or the equipment used in the provision of the facilities, it shall provide information on and offer these improvements to all participating carriers, including parent carriers, with equal time lines and on the same terms and conditions, subject to any technical constraints outside the control of the system vendor, and in such a way that there will be no difference in lead time for the implementation of the new improvements between parent and participating carriers.

Article 3a

1. (a) A parent carrier may not discriminate against a competing CRS by refusing to provide the latter, on request and with equal timeliness, with the same information on schedules, fares and availability relating to its own air services as that which it provides to its own CRS or to distribute its air transport products through another CRS, or by refusing to accept or to confirm with equal timeliness a reservation made through a competing CRS for any of its air transport products which are distributed through its own CRS. The parent carrier shall be obliged to accept and to confirm only those bookings which are in conformity with its fares and conditions.

   (b) The parent carrier shall not be obliged to accept any costs in this connection except for reproduction of the information to be provided and for accepted bookings.

   (c) The parent carrier shall be entitled to carry out controls to ensure that Article 5 (1) is respected by the competing CRS.

2. The obligation imposed by this Article shall not apply in favour of a competing CRS when, in accordance with the procedures of Article 6 (5) or Article 7 (3) or (4), it has been decided that the CRS is in breach of Article 4a or that a system vendor cannot give sufficient guarantees that obligations under Article 6 concerning unauthorized access of parent carriers to information are complied with.

Article 4

1. Participating carriers and other providers of air transport products shall ensure that the data which they decide to submit to a CRS is accurate, non-misleading, transparent and no less comprehensive than for any other CRS. The data shall, *inter alia*, enable a system vendor to meet the requirements of the ranking criteria as set out in the Annex. Data submitted via intermediaries shall not be manipulated by them in a manner which would lead to inaccurate, misleading or discriminatory information.
2. A system vendor shall not manipulate the material referred to in paragraph 1 in a manner which would lead to the provision of inaccurate, misleading or discriminatory information.
3. A system vendor shall load and process data provided by participating carriers with equal care and timeliness, subject only to the constraints of the loading method selected by individual participating carriers and to the standard formats used by the said vendor.

Article 4a

1. Loading and/or processing facilities provided by a system vendor shall be offered to all parent and participating carriers without discrimination. Where relevant and generally accepted air transport industry standards are available, system vendors shall offer facilities compatible with them.
2. A system vendor shall not reserve any specific loading and/or procesing procedure or any other distribution facility for one or more of its parent carrier(s).
3. A system vendor shall ensure that its distribution facilities are separated, in a clear and verifiable manner, from any carrier's private inventory and management and marketing facilities. Separation may be established either logically by means of software or physically in such a way that any connection between the distribution facilities and the private facilities may be achieved by means of an application-to-application interface only. Irrespective of the method of separation adopted, any such interface shall be made available to all parent and participating carriers on a non-discriminatory basis and shall ensure equality of treatment in respect of procedures, protocols, inputs and outputs. Where relevant and generally accepted air transport industry standards are available, system vendors shall offer interfaces compatible with them.

Article 5

1. (a)   Displays generated by a CRS shall be clear and non-discriminatory.
   (b)   A system vendor shall not intentionally or negligently display inaccurate or misleading information in its CRS.

2. (a)   A system vendor shall provide a principal display or displays for each individual transaction through its CRS and shall include therein the data provided by participating carriers on flight schedules, fare types and seat availability in a clear and comprehensive manner and without discrimination or bias, in particular as regards the order in which information is presented.

(b)   A consumer shall be entitled to have, on request, a principal display limited to scheduled or non-scheduled services only.

(c)   No discrimination on the basis of airports serving the same city shall be exercised in constructing and selecting flights for a given city-pair for inclusion in a principal display.

(d)   Ranking of flight options in a principal display shall be as set out in the Annex.

(e)   Criteria to be used for ranking shall not be based on any factor directly or indirectly relating to carrier identity and shall be applied on a non-discriminatory basis to all participating carriers.

3. Where a system vendor provides information on fares, the display shall be neutral and non-discriminatory and shall contain at least the fares provided for all flights of participating carriers shown in the principal display. The source of such information shall be acceptable to the participating carrier(s) and system vendor concerned.

4. Information on bundled products regarding, *inter alia*, who is organizing the tour, availability and prices, shall not be featured in the principal display.

5. A CRS shall not be considered in breach of this Regulation to the extent that it changes a display in order to meet the specific request(s) of a consumer.

Article 6

1. The following provisions shall govern the availability of information, statistical or otherwise, by a system vendor from its CRS:

(a)   information concerning individual bookings shall be provided on an equal basis and only to the air carrier(s) participating in the service covered by and to the subscriber(s) involved in the booking;

(b)   any marketing, booking and sales data made available shall be on the basis that:

(i)   such data are offered with equal timeliness and on a non-discriminatory basis to all participating carriers, including parent carriers;

(ii)   such data may and, on request, shall cover all participating carriers and/or subscribers, but shall include no identification of or personal information on a passenger or a corporate user;

(iii)   all requests for such data are treated with equal care and timeliness, subject to the transmission method selected by the individual carrier.

2. A system vendor shall not make personal information concerning a passenger available to others not involved in the transaction without the consent of the passenger.

3. A system vendor shall ensure that the provisions in paragraphs 1 and 2 above are complied with, by technical means and/or appropriate safeguards regarding at least software, in such a way that information provided by or created for air

carriers can in no way be accessed by one or more of the parent carriers except as permitted by this Article.

4. A system vendor shall, within three months of the entry into force of this Regulation, make available on request to all participating carriers a detailed description of the technical and administrative measures which it has adopted in order to conform with this Article.

5. Upon receipt of the detailed description of the technical and administrative measures which have been adopted or modified by a system vendor, the Commission shall decide within three months whether the measures are sufficient to provide the safeguards required under this Article. If not, the Commission's decision may invoke the application of Article 3a (2). The Commission shall immediately inform Member States of such a decision. Unless the Council, at the request of a Member State, takes a different decision within two months of the date of the Commission's decision, the latter shall enter into force.

Article 7

1. The obligations of a system vendor under Articles 3 and 4 to 6 shall not apply in respect of a parent carrier of a third country to the extent that its CRS outside the territory of the Community does not offer Community air carriers equivalent treatment to that provided under this Regulation and under Commission Regulation (EEC)No 83/91 (1).

2. The obligations of parent or participating carriers under Articles 3a, 4 and 8 shall not apply in respect of a CRS controlled by (an) air carrier(s) of one or more third country (countries) to the extent that outside the territory of the Community the parent or participating carrier(s) is (are) not accorded equivalent treatment to that provided under this Regulation and under Commission Regulation (EEC)No 83/91.

3. A system vendor or an air carrier proposing to avail itself of the provisions of paragraphs 1 or 2 must notify the Commission of its intentions and the reasons therefore at least 14 days in advance of such action. In exceptional circumstances, the Commission may, at the request of the vendor or the air carrier concerned, grant a waiver from the 14-day rule.

4. Upon receipt of a notification, the Commission shall without delay determine whether discrimination within the meaning of paragraphs 1 and 2 exists. If this is found to be the case, the Commission shall so inform all system vendors or the air carriers concerned in the Community as well as Member States. If discrimination within the meaning of paragraph 1 or 2 does not exist, the Commission shall so inform the system vendor or air carriers concerned.

5. (a) In cases where serious discrimination within the meaning of paragraph 1 or 2 is found to exist, the Commission may by decision instruct CRSs to modify their operations appropriately in order to terminate such discrimination. The Commission shall immediately inform Member States of such a decision.
(b) Unless the Council, at the request of a Member State, takes another decision within 2 months of the date of the Commission's decision, the latter shall enter into force.

Article 8

1. A parent carrier shall neither directly nor indirectly link the use of any specific CRS by a subscriber with the receipt of any commission or other incentive or disincentive for the sale of air transport products available on its flights.
2. A parent carrier shall neither directly nor indirectly require use of any specific CRS by a subscriber for sale or issue of tickets for any air transport products provided either directly or indirectly by itself.
3. Any condition which an air carrier may require of a travel agent when authorizing it to sell and issue tickets for its air transport products shall be without prejudice to paragraphs 1 and 2.

Article 9

1. A system vendor shall make any of the distribution facilities of a CRS available to any subscriber on a non-discriminatory basis.
2. A system vendor shall not require a subscriber to sign an exclusive contract, nor directly or indirectly prevent a subscriber from subscribing to, or using, any other system or systems.
3. A service enhancement offered to any other subscriber shall be offered by the system vendor to all subscribers on a non-discriminatory basis.
4. (a) A system vendor shall not attach unreasonable conditions to any subscriber contract allowing for the use of its CRS and, in particular, a subscriber may terminate its contract with a system vendor by giving notice which need not exceed three months, to expire not before the end of the first year. In such a case, a system vendor shall not be entitled to recover more than the costs directly related to the termination of the contract.
   (b) Subject to paragraph 2, the supply of technical equipment is not subject to the conditions set out in (a).
5. A system vendor shall provide in each subscriber contract for:
   (a) the principal display, conforming to Article 5, to be accessed for each individual transaction, except where a consumer requests information for only one air carrier or where the consumer requests information for bundled air transport products alone;
   (b) the subscriber not to manipulate material supplied by CRSs in a manner which would lead to inaccurate, misleading or discriminatory presentation of information to consumers.
6. A system vendor shall not impose an obligation on a subscriber to accept an offer of technical equipment or software, but may require that equipment and software used be compatible with its own system.

Article 10

1. Any fee charged by a system vendor shall be non-discriminatory, reasonably structured and reasonably related to the cost of the service provided and used and shall, in particular, be the same for the same level of service. The billing for the services of a CRS shall be sufficiently detailed to allow the participating carriers and subscribers to see exactly which services have been used and the fees therefore; as a minimum, booking fee bills must include the following information for each segment:

- type of CRS booking,
- passenger name,
- country,
- IATA/ARC agency identification code,
- city-code,
- city pair or segment,
- booking date (transaction date),
- flight date,
- flight number,
- status code (booking status),
- service type (class of service),
- PNR record locator,
- booking/cancellation indicator.

The billing information shall be offered on magnetic media.

A participating air carrier shall be offered the facility of being informed at the time that any booking/transaction is made for which a booking fee will be charged. Where a carrier elects to be so informed, it shall be offered the option to disallow such booking/transaction, unless the latter has already been accepted.

2. A system vendor shall, on request, provide interested parties with details of current procedures, fees and systems facilities, including interfaces, editing and display criteria used. However, this provision does not oblige a system vendor to disclose proprietary information such as software programmes.

3. Any changes to fee levels, conditions or facilities offered and the basis therefore shall be communicated to all participating carriers and subscribers on a non-discriminatory basis.

Article 11

1. Acting on receipt of a complaint or on its own initiative, the Commission shall initiate procedures to terminate infringement of the provisions of this Regulation.

2. Complaints may be submitted by:
   (a) Member States;
   (b) natural or legal persons who claim a legitimate interest.

3. The Commission shall immediately forward to the Member States copies of the complaints and applications and of all relevant documents sent to it or which it sends out in the course of such procedures.

Article 12

1. In carrying out the duties assigned to it by this Regulation, the Commission may obtain all necessary information from the Member States and from undertakings and associations of undertakings.

2. The Commission may fix a time limit of not less than one month for the communication of the information requested.

3. When sending a request for information to an undertaking or association of undertakings, the Commission shall forward a copy of the request at the same time to the Member State in whose territory the head office of the undertaking or association of undertakings is situated.

4. In its request, the Commission shall state the legal basis and purpose of the request and also the penalties for supplying incorrect information provided for in Article 16 (1).

5. The owners of the undertakings or their representatives and, in the case of legal persons or of companies, firms or associations not having legal personality, the person authorized to represent them by law or by their rules shall be bound to supply the information requested.

Article 13

1. In carrying out the duties assigned to it by this Regulation, the Commission may undertake all necessary investigations into undertakings and associations of undertakings. To this end, officials authorized by the Commission shall be empowered:

    (a)   to examine the books and other business records;

    (b)   to take copies of, or extracts from, the books and business records;

    (c)   to ask for oral explanations on the spot;

    (d)   to enter any premises, land and vehicles used by undertakings or associations of undertakings.

2. The authorized officials of the Commission shall exercise their powers upon production of an authorization in writing, specifying the subject matter and purpose of the investigation and the penalties provided for in Article 16 (1) in cases where production of the required books or other business records is incomplete. In good time before the investigation, the Commission shall inform the Member State, in whose territory the same is to be made, of the investigation and the identity of the authorized officials.

3. Undertakings and associations of undertakings shall submit to investigations ordered by decision of the Commission. The decision shall specify the subject matter and purpose of the investigation, appoint the date on which it is to begin and indicate the penalties provided for in Article 16 (1) and the right to have the decision reviewed in the Court of Justice.

4. The Commission shall take the decisions mentioned in paragraph 3 after consultation with the Member State in the territory of which the investigation is to be made.

5. Officials of the Member State in the territory of which investigation is to be made may assist the Commission officials in carrying out their duties, at the request of the Member State or of the Commission.

6. Where an undertaking opposes an investigation ordered pursuant to this Article, the Member State concerned shall afford the necessary assistance to the officials authorized by the Commission to enable them to make their investigation.

Article 14

1. Information acquired as a result of the application of Articles 12 and 13 shall be used only for the purposes of the relevant request or investigation.

2. Without prejudice to Articles 11 and 20, the Commission and the competent authorities of the Member States, their officials and other servants shall not disclose information of a kind covered by the obligation of professional secrecy which has been acquired by them as a result of the application of this Regulation.

3. Paragraphs 1 and 2 shall not prevent publication of general information or of surveys which do not contain information relating to particular undertakings or associations of undertakings.

Article 15

1. When an undertaking or association of undertakings does not supply the information requested within the time limit fixed by the Commission or supplies incomplete information, the Commission shall by decision require the information to be supplied. The decision shall specify what information is required, fix an appropriate time limit within which it is to be supplied and indicate the penalties provided for in Article 16 (1) as well as the right to have the decision reviewed by the Court of Justice.
2. At the same time the Commission shall send a copy of its decision to the competent authority of the Member State in the territory of which the head office of the undertaking or association of undertakings is situated.

Article 16

1. The Commission may, by decision, impose fines on undertakings or associations of undertakings from ECU 1 000 to 50 000 where, intentionally or negligently:
    (a) they supply incorrect information in response to a request made pursuant to Article 12 or do not supply information within the time limit fixed;
    (b) they produce the required books or other business records in incomplete form during investigations or refuse to submit to an investigation pursuant to Article 13 (1).
2. The Commission may, by decision, impose fines on system vendors, parent carriers, participating carriers and/or subscribers for infringements of this Regulation up to a maximum of 10% of the annual turnover for the relevant activity of the undertaking concerned. In fixing the amount of the fine, regard shall be had both to the seriousness and to the duration of the infringement.
3. Decisions taken pursuant to paragraphs 1 and 2 shall not be of a penal nature.

Article 17

The Court of Justice shall have unlimited jurisdiction within the meaning of Article 172 of the Treaty to review decisions whereby the Commission has imposed a fine; it may cancel, reduce or increase the fine.

Article 18

For the purposes of applying Article 16, the ECU shall be that adopted in drawing up the general budget of the European Communities in accordance with Articles 207 and 209 of the Treaty.

Article 19

1. Before taking decisions as provided for in Article 16, the Commission shall give the undertakings or associations of undertakings concerned the opportunity of being heard on the matters to which the Commission takes, or has taken, objection.

2. Should the Commission or the competent authorities of the Member States consider it necessary, they may also hear other natural or legal persons. Applications by such persons to be heard shall be granted when they show a sufficient interest.

Article 20

1. The Commission shall publish the decisions which it adopts pursuant to Article 16.
2. Such publication shall state the names of the parties and the main content of the decision; it shall have regard to the legitimate interest of undertakings in the protection of their business secrets.

Article 21

The provisions in Article 5, Article 9 (5) and the Annex to this Regulation shall not apply to a CRS used by an air carrier or a group of air carriers in its (their) own office(s) and sales counters clearly identified as such.

Article 21a

1. The system vendor shall ensure that the technical compliance of its CRS with Articles 4a and 6 is monitored by an independent auditor. For this purpose, the auditor shall be granted access at any time to any programs, procedures, operations and safeguards used on the computers or computer systems through which the system vendor is providing its distribution facilities. Each system vendor shall submit its auditor's report on his inspection and findings to the Commission at least once a year. This report shall be examined by the Commission with a view to any necessary action in accordance with Article 11 (1).
2. The system vendor shall inform participating carriers and the Commission of the identity of the auditor at least three months before confirmation of an appointment and at least three months before each annual reappointment. If, within one month of notification, any of the participating carriers objects to the capability of the auditor to carry out the tasks as required under this Article, the Commission shall, within a further two months and after consultation with the auditor, the system vendor and any other party claiming a legitimate interest, decide whether or not the auditor is to be replaced.

Article 22

1. This Regulation shall be without prejudice to national legislation on security, public order and data protection.
2. The beneficiaries of rights arising under Article 3 (4), Articles 4a, and 21a cannot renounce these rights by contractual or any other means.

Article 23

1. The Council shall decide on the revision of this Regulation by 31 December 1997, on the basis of a Commission proposal to be submitted by 31 March 1997, accompanied by a report on the application of this Regulation.
2. The Council shall review the application of Articles 4a and 6 (3), based on a report to be submitted, at the latest by the end of 1994, by the Commission. This

Regulation shall be binding in its entirety and directly applicable in all Member States.

ANNEX
Principal display ranking criteria for flights offering unbundled air transport products

1. Ranking of flight options in a principal display, for the day or days requested, shall be in the following order unless requested in a different way by a consumer for an individual transaction:
    (i)   all non-stop direct flights between the city-pairs concerned,
    (ii)   other direct flights, not involving a change of aircraft, between the city-pairs concerned,
    (iii) connecting flights.

2. A consumer shall at least be afforded the possibility of having, on request, a principal display ranked by departure or arrival time and/or elapsed journey time. Unless otherwise requested by a consumer, a principal display shall be ranked by departure time for group (i) and elapsed journey time for groups (ii) and (iii).

3. Where a system vendor chooses to display information for any city-pair in relation to the schedules or fares of non-participating carriers, but not necessarily all such carriers, such information shall be displayed in an accurate, non-misleading and non-discriminatory manner between carriers displayed.

4. If, to the system vendor's knowledge, information on the number of direct scheduled air services and the identity of the air carriers concerned is not comprehensive, this shall be clearly stated on the relevant display.

5. Flights other than scheduled air services shall be clearly identified.

6. Flights involving stops en route shall be clearly identified.

7. Where flights are operated by an air carrier which is not the air carrier identified by the carrier designator code, the actual operator of the flight shall be clearly identified. This requirement shall apply in all cases, except for short-term *ad hoc* arrangements.

8. A system vendor shall not use the screen space in a principal display in a manner which gives excessive exposure to one particular travel option or which displays unrealistic travel options.

9. Except as provided for in paragraph 10, the following shall apply:
    (a)   for direct services, no flight shall be featured more than once in a principal display;
    (b)   for multi-sector services involving a change of aircraft, no combination of flights shall be featured more than once in a principal display;
    (c)   flights involving a change of aircraft shall be treated and displayed as connecting flights, with one line per aircraft segment.
Nevertheless, only one reservation shall be necessary where the flights are operated by the same air carrier, with the same flight number, and where the air carrier requires only one flight coupon.

10.1. Where participating carriers have joint venture or other contractual arrangements requiring two or more of them to assume separate responsibility for the offer and sale of air transport products on a flight or combination

of flights, the terms 'flight' (for direct services) and 'combination of flights' (for multi-sector services) in paragraph 9 shall be interpreted as allowing each of the carriers concerned:
- up to a maximum of two
- to have a separate display using its individual carrier designator code.

2. Where more than two carriers are involved, designation of the two carriers entitled to avail themselves of the exception provided for in subparagraph 1 shall be a matter for the carrier actually operating the flight.

11. A principal display shall, wherever practicable, include connecting flights on scheduled services which are operated by participating carriers and are constructed by using a minimum number of nine connecting points. A system vendor shall accept a request by a participating carrier, to include an indirect service, unless the routing is in excess of 130% of the great circle distance between the two airports or except where this would lead to the exclusion of services with a shorter elapsed journey time. Connecting points with routings in excess of 130% need not be used.

The text continues with amendments which the EC has not incorporated in the above text.

COUNCIL REGULATION (EC) No 323/1999 of 8 February 1999 amending Regulation (EEC) No 2299/89 on a code of conduct for computer reservation systems (CRSs)

THE COUNCIL OF THE EUROPEAN UNION,

Having regard to the Treaty establishing the European Community, and in particular Articles 75 and 84(2) thereof,

Having regard to the proposal from the Commission,

Having regard to the opinion of the Economic and Social Committee (1),

Acting in accordance with the procedure laid down in Article 189c of the Treaty (2),

(1) Whereas Regulation (EEC) No 2299/89 (3) has made a major contribution to ensuring fair and unbiased conditions for air carriers in computer reservation systems, thereby protecting the interests of consumers;

(2) Whereas it is necessary to extend the scope of Regulation (EEC) No 2299/89 and to clarify its provisions and it is appropriate to take these measures at Community level to ensure that the objectives of the Regulation are met in all Member States;

(3) Whereas this Regulation is without prejudice to the application of Articles 85 and 86 of the Treaty;

(4) Whereas this Regulation is without prejudice to the application of Directive 95/46/EC of the European Parliament and of the Council of 24 October 1995 on the protection of individuals with regard to the processing of personal data and on the free movement of such data (4);

(5) Whereas Commission Regulation (EC) No 3652/93 (5) exempts agreements for the common purchase, development and operation of computerized reservation systems from the provisions of Article 85(1) of the Treaty;

(6) Whereas it is desirable to clarify the basis on which parent carriers should be charged for bookings they are required to accept from competing CRSs;

(7) Whereas it is necessary to clarify the basis on which CRSs charge for the services they provide for participating carriers and subscribers, in particular as regards incentives and in order to improve transparency;

(8) Whereas it is necessary to ensure that third parties carrying out services on behalf of a CRS are subject to the same obligations as the code imposes on that CRS;

(9) Whereas the code's CRS audit requirements should also be used to check data-protection requirements arising out of Directive 95/46/EC;

(10) Whereas it is necessary to specify the obligations of subscribers under the code so that the reservation services they provide for their customers are not inaccurate, misleading or discriminatory;

(11) Whereas express provision ought to be made for a defendant's right to be heard on matters to which the Commission takes objection;

(1) OJ C 95, 30.3.1998, p. 27.
(2) Opinion of the European Parliament of 15 May 1998 (OJ C 167, 1.6.1998, p. 293), Council Common Position of 24 September 1998 (OJ C 360, 23.11.1998, p. 69) and Decision of the European Parliament of 3 December 1998 (OJ C 398, 21.12.1998).
(3) OJ L 281, 23.11.1995, p. 31.
(4) OJ L 220, 29.7.1989, p. 1. Regulation as amended by Regulation (EEC) No 3089/93 (OJ L 278 11.11.1993, p. 1).
(5) OJ L 333, 31.12.1993, p. 37. Regulation as amended by the Act of Accession of 1994.

(12) Whereas the integration of rail services into the CRS principal display can improve the quality of information available to consumers and provide consumers with the best options for their travel arrangements;

(13) Whereas rail operators distributing certain well defined categories of their services through the principal displays of CRS should be subject to conditions comparable to those imposed on air carriers;

(14) Whereas information or distribution facilities offered by a carrier or a group of air carriers should not be subject to certain code provisions provided that such arrangements are clearly and continuously identified,

HAS ADOPTED THIS REGULATION:

Article 1

Regulation No 2299/89 is hereby amended as follows:

1. Article 1 shall be replaced by the following:

Article 1

This Regulation shall apply to any computerized reservation system, insofar as it contains air-transport products and insofar as rail-transport products are incorporated in its principal display, when offered for use or used in the territory of the Community, irrespective of:
- the status or nationality of the system vendor,
- the source of the information used or the location of the relevant central data processing unit,
- the geographical location of the airports between which air carriage takes place.

2. Article 2 shall be amended as follows:

(a) paragraph (l) shall be replaced by the following:

'(l) "subscriber" shall mean a person, other than a consumer, or an undertaking, other than a participating carrier, using a CRS under contract or other financial arrangement with a system vendor. A financial arrangement shall be deemed to exist where a specific payment is made for the services of the system vendor or where an air-transport product is purchased;'

(b) paragraph (m) shall be replaced by the following:

'(m) "consumer" shall mean any person seeking information about or intending to purchase an air-transport product for private use;'

(c) the following paragraphs shall be added:

'(q) "unbundled rail-transport product" shall mean the carriage of a passenger between two stations by rail, including any related ancillary services and additional benefits offered for sale or sold as an integral part of that product;

(r) "bundled rail-transport product" shall mean a pre-arranged combination of an unbundled rail-transport product with other services not ancillary to rail transport, offered for sale or sold at an inclusive price;

(s) "rail-transport product" shall mean both unbundled and bundled rail-transport products;

(t) "ticket" shall mean a valid document giving entitlement to transport or an equivalent in paperless, including electronic, form issued or authorised by the carrier or its authorised agent;

(u) "duplicate reservation" shall mean a situation which arises when two or more reservations are made for the same passenger when it is evident that the passenger will not be able to use more than one.'

3. Article 3a shall be amended as follows:

(a) paragraph 1(b) shall be replaced by the following:

'(b) The parent carrier shall not be obliged to accept any costs in this connection except for reproduction of the information to be provided and for accepted bookings. The booking fee payable to a CRS for an accepted booking made in accordance with this Article shall not exceed the fee charged by the same CRS to participating carriers for an equivalent transaction;'

(b) paragraph 2 shall be replaced by the following:

'2. The obligation imposed by this Article shall not apply in favour of a competing CRS when, in accordance with the procedures of Article 11, itEN Official Journal of the European Communities 13.2.1999 L 40/3 has been decided that that CRS is in breach ofArticle 4a or of Article 6 concerning parent carriers' unauthorised access to information.'

4. In Article 4(1) the following subparagraph shall be added:

'The principles stated in the first and second subparagraphs shall apply to rail services in respect of data provided for inclusion in the principal display.'

5. In Article 4a the following paragraph shall be added:

'4. The system vendor shall ensure that any third parties providing CRS services in whole or in part on its behalf comply with the relevant provisions of this Regulation.'

6. Article 6(1)(a) shall be replaced by the following:

'(a) information concerning identifiable individual bookings shall be provided on an equal basis and only to the air carrier or carriers participating in the service covered by and to the subscribers involved in the booking. Information under the control of the system vendor concerning identifiable individual bookings shall be archived off-line within seventy-two hours of the completion of the last element in the individual booking and destroyed within three years. Access to such data shall be allowed only for billing-dispute reasons.'

7. Article 6(1)(b) shall be amended as follows:

(a) point (ii) shall be replaced by the following:

'(ii) such data may and, on request, shall cover all participating carriers and/or subscribers, but shall include no identification, either directly or indirectly, of, or personal information on a passenger or a corporate user;'

(b) the following points shall be added:

'(iv) information is made available on request to participating carriers and subscribers both globally and selectively with regard to the market in which they operate;

(v) a group of airlines and/or subscribers is entitled to purchase data for common processing.'

8. Paragraphs (4) and (5) of Article 6 shall be deleted.

9. The following Article shall be inserted:

'Article 9a

1. (a) In the case of information provided by a CRS, a subscriber shall use a neutral display in accordance with Article 5(2)(a) and (b) unless another display is required to meet a preference indicated by a consumer.

(b) No subscriber shall manipulate information provided by a CRS in a manner that leads to inaccurate, misleading or discriminatory presentation of that information to any consumer.

(c) A subscriber shall make reservations and issue tickets in accordance with the information contained in the CRS used, or as authorised by the carrier concerned.

(d) A subscriber shall inform each consumer of any en route changes of equipment, the number of scheduled en route stops, the identity of the air carrier actually operating the flight, and of any changes of airport required in any itinerary provided, to the extent that that information is present in the CRS. The subscriber shall inform the consumer of the name and address of the system vendor, the purposes of the processing, the duration of the retention of individual data and the means available to the data subject of exercising his access rights.

(e) A consumer shall be entitled at any time to have a print-out of the CRS display or to be given access to a parallel CRS display reflecting the image that is being displayed to the subscriber.

(f) A person shall be entitled to have effective access free of charge to his own data regardless of whether the data is stored by the CRS or by the subscriber.

2. A subscriber shall use the distribution facilities of a CRS in accordance with Annex II.'

10. In Article 10 paragraphs 1 and 2 shall be replaced by the following:
'1. (a) Any fee charged to a participating carrier by a system vendor shall be non-discriminatory, reasonably structured and reasonably related to the cost of the service provided and used and shall, in particular, be the same for the same level of service. The billing for the services of a CRS shall be sufficiently detailed to allow the participating carriers to see exactly which services have been used and the fees therefore; as a minimum, booking fee bills shall include the following information for each segment:
- type of CRS booking,
- passenger name,
- country,
- IATA/ARC agency identification code,
- city-code,
- city pair of segment,
- booking date (transaction date),
- flight date,
- flight number,
- status code (booking status),
- service type (class of service),
- passenger name record (PNR) locator, and
- booking/cancellation indicator.
The billing information shall be offered on magnetic media. The fee to be charged for the billing information provided in the form chosen by the carrier shall not exceed the cost of the medium itself together with its transportation costs. A participating air carrier shall be offered the facility of being informed when any booking or transaction is made for which a booking fee will be charged. Where a carrier elects to be so informed, it shall be offered the option of disallowing any such booking or transaction, unless the latter has already been accepted. In the event of such a disallowance, the air carrier shall not be charged for that booking or transaction.
(b) Any fee for equipment rental or other service charged to a subscriber by a system vendor shall be non-discriminatory, reasonably structured and reasonably related to the cost of the service provided and used and shall, in particular, be the same for the same level of service. Productivity benefits awarded to subscribers by system vendors in the form of discount on rental charges or commission payments shall be deemed to be distribution costs of the system vendors and shall be based on ticketed segments. When, subject to paragraph 5 of Annex II, the system vendor does not know whether a ticket has been issued or not, then that system vendor shall be entitled to rely upon notification of the ticket number from the subscriber. The billing for the services of a CRS shall be sufficiently detailed to allow subscribers to see exactly which services have been used and what fees have been charged therefore.
2. A system vendor shall, on request, provide interested parties, including consumers, with details of current procedures, fees and system facilities, including interfaces, editing and display criteria used.

For consumers that information shall be free of charge and cover the processing of individual data. This provision shall not, however, require a system vendor to disclose proprietary information such as software.'

11. Article 19(1) shall be replaced by the following:
'1. Before taking decisions pursuant to Article 11 or 16, the Commission shall give the undertakings or associations of undertakings concerned the opportunity of being heard on the matters to which the Commission takes or has taken objection.'

12. Article 21 shall be replaced by the following:

'Article 21

1. Neither Article 5, Article 9(5) nor the Annexes shall apply to a CRS used by an air carrier or a group of air carriers:
(a) in its or their own office or offices and sales counters clearly identified as such;
or
(b) to provide information and/or distribution facilities accessible through a public telecommunications network, clearly and continuously identifying the information provider or providers as such.
2. Where booking is performed directly by an air carrier, that air carrier shall be subject to Article 9a(d) and (f).'

13. Article 21a(1) shall be replaced by the following:
'1. The system vendor shall ensure that the technical compliance of its CRS with Articles 4a and 6 is monitored by an independent auditor on a calendar year basis. For that purpose, the auditor shall be granted access at all times to any programs, procedures, operations and safeguards used on the computers or computer systems through which the system vendor provides its distribution facilities. Each system vendor shall submit its auditor's report on his inspection and findings to the Commission within four months of the end of the calendar year under review. The Commission shall examine those reports with a view to taking any action necessary in accordance with Article 11(1).

14. The following Article shall be added:

'Article 21b

1. Subject to this Article, this Regulation shall apply to the inclusion of rail-transport products.
2. A system vendor may decide to include rail services in the principal display of its CRS.
3. Where a system vendor decides to include rail products in the principal display of its CRS, it shall choose to include certain well-defined categories of rail services, while respecting the principles stated in Article 3(2).
4. A rail-transport operator shall be deemed to be a participating or parent carrier, as appropriate, for the purposes of the code, insofar as it has an agreement with a system vendor for the distribution of its products through the principal display of a CRS or its own reservation system is a CRS as defined in

Article 2(f). Subject to paragraph 5, those products shall be treated as air-transport products and shall be incorporated in the principal display in accordance with the criteria set out in Annex I.

5. (a) When applying the rules laid down in paragraphs 1 and 2 of Annex I to rail services the system vendor shall adjust the ranking principles for the principal display in order to take due account of the needs of consumers to be adequately informed of rail services that represent a competitive alternative to the air services. In particular, system vendors may rank rail services with a limited number of short stops with non-stop direct air services.

(b) System vendors shall define clear criteria for the application of this Article to rail services. Such criteria shall cover elapsed journey time and reflect the need to avoid excessive screen padding. At least two months before their application those criteria shall be submitted to the Commission for information.

6. For the purposes of this Article, all references to "flights" in this Regulation shall be deemed to include references to "rail services" and references to "air-transport products" shall be deemed to include references to "rail products".

7. Particular attention shall be given to an assessment of the application of this Article in the Commission's report under Article 23(1).'

15. Article 22(1) shall be replaced by the following:

'1. This Regulation shall be without prejudice to national legislation on security, public order and data protection measures taken in implementation of Directive 95/46/EC (OJ L 281, 23.11.1995, p. 31). EN Official Journal of the European Communities 13.2.1999 L 40/6.'

16. Article 23 shall be replaced by the following:

'Article 23

Within two years of the entry into force of this Regulation, the Commission shall draw up a report on the application of this Regulation which shall, *inter alia*, take account of economic developments in the relevant market. That report may be accompanied by proposals for the revision of this Regulation.'

17. The Annex shall be replaced by Annexes I and II set out in the Annex hereto.

Article 2

This Regulation shall enter into force on the thirtieth day after that of its publication in the *Official Journal of the European Communities*, with the exception of the new Article 10(1)(b) of Regulation (EEC) No 2299/89, which shall enter into force six months after the publication of this Regulation. This Regulation shall be binding in its entirety and directly applicable in all Member States.

Done at Brussels, 8 February 1999.
For the Council
The President
O. LAFONTAINE

EN Official Journal of the European Communities 13.2.1999 L 40/7

'ANNEX I
Principal display ranking criteria for flights (1) offering unbundled air transport
products

1. Ranking of flight options in a principal display, for the day or days requested, must be in the following order unless requested in a different way by a consumer for an individual transaction:
   (i)   all non-stop direct flights between the city-pairs concerned;
   (ii) all other direct flights, not involving a change of aircraft or train, between the city pairs concerned;
   (iii) connecting flights.

2. A consumer must at least be afforded the possibility of having, on request, a principal display ranked by departure or arrival time and/or elapsed journey time. Unless otherwise requested by a consumer, a principal display must be ranked by departure time for group (i) and elapsed journey time for groups (ii) and (iii).

3. Where a system vendor chooses to display information for any city-pair in relation to the schedules or fares of non participating carriers, but not necessarily all such carriers, such information must be displayed in an accurate, non-misleading and non-discriminatory manner between carriers displayed.

4. If, to the system vendor's knowledge, information on the number of direct scheduled air services and the identity of the air carriers concerned is not comprehensive, that must be clearly stated on the relevant display.

5. Flights other than scheduled air services must be clearly identified.

6. Flights involving stops en route must be clearly identified.

7. Where flights are operated by an air carrier which is not the air carrier identified by the carrier designator code, the actual operator of the flight must be clearly identified. That requirement will apply in all cases, except for short-term *ad hoc* arrangements.

8. A system vendor must not use the screen space in a principal display in a manner which gives excessive exposure to one particular travel option or which displays unrealistic travel options.

9. Except as provided in paragraph 10, the following will apply:
   (a) for direct services, no flight may be featured more than once in any principal display;
   (b) for multi-sector services involving a change of aircraft, no combination of flights may be featured more than once in any principal display;
   (c) flights involving a change of aircraft must be treated and displayed as connecting flights, with one line per aircraft segment. Nevertheless, where the flights are operated by the same carrier with the same flight number and where a carrier requires only one flight coupon and one reservation, a CRS should issue only one coupon and should charge for only one reservation.

10.1. Where participating carriers have joint-venture or other contractual arrangements requiring two or more of them to assume separate responsibility for the offer and sale of air-transport products on a flight or combination of

flights, the terms "flight" (for direct services) and "combination of flights" (for multi-sector services) used in paragraph 9 must be interpreted as allowing each of the carriers concerned
- not more than two
- to have a separate display using its individual carrier designator code.

2. Where more than two carriers are involved, designation of the two carriers entitled to avail themselves of the exception provided for in subparagraph 1 must be a matter for the carrier actually operating the flight. In the absence of information from the operating carrier sufficient to identify the two carriers to be designated, a system vendor must designate the carriers on a non-discriminatory basis.

(1) All references to "flights" in this Annex are in accordance with Article 21b(6). EN Official Journal of the European Communities 13.2.1999 L 40/8.

11. A principal display must, wherever practicable, include connecting flights on scheduled services which are operated by participating carriers and are constructed by using a minimum number of nine connecting points. A system vendor must accept a request by a participating carrier to include an indirect service, unless the routing is in excess of 130% of the great circle distance between the two airports or unless that would lead to the exclusion of services with a shorter elapsed journey time. Connecting points with routings in excess of 130% of that great circle distance need not be used.

ANNEX II
Use of distribution facilities by subscribers

1. A subscriber must keep accurate records covering all CRS reservation transactions. Those records must include flight numbers, reservations booking designators, date of travel, departure and arrival times, status of segments, names and initials of passengers with their contact addresses and/or telephone numbers and ticketing status. When booking or cancelling space, the subscriber must ensure that the reservation designator being used corresponds to the fare paid by the passenger.
2. A subscriber should not deliberately make duplicate reservations for the same passenger. Where confirmed space is not available on the customer's choice, the passenger may be wait-listed on that flight (if wait-list is available) and confirmed on an alternative flight.
3. When a passenger cancels a reservation, the subscriber must immediately release that space.
4. When a passenger changes an itinerary, the subscriber must ensure that all space and supplementary services are cancelled when the new reservations are made.
5. A subscriber must, where practicable, request or process all reservations for a specific itinerary and all subsequent changes through the same CRS.
6. No subscriber may request or sell airline space unless requested to do so by a consumer.

7. A subscriber must ensure that a ticket is issued in accordance with the reservation status of each segment and in accordance with the applicable time limit. A subscriber must not issue a ticket indicating a definite reservation and a particular flight unless confirmation of that reservation has been received.'

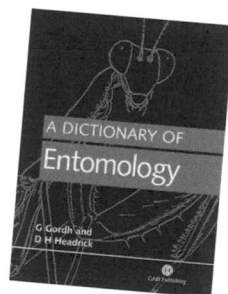